Flash 5 ActionScript Studio

David Beard
Michael Bedar
Sham Bhangal
Richard Chu
John Davey
Justin Everett-Church
Jamie MacDonald
Jose Rodriguez
Adam Wolff

friendsof

DESIGNER TO DESIGNER™

Flash 5 ActionScript Studio

© 2001 friends of ED

First printed in June 2001

Trademark Acknowledgments

Published by friends of ED
30 Lincoln Road, Olton, Birmingham. B27 6PA. UK.

Printed in USA

ISBN: 1-903450-35-7

Flash 5 ActionScript Studio

Credits

Authors David Beard, Michael Bedar, Sham Bhangal, Richard Chu, John Davey, Justin Everett-Church, Jamie MacDonald,, Jose Rodriguez, Adam Wolff

Content Architect Jon Hill

Editors Eleanor Baylis, Kristian Besley, Benjamin Egan, Julia Gilbert, Ben Renow-Clarke,Andrew Tracey

Technical Reviewers Jason Anderson, Konstantin Bereznyakov, Kim 'Bimmer' Christensen, Jeff Diamond, John Davey, J. Gahlord Dewald, Clifton Evans, Brian Eric Ganniger, Doug Hays, Brandon Houston, Michael S. Johnson, Stephen Kirby, Vicki Loader, William B. McIntyre, Glain Martin, Tim Payne, Mark Pusateri, Keyur Shah, Steven Skoczen, Gabrielle Smith, Eric Smollin, Jon Steer, Andrew Stopford, Kevin Sutherland, William L. Thomson Jr, Andrew H. Watt

Graphic Editors William Fallon, Katy Freer, Deborah Murray, David Spurgeon

Author Agent Sophie Edwards

Project Administator Thomas Stiff

Index Andrew Criddle, Simon Collins

Cover Design Katy Freer

Proof Readers Eleanor Baylis, Kristian Besley, Jez Booker, Luke Brown, Joanna Farmer, Laurent Lafon, Darren Lenihan, Fionnuala Meacher, Gaynor Riopedre, Joel Rushton, Thomas Stiff

Team Leader Joanna Farmer

Flash 5 ActionScript Studio

David Beard

David is a software developer and technology consultant. He is a founder of Wavelength Releasing llc, where he works with Flash, primarily as a web application medium. David's current efforts are devoted to the development of M.O.D.E – Multi-user Object Development Environment. MODE enables the development of real-time collaboration environments within standard web domains, and will use Flash in various aspects of its user interface and multi-user domain.

Michael Bedar

Michael C. Bedar is a freelance multimedia designer in Boston, MA. He is contributing author and assistant webmaster for www.flashaddict.com, and a founding member of the Boston Flash MMUG. His work can bee seen at FlashAddict, as well as at www.virtual-fx.net. Michael is a self-professed computer geek, and a devout Mac Evangelist. Michael enjoys reading books that have as little to do with reality as possible, and practicing martial arts. Michael's worst fear is that some day he will be forced to write about himself in the third person.

Sham Bhangal

Sham Bhangal originally started out as an engineer, specializing in industrial computer based display and control systems. His spare time was partly taken up by freelance web design, something that slowly took up more and more of his time until the engineering had to go. He is now also writing for friends of ED, something that is taking more and more time away from web design...funny how life repeats itself! Sham lives in Manchester, England, with his partner Karen.

Richard Chu   www.hview.com/Nethod/Main1.htm

Graduating from SUNY Fashion Institute of Technology in NYC as a traditional 2D artist, Richard fell in love with Flash when he saw his first animation on the web. He left print design and entered the world of web and multimedia, focusing on Flash and 3D design. Now working as a Senior Multimedia Designer at Nethod EURO RSCG Interaction, offering innovative multimedia solutions to the global life-sciences community. When not immersed in Flash design, Richard focuses on developing his 3D skills in hopes of one day becoming a great 3D animator. His current project is the redesign of Pfizer Health Solution's website, the new Flash enriched site will be launched in June 2001.

John Davey   www.developette.com

This is how it normally goes: "www.developette.com, developette, as in launderette, you know, like a place to air work and ideas. Flash & Generator; nothing else. Stuff for the BBC, Science Museum, Kelloggs, ASDA/Walmart, Digit Magazine, Internet Magazine." John Davey doesn't know why he started everything too late in life, why people call football, "soccer", why people think snowboarding is cooler than extreme skiing, why he can't do a double daffy any more, or why whenever he takes a straight line, everyone else zigzags. John says: "In the land of the blind, the one eyed is King! Put in the hours. Don't zigzag!"

About the Authors

Justin Everett-Church   www.infinitumdesign.com

I'm currently Interactive Director at Estudio.com, a studio specializing in Flash shows and games. You can see some of our work at shockwave.com (look for Regurge). When I'm not making games (and other neat stuff) there, I can be found at home playing games (purely for research), making effects for Flashkit, or hanging out in #flashhelp on IRC, a great place to talk to other Flashers. Prior to becoming a Flash devotee, I studied linguistics and foreign policy. This fantastically geekish life takes place in San Jose, California along with my very patient partner and two rather strange looking cats.

Jamie MacDonald   www.nooflat.nu

Jamie William Macdonald came across flash while studying for his masters in the film department at UCLA last year. He has recently moved home to England and is currently working in London, developing interfaces atrelevare.com. In his spare time Jamie updates his website, nooflat.nu.

Jose Rodriguez   www.JRVisuals.com

Born in Puerto Rico, Jose is the founder of JRVisuals (www.JRVisuals.com) which he runs from his apartment in the Bronx, New York where he lives with his wife Jennifer and son Julian. Jose is also developing a Collective of Media Developers under the name Media-OP (www.Media-OP.com) and currently runs the New York Metro Macromedia User Group (www.NYMMUG.org). His work combines programming, audio, and art into a seamless blend that has gained notoriety in the field for nearly a decade.

Adam Wolff

Adam Wolff is a game and interface designer who still believes in the promise of the tech industry. After living through the demise of two promising game companies -- Rocket Science and Purple Moon -- he joined Microsoft as a TV interface architect. He's now starting his own custom software company, Flatland Exports, which specializes in user-interface-heavy applications for devices and the Web.

Flash 5 ActionScript Studio

Palette
and
Table of
Contents

Flash 5 ActionScript Studio

CORE SKILLS

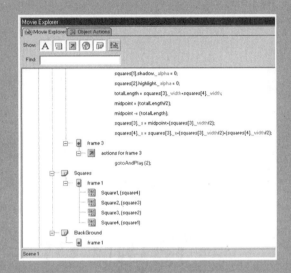

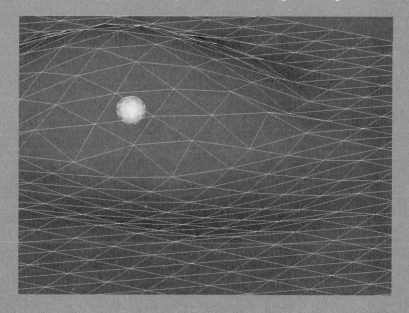

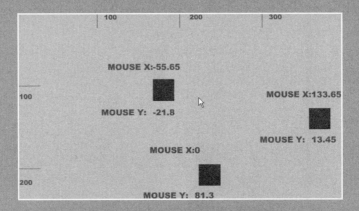

SPECIALIZATION

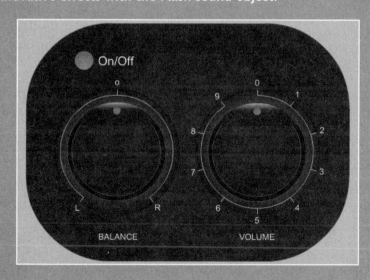

> Implementation of matrix methods for spatial transformations of inner 3D geometry.

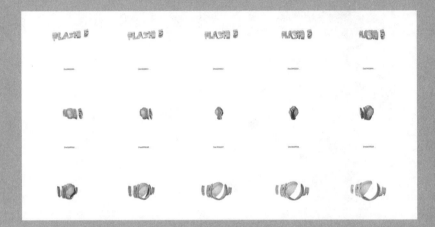

> Flash gaming: a new spin on an old skool title.

Utilizing Flash's new XML object to build enterprise level solutions.

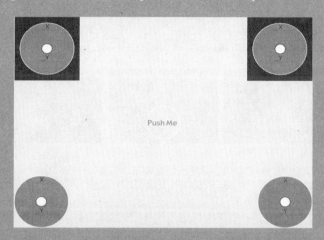

Designing dynamic interfaces with Macromedia Generator.

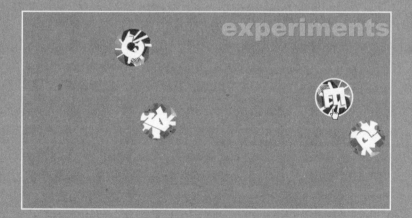

Flash 5 ActionScript Studio

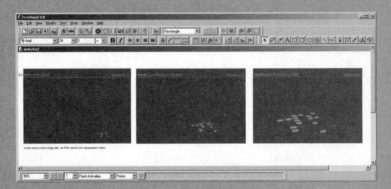

CASE STUDIES

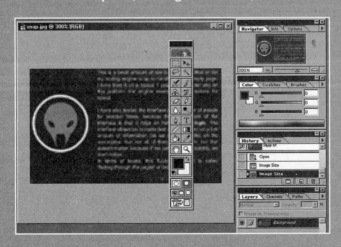

CHAPTER 15   XML FOR DATA AND DESIGN   595
JOSE RODRIGUEZ
    Dynamic data manipulation using XML.

Flash 5 ActionScript Studio

Table of Contents

Table of Contents

8   Sound Control   243

9   3D Flash   293

Table of Contents

Table of Contents

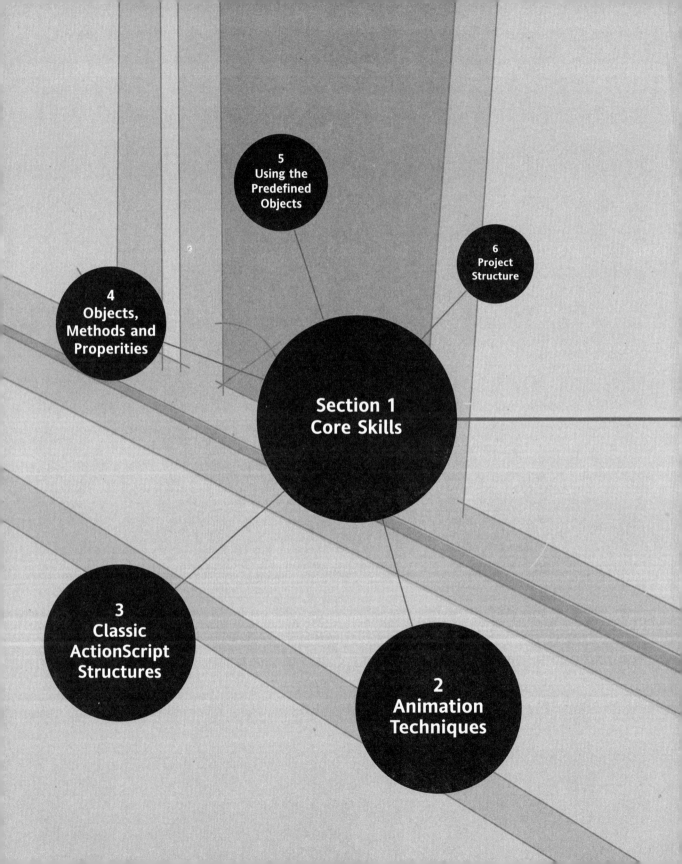

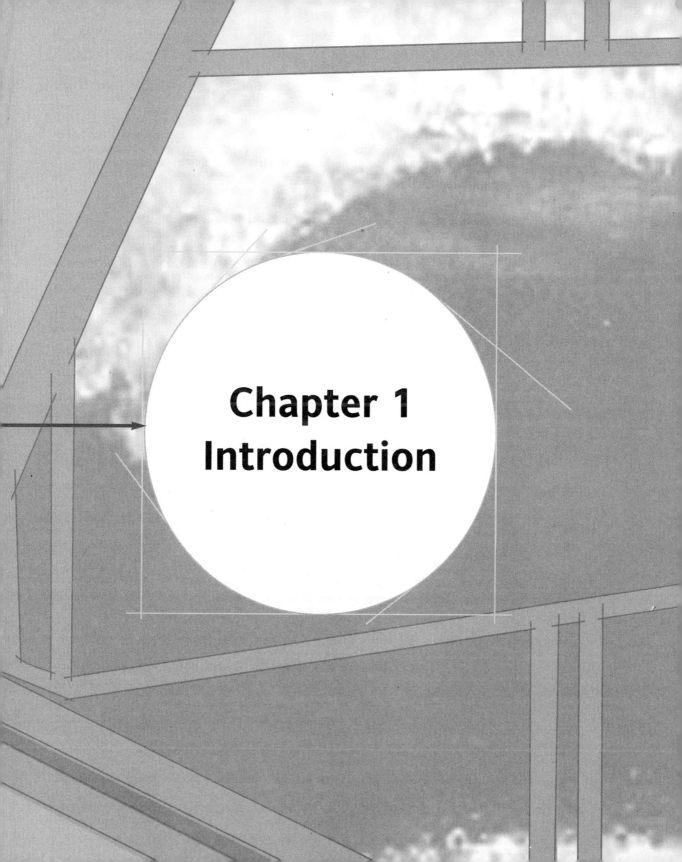

Chapter 1
Introduction

Scripting Language. It's not a very pretty name, but it can do some spectacularly pretty things, IF (and that's a big if) you know how to use it. Macromedia cottoned on to the whole pretty name thing early on and called their scripting language "ActionScript", which was much more exciting, but still didn't help with the "knowing how to use it" bit. That's where this book comes in.

This chapter is to serve both as an introduction to this book and what it's trying to do, and to bring you up to speed if you're coming to ActionScript from Flash 4. Flash 5 has been out for a while now – long enough for people to begin to realize its new power and flexibility; to see that it contains a mature, structured language; and to catch on that to get the most out of it, it needs to be fed mature, structured code. Unfortunately, mature, structured code is something that only mature, structured programmers know about, isn't it? Not any more, and with this book's help, hopefully never again. Flash 5 has heralded a new age of renaissance programmer-designers able not only to make beautiful and distinctive sites, but also to make them interactive in ways people had never dreamed about.

What's in it then?

This book is split into three main sections, covering core skills, specialization, and case studies. The aim is first to teach you the fundamentals of good ActionScript, then to go into those fundamentals in much greater detail, before giving you examples of how all of the new knowledge you've have gained fits into the real world. Every contributor to this book is a working web designer and/or coder who's learned the arcane arts of Flash the hard way. They're here to help you crack the code and unlock the secrets of great ActionScript programming.

Core skills
This is where we'll run through the underlying techniques and know-how that you need before you can start to write code that both performs brilliantly and reads well. We'll teach you how to make use of Flash's new structures and commands, what object-oriented programming is, and how it affects the ActionScript user.

Specialization
Here we'll go into detail on certain aspects of the core skills learned in the last section, showing how they can be applied to your projects through worked examples. We'll cover things like the new Sound and XML objects, how to build a true 3D array-based engine, using Generator to empower your Flash movies, and discovering how teamwork can send your creativity into orbit.

Case studies
This is where the gloves come off. These two case studies are examples of what good designers do best: making incredible and individual web sites, and explaining the method behind their madness. You'll discover how a unique interface is created from inception to inauguration, and how Flash's new addition of XML can not only revolutionize data communication, but also inspire site design. After this, it's down to you.

ActionScript's evolution, and what you need to know

In this book, we're assuming that you know your way around the Flash interface, and that you know what the basic building blocks of a Flash movie are. What you won't know all about is Flash 5 ActionScript. Maybe you've dabbled with the basic functions before, or you're still coming to terms with the transition from Flash 4, but you won't have looked into the more advanced aspects of the language. To aid in this, we'll quickly run through the ActionScript programmer's home – the Actions panel – and the new methods of ActionScript entry as well. We'll also glance at a few pieces of syntax with which you may not be completely familiar.

One thing we can say for sure is that ActionScript isn't what it used to be. Once, it took some of the best designers in the world to make those amazing, interactive sites that everybody wowed at. Now, most anybody can do it. Flash 5 has put tremendous power into the hands of designers and programmers alike, and the most powerful tool of all is ActionScript.

Yes, Flash 4 had actions as well, but they were nothing compared to this. Flash 5 ActionScript allows you to do much more than pretty graphics and animation; now you can make advanced applications too – things like games, screen savers, and weird math-based experiments. That's not to say that pretty graphics and animation are now redundant though – far from it. ActionScript gives you far greater control over traditional animation and events too, and it frees you from being tied to the timeline.

So what's new?

Rather than creating their own language from scratch, and going through all of the teething problems associated with it, Macromedia sensibly chose to integrate a widely used and syntactically mature language with Flash. The result is something so natural that it feels like it was always there, and yet it's such a radical step forward that you won't know how you survived without it.

JavaScript

So what was the radioactive spider that bit Flash 5? In a word, JavaScript. In a slightly more complicated word, ECMA-262. That's not the prototype for a new robot; it's the European Computer Manufacturers Association's document on their international, standardized version of JavaScript. If you've been hanging round the Web for a while, you've probably heard of JavaScript, and you may even be familiar with it. If you're not, don't worry: you don't need to know it in order to use ActionScript. If you *are* acquainted with JavaScript, then of course you'll recognize a few things here and there, but that's no reason to get complacent – ActionScript combined with Flash is a completely different can of clam chowder.

The combination of Flash's vector animation and built-in streaming technology with JavaScript's functionality is a very effective one. What JavaScript gives so generously to ActionScript is structure, and ease of use through standardization. Gone is the old slash notation for referencing movie clips; here instead is the new dot notation, bringing it into line with other languages, and replacing the colons and confusion of Flash 4.

Objects

Flash is now the proud possessor of an object-enabled programming language. This may sound a bit scary, and not at all designer friendly, but really it's nothing of the sort. Flash has *always* been based around objects; it just hasn't had the programming language to go with it. Now, when you tell a movie clip to play, you're *actually* utilizing a method of an object – and you're probably doing it without realizing it. We'll look into this subject in more detail, and at what it means for

Flash, in Chapter 4. Until then, it's enough just to keep this 'objects, methods, and properties' stuff in the back of your mind, and to realize that something big has changed.

Events

Another thing worth mentioning is that ActionScript is an *event-driven* language – and again, this is something that sounds rather formal, but is in fact something that you're probably already familiar with. Flash 4 had buttons, and the giveaway `On MouseEvent` action. For example, you could have a button that said:

```
On (Press)
    Go to and Play (10)
End On
```

This would make Flash wait for an event – in this case, a mouse click – before reacting, which here means going to frame 10 and starting to play. In Flash 5, you still have all of the old mouse events on buttons, but they're joined by the new clip events that can be added to movie clips. Some of these cover the same ground as mouse events, checking for things like whether the mouse has been clicked, but there are also some more specialized ones for detecting when movie clips have been loaded, or when data has been received from outside. This allows you to wait until a soundtrack movie has fully loaded before playing it, or until the contents of a `currentNews` text file have been received in their entirety before displaying the news page movie.

New methods of addressing and notation

One of the most noticeably different things between the two most recent versions of Flash is the change from slash syntax to dot syntax. The old method of writing paths has gone completely, but you shouldn't have any trouble at all switching over to the new regime. At its most trivial level, it's just the swapping of slashes and colons in old script for periods in new script, but its repercussions are wider reaching. Dot notation makes it much easier to get and set properties, because rather than needing Flash 4's separate `Get` and `Set Property` commands, you can now achieve all of the same effects simply by using the path. For example, to set the `X Position` of a movie clip instance called `Ball` to 100 in Flash 4, you'd have to write:

```
Set Property ("/Ball", X Position) = "100"
```

In Flash 5, you just need:

```
Ball._x = 100;
```

Immediately, you can see how much quicker and easier this is – and the same degree of simplicity can be found with variables. Instead of having to use a colon to reference a variable, you now just use a period, as you would with everything else.

The other major difference that this has made for people coming from Flash 4 is that there is no longer a `Tell Target` command – it has become obsolete with the new system of notation. A bit of a culture shock for Flash 4 users, perhaps, but those who started with Flash 5 won't understand what all the fuss is about. We'll use the same example of our `Ball` movie clip, but this time we'll tell it to start playing. In Flash 4, the code for this would be:

```
Begin Tell Target ("/Ball")
    Play
End Tell Target
```

But using dot notation in Flash 5, it's just:

```
Ball.play();
```

Which, you'll surely agree, is rather less tedious. Another, slightly more subtle artifact you might have picked up on is that there's been a semicolon appearing at the end of every complete line of Flash 5 code. This is *another* result of Flash 5's adoption of JavaScript. Semicolons are now used to terminate every statement in ActionScript – although, for now at least, don't worry if you forget to put them in, because Flash will add them for you.

The new interface

The new coding facilities of Flash required a new method of script entry to go with them. The old Actions tab in the Instance Properties window just couldn't cope any more, so what we have now is the Actions panel, a vaguely familiar interface that offers much more than it might at first appear. For starters, the list of actions is much longer than it was in Flash 4. Open up the Actions panel (Window > Actions), and click on the + icon. Now, instead of the list of 20 actions that you'd expect in Flash 4, you'll find 6 submenus – and in each of these you'll find long lists of actions, and even more submenus, with even more actions in:

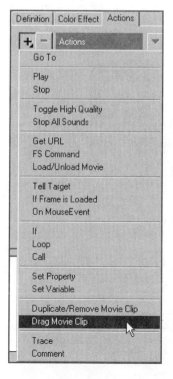 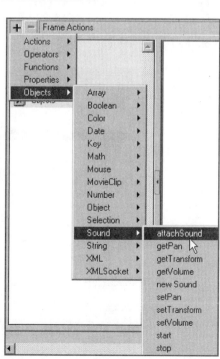

Although it's a lot bigger, you shouldn't be daunted by it: you don't need to know every command in order to be able to write good ActionScript. It's much more important that you come to an *appreciation* of what functionality is available, and where you're likely to find it when you need it. For the specifics, you can always turn to the online documentation; but if you don't know where to look, or what to look for, you'll be stumped.

As a way of introducing new users (and old Flash 4 users) to ActionScript, Macromedia built two modes of code entry into the Actions panel: Normal mode, and Expert mode. If you haven't seen it before, then we'll quickly familiarize you with Normal mode, but the rest of the chapters in this book will assume that you're using Expert mode, so we'll spend some time getting to know that as well.

Normal mode

Normal mode is a blessing for designers who are brand new to programming. It's a drag-and-drop environment that introduces you to the new language and its structure, while holding your hand all the way. Let's take a quick look at it.

Click on the first frame of the timeline, and then open up the Actions panel. First of all, make sure that you're in Normal mode by clicking on the triangle button on the right-hand side of the panel to open the fly-out menu and making sure that there's a check mark next to Normal Mode. (If there's not, then click on it so that there is!)

Normal mode is similar to script entry in Flash 4, in that it tells you what arguments (if any) a particular action takes. On the left-hand side of the panel you should see a list of actions, and at the top of this list should be Go To. Click and drag (you could also double-click) this into the blank area on the right of the panel:

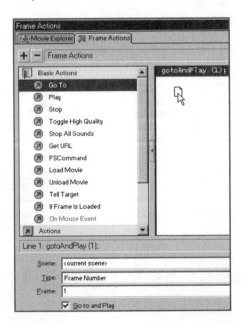

You should now have the following code in the window:

```
gotoAndPlay (1);
```

There should also be a set of options in the parameters area that will be familiar to you from Flash 4, allowing you to change things like whether to play a frame number or a label, whether to stop or play, and so on. Change the frame number to 5, and we'll be on our way.

Expert mode

Despite the name, Expert mode is basically the same as Normal mode, but without the parameters area, or the requirement to drag-and-drop actions. I'll explain why you'd want to use this when it seems to offer *less* than Normal mode in a minute, but first let's take a quick look at entering code here

Switch to Expert mode using the same menu you did for Normal mode, or by pressing Ctrl-E (it's Ctrl-N to switch back to Normal mode). Straight away, you should notice that the parameters area disappears. Click in the window to get a flashing cursor, then, on the line below the action that you entered in Normal mode, type:

```
gotoandplay (5);
```

You should see that the line you've just written is in black, whereas the line that you entered before is a fetching blue. This is because gotoAndPlay is a reserved action, and as such it must be typed correctly for Flash to understand it. To help you make sure that you're giving Flash the command that you want to, it will color the words that it recognizes. Actions and keywords are blue, properties are green, comments are magenta, strings are gray, and everything else is black.

Go back to your code, change the "a" of "and" to a capital letter, and the "p" of "play" the same, to read:

```
gotoAndPlay (5);
```

This line of code should now turn blue, just like the first one did.

You're probably thinking that using Normal mode was much easier than all this typing-things-in- and making-sure-you-capitalize-them-in-the-right-place malarkey, but hold on! You can make things a bit quicker and easier by using shortcuts.

Go back to your Expert mode code, and press Enter to start a new line. Now type the key sequence Esc-g-p-5 You should see the same gotoAndPlay command appear. The keyboard shortcuts for all of the actions are displayed next to their names when you click on the + button to view the drop-down menus containing all of the actions. Of course, you're never going to learn them all, but they're like any other application's keyboard shortcuts: you only tend to know the ones that you use most often.

If you're still not convinced by Expert mode, try this. Type the following into the code window:

```
_parent.myMovie._x = (this._y + _root._ymouse) * Math.random();
```

Don't worry about what it all means for now (basically, it just sets the x position of a movie clip in a very strange way), because that's not the point of this exercise. The point is now to go into Normal mode and try to enter exactly the same code. It's not quite fair if you don't know your way around the menus, but even if you did, you'd find yourself hard pressed to get it all in as quickly as you would just typing it.

If I still haven't won you over, then by all means use both entry techniques. I spend the majority of my time in Expert mode, but every now and then I'll come to use an action whose parameters I can't quite remember. In cases like this, I quickly switch to Normal mode, enter the action, and fill in the parameters area; and then switch back to Expert mode to continue working. I find this is the best solution for me, but the answer (as always) is to try everything and find what works best for you.

Other features of the Actions panel

There's more to the Actions panel than just entering code, though: there are also a lot of helpful features lurking in the fly-out menu where we found the Normal mode/Expert mode switch. Click on the button again to open up the full menu:

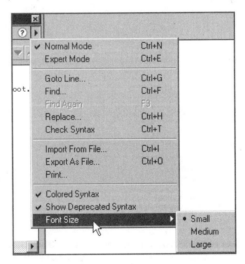

From here, you can see all of the other options. The Goto Line command is very useful for debugging, since Flash reports errors by telling you the line number that the error can be found on. Rather than counting through the lines of code to find the one in question, you can just use this command to go straight there. The Find and Replace options speak for themselves – although one thing worth pointing out is that they'll only work on the code that's currently in the window: you can't do a global movie search for something from here. We'll be looking at how you *can* do such a search later on.

I'll skip past the importing and exporting for now, but come back to it in just a second. The remaining options are fairly self-explanatory: Print will print out all of the code in the window, but as with Find and Replace, you can't print out the whole movie. It's always worth leaving Colored Syntax and Show Deprecated Syntax checked – the former highlights your code as we saw before, while the latter refers to the highlighted green actions that you may have seen in the list on the left-hand side of the Actions panel:

These highlighted actions are Flash 4 commands that have been replaced by more JavaScript-compatible actions in Flash 5, and they're not recommended for use. The reason that they're still here, and that they still work, is for backwards compatibility with Flash 4 code. The last option in the list is for changing the font size of the code displayed in the Actions window; set this to whatever your eyesight's happiest with!

Importing and exporting files

I said that we'd return to the two options that we missed out of that list, so we'll do so now – they were: Import From File and Export As File. They enable you to keep your code in a separate text file (in this case a .as file, though it's still just plain text), and then bring it into different movies as and when you need it. What this really means is that you can start to build up libraries of often-used code.

Take the example of a 3D program. If you've written an ActionScript 3D engine (as you will later in the book) for one application, and you want to use the same engine for another application, then the simplest solution would be to keep the code for your engine in an external file that can then be quickly incorporated into any project. Let's run through a quick example of how to do this.

Start a new movie, and type the following into the Actions panel for the first frame, setting up a variable:

```
sweaterColor = "red";
```

> *It's worth noting here that the single equals sign in Flash 5 is used solely as an assignment operator – that is, for assigning values to variables, and not as an equality operator, as it was in Flash 4. The equality operator in Flash 5 is now a double equals sign (==). We'll take a look at a few other operators later on.*

Next, create a static text box on the stage that says, "The color of my sweater is". Finally, create a dynamic text field next to this with the variable name `sweaterColor`, and place it next to the last text box against the right-hand edge. Now when you test your movie, you should see the words...

The color of my sweater is red

...on the screen. Once you've done this, save the file.

Go back to your line of code, and choose to export the file as a `.as` file in the same place as you saved the FLA. Once you've done this, delete the code that you wrote.

There are now two ways to get the code back into your movie. The first is to use the Import From File command from the Actions panel, which will bring the entire contents of the `.as` file back into the current frame. Try it, and you'll see what I mean.

The second option is to use the new `#include` command, which brings the entire contents of a specified text file into your project, but does so without actually displaying all of the code in the FLA. Let's run through this.

Go back to your code, and again delete everything that's there. Now type the following into the Actions panel for the first frame:

```
#include "fileName.as"
```

Where `fileName` is the name of the `.as` file that you exported earlier. If you run the file now, you should find that nothing has changed: the color of the sweater is still red, even though we don't seem to say anything about red sweaters in the script.

As I suggested earlier, this is extremely useful for building libraries of commonly used code, but it's also more specifically helpful because the `.as` files are just plain text files. This means that you don't necessarily need to have Flash with you to be able to change the script of a movie – you can just open up the AS file in your favorite text editor, and get typing. It also allows multiple people working on a project to write code for the same FLA. Theoretically, you could have an ActionScript-heavy movie that only had `#include` commands in it, if you wanted, and no other code! This won't make a difference to the size of the SWF file, as the code will all be added at compile time, but it would certainly make the FLA smaller – albeit more difficult to debug!

This brings us back to a couple of points that were mentioned earlier, and gives us a chance to look at one of the most important parts of programming: debugging.

New methods of debugging your code

In Flash 5, you can put your ActionScript code in numerous different locations – you're no longer just confined to frames and buttons. While this massively expands the amount you can do with ActionScript, it also makes it a lot harder to find things later on, when it comes to debugging your code. To help you in this task, the kind people at Macromedia created the Movie Explorer. This companion to the Actions panel (it's the tab right next door to it) is where you can view and print the code for your entire movie – but that's not all it does. Open it up and take a look; I've opened one of the FLAs from later in the book with it, so you can see the difference it makes on a large file:

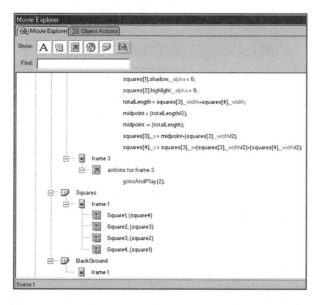

You can use the Movie Explorer to see a linear visual representation of *everything* that's happening in your movie. The buttons at the top can be used to toggle whether or not to show certain aspects of it, so if you only want to see the ActionScript, you can turn off everything but the Show Action Scripts button. If you want to see the frames and layers as well, then you can turn them on with the appropriate button, and so on. This is brilliant, because it lets you see what's going on in your movie quickly and easily, and you can search for things that you know are causing problems. For example, if you'd gone through your code manually, and changed the name of a variable from "green" to "blue" every time you found it, but your code wasn't working properly, you could come into the Movie Explorer and search for the word "green". Every time you saw the code, you could then replace it with "blue".

Just like the Actions panel, the Movie Explorer has a fly-out menu concealing most of its options. From this menu, you get the chance to copy and paste text, to find the instances of a specified movie, to rename and edit elements of the movie, and finally – perhaps most importantly of all –

it allows you to get a printout of all of the code in your movie, so that you can debug it or compare it to another movie.

What other means are there for debugging? The most obvious is the Debugger itself, but it's not always the most helpful, and different methods of debugging are useful in different situations. Most of the time, people's first resort is the Output window. This is the same as it was in Flash 4, and it will display a list of any problems that Flash finds in the code when it tries to compile and run it. Again, as with Flash 4, you can use the `trace` command to send things to the Output window, which is useful for jobs like keeping track of variables. What the Debugger does differently is to keep track of all of these things for you *in real time*, without you having to add any extra commands to your code. Here's an example of the Debugger in action:

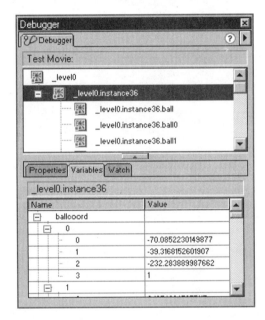

The only real problem with the Debugger is that it has been known to be a bit temperamental! The most surefire way that I've found of getting it to work is to go into the Publish Settings menu, and under the Flash tab, check the box next to Debugging Permitted. After doing this, test your movie, then right-click on the screen while it's running and select the Debugger option that should be right at the bottom of the menu. You can tell that it's worked when you see something appear in the window.

The great thing about the Debugger (once it's running) is that not only does it show you the variables and properties running in your movie in real time, *but you can also change them*. This means that if you want to see what that ball would look like were it slightly wider when it bounced across the stage, then you could just select the ball from the top window, click on the Properties tab, then find the _xscale property and double-click on it to change it. The ball would then immediately grow in size on the screen, with no need for you to go back into the movie and alter it there. It's worth bearing in mind, though, that the changes you make in the Debugger won't carry back into your movie, so if you *do* decide to keep a change that you made, you'll have to go back into the movie once you've finished debugging and change it.

Another handy thing that you can do from the Debugger is to set **watches** on certain variables, to make it easier to keep track of them. This means that you can compare variables running in different movie clips. To do this, just find the variable that you want to watch, and right-click on it: a mini-menu will pop up with Watch as its single option. Select it, and the variable will be added to the Watch window underneath the Watch tab in the Debugger. To add another variable to it, just follow the same process.

You can also debug your code before you even get round to testing the whole movie, courtesy of the built-in safety features and handholding of Normal mode. You may have noticed that sometimes, when you change from Expert to Normal, Flash won't let you do it, reporting an error in the code – it can be a useful way of catching problems. However, there's also a way that you can do this without having to switch back and forth. By pressing CTRL-T in Expert mode, you'll tell Flash to test the current code for errors. If any errors are found, a little box will pop up to tell you, and all of the error reports will be sent to the Output window. From here, you should be able to trace the error back to a specific line in the code, and hopefully erase it. It's not *always* that easy, but a lot of the time, it is.

Operators

To finish off, we'll take that promised tour around some of the new operators in Flash 5. As I said earlier, now that Flash 5 has adopted JavaScript, it has taken on some of the accepted operators and programming shortcuts of more established languages. We've already talked about the changes to the meanings of the single (=) and double (==) equals signs, but there are plenty more than that. Let's look at some of the more common ones.

Two that you'll come across very frequently are the increment (++) and decrement (- -) operators. These are most commonly found in loops with counters, but they can be used anywhere else too. The increment operator simply adds one to the variable it's applied to every time it's run, while the decrement operator does the opposite and subtracts one.

So, `i++` is the same as writing `i = i + 1` – it's just shorter. This doesn't look like much of a time saver with a small variable name, but when it includes a path as well, like...

```
_root.movieOne.variableOne = _root.movieOne.variableOne + 1;
```

...you start to notice the difference.

Another group of operators that you'll find useful are the addition, negation, multiplication and division assignment operators, written +=, -=, *=, and /=. Again, these are just programmer shorthand for longer common expressions, so `geoff + 4` is the same as writing `geoff = geoff + 4`.

One last common operator that has changed in the upgrade from Flash 4 to 5 is the *in*equality operator. This used to be <> (that is, "greater than or less than"), but it's now been replaced with the logical operator != (where "!" means "not", so you can read this as, "not equal to").

The operator changes aren't the biggest of the changes to Flash 5, but they are pervasive, and they can catch you out, so it's important to bear them in mind.

Conclusion

In this introduction we've touched upon the new nature of Flash 5 ActionScript, and what it means for the Flash programmer. Flash has taken a headlong dive into the world of mature scripting languages and managed to pull off an 8.7, which isn't a bad result for a first attempt. There's a lot left to learn, and a lot left for this book to teach you, starting with some familiar-looking animation techniques in the next chapter, and leading into an integrated, XML-based interface in the final case study. No one said that the path to the peak of ActionScript mountain would be an easy one, but it'll be exhilarating and rewarding, and that's all you can ask for. It's time to tie up this protracted introduction, and get on with the journey.

Layout conventions

We've tried to keep this book as clear and easy to follow as possible, so we've only used a few layout styles to avoid confusion. Here they are...

- Practical exercises will appear under headings in this style...

Build this Movie now

...and where we think it helps the discussion, they'll have numbered steps like this:

- Do this first

- Do this second

- Do this third, etc...

- When we're showing ActionScript code blocks that should be typed into the Actions window, we'll use this style:

```
Mover.startDrag (true);
Mouse.hide ();
stop ();
```

- Where a line of ActionScript is too wide to fit on the page, we'll indicate that it runs over two lines by using an arrow-like 'continuation' symbol:

```
if (letters[i].x_pos == letters[i]._x &&
➥     letters[i].y_pos == letters[i]._y) {
```

Lines like this should all be typed as a single continuous statement.

- When we discuss ActionScript in the body of the text, we'll put statements such as stop in a code-like style too.

- When we add new code to an existing block, we'll highlight it like this:

```
Mover.startDrag (true);
variable1 = 35;
Mouse.hide ();
stop ();
```

- Pseudo-code will appear in this style:

```
If (the sky is blue) the sun is out
    Else (it's cloudy)
```

- In the text, symbol names will use this emphasized style: symbol1.

- Interesting or important points will be highlighted like this:

> **This is a point that you should read carefully.**

- `file names` will look like this.

- Web addresses will be in this form: www.friendsofED.com

- New or significant phrases will appear in this **important words** style.

Code download

All of the source files for this book can be downloaded direct from the friends of ED website at www.friendsofed.com, from there go to the code section then follow the link to ActionScript Studio to find all the necessary files. If you have any problems with the source files or the downloading, then contact us using one of the methods detailed below and we'll to our best to help.

Support

If you have any questions about the book, or about friends of ED, check out our web site: there are a range of contact e-mail addresses there, or you can just use the generic e-mail address: feedback@friendsofed.com.

There are also a host of other features up on the site: interviews with renowned designers, samples from our other books, and a message board where you can post your own questions, discussions and answers, or just take a back seat and look at what other designers are talking about. So, if you have any comments or problems, write us, it's what we're here for and we'd love to hear from you.

OK, that's the preliminaries over with. On with the show...

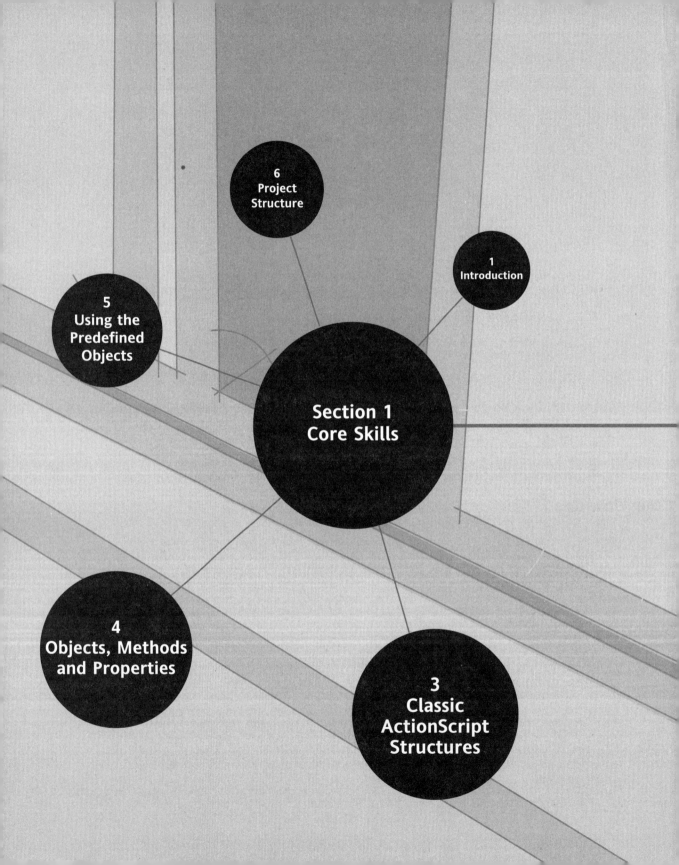

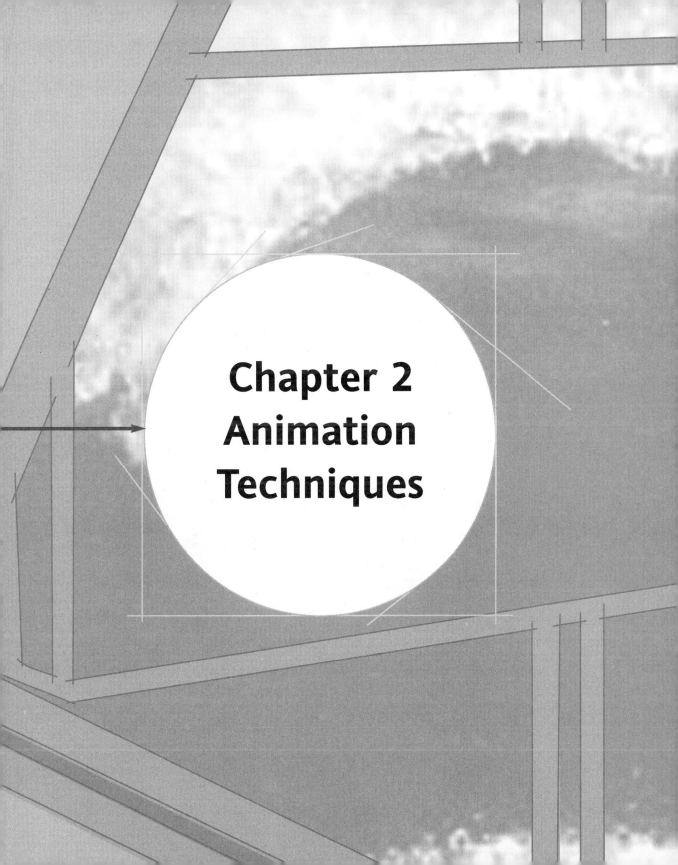

Chapter 2
Animation
Techniques

Whether you chose to read our little tour in Chapter 1, or you were already happy with the mechanics of ActionScript and the environment in which you write it, we're now going to assume knowledge of those things. Analyzing ActionScript as a programming language and a development environment is all very well, but if programming were our only desire, we'd be using Basic, or Java, or C++. We care about ActionScript because of what it can do for our Flash movies, and that's what we'll now begin to focus on.

In a book like this, where code might be held up as the be-all and end-all, a point worth making is that ActionScript is not always the right solution. It's instructive, therefore, to look briefly at what Flash can achieve *without* the use of ActionScript, so that we can start to see precisely where code might help in the creation of a Flash movie, and – just as important – where traditional, tween-based animation is the right way to go.

Traditional Animation vs. Dynamic Animation

If you speak to Internet users about Flash, most of them will say something like, "Yeah, Flash is cool. It does some great animations and stuff..." This reflects many casual surfers' understanding of Flash: it's an animation tool that's used for creating cartoons, banner advertisements, maybe a few buttons, that kind of thing. And of course, Flash is extremely good at these applications – they represent excellent ways of grabbing the audience's attention. A cartoon such as the one represented by the three images below is a fairly typical example of the genre:

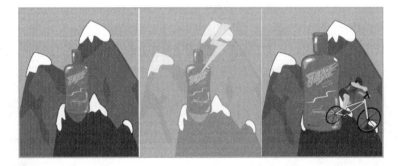

Of course, this has all the usual benefits that we associate with a Flash movie: with a SWF file size of around 50K, it's much easier on bandwidth than, say, an animated GIF file with the same content would be. Also, because it was created using vector graphics, it can be scaled to any size without loss of quality. But these are things you already know; what we need to examine here are the *characteristics* of this movie, so that we can see why it doesn't use ActionScript – and when your movies should.

This particular Flash movie was actually created last year by a friend of mine. If you hadn't guessed, it's an advertisement for a body wash geared towards athletes (we've changed the names to protect the innocent). Cursory examination of the movie's timeline would reveal movie clips that appear and disappear, sounds that come and go, motion tweens, and shape tweens. When you view the movie, you see an animation that starts at the beginning, runs to the end, and then begins again. That's what it was designed to do, and that's what it does.

If you were so inclined, it would be quite possible (once you or your colleagues had created the artwork) to use ActionScript, rather than tweening, to create a close facsimile of this movie. In the final analysis, the purpose of the code you write is to affect – directly or indirectly – the behavior of movie clips on the Flash stage. But in cases like this, I'd suggest that using ActionScript wouldn't make good sense. For a start-to-finish animation that doesn't require the use of numerous identical or similar movie clips, it's much easier for you and the others in your team to understand what's going on if you use 'visual' animation. And the greater the number of distinct images your movie needs (the cells of an animation, perhaps), and the less regular the movement you require, the more true that is.

However, creating animations like this is just one aspect of what's possible with Flash 5. The movie we've looked at here always does exactly the same thing: it doesn't attempt to keep the user's attention by changing its behavior from time to time, and it offers no opportunity for interaction. Of course, those things were never its goals, but there are countless other movies in which they *are* desirable, and it's then that ActionScript comes to the fore. Specifically, if you need your movie clips to interact with one another or with the user; if you want them to appear, disappear and replicate at times that aren't predefined; if you need them to move or behave according to the results of mathematical calculations; then ActionScript is the way to go.

Symbols

The production that is your beautifully crafted Flash animation is played out on a stage that involves many interwoven elements: levels, layers, timelines, frames, and symbols. The relationships between these elements are complex: levels and layers determine how things appear to pass behind one another; frames dictate the location of symbols or ActionScript code; and yet symbols – or at least, some symbols – contain timelines, which themselves are made up of layers and frames.

As ActionScript users, we're able to establish at least some control over all of this interplay, but our starting point for doing so is always through symbols – of which, as you know, Flash has three types: graphics, buttons, and movie clips. In this chapter, we're going to be focusing on the relatively straightforward task of getting objects on the stage to move at our bidding, so we'd better take a look at the options available to us in that regard.

Graphic Symbols

Graphic symbols are static elements in Flash – at least, as far as programming is concerned. When you place a graphic symbol on the stage, you can't give it a name – and without a name, there's no way for ActionScript code to get any direct control over it.

Button Symbols

Buttons are key interactive pieces of a Flash movie, and we know well that it's possible to attach ActionScript to buttons on the stage, with the intention (usually) of causing navigation of some kind to take place when the button is pressed. When it comes to animation, however, we encounter the same problem that we had with graphics symbols: the buttons on the stage don't have names, so we can't talk to them directly.

Movie Clip Symbols

Movie clips are another matter altogether. In terms of code-driven animation, and for a host of other reasons, they are the most important symbols in a Flash movie. For one thing, they can contain any number of other symbols (graphics, buttons, and even other movie clips), and they have their own timelines that run independently of the main timeline. For another, the movie clips that you place on the stage can have *names*, giving us the opportunity to communicate with, manipulate, and control them. If we want to see some ActionScript-driven animation, movie clips are the place to start.

Animation with ActionScript

As far as ActionScript is concerned, every movie clip symbol that you place on the stage and supply with a name is an instance of the Flash 5 `MovieClip` object. Each one of these instances has the same set of properties and methods that you can use to control how it appears, and how it behaves. Over the course of this book, you'll see many different techniques for creating and refining animation with ActionScript, but at heart they all come down to the manipulation of `MovieClip`'s properties and methods.

> *If the terminology is unfamiliar right now, don't worry about it. Hopefully, seeing it used in the cozy surroundings of some straightforward animation will give you a chance to become acclimatized before we assemble something more complex!*

Pushing a Movie Clip Around

Let's start the ball rolling, then, with a simple example of ActionScript being used to make a movie clip move around the stage. If you open the AS_ball.fla file in Flash, this is what you'll see:

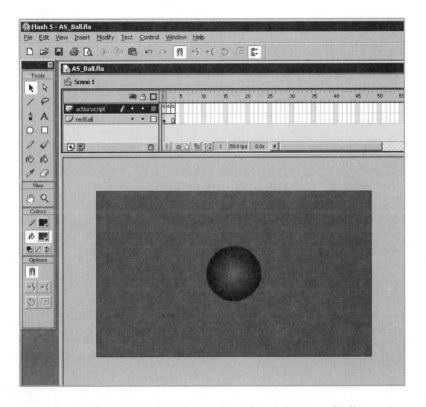

This, plainly, is a simple movie featuring two three-frame layers. redBall contains a movie clip (instance name: redBall) that looks a little like, well, a red ball, placed squarely in the center of the stage. If you test the movie, you'll see that the clip moves around the stage, appearing to bounce off the edges. However, there's no tweening going on here – one of the exciting things about ActionScript animation is that, as well as simply recreating many of the effects that are possible through tweening, we can imbue Flash movies with the ability to take decisions for themselves by using **conditional statements**.

The actionscript layer contains ActionScript code in all three of its frames, and it's through this code that the animation takes place. It doesn't work in a particularly difficult or unusual way, but it's still well worth looking at, because even a simple project like this introduces ideas that we'll see again and again over the course of the book.

Here's the ActionScript in frame 1:

```
xStage = 500;
yStage = 300;
xStep = 1;
yStep = 1;
```

This is initialization code that we'll only ever need to execute once. It defines four new variables that are potentially available for use from anywhere inside this movie. xStage and yStage are set to contain numbers that represent the size of the movie's stage, while the numbers in xStep and yStep will dictate how quickly the ball should move. The code in frame 2 then uses all of these variables:

```
redBall._x = redBall._x + xStep;
redBall._y = redBall._y + yStep;

if ((redBall._x + redBall._width / 2) >= xStage) {
    xStep = -xStep;
}

if ((redBall._x - redBall._width / 2) <= 0) {
    xStep = -xStep;
}

if ((redBall._y + redBall._width / 2) >= yStage) {
    yStep = -yStep;
}

if ((redBall._y - redBall._width / 2) <= 0) {
    yStep = -yStep;
}
```

This is where we use the if action to form four conditional statements that we supply to the movie clip as rules to be obeyed. Before that, though, the first two lines cause the position of redBall on the stage to change, by adding xStep and yStep to its _x and _y properties respectively.

The purpose of the conditional statements is then to keep the movie clip within the area of the stage. After each movement, we check to see whether the edge of the ball has reached or crossed the stage boundaries, using expressions like this one:

```
if ((redBall._x + redBall._width / 2) >= xStage)
```

In this movie, the ball's _x property represents the *center* of the ball, so it's not enough simply to examine where that is. To make decisions about the location of the *edge* of the ball, we have to bring another property – the _width of the movie clip – into play. By adding or subtracting half the width (in other words, the radius) of the ball from the coordinates of its center, we can determine where its top-, bottom-, left-, and right-most points are. If one of those has hit or crossed the boundary, we change the sign of one of the 'step' variables, and the ball begins to move off in the other direction.

Lastly, in frame 3, we have the following:

```
gotoAndPlay (2);
```

This call to `gotoAndPlay` just returns the movie to frame 2 every time Flash encounters it, so that the `redBall` movie clip instance will continue to update its position for as long as the movie is playing. It doesn't matter where you place the ball on the stage to start with, because that position never features in the calculations. The movie clip just keeps on bouncing off the walls.

No Strings Attached

While we're in this mood, open up `AS_ball2.fla`, and without looking too hard, give the movie a test spin, and you'll see... a bouncing ball that looks exactly like the one we had not two minutes ago! A quick glance at the timeline, however, will soon tell you that everything is not as it once was. For a start, it contains but a single frame:

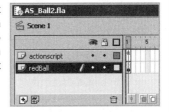

And if you take a look at the ActionScript code in frame 1, you'll see:

```
xStage = 500;
yStage = 300;

stop ();
```

The main movie is instructed to stop almost as soon as it starts, and yet the `redBall`, which is still located on frame 1 of the timeline, just keeps on moving. The answer, of course, lies with the `redBall` movie clip, whose timeline has a structure that you might find familiar:

What you're seeing here is what we described at the start of the chapter. The timeline of this movie clip runs entirely independently of the main timeline, which we know to have stopped (because we stopped it!). Before we declare ourselves satisfied and move on, though, this example has one last thing to show us. Look at the code from frame two of the clip:

```
_x = _x + xStep;
_y = _y + yStep;

if ((_x + _width / 2) >= _root.xStage) {
    xStep = -xStep;
}

if ((_x - _width / 2) <= 0) {
    xStep = -xStep;
}
```

continues overleaf

```
if ((_y + _width / 2) >= _root.yStage) {
    yStep = -yStep;
}

if ((_y - _width / 2) <= 0) {
    yStep = -yStep;
}
```

For the most part, this is simpler than what we had when we were controlling the ball from the main timeline, because we no longer have to specify the name of the clip whose properties we're manipulating. If we don't tell it otherwise, ActionScript assumes that we're referring to the clip containing this code, which is precisely what we want here. However, the lines that check the edges of the stage have something new:

```
if ((_x + _width / 2) >= _root.xStage) {
```

It wouldn't have made much sense to move the variables that contain the dimensions of the stage into this movie clip. It's the main stage that sets the size, so the variables belong there. However, by using _root, which is a special path that means, "Go back to the top of this hierarchy," we can access variables in movie clips that contain our own movie clip, just as we're doing here.

Movie Clip Properties

The effect we achieved in the last section used just three of the MovieClip object's properties – _x, _y, and _width – but there are many more, and they all hold values that say something about the state, the condition, or the appearance of a movie clip. All of these values can be interrogated from ActionScript code, and the majority can be changed in order to make something 'happen'. Learning what the properties of a movie clip describe, and what can be achieved by altering them, are the first steps towards a complete understanding of ActionScript-based animation.

Perhaps the easiest way to see a complete list of movie clip properties is to use the Debugger panel, which you can open via the Controls > Debug Movie menu item. This causes Flash to publish a movie in SWF format, and activate test mode.

If you do this for the original `AS_Ball.fla` movie, this window should appear:

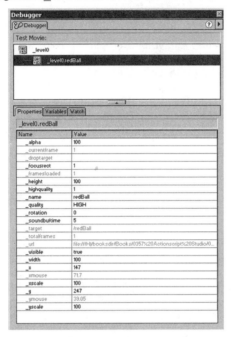

All movie clips – including the 'main' movie – have the same set of properties. The things that change from one movie clip to the next are their *values*. The list of 22 properties that you can see in the screenshot includes a few that are already familiar, some more whose purpose you can probably divine from their names, and perhaps one or two that are a little more mysterious – for now, at least. Unfortunately (from an author's point of view), there are at least three ways in which the properties can usefully be split into categories:

- Some of the properties may be read and changed by ActionScript code; there are others that can only be read.

- Some of the properties are directly related to the appearance of a movie clip on the stage; others hold values that are not immediately visible.

- *Most* of the properties have different values from one movie clip to the next, but there are just a few that affect the whole movie, whatever movie clip you change them from.

The split that provides the most even category separation is 'visible' against 'invisible', so that's how we'll do it here. As well as describing all the properties of the `MovieClip` object, however, the following tables include an extra column that fills in the other information: 'r' and 'r/w' indicate whether a property may be read, or both read and written to, by a user; while 'l' and 'g' describe whether a property is local or global in scope (that is, whether its value affects the entire movie).

Visible Properties

As explained before, the values of 'visible' properties have a direct consequence on the appearance of a movie clip. ActionScript animation involves widespread and frequent use of visible properties, and they're not difficult to understand:

Property	Attributes	Description
_alpha	r/w, l	The transparency of the movie clip, ranging from 0 (invisible) to 100 (opaque).
_height	r/w, l	The vertical dimension of the movie clip, in pixels.
_highquality	r/w, g	The anti-aliasing level of the whole movie. 0 means low quality, 1 means high quality, and 2 means best quality). This property is deprecated in Flash 5, in favor of _quality (q.v.).
_name	r/w, l	The instance name of the movie clip.
_quality	r/w, g	Taking the place of _highquality, this has four possible settings: LOW (not anti-aliased), MEDIUM (anti-aliased using a 2x2 grid), HIGH (anti-aliased using a 4x4 grid with some smoothing), and BEST (4x4 grid, anti-aliased, always smoothed).
_rotation	r/w, l	The orientation of the movie clip's y-axis, from 0 to 360 degrees, where 0 is vertical.
_visible	r/w, l	The movie clip's visibility on the stage, as defined by a Boolean (that is, true or false) value. If this property is false, movie clip is effectively disabled.
_width	r/w, l	The horizontal dimension of a movie clip, in pixels.
_x	r/w, l	The position of the movie clip's registration point on the x-axis of movie containing it.
_xscale	r/w, l	The horizontal scaling of the movie clip, as applied from its registration point, expressed as a percentage. A 100-pixel wide clip with its registration point at (0, 0) will become 50 pixels wide if you set _xscale to 50. The coordinates of the registration point do not change, however.
_y	r/w, l	The position of the movie clip's registration point on the y-axis of movie containing it. _yscale r/w, l The vertical scaling of the clip, as applied from its registration point, expressed as a percentage.

As you can clearly see, there's nothing about the appearance of a movie clip that you can't change by setting a property or two. However, you might also notice that there's a bit of a theme running through some of the descriptions: phrases like, "...of the movie containing it," are quite revealing, because they refer to the that the position, orientation, and scale of a movie clip are all expressed in numbers that make sense to the *container* of that clip. To see what this means, take a look at the following screenshot of the Spirals.fla project:

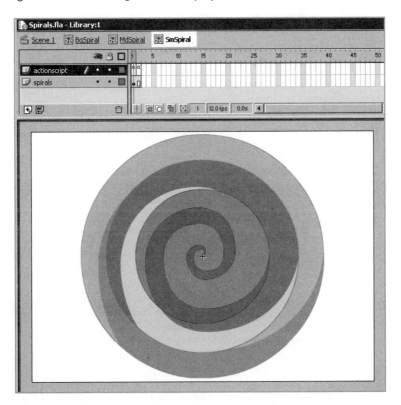

Here, the three spiral movie clips are arranged such that the large one contains the medium-sized one, and the medium-sized one contains the small one. It's a bit like one of those sets of Russian dolls; or you might hear it described as a grandparent...parent...child hierarchy. Either way, their timelines are set up so that each clip attempts to make per-frame amendments to its _rotation property – five degrees per frame clockwise for the inner and outer spirals, and five degrees counterclockwise in the case of the middle one. Before you read this, you might have expected testing this movie to result in all three clips spinning merrily away, but it doesn't.

What actually happens is that the middle wheel stays still, its counterclockwise movement being exactly balanced by the clockwise motion of its parent. Psychedelic!

Invisible Properties

In general, you'll use the 'invisible' properties of movie clips in decision-making code that causes changes in the behavior of your movies: "Where's the mouse?" "Has that movie clip loaded yet?"

Property	Attributes	Description
_currentframe	r, l	The number of the frame in the timeline where the playhead is currently located.
_droptarget	r, l	The path, *in slash notation*, of the movie clip over which this movie clip has been dragged.
_framesloaded	r, l	The number of frames that have been downloaded to the viewer's computer.
_name	r/w, l	The name of the movie clip instance.
_soundbuftime	r/w, g	The number of seconds for which streaming sounds should be buffered.
_target	r, l	The full path, *in slash notation*, of the movie clip instance.
_totalframes	r, l	The total number of frames in the timeline of the movie clip instance.
_url	r, l	The URL of the file from which the content of the clip came.
_xmouse	r, l	The coordinate of the cursor on the movie clip's x-axis.
_ymouse	r, l	The coordinate of the cursor on the movie clip's y-axis.

More often than not, these properties will be examined by the container of a movie clip, rather than by the movie clip itself.

Loading, Duplicating, Removing

The examples we've looked at so far have shared a number of common features, not least in terms of their structure. In every case, the movie clips that we've wanted to animate, or rotate, have been on the stage when the movie began. Of course, we could have changed things so that items sprang into life on frame 10, rather than frame 1, but we'd still be falling foul of one of the problems we identified with tween-based animation at the start of the chapter: the same things happen all the time, every time.

With ActionScript, it can be very different. You're not limited to working with the items that appear on the stage or the timeline at the beginning of a movie, because it's possible to load, duplicate, and remove movie clips from timelines dynamically. If you want to, you can load different clips into your movie, depending on the actions of a user, or the time of day, or completely at random. With a bit of careful planning, you could arrange it so that a user would have to come back to your site tens or even hundreds of times before they saw the same things twice.

Movie Clip Methods

Before we go ahead and look at some examples that demonstrate the techniques we were just discussing, it might seem a little odd that we haven't yet taken the time to look at the methods of the MovieClip object in the same way that we dealt with its properties. The thing is, though, that despite the fact that we introduced the MovieClip object with the useful fanfare of, "Properties tell us things about it; methods let us do things with it," we've been managing to make movie clips do some fairly interesting things without having to use methods at all. It's only now, when we're starting to think about what to do next, that our eyes are looking towards the methods for help again.

As we said a little earlier, animation in Flash 5 ActionScript is all about the MovieClip object, and the number and variety of its methods reflects that situation. Over the next few chapters, and starting right here in this one, we'll be looking ever harder at the MovieClip object, with a view to discovering exactly what it's capable of.

Duplicating and Removing Movie Clips

To begin our investigations of the more exciting methods of the MovieClip object (after all, we've been working quite happily with the likes of gotoAndPlay already), we're going to try to program the twin abilities of duplicating and removing movie clips on demand. Any time you need multiple movie clips that are identical or similar to one another, you can save yourself time by getting ActionScript to perform all those tedious copy operations for you. Used well, duplication can also significantly reduce the size of your SWF files, because no matter how many of them you have on stage, there's only one symbol in the Library.

The two methods of the MovieClip object responsible for duplicating and removing movie clips are duplicateMovieClip and removeMovieClip, and there are highly standardized ways of calling both. To demonstrate them, I put together duplicate.fla, whose picture you can see right:

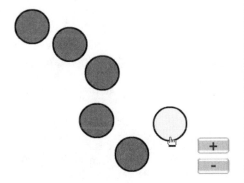

When the movie first appears, all you can see are a single circle, and the '+' and '-' buttons in the bottom right-hand corner. Clicking on the top button increases the number of circles on the stage (up to a maximum of six), while the lower button decreases their number (to a minimum of one). Most of the important ActionScript code resides in the two silver buttons, but in order to make the whole thing just a little more dynamic and interesting to look at, I put some in the circle too. (In fact, the initial circle is a movie clip that contains a button, getting us a useful hybrid that can be used with these `MovieClip` methods, but also has mouse-friendly button-handling features.) Here's the circle code, which you'll need to attach to the button inside the clip:

```
on (press) {
    startDrag ("");
}

on (release) {
    stopDrag ();
}
```

This is straightforward mouse handling that will be duplicated when we duplicate the clip... so it's about time we got on and did that. Here's the handler for the `on (press)` event that's attached to the '+' button:

```
on (press) {
    if (dupCount < 5) {
        dupCount++;
        _root["pinkButton"].duplicateMovieClip (
                        ➡"pinkButton" + dupCount, dupCount);
        _root["pinkButton" + dupCount]._x += 20 * dupCount;
        _root["pinkButton" + dupCount]._y += 20 * dupCount;
    }
}
```

That's not an enormous amount of code, but it does contain some new ideas, so we need to follow it through fairly carefully. `dupCount` is easy enough, though: it gets initialized to zero in the one-and-only frame of our main timeline, and thereafter ensures that we never make any more than five copies of the circle, by keeping track of how many exist at the moment. The really important line is this one:

```
        _root["pinkButton"].duplicateMovieClip (
                        ➡"pinkButton" + dupCount, dupCount);
```

Clearly, this is *where* duplication takes place, but how does it work? The first thing you need to know is that `pinkButton` is the instance name of the one circle that we have to place on the stage. Remember that, and take a look at `duplicateMovieClip`'s syntax:

```
MovieClip.duplicateMovieClip(newname, depth);
```

The easiest way to sort this out is to go from right to left. When you create a new movie clip on the stage, you give it a **depth**. The higher that number, the 'closer' it appears to the user. We're using `dupCount` to set it, so later copies will appear to be 'higher' than earlier ones.

Next, the new instances we're creating must have names, and we generate those by adding numbers to the end of the original instance name – so the first duplicate will be pinkButton1, then pinkButton2, and so on.

Finally, duplicateMovieClip demands that we call it as a method of an existing movie clip instance, here specified by _root["pinkButton"]. This notation, which (for reasons that will become clear later in the book) I call 'array notation', simply means, "The movie clip on the root timeline whose name is given by the string between the brackets." The same syntax is used to greater effect in the last two lines of the handler, which moves the newly created movie clip a little way away from its maker. When a movie clip is created by this method, it takes on all the property values of the clip that was duplicated, which means (among other things) that it occupies the same location. We move it just a fraction, so that the user can see the effects of their actions.

Having been through all that, the on (press) handler in the '-' button is much easier to cope with:

```
on (press) {
    if (dupCount >= 1) {
        _root["pinkButton" + dupCount].removeMovieClip ();
        dupCount- -;
    }
}
```

This checks dupCount to make sure that there's at least one clip around that can be deleted, and then proceeds to get rid of it by calling removeMovieClip, whose syntax is straightforward. With the duplicate gone, we decrement dupCount, and everyone's happy again.

The SwapDepths Method

Now that you've seen how to duplicate movie clip instances, and experimented with the sample file just a little, you may have noticed that there's something not quite right about the way your duplicated movie clips sit on top of each other: they maintain the levels that they were assigned by the duplicateMovieClip process. Happily, there's a solution to this slightly ungainly state of affairs, which is to use swapDepths:

```
MovieClip.swapDepths (depth);
MovieClip.swapDepths (target);
```

As you can see, there are two ways to use this method: you can either specify the depth you wish to attain explicitly, or you can specify a target movie clip with which to exchange depths. To try it out, we'll reuse duplicate.fla, with the following change to the code attached to the button embedded in pinkButton:

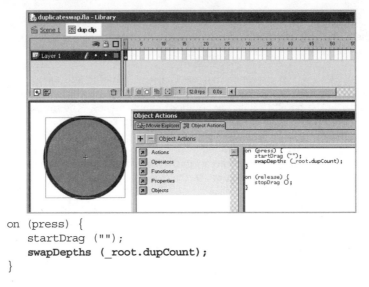

```
on (press) {
    startDrag ("");
    swapDepths (_root.dupCount);
}
```

This call to swapDepths without supplying an instance name works because we're calling it from inside the movie clip that we want to affect – and in the absence of any further guidance, that's exactly what Flash will do. As for the argument to swapDepths, we're providing an explicit depth: we know that _root.dupCount always holds the depth number of the 'highest' element on the stage, so it seems to make sense to reuse it here too.

Targets and Levels

On a few occasions in this chapter, we've talked about the idea that from an ActionScript point of view, there's not a great deal of difference between a Flash movie, and the movie clips it contains. At no point is this clearer than when we start to look at our final subject for this chapter: the methods at our disposal for loading one Flash movie into another, on demand.

Loading new movies from an external file is probably the easiest way of 'staggering' the download of your creation, so that users aren't left waiting around or – worse – giving up and going somewhere else instead. Rather than packing absolutely everything into a set of scenes, using the loadMovie method allows you to load your content piecemeal, on demand. If the user never goes near a part of your site, why should they have to download the data related to it? Thanks to loadMovie, they don't have to.

When you load a movie into your existing movie, you've a choice of two ways of doing so. You can load the movie into a **target**, or you can load it into a **level**. Though it sounds exciting, a target is actually just a movie clip that will be replaced by the movie you're loading – the name is a bit of a throwback to Flash 4, when all movie clips were referred to in code using the tellTarget command. The opportunities this offers, however, are certainly interesting, and you'll see more on this topic in Chapter 6.

Levels, on the other hand, are quite strange entities, and the first thing I should warn you is that regardless of what you may read or hear, there is no relation between the layers that we've been manipulating with swapDepths, and the levels we're talking about here. It's true that they both affect how far toward the 'back' or the 'front' of the stage things appear, but levels represent a different order of magnitude in that respect. You can stack the layers in a particular level as high as you like, but you'll never get in front of the next level up.

Loading into Levels

Your main movie – the one that appears when you double-click on the SWF – is *always* loaded into _level0. If you choose to do so, you can then load other SWF files into other levels, and the number you pick has a direct bearing upon whether the original movie will remain loaded in the browser, and how much of it you're able to see if it is. In the final example for this chapter, we're going to examine how we can communicate with the levels that contain the external movies we loaded, just as we've been doing so far with movie clips. Here are the rules that govern loading into levels:

Loaded Movie Levels

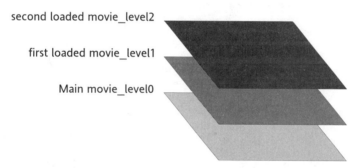

second loaded movie_level2

first loaded movie_level1

Main movie_level0

- The main movie (the one that will set the stage, and communicate with the rest of the external movies) will *always* be at _level0. Each subsequently loaded movie will occupy the next level in sequence, so the first loaded movie will be at _level1, the second at _level2, and so on.

- Movies at higher levels will overlap and/or obscure movies at lower levels.

- Loaded movies have transparent stages, which means that only the main movie at _level0 can determine the background graphic or stage color.

- Loaded movies set their position relative to the main movie from the top-left corner. Be careful when creating external movies that are smaller in size than the main movie.

- A movie loaded into _level0 will replace the original movie, but the size set by the previous movie will remain the same, regardless of the size of the movie being loaded, it will be centered and scaled to fit the original dimensions.

Here's a preview of the movie we're about to assemble. Open the file level_movie.swf:

The movie looks like a TV, with three buttons on the front, labeled movie1, movie2, and movie3. Test the movie by clicking on the buttons, and you'll see smooth transitions from between the scene that was there in the first place, and the one you selected. We'll now deconstruct this movie to see how the main movie can communicate with external movies that have been loaded into levels, just as though they were movie clips.

Open frame.fla, which you'll notice has only a blue border. This is the shell for the main movie. I'm sure you know how to create a similar border, so let's move on to the next step, and take a look inside movie1.fla. Here, you should see the layout and timeline exactly as in the screenshot below:

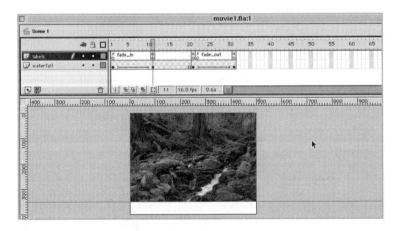

The movie contains a graphic symbol, with a tweened animation. If you study the animation, you can see it has a 'fade-in' introduction, then a 'fade-out' effect, using alpha values. The fade_out label here is very important, because we'll be using it to make the transition from one movie to the other. There's also a `stop` action at the end of each tweened animation, which is necessary to hold the playhead until the user decides to continue. If you open them up, you'll find that the other two movies (`movie2.fla` and `movie3.fla`) are set up in the same way.

Next, open `level_movie.fla`, and you should see something similar to the screenshot below:

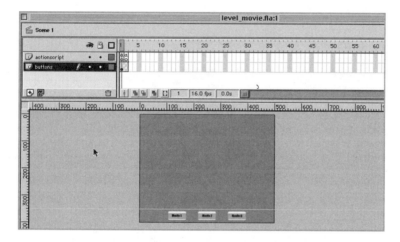

The ActionScript in frame 1 goes something like this:

```
loadMovie ("frame.swf", 4);
```

This `loadMovie` command brings the external movie `frame.swf` into level 4, which is the topmost level in our set-up.

Frame 2 is incredibly simple:

```
stop ();
```

It's just a `stop` action to hold the playhead at this particular frame, so that the user can interact with the movies. Now let's script the buttons:

Movie1:

```
on (press) {
    loadMovie ("movie1.swf", 1);
    _level2.gotoAndPlay ("fade_out");
    _level3.gotoAndPlay ("fade_out");
}
```

Movie2:

```
on (press) {
    loadMovie ("movie2.swf", 2);
    _level1.gotoAndPlay ("fade_out");
    _level3.gotoAndPlay ("fade_out");
}
```

Movie3:

```
on (press) {
    loadMovie ("movie3.swf", 3);
    _level1.gotoAndPlay("fade_out");
    _level2.gotoAndPlay("fade_out");
}
```

Each button has a loadMovie action that loads a movie corresponding to the name of the button. The tricky parts, if you can call them that, are the two lines following each of the loadMovie actions. Basically, they tell the external movies' playheads to go to and play the frame labeled fade_out, which will give a video-like transition when the action is triggered. That was pretty easy, wasn't it?

Conclusion

After this chapter, you should have sufficient understanding of the MovieClip object's properties to start to apply simple ActionScript to them, and be one step closer to creating complex interactivities in your Flash projects. The rest of the book will bring you more advanced knowledge, complex functions, and deeper coverage of other types of objects in Flash. Once you've learned all of them, you'll be ready to compete with the very best of the content on the Web today. Remember: always try to give something back to the Flash community and bring this technology to an ever-wider audience. Good luck!

Section 1
Core Skills

1
Introduction

2
Animation Techniques

4
Objects, Methods and Properties

5
Using the Predefined Objects

6
Project Structure

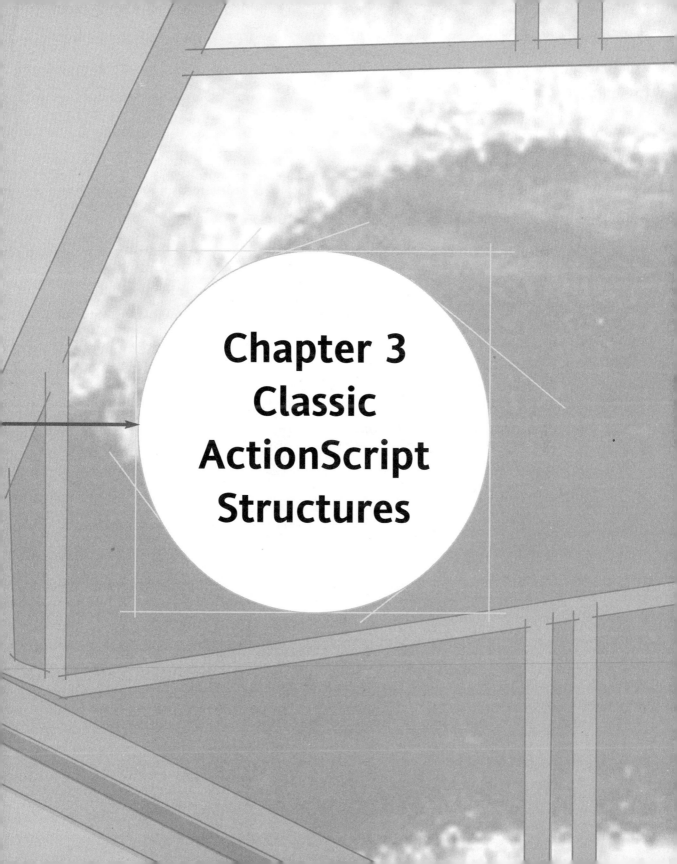

Chapter 3
Classic
ActionScript
Structures

As we've already begun to see, Flash 5 sometimes offers different approaches to solving the same problems, and you'll come across more situations where that's true as you progress. Our goal, of course, is to choose the right solution in each case. In this chapter, we'll be looking at three major themes in ActionScript programming – communication, control, and modularity – and examining what facilities are placed at our disposal with respect to each of them. You'll see some structures that you've seen before, some others you may not have encountered, and we'll talk about making the appropriate selection. Along the way, we'll step through the process of creating an advanced Flash application – namely, a hierarchical menu system.

Communication

Communication in your Flash movie – or more specifically, communication between different components in your movie – is the key to any kind of advanced interaction. In the previous chapter, you saw how code situated in the frames of the main timeline could send instructions and information to movie clips on that timeline through the use of dot notation, and how you can use _root and _levelN to talk directly to the main timeline of the current level, and any level, respectively.

In general, movie clips can be stored inside movie clips, inside movie clips, inside movie clips... to great depths, if you so require. While there are certainly limits on the extent to which this activity is useful, it can be a powerful technique if employed thoughtfully, as we'll see. In order to take maximum advantage of it, though, we'll need a means of communication that allows one movie clip to communicate directly with any other, and that's what we'll look at first.

Every movie clip on your stage has a property called _parent that can be used to refer to the movie clip that contains it. To see how that might come in handy, the figure below represents a Flash movie that has four 'tiers' of movie clips, some of which (on an individual basis) have the same names. The structure of the diagram shows that each one can be identified unambiguously from the _root timeline, but _parent gives us another way to accomplish the same task.

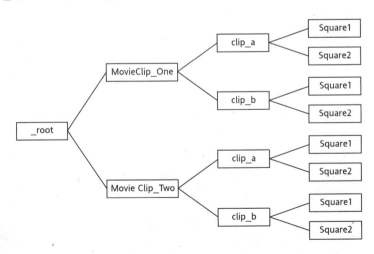

In the examples that follow, imagine that we're writing code in a frame of the movie clip at the top center whose full path is `_root.MovieClip_One.clip_a`. The following table shows the full paths of some of the other clips in the figure, along with a **relative path** that can be used to identify each one uniquely, *from our given starting point*.

Target	Path from _root.MovieClip_One.clip_a
`_root.MovieClip_One.clip_a.Square1`	`Square1`
`_root.MovieClip_One`	`_parent`
`_root.MovieClip_One.clip_b`	`_parent.clip_b`
`_root.MovieClip_One.clip_b.Square2`	`_parent.clip_b.Square2`
`_root`	`_parent._parent`
`_root.MovieClip_Two`	`_parent._parent.MovieClip_Two`
`_root.MovieClip_Two.clip_b`	`_parent._parent.MovieClip_` ➥`Two.clip_b`
`_root.MovieClip_Two.clip_b.Square1`	`parent._parent.MovieClip_Two.clip_` ➥`b.Square1`

As you can see, there's a unique path from any given movie clip to any other, just as there's a unique path from `_root` to any movie clip. For *any* two movie clips, one will be the 'parent' (or grandparent, or...) of the other, or else there will be a movie clip of which they are both 'children' (or grandchildren, or...). You simply need to find that common movie clip, and construct your path through it.

So now we've got two ways of doing more-or-less the same thing, but what has it gained us? Certainly, the relative path is sometimes shorter than the full path, so perhaps we should try to save some typing by using it when that's the case? That's not a great idea, and it's not what relative paths are for. Instead, imagine that the movie represented by the diagram is so fantastic that you want to use it in another project you're working on – one in which, however, it won't be starting on the main timeline. Wherever you put it, it's a good bet that `_root` in the diagram won't be `_root` in the new project, so any full paths you've used won't work properly. Paths using `_parent`, on the other hand, will be blissfully unaware of the change.

Example Menu System Part I

At the beginning of the chapter, I promised that we'd look at a hierarchical menu system. We'll start that project now, and add to it as we go along. The finished menu will look something like this:

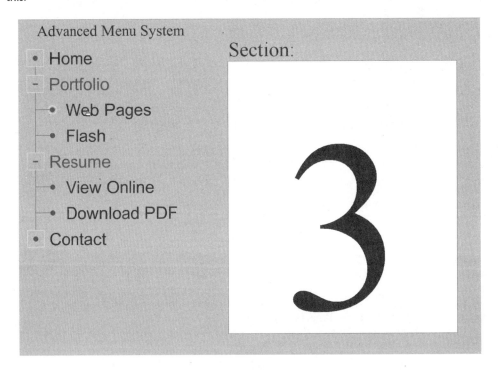

You've probably seen menus something like this before – they're usually built by creating a movie clip for each main menu item, and then placing a movie clip for each of *that* menu item's submenus inside it, on frame 2 (for example). This means that to build a menu, you need a unique movie clip for each menu, and one for each submenu. That sounds like a lot of work, especially if we want to make changes down the road. And whenever something does sound like it's more work than it ought to be, the chances are that we're considering it in a less-than-optimal way.

The best way to create a menu system would be to have *one* menu item movie clip, which would then be duplicated for every menu and submenu item. Even better would be if we could set all of this up in such a way that we could change the structure of our menu at any time – perhaps even on-the-fly. The question is: How do we begin to go about creating such a thing? You can probably guess that the solution's going to involve the relative paths we just looked at, but before we dash headlong into writing ActionScript, we need to create the pieces that will make up our menu.

As you'd expect, all the code for this example is available for download from the friends of ED web site, in the file called `Advanced_Menu.fla`. If you'd rather follow along with the development, though, kick off a nice, fresh Flash project, and create a new movie clip in which the finished menu will eventually be stored. I called mine Advanced Menu System.

We're also going to need a movie clip that will be used as the template that will be duplicated to create all the menu items in our menu. The movie clip that we'll be duplicating in order to build up the menu structure will be called MenuItem, and it will be the *only* thing that we need to build our menu. Basically, it will consist of three components: a dynamic text field to display our menu labels, a button that will capture mouse events, and a graphic to represent our button. Because we'll be using instances of the same movie clip for different types of menu items, it will need a little versatility. Specifically, the menu will have four different 'states': a main menu item that has no submenu items, one that can be opened, one that can be closed, and a submenu item:

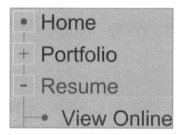

In the MenuItem movie clip, rename the first layer Actions and create four consecutive keyframes, placing a `stop` action on each. Then, create a new layer called Text, and place on it a dynamic text field with the variable name `text` in the Text Options panel. This will be the field we use to hold the text labels that we'll define later. Use the align tool to center the text field in the frame.

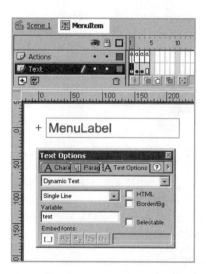

Also in this movie clip, create new layers called Symbol and BG. You can place graphics on these layers for each of the types of menu item that we need, each symbol in a separate frame. I made a gray square containing a plus sign if the menu can be opened, followed by a minus sign if the menu can be closed. Non-expanding menus will have bullets, while submenus will have bullets without the square background. Of course, these graphics are completely up to you, and have no effect on the broader operation of the menu.

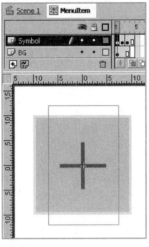
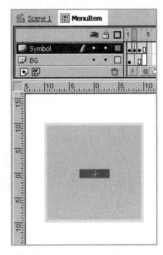
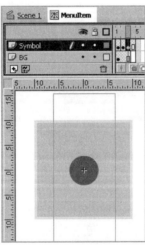
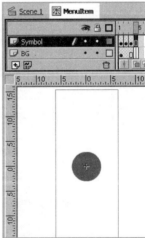

The last layer we'll need is called Buttons, and you can guess what it will hold. The button will cause something different to happen, depending on the state of the menu item at the time it's pressed, so you'll need to insert keyframes on frames 1, 2, 3, and 4 of this layer. As for the thing itself, create a new button symbol, call it Node Trans Button, and draw a rectangle in its 'hit' state that's the same size as your text field; this results in the creation of an 'invisible' button. On the stage, you'll see that the position of the button is indicated in cyan:

+ MenuLabel

As the final step for now, place your Menultem movie clip in the Advanced Menu System movie clip we made earlier, in a new layer called menu. Hang on to this until later on, when we'll add the frame scripts and button actions that make the menu come to life.

Control

All of the examples you've seen in this book so far have involved timelines containing single movie clips, but it's not hard to imagine a project with a timeline featuring multiple clips that all need to be animated at once – say, four balls bouncing around, rather than just one. It's not exactly a realistic example, but somewhere in such a movie, you might end up writing code that looked a little bit like this:

```
ball_1._x += xSpeed;
ball_1._y += ySpeed;

ball_2._x += xSpeed;
ball_2._y += ySpeed;

ball_3._x += xSpeed;
ball_3._y += ySpeed;

ball_4._x += xSpeed;
ball_4._y += ySpeed;
```

I don't know about you, but I got sick of typing that about halfway through. It got the job done all right, but there are two big problems just waiting to get you. First, imagine the amount of code you'd need for ten balls, or a hundred. Second, it's hard to change: imagine that I just finished coding the movement for 250 balls, and then decide that I want them to follow each other, instead of moving in straight lines.

While Loops

Looping is an idea that's new neither to programming in general, nor to Flash in particular, and the kind of thought experiment detailed above is one that's often brought out to demonstrate why loops can be useful. The idea is that having identified a longish series of commands that all perform a similar task, and/or look extremely similar to one another, you can write code that deals with the repetition for you. Here, for example, the four pairs of statements differ only in the numbers 1, 2, 3, 4 that appear. If we can make ActionScript count up to four, executing *one* pair of lines as it goes, we'll save ourselves some effort. Without further ado, here's the solution:

```
ball_counter = 1;
num_balls = 4;

while (ball_counter <= num_balls) {
    this["ball_" + ball_counter]._x += xSpeed;
    this["ball_" + ball_counter]._y += ySpeed;
    ball_counter++;
}
```

This is a `while` loop, and there's a good chance it will be familiar – for one thing, it's changed little since Flash 4; for another, `while` loops are shared by very many programming languages, so you could well have come across them elsewhere. In these few lines of code, though, we've got a couple of things to talk about. First, there are the mechanics of the loop itself. Second, there are the two lines that make up the action we were writing the loop for in the first place.

If this is going to work, we need to count from 1 to 4, so we set up variables holding those values before the loop begins. The nature of the `while` loop is then that the three statements contained between the braces will execute over and over again, *until* the expression in parentheses ceases to equate to a Boolean `true` value. In that respect, the last of the three lines in the **body** of the loop is important – if an expression featuring two variables is to change in value, at least one of those variables must be changing, and that's what's going on here.

The test represented by the expression, which is known as the **loop condition**, is conducted at the start of every loop. This means that it's possible to have a `while` loop that doesn't execute at all, if the condition turns out to be `false` straight away. Here, the condition becomes `false` when `ball_counter` reaches 5, and no further execution of the loop occurs after that time. Don't worry, though: there are plenty more where this one came from!

What, then, of that repetitive animation code we started with? For its appearance in the loop, it looked like this:

```
this["ball_" + ball_counter]._x += xSpeed;
this["ball_" + ball_counter]._y += ySpeed;
```

How about that? We've found another use for the 'array notation' technique for addressing movie clips that you first saw in the previous chapter! On each iteration of the loop, the expression between the square brackets becomes the string `"ball_1"`, `"ball_2"`, etc. A change, though, is that by specifying `this` rather than `_root` in front of the square brackets, Flash will attempt to access children of *this* movie clip, rather than children of the root timeline.

> *The ability to refer to the current timeline with* `this` *is a more useful device than you might at first imagine it to be, and though this may have been the first time you've seen it, it surely won't be the last.*

In partial summary, then, these six lines of code will run through the four balls and adjust their x and y positions, just like that long list we saw before. The real charm, though, is that if we had five, ten, or a hundred times as many balls, we'd need to change the value of one variable. If we wanted to change the *behavior* of all the balls, that would be a little harder: we'd have two lines to edit!

For Loops

Since we're on the subject of making our code neater, tidier, and easier to maintain, let's see if we can't shave a few more lines off our ball movement routine. As you know, while-type loops were the only ones available in Flash 4, but they make up just half (or, arguably, a third) of the looping capabilities of Flash 5 ActionScript. Thanks to its alignment with JavaScript, we now have for loops to play with as well.

Before we look at the syntax, I should say that because there are now two kinds of loops to choose from, questions inevitably get asked about which one is better – and you'll see people recommending one or the other in particular circumstances. As we'll see in a moment, though, the two are entirely equivalent, and which you decide to use is really a matter of familiarity and personal preference, rather than one of performance.

A for loop does exactly the same things as the iterative while loop that we were just working with – that is, it initializes a counter variable, describes a conditional test based on that variable, and increments that variable. The difference is that it does all three on one line! Let's look at the two loops together.

A while loop:

```
i = startValue;
while(i <= endValue) {
    ...
    ...
    i++;
}
```

A for loop:

```
for (i = startValue; i <= endValue; i++) {
    ...
    ...
}
```

These two are completely equivalent in function – the `for` loop just saves space, and looks a bit neater. Just for exercise, let's rewrite that ball moving code again, this time using a `for` loop:

```
num_balls = 4;

for (ball_counter = 1; ball_counter <= num_balls; ball_counter++)
{
    this["ball_" + ball_counter]._x += xSpeed;
    this["ball_" + ball_counter]._y += ySpeed;
}
```

I've just taken the parts of the `while` loop that were spread across three line of code, and compressed them into the one line. If you find this to be cleaner and neater than the `while` version, go ahead and use it; if not, that's fine too.

For..In Loops

When I 'argued' over whether `while` represents a half or a third of ActionScript's looping capabilities, the cause was a variant of the `for` loop that will become increasingly valuable as we begin to work with ActionScript objects in our Flash projects. It's probably easiest for me to describe the `for..in` loop if I first show you how it affects our favorite ball-animating routine:

```
for (ball in this) {
    this[ball]._x += xSpeed;
    this[ball]._y += ySpeed;
}
```

No, I haven't missed anything out. `for..in` isn't always the right solution – sometimes, for example, you really do need a counter variable – but in the right place, it can be very efficient indeed. What's happening here is that one by one, a reference to each of the movie clips in `this` timeline is assigned to `ball`. (In fact, you could call `ball` anything you like – with `for..in`, it doesn't matter.) That reference then gets used in the body of the loop, as before. When it has visited all the movie clips, the loop ends.

Actually, I've cheated a *little* here: `for..in` actually goes through all the *objects* in `this`, but since this little example doesn't mention anything other than movie clips being present, the technique is valid. If we couldn't be certain of that, there would be a few more hoops to jump through. The reason why it's potentially so useful is that in the right circumstances, you don't need to keep hold of a `num_balls`-type variable, and you can do away with having to assemble names from strings and numbers. It's a precision tool, rather than a blunt instrument, but it can save you time and effort.

Arrays

Over the course of the next couple of chapters, we'll be looking at all of the built-in objects that are available to you as a Flash 5 ActionScript programmer. One of these objects, however, is so enormously useful that it's a shame to wait until then – so we won't!

On a couple of occasions so far, we've referred to the technique of specifying the paths to movie clips by using square brackets as "array notation", without ever really describing what that meant. The term is not an official one, but it seems appropriate because it does bear a reasonable resemblance to using **arrays** in ActionScript. That, in turn, begs the question: What exactly is an array? To answer that question, we need to take a short backward step and ask: What exactly is a movie clip?

It might seem a strange thing to ask, but what I'm getting at here is that the `MovieClip` object is a complete toolkit for dealing with movie clips from code – the methods and properties of the object allow you to do and discover just about anything you could ever want to do with a movie clip. `Array` is another of Flash 5 ActionScript's built-in objects, and in similar fashion, it provides all kinds of facilities for dealing with arrays. Simply put, an array is a way to store a bunch of similar things in a single data structure, indexed by number – making them particularly apt for use with looping techniques. Let's see how.

One of the first things you need to know about arrays is that they're not just 'there' when you need them. Instead, you have to create an array of your own by using the `new` command, like this:

```
daysOfWeek = new Array("Mo", "Tu", "We", "Th", "Fr", "Sa", "Su");
```

With that line, you've created an array containing seven strings that might just come in handy were you ever to receive some data that represented the day of the week as a number. This is because, in order to 'get at' the values in the array, you use code like this:

```
day = daysOfWeek[4];
```

There (at last) are those square brackets, and you should also be aware that arrays start counting at zero, so the result of the above would be that `day` contains the string `"Fr"`. Conversely, if you ever decide that you *really* don't like Mondays, and things would be better all round if there were two Sundays instead, you could do this:

```
daysOfWeek[0] = "Su";
```

We'll be introducing some more demanding uses of the `Array` object as we progress, and as usual – once you know what you're looking for – the online documentation is a useful resource. As a final example before we continue, here's how you might access the array using a loop:

```
for (i = 0; i < daysOfWeek.length; i++) {
    trace(daysOfWeek[i]);
}
```

The length property of an array returns the number of **elements** in the array, and were you to assemble the sample code here into a movie, the names of the seven days of the week (abbreviated) would be sent to the output window.

Example Menu System Part II

In our menu system so far, we've created the movie clip pieces that we'll need. The next step is to define exactly what our menu will look like. To accomplish this, we need to figure out a way to represent our menu as a data structure – and since you now know how to use arrays, they would seem to fit the bill. To start out, I'm going to create an empty array called num_menus that will eventually store the structure of my menu:

```
num_menus = new Array();
```

The 'rows' of the menu (there were four in the screenshot at the start of the chapter: Home, Portfolio, Resume, and Contact) will be represented by an element of this array. Each of these 'rows' will have a main menu item, and zero or more submenus. Now, just as a movie clip can contain movie clips, which can contain further movie clips, so an array can contain other arrays, and we can use this idea to assemble the structure we're after.

The elements of our num_menus array are going to store arrays of strings that will be used as labels for the menu items whose positions they occupy. That probably sounds more confusing in words than it is in code; what I mean is that the sample menu, for example, would be set up like this:

```
num_menus[0]  =  ["Home"];
num_menus[1]  =  ["Portfolio", "Web Pages", "Flash"];
num_menus[2]  =  ["Resume", "View Online", "Download PDF"];
num_menus[3]  =  ["Contact"];
```

Hopefully, you can see how this arrangement reflects the appearance of the menus on screen, and you should also notice that in creating these new arrays, we haven't had to call new Array. Using a pair of brackets around the comma-separated list of values works just as well, and it's a neat technique to use when you're creating an array with a small number of known values.

To recap, we now have an array whose elements contain arrays, each of which contains one or more strings, which are the labels for the menu items. An array that holds other arrays is known as a **two-dimensional array**. Having done this, we're in a position where we know (or can find out using ActionScript) how many items our menu will have, the relationships between those menu items, and their names. In order to have a functional menu, we need to provide one more piece of information: we need to say what happens when a menu item gets clicked. Here are the rules:

- When we click on a main menu item that has submenus, it should reveal those submenus, thus causing the menu to expand

- Similarly, clicking it again should close the menu by hiding those submenu items

- Clicking on a submenu however, or a main menu that doesn't have any submenus, should be able to affect some other object, external to the menu

Normally, the menus in a Flash movie will navigate either to another location on the main timeline, or to the timeline of another movie clip. In our menu, we'll allow the user to specify both a target movie clip *and* a target frame for each terminal menu item. We'll talk about how to add the functionality that actually performs the navigation later, but for now we need a place to store this extra information. We *could* modify our array to accommodate *three* items of information per index, by using a movie clip or yet another array, but instead we're going to create two analogous arrays, one for each of these pieces of information. This will work out better for us in the long run for many reasons, not the least of which is readability.

Thus, we will make an array called target_menus, and another called goTo_menus. Furthermore, we'll populate them so that the structure of each is identical to that of num_menus. In the example below, I'm telling my menu that all of the menu items will be affecting a movie clip whose path from the _root level is test:

```
target_menus = new Array();
target_menus[0] = ["test"];
target_menus[1] = ["none", "test", "test"];
target_menus[2] = ["none", "test", "test"];
target_menus[3] = ["test"];

goTo_menus = new Array();
goTo_menus[0] = ["1"];
goTo_menus[1] = ["none", "2", "3"];
goTo_menus[2] = ["none", "4", "5"];
goTo_menus[3] = ["6"];
```

Now we have all the information we need in order to start building our menu. However, we're going to pause here for a while in order to talk about some more ActionScript structures that we'll need before progressing any further, which we will see again at the end of the next section.

Modularity

We've already talked in this chapter about not repeating work unnecessarily, and in this section we'll discuss how to write ActionScript code in ways that can centralize your code, making it easier to understand, easier to update, and generally giving you more control over your movie.

Writing loops enables us to repeat the same set of operations lots of times, in a single place. What if we wanted to do the same thing again from somewhere else in the movie, inside or outside of a loop? You might suggest cutting and pasting the code from one place to the other, but there are two huge reasons why that's a bad idea:

- All those repeated blocks of code will inflate the size of your movie.

- If you find something wrong with the repeated code, or if you decide to improve it, you've got to remember to change it faultlessly, everywhere. That's just asking for trouble.

Naturally, there *is* a solution for this scenario, and it's one that will become ever more useful in all kinds of contexts. Enter **functions**.

Functions

The ability to write a self-contained function is one of the most useful additions to ActionScript in Flash 5. As well as the advantage stated above, functions can be used as a way of making your code more readable, and to simplify complex operations. Let's look at how we can define a function, and at a few ways they can be used.

Function definitions always start with the `function` command, followed by the name of the function, and a list of **parameters** in parenthesis. Lastly, a pair of braces encloses the lines of code that make up your function, just as they enclose the body of a loop. We can summarize this list of rules as follows:

```
function funcName(parameter1, parameter2, ...) {

    ...function body...

}
```

Functions are enormously versatile, and it's difficult to do them justice in a short introduction – you'll get a much better feel for them when we begin to use them in our examples. However, it's worth looking quickly at a couple of the more prominent features. When you call a function that you've written, it looks exactly like calling one of ActionScript's built-in functions or methods, and that gives something of a clue to the options you have while creating you own.

For example, a method like `gotoAndPlay` requires that you provide it with an argument: the number of the frame you want to go to. If the function you're writing needs to be given an argument in order for it to work, you need to specify a parameter in the definition. We'll look at an example of that in a moment, but first we'll consider something else, and treat the two together in an example.

Code that calls `gotoAndPlay` looks unlike code that calls, say, `getBytesLoaded`, because in the latter case you're expecting the method to return some information to you. It's the difference between this:

```
myClip.gotoAndPlay(3);
```

And this:

```
bytesSoFar = myClip.getBytesLoaded();
```

To return values from your functions, you need to use the `return` command – and with that, it's time for a quick demonstration. Sometimes, it's useful to know the precise distance between two points, and one of the quickest ways to work that out is to use Pythagoras' theorem. Here's a function that returns the sum of the squares of two numbers that will accept as arguments:

```
function sumOfSquares (a, b) {
    return (a * a) + (b * b);
}
```

In the body of the function, you can refer to the values that are passed to you as arguments, by the names that you gave to the parameters. A typical call to this function would go something like:

```
distanceSq = sumOfSquares(3, 4);
```

After which, with a bit of luck, `distanceSq` should be set to 25. As I said at the start of this discussion, though, the best way to learn about functions is to encounter them in the wild, so let's keep moving for now.

Event Handling

One of the first things you learn when you begin to program ActionScript is that the code you write gets executed as a result of 'something happening'. You place some code in a frame on your timeline, and a few movie clips move around when the movie enters that frame. You attach some code to a button, and the movie skips to another frame when that button is pressed. These are the places where we've been writing our ActionScript in this book so far.

In terms of what we're about to discuss, the **event handlers** that we attach to buttons (like `on (press)` and `on (release)`) are key, because events lie at the heart of interactivity in Flash. Events are flying all over the place while your movie is playing, but nothing will happen as a result *unless* you've specified a handler. Back in Flash 4, your ActionScript code could only respond to the events associated with buttons, but in Flash a new type of event, the **clip event**, makes its debut.

Clip event handlers can be attached to any movie clip on the stage by the same means that button event handlers are attached to buttons: you select the movie clip, and type your code into the Actions panel. There are a total of nine events that you can look for and act upon, using handlers that take the form onClipEvent (*clipevent*). Here's a quick description of each:

load and unload: These events only occur once each in the lifecycle of a movie clip, when the movie clip is loaded and unloaded respectively. load is very useful for initializing the values of variables and defining functions that you'll need later in that movie clip, while unload can be used to clean up when a movie clip is deleted, or to trigger the loading of another movie clip.

enterFrame: This event occurs every time the playhead passes over a frame containing the movie clip. This event is most often used to create a single-frame loop, and it can also be used to centralize a frame script that would otherwise appear on multiple frames.

mouseMove: This event occurs every time the mouse is moved. This handler is very useful any time you have motion in your Flash movie that changes based on the mouse position, allowing you to update that motion only when the mouse actually moves.

mouseDown and mouseUp: These events are similar to the mouse events, press and release respectively, but they're not limited in scope to a specific area. Instead, they're triggered whenever the mouse button is activated. These events can be used to make a movie behave like a button, and they're handy to have around in Flash game creation.

keyDown and keyUp: Similar to the last two, these handlers detect key presses and releases. They're useful in any application where you want to allow either keyboard control of your movie, or text entry without a text field. You can also use the keyUp event to see how long a certain key is pressed, or to detect if multiple keys are pressed at the same time.

data: The last event is a little unusual, because it occurs every time something is loaded into the movie from an external source, whether that something is a set of variables from a text file, or an external SWF. It's extremely useful when you're dealing with some of the advanced Flash communication techniques that you'll be seeing later in the book.

Event Handling Example

Now that we know what the clip event handlers are, let's try an example. One thing that's always frustrated me in Flash is the limited functionality of the button, which is a remnant from a time in Flash before ActionScript. They work fine for simple movies, but they can't be addressed as objects, which makes them unfit for many dynamic applications. If you've ever tried to label a set of buttons dynamically, you may know what I mean. In this example we'll build a movie clip that behaves like a button. To get started, create a new Flash movie – I called mine MC-Button.fla.

In this new movie, create a new movie clip called MovieClip Button – and inside this, create two consecutive keyframes on the first layer: one for the 'up' state of your button, and one for the 'down' state. Place a stop action on each of these frames.

The button will perform a toggle operation, so we need a graphic on each of these frames to correspond with the state. You can draw a button or switch if you want, but as a minimum you should create a static text field with the word Up or Down in it, accordingly. I decided to make my button look like a futuristic light switch.

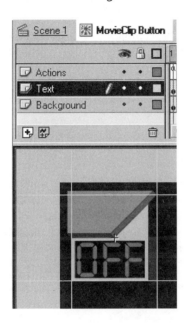 

Go back to the main timeline and drag your new movie clip onto the stage. Without deselecting the movie clip, open the Actions panel. Now, to start out our script, we need to write the clip event handler – *any* script code that resides 'on' a movie clip *must* be inside a handler. For this example, we'll be using mouseDown:

```
onClipEvent (mouseDown) {
}
```

This handler will be called any time the mouse button is pressed in the presence of this movie clip. Since we're making a 'button', we're only interested if the mouse is pressed while it's over *our* movie clip, so we need a way to filter out any other mouse presses – and to do that, we can use the MovieClip object's hitTest method.

You'll see more of hitTest later in the book, but for now you just need to know that when we pass in the current mouse coordinates from this movie clip, it will return true only when the mouse is over the movie clip. Notice that I've had to target the mouse position from the _root level – if I left the _root keyword out, I'd get the mouse's position relative to the movie clip, which would be a few hundred pixels off. The script below will only execute any code in the if statement if the mouse is pressed while it's over the movie clip.

```
onClipEvent (mouseDown) {
  if(this.hitTest(_root._xmouse, _root._ymouse, true)) {
    }
}
```

Event-wise, the movie clip is now behaving a lot like a button, but we want it to swap graphics too. Inside that `if` statement, we need to check to see which of its two frames our movie clip is in, and then send it to the other. We can do this with the addition of an `if..else` statement:

```
onClipEvent (mouseDown) {
    if(this.hitTest(_root._xmouse, _root._ymouse, true)) {
      if(_currentFrame == 1) {
          gotoAndPlay (2);
        } else {
          gotoAndPlay (1);
        }
    }
}
```

If you test your movie now, the button should be fully functional – all it needs now is something to toggle. Keeping with the light switch idea, I made a new layer in my main movie with two consecutive keyframes, each with a `stop` action. I drew a square as big as the movie in each frame, filling the first square with black, and the second with a white gradient. I want my button to toggle between these two frames, to make it look like a light is being turned on. In my script, the change could not be easier: we just tell the movie clip's `_parent` – the main movie in this case – to go to the correct frame.

Here's the complete script:

```
onClipEvent (mouseDown) {
    if(this.hitTest(_root._xmouse, _root._ymouse, true)) {
        if(_currentFrame == 1) {
          gotoAndPlay (2);
          _parent.gotoAndStop (2);
        } else {
          gotoAndPlay (1);
          _parent.gotoAndStop (1);
        }
    }
}
```

Clip events are incredibly useful scripting entities, and you'll find yourself using them ever more frequently. If you're ready, we will now move on to finish our menu system in the next section.

Example Menu System Part III

At last, the time has come to finish our menu. To review, so far we've built a menu movie clip that we know will be used throughout our menu. We've also constructed three arrays that hold the data we'll use to populate our menu. Now that all the preparation is done, it's time for the fun to begin. We have three tasks ahead of us.

- We already have a movie clip to represent a menu item in our movie, but we need to create and customize instances of our MenuItem movie clip to hold all the necessary functionality

- We need to write some code that will use the input arrays to create and populate the instances from step one

- We need to write functions that will operate our menu, including a function to draw the menu, and a function each to open and close a main menu item

Initializing the MenuItem Movie Clip

In order to populate our menu with movie clip instances, and to give each of the movie clips we create the necessary information, we need to write an initialization routine that will first duplicate a MenuItem movie clip, and then initialize it. The question is, what type of information should we put into the movie clip? We know that we'll need to include the information from our three input arrays, which we'll call label, target, and frame. We're also going to include some information that will help us to keep track of where each menu is in relation to the others in the overall structure, so row and col will be used to store its position in a two-dimensional array of menu items that we'll be constructing later, and counter will store an ID number for each MenuItem instance.

Therefore, following on from the arrays that we created in frame 1 of our Advanced Menu System movie clip, the initialization function starts out like this:

```
function newMenuItem(label, row, col, counter, target, frame) {
    duplicateMovieClip(menu, "menu" + counter, 200 * counter);
    menuItem = this["menu" + counter];
```

The first step in this function is to duplicate the single instance of the MenuItem movie clip, named menu, which I've placed outside the visible area of the stage. This movie clip is temporarily copied into a variable called menuItem. Next, we need to store the arguments that were passed into this creation function as variables inside the new instance of the movie clip:

```
menuItem.row = row;
menuItem.col = col;
menuItem.men_num = counter;
menuItem.target = target;
menuItem.frame = frame;
menuItem.text = label;
```

Last, but not least, we need to return the completed movie clip instance from the function. Now we can create new menu items in our movie, and not only will the data structure be set up for us, but the movie clip duplication will be handled as well, all in the one place. Being able to 'factor out' code like this is precisely why functions are so useful.

```
    return menuItem;
}
```

Before we move on, there's a very small helper function that's located at this position in the code, and now seems as good a time as any to mention it. In a little while, we'll have to revisit our MenuItem movie clip to add some actions to the buttons that we placed on its timeline. The button event handlers are going to call a function that will use the target and frame information to cause navigation to occur. Here's that function now:

```
function link(target, frame) {
    _root[target].gotoAndStop(frame);
}
```

Building the Menu

The next step in our movie is to use our new function, together with the input arrays we defined earlier, to create a menu. Throughout the creation process, we're going to maintain the two arrays I mentioned before: one, called menus, to hold our MenuItem instances; and another, called MenuItems, to act as a lookup table to access the instances by ID number. This may sound confusing, but the idea is simply to enable us to have the best of both worlds. When we want to know how the menu should look as a structure, we use menus; when we want to treat the whole thing as a single list, we use MenuItems. We'll also be using a variable called menu_counter to keep track of the current menu during the creation process. Let's go ahead and set these three things up now.

```
menus = new Array();
MenuItems = new Array();
menu_counter = 0;
```

If you recall the structure of our input array, you'll remember that it's actually two-dimensional. That sounds as though it might be tricky to use, but it's actually quite straightforward: the notation you use for access is simply extended, so that myArray[3][4] would refer to the fifth element of the array that's stored in the fourth element of myArray. (Remember, array indices are zero-based.)

In order to navigate a two-dimensional array, we need to use nested for loops – that is, one loop is placed inside the other, so that the 'inner' loop executes completely for every single iteration of the 'outer' loop. By using different index counters in each loop, we can access every part of our two-dimensional array. Let's look at the first part of our two for loops:

```
for(i = 0; i < num_menus.length; i++) {
    menus[i] = new Array();
    for(j = 0; j < num_menus[i].length; j++) {
        menu_counter++;
```

The first `for` loop is going to step through each array in `num_menus`. Inside that `for` loop, the first thing we do is to add an array to `menus[i]`. Now we can step inside `menus[i]` with a second `for` loop, and populate it with information from the three input arrays. The second `for` loop uses the length of `num_menus[i]` to iterate through the sub-arrays. Notice that we're incrementing `menu_counter` every time we run through the second loop – we'll be creating a new `MenuItem` instance every time we go through the loop, and we need to keep track of their ID numbers.

The next line uses the initialization function we defined above to create a new `MenuItem`:

```
menus[i][j] = newMenuItem(num_menus[i][j], i, j,
  ➥menu_counter, target_menus[i][j], goTo_menus[i][j]);
```

This is pulling in information from all three of the input arrays, in order to get all of the relevant information. Now that the `MenuItem` instance has been created, a reference to it is copied into `MenuItems[menu_counter]`. Think of this as a cross-reference system.

```
MenuItems[menu_counter] = menus[i][j];
```

Coming to the end of the creation code, we need to set a variable called `isOpen` in each instance that we'll use later in the `openMenu` and `closeMenu` functions. For now, just set it to `false`:

```
menus[i][j].isOpen = false;
```

The last thing we need to do to finish our menu is to decide what frame to set the movie clip to. This is decided by two `if` statements. The first `if` checks to see if this instance is in fact a submenu item, by testing if `j` is greater than zero. If it is, the movie clip is sent to frame 4. The second `if` statement, which is outside the second `for` loop, checks to see if the instance is a main menu item that has no submenus, in which case it's sent to frame 3:

```
        if(j > 0) {
            menus[i][j].gotoAndStop(4);
        }
    }
    if(num_menus[i].length == 1) {
        menus[i][0].gotoAndStop(3);
    }
}
```

We've now finished all the code that describes what the menu *is*. If you ran your movie now, however, it would look a little scary. We have not yet told Flash how we want to *display* the menu. To remedy this, we will write a drawing function, called `drawMenu`.

Positioning the Menu

The `drawMenu` function does one thing: it goes through the `menus` array, and positions each movie clip in the appropriate place. As you'd expect from any code that goes through `menus`, `drawMenu` has two nested `for` loops. Basically, it goes through the array, draws each main menu item, checks to see if each menu is open, and decides whether to draw that menu's submenus based on the answer. All along, it uses a variable called `v_offset` to increment the `_y` values of each successive menu item. After it draws each item, it will increment `v_offset` with that item's height. Take a look at the code:

```
function drawMenu() {
    v_offset = -150;
    for(var i = 0; i < num_menus.length; i++) {
        menus[i][0]._y = v_offset;
        menus[i][0]._x = 0;

        v_offset += menus[i][0]._height;
        if(menus[i][0].isOpen == true) {
            for(var j = 1; j < num_menus[i].length; j++) {
                menus[i][j]._y = v_offset;
                menus[i][j]._x = menus[i][0]._x + 20;
                v_offset += menus[i][j]._height;
            }
        }
    }
}
```

Once this function has been defined, it's a good idea to call it once, to set the ball rolling. In future, it will be called every time a menu item is clicked on.

Accessing the Submenus

Moving on, we have only two more functions to write: the ones that open and close the menus. Our main menu items need to be able to expand and contract their submenus, which they do by calling `openMenu` and `closeMenu` respectively. These functions are almost identical, one reversing the action of the other. The menu that is clicked will call these functions, at the same time passing its own `menu_num` to the function:

```
function openMenu(menu_num) {
    MenuItems[menu_num].isOpen = true;
    for(var k = 1;
            k < num_menus[MenuItems[menu_num].row].length; k++) {
        menus[MenuItems[menu_num].row][k]._visible = true;
    }
    drawMenu();
}
```

Both functions operate by accessing the menu item that corresponds to the parameter passed into the function. (Remember that MenuItems is a linear array containing all of the menu items that are in menus.) They each set the isOpen variable in the menu in question, openMenu to true, closeMenu to false. They also render the submenus visible or invisible, as appropriate.

```
function closeMenu(menu_num) {
    MenuItems[menu_num].isOpen = false;
    for(var k = 1;
            k < num_menus[MenuItems[menu_num].row].length; k++) {
        menus[MenuItems[menu_num].row][k]._visible = false;
    }
    drawMenu();
}
```

Congratulations, you have now finished this frame script! If you test your menu now, it should draw properly. What else is there left to do?

Activating the Buttons

There's actually only one small task left to perform: the activation of the buttons. If you remember, we placed a button in the MenuItem movie clip, but we never added any actions to it. Now that we have to define all of our functions, we can go back into that movie clip and finish the job.

Open the MenuItem movie clip, and select the button on the first keyframe. Add an on (release) handler to the script, inside of which we need to write two lines of code, as shown here:

```
// Frame 1 Button Script
on (release) {
    _parent.openMenu(men_num);
    gotoAndStop (2);
}
```

The first line inside the handler calls the open function we just defined back in the main movie clip, while the second line tells the clip to go to frame 2. In this way, the movie clip is toggled between open and closed states.

Here's the script for the button on frame 2:

```
// Frame 2 Button Script
on (release) {
    _parent.closeMenu(men_num);
    gotoAndStop (1);
}
```

The button script on frames 3 and 4 is slightly different, because it calls our `link` function, specifying the target movie clip, and the frame within that target. Here's the script:

```
// Frames 3 and 4 Button Script
on (release) {
    _parent.link(target, frame);
}
```

After you've completed these additions, you're ready to test out your menu. One thing you'll need in order to do so is a movie clip that the menu can drive. You can either make your own, or take a look at mine in the source file. The movie clip you need should have the instance name `test`, to go along with the data we hard-coded into our input arrays. It should have `stop()` actions on the first ten frames or so, and have some visual indication that those frames are different.

When your test movie is set up, you can experiment changing data in the input arrays. Want another menu? Just add one to the arrays. Now that you've put a bit of work into creating a robust menu system, you can adapt it to almost any need. Of course, editing three arrays is not very user friendly, is it? Never fear; in the next section, we'll discuss the **smart clip**, and how it can make your life (and your menu) much, much better.

Smart Clips

In order to allow Flash developers to create content that could be distributed more easily, Macromedia created smart clips. A smart clip is a special type of movie clip with editable parameters that can be changed on a per-instance basis, through the movie clip's Properties window. By using smart clips, developers can present other Flash users with user-editable parameters, while insulating them from the inner workings of the movie clip.

Creating a smart clip from a movie clip is fairly straightforward. Programming a movie clip so that it's *useful* as a smart clip can be more difficult. Whatever effect you're building, you need to make it so that it's easily customized by editing variables. For example, if you're making a custom button or interface element that you wish to turn into a smart clip, you should think about what aspects a designer might want to change. Any text or labels should obviously be dynamic, but what about the function that gets called when someone clicks your button? Is it versatile enough for others to use in their movies? What about the graphics? Can they be edited? Should you include different styles? All these considerations affect how much work you need to do to get your smart clip up and running. Of course, the biggest question to ask when designing a smart clip is whether it will be useful, for you and/or for others.

A Basic Movie Clip Chaser

To move from the abstract to the practical, and in order to demonstrate how a smart clip is created, we're going to take a simple gravitational 'chaser' effect and convert it into a smart clip. A movie clip chaser, if you haven't seen one before, is when one movie clip follows another around the screen, usually in such a way that it lags behind when the lead movie clip is in motion.

For this system, you need one movie clip that contains the effect, and two movie clips·containing graphics: one to lead, and one to follow. The motion is guided by a simple three-frame script, and contains two variables that control the type of motion in the effect.

We'll first build the effect in a movie clip, and then convert that into a smart clip. Start with a new project (I called mine SC-Follow.fla), in which you should create a new movie clip named Attraction. This movie clip will house our effect, and while you might not want to see it in production code, it helps to give it some kind of representation here. Place a static image of some kind in its existing layer, and then create a second layer called Actions, adding two new consecutive keyframes after the first.

Now create two movie clips; one named Lead, the other Follow. Inside each, draw some sort of graphic. What you draw is unimportant, but try to keep them small. (I used a gradient ball and a circle.) Then, place instances of both movie clips on another new layer in the Attraction movie clip. Name their instances Lead and Follow accordingly.

Our movie clips are set up, so we need to write the motion script. In order for one movie clip to follow the other, the first clip needs to be moving in some way. There are many ways you could achieve this, but for simplicity's sake we're just going to attach it to the mouse in the first frame of the Attraction clip. Also in this frame, we set up two variables. speed describes what part of the distance between the two clips the follower will travel per cycle: the higher the value, the smoother the animation – but the slower the follower moves as well. You may want to increase the frame rate of this movie to 30 fps or so. The air_friction variable describes how much energy the follower loses each cycle. A value of 1 will cause the follower to orbit perpetually; I find that values between 0.9 and 0.45 work well.

```
speed = 2;
air_friction = 0.7;
startDrag (Lead, true);
Mouse.hide();
```

> I'm also using the Mouse.hide() function, purely for aesthetic value.

In the second keyframe, we can then go on to write the main motion routine. The script itself is fairly straightforward. First, it calculates the *x* and *y* differences between the two movie clips. It then uses the `speed` and `air_friction` variables to increment first, and then to erode the follower's rate. The rate is then used to update the position of the follower.

```
Xdiff = Lead._x- Follow._x;
Ydiff = Lead._y- Follow._y;

Follow.x_rate += Xdiff / speed;
Follow.y_rate += Ydiff / speed);
Follow.x_rate *= air_friction;
Follow.y_rate *= air_friction;

Follow._x += Follow.x_rate;
Follow._y += Follow.y_rate;

updateAfterEvent(mouseMove);
```

The last line of the script calls the `updateAfterEvent` function to help keep the animation running as smoothly as possible. Lastly, add a `gotoAndPlay(2)` command to the third keyframe. This will cause the motion script to loop forever. If you test your movie clip, you'll see that the follower movie clip will move toward the lead movie clip, which is of course following the mouse.

Converting to a Smart Clip

Now that we have our effect up and running, it's time to turn it into a smart clip that will work with *any* two movie clips. We don't want to force people who use our smart clip to open it, so we need to take the 'lead' and 'follow' movie clips out of the 'effect' movie clip. First, then, delete the two movie clips from the Attraction movie clip's timeline (not the Library!).

Next, click out to the main timeline, and place the Lead and Follow movie clips on a new layer each. Give them instance names of `clip_one` and `clip_two` respectively. Once you've done that, right-click on the Attraction movie clip in your library, and use the library pop-up menu to select Define Clip Parameters.

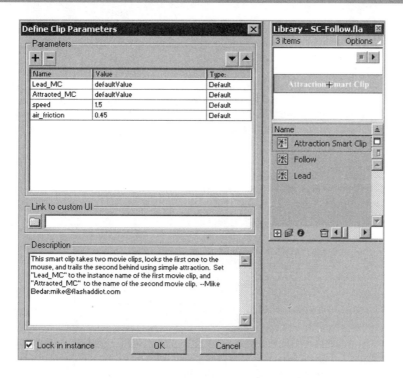

This is where we perform the magic that turns a movie clip into a smart clip. As we do so, you might notice that the icon in the Library changes from a movie clip icon to a smart clip icon. Follow the figure and make your dialog look like the one above. As you proceed, you'll surely realize that parameters you're creating have names that we used in our scripts.

Once you've defined them, clip parameters behave a bit like an extra set of properties – that is, they're common to all instances of the smart clip, just as all movie clip instances have the standard set of properties. Once the instance exists, you can read and write the values of the smart clip parameters, just as you would for standard properties.

We now need to edit our script to take advantage of the smart clip's capabilities. In frame 1, we can delete the declarations of speed and air_friction, because we will now be pulling this information from the smart clip's parameters. Also, since the movie clips we wish to affect are now one tier *above* this timeline, we need to re-target the script. Instead of using a complicated reference many times, however, let's make local aliases for the two movie clips. For that, we'll need to use the values from the first two parameters of the smart clip to create paths to the two movie clips. In the first frame of our smart clip, write:

```
Lead_MC = _parent[Lead_MC];
Attracted_MC = _parent[Attracted_MC];

startDrag (Lead_MC, true);
Mouse.hide();
```

Notice that we're actually writing over the values we get from the smart clip, by using those values to calculate paths to the Lead and Follow movie clip instances. With these simple modifications made, everything else should fall into place.

Something that's not immediately obvious, however, is how to *use* a smart clip, now that you've gone through the trouble of making one. Let's try this one out. Go back to your main timeline and select the smart clip. Go to the Window menu, and choose Clip Parameters from the Panels submenu. This will open up the user interface to a smart clip. You should see something similar to the fields you defined a few minutes ago.

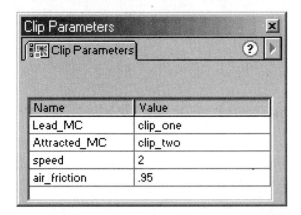

In order to associate the clip_one and clip_two movie clips with the smart clip, you need to type their names into the fields. The speed and air_friction fields should already have default values, but you're free to modify them. When you're ready, test your movie. The general effect should be the same as before. To show the power of the smart clip, try reversing the names of the movie clips in the Clip Parameters dialog. This should make the 'lead' movie clip chase the 'follow' clip.

Example Menu System Part IV

Now that we know how to make a smart clip, wouldn't it be great to make our advanced menu just a little bit *more* advanced, by making it 'smart' too? The problem is that while the standard Clip Parameters dialog is fine for a mouse trailer, it leaves a lot to be desired for a tool to build a dynamic menu. The idea is to make it easier, right? The last thing we want to force people to do is trudge through a clunky spreadsheet-like interface to define something like a hierarchical menu. What we need instead is a way to let our users build a menu *graphically*.

Thankfully, smart clips provide a way to do just this, because the come pre-packed with the ability to use custom interfaces. These interfaces, which are actually self-contained Flash SWF files, can contain anything you want, from a pretty way to present a few options, to intense interactive environments. For instance, if I'd wanted to make a custom interface for the mouse trailer example we just did, I would be able to let people use a slider to set the speed, instead of having them enter a number in the standard dialog. Taking the next logical step, I could even write some code in my custom interface to make sure that only values in a certain range were accepted, giving myself more control over how my smart clip is used.

Custom interfaces are a lot easier to create than you may think, but as with smart clips, you have to be careful not to let the process involve more work than the effect you're trying to control in the first place. When you make a custom interface, the goal is to transfer data from the interface to the smart clip as quickly and efficiently as possible. In the mouse trailer example, that data would be those four variables, and no more. In the much more complex example of the menu, however, we have three multi-dimensional arrays to transfer. The goal becomes to construct these arrays, and then bring them over to the smart clip.

But just how does information pass from the interface into the smart clip? The one requirement of a custom interface is that it must contain at its root level a movie clip called xch. This 'exchange' clip is solely responsible for communication between the interface and the smart clip. Basically, any variable that's in the xch movie clip is instantly available in the smart clip – but there are a few restrictions. First, the 'exchange' movie clip should *only* contain variables you want to transfer to the smart clip. It should not contain any graphics, movie clips, complex objects, or multidimensional arrays. It definitely should not contain any functions. These limitations mean that you must really plan how to get data from one movie to another – we cannot, for instance, pass our menu arrays through the 'exchange' clip, which is one of the reasons why I built the menu using those three arrays, instead of one array of more complicated objects. As it is, we're still going to have to do some translating at either end to get our menu data through.

We're now going to set out to make an interface for our menu. When we were coding our menu, we were building that menu from an array. Now, in the custom interface, we are going to build an array from a menu. I'm not going to go into quite the level of detail concerning how the menu-building code works as I did in the main menu example, since the aim of this section is to teach you how to use the xch movie clip in a custom interface, not how to make a menu maker. Besides, the code for building an array from a menu is remarkably similar to the code for building a menu from an array, if a little backwards.

Getting Started

Open up a new Flash movie, and once Flash has done its thing, create a movie clip called Exchange. Drag it from your library onto the stage, and give it an instance name of xch. The instance name must be typed correctly for this to work.

Create a new movie clip called MenuItem. Sound familiar? Inside this movie clip, you'll need to arrange three input text fields as best you can in a small space. Name them text, target and frame. These will be used to enter the corresponding information for each menu item.

Also in this movie clip you'll need two bigger buttons: an add menu button, and a delete menu button. Here are the mouse-event handlers for the two buttons; don't worry about the functions they're calling, as we'll be writing those shortly.

Add menu item button script:

```
on (release) {
    _parent.addMenu(row, "subMenu")
}
```

Delete menu item button script:

```
on (release) {
    _parent.deleteMe(myNum);
}
```

Back in the main timeline, you will need two more buttons (you can use the same symbols): one to add a menu *row*, and the other to delete one. Again, here are the handlers:

Add menu row button script:

```
on (release) {
    addRow();
}
```

Delete menu row button script:

```
on (release) {
    deleteRow();
}
```

As you can see from all of those calls, we have a few functions to write. Now that the movie clips and buttons are taken care of, we can concentrate on the main movie script. As you can probably guess at this point, the first thing we need to do is define some data structures. In fact, we need to create the four arrays that will correspond with those in our menu movie. Here are the declarations:

```
menus = new Array();
targets = new Array();
frames = new Array();
menuItems = new Array();
```

The arrays are starting off empty, since we haven't added any menus yet. We are also going to use two more arrays to help us keep track of the various menus that we'll be creating at runtime. These arrays are somewhat like the cross-reference array we used in the menu movie.

```
menuLookup = new Array();
menuItemLookup = new Array();
```

Everything from this point on is a function. In fact, there are five functions to define, four of which you've seen already in the button handlers. First, we'll define a function that will allow us to add a submenu to an existing menu row. This is by far the most complicated, partly because it needs to duplicate a movie clip and place it on the screen. The addMenu function takes the row to which the menu is being added, and a temporary label for the menu item to display.

```
function addMenu(menu, label) {
```

The next section of code goes through all the arrays we need to maintain, and updates them accordingly.

```
if(menus[menu].length < 6) {
  menus[menu][menus[menu].length] = label;
  targets[menu][menus[menu].length] = "";
  frames[menu][menus[menu].length]= "0";
  menuLookup[menuItems.length] =
    ➠menus[menu][menus[menu].length];
  menuItemLookup[menu][menus[menu].length-1] = menuItems.length;
```

Then it's time to duplicate a new *menu item* movie clip. After it's duplicated, the new menu item is placed in the menuItems array. It is then initialized with information regarding its place in the overall menu, as well as with default values for target and frame.

```
duplicateMovieClip(menuItem,
  ➠"menuItem" + menuItems.length, menuItems.length);
menuItems[menuItems.length]=this["menuItem"+menuItems.length];
menuItems[menuItems.length].myNum = menuItems.length;
menuItems[menuItems.length].row = menu;
menuItems[menuItems.length].place = menus[menu].length-1;
menuItems[menuItems.length].target = "_parent";
menuItems[menuItems.length].frame = 0;
```

Finally, it's time to use the *menu item*'s data to place it on the screen:

```
menuItems[menuItems.length]._x =
  ➠(menuItem._width - 22.5) *
menuItems[menuItems.length].place;
  menuItems[menuItems.length]._y =
  ➠(10 + menuItem._height) * menuItems[menuItems.length].row);
  menuItems[menuItems.length].text = label +":" +
  ➠menuItems[menuItems.length].row +"_" +
  ➠menuItems[menuItems.length].place;
  }
}
```

If you made it this far, you can breathe a sigh of relief, since most of the work is done in the addMenu function. Next up is addRow.

This function is fairly straightforward: it simply creates a new array in the next position in the existing arrays, and then calls addMenu to start the row off:

```
function addRow() {
    if(menus.length < 17) {

        menus[menus.length] = new Array();
        targets[targets.length] = new Array();
        frames[frames.length] = new Array();

        menuItemLookup[menus.length] = new Array();
        addMenu(menus.length, "Header " + menus.length);
    }
}
```

The next two functions are the opposite of the first two. Luckily for us, deleting a menu is much easier than creating one. To delete a single MenuItem instance, deleteMe uses the Array object's pop method to take the last MenuItem instance off the row in question. The row itself is determined by using the triggering movie clip's row variable, which was set when the MenuItem instance was created. The MenuItem movie clip itself is then deleted. Remember, just because you remove the reference in our array to a movie clip, it doesn't mean that the movie clip goes away. To get rid of it, you have to use removeMovieClip.

```
function deleteMe(menuNum) {
    if((menus[menuItems[menuNum].row].length - 1) >= 1) {
        temp = menus[menuItems[menuNum].row].pop();
        temp = targets[menuItems[menuNum].row].pop();
        temp = frames[menuItems[menuNum].row].pop();
        removeMovieClip(menuItems[menuItemLookup[menuItems
          ➥ [menuNum].row][(menus[menuItems[menuNum].row].length)]]);
    }
}
```

Deleting a row is even easier. All we do is iterate through the row, and remove all the movie clips. Then we simply pop the entire row off our arrays. Notice that when we want to deal with individual menu items, we use both indices on our array, but when we are dealing with a row, we only use the first.

```
function deleteRow() {
    for(i = 0; i < menus[menus.length].length; i++) {
        removeMovieClip(menuItems[menuItemLookup[menus.length][i]]);
    }

    temp = menus.pop();
    temp = targets.pop();
    temp = frames.pop();
```

```
            if(menus.length == 0) {
                addRow();
            }
        }
```

At this point, the menu-builder is almost done. All we need is a function to call that will take all the data from our menu builder and place it in the exchange movie clip in a usable form. Thus, we have the function, setXCH(). This function looks at our beautifully constructed menu and pulls out all of the important information. Since we can only transfer one-dimensional arrays to our smart clip, it flattens the information out into separate one-dimensional arrays.

```
        function setXCH() {
            xch.num_menus0 = menus.length;

            for(i = 0; i < menuItems.length; i++) {
                menus[menuItems[i].row][menuItems[i].place] =
                                                ➥menuItems[i].text;
                targets[menuItems[i].row][menuItems[i].place] =
                                                ➥menuItems[i].target;
                frames[menuItems[i].row][menuItems[i].place] =
                                                ➥menuItems[i].frame;
            }

            for(i = 0; i < menus.length; i++) {
                xch["num_menus" + i] = menus[i];
                xch["target_menus" + i] = targets[i];
                xch["frame_menus" + i] = frames[i];
            }

            trace(menus)
        }
```

Last, we call addRow at the end of our script, simply so that there is something there when the user opens up the menu-builder. We could call it a few times if desired, to give them a head start.

```
        addRow();
```

That about finishes the functionality for our interface. The only thing left to do is make a button that will call the setXCH() function. You can label this button Make Menu, or something similar. Just place it in your interface, and have it call setXCH() when clicked. Publish this movie, and place the resulting SWF file in the same directory as the menu movie. If you're confident that you did everything correctly, you can close this movie. Open up the menu movie so that we can make our menu a smart clip.

In the menu movie's Library, duplicate the Advanced Menu MC and name the copy Advanced Menu SC. Select the new clip in the Library and then choose Define Clip Parameters from the library menu, just like we did with the mouse trailer effect. This time, however, ignore the spreadsheet fields, and type in the name of your custom interface into the input field Link to custom UI. Make sure you include the file extension. You can then close this dialog.

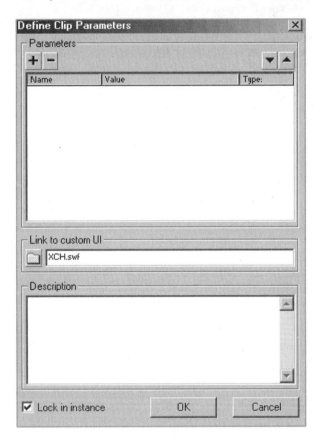

Now, place the smart clip on the stage, in place of the old movie clip. We need to make a minor modification to the main script in order for our menu to see the data that will be coming from the user interface.

Before we decided to use a smart clip, we described our menu by using three arrays. The main script in the menu movie clip starts off with this hard-coded description. Now that we're pulling this data in from the smart clip, setting up these arrays is no longer necessary. Instead, we need to take the information provided by the smart clip, and make it look like the arrays that the rest of the code is expecting. This can be done simply by using the smart clip information to reconstruct our arrays. It would have been nice to pass the arrays intact from the smart clip, but the limitation of passing only one-dimensional arrays makes this extra step necessary.

Open up the main script in your smart clip, and erase the three array declarations. Here is the code we're going to replace them with:

```
num_menus = new Array();
goTo_menus=new Array();
target_menus=new Array();

for(i = 0; i < num_menus.length; i++) {
    num_menus[i] = this["num_menus" + i];
    goTo_menus[i] = this["frame_menus" + i];
    target_menus[i] = this["target_menus" + i];
}
```

All this script is doing is creating two-dimensional arrays out of a set of one-dimensional arrays. The smart clip passes in a variable like num_menus5, which this script would place in num_menus[5].

With that final modification complete, we're now ready to try out our smart clip. Select it on the stage and open the clip parameters palette. You should see the custom interface we designed. If you don't, you may need to re-link the SWF file in the Define Clip Parameters panel. You may need to resize this panel as well, since the menu builder movie is a bit bigger than the standard interface. Try building a menu, and then hitting your Build Menu button. Nothing will happen right away, but when you publish your menu movie, the data from the custom interface should be used to build a menu. This data is persistent until you press that Build Menu button again.

If all has gone well, you should take a second to bask in the accomplishment. Not only have you made a really difficult project come alive, but you have also taken that huge step from a developer making content for Flash's end users (people viewing Flash content on the Web), to a developer making content for other Flash developers. Smart clips open up a new world of sharing work and ideas. Think about any cool effect you have ever made, and think about how you could make that effect infinitely reusable by making it a smart clip. I am sure that you can even think of a few ways to make this menu smart clip more useful.

Conclusion

This brings us to the end of our discussion of some classic ActionScript structures being used in innovative ways. If you've made it this far, you should have a fairly good idea of how complex programs can be constructed in Flash. More importantly, I hope you can see from this new perspective how much more there is to *do*. Sure, you now have all of the tools necessary to turn your ideas into hard code; but as I said earlier, the possibilities are endless.

2
Animation
Techniques

3
Classic
ActionScript
Structures

1
Introduction

Section 1
Core Skills

6
Project Structure

5
Using Predefined
Objects

Chapter 4
Objects, Methods, and Properties

Object-oriented programming (OOP) in Flash is easy, and don't let anyone tell you otherwise. It's even easier if you've never come across it in another programming language before, which sounds like a contradiction in terms, but I assure you it isn't. If you know how to use dot notation, and you know what a movie clip is, then you're already halfway there (although we'll probably destroy your understanding of movie clips in the next couple of pages). What's difficult about OOP lies in understanding how to use it to its full potential, and why you'd want to. That understanding is what will take your ActionScript coding to the next base – and once you start unconsciously thinking in OOP terms, you'll be hitting home runs.

It's quite possible to program ActionScript without a complete understanding of what objects are, and how they work. However, to use all of the new power in Flash 5 to create truly stunning effects, that knowledge is vital. Don't let that scare you though, because once you understand the general techniques for creating and controlling an object, you'll know how to create and control *any* object. Once again, Flash 5's dot syntax is the key to the puzzle.

Classes, Objects, Methods and Properties

If you've ever come across object-oriented programming before, in another language, then you may at first be slightly confused (or even irritated) by Flash terminology. In traditional OOP, you have two main structures: the **class** and the **object**. In Flash, there are also two main structures, but in this case they're called **object** and **instance**. Now, you may have noticed that the word "object" appeared in both of those descriptions, and you may therefore be thinking that an OOP object is the same as a Flash object. If only it were that easy. An OOP class is the equivalent of a Flash object, and an OOP object is the same as a Flash instance. Confused yet? The easiest thing to do here is for us to step out of the frame completely, and make up our own name for the whole shebang. From now on, don't think of it as OOP, think of it as IOP: instance-oriented programming. That'll either muddy things even more, or else clear them up a bit. Hopefully, it'll be the latter.

We'll be sticking to the Flash terminology in this chapter, so if you've encountered OOP before, you can put your learned terminology down and prepare to begin again. If you *haven't* come across it, then you'll be wondering what we were talking about in that last paragraph. Not to worry: this chapter will act as both an introduction to the novice, and a re-evaluation for the veteran. Enough of this introduction already – let's get learning!

The Basics

You've probably come across the word "object" before in your Flash travels – there's a menu full of them in the Actions panel – but you probably don't know *exactly* what it means. Let's take another look at that menu:

Under the `MovieClip` object submenu, there's another menu containing a list of actions that can be used with movie clips. This may have given you the impression that an object is just a container for a group of commands with related functionality. This is kind of right, but not

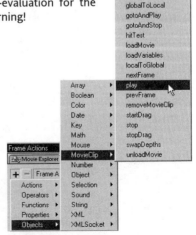

quite. An object is actually one step simpler than this: it's just a container, something that allows you to hold multiple pieces of data.

That's still not the *full* story, though, because objects also let you arrange that data in ways that make it easier to work with. There's usually a lot of abstract, conceptual stuff bandied about when people discuss objects, but we'll skip that and start with an object that we know you're familiar with: the MovieClip object.

You already know movie clips as, well, movie clips, but you probably haven't fully considered them as objects. Although movie clips are the only *visual* objects, they are still just objects: they're collections of data that happen to be displayed visually. When they start to talk about objects, programming books seem to have a habit of drifting off into discussions that compare them to physical things (for some reason, cars seem to be a particular favorite), but here we're going to describe objects, methods, and properties in Flash terms – and initially, we don't need to look any further than the movie clip.

Objects and Instances

Looking at movie clips from this angle, the first thing to notice about them is that in terms of their structure, they are all fundamentally the same. They still have _xscale, _yscale, _alpha, and all the other properties that we know and love. This is a common *template* of features that we expect all movie clips to have, and this standardization makes life a lot easier for us, because given *any* movie clip, we automatically know how to work with it. In Flash terms, this movie clip 'template' is called an **object**. We saw a list of all of the predefined templates in Flash earlier, under Objects in the Actions panel.

We also know that when we have a movie clip on the stage, we give it an instance name. What, then, is the 'instance' part? An instance is simply an object in the flesh. The MovieClip object is an unrealized possibility that only becomes definite when you drag it kicking and screaming into your movie. When it's born, you give it a name, a fact that makes it *unique*. Once you've given a name to a movie clip, you can differentiate it from other movie clips simply by using that name. The process of giving a name to an instance goes by the term **instantiation** – but again, why get tangled up with nomenclature? If you'd rather remember it as "entering something in the Name field of the Instance panel," you won't be hurting anyone. If you're starting to get the feeling that you've heard all this before, expressed in a slightly different way, then good! That's exactly as it should be.

Here's a question that may have crossed your mind, though: From the above discussion, if we instantiate an object by giving it a name, then a movie clip can't be an object all the time, because we can define a movie clip without naming it. If it doesn't have an instance name, then it's not a unique entity, and therefore it can't be an object.

It's a good question, but it's based on a flawed assumption. *You* might not give every movie clip an instance name, but *Flash* does. Open any FLA you've created in the past, then test it and use the Debug > List Objects menu to see the objects present in that movie. You'll see that the first movie clip to which you haven't given an instance name will be called instance0, the second will be called instance1, and so on. In the Flash 4 file I've opened, the Debugger is currently showing instance2837 and 2838 (that was some web site!). Every movie clip on your stage really does have an instance name, because behind your back Flash is making absolutely sure of it! This doesn't affect the way you work, but it does let you see how Flash is working behind the scenes – and knowing that will come in very handy as we progress.

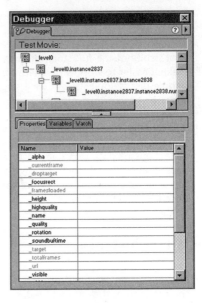

There are three broad categories that the predefined objects can be divided into. First, there are the ones that you only ever need one of, and which are always available to you in Flash, such as Math, Key, and Mouse. Then, there are the ones that instantiate themselves as and when you need them, such as MovieClip, Number, String, and Boolean. Last, there are the ones that you have to instantiate explicitly, like: Color, Sound, Date, and Object.

We'll look into the object definitions and their uses later on in this and the following chapters, but first we'll look into the other two structures on our list: methods and properties.

Methods

A **method** is just that: a method for doing something with an object. The relationship between objects and methods can be compared to that between nouns and verbs; the object is the noun or 'individual thing', while the method is the verb or 'action I want this thing to perform'. So if we have a movie clip on the stage with the instance name bill, we can use the code bill.play from the main timeline to start bill playing. play is a method of the MovieClip object, and it can be used with any instance of that object to make it play.

Earlier in the discussion, I talked about movie clips having a standard structure that we can apply standard techniques to when we create them. Well, software methods work on the same principle: because Flash knows what to expect of each predefined object, it gives us a set of standard methods to work with them.

As we just saw, the standard syntax for applying a method to an object looks like this:

```
object.method(arguments);
```

Where *object* is the object that the method will be applied to. This name needs to contain enough information for Flash to be able to reference a *unique* instance, so if there's a risk of ambiguity, you may need to include a path to the instance as part of this term.

Again, I can hear your arguments already, because you and I both know that we can use commands like `stop` without specifying an *object* at all. Once again, though, this is an illusion maintained by Flash, which *always* uses the *object.method()* syntax, *even if you don't*. In order to understand when you do and don't need to specify the *object* to which a *method* will be applied, you need to know the rules that Flash applies, and that's what we'll look at here.

In the particular case of the `stop` action, Flash is actually executing the following:

```
this.stop();
```

By quietly adding 'this' as the instance name, Flash is assuming that any call to `stop` for which the programmer doesn't specify otherwise means "stop the playback of the movie clip instance that this `stop` action is attached to".

Something else that's important to keep in mind is that in Flash, there are cases where methods and actions have the same name, but behave slightly differently. When you call a method, an assumption is made that an instance name will be specified – and if you don't do it, Flash will. If that sounds a little vague, a good example is provided by `duplicateMovieClip`.

When expressed as an action, `duplicateMovieClip` looks like this:

```
duplicateMovieClip(target, newName, depth);
```

When expressed as a method, on the other hand, `duplicateMovieClip` looks like this:

```
target.duplicateMovieClip(newName, depth);
```

target is no longer required as an argument, because it has already been expressed as part of the notation, cutting the number of required arguments down to two. But so what? What does this new way of saying the same thing give us over the less fussy Flash 4 way? Well...

- You understand what dot notation actually is, and see its inherent simplicity if (and only if) you embrace the object-oriented approach. Dot notation is integral to it.

- Irrespective of how you choose to write it, the `object.method(arguments)` is always the one that Flash actually uses. If you use the 'action' version of `duplicateMovieClip`, that's not what will be compiled – Flash will turn it into the method-based format, because that's the way it thinks. Getting closer to Flash means dreaming in the same colors Flash dreams in, and that palette is object-oriented.

- Where action- and method-based versions of the same thing exist, the former is there for the sole purpose of compatibility with Flash 4. It is entirely possible that such variants will become deprecated and disappear in future revisions of Flash, so for the continued use of your code, the word is to learn the structures that will last the course.

● The *object.method(arguments)* structure is consistent with the way you use any other objects in Flash, and being consistent is important. From ActionScript's point of view, there's nothing 'special' about a movie clip, so why treat it as though it's somehow different? If you think there should be a command to do something, you can usually guess what it will look like before you find it, because it will conform to the same structure. There are no commands with novel syntaxes in an object-based system!

Properties

Going back to our grammatical analogy, in which objects and methods were nouns and verbs respectively, a property is an *adjective* because it describes something about the object, such as its length, its height, its visibility, and so on.

Most movie clip properties can be set and retrieved directly using the `object.property` dot notation that we know and love, for example:

```
retrievedStagePosition = movieClip._x;
movieClip._x = setStagePosition;
```

However, this is not a universal rule – there are some properties that require a small amount of internal calculation before they can be retrieved. The reason for this can vary, but it's usually to do with the fact that something has to be done or calculated before the property value can be manipulated (such as setting a `Sound` object's volume property, which may have to be converted from an internal value before we can use it on a 0 to 100 scale).

A good example of this happening in the `MovieClip` object is provided by the `getBytesLoaded` and `getBytesTotal` methods, which can be used to give you the number of bytes loaded and the total download size for the current SWF file, if you target the `_root` movie clip:

```
onClipEvent (enterFrame) {
  percentLoaded =
    ➡ (_root.getBytesLoaded() / _root.getBytesTotal()) * 100;
}
```

This will give us what we're *really* trying to measure: the actual *proportion* of the file downloaded so far. You can easily modify this so that your pre-loader also tells you the total download size, and gives you a reading of the form:

```
83% of 120K downloaded.
Estimated time left 6 seconds...
```

Now that we've had a good look at objects, methods and properties in terms of the easy-to-understand movie clip object, we'll move away from graphical objects towards the real meat: data objects. We'll look at the creation and use of structured data using objects and methods. Later chapters will move on from this discussion to look at more specific objects, such as the `Color`, `Sound`, and `Math` objects.

Strings, Numbers, and Booleans

After all that talk of classes, objects, instances, methods, and properties, isn't it good to be back where you feel comfortable? Strings, numbers, and Boolean values – you add them; you multiply them; you perform logical checks on them. You couldn't possibly change how they work, because every movie, every program would be broken overnight. So that's all right then.

Well, that's true. Strings, numbers and Booleans *do* work like they always have, and they probably always will... but in Flash 5 ActionScript, you can *also* treat them like objects – and by doing so, you avail yourself of some powerful extra functionality.

Numeric and Boolean objects have only one real method to speak of: toString. This converts a Boolean or a numeric value to a string:

```
x = 30;
y = x.toString();
```

The result of these two statements is that y contains the string "30". When you apply toString to a number, you can also specify a different base for your conversion:

```
x = 30;
y = x.toString(16);
```

This time, the number 30 is first converted to base 16, and then converted to a string – so y becomes equal to "1e". This could be useful if you were doing something that allowed the user to create a color using red, green, and blue sliders (via the Color object, which you'll meet in the next chapter) and then read off the hexadecimal value that's required for HTML and JavaScript.

To convert a string back into a Boolean value, or a number, you use the Boolean and Number functions respectively. There's seldom a need to use them in new projects, but if you import an old Flash 4 FLA into Flash 5, you'll see these functions cropping up all over the place. The reason for this is that while Flash 4 tended to assume that all variables contained numbers (unless you told it otherwise), Flash 5 makes a stab at guessing what kind of value a variable holds, based on how you've tried to use it. If it gets this wrong while you're developing a project, you can take steps to fix it, so that's not a big problem. For a Flash 4 project to be *guaranteed* to work unamended, though, it has to take precautions – and that means wrapping a lot of code with Number functions.

Further proof of Flash 5's willingness to interpret what kind of value a variable contains based on context comes when you try to add things together using the + operator. For the three 'basic' types we're discussing in this section, the results are as follows:

```
String + {anything} = String
Number + Boolean = Number
Number + Number = Number
Boolean + Boolean = Number
```

If numbers and Booleans have gained only a little from their new object status, the same can't be said of strings. The `String` object has an additional property – `length` – and a good many methods that enable strings to be sliced and diced in a number of different ways. We'll wait until the next chapter before covering the manipulation of string methods in detail, but just to whet your appetite, here's a quick taster. To see the `length` property of a string, you'd write something like:

```
mystring = "hello world";
len = mystring.length;
```

This pair of statements would result in `len` being set to 11 – and once your code has that, you can do all kinds of things. The simple example below will extract the first word from the string "hello world", so that `firstWord` is set to "hello".

```
mystring = "hello world";
firstWord = "";
for (i = 0; i < mystring.length; i++) {
  char = mystring.charAt(i);
  if (char != " ") {
      firstWord = firstWord + char;
  } else {
      break;
  }
}
```

The `length` property is used as the test condition in the `for` loop that checks every character in turn via the `String` object's `charAt` method. If the character at position `i` is not a space, it's added into the end of `firstWord`. If it *is* a space, we stop the loop with a `break` statement. Notice here that the first character position in a string is 0, not 1.

You'll notice above that we never seemed to formally instantiate the `String` object. You can get away with simply initializing a variable with a literal, such as:

```
myString = "hello";
```

And then you can immediately start treating the variable as though it contains an object (in this case, a `String` object):

```
x = myString.length;
```

Flash realizes that you want to use a `String` object here, and will have already created the appropriate structure, so you can be sure that the property you're assuming exists here (`length`) actually *does* exist.

In the case of the `Array` and `Object` objects (and many of the others you'll meet properly in the next chapter), you have to do something a little more complicated. Before you can just go ahead and place data into an instance of the object, as shown above, you have to create (or **construct**) the instance. This is because some of the built-in objects are more complex than the simple data types we've met so far, and there are a number of different ways we can configure them when we construct them. This is actually a Very Good Thing, because rather than mess about with the previous object types to contain our data, we can now define objects that reflect the way our data is. Because of all this flexibility, Flash doesn't know exactly what we want defined, so we have to do it all explicitly. Flash can make no assumptions behind the scenes and hold our hands as it has done up to now; we are finally looking at object-oriented programming head on!

The Object Constructor

Defining a new object is actually very easy. We use ActionScript's new action:

```
myObject = new Object();
```

This creates a generic object called myObject, of the class Object. The Object object is a multipurpose device for creating one-off, lightweight, custom objects that you might need from time to time in your movies. (For example, you'll need one to call the localToGlobal and globalToLocal methods of movie clips, as we'll see in the next chapter.) This object is created with two default methods – toString and valueOf – but apart from those, you're free to create your own.

This chapter will concentrate on the Object object for now, but later on we'll look into the Array object as well, because it has a structure that's fundamentally different from the Object object, in that Arrays are indexed lists, and Objects have a definite hierarchy. We'll leave all the other objects to a later chapter, because you will first need to know a bit more about objects in general, and the Object object is the closest thing to a general object that there is.

Populating the Object

Once you've defined your empty object, you can start to initialize it – and at this stage, I think it's about time we started looking at objects up close and in the wild. You can see the final FLA for this exercise by looking at bouncy.fla.

In a new movie, add the following script to frame 1 of the main timeline:

```
screen = new Object();
```

And then test your movie. Use the Debug > List Variables menu to generate a listing in the Output window:

```
Output
Generator Installed                                    Options
Level #0:
  Variable _level0.$version = "WIN 5,0,30,0"
  Variable _level0.screen = [object #1] ()
```

You can immediately see that, unsurprisingly, a variable called screen has appeared. You can also see that it contains an instance of our object. We'll use our new screen object to tell us about our Flash stage's screen area by defining the edge limits, as shown in this diagram:

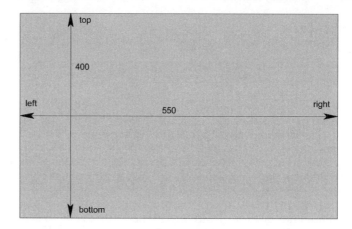

We'll then use the screen object in an animation, so that our controlling script will use this and other scripts such that our animated elements never stray outside the screen area.

Looking at our data, we see that there are two directions: x and y. The x direction is 550 pixels wide, and the two extreme edges in this direction are the stage's *left* edge and *right* edge. The y direction is 400 pixels high, and the two extreme edges are the *top* edge and the *bottom* edge.

We can define these four measurements as being a part of our screen object by using the same dot notation that we'd employ if screen were a MovieClip, rather than an Object:

```
screen.top = 0;
screen.bottom = 400;
screen.left = 0;
screen.right = 550;
```

You can place *any* object inside here; it's exactly the same as nesting movie clips inside movie clips on the stage, except that here we're doing it in code. We don't need to do it in this example, but if you wanted to add a new property that told you whether the screen was empty or not, you could easily add the following Boolean value:

```
screen.empty = true;
```

If you were creating a web site with multiple SWFs, and each one had its own screen object, a good idea might be to add a version number, so that the _level0 SWF could check that all the SWFs were the same revision:

```
screen.version = "1.2.4.beta";
```

_level0 could then check any loaded level against its own revision number:

```
if (_root.screen.version != _level2.screen.version) {
  _root.diagnostic = "version control error"
  _root.stop();
}
```

Here, we've used the structure of objects to set up a definite naming convention. By placing the dimensions of the screen in their own namespace, you are now free to use variables like height and width without any fear of name clashes.

Anyway, the code we're looking at right now is this:

```
screen.top = 0;
screen.bottom = 400;
screen.left = 0;
screen.right = 550;
```

If you add these lines beneath the line where we created the screen instance, and then look at the variables again, you should see this:

top, bottom, left, and right are now properties of screen. Although this is the way of initializing an object that you'll feel most at home with initially, there is a shorthand means of doing the same thing, which occupies just one line:

```
screen = {top:0, bottom:400, left:0, right:550};
```

Flash will automatically create a new object when it finds something assigned inside curly braces. The {} braces are called **object initializers**, and they're a quick way of expressing the same operation that we performed with dot notation above.

Now that we have this object, how can we use it? Well, we've created a simple object whose properties contain the screen dimensions. We can easily use this object to keep an animation from traveling outside the visible screen.

In the same project, draw a simple black circle with no outline stroke (omitting the stroke makes for a slightly faster animation).

Make it a movie clip with F8, and attach the following script to it:

```
onClipEvent (load) {
  directionX = Math.random() * 20 - 10;
  directionY = Math.random() * 20 - 10;
}

onClipEvent (enterFrame) {
  _x += directionX;
  _y += directionY;
  if ((_x < _parent.screen.left) || (_x > _parent.screen.right)) {
      directionX = -directionX;
  }
  if ((_y < _parent.screen.top) || (_y > _parent.screen.bottom)) {
      directionY = -directionY;
  }
}
```

You'll notice that we've used a method of the Math object here; all this does is give us a random decimal number from 0 to 1.

Copy the circle movie clip, and paste it onto the screen three or four times. With Modify > Movie, increase the frame rate to 18, and test the FLA. You'll see the balls bounce about via the property-based animation instigated by the enterFrame handler script's first two lines:

```
  _x += directionX;
  _y += directionY;
```

These lines continually add the directionX and directionY values to the _x and _y properties of each ball instance. If any ball hits one of the limits defined by screen, the appropriate direction is reversed, resulting in an apparent 'bounce' effect.

What we've done is to create an object that defines our screen area. This object has a structure that matches our screen perfectly: the Flash screen has four boundary values that we're interested in, and the screen object has four properties that reflect these same values, even though it's just *one* object.

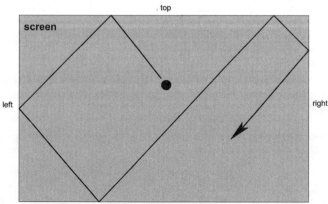

If we wanted to, we could create further `Object` objects – perhaps, for the sake of example, we could create an object called `bouncyBall`, which would have properties `xPos`, `yPos`, `xDirection`, and `yDirection`, instead of the several variables it has now. We would then no longer be thinking in terms of bouncing balls, but the interaction between the objects that are defining the animation. We would now think in terms of:

```
screen.top
screen.bottom
screen.left
screen.right

bouncyBall.xPos
bouncyBall.yPos
bouncyBall.xDirection
bouncyBall.yDirection
```

We have *abstracted* our problem, such that we can fully define it in terms of just two objects. We're no longer worried if the screen size changes, because our `screen` object will take care of that. What we *are* worried about is that:

- `bouncyBall.xPos` is always between `screen.left` and `screen.right`, and that if it isn't, we should change the sign of `bouncyBall.xDirection`, and

- `bouncyBall.yPos` is always between `screen.top` and `screen.bottom`, and that if it isn't, we should change the sign of `bouncyBall.yDirection`.

Learning this type of portable programming early on will stand you in good stead for your next steps in multimedia design, if you decide to advance to a more powerful platform such as Director.

A second important point is that the use of objects allows us to apply methods to the whole object (that is, to its properties) that stops us having to look inside the object.. We would achieve this by defining a standard method such as `collision`, and applying it like this:

```
screen.collision(bouncyBall);
```

Our object properties become hidden from us (because the method deals with all that stuff), and we no longer even have to look inside our objects; they become abstracted further and their internal complexity (or *properties*) become something we no longer have to consider. We just set all the objects and methods up and that's it!

Arrays

Arrays are enormously useful for storing, sorting, and searching through lists of data. The data can be anything from numbers to strings to movie clips, or indeed a mixture of them all, although normally they would all be of one type. An array is useful where the position of any data item in the list is significant.

Arrays are somewhat superceded in many cases by `Object` objects. You have to make more changes to the code with an array if the format of your data changes at all, and this change can be major, whereas with an object you usually only have to make changes to the code that looks after the affected properties. `Object` objects are easier to use with functions, and allow you to change your data quickly using *constructors* (which we will look at later), whereas arrays are extremely inflexible to changes in data structure.

Arrays' real advantage comes from the fact that they don't really need an object-oriented approach to be used (even though they're classed as true objects, in that they need to have an empty object assigned to them before they can be initialized with data). Rather than using lots of user defined functions and methods, an array-based implementation can be coded up using just a few loops and some of the predefined array methods to sift through the list. The following sections detail typical examples of their use.

Array of Strings

By keeping track of the position of an item in a list, you can perform conversions between a number and something associated with it. To be able to convert from the number representing the month, to a string containing the name of the month, you might set up a simple array of strings like this:

Item in array	Month
0	"January"
1	"February"
2	"March"
3	"April"
4	"May"
5	"June"
6	"July"
7	"August"
8	"September"
9	"October"
10	"November"
11	"December"

If you had a month 6, you would look at the array item number (6-1) ="June" to convert this number to a string.

Linked or Indexed Arrays

Sometimes, you want to search between linked lists. For example, if I wanted to keep a record of books and who wrote them, you might have the following setup:

Item in array	Book	Author
0	"Foundation ActionScript"	"Sham Bhangal"
1	"Flash 5 Dynamic Content Studio"	"Various"
2	"New Masters Of Flash"	"Yugo Nakamura et al"

This could easily be set up as an array of books objects with the following code:

```
books = new Array();
books[0] = {name:"Foundation ActionScript", author:"Sham
➥ Bhangal"};
books[1] = {name:"Flash 5 Dynamic Content Studio",
➥ author:"Various"};
books[2] = {name:"New Masters of Flash", author:"Yugo Nakamura et
➥ al"};
```

If I wanted to know who wrote Flash 5 Dynamic Content Studio, I would search through the books array until I found the element with that string stored in its name property, and then retrieve the string stored in its "author" property too.

Coordinate Systems

The storage of the (x, y) positions of a number of related movie clips could be stored in two arrays, as follows:

Item in array	xPos	yPos
0	23	6
1	45	17
2	56	-14

Here, the position in the list is the offset to the (x, y) coordinate of any given point. For example, to find the (x, y) coordinates of the second point in the list, you simply look at the second item in both arrays, item 1, which would give you point (xPos, yPos) = (45, 17). This could be simply defined with an object that has two arrays as properties:

```
myObject = {x:[23,45,56], y:[6,17,-14]};
```

Unlike many other languages, Flash doesn't require you to define the maximum size of your array up front, which can be a good thing – but watch out that your array isn't growing out of control and eating up memory behind your back, because this will probably kill the Flash plug-in. People always seem surprised when they hear a warning like this as they're sitting in front of their 4 GHz speedwhizz™ quad processor powerhouse, but it only takes a quick coding slip-up to bring them to their knees.

There are a number of applications that arrays tend to be very good at: working with strings (because arrays are a good thing to keep strings in while you're chopping and changing them), and creating tables of data. The example we'll look at once we've got functions under control will attempt to show how to create a collision detection system that uses a lookup table. This uses the simplicity of arrays to create a quick way of detecting collisions between many movie clips.

Functions

The major role that functions have to play when we're creating custom `Object` objects is that they allow us to do a number of things quickly, including:

- Creating and initializing a number of uniquely named but internally identical objects.

- Creating custom methods to go with our custom objects.

Before we start to extend ourselves, though, there are a few rules you must follow when setting up and using functions in Flash:

- If the function is defined in the same frame as the line that first calls it, the function *must* be read by Flash first – otherwise, it won't be defined when the call is made.

- If the frame containing the function is on the same timeline as a frame that calls the function, the function must be on a frame that precedes the calling script, and the keyframe containing the function definition must still exist.

- If the frame containing the function definition is on a different timeline from the script that calls it, the calling script must use the full path to the timeline, and the function definition must still exist on that timeline when this occurs.

- If the body of your function needs to create a variable, and unless you're otherwise certain, be sure to declare it with the `var` keyword, like this: `var name = value;` Normally, the variables you create in ActionScript are global, which means that they can be accessed from anywhere in a movie, as long as the timeline that created them still exists. Using `var` creates local variables that last only for the lifetime of the code block in which they're stored, which is usually what you want.

You've probably noticed that this is the same set of rules that apply when we're trying to get at the value of a variable: if the variable isn't there, or you're looking in the wrong place, or it isn't defined, you're not going to get it!

Have a look at `petals.fla`, which I wrote for the lovelorn. Touch the petals and whisper after me, "She loves me, she loves me not..."

The timeline for this FLA looks like this:

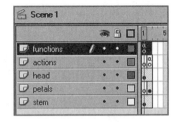

The functions layer contains the definition of the function that causes our petals to disappear. The actions layer contains a simple stop action at frame 2, to stop the main timeline from going any further. The head and stem layers contain the flower head and stem graphics, while petals contains our magic, disappearing petals. The script to do this makes use of our function, and to make *absolutely* sure that the function will be defined by the time I call it, I have placed the petals on frame 2, the frame after the function definition.

Okay, graphics first.

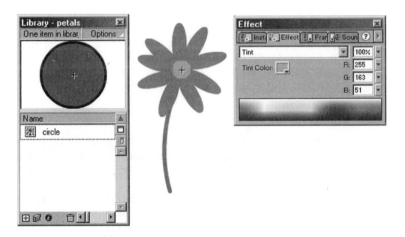

The whole flower, except the stem, is made up of instances of the circle movie clip, which is simply a circle that gets tinted, stretched, scaled, and rotated to produce my floral *trompe l'oeil* masterpiece that would make even Vincent envious.

Notice that none of the petals has been given an instance name. This is a little trick of mine that I've alluded to previously, but am actually using now: *If I don't give a movie clip an instance name, Flash will.* That I don't know the instance names might have been a problem, were it not for the fact that I don't actually care: my ActionScript will control the instances anyway, as you'll see.

Each of the red petals has a simple script attached to its `enterFrame` event:

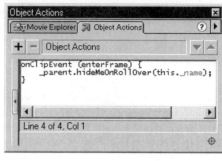

Each petal is calling the `_parent.hideMeOnRollOver` function with an argument `this._name`, which is the instance name of the current petal.

The function on frame 1 looks like this:

```
function hideMeOnRollOver (me) {
  if (_root[me].hitTest(_root._xMouse, _root._yMouse, true)) {
    _root[me]._visible = false;
  }
}
```

This function uses the movie clip method `hitTest` to see if a collision between the cursor and the petal movie clip has occurred. The key to it is my use of the `me` argument in the `object` part of the `object.method` syntax, which definitely bears some further explanation.

I am using `_root[me]` to identify the object whose `_visible` property I'll set to `false`. Each petal is calling the function with `this._name`, which is essentially saying, "the name I am known by". This is substituted for `me` in the function, which is used to form the path to the originating movie clip: `_root.theNameIAmKnownBy`. If the `hitTest` method evaluates as `true`, the function hides the original petal instance by making its `_visible` property `false`.

The final FLA is pretty cool, not only because the number of petals has been selected so that she always ends up loving you, but that there is the basis of a very powerful programming style here, and it is one that results in some sparse ActionScript: the whole effect is driven by the function itself, just three lines of code!

Using Functions with Arrays

The following movie is designed to demonstrate collision detection using arrays. As I mentioned earlier, the good thing about using arrays is that despite the advantages of more structured objects, they are simple, and if used properly can result in fast performance. Their combination with loops, and numerical indices, is also crucial to this example.

Have a look at `arrayTable.fla`. I haven't added all the bells and whistles yet to allow you to see the data at work, but we can use the debugger to see what is happening (and it's far more compact than the multitude of text fields we would have to show otherwise).

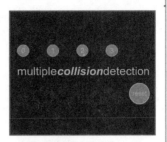

With the debugger active, you will see the following data:

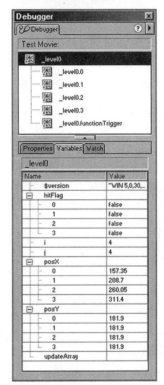

The example features three arrays: `hitFlag`, `posX`, and `posY`. Each of the three arrays has four items, numbered (as usual) 0 to 3. The two "`pos`" arrays hold the positions of the movie clips we are looking at for collisions – if one is detected, the appropriate elements of `hitFlag` will change to `true`.

The little numbered circles on the stage are draggable, and dragging them into each other will result in the two corresponding flags in `hitFlag` becoming `true`. The picture below shows the `hitTest` array's values when the movie clips labeled 2 and 3 hit each other:

	hitFlag	
	0	false
	1	false
	2	true
	3	true
	i	4

multiple**collision**detection

To clear the collision detection flags, simply press the reset button (although if used in anger, the individual animated objects would do this for their own collision flags, after they had moved away from their collision).

If you tried the sort of system shown here using Flash's inbuilt collision detection, you'd quickly realize that the latter is only really designed for collisions between one 'hitter' and one 'target', or possibly one 'hitter' and a number of targets. It's not really set up the situation where any movie clip is allowed to hit any other, as happens within animated effects involving particles, complex interfaces, or games.

As far as the project is concerned, the first thing to look at is the main timeline:

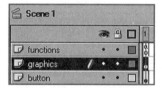

The `functions` layer contains our function, and its associated lookup table. The `graphics` layer contains our draggable movie clips, and the `button` layer contains the Reset button.

The script in the `functions` layer sets up a collision table consisting of movie clip (x, y) coordinates, as stored in `posX`, `posY`. (The movie clips themselves update these values, and we'll look at how this is done in a moment.) The final array, `hitFlag`, contains a set of Booleans all initialized to `false`.

The `updateArray` function looks at the `posX` and `posY` values to see if any movie clip's coordinates are within 20 pixels (in both directions) of any others'. If this is the case, then the `hitFlag` of both movie clips is set to `true`, denoting a collision. In a real application, the movie clips would be animating themselves, and would be constantly looking at this flag to see if they have collided. If they saw a `true`, one of a number of things might happen:

- One movie clip would change direction away from the other, probably by reversing its direction of travel. If both movie clips did this, you'd get what would look like a collision between billiard balls.

- One or both of the movie clips would be made to explode (I guess we're thinking about games in this option!).

■ One of the movie clips would perform some sort of navigation task, as part of a novel web site interface design. Although you might have difficulty seeing why an interface could require this sort of code, once you know how to do this sort of thing, the weird interfaces come out thick and fast!

An important thing to notice about the way the function works is the use of the `array.length` property to see how many times we need to loop to in order to cover all the array elements. Also, notice that the first `if` stops a movie clip from detecting collisions with itself – a common mistake to make in this sort of system.

```
// Define global collision table
posX = new Array();
posY = new Array();
hitFlag = new Array(false, false, false, false);

function updateArray () {
  for (i = 0; i < hitFlag.length; i++) {
     for (j = 0; j < hitFlag.length; j++) {
        if (i != j) {
           if (Math.abs(posX[i] - posX[j]) < 20) {
              if (Math.abs(posY[i] - posY[j]) < 20) {
                 hitFlag[i] = true;
                 hitFlag[j] = true;
              }
           }
        }
     }
  }
}
```

So what invokes this function? Well, we actually want the collision lookup table to be updated in every frame, and to do this I've attached the following script to a dummy movie clip (you can see it at the top left corner of the stage, just outside the stage area):

```
onClipEvent (enterFrame) {
  _root.updateArray();
}
```

Why do we want to update it every frame? Admittedly at this stage in the example we don't need to, but imagine the balls were actually constantly moving meteors in a game… that's what I was thinking when I made this example.

Finally, there are the movie clips themselves. The first problem we need to address is, "How do we know which movie clip is which?" Second, and even more importantly, "How do they know where their slot is within the collision table?" The answer to both is easy: they use their own name as an index into the table! The movie clip instances are called "0", "1", "2" and "3", as you'll see if you look in the top pane of the debugger.

Each movie clip has the following events attached to it:

```
onClipEvent (load) {
  me = Number(this._name);
  stop ();
}

onClipEvent (enterFrame) {
  _root.posX[me] = this._x;
  _root.posY[me] = this._y;
}
```

The load event handler looks at the movie clip's _name, and converts it from a string value to a number with the Number action. As well as being the place in the lookup table where the enterFrame event handler sends its current position (so that the updateArray function can check this movie clip's position against the other clips for collisions), the me variable is also displayed in the center of each movie clip; it's the number that appears to identify each movie clip circle. Sneaky, and altogether a much nicer set of techniques to learn than the 'arrays are good for cutting up strings within loops to create new strings and searches within larger strings' train of thought we could have gone down... good job this is a design book, then!

Using Functions in Object Creation

Once you get into the habit, you'll find all kinds of places where user-defined objects fit the movie you're creating – there will be some more examples over the course of this book. Sometimes, the solution you've come up with may require very many objects, or some with a large number of properties and methods. In that case, rather than laboriously having to add properties and methods to each new object in turn, we can use functions to create and initialize objects for us.

An example of this might come in the realm of real-time 3D geometry. To define a point in 3D space, we have to specify three positions: an x-coordinate, a y-coordinate, and a z-coordinate.

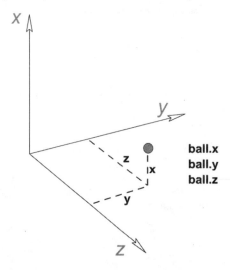

To specify a 3D position for our point, we might think of creating an object with properties called x, y, and z. To create a general function that will create an instance of such an object for us (a function of this type is called a **constructor function**), add the following code to frame 1 of a new movie:

```
function position3D (xPos, yPos, zpos) {
  this.x = xPos;
  this.y = yPos;
  this.z = zPos;
}
```

This function will add properties called x, y, and z, initialized to the values xPos, yPos, and zPos, to the newly created instance. To use this constructor to create a couple of new objects that can store 3D position data, add the following lines to the end of your script:

```
ball = new position3D(12, 34, 56);
origin = new position3D(0, 0, 0);
```

This will create new 3D position objects called ball and origin, as shown in the Debugger window if you test the movie in debug mode:

Properties	Variables	Watch	
_level0			
Name		Value	
$version		"WIN 5,0,30,0"	
ball			
x		12	
y		34	
z		56	
origin			
x		0	
y		0	
z		0	
position3D			

Suppose that you got your 3D engine working, and the origin and ball were correctly positioned in your 3D world, and you were really pleased with it, until a colleague mentioned that a bit of movement might not go amiss. Oh dear. You would have to start again, right?

Wrong. You can make your objects grow to accommodate the new situation, as illustrated in the diagram below. I've tacked something new onto the ball object: a property called speed.

To create motion in 2D animation, you have to add something to x and y. To get 3D motion, then, I have to add something to x, y, *and* z, and this needs to be reflected in the structure of my position3D object, as modified to handle things that move.

If I wanted to initialize my object to move straight upwards, as shown, with a speed of 5 units, it would mean defining a speed with x, y, z components of 5, 0, and 0 respectively:

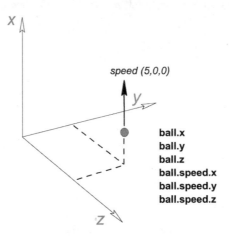

To add this new information to my 3D position object is actually a walkover. To frame one, add the second constructor shown below:

```
function position3D (xPos, yPos, zpos) {
     this.x = xPos;
     this.y = yPos;
     this.z = zPos;
}

function speed3D (xVel, yVel, zVel) {
     this.x = xVel;
     this.y = yVel;
     this.z = zVel;
}
```

To create the updated data object, you need to add the following lines to your object initialization:

```
ball = new position3D(12,34,56);
origin = new position3D(0, 0, 0);
ball.speed = new speed3D(5,0,0);
```

If you run the movie in debug mode now, you'll see that the structure of the `ball` object is now ready for the future of motion graphics in true 3D:

There are a couple of important points to notice here:

- The constructor that we used to add `speed` created a new `speed3D` object, but it knew that it was already in an existing object and added to that existing object to create a more advanced version of `ball`.

- Any functions (or, for that matter, methods, which we'll see in the next section) that were created to cater for the speed-less version of the `ball` instance will still work with the new version with `speed`. This means that you can build up your 3D world over time. You'd first build a static 3D viewer, with all the objects correctly drawn in 3D space, but there would be no motion. Once you were happy with that, you simply extend your objects with constructors, and write new functions that specifically deal with the new properties.

If you developed this train of thought, you could easily change the 3D routines that this route will create directly into a set of methods that act upon the `_x`, `_y` and `_xscale`, `_yscale` movie clip properties. You then have a portable engine that will act as a wrapper over the top of the standard `MovieClip` object to create 2D animation, plus the additional scaling to simulate depth. The use of the `Object` object in creating a wrapper that abstracts away from the standard `MovieClip` object, by sitting between the main code and the underlying `MovieClip` object, is discussed later in Chapter 14, where we create a zooming window object that acts as a wrapper for the `MovieClip`.

A major advantage of objects is that you don't have to rewrite old code if all you're doing is adding new functionality. You just add new data structures to your objects, and functions that will handle them! This is a side effect of object-oriented design: *truly modular code*. We're not talking about the Flash halfway house where you build modular movie clips, but rather about code that you can add to at any point, in a structured way. This is why you should use objects in preference to almost anything else in large projects. It isn't just cleverer; it's quicker, and therefore cheaper in the long run!

As a final exercise, you might want to have a think about why we didn't actually need to create the new constructor *speed3D*, and that this object construction script would have worked just as well:

```
ball = new position3D(12,34,56);
ground = new position3D(0, 0, 0);
ball.speed = new position3D(5,0,0);
```

For anyone out there with an inkling of trigonometry and how to set up look up tables to create fast 3D transformation routines, go for it! I haven't seen a true, object-oriented 3D engine out there yet, but it's only a matter of time... bet I don't write it before some of you do, though.

We're not quite there yet – there are even cooler things to come. We want to stop using functions, and do something even better: we want to define our own *methods*, allowing us to add new commands to ActionScript as we see fit, and changing the programming environment to fit in with the data objects we have created, rather than us having to fit in with it. It's all about creating wrappers over the `Movieclip` object to make it act like a bespoke graphic object – in the following case, a fluxDot. I'm deliberately avoiding the sentence, "We're changing the `MovieClip` into a new object", because that *isn't* happening. We're creating wrapper objects that sit between us and the movie clip – abstraction again.

Creating Methods

To turn a function into a method is actually very easy: you simply attach a function to an object. I could go on about a function that calculates the area of circles, and then make that function a method, but there's really no point. There may (possibly) be one person who actually wants to calculate circle areas in Flash using functions, but I refuse to believe that this same person would just *love* to do the same thing by creating methods. How about this as a better alternative: What if we designed some methods that created semi-intelligent animation?

Right then, have a look at `fluxdots.fla`. I don't really know what a fluxDot is (I just made the name up twenty minutes before writing it down), but I know what it appears to do:

A fluxDot is a little particle that seems to be dragged about by a number of magnetic forces. First, it seems to like the company of other fluxDots, and will generally try to congregate with them, unless something more interesting comes along. For example, it also seems to be attracted to a particular point in the center of the screen, which for the sake of argument we will call *home*. Finally, it seems to have a love-hate relationship with the mouse cursor. It usually hates being anywhere near the mouse, but just occasionally it gets a little braver – but not *too* brave.

The interaction of these three attractive/repulsive forces can create some dynamic patterns if you let it, particularly if you move your mouse in certain ways, and you can almost feel the forces that are pushing and pulling the poor little fluxDots around.

fluxDots are actually a little Flash 'toy' that came about while I was taking a short break from writing the earlier parts of this chapter. In terms of programming, though, they're pretty unusual in that they have their own ActionScript objects, and a couple of methods defined.

The object is called `sprite`, and it has two methods:

- `Sprite.repel` creates the fluxDot repel animation. This method tends to make a fluxDot hate the mouse cursor.

- `Sprite.attract` creates the fluxDot attraction animation. This is the method that the fluxDot uses to get back home.

Just in case you're interested, what's actually happening here is that there are two radial fields: one is centered on the mouse, and is repulsive; while the other is strongest around the center of the screen (`home`), and this is attractive. By superimposing the effects of these two forces, we're creating a nonlinear, attractive/repulsive surface across the face of the screen – it's rather like marbles moving on a rubber skin surface, with one area pushed down (home, because the marble tends to roll down the hole created) and the other pushed up (the cursor position, because the marble tends to move away from the slope created). When you stare at the screen, you're looking down on the surface from above, but if you took a more oblique view, the fluxDot's world would be as shown below:

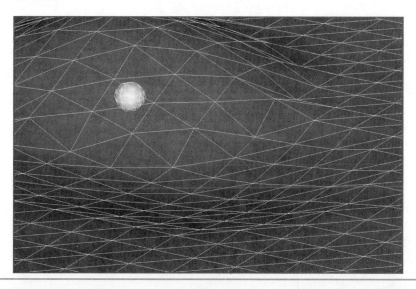

This setup is based around **topology**, a branch of math that looks at equations in terms of 3D sections, and maps the 'most likely path' a process would follow through the 3D landscape – rather like a ball rolling about along the peaks and troughs of the terrain.

Playing with attraction and repulsion is something that also has its roots in topology, and the reason why I wanted to animate such a strange world is that it's actually not as strange as it sounds: topology, and the interactions of repulsors and attractors, were the math tools that led scientists and mathematicians to stumble on a particular type of motion that had never been seen before: **chaotic motion**. I figured that this would be a suitable grand vision to add object-oriented design into, and that setting up this world might be a way to visualize my understanding of chaotic motion.

> *As an aside, if you want to know the sorts of thought processes that go into deciding on these strange flights of Flash fantasy, I talk about a typical thought process in detail when we look at designing an advanced Flash interface from scratch later in the book.*

The first thing to notice about the project is that I've done away with the idea of calling a function in a frame after the one in which it's defined, because although I've got a number of function calls in frame 1, they're all attached to `enterFrame` handlers in my little fluxDots that won't execute until the SWF has run through one frame. This is because the first event to occur will be `load`:

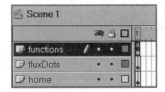

The home layer just contains some static graphics that make up the background, so we won't consider it here. The first bits of code that we *should* look at are the event scripts attached to the fluxDot itself. You might have trouble locating it, but you should find it just off the bottom right corner of the stage, near the *fluxdots* text:

fluxDot

Select the dot (it's actually a single instance of the dot movie clip), and open the Actions panel to see the code:

```
onClipEvent (load) {
  sprite = new Object();
  sprite.repel = _root.pushMe;
  sprite.attract = _root.pullMe;

  if (_name == "dot") {
    for (i = 0; i < 40; i++) {
      this.duplicateMovieclip("dot" + i, i);
    }
  }
}

onClipEvent (enterFrame) {
  sprite.repel(_name);
  sprite.attract(_name);
}
```

The first thing we do (via *a* load event handler) is to create a new object called sprite, with what look like two properties: repel and attract. These assigned with two things that appear to be variables: _root.pushMe and _root.pullMe. We'll look at pushMe and pullMe in a moment, but I can tell you now that they're not variables; they're *functions* – and notice that they're referenced without any arguments. After this has been done, I've written a for loop that duplicates my little square fluxDot 40 times.

The enterFrame event handler contains the script that does the main work of the animation... but the script is almost empty, and consists of just two actions!

These two actions are methods of the sprite object. Don't bother looking for this object or its methods in the ActionScript reference book, though, because they're not there – they're special commands to do with creating fluxDot topology-based animations, and I defined them myself. You can use them in your FLAs, and one day you might want to look at more complex methods of the sprite object, but for now I'll show you just the fluxDot methods.

The code that actually defines these actions is in the pushMe and pullMe functions, and they're in the functions layer. Have a look at the script on frame 1:

```
screen = new Object();
screen = {left:0, right:550, top:0, bottom:400};
screen.centerX = screen.right/2;
screen.centerY = screen.bottom/2;
//
function pushMe (me) {
    xDiff = [me]._x-_xmouse;
    yDiff = [me]._y-_ymouse;
    if (Math.abs(xDiff+yDiff)<100) {
        if (xDiff>0) {
            _root[me]._x += (100-xDiff)/10;
        } else {
            _root[me]._x -= (100+xDiff)/10;
        }
        if (yDiff>0) {
            _root[me]._y += (100-yDiff)/10;
        } else {
            _root[me]._y -= (100+yDiff)/10;
        }
    }
}
//
function pullMe (me) {
    distX = _root.screen.centerX-_root[me]._x;
    distY = _root.screen.centerY-_root[me]._y;
    _root[me]._x = _root[me]._x+distX/20+Math.random()*4-2;
    _root[me]._y = _root[me]._y+distY/20+Math.random()*4-2;
    _root[me]._xscale = (distX+distY)*4;
    _root[me]._rotation = DistY;
}
```

Line 31 of 31, Col 1

The first part of this code creates an object we've met before: screen. This is one of my favorite objects, because it always tells me something rather important: my stage area. If I ever change the stage area, all I have to do is alter the values in the braces, and I'm done. I don't usually have to do this, however, because most of the time I accept the default stage size and alter the scale sizes in the HTML. This has a number of advantages, the main one being that the Flash environment seems to work best with a stage area of this size, and I don't get cluttered screens and scrollbars all over the place if I try to set a bigger stage. Another advantage is that over time, you get a feel for how much you have to scale the movie window to see what the SWF would look in *all* the standard browser window sizes, which is a neat skill to develop. Finally, accepting the default size gives you a FLA that is the right ratio of height to width as a standard monitor. Those of you who know better will be jumping out of your seats and telling me how wrong I am right now, but hear me out before you pass judgment. I know that the average screen is a 4:3 proportion, but if you include the top and bottom browser menu bars, you'll be left with about the right proportion, so I never have to reach for a calculator in order to work out new screen sizes that follow the same proportions.

```
screen = new Object();
screen = {left:0, right:550, top:0, bottom:400};
screen.centerX = screen.right / 2;
screen.centerY = screen.bottom / 2;
```

The next thing I do is to define the two functions. How these work isn't really important here, but the way they're defined, and what they do with their single arguments certainly is. In outline though, pushMe is looking to see if me is within 100 pixels of the mouse – and if it is, me is pushed away from the mouse with a force proportional to the distance between me and the mouse.

The argument me is used to form a path _root[me], and this is used to access the properties _root.me._x and _root.me._y for the purposes of animation. If I'd wanted to, I could have also made the variables xDiff and yDiff local to the function, but I don't like doing this because I prefer optimized code with the minimum instructions when I am creating real-time animations. If these had been local variables, Flash would have to create them and clear them every time the function ran. The function is involved in the animation of 40 fluxDots so Flash would have to do this 40 times for every frame. The movie's running at 18 fps, so you can see that's a lot of variable creation/clearing going on. The easiest solution that I can come up with here is just to leave them as global variables. In a lot of occurrences, this would be a bad decision, but I think that here it was justified by the extra burst of speed it created:

```
function pushMe (me) {
  xDiff = [me]._x - _xmouse;
  yDiff = [me]._y - _ymouse;

  if (Math.abs(xDiff + yDiff) < 100) {
    if (xDiff > 0) {
      _root[me]._x += (100 - xDiff) / 10;
    } else {
      _root[me]._x -= (100 + xDiff) / 10;
    }

    if (yDiff > 0) {
      _root[me]._y += (100 - yDiff) / 10;
    } else {
      _root[me]._y -= (100 + yDiff) / 10;
    }
  }
}
```

The pullMe function does something similar to pushMe, but it's a weaker force. Thus, if the mouse is nearby, the fluxDots like to get away from the mouse more than they like to get home. However, distance plays a part in the equation, and if the mouse manages to get a fluxDot too far away from home, the dot will feel a much larger compulsion to get home, and will fight stronger against its mouse hatred.

A wildcard in all of this is a random quantity that I've thrown into the motion pot for good measure. This creates small differences in the individual fluxDots' positions, meaning that each one has a slightly different set of forces acting on it. Sometimes, this difference becomes magnified, you'll see a blob of fluxDots split into two different blobs, and each one will find a different route home. This tiny variation can potentially become huge over time and distance, and it's at the heart of chaotic behavior. It is the small force of a butterfly flapping a wing in one continent that can grow and cause a hurricane thousands of miles away in another part of the world. It may be just a Flash toy, but the motion has meaning.

Notice that the function uses absolute paths throughout – it even references the screen object by an absolute path, despite the fact that they're actually located in the same frame. This is because the actual location of the method defined in each fluxDot is dependent on the location of the fluxDot, and not the location of this function definition. Because I don't know where this function will actually be called from, I make all the paths absolute, so it doesn't matter. If you don't want this to happen, you would have to define sprite in this frame, and then call your new methods with _root.sprite.method();. Although this would now mean that you can reference screen by its relative path within pullMe, I don't like the fact that my new methods have to contain a full path to this function, and they don't look like true ActionScript methods anymore. If in doubt, set it up the way I have; it looks better in your main code sections.

```
function pullMe (me) {
  distX = _root.screen.centerX - _root[me]._x;
  distY = _root.screen.centerY - _root[me]._y;
  _root[me]._x = _root[me]._x + distX / 20 +
➥ Math.random()*4-2;
  _root[me]._y = _root[me]._y + distY / 20 +
➥ Math.random()*4-2;
  _root[me]._Xscale = (distX + distY) * 4;
  _root[me]._rotation = DistY;
}
```

And that's everything in this FLA.

Parting Shots

In this section, I've tried to steer away from the standard programming textbook, "Let's build a function that returns miles expressed in kilometers," clichés. That's because this book has *Designer to Designer*™ stamped on the cover.

My goal for ActionScript is that it lets me realize the creative thoughts in my head, and put them down on the Flash motion canvas. I've tried to demonstrate object-oriented design and the use of custom methods not as a clever programming technique, but as a tool to mold the ActionScript environment to the way *you* as a designer need it to work before you can start building creative and dynamic motion graphics, rather than just swathes of clever code. I hope you share that sentiment, despite the somewhat chaotic results that can ensue.

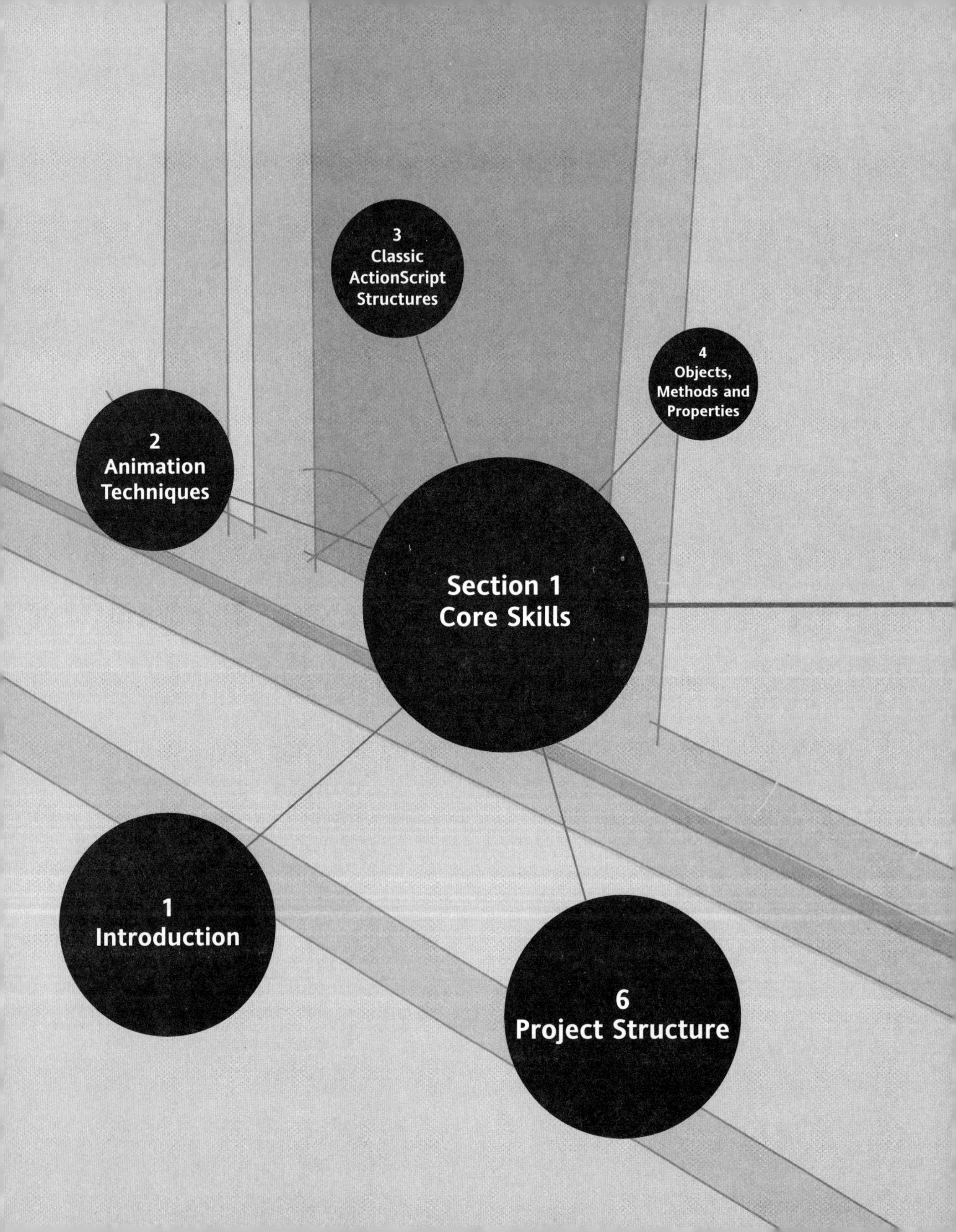

3
Classic
ActionScript
Structures

4
Objects,
Methods and
Properties

2
Animation
Techniques

**Section 1
Core Skills**

**1
Introduction**

**6
Project Structure**

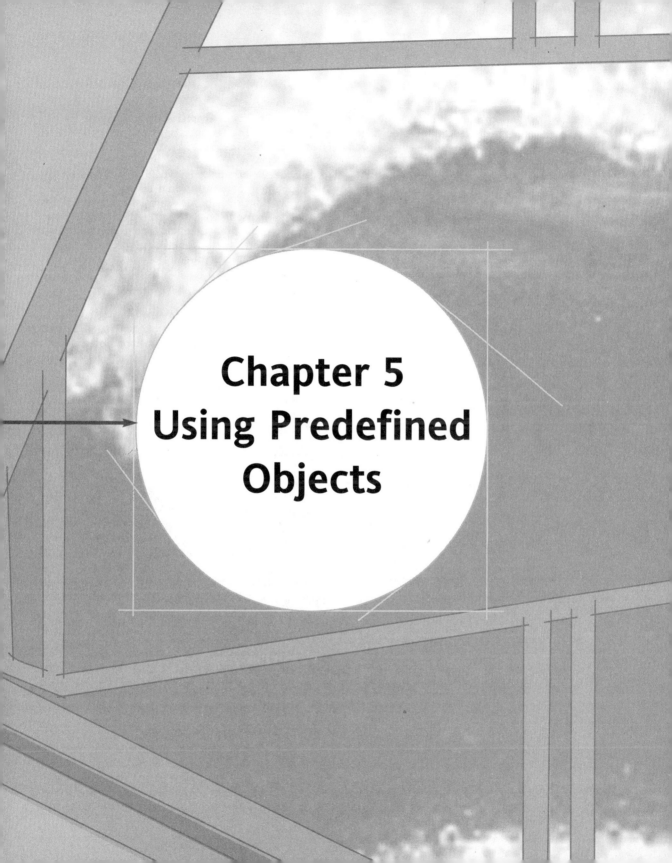

Chapter 5
Using Predefined Objects

In this chapter, I'll be extending our discussion of objects in Chapter 4, by introducing Flash's predefined objects. The predefined objects are, as their name suggests, objects with properties and methods that have already been defined within Flash.

Some of these methods are what I would describe as oblique, in that you'd be very unlikely to create an object with similar methods and properties yourself. It would be pretty difficult to create the method that tells a movie clip to play from scratch, for example. There are other methods, though, that you could put together yourself: `movieClip.localToGlobal`, for example, which you could construct using a combination of other methods and properties of the `MovieClip` object, or the `String.charat` method, which could be reproduced using `String.substr`. These methods are great shortcuts, and save you a lot of work. Together, the objects and methods that come with Flash provide baseline functionality. Some of the methods are essential, and others are there as handy shortcuts that save you time and effort.

We'll work through most of the predefined objects in Flash in this chapter, looking at how each object can be used in real-world development, and covering as many of their methods and properties as possible. Rather than an exhaustive listing of the methods, the emphasis here is on these objects as they are used practically, and you'll notice how the use of most objects will also draw on the methods and properties of other objects. We'll look at:

- The `String` object: checking the content of strings

- The `Array` object: storing and manipulating data

- The `Key` object: capturing real-time user interaction

- The `Color` object: for dynamic color control

- The `MovieClip` object: the functional backbone for using all of the other objects

Before we begin, a word about the examples. Most of the examples we'll work with here are constructed with the frame rate set at 30 fps, and all objects and code should go on frame 1 of the timeline (unless otherwise mentioned). Use layers whatever way you're used to, but be aware that it is common practice to put all actions on the topmost layer so that you can ensure that all the other elements of your movie, graphics etc., can be loaded before the actions execute. So, let's begin.

The MovieClip Object

Flash's `MovieClip` object allows you to access and manipulate the appearance and behavior of a movie clip; despite the fact that it appears unique in Flash, it's really just an object like any other. It comes with a number of properties, (width, height, and so on), and a collection of predefined methods.

The major distinction between the `MovieClip` object and most of the other objects is that you handle its creation through Flash's graphical user interface, rather than instantiating it through ActionScript. When you create an instance of a movie clip and drop it on the stage, you are in effect creating a `MovieClip` object. As many of the `MovieClip` methods and properties have already been discussed in earlier chapters, I'll just deal with a few of the more complex methods here:

- duplicateMovieClip

- attachMovie

- localToGlobal and globalToLocal

- getBounds

- hitTest

MovieClip.duplicateMovieClip

The MovieClip.duplicateMovieClip method allows you to specify an instance of a movie clip and duplicate it while the movie is playing. It takes two parameters, newname and depth, which specify the instance name that the duplicated MovieClip will be given, and the depth at which the new instance will be placed. Unless these parameters are unique, the duplication may overwrite any instance with the same name at that level.

Duplicating a Movie Clip

1. Put a movie clip on stage, call it flake and add the following code to the main timeline at frame 1:

    ```
    for(i=1;i<31;i++){
        flake.duplicateMovieClip("flake"+i, 10);
    }
    ```

    This loop duplicates the movie clip flake on the stage, giving each new instance the name flake with the value of i, appended to it. So when it is run, the new movie clips will be named flake1, flake2, and so on.

    If you try the code out, though, you'll see that nothing appears to happen. This is because the depth parameter is the same for each duplicated clip, and so each flake that is duplicated will overwrite the previous one, leaving us with only flake, our original clip, and flake30, the last duplication. List the objects in the test window to see.

2. Now amend the code so that it creates the new movie clips at different depths, using the value i that is incremented in the for loop to specify a new depth for each movie clip:

    ```
    for(i=1;i<31;i++){
        flake.duplicateMovieClip("flake"+i,i);
    }
    ```

    You now have thirty new instances of flake, named flake1 to flake30. At the moment each clip is positioned one on top of the other, so it might not look as if they have duplicated. Select list objects in the test movie environment, either selecting it from the debug dropdown menu or by pressing <CTRL>+L to check that all the duplications have been made.

> *Each duplicated movie clip takes on the properties of the instance that is being duplicated, including actions and clip events (but not variables).*

3. Let's amend the code so that each of the duplicated clips is positioned differently. We'll put each new instances in a random position as they are created, by adding the following clip event to the original instance, flake, so that it will be called each time the clip loads, i.e. when it is created:

```
onClipEvent(load){
    _x= Math.random()*550;
    _y= Math.random()*400;
}
```

We're using the Math.random method, which gives us a random decimal number somewhere between one and zero. The code multiplies a randomly generated number by 550 to give us a new _x coordinate, which will give us a number somewhere between 0 (0*550) and 550 (1*550). The new _y coordinate position is calculated the same way, but multiplying by 400 instead, putting the clip somewhere between 0 and 400 on the y axis.

4. If you try it out, you'll see that the code distributes the clips quite widely around the stage:

We can modify the code to concentrate the movie clips in the middle off the stage. Let's have them appear between 225 and 325 on the x-axis and 150 and 250 on the y-axis:

```
onClipEvent(load){
    _x= 225+Math.floor(Math.random()*100);
    _y= 150+Math.floor(Math.random()*100);
}
```

This code uses another method of the Math object, Math.floor, which takes a number and rounds it down to the nearest integer. So, for example, if Math.random returns 0.333, and we multiply that by 100, which would equal 33.3, and then round it down, we'd get 33.

Although it's not strictly necessary here, it does mean that each movie clip will be placed on a whole pixel, and it keeps things neater, because Math.random can return a number with up to 15 decimal places. Test the movie again to see the effect:

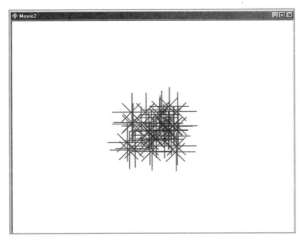

5. Now if we wanted each of the flakes to spin we can add the following code to the flake movie clip, underneath the first onClipEvent:

```
onClipEvent(enterFrame){
    _rotation+=Math.random();
}
```

This means that each frame after the clip loads we are adding a random number between 0 and 1 to the rotation property of each movie clip. Note that using code like this, each movie clip is entirely responsible for its own positioning and for its own movement:

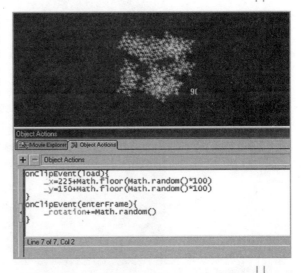

The duplicateMovieClip method depends on the target movie clip being at the same location of the duplicates you want to create, either on the stage or inside another movie clip. If you want to create your new movie clips from a movie clip in the Library instead, you can use the attachMovie, which allows you to create duplications of the movie clip inside the Library and place them wherever you want.

MovieClip.attachMovie

This method gives you much more flexibility. To use it, you need to first create a linkage on the movie clip that you want to attach using the Library.

> *Linkage controls the relationship of a symbol to its instances. Ordinarily, a symbol can only be exported as an instance of the original symbol, but linkage allows a symbol to be gathered from other sources or exported as the symbol itself, so it's no longer subject to the symbol-instance relationship.*

Using MovieClip.attachMovie

1. Using the same movie you've been working on, create a linkage by right clicking on the symbol in the Library and select Linkage, or selecting Linkage from the Library dropdown menu. Once the linkage dialogue box has opened, check Export this symbol and enter a name, or an Identifier, for the symbol. Call it flake:

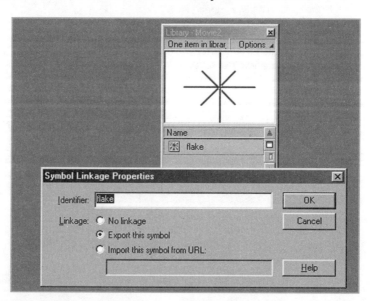

2. We'll create another movie clip, and attach the flake movie clip inside it. Create a square and put it on stage, naming the instance square.

We could simply attach the flake movie clip inside square, on the main timeline using this code:

```
square.attachMovie("flake","flake",1);
```

This would look within the exported symbols for one with the identifier flake, and then create an instance of the specified symbol inside square at level 1, naming the instance flake. The clip would be placed at the center point of square.

We're going to do something a bit more interesting though, and put the code in an onClipEvent on the square movie clip, rotating the clip at the same time. This code attaches an instance of the symbol exported as flake, puts it in the center of the movie that the code is attached to, and then rotates it 10 degrees every frame.

```
onClipEvent(load){
    this.attachMovie("flake","flake",1);
}
onClipEvent(enterFrame){
    flake._rotation+=10;
}
```

Test your movie.

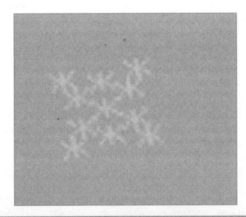

> *When you're using the* attachMovie *method, note that the attached instance can't have any* onClipEvent *actions attached to it, because it doesn't appear until the movie is exported. The only way around this is to attach a movie clip with another movie clip inside it and attach the* onClipEvent *actions to that, using the attached movie as a wrapper. You can still, of course, put actions on the timeline of the attached movie.*

Now we've started putting clips inside other clips, another issue arises: how do we find the inner movie clip's coordinates?

If, for example, you've nested Clip 1 inside Clip 2, and you access Clip 1's _x and _y properties, they will be expressed relative to the clip's _parent, Clip 2.

Take a look at the following diagram:

0,0 of stage

local co-ords: (80,20)
global co-ords: (160,70)

local co-ords: (80,50) | **CLIP 1: ON STAGE**
global co-ords: (80,50)

CLIP 2: INSIDE CLIP 1

Clip 1 is placed directly onto the stage and so its local coordinates are the same as its **global** coordinates (80,50). Clip 2 is placed at (80,20) within Clip 1. While we could calculate Clip 2's global coordinates by adding its local coordinates to the global coordinates of its parent, when you're dealing with clips nested several levels deep, the calculations can get complicated pretty quickly, and this is where the localToGlobal method comes in handy.

MovieClip.localToGlobal

The localToGlobal method allows you to find out the global coordinates of a clip, by retrieving the local coordinates of an object and transforming them into global coordinates. You might find this useful if, for example, you need to position a movie clip on the main stage relative to a clip that is inside several other clips.

In order to transform an object's coordinates from local to global, we have to store both of these points in an object created for that purpose. Once the object has been created, we need to set two variables to hold the _x and _y positions. Although the ActionScript dictionary does not point this out, this method will not function properly unless the variables inside the object are called 'x' and 'y', and the object contains both of these elements:

```
points=new Object();
points.x=_x;
points.y=_y;
```

There's something else you need to know as well. This line of code, that looks like it should work:

```
localToGlobal(points);
```

In fact doesn't: you'll get the global _x and _y position of the clip's _parent returned, instead of the global x and y positions of our clip. The solution to this is to use:

```
_parent.localToGlobal(points);
```

Now points.x equals the global _x position and points.y equals the global _y position.

Working with the localToGlobal method

1. To see this method in action, put together a file with three movie clips a, b and c. Give each movie clip a button with the following actions:

```
on(press){
    this.startDrag(false);
}
on(release){
    stopDrag();
}
```

So, when the button is pressed, the movie clip will be dragged, stopping when the button is released.

2. Now put movie clip b inside movie clip a, and then movie clip c inside movie clip b, and finally put an instance of a on the stage. If you test the movie at this point you'll see that when you drag a, b and c are dragged as well, and when you drag b, c is dragged too.

3. Next add two dynamic text fields within all three movie clips a, b and c, and give them the variable names myx (which will show the local _x position) and myxglobal. You could also add labels to identify which is which.

4. Now we can set the code that will compute the local and global _x positions of each clip. Select the instance of each movie clip (click on a on the main stage, then click on b within a, and then c within b) and add the following code:

```
onClipEvent(load){
    points=new Object ;
}

onClipEvent(mouseMove){
    myx=_x
    points.x = myx;
    points.y = _y;
    _parent.localToGlobal(points);
    myxglobal=points.x;
    updateAfterEvent();
}
```

This code creates a new object called `points` when the clip first appears. From then on whenever the mouse moves (so whenever the objects are dragged) the clip's `_x` and `_y` positions into the `points` object, and then performs the `localToGlobal` function on this new set of points. Then the global x value from the `points` object is assigned to the variable `myglobalx`, and so it appears in the text field. The final line `updateAfterEvent` is there to keep the dragging smooth.

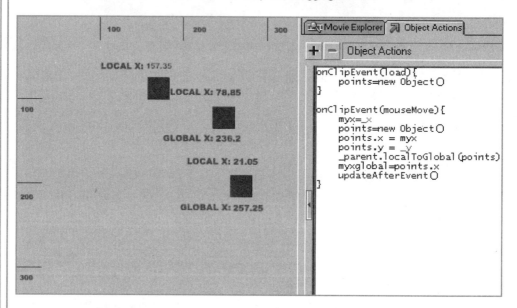

5. To test this, put a movie clip called "d" on the stage and keep it aligned to the right hand side of clip `c`, by putting another movie clip on the stage and assigning it the following code:

```
onClipEvent(mouseMove) {
    _x=_parent.a.b.c.points.x+100;
    _y=_parent.a.b.c.points.y+100;
}
```

MovieClip.globalTolocal

As you might expect, globalToLocal does the opposite of localToGlobal; it translates the global coordinates of a stage-level object into the local coordinates of a movie clip. It is set up in the same way as localToGlobal: by creating an object containing two variables, x and y and applying the localToGlobal method to it. We'll adapt the previous example to illustrate this, using it to determine the distance of the mouse from a movie clip – in other words, expressing the mouse's (global) co-ordinates in the (local) coordinate space of the movie clip.

Working with the globalToLocal method

6. First we need to change all the text field variables in the a, b, and c movie clips to `mousexdist` and `mouseydist`.

7. Now change the code to make these fields display the x and y distance of the clip from the position of the mouse. Attach this code to each clip:

```
onClipEvent (load) {
    points=new Object();
}

onClipEvent (mouseMove) {
    points.x = _root._xmouse;
    points.y = _root._ymouse;
    _parent.globalToLocal (points);
    mousexdist=_x-points.x;
    mouseydist=_y-points.y;
    updateAfterEvent();
}
```

8. Next delete the d movie clip from the stage, and test your movie. This behaves in the same way as the `localToGlobal` example, taking the global position of the mouse and putting it into the `points` object. The `globalToLocal` method then converts these coordinates into the coordinate space of the movie clip. Finally, subtracting the local mouse position from the position of the clip sets the `mousexdist` and `mouseydist` variables.

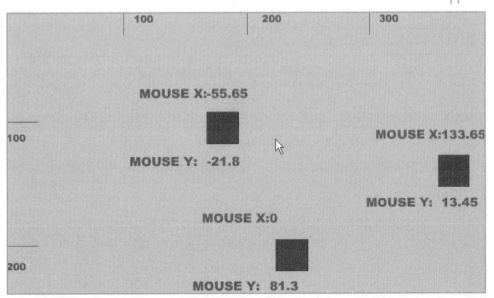

MovieClip.getBounds

A movie clip's **bounding box** is essentially a square that contains all of the graphic elements inside a movie clip. The `getBounds` method returns the coordinates of the four corners of the bounding box in relation to the coordinate space that is specified. The `getBounds` method returns an object with four properties, `xmin`, `xmax`, `ymin` and `ymax`. `xmin` represents the furthest point left at which content appears in the movie clip, `xmax` returns the furthest point right. `ymin` returns the furthest point up at which content appears in the movie clip and `ymax` returns the furthest point down.

In this diagram, the dotted line represents the bounding box with the values returned by the `getBounds` method:

While `getBounds` might initially appear a slightly obscure method, there are many times when it comes in useful. If, for example, you're attaching multiple movie clips within another movie clip, it can get difficult to keep track of exactly where they all are. Using `getBounds` allows you to determine exactly what the boundaries of these objects are on stage.

We'll work through an example next that sets a movie clip containing 4 draggable movie clips. We'll use `getBounds` to draw a square, a representation of the bounding box, around the edge of these movie clips.

Working with the getBounds method

1. First of all we need to create our draggable movie clips, which we'll call `square`. Draw a graphic and put a blank button on top of it, adding the following code to activate and deactivate the drag function:

    ```
    on(press){
        this.startDrag(false);
    }
    on(release){
        stopDrag();
    }
    ```

2. Now create another movie clip, `holder`, and drop several instances of the `square` movie clip inside (I've used four, but you can use as many as you like).

3. Now put `holder` on the stage, with the instance name `holder`, and add the following code to retrieve the bounds of the `holder` clip (`this`) relative to the main stage:

```
onClipEvent(enterFrame){
    borders=this.getBounds(_root);
    _parent.xmax=borders.xmax;
    _parent.ymax=borders.ymax;
    _parent.ymin=borders.ymin;
    _parent.xmin=borders.xmin;
}
```

4. Put four dynamic text fields on stage, and give them the variable names, xmin, ymin, xmax and ymax, to display the changing values of the bounding box as the squares are dragged. You can also use two more text fields on stage with variables names holder._x and holder._y, so that you can see that the xmin and ymin values are not in any way related to the _x and _y values of the holder clip.

5. We'll use the values retrieved to make an outline appear around the squares, to create a visual representation of the bounding box. Create another movie clip, called boundingbox and inside it draw the outline of a square, it doesn't matter how big, just don't include any fill. The top left of this square should be placed at the registration point within the movie clip.

    Now put the clip on stage and name the instance bounder. To represent the bounding box, the _x position of bounder should be xmin and the _y position ymin (if you look back at the diagram on the previous page you'll see that the coordinates of the top left of the bounding box are (xmin,ymin)).

    To set the width of bounder we'll use xmax-xmin, and to set the height ymax-ymin, as these represent respectively the distance from the left edge to the right edge and from the bottom to the top. So we now add this code to the bounder movie clip, after the existing code but within the onClipEvent(enterFrame):

```
_parent.bounder._x=borders.xmin;
_parent.bounder._y=borders.ymin;
_parent.bounder._width=borders.xmax-borders.xmin;
_parent.bounder._height=borders.ymax-borders.ymin;
```

    The complete statement now looks like this:

```
onClipEvent(enterFrame){
    borders=this.getBounds(_root);
    _parent.xmin=borders.xmin;
    _parent.ymin=borders.ymin;
    _parent.xmax=borders.xmax;
    _parent.ymax=borders.ymax;
    _parent.bounder._x=borders.xmin;
    _parent.bounder._y=borders.ymin;
    _parent.bounder._width=borders.xmax-borders.xmin;
    _parent.bounder._height=borders.ymax-borders.ymin;
}
```

Test the movie. You should find that the bounding box will resize itself to contain all the `square` movie clips as they are dragged.

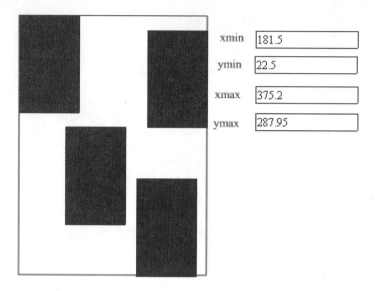

xmin	181.5
ymin	22.5
xmax	375.2
ymax	287.95

MovieClip.hitTest

This uses the bounding box to detect collisions, so it's very useful for games as well as other applications. We'll look into `hitTest` in more detail in the coming chapters, but one thing that's worth bearing in mind is that it will only recognize a collision if the two movie clips overlap in a frame that Flash renders. For example, movie clip `a` might pass over movie clip `b` between frames, and no hit would be registered.

For example `hitTest` would fail in the following diagram, as the collision would occur between the second and third frames. If you were using `hitTest` to register a collision and then send the circle back in the opposite direction, the circle would have in this instance gone straight through the rectangle.

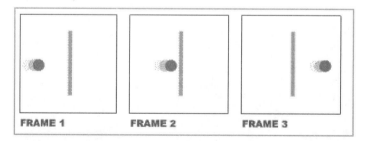

This is a definite limitation to the `hitTest` method, and you should bear it in mind if you're developing games that depend on the accurate testing of collisions. In these scenarios you might want to use some other method of collision detection as a backup, for instance, using the angle of motion to detect whether a clip's trajectory takes it through another clip.

Form Validation: the String object

The `String` object is something you'll find useful whenever you're dealing with non-numeric data, although you can also use the methods of the string object on data types that are not strings, for example numeric variables or Boolean values.

You can use the methods of the String object without explicitly creating an instance of it first – a temporary string object is created when the method is called, the method performed and the object discarded. Most methods will automatically convert these to string literals before they execute, but some, notably `String.substr`, require you to convert the data to a string manually, using the `toString` command (by using `variable.toString`).

I'm going to be using quite a few methods of the String object next, creating an application that tests the validity of data entered into a form. The validation we'll work with here is rough, but it does demonstrate some of the possible uses of the methods of the string object.

Testing data for validity

1. First create a form with five input text fields, and give them the variable names `forename`, `surname`, `dob`, `phone` and `email`. Then add a button to call a validation function, which we'll build next:

    ```
    on (press) {
    for(i=1;i<=5;i++){
        this["indicator"+i]._visible=0;
    }
    on(release){
        validate();
    }
    ```

2. We'll build the validation function next, but first we have to decide what will constitute a correct entry for each field, so that we can test for those conditions. Here are the rough tests I'll be working with:

forename / surname	For these two all we can really do is check that there's at least one character in each field and that all characters are letters, either lower or upper case.
dob	Here we can be more specific. The length of the entry will be set to eight characters (which we can also set as the maximum length of the text-field). All characters should be numbers. To constitute a valid date of birth the first two digits should be a number between 1 and 31, the third and fourth digits between

1 and 12, and the final four digits should be somewhere between 1880 and 2020 (more or less).

phone — Unless members of your target audience are likely to have consistently formatted telephone numbers, like a three-figure area code followed by a seven-figure number, it's best just to check that all the characters in this string are numbers.

email — It's hard to be definite about email addresses, as valid addresses can be in different formats, (ji@ozs.com or loo.pac@cop.org.uk example). There are only a couple of things that we can check for definite: that there's an '@' character at some point after the first character, and a dot at least two characters after it.

Now we need to translate the requirements for valid entry into ActionScript. I'll go through the process for each field and then we'll put the whole thing together at the end.

For the surname and forename fields we'll use `String.CharCodeAt` to check that each character is a letter. The `charCodeAt` finds the ASCII value for a character at a specific location within a string; `mystring.charCodeAt(3)` will return the ASCII value for the fourth character in the string called `mystring` (remembering that with strings, as with arrays, the numbering of characters always starts at zero).

3. What we need to know is which ASCII values correspond to letters. If you don't have an ASCII table to hand you can generate one like this:

```
for(i=33;i<=255;i++){
    val=String.fromCharCode(i);
    trace("Ascii value "+i+" refers to letter "+val);
}
```

The `String.fromCharCode` method returns the character corresponding to the ASCII value inside the brackets, so this loop runs through the numbers from 33 to 255 and uses the `fromCharCode` method to return the character for each of these ASCII values, using the `trace` command to print this to the Output window.

If you run this now, you'll see that upper case letters fall between 65 to 90 inclusive, and lower case letters are 97 to 122 inclusive. So we'll need to check that each character in our string has an ASCII value either between 65 and 90 or between 97 and 122. We should probably also allow spaces (" ") in the string (ASCII value = 32).

4. We'll create our own custom method to add to the `String` object, enabling us to call it for any string (like any other method). This approach allows us to use `this` inside the function to refer to the string, rather than having to send the name of the string into the function as a parameter. The syntax for adding a method to an object looks like this:

```
String.prototype.isLetters = function(){
};
```

Then we can define our function as usual between the curly braces. We should first check that the length of the string is at least one character:

```
if(this.length<1){
    return false;
}
```

If the length of the string is less than 1, the function will stop executing immediately and return `false`. Then we'll loop through each character checking that its ASCII value is within the bounds we set out:

```
for(i=0;i<this.length;i++){
    code = this.charCodeAt(i);
    if (code>64 && code<91 || code>96 && code<123 || code==32) {
    }else{
        return false;
    }
}
return true;
```

The loop executes once for each character in the string. It creates a variable, `code`, which contains the ASCII value for the character, and then checks that the value of the character is either between 65 and 90 or between 97 and 122. If it isn't it returns `false` and the function ceases; if it is, it carries on to check the next character. As long as the loop runs though without returning `false`, the final value will be `true`. Altogether the loop looks like this:

```
String.prototype.isLetters = function(){
    if(this.length<1){
        return false;
    }
    for(i=0;i<this.length;i++){
        code = this.charCodeAt(i);
        if (code>64 && code<91 || code>96 && code<123 ||code==32) {
        }else{
            return false;
        }
    }
    return true;
};
```

You can test the function by adding it to a frame, and concluding it with this code:

```
mystring="anycombinationoflettersandnumbers";
if(mystring.isLetters()){
    trace("this string is all letters");
}else{
    trace("this string is some combination of letters and
numbers");
}
```

Change the value of mystring, and test the movie to see the validation at work.

5. Now we have a method that checks that any given string is composed entirely of letters, for the surname and forename fields, we should create another to check strings that should be entirely composed of numbers. We'll be able to use this for the phone and the dob fields.

While we could build it in the same way as we did the isLetters function, and check each character in turn, there's a simpler way:

```
String.prototype.isNumbers = function(){
    if(this.length<1){
        return false;
    }
    if(this*1){
        return true;
    }else{
        return false;
    }
};
```

As with isLetters we're first checking that the string has at least one character. Then we're asking whether this*1 is true or not. If the character is a number, this*1 will equal the number and so equate to true. If it's a combination of letters and numbers or just letters, it will equal NaN (not a number), and equate to false. This is a much quicker way of doing things than looping through each character in turn.

So to check if the telephone number entered is composed of numbers, all we need to write is:

```
if(phone.isNumbers()){
    trace("phone number is valid");
}
```

However, as it is, spaces will throw the function, so if someone entered 01212 121232, they would be told that their entry is not valid. If you want to allow for spaces, you'll need to modify the isNumbers method to behave as the isLetters method, and check that each character is either a number or a space. That would look like this:

```
String.prototype.isNumbers = function(){
    if(this.length<1){
        return false;
    }
    for(i=0;i<this.length;i++){
        code = this.charCodeAt(i);
        if (this.charAt(i)!=" " && code<48 || code>57) {
            return false;
        }
    }
    return true;
};
```

This loop checks that each character is either a space (" ") or that its ASCII value is between 48 and 57 (the ASCII values for numbers), and if not, returns `false`.

6. While just checking that the string entered in the `phone` field is numeric is sufficient, we can be more specific about the format for the date of birth check; we'll check that the first two characters are numbers between 1 and 31, that the third and fourth characters are numbers between 1 and 12, and that the final four characters numbers that fall between 1880 and 2020 (for the sake of argument).

We'll use the `String.substr` method, which allows you to specify a span of characters within a string. This code, for example, should trace `fire`:

```
title="indoor fireworks";
section=title.substr(7,4);
trace(section);
```

The numbers inside the brackets specify where the selection starts and how long it should be. In this example the section starts with the seventh character (as strings are zero-based) and takes that character and the following three characters starting from that point to make four, so the trace outputs `fire`:

"TITLE": A VARIABLE WITH ITS INDEX NUMBERS: **INDOOR FIREWORKS**
0 1 2 3 4 5 67 8 9 10 11 12 13 14 15

TITLE.SUBSTR(7,4) EXTRACTS FOUR
CHARACTERS, STARTING AT INDEX NUMBER 7: **INDOOR** **FIRI**
0 1 2 3 4 5 67 8 9 10 11 12 13 14 15

Before we check the individual parts of the string, though, we need to make sure that the string has eight characters and that the are all numeric:

```
if (dob.length == 8 && dob.isNumbers()){
    trace("right number of characters and all numbers");
}
```

As long as the loop returns `true`, then we'll go on to check subsections of the string. The first two characters will reference the day, (`dob.substr(0,2)`), the third and fourth the month (`dob.substr(2,2)`) and the last four characters the year (`dob.substr(4,4)`), so:

```
if (dob.length == 8 && dob.isNumbers()){
    if (dob.substr(4, 4)>1880 && dob.substr(4, 4)<2020) {
        if (dob.substr(0, 2)<=31) {
            if (dob.substr(2, 2)<=12) {
                trace("dob is a valid date of birth");
            }
        }
    }
}
```

7. The final string to check is the email address. The first thing we need to do is check that the string contains one at character, with at least one character in front of it. We can use the `String.indexOf` method for this check, which returns the position of the first instance of a particular character in a string. This is the code that will check that there is an @, and that it is at least the second character:

```
if(email.indexOf("@")>0){
    trace("email contains an @ with at least one character before
    ➥it");
}
```

We'll also check that there is only one @ in the string, using the `String.lastIndexOf` which returns the last instance of a particular character in a string. So long as there is only one at, `email.indexOf("@")` will equal `email.lastIndexOf("@")`:

```
if(email.indexOf("@")>0 &&
    ➥email.indexOf("@")==email.lastIndexOf("@")){
    trace("email contains one @ with at least one character before
    ➥it");
}
```

We can also check that the last dot in the string comes after the at, and that there are at least two characters between the symbols:

```
if(email.lastIndexOf(".")>email.indexOf("@")+1){
    trace("last dot at least two characters after @");
}
```

Finally, we'll make sure that there are at least two characters after the final dot (as all valid domains have two characters):

```
if(email.lastIndexOf(".")>email.indexOf("@") &&
    ➥email.lastIndexOf(".")<email.length-1){
    trace("last dot at least two characters after @ and two
```

➥characters before the end of the string.");
}

Altogether, then, our code for validating the `email` variable filled by the input field looks like this:

```
if(email.indexOf("@")>0 && email.indexOf("@")==
➥email.lastIndexOf("@")){
  if(email.lastIndexOf(".")>email.indexOf("@") &&
➥email.lastIndexOf(".")<email.length-1){
    trace("a valid email");
  }
}
```

8. We also need to consider how we should let users know that one or more of the fields contain invalid information. Unfortunately the Flash `Selection` object only allows one text field to be highlighted at a time, and we're trying to do something a little different here, by checking all the fields at once.

We'll create an indicator movie clip, an arrow or whatever you prefer, and put an instance of this movie clip next to each text field, naming them `indicator1`, `indicator2`, and so on. These clips will begin by being invisible, and we'll toggle their visibility if the field is invalid. This is all that's needed:

```
for(i=1;i<=5;i++){
    this["indicator"+i]._visible=0;
}
```

You may recognize this code from the validate button earlier. We're initializing it here to turn all of the indicators invisible to start off with, and then resetting them every time you click the button to recheck the variables.

9. Now that we have all the components we need for the form validation, we should integrate them into the `validate` function we've set to be called when the submit button is pressed. The simplest way to do this will be to have the `validate` function call the individual functions that check the email address, date of birth, and so on. So let's take the code we've already written to check each field and put it inside functions:

```
String.prototype.isLetters = function(){
    if(this.length<1){
        return false;
    }
    for(i=0;i<this.length;i++){
        code = this.charCodeAt(i);
        if (code>64 && code<91 || code>96 && code<123 ||code==32) {
        }else{
            return false;
        }
    }
    return true;
```

continues overleaf

```
};

String.prototype.isNumbers = function(){
    if(this.length<1){
        return false;
    }
    if(this*1){
        return true;
    }else{
        return false;
    }
};

function chkforename(){
    if(forename.isLetters()){
        return true;
    }
}

function chksurname(){
    if(surname.isLetters()){
        return true;
    }
}

function chkphone(){
    if(phone.isNumbers()){
        return true;
    }
}

function chkdob(){
    if (dob.length == 8 && dob.isNumbers()){
        if (dob.substr(4, 4)>1880 && dob.substr(4,4)<2020) {
            if (dob.substr(0, 2)<=31) {
                if (dob.substr(2, 2)<=12) {
                    return true;
                }
            }
        }
    }
}

function chkemail(){
    if(email.indexOf("@")>0 && email.indexOf("@") ==
➥email.lastIndexOf("@")){
        if(email.lastIndexOf(".") >email.indexOf("@") &&
➥email.lastIndexOf(".")<email.length-1){
            return true;
        }
```

```
        }
    }
```

10. Now we put together the validate function which will call each of these functions in turn. For each one that does not return `true` we need to toggle the visibility of its indicator. If any of them are `false` we won't submit the data. Instead, we'll have a text field on stage, called `status` which we'll use to display a message to the user, letting him or her know either that the data has been submitted successfully, or that changes need to be made:

```
function validate(){
    var notvalid;
    if(!chkforename ()){
        indicator1._visible=1;
        notvalid=1;
    }
    if(!chksurname ()){
        indicator2._visible=1;
        notvalid=1;
    }
    if(!chkphone ()){
        indicator3._visible=1;
        notvalid=1;
    }
    if(!chkdob ()){
        indicator4._visible=1;
        notvalid=1;
    }
    if(!chkemail ()){
        indicator5._visible=1;
        notvalid=1;
    }
    if(notvalid){
        status="INVALID DATA - CORRECT MARKED FIELDS";
    }else{
        status="DATA IS VALID - YOUR DATA HAS BEEN SUBMITTED";
        delete dob;
        delete forename;
        delete surname;
        delete phone;
        delete email;
    }
}
```

FORNAME:

Bill

SURNAME:

Flanders

DOB:

16081968

PHONE:

084571264891

EMAIL:

support@friendsofed.com

SUBMIT

STATUS:

That's all there is to it. Obviously the data isn't actually going anywhere, as yet, but you get the idea.

Clearing Form Fields: The Selection Object

Before we move on to using the Array object to store the data entered, I just want to briefly cover using the Selection object to remove information from a form field while it is active. (You can also use the Selection.setFocus method of the Selection object to highlight any text fields which contain incorrect data, but as it only allows you to highlight one field at a time that's not much use to us, here, so we'll stick with using indicator movie clips.)

The method we are going to use here is Selection.getFocus. This method returns the text field with focus, that is, the text field that is currently in use. We could access the text field with focus and check that it still contains its original information, (if dob still contains DDMMYYYY, for example), and if it does, simply remove that information. The downfall of that method is that it won't clear the field if the user is making a correction.

We'll use a timer instead. We start the timer when the mouse button is pressed and then check it again when the mouse button is released. If it is a short click, then we'll reset the text field. If it is a long-click then the user is probably highlighting an area of the text field to edit, and so we'll leave the information intact.

Clearing fields using a timer

1. First of all we need to create an empty movie clip, which we'll call `clipevents` and put on the stage. To get the timer working first, add the following code to the movie clip:

    ```
    onClipEvent (mouseDown) {
        click=getTimer();
    }

    onClipEvent (mouseUp) {
        if (getTimer()-click<150) {
            trace("short click");
        }
    }
    ```

    The `getTimer` function returns the number of milliseconds elapsed since the start of the movie. We're setting a variable, `click`, to hold the number of milliseconds that have elapsed between the user pressing the mouse button and releasing it. If the press is less than 150, then it was a short click.

2. Now we need to add the commands to check which text field is selected and then remove the data from it.

    ```
    onClipEvent (mouseDown) {
        click=getTimer();
    }

    onClipEvent (mouseUp) {
        if (getTimer()-click<150) {
            a=Selection.getFocus();
            eval(a)="";
        }
    }
    ```

    The `Selection.getFocus` method returns the name of the variable that is focused as a string, and so to modify the variable we need to use `eval(a)` and set that to equal nothing (`""`).

So, now we have the data inside Flash, we need to be able to do something with it. We'll use the `Array` object to work with the data.

Storing Data: The Array Object

An array is, essentially, a collection of data, usually indexed in numbered form. Arrays are useful whenever you need to store a number of pieces of related data. If, for example, you had a list of people's names that you wanted to store, it's simpler to collect them all together in an array, where each name is a separate element and has a unique identifying index number, than have separate variables for all of them.

There are a number of different ways in which we can set up arrays. Here are three ways of writing the same array:

Array 1

```
names= new Array();
names[0]="lewis";
names[1]="pontecorvo";
names[2]="clouzot";
```

Array 2

```
names=new Array("lewis","pontecorvo","clouzot");
```

Array 3

```
names=["lewis","pontecorvo","clouzot"];
```

Each of these short lines of code would give you an array like this:

```
0:"lewis",
1:"pontecorvo",
2:"clouzot"
```

How you set up your arrays is really up to you and which method you prefer; sometimes the first might be useful to see all the entries set out clearly, while the third version obviously requires less typing.

> *Note that, as with the string object, the indexing of arrays is zero based, in other words, the first element is numbered zero.*

Once you have set up an array, you need to be able to access the values it holds. You do this by referring to the elements of an array using the array name, followed by the index number held in square brackets (square brackets are know as the array operator).

```
numbertwo=names[1]; // numbertwo equals "pontecorvo"
```

We can also use a variable to decide which element of an array is accessed:

```
personnumber=Math.Floor(Math.random()*4);
personpicked=names[personnumber];
trace("personnumber= "+personnumber);
trace("personpicked= "+personpicked);
```

In the form example we dealt with data input of data, so now I want to show you how you can use the array object to organize that data and deal with it logically. After each person's data is submitted we will enter that data into an array and I will demonstrate how the methods of the array object allow us to arrange and keep track of that data.

Working with the collected data

In the example so far, you'll remember that we have five different variables containing data we want to store about each person. We'll need to construct our data storage so that we can refer to a person in our array and then the contingent data: forename, surname, and so on. We'll also build in a system that allows us to see the values for each person as they are submitted.

A good way to do this is to create a new movie clip for each person, containing a text field with all of the information for the person. We'll also set variables within the movie clip for each of the fields we have set. The name of the movie clip will then be added to an array and by targeting the movie clip in the array we can then gain access to the submitted values.

1. So, create a new movie clip to display the information. All this needs to be is a dynamic text field, with the variable named description. We'll use the attachMovie method, so we need to set the linkage of the movie clip as we did earlier. Check Export as symbol, and set the identifier to display.

2. Next we need to create our function to store the data and attach the movie clip. We'll call this storedata. This function will be called after the data has been submitted and its validity has been checked. We'll call the function from within the final section of the validate function we created earlier. The end of the validate function should now look like this:

    ```
    status="DATA IS VALID - YOUR DATA HAS BEEN SUBMITTED"
    storedata();
    delete dob;
    delete forename;
    delete surname;
    delete phone;
    delete email;
    ```

3. Now we can create the storedata function. It will attach the movie to the main stage, then set the variables inside the movie clip to hold the data for each person, and finally set the description variable for the text field, in order to display the information.

    The first part of the function should be familiar from the MovieClip section of the chapter. We attach an instance of the movie clip with the identifier display to the main stage. Every time the function is called it increments the variable count so that the movie clips are named sequentially (display1, display2, and so on) and to ensure that each movie clip is on a different level:

    ```
    count++;
    _root.attachMovie("display","display"+count,count);
    ```

After that we use methods of the string object to ensure that the name fields have the correct capitalization:

```
surname=surname.charAt(0).toUpperCase()+surname.substr(1,surname.
➥length-1).toLowerCase();
forename=forename.charAt(0).toUpperCase()+forename.substr(1,
➥forename.length-1).toLowerCase();
```

The code breaks down like this:

`surname.charAt(0)`	Refers to the first character of the string surname, (the 'character at' position zero in the string)
`surname.substr(1,surname.length-1)`	Refers to the section of the string surname which starts at the second character and continues to the end of the string (recalling that strings are zero-based)
`toUpperCase()` and `toLowerCase()`	Converts the specified strings to upper case or lower case characters respectively

So, to summarize, the code takes the first character of `surname`, converts it to upper case, then appends to it the rest of the characters of `surname`, which are converted to lower case.

4. We then go through each of the variables set in the form and create a corresponding variable within the movie clip we have created. Note how we're now using the count variable, which we used to create the instance of the display movie clip to refer to it:

```
_root["display"+count].forename=forename;
_root["display"+count].surname=surname;
_root["display"+count].phone=phone;
_root["display"+count].dob=dob;
_root["display"+count].email=email;
```

Next we add all of the fields together to make one long string to display in our movie clip:

```
_root["display"+count].description=forename+" "+surname+" "
➥+dob+" "+phone+" "+email;
```

5. Finally we need to add our movie clip to an array. Before using an array it has to be initialized, so right at the top of all the code we add:

```
people=new Array();
```

This sets up the array when the movie is initialized, and sits empty until we add elements to it. At this stage we want to add our movie clip to the array. We'll use the push method, which pushes a value or a string onto the end of an array. So the command:

```
people.push(_root["display"+count]);
```

takes _root["display"+count] and adds it to the end of the people array.

Here's the function so far:

```
function storedata () {
    count++;
    _root.attachMovie("display","display"+count,count);
    //Format the surname and forename fields
    surname=surname.charAt(0).toUpperCase()+surname.substr(1,
➡surname.length-1).toLowerCase();
    forename=forename.charAt(0).toUpperCase()+forename.substr(1,
➡forename.length-1).toLowerCase();
    //Set the data variables within the MovieClip
    _root["display"+count].forename=forename;
    _root["display"+count].surname=surname;
    _root["display"+count].phone=phone;
    _root["display"+count].dob=dob;
    _root["display"+count].email=email;
    //Set the variable to display the data;
    _root["display"+count].description=forename+" "+surname+"
➡"+dob+" "+phone+" "+email;
    //add MovieClip to Array
    people.push(_root["display"+count]);
}
```

If you run the function like this you'll find that although it works, but we haven't positioned the movie clips and so they appear one on top of the other. If you try submitting three people's data, and then list the variables, you'll see that the array has been created and contains the names of the movie clips as follows:

```
Variable _level0.people = [object #15] [
   0:[MovieClip:_level0.display1],
   1:[MovieClip:_level0.display2],
   2:[MovieClip:_level0.display3]
]
```

You'll also see that each movie clip contains the pertinent data for each person.

We can now access the data for each movie clip through the array. For example, in this instance people[0].surname would be equivalent to _root.display1.surname. You might reasonably ask what the benefit of storing them in this way is, as after all, the movie clips are named sequentially anyway. Well, there are many advantages to doing things in this way: if, for example, we wanted to remove clips from the middle of the sequence, in order to maintain the sequence we would have to go through the clips incrementing or decrementing their index numbers. Using the methods of the `Array` object we can remove element one and element two will become element one. We can also use the `Array` object to do things like sort our list, or cycle through it.

6. Before we get into sorting the array, though, we need to take care of the positioning of the movie clips we're creating. We need to position each movie clip according to its position in the array, with `people[0]` at the top, then `people[1]`, and so on.

    Because of the way I have set it up, we need to have the top movie clip, (`people[0]`), at 157 on the y-axis, and each following entry an extra 12 pixels down. So, each movie clip needs to have a `_y` position of 157 plus 12 multiplied by its position in the array; `array[0]` will be at 157, `array[1]` at 169, `array[2]` at 181, and so on.

    We'll pass the function two parameters, the path to the movie clip itself and its position in the array. Here's the function:

    ```
    function position(entry,arraypos){
        entry._y=157+arraypos*12;
    }
    ```

7. Now we need to add the following call to the function as the final line of the `storedata` function.

    ```
    position(_root["display"+count],people.length-1);
    ```

    The name is the movie clip we have just created, and `people.length-1` refers to its position in the array (as the clip has just been added to the end of the array we know that it is the last element).

    If you test the movie now, and submit some entries, you'll see that the information will display properly, each entry one after the other. Now to add some functionality to what at the moment is just a list of entries.

    The first thing to tackle is removing an item from the list. We'll create a new function called `removeentry` to handle this. What the function should do is find the relevant movie clip and then remove its corresponding entry from the `people` array.

    We'll put a button inside the display movie clip that we're duplicating and call the `removeentry` function when the button is pressed, sending the path to the movie clip as a parameter.

8. So first of all create a button and put it inside the display movie clip (in my example I've used an invisible button). Attach the following code to the button:

    ```
    on(release){
        _root.removeentry(this);
    }
    ```

When the function is called we need to ascertain its position in the array and then remove the movie clip. The quickest way to do that is to loop through the array and check each element to see if it corresponds to the movie clip the function is called from. The `Array.splice` method of the array object is just what we need here. This method is quite flexible and can be used to insert elements into the middle of an array as well as to delete them, but in this case we only need to worry about removing elements.

9. In this case we use splice with two parameters, the first referring to the position within the array where we want the deleting to begin, and the second referring to the number of elements to be deleted. Here's the function:

```
function removeentry(entry){
    for(i=0;i<people.length;i++){
        if(people[i]==entry){
            people.splice(i,1);
            entry.removeMovieClip();
        }
    }
}
```

The `for` loop tackles each of the elements in turn (from 0 to the end of the array) checking whether its entry is the same as the movie clip that we have sent as a parameter (`entry`). If it is we then use splice to remove that element from the array. For example if `people[4]` is our movie clip, the function will remove the element of the array with the index number 4. Finally we remove the movie clip.

If you test this you'll find that although the element is being removed effectively, the elements still need repositioning on the stage, as their index numbers have changed. To do this we'll create another function called `arrangeall`.

10. Here's the function. This will loop through all the elements in our array and call the position function that we have already created for each of the elements:

```
function arrangeall(){
    for(i=0;i<people.length;i++){
        position(people[i],i);
    }
}
```

Now, if you test it again, you'll find that you can add or remove the entries and the rest will shuffle up to accommodate the changes. This is because we are positioning each clip based on its index number in the array, and when we use the `splice` method to remove an element, all of the other elements are automatically renumbered.

If you want to test this section in isolation, try the following code and then list the variables:

```
names = new Array();
names[0]="argento";
names[1]="verhoeven";
names[2]="hellman";
names[3]="carpenter";
names.splice(2,1);
```

You'll see that initially the elements are numbered 0 to 3. When element 2 is removed the elements are numbered 0 to 2.

The next functionality that we'll implement is the ability to cycle through the entries. To visualize how this works, think of the entries forming a stack. As we add an element it goes on top of the stack using the `Array.push` method. To cycle through we want to remove an element from the top of the stack and put it to the bottom, or remove an element from the bottom of the stack and put it to the top. `Array.push` will clearly come in useful here, but we'll also need to use `Array.pop`, `Array.shift` and `Array.unshift`.

> `push` *and* `pop` *perform operations at the end of an array, and* `shift` *and* `unshift` *perform operations at the beginning of an array; so you can think of these methods as pairs*

You've already come across the `push` method that adds an element to the end of an array. The `pop` method removes an element from the end of an array, `shift` removes the first element of an array, and `unshift` adds an element to the beginning of an array:

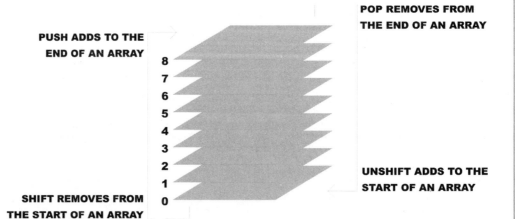

PUSH ADDS TO THE END OF AN ARRAY

POP REMOVES FROM THE END OF AN ARRAY

UNSHIFT ADDS TO THE START OF AN ARRAY

SHIFT REMOVES FROM THE START OF AN ARRAY

8
7
6
5
4
3
2
1
0

So to cycle forward through an array, we need to pop the last element, and then unshift it so that it becomes the first element. To cycle backwards through the array we need to shift the first element, and then push it to the end of an array. So, let's put them to use.

11. First of all we need to add two buttons to the stage, one to cycle backwards and one to cycle forwards. We'll create functions for cycling backwards and forwards, and the buttons will call those functions. Put this code on the forward button:

```
on(press){
    cycleforward();
}
```

...and this on the backward button:

```
on(press){
    cycleback();
}
```

12. Now we'll create the functions. To cycle forward we need to remove the last element of the array using pop and then add it to the beginning of the array using unshift. You can use a variable to help with this, as I have done in this code (the variable nextperson):

```
function cycleforward(){
    var nextperson=people.pop();
    people.unshift(nextperson);
}
```

In fact, though, we can manage without:

```
function cycleforward(){
    people.unshift(people.pop());
}
```

This second version removes the element from the end and puts it to the start within one statement, a much more compact way of doing things.

Of course after we do this we need to arrange everything properly, so we need to call the arrangeall function.

```
function cycleforward(){
    people.unshift(people.pop());
    arrangeall();
}
```

13. The `cycleback` function will work in exactly the same way, but using `shift` and `push` instead of `pop` and `unshift`:

```
function cycleback(){
    people.push(people.shift());
    arrangeall();
}
```

If you test this now, the cycling backwards and forwards should work fine.

14. We'll use one more function to allow us to reverse the order of the array. This is very simple, and uses the `reverse` method of the array object. Just put a button on stage and add this code:

```
on(release){
    people.reverse();
    arrangeall();
}
```

That should work straight away without any more effort.

Finally, we'll implement a couple of `sort` methods, to sort the data by surname and by date of birth. If you use it as is, the `sort` method of the `Array` object sorts an array into alphabetical or numerical order. For example, if you had an array like this...

```
names = new Array();
names[0]="argento";
names[1]="verhoeven";
names[2]="hellman";
names[3]="carpenter";
```

...and used the `sort` method...

```
names.sort();
```

...and tested the movie, (using list variables), the `names` array would come out like this:

```
Variable _level0.names = [object #1] [
    0:"argento",
    1:"carpenter",
    2:"hellman",
    3:"verhoeven"
]
```

Used this way, then, the `sort` method would not be that useful to us, as that would just sort our movie clips alphabetically. To `sort` the array differently requires us to create our own custom function to pass to the `sort` method. It's simpler than it sounds!

We'll send the custom function two parameters, a and b, and tell the sort method what order to put these two elements in. The method will return -1 if a should appear before b, 1 if b should appear before a, and 0 if the two should be seen as equivalent.

We'll never actually see these values, as they will be returned to the sort method, giving it a scheme to refer to when sorting the array – a way to compare and arrange the elements.

15. We'll start by creating a function to sort the elements by surname. First of all we need a "sort by surname" button. Put it on the stage and add the following code to it.

```
on(release){
    people.sort(bysurname);
    arrangeall();
}
```

Note that where previously the brackets after sort were empty, instructing sort to use its default method of ordering, here we used the parameter bysurname, telling the sort method to look for this function in order to determine how the sorting should be carried out.

Now to the method. In the function a and b will refer to two elements of the array, our movie clips, and a.surname and b.surname will refer to the surname variables of these movie clips:

```
function bysurname(a,b){
    if(a.surname>b.surname){
        return 1; //a should be placed after b
    }else if(a.surname<b.surname){
        return -1; //b should be placed after a
    }else{
        return 0;
    }
}
```

So, if movie clip a had the surname johnston, and movie clip b the surname hampshire, the function would return 1 because johnston is greater than hampshire, and johnston will be placed after hampshire in the array.

16. Now to sort by date of birth. We'll need a button, as before:

```
on(release){
    people.sort(bydob);
    arrangeall();
}
```

Sorting by date of birth is more complicated than by surname, as we need to compare several things: the years, and then if they are the same, the months, and then finally if they are the same, we will need to compare the days. This complexity is compounded by the fact that we don't have separate variables for year, month and day of birth. To get around that we'll use `String.substr`:

For year we can use `dob.substr(4,4)`
For month we can use `dob.substr(2,2)`
For day we can use `dob.substr(0,2)`

Here's the code. It might look slightly confusing at first, but it essentially operates as a series of conditional statements, comparing first the year, then the month and then the day. If at any point the values of `a` and `b` are different, the loop will exit:

```
function bydob(a,b){
    //compare years
    if(a.dob.substr(4,4)>b.dob.substr(4,4)){
        return 1;
    }else if(a.dob.substr(4,4)<b.dob.substr(4,4)){
        return -1;
    }else{
        //Years are same so compare months
        if(a.dob.substr(2,2)>b.dob.substr(2,2)){
            return 1;
        }else if(a.dob.substr(2,2)<b.dob.substr(2,2)){
            return -1;
        }else{
            // months are the same, so compare days
            if(a.dob.substr(0,2)>b.dob.substr(0,2)){
                return 1;
            }else if(a.dob.substr(0,2)<b.dob.substr(0,2)){
                return -1;
            }else{
                // year, month and day are the same so return 0.
                return 0;
            }
        }
    }
}
```

And that's all there is to it. Try your movie out.

The Math Object

We've already been using methods of the `Math` object in our other examples, so here I'll just investigate a couple of its other methods that we can usefully employ. I'm going to construct two examples, the first using the `Mouse` object, and the second demonstrating how to use `Math.abs` to terminate motion when an object has reached its destination.

Working with angles and distances

In this example we'll construct a custom cursor application in which the cursor turns to face whichever object it is closest to. We'll use `Math.atan2` to compute the angles and `Math.sqrt` to compute the distance between the current mouse position and each of the objects.

1. First create a movie clip containing a custom cursor. Drag it on the stage, name it pointer, and then attach the following code:

```
onClipEvent (load) {
    Mouse.hide();
}

onClipEvent (mouseMove) {
    _x = _root._xmouse;
    _y = _root._ymouse;
}
```

We're using the `hide` method of the `Mouse` object to hide the normal cursor when the clip first appears. From then on, when the mouse moves, the movie clip containing the custom cursor moves with it. In other words, we set the movie clip's `_x` position to equal the mouse's `_x` position, and the movie clip's `_y` position to equal the mouse's `_y` position. So far so good.

2. Now add our objects to the stage. Create a movie clip containing a graphic of some sort and put five instances of it on stage, naming them sequentially, (object1, object2, and so on).

We'll create a function to check which of the objects is closest to the mouse position. We'll check how far each object's `_x` and `_y` positions are from the mouse's `_x` and `_y` position, and use these values to compute the distance from the object to the mouse.

We'll call the function `calcdistances` and put it on the main timeline. Create a new layer to hold all your actions, and insert the following code there on the first frame:

```
function calcdistances(){
    for(i=1;i<=5;i++) {
        xdist=this["object"+i]._x-_root._xmouse;
        ydist=this["object"+i]._y-_root._ymouse;
        this["object"+i].totaldist =
    ➥Math.sqrt((xdist*xdist)+(ydist*ydist));
    }
}
```

This code sets variables within each object containing its total distance from the mouse – object1.totaldist=20, object2.totaldist=40, and so on. The `totaldist` figure is arrived at by using Pythagoras' theorem, which I've quickly sketched out below. Pythagoras' theorem basically states that with a right angle triangle, the square of the hypotenuse (longest side) is equal to the sum of the squares of the two sides, so in the picture below, (3*3)+(4*4)=(5*5).

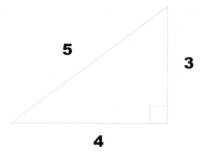

So to find out the distance from each object to the mouse we add the x distance squared to the y distance squared, which gives us the total distance squared, and we then find the square root of this sum to obtain the total distance (un-squared).

3.   Next we add a call to the `calcdistances` function on the `pointer` clip:

```
onClipEvent (mouseMove) {
    _x = _root._xmouse;
    _y = _root._ymouse;
    _root.calcdistances();
}
```

Here we are computing each object's distance from the mouse. Now we need something to check which of these is smallest. To do that we're going to modify the `calcdistances` function, adding some new lines to the code we just entered. The new lines are highlighted:

```
function calcdistances(){
    closestobject=this.object1;
    for(i=1;i<=5;i++) {
        xdist=this["object"+i]._x-_root._xmouse;
```

```
      ydist=this["object"+i]._y-_root._ymouse;
      this["object"+i].totaldist=
➡ Math.sqrt((xdist*xdist)+(ydist*ydist));
      if(this["object"+i].totaldist<closestobject.totaldist) {
         closestobject=this["object"+i];
      }
   }
}
```

The new lines set a variable called closestobject containing the path to whichever clip is closest. Before the loop starts, we set it to object1, as the way the code works is to go through each of the objects checking whether its distance from the mouse is less than the clip that is currently set as the closestobject. As we loop through the objects, each one checks whether its totaldist is less than the closestobject's totaldist and, if it is, it becomes closestobject itself. We could achieve the same results by adding each object's distance from the mouse to an array and then sorting that array to find the clip with the smallest distance variable, but it seems like that our method is probably more economical.

Now we have used the calcdistances function to find out which movie clip is closest to the mouse, we need another function that will calculate the distances on the x and y axes between the closest object and the mouse, and then calculate the angle between them in order to rotate the cursor to point at the object.

4. On the main timeline, on the first frame, add the code:

```
function calcangle(){
   var deltax = _root._xmouse-closestobject._x;
   var deltay = _root._ymouse-closestobject._y;
   angle = Math.atan2 ( deltay, deltax );
   angle/=( Math.pi/180 );
   return angle;
}
```

and then add this code to the *pointer* movie clip:

```
onClipEvent (mouseMove) {
   _x = _root._xmouse;
   _y = _root._ymouse;
   _root.calcdistances();
   _rotation = _root.calcangle();
}
```

To compute the angle between the object and the mouse we use Math.atan2, using the distance between the mouse and the object on its x and y axes as the parameters. This returns the angle as a radian, which the final line of the function converts to a degree by dividing it by (Math.PI/180). We then add a call to the function from the *pointer* movie clip and set the rotation to the value returned by the function (angle).

5. And that's all there is to this example finished. As a final touch, you could add a button with the following code to the object movie clip:

```
on (rollOver) {
    mouse.show();
    _root.pointer._visible = 0;
}

on (rollOut, dragOut) {
    mouse.hide();
    _root.pointer._visible = 1;
}
```

Now on rollover the original mouse will reappear and our custom cursor will be hidden. On rollout our custom cursor is restored.

Math.abs and programmatic movement

In this next example we'll use math.abs to terminate programmatic movement when a movie clip in motion reaches its destination. So, the first thing we have to do is create the programmatic motion.

1. Create a movie clip with some kind of graphic in it and place it on stage.

We're going to have the movie clip follow a user click, so we need a mouseDown handler to store the _x and _y positions of the mouse when it is clicked, and an enterFrame handler to move the movie clip. Both of these need to be attached to the movie clip instance:

```
onClipEvent (mouseDown) {
    targetx=_root._xmouse;
    targety=_root._ymouse;
}
onClipEvent (enterFrame) {
    xdif=targetx-_x;
    _x+=xdif/5;
    ydif=targety-_y;
    _y+=ydif/5;
}
```

The `mouseDown` code is fairly self-explanatory; we're storing the mouse _x and _y position in the variables `targetx` and `targety`.

In the `enterFrame` handler we are first computing the distance between the target position (`targetx` and `targety`) and the actual position (_x and _y), and then adding a fraction of that difference to the current position. Every frame, the distance between the object and its target is reduced by a fifth. So if it starts off 500 pixels away, it will then be 400 pixels away, then 320 pixels away then 256 pixels, etc. This produces an easing out effect.

The problem with the code at the moment is that it will carry on forever. If you put an extra line within the `enterFrame` handler:

```
trace(xdif);
```

You'll see that the difference gets smaller and smaller and smaller. Obviously if we were dealing with a large number of clips this would become quite processor intensive, with large number of movie clips moving almost infinitesimal amounts. To deal with this we need to say that when the difference between the movie clip's position and its target position on the x and y axes is less than a certain amount, put it to its target position and stop it moving. The problem that we run into here is that we can't say...

```
if(xdif<0 && ydif<0){
    //stop moving;
}
```

...because the movie clip might be moving from right to left, which would mean that `xdif` would always be less than zero. We can use `Math.abs` to solve this problem. This method returns the absolute value of any number, that is to say if it is passed a positive number it will return that number, and if it is passed a negative number it will return its positive equivalent, that is to say the same number multiplied by -1. We can now say:

```
if(math.abs(xdif)<0.2 && math.abs(ydif)<0.2){
    //stop moving;
}
```

This in effect means that if the clip is within 0.2 pixels left and right of the target, and the clip is within 0.2 pixels above and below the target, the code will stop running.

2. So here is the modified code that will do what we want:

```
onClipEvent(mouseDown){
    targetx=_root._xmouse;
    targety=_root._ymouse;
    active=true;
}
onClipEvent(enterFrame){
    if(active){
```

continues overleaf

```
        xdif=targetx-_x;
        _x+=xdif/5;
        ydif=targety-_y;
        _y+=ydif/5;
        if(Math.abs(xdif)<0.2 && Math.abs(ydif)<0.2){
            _x=targetx;
            _y=targety;
            active=false;
        }
    }
}
```

Now when the user clicks we set the Boolean `active` to `true`. While `active` is `true` the movement code runs, until it gets to within 0.2 pixels of its target on the x and y axes, at which point the clip is positioned exactly at its target and the Boolean `active` is set to `false`, meaning that the code will no longer run until the mouse button is pressed again.

The Key Object

The Key object is another object that does not require initialization; its methods can be utilized immediately. The key object has four methods:

```
Key.getAscii
Key.getCode
Key.isDown
Key.isToggled
```

It also has a number of properties, such as `Key.DOWN` and `Key.ENTER`. In this next section I'm going to look at two applications of the `Key` object, the first enabling the input of text without the use of an input text field, and the second the use of keys to control the movement of an object, a possible gaming application.

Capturing keystrokes

Being able to capture keystrokes and represent on screen the character referred to by the key pressed is pretty handy for creating the text effects that kids love nowadays. To do this we need to get the ASCII value of the key when it is pressed and then convert it back into the relevant character.

There is a method of the key object that allows us to do this, `Key.getAscii`. Once we have captured the ASCII value, we can use the `String.fromCharCode` method to covert this ASCII value back to something recognizable.

1. So to start off we need to do two things, first put a multiline dynamic text field on the stage and give it the variable name `text`, making sure that Word wrap is checked and

that selectable is unchecked. Next create a blank movie clip called `clipevents` and drop it onto the stage.

2. Now the code we need is fairly simple. For this example we'll use the `clipEvent` handler `keyDown`. This handler is activated whenever a key is pressed. First of all to capture the key press and return its ASCII value we can use this code attached to the `clipevents` movie clip:

```
onClipEvent(keyDown){
    trace(Key.getAscii());
}
```

That should return the ASCII value of the key pressed.

3. Now to convert that into its corresponding character we use `String.fromCharCode`

```
onClipEvent(keyDown){
    trace(String.fromCharCode(Key.getAscii()));
}
```

That should now trace the correct characters for each key pressed.

4. Finally we need to add this character to the `text` string each time:

```
onClipEvent(keyDown){
    _parent.text+=(String.fromCharCode(Key.getAscii()));
}
```

Now what you type should appear in the text box as you type it.

One thing to bear in mind with anything using key presses is that the window must be focused for it to work properly. Bearing that in mind it's probably worth including some kind of instruction to click on the screen before starting. The least intrusive way to do this is to just have a click to start button or something like that.

Using the Key object for gaming

This is just a quick example of how you might begin to construct a game using keyboard control with Flash. The basic set-up will be an object with movement controlled by the cursor keys. Each cursor key will increase its speed in the relevant direction.

1. First of all, set up a movie clip with a graphic in it, and put it on the stage.

2. Now for the code. We'll make each cursor key increase the speed in a different direction, so we'll use a different if statement for each. First of all we need to get the key codes for each cursor. There is a table of these codes in the ActionScript reference: down is 40, right is 39, left is 37 and up is 38.

So, put this code on the movie clip:

```
onClipEvent(enterFrame) {
    if(Key.isDown(40)) {
        yspd+=2;
    }
    if(Key.isDown(39)) {
        xspd+=2;
    }
    if(Key.isDown(37)) {
        xspd-=2;
    }
    if(Key.isDown(38)) {
        yspd-=2;
    }
}
```

This code checks if each cursor is down and adjusts the speed accordingly.

3. Now we need to add code to move the graphic. We want this code to do several things. First of all we need to apply friction to the motion. We do this by multiplying the x and y speed variables by a fraction (0.95 works). We then need to reposition the movie clip, adding the x speed variable to the _x position and adding the y speed variable to the _y position. This is entered after the previous code, within the clipEvent handler:

```
xspd*=0.95;
yspd*=0.95;
_x+=xspd;
_y+=yspd;
```

If you try the code like this you'll see that it works after a fashion, but the clip is easily lost off-stage.

4. To tackle this we need to add some kind of wraparound. The way we'll do this is to check what position the clip will move to next, and if that is offstage in any direction, we need to send the clip to the other side of the stage. Remove the previous code and put this on the clip instead:

```
xspd*=0.95;
yspd*=0.95;
//set variables for next _x and _y positions
nextx=_x+xspd;
nexty=_y+yspd;
//Check if the clip will move offstage (stage is 550 X 400)
if(nextx+0.5*_width<0){
    nextx+=550;
}
if(nextx-0.5*_width>550){
```

```
        nextx-=550;
    }
    if(nexty+0.5*_height<0){
        nexty+=400;
    }
    if(nexty-0.5*_height>400){
        nexty-=400;
    }
    //Update _x and _y
    _x=nextx;
    _y=nexty;
```

In checking if the clip has moved offstage we're adding and subtracting half of the height and width to make sure the clip has completely moved outside the bounds. If we did not add this half of the clip would still be visible on stage.

You may have noticed that in our first example we used `onClipEvent(keyDown)` to check the last key pressed, but in this example we used `onClipEvent(enterFrame)` to check whether each key is down.

The reason for this is that the `enterFrame` method seems more responsive and better at capturing multiple key presses. Here's a modification of our code using `clipEvent(keyDown)` and `Key.getCode`. The `Key.getCode` method returns the key code of the last key pressed, so we use the same code values as our previous method.

5. If you replace the code we had on our movie clip earlier with the following, you'll see how the previous method seems a lot more responsive:

```
onClipEvent(keyDown){
    if(Key.getCode()==40) {
        yspd+=2;
    }
    if(Key.getCode()==39) {
        xspd+=2;
    }
    if(Key.getCode()==37) {
        xspd-=2;
    }
    if(Key.getCode()==38) {
        yspd-=2;
    }
}

onClipEvent(enterFrame){
    xspd*=0.95;
    yspd*=0.95;
    nextx=_x+xspd;
    nexty=_y+yspd;

    if(nextx+0.5*_width<0){
```

continues overleaf

```
            nextx+=550;
        }
        if (nextx-0.5*_width>550) {
            nextx-=550;
        }
        if (nexty+0.5*_height<0) {
            nexty+=400;
        }
        if (nexty-0.5*_height>400) {
            nexty-=400;
        }
        _x=nextx;
        _y=nexty;
    }
```

The code is essentially the same, but it checks if a key has been pressed when Flash registers a key press, instead of checking whether each key is down, as in the previous version.

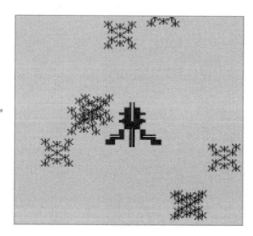

Before we move on to the date object I just want to discuss a few other issues that might arise in the use of the Key object and how to get around them.

The numerical keypad

Numerical keypads represent an interesting problem, as using Key.getAscii returns 0 for all of the keys, and Key.getCode returns different values depending on whether NUMLOCK is on or not: if NUMLOCK is off, the keys return the same key codes as the cursor keys that they represent; if NUMLOCK is on, the numbers on the keypad return different values to the numbers on the main keyboard. So if you needed to check whether 1 was pressed on the keypad or the main keyboard you would need to check both separately (97 is the code for 1 on the keypad and 49 is the code for 1 on the main keyboard):

```
onClipEvent (keyDown) {
```

```
            if(key.getCode()==49 || key.getCode()==97) {
                trace("1 pressed on either keyboard or keypad");
            }
        }
```

Of course, even with this amendment there is still a problem: if NUMLOCK is off, 1 on the numeric keypad will return the value for 'END', 35. What you could do in this situation is add another conditional that states if NUMLOCK is off, also check if 'END' is pressed. The method to check if CAPSLOCK or NUMLOCK is on is Key.isToggled, with the relevant key code in the parentheses. The code for NUMLOCK is 144, and we need to check that it is not toggled:

```
onClipEvent(keyDown){
    if(key.getCode()==49 || key.getCode()==97) {
        trace("1 pressed on either keyboard or keypad");
    }else if(!Key.isToggled(144) && Key.getCode()==35){
        trace("num lock is off and end has been pressed");
    }
}
```

You can also use Key.isToggled to instruct the user to tell the user to turn off their CAPSLOCK or NUMLOCK.

Key.getAscii

We've already worked with Key.getAscii, but I want to reiterate how helpful this method can be if you need to distinguish between upper case and lower case letters. Say, for example, you need to have different actions occur depending on whether the letter pressed is a lower case or upper case 'A'. Key.getCode returns 65 for both 'A' and 'a', so if you wanted to check whether the 'a' is lower case, you would have to check both that caps lock is turned off and that the shift key is not being pressed:

```
onClipEvent(keyDown){
    if(key.getCode()==65) {
        // "a" or "A" was pressed
        if(!Key.isToggled(20) && !Key.isDown(16)){
            //!key.isToggled(20) means that caps lock is not on
            //!key.isDown(16) means that shift is not pressed
            trace("lower case a was pressed");
        }
    }
}
```

Contrast that with this method using Key.getAscii (the ASCII value for a lower case a is 97):

```
onClipEvent(keyDown){
    if(key.getAscii()==97) {
        // lower case "a" was pressed
    }
}
```

That's a lot cleaner and simpler. It should be noted that the use of `getAscii` is not always appropriate as certain keys, such as the enter key and cursor keys, do not return values. It's important to test thoroughly before picking which method you're going to use.

The Date Object

With Flash 4, any attempt to include the current date/time in a movie involved a lot of JavaScript and was rather time-consuming. Now we have the `Date` object, and it's a much simpler matter. In this section, I'll show you a couple of practical examples of its use. First I'll show you how to use the `Date` object in combination with the `Array` object to display the current date, and then I'll show how we can use the it in combination with the `Sound` object to create a speaking clock!

Using the Date Object and the Array Object Together

1. The `Date` object needs to be initialized before its use, so that's the first thing to do. Put this code on the first frame of the timeline.

```
mydate = new Date();
```

Once we have done this, we can retrieve the month, day, date, hours, minutes, seconds and milliseconds either in local time or in GMT (Greenwich Mean Time).

2. If you add the following code to the timeline, it will display in the Output window the current hours on your system and then the current hour of the day in London. Note that `getUTCHours` is still referring to your system clock, using your system time zone settings:

```
trace(mydate.getHours());
trace(mydate.getUTCHours()); //GREENWICH MEANTIME
```

That's fairly simple, and the same applies to `getMinutes`, `getSeconds` and `getMilliseconds`. They all return the numbers we're looking for.

If, however, you want to display the date like this:

Tuesday, 14th March, 2001,

Then you start running into difficulties. If we trace `mydate.getDay` it will return a number from 0 to 6 corresponding to the day of the week (this is zero-based as with the `String` and `Array` objects). What we need to do, then, is use an array to associate each number with the corresponding day of the week. Something like this:

```
daysoftheweek =[ "Sunday", "Monday", "Tuesday", "Wednesday",
"Thursday", "Friday", "Saturday" ];
```

It creates an array like this:

```
0:"Sunday",
1:"Monday",
2:"Tuesday",
3:"Wednesday",
4:"Thursday",
5:"Friday",
6:"Saturday"
```

As you can see, the numbers now correspond to the days of the week. If it's a Sunday, getDay will return 0 and daysoftheweek[0] is Sunday.

3. So we can now do this:

```
daysoftheweek =[ "Sunday", "Monday", "Tuesday", "Wednesday",
   ➡"Thursday", "Friday", "Saturday" ];
mydate= new Date();
daynum=mydate.getDay();
actualday=daysoftheweek[daynum];
```

This retrieves the number of the day from the date object (daynum) and then puts the corresponding value from the array daysoftheweek[daynum] into the variable actualday. The same principle applies for setting the name of the month:

```
monthsoftheyear=["January", "February", "March", "April", "May",
"June", "July", "August", "September", "October", "November",
"December"];
mydate= new Date();
monthnum=mydate.getMonth();
actualmonth= monthsoftheyear[monthnum];
```

The next problem we come up against is the suffix for the date in the month, in other words, how to make Flash display 14th and 2nd instead of just 14 and 2.

We can do this using an array containing the suffix corresponding to each date.

Note that the getDate method returns a number from 1 to 31 and the index numbers in our array will range from 0 to 30, so we use datenumber-1 to access the correct suffix:

```
suffixes=["st", "nd", "rd", "th", "th", "th", "th", "th", "th",
   ➡"th", "th", "th", "th", "th", "th", "th", "th", "th", "th",
   ➡"th","st", "nd","rd","th", "th", "th", "th", "th", "th", "th",
   ➡"st" ];
mydate= new Date();
datenumber=mydate.getDate();
daysuffix = suffixes[datenumber-1];
trace(datenumber+daysuffix);
```

The trace should now return the number of the current day along with the correct suffix.

4. Now we can put everything together to display the current date properly formatted:

```
daysoftheweek =[ "Sunday", "Monday", "Tuesday", "Wednesday",
➥"Thursday", "Friday", "Saturday" ];
monthsoftheyear=[ "January", "February", "March", "April", "May",
➥"June", "July", "August", "September", "October", "November",
➥"December" ];
suffixes=[ "st", "nd", "rd", "th", "th", "th", "th", "th", "th",
➥"th", "th", "th", "th", "th", "th", "th", "th", "th",
➥"th", "st", "sn", "rd", "th", "th", "th", "th", "th",
➥"th", "st" ];

mydate = new Date();
year=mydate.getFullYear();
monthnum=mydate.getMonth();
datenumber=mydate.getDate();
daynum=mydate.getDay();
actualday=daysoftheweek[daynum];
actualmonth= monthsoftheyear[monthnum];
daysuffix = suffixes[datenumber];
displaydate=actualday + ", " + datenumber + daysuffix + " " +
➥actualmonth + ", " + year + ".";
```

The last line of code puts all of the individual variables together into one long string.

5. Now if we put a text field on stage for the variable `displaydate`, the date will display as specified.

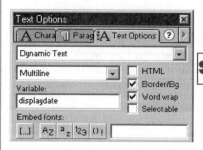

Saturday, 12th May, 2001.

Creating an Analogue/Digital Speaking Clock

Next we'll create a combination clock, one that displays the time in both analogue and digital formats and speaks the time on command. We're essentially taking the data provided by the `Date` object and displaying it graphically and aurally:

1. First we set up a `Date` object and create a function to update the values of hours, minutes and seconds. On the main timeline, add this code to frame 1:

```
function getTime () {
    time = new Date();
    hours = time.getHours();
    minutes = time.getMinutes();
    seconds = time.getSeconds();
}
```

This function will update the values of hours, minutes and seconds whenever it is called.

2. Next, we'll display that information as an analogue format. For this we need three movie clips, one for the clock outline and two for the clock hands. The clock hands should both be straight lines going straight up and originating from the registration point like this:

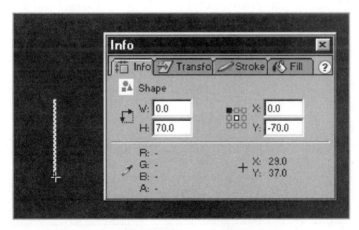

3. We now put these three objects on stage, naming them hourhand, minutehand and clockface. The two hands should be placed at the center point of the clock, using the info panel or the align panel, whichever you prefer.

4. Now we have to move the hands to display the correct time by setting their rotation to the appropriate point. There are 360° in a circle and 60 minutes in an hour, so each minute corresponds to a 6° shift around the circle. So we add this to the function:

```
minutehand._rotation=minutes*6;
```

For hours we can say that there are 12 hours in 360° and so each hour corresponds to a 30° shift around the circle, but we want it to change gradually with the minutes rather than jump 30° once every hour, so we use this:

```
hourhand._rotation=(hours*30)+(minutes/2);
```

Each minute adds half a degree to the rotation of the hour hand. To see this working we need to call our `getTime` function. Add this code to the `clockface` movie clip:

```
onClipEvent(enterFrame){
    _root.getTime();
}
```

Next we'll create a digital display to go alongside this. The thing to bear in mind here is that we always want to display two digits, so that if it's nine minutes past seven we display 7:09 and not 7:9.

5.   To this end we'll create a separate variable in the getTime function in frame 1 for the digits that are displayed for hours, minutes and seconds:

```
if(minutes<10) {
    minutesdisplay="0"+minutes;
} else {
    minutesdisplay=minutes;
}
if(seconds<10) {
    secondsdisplay="0"+seconds;
} else {
    secondsdisplay=seconds;
}
if(hours>12) {
    hoursdisplay=hours-12;
} else {
    hoursdisplay=hours;
}
if(hoursdisplay == 0) {
    hoursdisplay = 12;
}
if(hoursdisplay<10) {
    hoursdisplay = " "+hoursdisplay;
}
timedisplay = hours+" : "+minutesdisplay+" : "+secondsdisplay;
```

If the `minutes` or `seconds` variables are below 10, we put a zero in front of them for display purposes, otherwise we use the value itself. If the `hours` variable is greater than 12 we subtract 12 from it so that we display time in 12-hour format rather than 24-hour. If `hours` is less than 10 we add a space in front of it to keep the layout even.

6.   Once again, put a dynamic text field called `timedisplay` on the stage, and we have a working analogue and digital clock.

Now for the tricky part, making the clock speak. We need to consider how each figure will be spoken. Firstly hours will be a number between one and twelve. We can use this figure to trigger the respective sound. Minutes are different. To avoid having to include separate sounds for each number from one to sixty we can consider how each number is made up. The numbers from one to nineteen require separate sounds. For twenty and above we can use a combination of the tens figure (twenty, thirty, etc.) and the numbers one to nine.

7. With that in mind, we need to create separate variables for the tens and units of the `minutes` variable, so we add the following code to our function:

```
mintens = minutesdisplay.toString().substr(0,1);
mintens *=10;
minunits = minutesdisplay.toString().substr(1,1);
```

So if `minutesdisplay` equals 23, `mintens` will equal 20 (the first character multiplied by ten) and `minunits` will equal 3(the second character).

Note that we have to turn our numeric variable into a string using the `toString` method before invoking the `String.substr` method.

Now, if the minutes are over twenty we will know to play first the sound for `mintens` (twenty) and then the sound for `minunits` (three, for example).

8. The final thing to add here is another conditional to set whether it is currently am or pm.

```
if (hours>11){
    pm = true;
} else {
    pm = false;
}
```

9. At this point, it is probably wise to bring in the sounds we want to use. I've imported a `.wav` file for each number we need. Because we're not including the separate sounds on a timeline, we need to make sure they're exported. To do this, right-click/CTRL-click on the sound and select linkage. Then check Export this symbol and give each number an identifier (such as 0 for "zero", 20 for "twenty" etc.) as we did for `MovieClip.attachMovie` earlier.

Now we have to work out how to trigger the different sounds in the right order. Ideally, one would want to create a list of the sounds to play in order and then play them sequentially with each starting as the previous one finishes. Unfortunately, Flash's sound object does not provide a property for the length of each sound or a flag to indicate whether it is still playing and so we cannot do it this way. Considering this, the best option is to create a series of triggers in a movie clip to set off each sound. When the clip plays through each sound will be played in turn.

10. Create a new movie clip, put it on the stage and give it an instance name of `sounds`. On the clip, attach the following code:

```
onClipEvent(load){
    speak=new Sound();
}
```

This will create a new Sound object within our movie clip. Once we have initialized this object, we can use the methods of the sound object, attachSound and Start, to play the different numbers.

11. Now, inside the sounds movie clip add three blank keyframes, and add a stop action to the second one.

12. Put the following on the third frame:

```
hoursdisplay = Number(_root.hoursdisplay);
/* in order for the hours figure to display properly when it is
only a single digit, we may have put a space in front of it which
would have turned it into a string. The number method turns it
back to a number.*/

minutes = _root.minutes;
mintens = _root.mintens;
minunits = _root.minunits;
pm=_root.pm;
```

Now when this clip is told to play, it will hit the third frame and create local variables for the global variables hourssound, etc. We do this to guard against the variables changing as we run through this clip (if the minutes or hours change for example).

On the fourth frame we put:

```
speak.attachSound(hoursdisplay);
speak.start();
```

What this does is check through the symbols that have been exported for one whose name is equivalent to hourssound, attaches it to our sound object and then tells it to play.

13. To test this put a button inside the clock face with these actions:

```
on(press) {
    _root.sounds.play();
}
```

Now every time we press the button, it tells the sounds movie clip to play and triggers the hours sound.

Dealing with the minutes is slightly more difficult and requires a little logical thinking. There are four different possible situations:

- case1: If minutes is between 1 and 9, we want Flash to play 0 and then play the minutes figure.

- case 2: If minutes is between 10 and 19, or it equals 20, 30, 40 or 50, we want it to just play the number itself.

- case 3: If minutes is between 21 and 29, 31 and 39, 41 and 49 or 51 and 59, we want it to play first the tens figure (20, 30, etc.) and then the units figure.

- case 4: if minutes equals 0 we want to skip minutes and just play pm or am

14. So, let's go back into our **sounds** clip, convert these four cases into conditional statements and put them on the tenth frame (leaving a delay in frames on the timeline to allow the hours sound to play out):

```
if(minutes<10 && minutes>0) {
    gotoAndPlay("case1");
}
if(mintens==10 || minunits==0 && minutes!=0) {
    gotoAndPlay("case2");
}
if(mintens>10 && minunits!=0) {
    gotoAndPlay("case3");
}
if(minutes==0) {
    gotoAndPlay("case4");
}
```

Now we need to split the timeline into four separate sections, creating labeled frames for each of those cases, and then adding the actions. This is how they should be set up:

- case 1: First frame plays 0, leave some frames and then play minunits, leave some frames and then skip to play am or pm

- case 2: First frame plays minutes, then leave some frames and skip to play am or pm

- case 3: First frame plays mintens, leave some frames, then play minunits, leave some frames and skip to play am or pm

- case 4: First frame skips straight to play am or pm

15. Now the code for each section. The actions should be placed on one layer, with a label for each section placed on the layer above, on the same frame as the first action of each section.

case 1
First Frame (frame 12):

```
speak.attachSound("0");
speak.start();
```

Second Frame: (frame 17)

```
speak.attachSound(minunits);
speak.start();
```

• case 2
First Frame (frame 32):

```
speak.attachSound(minutes);
speak.start();
```

case 3
First Frame (frame 48):

```
speak.attachSound(mintens);
speak.start();
```

Second Frame (frame 55):

```
speak.attachSound(minunits);
speak.start();
```

case 4
First frame (frame 77):

```
gotoAndPlay("meridian");
```

meridian (frame #83):

```
if(pm) {
    speak.attachSound("pm");
    speak.start();
} else {
    speak.attachsound("am");
    speak.start();
}
gotoAndStop(2);
```

At the end of each section, on frames 31, 47 and 70, add:

```
gotoAndPlay("meridian");
```

...so that when the section has finished it plays pm or am.

The spacing of the frames is a matter of trial and error, as this method is using the timeline to crate a delay between sounds. My finished timeline looks like this:

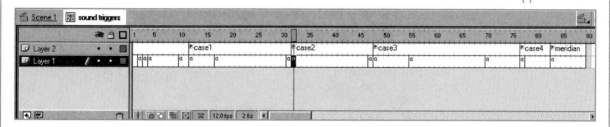

Run the movie... That's magic!

The Color Object

The `Color` object is another useful addition to Flash 5. Whereas previously, you would have had to set up color transformations using a motion tween between two colors in advance, now you can set and transform color dynamically through the use of the color object. I've used a red movie background throughout my examples, so you may have to alter some of the color transformations so that you can see them clearly if you use a different color.

Although it might seem that color should be accessible as a property of a movie clip – in the same way as `_alpha` for instance – it is, in fact, a separate object that has to be initialized before you can use it. Once we've done this, we can access and set the colors of a movie clip through the `Color` object. Setting up an object is simple, taking only one line of code:

```
mycolor=new Color(instance_name);
```

Once this has been initialized, we can access the various methods of the `Color` object: `setRGB`, `getRGB`, `setTransform` and `getTransform`.

We'll begin with the basics: changing the color of a movie clip. To do this we use the `setRGB` method. Once we have set up a `Color` object for a movie clip we can then set its color using:

```
mycolor.setRGB(colorvalue);
```

To test this, put a movie clip containing a red graphic on stage and then attach the following code to it:

```
onClipEvent(load) {
    flakecol=new Color(this);
    flakecol.setRGB(0xFFFFFF);
}
```

As soon as the clip loads we create a new `Color` object for the clip, `flakecol` and then use the `setRGB` method to set its color to white (#FFFFFF).

The `0x` in front of the hex number converts the hex number to its decimal equivalent. For example if you set a variable to 0xFF it will equal 255.

A second, and possibly more useful method of using setRGB is to deal with the red, green and blue components separately, as numbers from 0 to 255. Again, to turn our movie clip white as it is initialized, you can attach the following code to it:

```
onClipEvent(load) {
    flakecol=new Color(this);
    red=255;
    green=255;
    blue=255;
    flakecol.setRGB(red<<16 | green<<8| blue);
}
```

This method uses bitwise shifting to transform the individual numbers into a form accepted by the setRGB method. Essentially, bitwise shifting involves interpreting an argument as a collection of bits rather than a single entity. There is not the space here to go into how this is working, but if you wanted to check this, you could try the following code:

```
bitwisevar= 255<<16 | 255<<8 | 255;
hexvar=0xFFFFFF;
```

You'll notice that the two processes produce the same result.

Dynamic Fading

We've looked at two very simple ways in which you can set your movie clip to a specific color instantly. In practice, though, you'll probably want to know how to fade to this new color in gradually, and that's what I'll walk though next.

In order to do this we need to treat the red, green and blue components of the color separately, so we can gradually change each from their starting value to their target value. We could do this by using hex colors, but then we'd have to convert them back and forth between hexadecimal numbers and decimal numbers, and that takes up processing time. To keep our code efficient, it is best to start with red, green and blue values from 0 to 255, and use bitwise shifting to feed them into the setRGB method.

Color Fading

In this example, we'll fade a movie clip from white to orange. We'll start with the code we looked at earlier to set an object's color to white, and we then add target values for red, green and blue (the values that we want to fade to).

1.   To find the RGB values of the destination color, use the Mixer panel in Flash, set to RGB, and select the color from the bar at the bottom – its values will appear in the R, G and B boxes on the right. To make fine adjustments, use the slider bar to the right of each box. The code looks like this:

```
onClipEvent(load) {
    flakecol=new Color(this);
    red=255;
    green=255;
    blue=255;
    flakecol.setRGB(red<<16 | green<<8| blue);
    targetred=204;
    targetgreen=102;
    targetblue=51;
}
```

2.   Now that we've set the initial color of the movie clip and the color we want it to fade to, we need some script to handle the transition between them. A good method of doing this is to get the difference between the two values and then add a fraction of that difference to the current value. If we do this every frame, the color will gradually approach the target color. Look at this code:

```
onClipEvent(load) {
    red=0;
    targetred=255;
}

onClipEvent(enterFrame) {
    difference=targetred-red;
    red+=difference/10;
    trace("difference= "+difference);
    trace("red= "+red);
}
```

If you were to test it, you'll see that red gradually increases and difference gradually decreases until red equals targetred. If we reduce the figure (10), the increment will be faster and if we increase it, it will be slower:

```
Output                                        ×
                                      Options
difference= 255
red= 25.5
difference= 229.5
red= 48.45
difference= 206.55
red= 69.105
difference= 185.895
red= 87.6945
difference= 167.3055
red= 104.42505
difference= 150.57495
red= 119.482545
difference= 135.517455
red= 133.0342905
difference= 121.9657095
red= 145.23086145
difference= 109.76913855
red= 156.207775305
difference= 98.792224695
red= 166.0869977745
difference= 88.9130022255
```

3. Lets now take this principle and apply it to our original red, green and blue values. Note that here, the value 10 has been replaced with a variable `incrspeed` to enable us to adjust it more easily across the three RGB values:

```
onClipEvent(load) {
    flakecol=new Color(this);
    red=255;
    green=255;
    blue=255;
    targetred=204;
    targetgreen=102;
    targetblue=51;
    flakecol.setRGB(red<<16 | green<<8| blue);
    incrspeed=10;
}

onClipEvent(enterFrame) {
    difference=targetred-red;
    red+=difference/incrspeed;
    difference=targetblue-blue;
    blue+=difference/incrspeed;
    difference=targetgreen-green;
    green+=difference/incrspeed;
    flakecol.setRGB(red<<16 | green<<8| blue);
}
```

You can modify the red, green and blue values in the code to create a fade start and finish point for any valid RGB color.

Once you've set the color of an object using `setRGB`, you can then retrieve that value using `getRGB`. This might be useful when, for example, you need to check if two clips are the same color.

4. To get this figure and convert it to a hex number, use this following code:

```
currenthex=mycolor.getRGB().toString(16);
```

In this code, `toString(16)` is used to convert the number returned by `getRGB` into a hexadecimal number.

If you insert the following lines into the dynamic fade we just wrote, you can trace the hex value at any point in the fade:

```
currenthex=flakecol.getRGB().toString(16);
trace("current hex value = "+currenthex);
```

Color.setTransform and Color.getTransform

While setRGB can be very useful when you need an object to be a definite hex color, it has definite drawbacks. Try dropping a photo into our color fade example above, for example, and you'll see that it renders it as a solid block of color – not a very useful effect.

With setRGB, all colors within a movie clip are changed to the RGB value specified and all detail is lost. Whenever you need to dynamically tint or adjust the color of a detailed object, you are much better using setTransform.

The setTransform method takes eight separate parameters:

```
ra: red percentage (-100 to 100)
rb: red offset (-255 to 255)
ga: green percentage (-100 to 100)
gb: green offset (-255 to 255)
ba: blue percentage (-100 to 100)
bb: blue offset (-255 to 255)
aa: alpha percentage (-100 to 100)
ab: alpha offset (-255 to 255)
```

You might notice here that it looks as if we could use setTransform() to affect the alpha of a movie clip: well, you can. Any changes made to the alpha values of a color object using a setTransform() are reflected in the _alpha property of the relevant movie clip.

To use setTransform(), the various parameters need to be set in a new object that can be plugged into the setTransform method:

```
mycol=new Color(myMovieClip);
colorTransform= new Object();
colorTransform.ra= 50;
colorTransform.rb= 90;
colorTransform.ga= 20;
colorTransform.gb= 100;
colorTransform.ba= 30;
colorTransform.bb= 70;
colorTransform.aa= 80;
colorTransform.ab= 9;
mycol.setTransform(colorTransform);
```

The setTransform method takes each of the values from the colortransform object that we have set up and uses them to create its transformation. You could also set up the object like this:

```
mycol=new Color(myMovieClip);
colorTransform= {ra: '50', rb: '90', ga: '20', gb: '100', ba:
'30', bb: '70', aa: '80', ab: '9'};
mycol.setTransform(colorTransform);
```

Although it might look a bit mysterious at first, (especially with the ActionScript dictionary being rather enigmatic as to what they mean), if you look at the Advanced section of the Effects panel (as in the screenshot below), you'll notice a correspondence.

> *Each of these parameters is equivalent to the transformation that this panel performs on a stage object; with the values on the left equivalent to the percentages, and the values on the right equivalent to the offset values.*

So, in the screenshot below you can see that the transform values that we were setting dynamically can be reproduced manually on a stage level object in Flash.

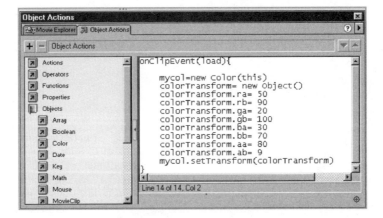

So this is useful. It means that we can produce a certain tint using the Advanced panel within the authoring environment, and then dynamically set an object to fade to that exact tint. In fact, this can be taken even further. While the ActionScript dictionary states that `getTransform` retrieves the value of the last `setTransform` call, this method can actually be used to retrieve color transformations that we have set on the stage in Flash using the advanced panel, as long as we first set up a `Color` object for the movie clip.

Color Transformations

1. To test this, put a movie clip on the stage, call it object1, change it to whatever color you want using the Advanced panel, and then attach the following code to the movie clip:

```
onClipEvent(load){
    mycol=new Color(this);
    originaltransform = mycol.getTransform();
}
```

If you list your variables when you test the movie (CTRL+ALT+V) you'll see that you've created a new object, `originaltransform`, which contains the separate values that combine to create the transformation.

We can do a test to prove this.

2. Add another instance of the same movie clip to the stage, call it `object2` and don't apply any transformation to it.

3. Then change the code on the original movie clip to this:

```
onClipEvent (load) {
    mycol=new Color(this);
    originaltransform = mycol.getTransform();
    secondcol=new Color(_parent.object2);
    secondcol.setTransform(originaltransform);
}
```

The code now retrieves it's own value and puts it into the `originaltransform` object (the first two lines). It then creates a new color object for the second movie clip and sets the transform of the second object to `originaltransform`, its own set of transform values.

The effect is to dynamically set the tint of the second object to the tint we manually applied to the first object within the authoring environment. If you play around with this you'll see that this method does not just work with the advanced section of the Effect panel, but the Tint, Brightness, and Alpha sections also have effects on a movie clip's transform object.

Now you've seen how that works, we can set up a number of instances of a movie clip with different color effects on stage and have another clip fade to reproduce those same effects on a rollover, for example.

4. Let's try it. First we need to set up our objects on the stage, all instances of the same movie clip. They should be named in some kind of consistent fashion (object1, object2, etc.) with the movie clip that you want to fade called something different like fadingclip.

5. Apply different color effects to each of the movie clip's objects using the Effects panel.

We'll use a different method of coding for this example. We'll create a new method of the `MovieClip` object, which will get its transform value and put it in a new object.

6. Put a button inside the 'object' movie clips. The button will call a function that sets the movie clip's own transform values to a new set of values, which the `fadingclip` will fade to:

```
on(rollover) {
    makeactive();
}
```

On the main timeline, add:

```
MovieClip.prototype.makeactive=function() {
    _root.tempcolor=new Color(this);
    _root.fadingclip.targetvalues=_root.tempcolor.getTransform();
}
```

This code creates a temporary color object for the clip that is rolled over. It retrieves the set of transformations that have been applied to it using the `getTransform` (as we did earlier). It then creates an object, `targetvalues`, in the `fadingclip`, which holds a reference to its own transform values for the `fadingclip` to fade towards.

7. Now, to finish off, we need to add code to our `fadingclip` to make it fade to the specified value. Using the same principle we discussed earlier, of gradually decreasing the distance between a value and its target, add the following code:

```
onClipEvent(load) {
    mycol=new Color(this);
    targetvalues=mycol.getTransform();
    speed=10;
}

onClipEvent(enterFrame) {
        mytransform=mycol.getTransform();
        mytransform.ra+= (targetvalues.ra-mytransform.ra)/speed;
        mytransform.rb+= (targetvalues.rb-mytransform.rb)/speed;
        mytransform.ga+= (targetvalues.ga-mytransform.ga)/speed;
        mytransform.gb+= (targetvalues.gb-mytransform.gb)/speed;
        mytransform.ba+= (targetvalues.ba-mytransform.ba)/speed;
        mytransform.bb+= (targetvalues.bb-mytransform.bb)/speed;
        mytransform.aa+= (targetvalues.aa-mytransform.aa)/speed;
        mytransform.ab+= (targetvalues.ab-mytransform.ab)/speed;
        mycol.setTransform(mytransform);
}
```

Try it out.

The difference between each attribute in the `mytransform` object, and its counterpart in the `targetvalues` object is being calculated in each frame, and a fraction of that value added, so the colors of the object gradually fade to those of the target. You can amend the speed of this fade by changing the value of the speed variable.

Conclusion

We've covered a lot of ground in this chapter. I hope that you've have gained some insight into the different ways that the predefined objects in Flash can help you solve a number of design problems, and allow you to create all sorts of effects. The more familiar you get with the many different methods of each object, the easier authoring with Flash will become.

I'd recommend that you work through the ActionScript dictionary, checking out the entries for each method, and constructing your own sample files to see how they work. Even if they at first might seem a bit obscure, like the `charCode` methods of the `String` object, they often turn out to be essential to get around some problem or other. Having solid background knowledge will give you a good idea where to start when you're confronted with difficulties.

I'd also suggest that you try to combine the FLA you've worked with in this chapter, bringing the exercises together. You could, for example, try building on our game example. There are several ways that you could use techniques from other sections of the book to extend this into a fully-fledged game: you might use the orientation code from the math example to make the movie clip point in the direction it's traveling, or even change it so that the cursor keys rotate the ship and apply thrust in the direction it's facing. You could try modifying the first keystroke example into a dynamic text effect, duplicating movie clips containing the letter whose key was pressed. Or you might come up with something completely different. Try playing with the code, seeing what effect changing numeric values gives you, and if, at any point you're not sure what's going on, you can always use `traces` to keep track of things.

4
Objects,
Methods and
Properties

5
Using the
Predefined
Objects

3
Classic
ActionScript
Structures

**Section 1
Core Skills**

2
Animation
Techniques

1
Introduction

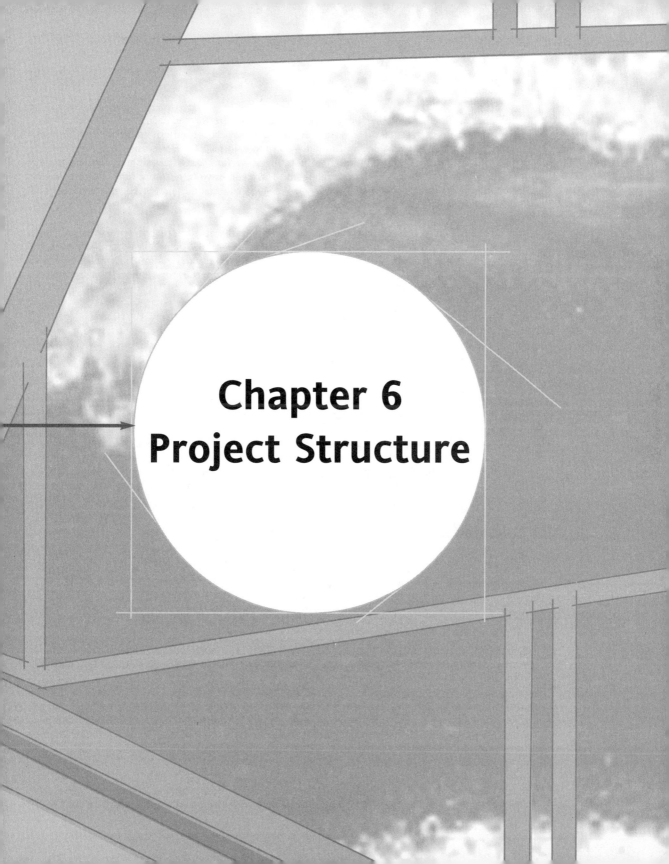

Chapter 6
Project Structure

I remember my first Flash movie. It consisted of buttons that performed navigation between a few scenes, and within each scene there were more buttons that caused various animations and other rich media to start up. It was nice and simple – so simple, in fact, that I was able to build it more or less on the fly, with no forethought other than sketching out the graphics and the style beforehand. In those days, sideways scrolling and Flash games were no more than a pipedream. Flash had little scripting power beyond a few 'goto'-type commands, and there were certainly no variables or advanced ActionScript structures.

Things have moved on since then. Flash has revolutionized web site creation with some much-needed interactivity. ActionScript has finally grown up into a fully object-based and structured language, opening up all sorts of new avenues in terms of web site navigation. The movie clip has now attained the heady status of an *object*, with a full set of properties for designers to use, rather than the old, limited, timeline-based animation methods.

With this increase in versatility, though, comes something else: complexity. We have gained the freedom to design that results from a richer environment, but to make the best of it we have to plan ahead. It's not uncommon for designers to get scared off when they start to see words like *modular design* and *hierarchy* (and all the other stuff that sounds a little too much like programming) being bandied about, but it's really not that bad, as you'll soon see.

In this chapter, we'll explore the fundamentals of planning (and building) a Flash 5 FLA. When the word 'structure' appears in a chapter title, it can mean reams of wholly theoretical text, and lists of instructions: do this; avoid that. But I don't think that kind of thing is practical enough to be useful to anyone. Instead, in the second part of this chapter, I will describe a brief introductory game plan, and then dive straight into the creation of a moderately complex, moderately creative Flash movie, showing how it was all planned and structured for fast and efficient coding. As a Flash professional who often needs to get things done in a hurry, the ability to do that reliably is an attractive proposition.

Initial considerations

There are two driving forces that define what the structure of a Flash movie will be: its content, and its audience.

Content

Web sites exist to provide content to their viewers. They may be factual resources, part of a retail front end, or for entertainment purposes. The needs of the user define the type of content, which in turn largely defines the layout of the site.

For example, a factual resource needs to allow the user to get to information quickly, perhaps giving the latest news and updates the greatest priority. An entertainment site is able to deliver the information in a very different way, because the content and interface are one and the same. The interface itself provides part of the site's entertainment value, and is therefore actually part of the content in its own right.

A related consideration is the demand on bandwidth imposed by the content. A web site advertising an upcoming movie would tend to be very visual, and animation intensive. If the user is not to be faced with long pauses, methods of managing long download times need to be formulated and embedded into the site's structure. If they're not addressed, issues like these are highly likely to cause users to click away.

Sometimes, the content you're provided with by your client may simply be unsuitable for a web audience. Web surfers are notoriously resistant to any form of hard sell, and will quickly go elsewhere if all they see is a re-run of the TV commercial for Brand X soap. The average surfer is used to having something interactive to play with. In fact, this may be one of the reasons that Brand X chose to go with a Flash designer, and the structure of your final site needs to reflect this level of expectation: a simple, scene-based Flash site, with a few navigation buttons, could be commercial suicide for the professional designer. We would need to create web-based content that was different from (but complemented) the TV commercials.

Audience

The expectations and abilities of the audience you are going for need to be considered too. A high-bandwidth showcase site aimed at other designers is somewhere you can really go to town, but if you try the same trick on a site aimed at the typical user on the end of a 56K modem line, the initial download time may cause almost all your visitors to go elsewhere at the preloading screen. Again, the movie's basic structure can help reduce this problem, via intelligent use of the streaming facilities available to Flash.

Overall site structure

An early choice to make is what the overall structure of the site will be. It's important to get this right, because some of the simpler structures make it difficult to implement complex designs, while some of the more involved ones may be overkill for basic sites, resulting in unnecessarily long development times. To begin with, then, I will introduce all the site structures commonly used within Flash sites.

Although the first few designs listed here are likely to come as nothing new to you, some of the later structures might be. Therefore, I'll treat the former fairly quickly, and concentrate in more depth on the new structures that can be useful to the advanced Flash movie creator.

Movies based on a single timeline

A single movie with a single timeline is the structure adopted by most Flash beginners, and consists of content attached directly to the main timeline. In the example timeline shown below, frames 1 to 28 make up the first 'page' of the movie: the movie will run from frame 1 to frame 28 (stopping only because frame 28 has a `stop` command attached to it), and further pages can be accessed by jumping to labels such as `main` and `about`, usually via buttons with `goto` actions attached.

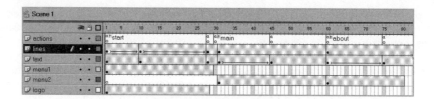

> *It's possible to clean up a timeline like this somewhat by using scenes; the one above could, for example, be split across at least three scenes called* start, about *and* main.

This structure is not *just* for beginners though, because it has at least one very big benefit: the lack of any subsidiary movie clips means that each frame will play as soon as it streams in (movie clips don't start playing until the whole movie clip timeline has loaded). Even for the Flash expert, this has particular advantages in applications such as banner adverts, where you want a slim download that starts running as soon as possible. It's also useful as a component of movies that use multiple levels, which we'll examine in more detail shortly.

Otherwise, however, the single timeline structure is fairly limiting to the ActionScript programmer, simply because ActionScript and streaming are two things that don't go together very well. The trouble is that attempting to jump to a frame that hasn't yet loaded causes the Flash player to go to the last loaded frame, which can be anywhere – and that kind of behavior would normally be fatal to an ActionScript movie.

Movies based on movie clips

Rather than placing motion tweens directly on the main timeline, it's usually better to create animations and other media content as movie clips. Doing so has three major advantages:

- It tidies up the timeline significantly, making it much more compact:

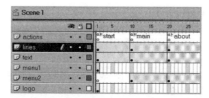

In this timeline, the tweened animations are now in movie clips sitting on the main timeline at frames 1, 10, and 20, so there is no need for any tween keyframes.

- The second advantage becomes apparent when you start using ActionScript: the movie clip timelines can run independently of the main timeline, and they can be stopped or made to play from the main timeline via commands such as `instancename.play`, `instancename.gotoAndPlay`, or `instancename.stop`.

- Movie clips can themselves be animated - that is, as well as having animations within the movie clip, you can animate the movie clip itself (moving it around the stage, for example). This is done by controlling movie clip properties from ActionScript, as we touched on in Chapter 2, and will expand upon in Chapter 9.

This structure is more conducive to the implementation of page-based sites (the 'pages' in this example are start, main, and about).

Movies based on multiple timelines

A movie that uses multiple timelines has movie clips sitting on the main timeline in just the same way as the movie clip based movie above, but it doesn't necessarily stop there: you can have further levels of embedded movie clips. This allows you to use advanced structures in which tasks are broken down into a number of different functional blocks, and then to implement those blocks as separate embedded movie clips.

Most developers of ActionScript-heavy movies (the author included) use this method in preference to the previous ones we've discussed, because it creates a more compact and efficient movie. In particular, it allows you to create modular code, which is more reusable and allows the use of common function routines.

(Although the movie can no longer stream in, this isn't a problem because ActionScript-based movies are not generally built with streaming in mind.)

This design forms the basis of *all* Flash movies that are ActionScript monsters – the games and sideways scrolling types that I mentioned at the start of the chapter, for example. Because it's the most versatile, it's also the one I will illustrate in the later example. Once you get your head round it, you'll find that it's actually the *easiest* to code up when you're writing ActionScript-heavy movies.

To make this kind of movie work well, there is a subtle twist you can use, which is to arrange (where possible) for each movie clip to control its parent. This is a major advance over a structure based only on movie clips, because you don't need to know the instance name (you instead refer to the _parent).

The next three types of movie structure are really just modifications of what we've already covered: they are ways of addressing bandwidth or content issues, and are typically employed to make use of Flash's streaming abilities to reduce download times, or to split up the overall content into separate chunks that are downloaded on demand.

Movies based on multiple windows

Movies that use multiple windows were a favorite of early Flash developers, but a cynical public is now quite likely to find them annoying, especially if the technique is overused. Examples of this design type are made up of a series of SWF movies, each of which is loaded on request into a new browser window (sometimes called a **pop-up window**). They are frequently found in Flash-based web advertising (in place of the more traditional animated GIF banner), because they allow the ad to stream in the background, without causing annoying pauses in the main browser window.

As suggested above, it's a good idea only to use this effect once or twice in a Flash web site, because you can quickly cover the desktop with open windows. Some Flash designers have started to use a *single* pop-up that's called from a HTML page and then hosts the whole Flash site. This is perhaps the best way to use a pop-up, particularly if the Flash site takes a while to load – surfers can busy themselves with whatever's going in the original window while they wait for the pop-up to fill with a multimedia extravaganza. You may need to make it obvious that the pop-up *is* the main movie, so that the user doesn't close it, thinking it to be another commercial.

To create a pop-up window, you need to set up a bit of JavaScript in the HTML file that hosts your Flash movie. Don't worry: it's really only one line, which uses the open method of the JavaScript window object. The simplest function you could write, which needs to be placed inside the HTML document's <HEAD> element, looks like this:

```
<HTML>
    <HEAD>
        <TITLE>Harry Hard</TITLE>
        <META http-equiv="Content-Type"
                content="text/html; charset=iso-8859-1">
        <META name="Creator" content="boy@Futuremedia">
        <SCRIPT language="Javascript">
            function popUp(url, name, attributes)
            {
                window.open(url, name, attributes);
            }
        </SCRIPT>
    </HEAD>

    ...
```

This function can then be called from within Flash 5 ActionScript, via a command such as:

```
on (release) {
    getURL ("javascript:popUp ('tips_for_deejays.htm',"+
        ➡ "'HarryH', 'toolbar=no, location=no," +
        ➡ "directories=no, status=no, menubar=no," +
        ➡ "scrollbars=no, resizable=0, height=520," +
        ➡ "width=790, top=50, left=50')");
}
```

The command is issued here as part of a getURL action attached to a Flash button. It will open up a new browser window titled HarryH, containing the page tips_for_deejays.htm (which of course can be a HTML document with a Flash SWF embedded inside it). To make the browser pop-up look less cluttered, we also suppress some of the features of the window that would normally appear (menu bars and scroll bars), and specify where and how large it should appear on the screen.

Movies based on multiple levels

Basing a movie design on multiple levels means creating a principal Flash movie with additional SWFs that will be loaded up as required. The benefit of this is that the need for a major download during initial loading of a movie is minimized; alternatively, you can arrange for bandwidth-heavy media (such as sound, and large animations) to be loaded up separately from the main movie interface, and only when requested by the user (contributing greatly to the impression of a well thought-out site).

Levels exist as stacked SWFs, with the items on one layer obscuring those on any levels below it. However, any buttons on a lower level will still be active, even though they may be hidden. I like to think of levels as sheets of glass: the bottom level has a 'back', but you can see straight through the others, so the lower levels can be seen.

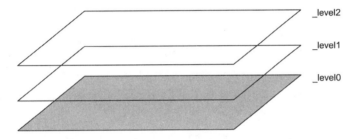

It isn't possible to assume that each level can be treated as a standalone movie in its own right – some thought needs to be given to how the levels will interact. If you *want* levels as standalone movies, then you need to consider the structure based on multiple windows, above.

Using levels to stagger loading is used to good effect in Eric Jordan's 2Advanced (www.2advanced.com)*, and at* www.freshfroot.com*. It's also used in Foundation ActionScript (also published by friends of ED), and you can see the project created in that book at* www.stundesign.com.

To load a SWF into a level, you first prepare your separate SWFs as you would normally (noting that they are 'transparent'). Then, you load the SWF by using `loadMovie`, as shown in the Actions panel below:

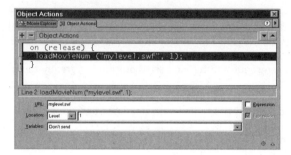

Levels are quite straightforward, and you had a good look at them in Chapter 2, but there are a few things to remember when using them that can still catch you out if you're not careful:

- Within each level, you can refer to the root timeline in two ways: `_root` or `_leveln` (where `n` is the level this timeline is loaded at). To refer to *another* level, you must use `_leveln`.

- The first parameter to `loadMovie` is not merely the *name* of the movie to be loaded, but its *URL* – so make sure the path is correct as well!

- Loading into a level that already has content overwrites the existing content.

- The stage size, background color, and frame rate is defined by the first level (`_level0`), and cannot be changed by subsequent levels.

Although levels can be unloaded when they are no longer needed, a more sophisticated technique is **parking**. Here, each level has a blank frame (usually the first) with a `stop` action attached to it. If you want to hide a level, just send it to the `stop` frame, and it disappears (it's said to be "parked"). You can bring it back into view by doing a `_leveln.gotoAndPlay` (or even just a `_leveln.play`).

The beauty of this is that once the main level (`_level0`) has loaded, you can load further levels in the background, without any interaction from the user. Thus, you're able to separate the main movie from the multimedia graphics and sound. This technique is one that I apply often to loading a web site soundtrack. Another advantage of parking levels is that they're always in the cache and ready to go when the user requests them, so the user never has to wait for a particular section of the site to load.

Movies based on multiple targets

For the ActionScript programmer, there's actually a better strategy for handling several SWFs at once, which is to use multiple *targets*. This structure is almost identical to using multiple levels, except that this time, new content is loaded into *movie clips*, rather than levels.

When you load content into a target (that is, a ready-made movie clip), the movie clip's existing timeline is replaced by the new content. This has a number of potential advantages, and allows you to do things you never thought possible with Flash movie clips. Here's why:

- The target exists and can be referenced even when it's empty and no content has yet been sent to it. This is a subtle point, but it means that any ActionScript referring to the target can do the same thing irrespective of whether the target actually contains anything, so you don't need to check for content beforehand. You could even arrange for your 'empty' movie clips to start their lives with loading messages that will be replaced by the actual content when they are 'filled', which is a pretty neat solution. Levels, on the other hand, only come into existence when content is loaded, so they're less flexible.

- Because the target movie clip is really just an ordinary movie clip, you can fill it with *whatever you want* prior to loading new content. We'll use this property in a simple example in just a moment.

You can now simulate movie clips with scenes, by loading SWFs that were built with multiple-scene FLA structures. It works because the scene structures (and, for that matter, the layers) are all stripped out in the final SWF, so the Flash player doesn't really 'recognize' scenes as anything at all. Additionally, you can have embedded (or nested) movie clips in your loaded content, in the same way as in a normal SWF – which means that unlike loaded _levels, you can have nested levels, because the nested movie clips can themselves be load targets! This is a very advanced loading strategy, and I haven't seen it used by many people – perhaps it's a well-kept secret!

There is a fundamental difference between a level and a target, and it lies in how they interpret _root. In a level, a _root path means _leveln – but because a target is essentially the same as a normal movie clip, _root there means just that: the _root of the main timeline, or _level0. This is *good*, because whenever you use _root within this structure, you're always referring to the same timeline. You can easily implement global variables across loaded SWFs, which is a big plus for structured programming.

> *A problem to watch out for is that the content loads into an instance of the target, and not into the library version of the movie clip. This means that if the instance disappears from the timeline, you lose the content. In practice, however – and now you've read this warning – this is unlikely to give you sleepless nights.*

Using multiple targets

One of the things that HTML can do but Flash can't (directly) is to have two versions of an image: you have a low-resolution version (HTML programmers call this the `lowsrc`), and a high-resolution one. The first of these can be made to load straight away, while the better quality version comes in later.

When designing Flash-based online portfolios, wouldn't it be nice to have something similar at your disposal? Something like, for example, a gallery of static images that are replaced immediately by Flash animations at the click of the user's mouse button? When you load your content into a target, it's a piece of cake.

Have a look at `resolution.fla`, which features a movie clip called Picture that contains the image you can see below. It's pretty small, which means that it's low-bandwidth – even a fairly sizable collection of such images wouldn't take long to download. It may not be the all-singing, all-dancing animated content we're used to, but it will certainly appear on the screen quickly enough.

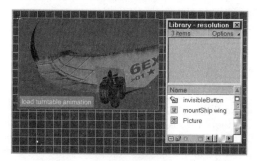

When the user clicks on the invisible button within Picture, however, the following attached script is executed:

```
on (release) {
    loadMovie ("hiRes.swf", this);
}
```

Last time you saw `loadMovie`, we specified a *level* as the second argument. This time, we're giving it the *path* of a target movie clip into which we want the new movie to be loaded. By using `this`, we're saying that the new movie should replace the current one. The SWF identified by the first argument could be anything at all: a higher resolution bitmap, a bit of video, or a complex tween animation. In this case, I've created a Swift3D animation using the same basic m3D model shown in the original image:

Test `resolution.fla` from a location that also contains the file `hiRes.swf`, and you'll see that the image is replaced by the animation when you click on the button. Notice that the invisible button and the load turntable animation text are overwritten by `hiRes.swf` when it's loaded in.

The beauty of this method is that Picture could be a movie clip that my ActionScript is in the process of animating (an image in a sideways-scrolling presentation, perhaps, animated by changing `picture._x` and `picture._y`). At first, it would contain the image, but the user could elect to say, "Never mind the bandwidth, give me the multimedia." The site then has to load the animation, but the ActionScript concerned with the scrolling doesn't care, because the instance name remains the same. It would continue to move the new animated content within the presentation regardless.

Get the feeling that this would be a really good way to create a site whose graphics were enhanced for high bandwidth users while supporting low bandwidth ones as well, all within the same SWF? Now wouldn't that be a cool and thoughtful feature...

Structuring the code

A second major task is designing the code portion of the movie. Regardless of what some people might have you believe, being good at programming isn't about being good at math – it's about getting a plan laid down before you start, and deciding on general structures to implement, and doing all this *before* you reach for the keyboard. This kind of forethought goes a long way to facilitating the creation of well-structured ActionScript code, and Flash 5 has a number of new commands that allow coding to proceed in this manner.

Unfortunately, if you get it wrong, Flash 5 also allows you to write a real rats' nest of code – one of those jobs where it works in the end, but if someone asked you to do it all again from scratch, you wouldn't have a clue. For a while, you might be able to hide this kind of thing behind some cool graphics, but as you advance, and being able to design tight little routines to create ActionScript-based interfaces and games becomes a must, you've got to sit back and have a think before you start.

At this level, a particularly useful design method is to create small, self-standing effects or routines that can be combined later to build the final product. These can be implemented in two ways, to make it easy to incorporate them into a finished movie design:

- For graphical effects, the technique is to use a movie clip that plays the role of a ready-built 'code container'. Not only does this allow you to write code that is self-contained, but also if you use **relative paths** (such as `this` or `_parent`) rather than specific instance names or absolute paths (like `_root` or `_leveln`), the movie clip becomes generalized. Its effect can then be applied to any other movie clip.

■ For pure code sections, consider implementing these routines as functions. These can be saved either in movie clips, or as text files. If you choose the latter method (recommended because it allows you more flexibility), remember that the ability to export or import ActionScript as text files is available from the Actions window, as shown below:

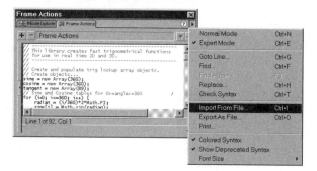

In programming circles, this style of coding is called a 'bottom-up' methodology, because once you've conceptualized your overall movie design in terms of what you want it to do, you code it by breaking up the "what you want it to do" into little building blocks and solving each in turn, using each building block in the final FLA to start from the bottom and slowly build up the complexity.

This method has another added advantage: if you adopt this style of coding, you'll soon realize that many of the better resource sites contain large numbers of FLAs that are also written this way, so not only can you submit your works in progress to enliven the Flash community, but also (copyright permitting) you can use other designers' routines in your own projects.

Putting it into practice

Network television loves makeover shows. If you've never seen one, they tend to involve members of the public having their appearance, garden, house, etc. 'transformed' by 'experts' over the course of a program. This is sometimes done against the clock, building to a crescendo of excitement as the deadline approaches and the glue hasn't dried yet, or the homeowner decides to come back early, or Becky from Minnesota still looks plain.

At Christmas last year, one of my crackers burst open to reveal a puzzle made up of a few plastic triangles, the idea being to arrange them so that they form a big square. I don't know about you, but I find that inspiration for Flash designs can come from anywhere, at any time, and as soon as I saw it I knew that the puzzle had potential. I saved it in a drawer to play around with later.

Later that Christmas, when I'd grown tired of television and the usual family anecdotes, I turned my attention to coding up the puzzle as a Flash FLA. Because I was doing this just for fun (the puzzle was never going to see the light of day, until I planned this chapter), I wanted to complete it in an evening — so, like the best makeovers, I had a time limit. That limit made the planning it in an evening – so, like the best makeovers, I had a time limit. That limit made the planning process crucial, and the project an ideal example of the things I've been recommending so far.

With its great graphic interfaces, Flash can be very alluring, and I've conversed with users on the Flash newsgroups who say things like, "I have a Flash FLA that's 90% complete, but I can't get this bit working, can you have a look at it?" When I examine some of these, the 90% that's "complete" is the meticulously crafted graphics for the interface. The 10% that's not working is the fundamental ActionScript code that's supposed to drive it all! Sometimes, I wish I could just say, "This is not the optimal solution – you need to do it this way, and that means you have to redo all the graphics as well," but of course I can't. Instead, we have to go through a longwinded and unattractive bit of code that's more a hack than a fix, and the resulting movie doesn't so much run as limp along.

I like to think of planning and structuring on the same terms: as an intellectual exercise, rather than 'the boring bit that goes at the beginning of the FLA building process'. By following this example, I hope you'll see that my thought processes follow a stepwise progression, solving each part of the problem in turn. Most of all, though, I hope you'll see that it was fun. Let's get down to it.

The initial brief

In a nutshell, the puzzle looks like this:

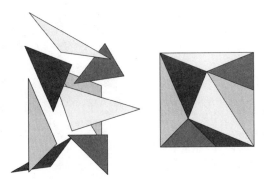

The triangles can actually be arranged into a number of different shapes. In this case, you have to make a square, but the instructions that come with the puzzle depict all sorts of shapes to be made – different-sized quadrilaterals, and crosses that get harder as you have to use more and more of the pieces.

So far, then, I had an idea for my content. In a real project, this would be the client's brief (that is, what the client wants, with no real description of how to do it). It's not normally the specification I want to work to, because it takes no account of the limitations and advantages of Flash, or of computers in general. The next stage is to massage this brief, working out the limitations that you'll face when building it with Flash.

As an aside, my initial brief is a good one because it takes no account of how to solve the problem. At this stage, I have not made myself think and plan in a blinkered way by considering only those things that can be done in Flash. By stepping beyond Flash design, I'm thinking about the implementation as a general design problem, rather than going straight into coding.

Think about your goal in terms of what you want to achieve, not what you have. This is the creative part of the design, so go to town: take all the input you need (creative and technical), and don't worry if it doesn't fit with what Flash can and can't do.

Building a working specification

Before the puzzle brief can become a working specification, there are a few limitations and pitfalls that must be addressed early on. The first problem is that with my plastic pieces, I can arrange the shape anywhere on the table – but allowing the same freedom in Flash would make it difficult to tell when all the triangles were in the right place, and the puzzle had been completed. I decided that the best way to solve this problem would be to fix the area on the screen in which the puzzle has to be assembled by using an outline:

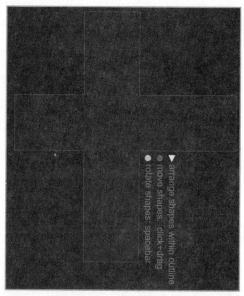

You've probably noticed that this is a slightly lopsided-looking cross. In fact, this is not due to my lack of hand-eye coordination, but done on purpose to solve the second problem in the brief. With my plastic puzzle pieces, I can fit the same shape within the same square outline in four different ways, by rotating the positions of the pieces by 90 degrees:

Although I can see that this is really the same solution, a computer is not imbued with the same degree of intuition. It would need to treat these as four different solutions, or as one solution with three transformation functions applied. Either way, detecting a valid solution is now harder, because there are multiple answers. The easiest way out here is somehow to fix the shape so that the player cannot create a rotated solution. This is a simplification of my puzzle to avoid a potential problem, and something you need to get used to doing.

After some thought, I realized that rotation is only possible if the final shape is symmetrical. All I had to do was make sure that my shape was not symmetrical, and rotation would no longer be an issue. The shape I decided to use was a lopsided cross – it isn't symmetrical, and rotating the pieces within the target outline doesn't work, because the shape formed by doing so no longer fits.

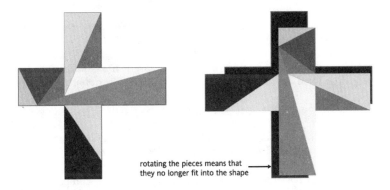

rotating the pieces means that
they no longer fit into the shape

Following on from this, if any triangles are congruent (that is, they're the same shape), or have rotational symmetry, they can be placed on the board in two different places, or in more than one orientation, making the detection of a winning solution more difficult. I realized that I'd have to make sure that all the tiles were different, making for only one solution to detect. (This is another facet of our initial simplification: I am constantly looking to alter the puzzle so that there is only one possible solution, because this is the easiest to detect.)

There is a final problem, which took the longest time to solve, but turned out to have the easiest solution. My plastic tiles are real: they can be picked up and moved around. My digital tiles are not, and they move around on a 2D screen. This poses a problem to do with ergonomics.

Flash gives each tile a depth that you can vary within a layer by using Modify > Arrange. Once your instances are on the stage, however, it's actually quite difficult to change this depth, and this causes problems such as the one shown below. If you were moving the smaller tile 'over' the larger one, you'd expect it to move in front of the unselected piece. However, if the unselected tile were at a higher depth than the one being moved, the latter would appear to pass behind the former, which looks quite wrong. Frankly, it would be shoddy design.

selected

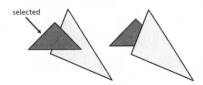

There are two solutions to this issue: a longwinded technical one, and a simple creative one. The longwinded solution involves swapping depths and all sorts of hocus pocus that I don't want to go into here. The simple solution came about through a bit of lateral thinking: make the tiles appear to be of colored glass, such that you can always see through them. Depth is then no longer a problem, because no tile is ever obscured by another.

Anyway, I hated the first solution, and loved the second one.

So far, this section has covered all the clever stuff in the final design. It contains all the creative design input, and the actual coding will be an easier task with no surprises (or at least, fewer surprises) now that I've come up with a path to the solution that circumvents all the pitfalls I could think of. It took me a couple of hours to get from playing with the tiles to this point in the proceedings. That's an awful long time to have nothing concrete to show the boss, but it's a crucial process if what you're trying to come up with is a novel design. I can now build a working specification, which looks something like this:

1.   The puzzle consists of a number of semitransparent triangular shapes that have to be arranged to form a cross whose exact size and shape is defined by an outline.

2.   Flash will shuffle the triangles at the start of the puzzle.

3.   The tiles may be moved by click-dragging the mouse cursor over the selected shape, and rotated (in steps of 90 degrees) by using the spacebar.

4.   The user has to place all the triangles within the cross to complete the puzzle. There is only one way to do this, and Flash will detect it by looking at the orientation and position of each tile, and seeing if it matches the orientation and position of the tile in the solution. If this is true for all the tiles, the solution has been reached.

Now I've got a specification I can work to. Notice that I still haven't gone anywhere near Flash yet, but I can already see that I've broken the back of the problem. That's the magic of planning a structure before you start! If you want to peek at the game before we discuss the code, you can have a look at the final FLA in shape.fla.

Look at the brief, identify all the potential coding pitfalls you can, and add the solution to each back into the brief as you go, thus refining it. You're through with this stage when you feel that you've addressed all the major issues regarding the final implementation. Then you're set to start the coding process. Where answers become difficult to find, try simplifying the initial problem.

Don't worry about catching absolutely *everything* before you start. As you'll soon see, I missed a few things in this project, but pre-empting the majority of problems is a real boon when coding begins.

If, when you started reading this chapter, you were expecting me to take the high ground and tell you to use flowcharts and logic diagrams, you can relax. Through the process I've described here, we're starting to move towards the point where we can break a task into easy-to-digest chunks that don't need that kind of analysis. It means that your detailed plans for each code section will be small (typically, mine are of the 'back of a napkin' variety). One of my reasons for thinking this way is that your clients aren't paying you to draw a set of pictures that look like they belong in a C++ programming manual – they're paying you to build an FLA.

Modular coding

Although knowing how the puzzle works is a useful thing to learn (it could form the basis of other things, such as jigsaws with moving triangles that have to fit into a certain pattern), I am more interested in showing *why* and *how* it was built the way it is. The easiest way to approach this challenge is to start with one triangle and get that working, and then to move on to the full game with lots of triangles. There are a number of functions we need to write, and these are:

- The ability to tell Flash what the triangle's 'finished' position is, and for it to be randomly shuffled at the start of the game, so that it's not at that position.

- The ability for the user to drag and drop the triangles.

- The ability to rotate the triangle when it's selected.

- For Flash to realize when the user has dropped the triangle in the correct position.

We could happily code each of these as a separate function... but going back to what we've been looking at in this chapter, we can go one better than that: we can code it up in a modular fashion, via embedded movie clips. This will save a lot of time, because if we can write modules to perform each function on *one* triangle, we can just as easily apply the same thing to *n* triangles. That's the beauty of modularity.

The way to handle writing this FLA is to take it in logical steps, something like this:

1. Create the board with one tile. Add the basic functionality to the one tile, and get it moving.

2. Add each of the advanced functions to the tile in turn, using modular movie clips.

3. Add the other tiles, adding the same functions to each.

4. Change the main program to be able to handle all the tiles, and to realize when the user has dropped the last triangle in the correct position (which means that the puzzle is completed).

5. Find another source of inspiration by pulling some more crackers!

Dragging the tile

Have a look at shape01.fla, which represents the first step in the process: it contains the graphics for a one-tile game. The board is a rectangular outline in the center of the stage, and there's a single tile that fits over it. The tile has been given an _alpha property of 30%, making it semitransparent, and giving us our 'colored glass' effect.

While playing with this file, I realized that it might be a good ergonomic idea to increase the `alpha` value when the tile is selected, so that it gains 'I am selected' prominence. Little ideas like that are easy to implement at this early stage, because I have a simple file to play with.

The ActionScript in this file is extremely simple. The main timeline has three layers called actions, tile, and board. Predictably, the tile and the board are in the bottom two layers, while the actions layer contains my script. The code in frame 1 sets two variables: `alphaSelect`, which will be the alpha value of a selected tile; and `alphaUnSelect`, representing the alpha value of an unselected tile.

```
alphaSelect = 70;
alphaUnSelect = 30;
stop ();
```

The code to handle dragging, and changing the alpha value, is located in the button inside the movie clip:

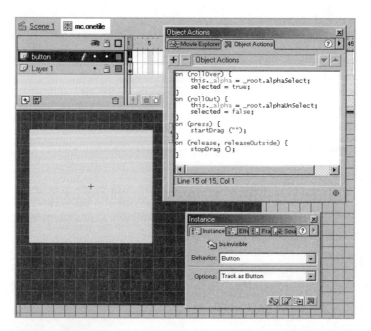

All this does is to attach drag functionality to the press and release button states, and an alpha-changing routine to the rollOver and rollOut button states.

Notice that this initial FLA is very simple, and represents very little effort. It has to be, because *it might be wrong*. A common mistake when starting to assemble a movie, is to build up all the graphics, and the 'stuff that's most interesting', straight away. This has the unfortunate effect of tying a lot of effort into your first attempt, before you know it's definitely the right way to go. You end up chopping and changing it to make it work, and you can't just discard it because it represents too much work invested, so you end up with a less than perfect final result.

> *Start coding on FLA files that contain the essence of the problem, and no more. It's better to have several small test programs than a single big one, because it speeds up development of each individual feature, and constrains the effects of errors.*

So to recap, our design so far has one moving tile. Much more importantly, though, we have a skeleton environment to which we can add the rest of our functional modules. The next thing we need to be able to do is shuffle the position of the tile away from the 'winning position'.

Shuffling the Tile

Have a look at shape01a.fla. I've added a couple of variables on frame 1 of the main timeline to specify the screen area that the tiles are dropped into, and there is now a strange-looking movie clip called ma.initTile in the library:

This movie clip is an ActionScript-only movie clip – it contains only one frame, which has only a script attached. In a moment, we'll take a closer look at it, but first I'd better explain the ma, bu and mc prefixes I'm using:

- ma means, 'movie clip, ActionScript'. It's a movie clip that has been used to hold a piece of ActionScript, and contains no graphics. I'm using the movie clip as an ActionScript container, or code module.

- bu and mc are used to denote standard button and movie clip symbols.

I use this system in my Flash projects for two main reasons. First, it makes it possible for me to differentiate between different types of movie clip easily (ma, mc, and not used here, ms – 'movie clip, smart clip'). Second, the Library lists symbols in alphabetical order, so using these prefixes forces it to group symbol types together in each folder, making it easier for me to navigate within the Library as it gets bigger.

Anyway, the ma.initTile movie clip has the following script in frame 1:

```
// Initialize this tile's starting position and angle
_parent.xStart = _parent._x;
_parent.yStart = _parent._y;
_parent.rStart = _parent._rotation;

// Change alpha to avoid overlapping problems
_parent._alpha = _root.alphaUnSelect;

// Shuffle this piece
_parent._x = Math.round(
    ➥ Math.random() * (_root.screenX - _root.border)) +
    ➥ _root.border;
_parent._y = Math.round(
    ➥ Math.random() * (_root.screenY - _root.border)) +
    ➥ _root.border;
_parent._rotation = Math.round(Math.random() * 3) * 90;
stop ();
```

This code:

- Captures the tile's initial position and angle, and places them into xStart, yStart (x and y position), and rStart (start angle, which will always be 0, but this may change later in the development)

- Changes the tile's _alpha property to our predefined 'unselected' value

- Places the tile randomly within a defined area (which is the stage area minus a border area)

The important thing to notice here is that everything the movie clip does is directed to its _parent, which could be *any* movie clip. This makes the new code *modular*, because all I have to do is drop ma.initTile into my test tile, and it will be shuffled at the start of the movie. I can do this to any tile I happen to create, and I'll be able to do it to movie clips that I haven't even designed yet, which will be in other sites I develop.

You can see how it works by taking a look at the mc.onetile movie clip. My modular script movie clip ma.initTile is sitting inside it, and you can see ma.initTile as the little dot in the figure right. Flash shows all movie clips with no graphics in their first frame like this.

Well, we now have a tile that can be shuffled, but what do we need to develop next? My brief said that I needed to be able to rotate a tile as well as drag it, and the way I went about adding this functionality is important: I didn't add it to shape01a.fla, but started again from the basic skeleton, shape01.fla, and added it to that. In this way, I am coding up one thing at a time, I don't get complex or subtle errors due to interactions with existing code, and I can always stay focused on the thing I'm currently doing.

Rotating the tile

Have a look at `shape01b.fla`. This includes the rotation function as a new movie clip, `ma.rotateTile`, but is otherwise almost identical to `shape01a.fla`. The only other thing I've done is to give my tile two colors, so that I can easily see the rotation taking place:

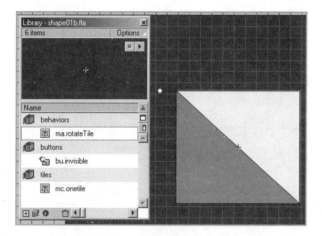

Again, the code I'm adding here is fairly straightforward; it's the way I am adding it that's the issue. Still, just in case you're curious, here are the guts of the movie clip:

```
spaceKey = Key.isDown(Key.SPACE);
if (spaceKey) {
    rotation = _parent._rotation;
    rotation = rotation + 90;
    if (rotation > 270) {
        rotation = 0;
    }
    _parent._rotation = rotation;
}
```

This code section uses the new Flash 5 `Key` object to look for the spacebar being pressed, making `spaceKey` true if it is. In that event, the tile is rotated by 90 degrees – or rather, the `_parent` movie clip is rotated, which is *probably* the tile, but could be anything at all. If I put this movie clip on the main timeline of a movie, it would be the whole movie that started rotating! (Try it, if you don't believe me.)

So now we have *two* modular bits of code, encapsulated within two movie clips. If you look at my original breakdown of what I needed to code, there's only one thing left to do, and that's to detect when the tile has been placed in the correct (or 'winning') position.

Detecting a winning position

Have a look at my final test file, shape01c.fla. This includes the initial skeleton, with the added code module required to detect a winning position. You may remember that one of my concerns at the initial design stage was that there should be no symmetry, as this would make the detection of a winning position too difficult. Well, that gets used in this file, because the game board is no longer a symmetrical rectangle, but an asymmetrical, triangular shape.

This time, the FLA includes our two previous code modules, plus the new one that detects when the tile is in the winning position (it's called ma.detectDone). When you publish and play the FLA this time, all three ma modules are working simultaneously!

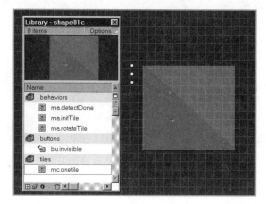

Individually, my three modules are simple little bits of code, but when they're all dropped into the mc.oneTile movie clip, their respective actions are all conferred upon the tile. It will rotate as specified by ma.rotateTile; it will initialize and shuffle itself as specified by ma.initTile; and it will detect when it is in the winning position via ma.detectDone. This is the power of modular design.

The ma.detectDone module works by looking at the tile's initial position (which is the 'winning position', as created by the ma.initTile module via the variables xStart and yStart). It looks to see if the tile is placed within five pixels of this winning position, and signals to the main timeline when it is via _root.gameStatus, which is being used by the main timeline to drive the little text box shown in the pictures below. The rotation angle also has to be right, but since this is always 0 at the start, I haven't used rStart, but simply used zero instead.

```
xError = Math.abs(Math.round(_parent._x - _parent.xStart));
yError = Math.abs(Math.round(_parent._y - _parent.yStart));

// Check if tile is in the right place
if ((xError < 5) && (yError < 5) &&
➥ (_parent._rotation == 0) && (!done)) {
   _root.gameStatus = "done it!"
   done = true;
}
// Check if tile has been moved from the right place
if (done && ((xError > 5) || (yError > 5) ||
➥ (_parent._rotation != 0))) {
```

```
        _root.gameStatus = "not yet..."
        done = false;
}
```

Notice that the five-pixel limit means Flash is a little tolerant of where you put the tile. It's happy if you're slightly out, which is great if you think that all this 'big tiles and bright colors' stuff may have applications in teaching programs for the small people in kindergarten, whose mouse control is about as good as that of oldsters like me.

By coding each bit separately, we have kept our problem simple for longer, as we tackle each small chunk at a time. This means that less planning is required in the long run, because each code section is small and manageable – I could more or less work them out in my head, without having to use big software planning diagrams.

As well as the ease with which I managed to reach this point (each FLA from shape01a.fla to shape01c.fla took about 30 minutes, which means that my makeover is proceeding right on time!), the resulting FLA is structured and modular by default, because that's the way I wrote it. In essence, what I've done is to build a modular software hierarchy.

Listen carefully. Here comes the science...

The lowest level here is the main timeline – the _root or 'global' level. The next level up comprises the movie clips that sit on the main timeline, which can be thought of as mini-timelines in their own right – they contain everything they need to do their thing. I call this the 'local' level. Above that are the specialized bits of code that are plugged into each movie clip's local level, to make the movie clip perform specific actions. If you like, you can think of it as the 'module' level (or, if you consider the movie clip as being an 'object-like' structure, the module level is a bit like a method level, and this is shown by the pathnames that mirror what you would expect in other languages like JavaScript and C++ – movieclip.module).

It's interesting to think about the data flow through this hierarchy, which is *towards* the root, rather than *away* from it. This is a prerequisite for true modularity: as the arrow shows in the diagram, the data flow doesn't need to know instance names, because the next level down can always be referred to by the general path _parent, making it a generic data path, and much more flexible as a result.

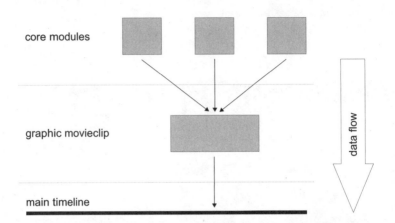

core modules

graphic movieclip

main timeline

data flow

> *In large, advanced ActionScript projects, a code structure is important. Through this example, I've introduced you to the most efficient one, but there are a few others too. The rule is to choose one of them and stick to it, or the lack of structure or well-defined data flow directions will quickly bog you down.*

Putting it all together

The pieces of code needed to create the final FLA are all now developed, and the structure has fallen together. You can see this in the final FLA (shape_final.fla), where each tile is almost exactly like our test tile. (There's a little masking going on so that the buttons only work within the triangle tile areas, but that's about it.) The main timeline knows when the puzzle is complete by counting the number of tiles that are in the right position, by means of a new variable called tilesDone. This is initialized along with the other variables in frame 1 of the main timeline:

```
alphaSelect = 70;
alphaUnSelect = 30;
screenX = 550;
screenY = 400;
border = 50
tilesDone = 0;
```

By adapting ma.detectDone, we can increase this variable each time one of the tiles is placed in the correct position:

```
xError = Math.abs(Math.round(_parent._x - _parent.xStart));
yError = Math.abs(Math.round(_parent._y - _parent.yStart));

// Check if tile is in the right place
if ((xError < 5) && (yError < 5) &&
➡ (_parent._rotation == 0) && (!done)) {
```

```
        _root.tilesDone++;
        done = true;
    }

    // Check if tile has been moved from the right place
    if (done && ((xError > 5) || (yError > 5) ||
➥ (_parent._rotation != 0))) {
        _root.tilesDone—;
        done = false;
    }
```

When tilesDone == 9, the player has won.

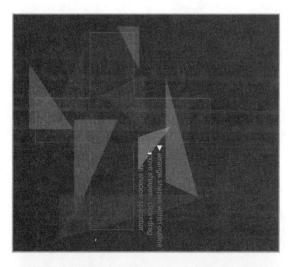

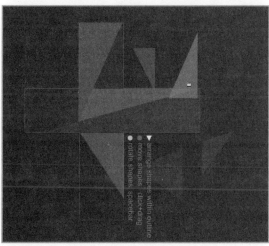

So, how did I do? Well, from start to finish, this FLA took approximately four and a half hours, which is about as long as I wanted for my 'Construct a Flash Puzzle in an Evening' makeover. By designing and planning in a structured way, and creating an FLA structure that mirrors my thought processes (allowing me to tackle each problem alone, in turn), I was able to move forward quickly and efficiently without wasting time.

Now that I've generated this FLA, I can go to town with the graphics, which would potentially be the next step. I've got an inkling that it will look a lot better with a 3D board and tiles created in Electric Rain's *Swift3D* program, for example, such that the whole thing is played in an isometric view. To animate the pieces in the new program, all I'd have to do is drag my ma movie clips across, and all the code would be there. It's easy when you don't put the cart before the horse. The code's done, and now is the time for me (or you) to play with the graphics.

Conclusion

Typical Flash site design follows a path something like this:

- You decide about the content, in terms of things like, "Is it bandwidth heavy or light?" and, "Does it need changing often?"

- You think about the requirements of the audience, and flesh out your ideas for an appropriate delivery interface. In doing so, you balance the need to confer information quickly against the need to create a visually/aurally special site – complete with all the sliding, scrolling, 3D, drop-down, window-based interface design that's expected of a cutting-edge Flash site.

- You don't implement the interface straight away, but write and test a small FLA to prove the concept is viable, or look at a couple of other sites and see that it is possible.

In this chapter, you've seen a technique for building jigsaws and similar puzzles in Flash. But you've also seen something more fundamental: the design considerations that go into creating such a project in Flash and ActionScript, and a general method of giving the final FLA a structure that's consistent with the needs of the working Flash designer who needs to move quickly to satisfy the needs of the client in a cost-effective way. To extend the cost effectiveness further, we've designed in a high level of code reusability, ensuring that we are not constantly reinventing the wheel.

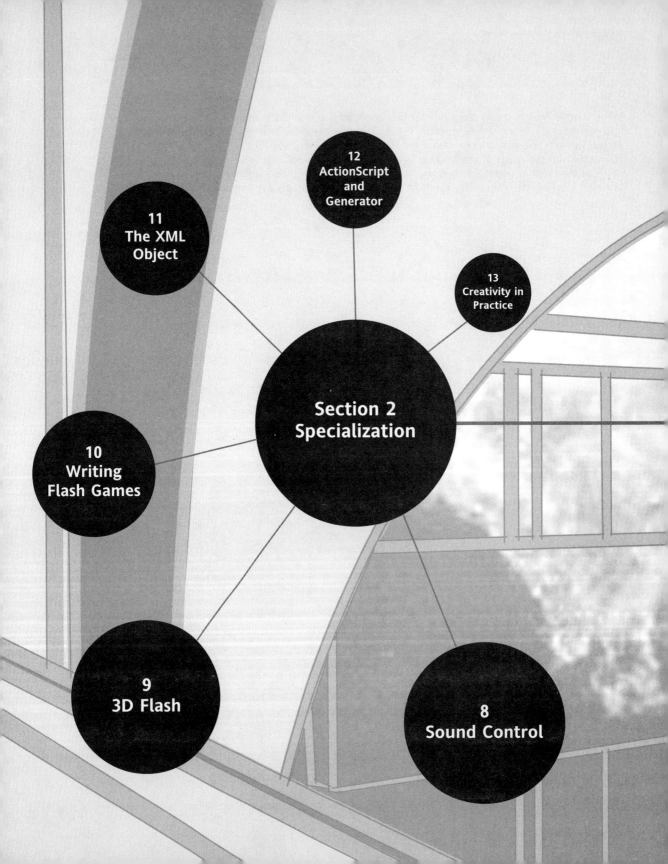

Chapter 7
Advanced
Interface Design

One of the major reasons for gaining a thorough understanding of ActionScript is that it allows you to move beyond Flash's built-in elements for creating user interfaces (which for the most part consist of simple buttons), and instead create advanced interfaces that slide, pop up, or enable the user to navigate around in a 3D space. Advanced interface design is one of the things that lifts a typical Flash design from its HTML-based cousins, so skills in this area are likely to be those that most distinguish you from your peers.

This chapter is split into three parts:

- A short discussion of interface ergonomics.

- A journey through the fundamental programming techniques that form the building blocks of advanced interfaces. This includes smart clips, drag-and-drop, collision detection, and mouse interaction via properties rather than button actions.

- The lowdown on how to combine these building blocks to create some Flash interface elements that are the equal of any used on the Web.

Ergonomics

When it comes to web design, a lot of people point straight to the issue of **usability**. To do so, however, is to ignore the fact that some interfaces have intrinsic *entertainment* value, even though they're not the quickest and easiest to navigate. An interface for Warner Brothers™, for example, might have slapstick animations involving Elmer Fudd™ and a large mallet, so that when the user clicks on a button, nothing happens until Elmer runs on screen and gives it a good whack. Occasionally, the mallet might not do the trick, so it's off to get the Acme box of dynamite... or I could have Daffy Duck telling me that I'm despicable if I decide to leave.

Of course, these elements would slow down the interface, but adding a super-fast (and often soulless) interface would remove the playful element that is ideally suited to this environment. The important point for designers is to consider not only efficiency and practicality, but also something else: maintaining a balance. This is an important point to remember as we continue to discuss usability. Creative design has many avenues that are closed in traditional ergonomic design, but that doesn't mean you can't follow them. Sometimes, good web design is about creating an experience that's not so much about presenting options, but about producing an organic and almost cinematic environment that involves exploration, surprise and humor on a narrative journey through the content.

Defining Usability

Some years ago, I was involved in designing user interfaces for some pretty important industrial applications, involving nasty stuff like hydrochloric acid and processes such as refueling a nuclear reactor. In cases like these, usability has to be considered very carefully indeed. Here's my checklist based on that experience; during my time as a web designer, I have found that all of the issues it raises are just as relevant to good web design.

- **Intuitive controls.** The user should understand intuitively what a control does, and always be able to see a way forward (or backward) through the content of your site.

Intuitive controls form a major topic in their own right, and involve lots of sub-issues such as standardization, clarity, unambiguous functionality, and so on.

- **Responsiveness.** The user should know when a control is working, and see a response to their actions quickly. That's one to remember when the user presses a button halfway through your site's download process.

- **Efficiency and speed of interaction.** The speed at which the interface allows the user to make changes should be consistent with the process being controlled. Efficiency and a quick response are vitally important in some interfaces (when you drive a car, for example, the steering wheel and pedals are easily accessible and have an immediate effect), but at other times it can be important to *slow the user down*, so that they take time to look at the content, and don't just click through it. The procedure for airline preflight checks takes this into account, and so too should web site interfaces that involve cash transactions, or legal imperatives. Usability isn't always what you first think it is!

- **Feedback.** Controls should 'feel' real, giving positive indication of correct activation. Where controls are simulated (which is always the case in web design), the feedback should simulate the action of real buttons, complete with click sounds, or a change of graphical appearance (the most common form being the rollover).

- **Significance and implied order.** Important controls should be given visual priority. Where controls are designed to be used in a series of linked actions, the order of controls (from top to bottom or left to right – or otherwise, depending on cultural norms) should imply that sequence. Furthermore, the apparent significance should change to reflect changing conditions.

- **Filtering.** Controls should not present options that are not valid or sensible for the next step in the process. This can be done via changing significance, or through the provision of a hierarchy of options.

- **Accessibility.** As far as is reasonably possible, the controls you define should do more than simply assume the norm. For example, it's a fact that around a fifth of all men are at least partially colorblind – and I try to take this into account when I'm designing. All it takes is to make sure that affected colors are never the same brightness where they overlap. You don't have to change much, but a little thought can go a long way.

These are perhaps the main considerations for *any* interface that needs to be designed, but keep in mind what I said earlier about usability, and the fact that as web designers we have creative horizons that make it acceptable to bend the rules. There are interfaces in which, for example, the links and buttons are hidden, reacting only when the user has found them. This is the designer creating the web site as an area to be *explored*, and intentionally making it a little tricky to use. If you're going to break the rules, though, you have to understand them to begin with.

Graphic Design

In many ways, web design is a progression from traditional graphic design. Even though web design generally involves multiple media, the old print-based rules still hold true, and they should be applied in order to bring out form and proper weighting. A detailed discussion on graphic design would fill this book, but that still wouldn't be the best way to learn about it. From advertising, magazines, and television, right down to the beer mats at the bar you went to last night, our everyday environment is full of graphic design. If you like the look of something, stick it in your scrapbook, or make a note of it for later inspiration.

Now that we have some idea of the broad goals we're looking to achieve in our interfaces, let's get our hands dirty and start building. Although there's a near-infinite variety of *possible* Flash interfaces, I'll try to build up a checklist of the basic building blocks that feature in a great many of them. We'll start with an investigation into how smart clips can be used to build up interfaces, and then go on to see how the ubiquitous invisible button can help too. Finally, we'll look at a typical 'designer' Flash interface, complete with button-less navigation.

Smart Clips

To make them easier for the user to identify and work with, graphical user interfaces are invariably made up of a set of common components like check boxes, scroll bars, and drop-down menus. These components will generally appear similar whenever you see them – take a quick look at your operating system to see what I mean. The only real difference between these components is the data they feature – the actual functionality is the same throughout.

Smart clips, which you first saw back in Chapter 3, work on the same premise: you have a 'standard' movie clip, but you vary the associated data on an instance-by-instance basis. In this section, I'm going to build up a typical interface element to get you into the habit of using smart clips in this way, but remember that once you've grasped the idea, there is nothing stopping you from building an entirely modular graphic interface.

This exercise is quite a long one, so it might be best to get yourself a nice cup of coffee before you start it! Remember, though, that you only have to do the hard work *once* for each kind of graphic element – when it's all set up, you can simply drag it into *any* FLA, configure it, and you're away!

Designing a Drop-down Menu

For this particular trick, I'll create a menu bar that's functionally similar to the sort of thing you see in applications such as Flash itself. On my Windows-based machine, for example, the menu bar looks like this:

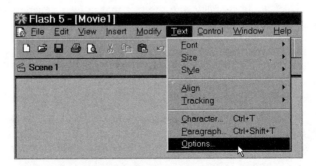

There are a number of main menu titles, and when you click on one, a drop-down menu with related options appears. This is a very efficient way of displaying a lot of options on a single screen, and much better than using ordinary buttons – to display the same number of options that Flash has tucked away in its drop-down menus using simple Flash buttons would require well over 100 of them!

Here's my Flash version of a Windows-style menu bar, which we'll start to assemble in a moment. It contains three main titles, and clicking on them allows you to see up to fifteen different options:

The three menus here are actually instances of the same smart clip, making this a pretty bandwidth, and effort, friendly way of going about interface design.

> *The completed menu element smart clip project is included with the downloadable files for this book as* `interface01.fla`. *The example shown above is also included, as* `interface01a.fla`.

Creating a Drop-down Menu Movie Clip

To begin producing the smart clip, the first thing I needed to do was to create the basic 'main title' element and its associated drop-down menu. If you want to follow my procedure exactly, start a new Flash movie, create a new button symbol called menuStrip, and draw a long thin rectangle (as shown on the following page) for the 'up' state. You should also place a highlighted (that is, a brighter or more colorful) version of the same rectangle in the 'over' state. Leave the other states blank (but don't put a blank keyframe in them), so that the 'down' and 'hit' states are the same as the 'over' state. The rectangle should be wide enough to accommodate the longest text you're intending to use in the menu.

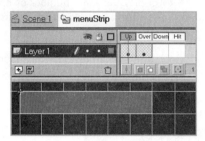 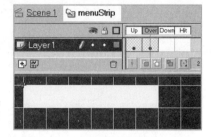

To make life easier, I created my rectangles with View > Grid > Show grid and Snap to grid turned on. Once you've created the button, test it to make sure that it changes to its highlighted state when you roll over it.

Next, create a new movie clip called menuClip, and create within it three layers: actions, text, and buttons. In the next few steps, we'll create the 'unselected' (that is, unopened) menu in frame 1 of this clip, and the 'selected' menu in frame 2.

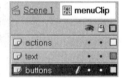

The 'unselected' menu will consist only of the title bar, so in frame 1 of the buttons layer, add a menuStrip button. In frame 2 of the same layer, add five more buttons arranged in a column, as shown. As you can probably tell, I've used the 'snap to grid' functionality to make placement easier:

 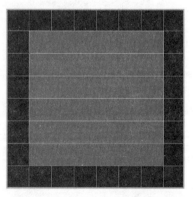

Next comes the text layer. We want different menus to contain different text, and the only way we can do that is by using dynamic fields. Lock the buttons layer, and on frame 1 of the text layer, add a dynamic text field that covers the button rectangle. It's important that you make the text field unselectable, by un-checking the Selectable box in the Text Options tab, as shown below. (If you don't, we'll be unable to select the button below it when we run the FLA.) For this exercise, I've used 12 point Arial Bold text – in this font, the default textbox covers the button rectangle almost completely, with no need for resizing. Give the dynamic text field a Variable name of `title`.

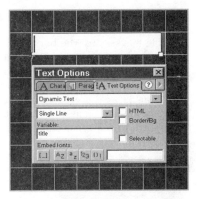

Just to make sure that things are progressing smoothly, the timeline of your menuClip should now look like this:

Now you need to add a keyframe at frame 2 of the text layer. When you look at this frame, you'll already have the text field that you just placed over the first button, so you can copy and paste it five times such that it covers all the other buttons as well. Change the text style in the lower five fields to Normal, and rename the Variable fields to `menuText1` to `menuText5`. These variable names will be smart clip parameters, and any text later assigned to these variables will appear as titles in the menu.

> *When not selected, the text fields become hard-to-see dotted rectangles, so in the picture below I've clicked inside the last text box with the text tool, just to prove that it's there.*

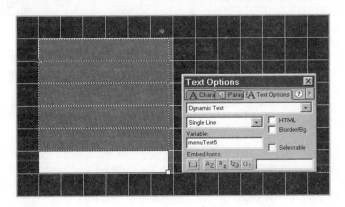

Believe it or not, these are actually all the graphics we need to create. Now we can get on with the fun part, which is to add the ActionScript that drives it all! Firstly, we'll need to add a 'toggle' variable that tells us whether the menu is selected or unselected, so that it closes when we're no longer over any part of it. The menu will also close once you've made a selection. (This is what happens in the drop-down menus of most operating systems.)

The variable we'll use to achieve this functionality is a Boolean called menuSelect. When the menu is opened, menuSelect is set to true. The menu will 'close' if menuSelect becomes or is false, which will occur only when:

- A selection is made from the drop-down menu, or

- A button is rolled out of, and the cursor does not roll onto another button

Any changes in the value of menuSelect are *always* due to some interaction between the user and the buttons in the menu, and we'll look at the code that makes those changes shortly. First, though, we can add the ActionScript that *detects* such changes, which resides in three keyframes of the menuClip's actions layer. This is what needs to go in frame 1:

```
menuSelect = true;
stop ();
```

This initializes our menuSelect variable, and stops the movie clip in its 'closed' state. The movie clip will remain here until told to proceed as a result of frame 1's single button being pressed. When it does eventually reach frame 2, which contains the 'open' menu, this code is executed:

```
if (menuSelect == false) {
    gotoAndPlay (1);
}
```

Enter the code on frame 3 which will loop us back to frame 2.

```
gotoAndPlay (2);
```

...the menu will appear 'open' until menuSelect is set to false, at which time the movie clip returns to frame 1 and the process begins again.

To prevent any unpleasant flickering, extend the text and buttons layers up to frame 3, so that your menuClip timeline looks like this:

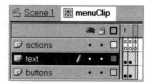

Before we begin to consider the detail of turning this movie clip into a smart clip, we need to add ActionScript that performs the tasks we require to the buttons. For this part, lock the text layer, so that you don't select the text instead of the buttons beneath it. Then, in frame 1 of buttons, add the following code to the single button it contains:

```
on (release) {
    play ();
}
```

When the mouse button is released, this causes the movie clip to start playing at frame 2, and so to display the 'open' menu. To the top button in frame 2 of the buttons layer, then, you should attach the following:

```
on (release) {
    gotoAndPlay (1);
}
on (rollOver) {
    menuSelect = true;
}
on (rollOut) {
    menuSelect = false;
}
```

If the user clicks on the top item in the menu for a second time, we 'close' it immediately by returning to frame 1; this further mimics the behavior of an operating system menu. The other two event handlers control the value of menuSelect: When we're over the button, menuSelect becomes true; when we roll out, it becomes false.

To see exactly how mouse movement affects the value of menuSelect, this is a good place to use the Flash debugger. Dropping the movie's frame rate right down to about 1-5 fps allows you to see clearly what's happening.

My plan is for each of the five buttons that comprise the menu options to 'close' the menu when any one of them is selected, and to cause the parent movie (that is, any movie into which this clip is embedded) to move to a new frame (identified by a label). We also want the menu to remain 'open' if the user moves the mouse 'up' or 'down' the menu, so we have to keep control of menuSelect too. This is the ActionScript that belongs in the first of these buttons:

```
on (rollOver) {
    menuSelect = true;
}

on (rollOut) {
    menuSelect = false;
}

on (release) {
    gotoAndStop (1);
    _parent.gotoAndStop(menuLabel1);
}
```

Buttons 2 to 5 are almost identical, so you can copy and paste the script across. The only thing that changes is the menuLabel*n* variable, which becomes menuLabel2, 3, 4, and 5 in the other four buttons. The script for the last button is therefore:

```
on (rollOver) {
    menuSelect = true;
}

on (rollOut) {
    menuSelect = false;
}

on (release) {
    gotoAndStop (1);
    _parent.gotoAndStop(menuLabel5);
}
```

We now have a working drop-down menu. It hasn't been populated with data yet, but if you run it you'll at least see the correct functionality. At first, there's a rectangle that becomes highlighted if you roll over it:

If you click on the rectangle, a drop-down appears, and rolling over any of the items in it results in that rectangle being highlighted. Clicking on any rectangle then makes the drop-down menu disappear, as does rolling out of the menu altogether:

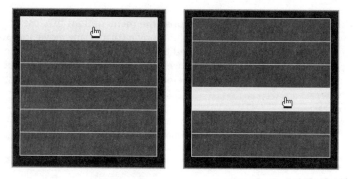

The reason *why* our menu currently has no data on it is because all the variables we've used in the ActionScript code are currently undefined. In the next section, we're going to fill in the gaps by turning our movie clip into a configurable smart clip.

Turning the Movie Clip into a Smart Clip

To define our variables and set up our movie clip as a smart clip, we need to use the Define Clip Parameters window that you can display by right/Ctrl-clicking on the menuClip movie icon in the

Library, and **selecting** Define Clip Parameters... from the drop-down menu. In order to allow instances of our smart clip to be customized according the project at hand, the clip parameters we're going to specify are:

- title, which is the text that will appear on the menu when it's 'closed'

- menuText1..5, which are the five text fields associated with the five drop-down menu items

- menuLabel1..5, which are the names of labels on the smart clip's parent timeline to which each button will direct the movie

It's a reasonable idea to supply default values for the button captions, but not for the labels, because it's impossible to know what might make sense for those. Additionally, I wrote a few words in the Description field to remind me how the clip works, and made sure that the Lock in instance check box was checked. (I'll explain the reason for that when we actually use the smart clip in anger, in a moment.) My completed list looked like this:

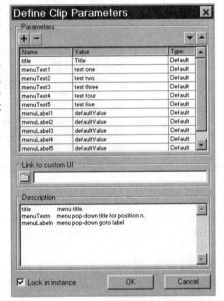

If you now drag a new instance of the newly formed smart clip onto the main stage, you'll see the following when you test the movie:

As you'd expect, the menu now displays the text Title when in its 'closed' state, and clicking on it reveals the options text one to text five, as shown. If you test the movie and *don't* see this, check your spelling in the Define Clip Parameters window against the variable names in your ActionScript code – there's probably a spelling mismatch.

Once there's an instance of the smart clip on the stage, you can change the parameters on a per-instance basis in the Clip Parameters panel, which you'll find at Window > Panels > Clip Parameters. For example, I've configured the one below to contain some navigation options that would be needed by a typical homepage:

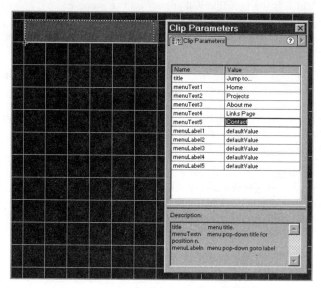

Notice here that you're not allowed to change the Name fields – this comes as a result of us checking that Lock in Instance box to which I drew your attention earlier. Un-checking that box would allow you to change the names in the Clip Parameters panel, but doing so would run a high risk of breaking code elsewhere in the movie... so leave it checked!

Using the Smart Clip in a Movie

As the final part of this demonstration, it's time to put this smart clip to work, and show how to use the menuLabel*n* clip parameters to create navigation. With the Clip Parameters window still open, take a look at interface01a.fla, which uses three instances of our drop-down menu smart clip. On the main stage, select the leftmost menu, and you'll see something like this:

The `title`, `menuText`*n* and `menuLabel`*n* parameters have all been given values. `title` and `menuText1..5` set the contents of the dynamic text boxes of the drop-down menu, so our first fully customized, smart clip generated menu looks like this:

The `menuLabel`*n* parameters refer to labels in the actions layer of the main timeline:

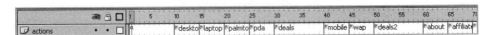

When any of the buttons (or drop-down menu items, as they have become) is pressed, the `on (release)` event will perform two `goto` commands:

- A `gotoAndStop (1)` command that will put the menu back to its closed state.

- A `_parent.gotoAndStop (menuLabeln)` command that actually causes the navigation jump to occur. The main timeline will jump to the label assigned to each `menuLabeln` parameter.

A point to note here is that sometimes, you might not want to use all five drop-down options. That's all right, though, because a `goto` action with an undefined clip parameter will not jump anywhere, and no navigation will occur. This fact is used in the Communications menu, where I didn't need all five items. Instead, I just defined the text for some of the buttons as – – –, and left the associated clip parameters set to `defaultValue`.

In practice, you'd probably have a movie clip at the position of each label, and these would typically load content into a Flash level. Because the use of smart clips makes for a lean file size (a paltry 5K on this occasion), you'll end up with a front end that loads quickly, and specific content that loads up on demand.

Ideas for Future Development

For me, part of the charm of this smart clip is that it was fairly straightforward to develop, and it's extremely easy to use. Because each menu item simply calls `_parent.gotoAndStop` in order to achieve its effect, you can drop an instance of this clip in any movie you like, and (provided that you've gone to the relatively small effort of labeling some frames) it will work straight away without further modification. As will become apparent in later examples, that's a feature I often seek to provide in the reusable Flash 'components' I develop.

You're probably already thinking, though, about ways in which it might be possible to improve or further customize the behavior of this clip, so here are a couple of ideas to get you started. One area where it might be nice to make some changes is in how the smart clip handles 'empty' menu items – those blank lines are a little cumbersome, and they'd become positively intrusive if you were to amend the menu to have eight, twelve, or even more items by default. A possible solution here would be to use movie clips *containing* buttons (rather than just buttons) as the menu items, and to set the `_visible` property of any clip without a label to `false`.

Another thing you may have noticed is that the menu still doesn't behave *exactly* like an operating system menu. The latter tend not to 'close' as soon as the cursor leaves them – rather they do so as a result of the mouse being clicked outside them. The change required to make that happen is simple, but it does break some of the 'out-of-the-box' functionality of the smart clip, because you need to add event-handling code on a per-instance basis. The trick is to remove the code from frame 2 of the actions layer of the smart clip, and add the following to each *instance* of the clip you use in your movie:

```
onClipEvent (mouseDown) {
    if (!menuSelect) {
        gotoAndStop (1);
    }
}
```

This trade-off between the per-instance technique of event-handling and the convenience of dealing with everything inside a 'plug-in-and-go' movie clip is one that will rear its head on more than one occasion in this chapter, and while I tend to prefer the second option, it's down to you to decide what works best for you in your projects.

The above notwithstanding, if you want to build advanced interfaces, the word is to build as many elements as you can with smart clips. You don't even have to have a final movie in mind – just trying to create all sorts of smart clip widgets is a worthwhile job in itself. I have a folder that's full of little interface bits and pieces, and when the time comes to build a new interface, all I have to do is delve in there and build something up with some of my ready-made smart clips, chopping and changing as I go. When you're working for a client, this practice carries huge advantages: initial development time goes right down, allowing you to concentrate on the fine tweaking that will make the site great, and get you noticed.

Buttons

The **invisible button** is one of the most-used buttons in advanced interface designs, and I know of no professional Flash web designer that doesn't use them all over their creations. At a recent FlashForward seminar, Joshua Davis (of www.praystation.com, and several other sites) went so far as to say that it's the *only* kind of button he uses!

An invisible button is one for which only a 'hit' state is defined – the other states are left blank. To make one, simply create a new button, and insert a keyframe into the **'hit' state**. The contents of this state will then define the area where the invisible button will function, as this simple square from interface02.fla shows:

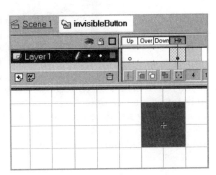

Although there's nothing in the 'up', 'over', or 'down' states, the 'hit' area is active, and this button works rather like an invisible pad. When you're over it, the cursor will change to denote the presence of a button, but there will appear to be nothing under the cursor, because the button has no physical appearance – it is invisible and ghostly!

If you create an invisible button in the way shown above (I called mine invisibleButton) and then drag it onto the main stage area, you'll see something like this:

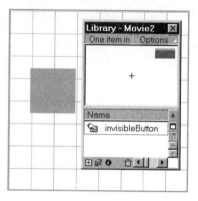

The invisible button's 'hit' area is shown on screen as a semi-transparent shape, although when you run the FLA, you won't see anything.

What use is an invisible button? Well, it means that you can turn *anything* on the stage into a button, just by placing an invisible button over it. In the example below, we'd normally have to create a separate button for each of the items in our web site menu. If we use our invisible button, however, we can simply 'cover' each piece of text with it. When you run this FLA, there will appear to be several text buttons, when in fact there's just one invisible button!

If you're watching closely, you might have picked up on the main flaw in using an invisible button in this way: the lack of visual feedback to show that a button has been pressed. You can overcome this by adding *sound* to the invisible button's 'hit' state simply by attaching a bleeping or clicking sound to it. I've just attached one to the 'hit' state, but you can add them to any of the other states too, depending on what you want to draw attention to.

The real benefit of invisible buttons, though, is that they can be used as much more than 'just' buttons. Because they're invisible, they really start to shine in complex interfaces, where you don't want a button so much as a 'detection pad' for things such as scroll bars, draggable areas, or rollover detection. We'll use invisible buttons a lot in the interface building blocks that follow, so you need to be familiar with creating and using them. An example of the menu above, complete with multiple uses of an invisible button and audio feedback, is included as `interface01.fla`.

> *Flash provides a number of advanced button types that you can access using* Help > Samples... > Advanced Buttons.fla. *The invisible button is used in all of them, so you can see that it's a very useful technique to remember.*

Drag-and-Drop, Collision Detection, and Goal-based Animation All in One

For further proof of just how useful invisible buttons can be, we'll be employing them in the very next example. In it, I'll try to demonstrate that graphic user interfaces that use drag-and-drop are particularly intuitive, and therefore well worth exploring. In support of this argument, we'll be assembling a drag–and–drop interface that permits the dragging of icons about the screen.

The goal of this particular exercise is to create a drag–and–drop interface for the download of music files. These files will be represented by appropriate icons that leave us in no doubt about what they are – and when we 'pick up' each icon, we should receive clear feedback about what the file contains.

Designing the Interface

A good analogy for this functionality would be selecting a particular piece of vinyl from my record collection: to choose a record, I pick it up and look at the label; if I want to play it, I move it across to my record deck and set the thing going. It would be nice if we could do the same thing with online MP3 files, so in my movie:

- Each MP3 file will be represented by a record graphic

- If we 'look' at a record by clicking on it, we should see the record label for that disc

- If we drag the record to a 'turntable' area, the download should proceed

By drawing this parallel, we are creating an intuitive system, because we are mapping the easier and well-known practice of playing records to the more difficult and less well-known task of downloading digital music from the Web.

In any drag–and–drop system, the central requirement is the ability to know when the graphic being dragged has been dropped onto something important (such as the trashcan, when you want something to be deleted). However, it can be a bit more complicated than that:

- It requires knowing how to detect a collision.

- You need to define what happens if the user drops the graphic in the 'wrong' place. In this instance, we'll get the graphic to 'snap' back to its initial starting point, which keeps our interface nice and tidy, regardless of what the user does. (If only they'd built my apartment to do the same thing!)

You can see the final interface we'll be creating in the project file interface03c.fla. To select an MP3 file, you simply pick up a record and drag it to the target at the bottom left of the stage. However, if you drop it somewhere other than the active area, the record seems to 'know' that something's gone wrong, and returns in a fluid movement to its starting position.

Its almost as if the records were attached to their starting positions via a bit of elastic: put them in the right place, and the elastic is broken – but if they're dropped in the wrong place, the elastic drags them back. This is **goal-based animation**: the interface element is making decisions based on two possible outcomes, and this is key to building 'intelligence' into an interface.

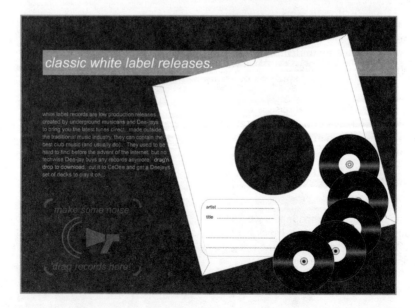

Creating a Drag-and-drop Movie Clip

My initial interface (with just the drag–and–drop functionality) is included in the files for download as `interface03.fla`. The starting point here was the draggable record icon (actually, it's a movie clip) that consists of a record graphic symbol called i-record, and an invisible, circular button called invisibleButton:

The movie clip is assembled like this: Create a new movie clip called record, and give it two layers: graphic and button. You should place i-record in the lower layer:

In the button layer, add the invisible button, scaling it so that it completely covers the underlying record:

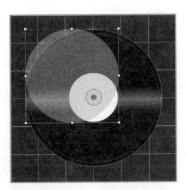 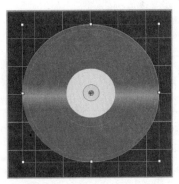

Select the button (you'll have to lock the graphic layer) and attach the following script to it:

```
on (press) {
    startDrag ("");
}

on (release, releaseOutside, rollOut, dragOut) {
    stopDrag ();
}
```

The `startDrag` action doesn't require any arguments in this situation. If you want to, you can specify the name of another clip that should be dragged, but if you leave this out, a target path of `this` is assumed, which is the timeline from which the command is issued. On this occasion, that means the record movie clip's timeline, and so it's the record clip that gets dragged.

With the record movie clip now assembled, you can arrange a number of instances of the clip on the main timeline, as shown below, starting with the 'highest' first. When you test the FLA, you'll notice (among other things) that only one record can be picked up at a time, and although that may sometimes seem like a limitation, it's a definite asset in applications like this – it ensures that you don't drag all the overlapping records at once.

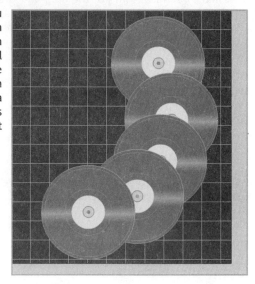

Another Smart Clip

Now that we have our draggable records, it's time to add some of the more advanced features we talked about at the start of this example. One of the things we specified was that choosing a record should cause its 'label' to be displayed. This will be different for each instance of the record movie clip, so... yes, you guessed it: smart clips are the order of the day.

`interface03a.fla` contains the record movie clip transformed into a smart clip, and the addition of the final movie's background assets. There is also a major functional addition: when you start dragging a record, the label on the 'sleeve' changes to contain information about the currently active record:

To differentiate the two in my head, I renamed the record movie clip to recordClip, signifying that it's about to become a smart clip, and I'd encourage you to choose a naming convention that suits you too. After that, you just need to make this fairly simple change to the invisible button's script code:

```
on (press) {
    _parent.label.artist = artist;
    _parent.label.title = title;
    _parent.label.notes = notes;
    startDrag ("");
}

on (release, releaseOutside, rollOut, dragOut) {
    stopDrag ();
}
```

In the new code, label is the instance name of the new sleeveLabel movie clip that will display information about this 'record' to the user. artist, title and notes are the variable names of dynamic text boxes inside that clip.

The artist, title, and notes that appear to the *right* of the assignment operators (=) are clip parameters of the new recordClip smart clip that we'll configure next – along with another parameter called url that represents the download location of our MP3 files, because we'll need that too. Here are all four definitions:

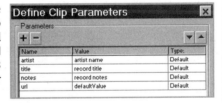

The sleeveLabel movie clip consists of a background graphic with three dynamic text boxes, as described above:

White label recordings are usually low production runs prepared by enthusiasts, and typically have handwritten labels. To emulate this aesthetic, I've used a font called Handwriting; you should install it, or choose something similar, if you want to achieve the same effect.

When you place this movie clip onto the stage, you must remember to give it the instance name `label`, so that the `_parent.label` paths we used in the `on (press)` handler work correctly:

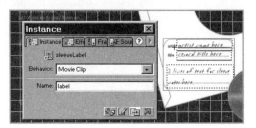

If any of the sleeve label's fields fail to show up, check that the ActionScript attached to the buttons is consistent with Define Clip Parameters window, and that the path to the `label` instance is correct. After that, it's on to the next part.

Creating and Using Behaviors

Our penultimate stage is `interface03b.fla`, which contains another of the features required by our brief: the ability for the records to 'snap' back and return to their original position when dropped. How exactly do we implement this? Well, a good technique is to add embedded movie clip modules, which I call **behaviors**, to your movie or smart clips. Behaviors are movie clips that have no graphical elements – just frames containing ActionScript code.

Behaviors are placed *inside* other movie clips, and communicate with them exclusively through the use of the `_parent` path, so that there is no dependence on the name of the parent, or of the behavior. For example, if the behavior wanted to cause its host movie clip to move, it would use the `_parent._x` and `_parent._y` properties. The behavior can examine and affect its parent without any need for cooperation in these respects.

If you've read some of the other friends of ED Flash books, or snooped around the right web sites, you'll probably have seen this kind of structure before. It's very powerful, and you'll find it used in many advanced ActionScript setups. It has the following advantages:

- Instance names are never used, and are not required. In essence, we've recreated the old Flash 4 `tellTarget` functionality without needing instance names!

- You can code behaviors separately, and even build up a library of useful ones, plugging them into movie clips whenever you see fit. Behaviors are modular, and can be reused.

- You can use more than one behavior in a single parent to create complex effects. Behaviors work in parallel, and their effects are additive.

Smart Clips that Snap

Exactly how to do this, and why it's worth doing, becomes most obvious by going ahead and putting together an example, so let's get on with it! The movie clip I'll build is called returnBehavior, and its name describes it completely: it's a behavior that causes a dragged movie clip to snap back to its original position when a message from its _parent tells it to do so. (Here, the "original position" is the location of the _parent movie clip on the stage when the returnBehavior is first invoked.) Here's what it looks like:

You can see that this behavior consists of a simple timeline with three frames, and in fact this is a typical structure for a behavior. Frame 1 is an initialization frame, frame 2 contains the main code, and frame 3 sets up a loop back to frame 2 with a simple goto instruction.

What do we need to initialize? Well, we need to know where the record has to snap back to when it's released, which will be its starting position. I've created variables called xHome and yHome to store the coordinates of this position, and because the behavior will be embedded inside recordClip, I can retrieve the starting position simply by looking at the _x and _y properties of the _parent:

```
xHome = _parent._x;
yHome = _parent._y;
```

exert initial values

This is therefore the initialization script that needs to go into frame 1.

Frame 2 contains the actual snap-back code, which employs a set of conditional statements. The first thing we need to ask is, "Do we need to snap back?" The behavior isn't in a position to work this out (it simply *performs* the snap), but it can use a 'flag' variable that the parent movie clip will set whenever snapping is required. I called this variable snapBack, and since it will reside in the parent, we have to use _parent.snapBack to get at it. The rest of the code is then made to run only if snapBack is true; once we've looked at the snap-back code below, we will create the snapback variable.

As soon as we see that snapBack *is* true, we need to move the parent movie clip back to (xHome, yHome), *unless it's already at (xHome, yHome)*. The next two if statements check for this by looking at whether we are within one pixel of the starting coordinates. If we're further away than that, the behavior moves the parent closer to xHome, or yHome, or both:

```
if (_parent.snapBack) {
    x = _parent._x;
    y = _parent._y;

    if (Math.abs (x - xHome) > 1) {
        x = x + ((xHome - x) / 4);
        _parent._x = x;
    }
    if (Math.abs (y - yHome) > 1) {
        y = y + ((yHome - y) / 4);
        _parent._y = y;
    }
}
```

get posi. of x & y.

If new Pos is less than x home {

The parent is moved via the statements $x = x + ((xHome - x) / 4)$ and $y = y + ((yHome - y) / 4)$. These expressions look at the difference between where we are and where we want to be ($x - xHome$ and $y - yHome$), and move us one-fourth of that distance each time they're executed. As we get closer to $xHome$ and $yHome$, this distance decreases, causing a deceleration that looks a lot like real-life movement against an opposing force. The 4 in the expression directly affects the return speed – setting it higher will slow snapping down, while and setting it lower will speed things up.

To ensure that the behavior monitors `snapBack` on a constant basis, frame 3 is simply:

```
gotoAndPlay (2);
```

Using this movie clip just involves placing it on recordClip's timeline, and creating the `snapBack` variable that it interrogates. With regard to the latter, we need `snapBack` to be `false` when we start and whenever we try to drag a record icon, and `true` whenever we drop the icon. To make things clearer, we can set up some new layers, so go into the recordClip smart clip and add two new layers, actions and behaviors, as shown here:

In frame 1 of the actions layer, add this:

```
snapBack = false;
stop ();
```

You've already attached some actions to the invisible button, but now we need to add a `snapBack = false` to the `on (press)` part, and a `snapBack = true` to the `on (release, releaseOutside, rollout, dragOut)` part. When that's done, your button's script will look like this:

```
on (press) {
    _parent.label.artist = artist;
    _parent.label.title = title;
    _parent.label.notes = notes;
    snapBack = false;
    startDrag ("");
}

on (release, releaseOutside, rollOut, dragOut) {
    stopDrag ();
    snapBack = true;
}
```

Finally, drop the returnBehavior movie clip into the behaviors layer. It will show up as a small, white, filled circle, as shown below (mine is placed to the top left, although this location is unimportant).

Test the movie now, and you'll see the 'snap back' take place: as soon as you release a record, it will animate itself back to its starting position. If you're feeling adventurous, you might also want to add a second behavior (called, say, rotateBehavior) that makes the record spin as it snaps.

Collision Detection

The last thing that we *need* to add to this example is the code that detects collisions and loads files. When a record is dropped over a certain area, we want to start downloading that particular recording's MP3 file. This is a two-stage process:

- We need to define the area to be 'hit' in our collision

- We need to set up hit detection in the 'hitter', which in our case will be a record clip

The final version of my interface is in interface03c.fla, and you might have taken a peek at it when we started. However, I haven't given it valid URLs or files to download, so running it can cause the SWF to attempt downloads that won't work. If that happens, just cancel the operation.

Our target area doesn't have to be anything more complicated than a movie clip with an instance name – the instance name is required to tell Flash what we want to detect a collision with. Here's my hit area graphic, which is a movie clip called download.

Drag this onto the stage in the same layer as the background artwork (this is called backdrop in the example FLA), give it an instance name of download... and that's it! All we need to do now is detect when our records collide with it.

In the recordClip smart clip, you need to change the script in the invisible button for the on (release, releaseOutside, rollOut, dragOut) event. The new code will detect a collision between the movie clip we're in, and the download instance we just created on the main timeline – which is the _parent of this smart clip.

```
on (release, releaseOutside, rollOut, dragOut) {
    stopDrag ();
    if (hitTest(_parent.download) && !snapBack) {
        snapBack = false;
        play ();
    } else {
        snapback = true;
    }
}
```

In order to work, the hitTest method of the Flash 5 MovieClip object needs to know the instance paths of both the 'hitter' and the 'hit area'. However, it takes the first of these from its current context (that is, the movie clip it's being called from), which means that this code uses only a single explicit instance name. This is a very useful trick when you want to detect collisions in more dynamic situations, especially games, where you have no hope of knowing all the instance names involved.

On this occasion, the hitTest method is used as a condition in our if statement, which does one of two things:

- If a collision is detected, *and we're not already in the process of snapping back*, our condition becomes true and we set snapBack to false. (This inhibits our 'snap back' behavior; the record will stay where it was dropped.) We also cause the recordClip timeline to start running by calling play ().

- If a collision is not detected, then we want our record to snap back, and specify this by setting snapBack to true.

What do we see when our timeline starts to play? Just at the moment, nothing at all, so extend the layers as shown:

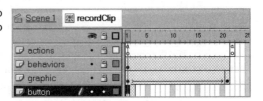

Frame 22 of the actions layer then contains our actual download script that loads the file via a call to getURL – to make it perform the file download, you need to specify the url clip parameter to be something of the form www.address.com/filename.

```
getURL (url);
stop ();
```

Before that takes place, however, I've added a motion tween to the graphic layer that contains an alpha transition, so that the record slowly disappears once a hit is detected.

You'll notice that the collision detection is a little iffy at times, and it may even detect a 'hit' when you think there's no overlap. This is because ActionScript is detecting intersections of the movie clips' **bounding boxes** – this is the area you see outlined when you select a movie clip on the stage. In the next exercise, we'll use a more advanced form of hitTest collision detection, but for now we'll stick with what we have, because it's good enough for the needs of the current interface.

You've seen a lot in this last exercise, from conditional, goal-based animation (the snap back), to collision detection of interface elements (and how to use this together with simpler things like drag-and-drop to make for an intuitive and open interface). Not only is it easy to do, but I just like playing with interfaces like this... stupid things like, "Can I keep all the records moving at the same time by dragging and dropping them quickly, one after another?" or trying to break the 'snap back' animation by trying it at odd angles.

From a programming perspective, the use of behaviors along with Boolean flags to run/inhibit them makes for an easy and consistent way to build up complex code, while still keeping it all well-structured and straightforward to modify.

Alternative Techniques

It can be argued that the structure of the behaviors I've used in this and other projects is a little 'old-fashioned', and that it would be preferable to make use of the movie clip events that Flash 5 makes available. This change in approach is quite possible, and it's closer to the way things are done in Macromedia Director, but it again has implications for reusability: you lose the convenience of 'dropping' a behavior into just *any* movie clip and seeing it work, because you have to add the event-handling code to each behavior instance.

If that sounds complicated, though, it really isn't – this project can be converted to use clip events in just a couple of steps. First, you need to remove all three frames from the returnBehavior clip, so that it's completely empty. Then, in the recordClip, select the instance of the behavior and add the following ActionScript code:

```
onClipEvent (load) {
    xHome = _parent._x;
    yHome = _parent._y;
}

onClipEvent (enterFrame) {
    if (_parent.snapBack) {
        x = _parent._x;
        y = _parent._y;

        if (Math.abs(x - xHome) > 1) {
```

```
        x = x + ((xHome - x) / 4);
        _parent._x = x;
    }

    if (Math.abs(y - yHome) > 1) {
        y = y + ((yHome - y) / 4);
        _parent._y = y;
    }
  }
}
```

The first event handler (`onClipEvent (load)`) is called the first time Flash sees the movie clip, and so takes the place of our initialization fame. The second handler is called all the time – that is, in every frame. There's therefore no need for any 'loop' code in this setup, and the modified movie behaves in the same way as the original. It's useful to know how this technique works, because it looks likely that it will become recommended practice, but I for one will be reluctant to give up that extra reusability that behaviors provide!

Interfaces that Don't Look like Interfaces

For this final example, we'll look at interfaces that don't look like interfaces.

What?

Let me explain...

There's a recent tendency in Flash to build creative interfaces that don't emulate the standard button, or window-based interfaces. In fact, the more way-out wacky it is, the better. You've probably seen them: when they first appear, you think, "What on *Earth* is that? I asked for a web site!" Then you look a bit more carefully, and comprehension dawns, and you think, "Well, it's different..." Hopefully, once you've figured it all out, you start to think it's *cool* too.

In this section, we'll deconstruct an interface that looks nothing like an interface. What's more, it doesn't even *work* like an ordinary point-and-click interface – for a start, there are no buttons. There's a lot of creativity that goes into designing an interface that doesn't look like an interface, and it can be difficult because:

- To be worth doing, it has to be something that hasn't been done before

- Users have to recognize it as an interface, despite having never seen anything like it

- It has to be intuitive enough, despite points 1 and 2, for no instructions to be required (that would defeat the point of an interface)

Before we go on, I should say that the following interface took me half a day to create. 75% of that time was spent with Photoshop and a Wacom pen, just doodling ideas and thinking, "Will that work?" In fact, I built an additional interface that had a rotational theme, complete with gravity and arcs and stuff, but it just wasn't intuitive. The final FLA, `interface04.fla`, was my second attempt – and once I'd defined it and was happy with my idea, the whole thing just came together programming-wise. Good, creative interface design is like that: design is the important part.

You can have a look at the final goal of this exercise right now, and because it's an interface that you're unlikely to have seen before, it would be a good idea to have a play before I describe how it was done. You'll need to understand the final goal for any of the rest of this chapter to make sense!

The interface consists of a ball on a board. Using your mouse, you have to coax the ball into one of the exits in order to navigate to a particular option. The ball is made of steel, though, and it takes a while to get going – it follows you with a delay, making it hard to control at times. If your ball falls off the edge of the board, you start again.

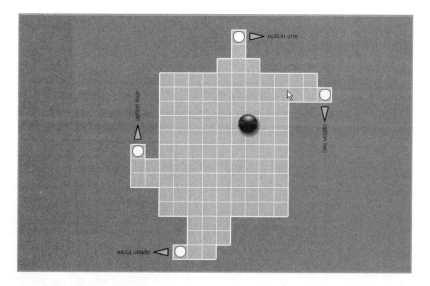

This "board" is based on an old game that used to be popular when I was a kid (the pre-computer 1970s). You had a wooden maze with a hole at the exit, you put a marble at the start, and you had to tilt the maze to move the marble into the exit hole, avoiding the edges of the maze. My maze is not difficult, but it's easy enough to make it more of a challenge if you're minded to do so. Make it sufficiently hard, and you have a game rather than an interface, which is actually a fundamental point: the interface is fun in itself, and will keep people at your site (or your client's site) for longer, because they're taken by the interactive-play potential of it all.

Because it starts straight away, it only takes a couple of mouse movements to work out what's going on (even if you're young enough to have spent a wooden-toy-free childhood), making it pretty intuitive.

In terms of programming, there are a few things that are special about this interface:

- Instead of button clicks, it uses the advanced form of the hitTest collision detection method we used earlier

- It steals a trick called **collision** (or **sprite**) **maps** from the world of computer games, specially redesigned for use in Flash

- It uses a modified version of the record icon's movement, which we met in the previous exercise

From these observations, you might start to suspect that this interface is really just a more creative version of the MP3 interface above – and you'd be right. In fact, you've now learned about most of the basic building blocks of advanced interfaces. For example, you understand that buttons can be 'mouse detection devices'; you've used smart clips; and you've programmed motion that models real physics, goal-based animation, and behaviors. The real challenge in creating advanced interfaces is to design an interface using these building blocks.

The first thing I created was the board, which is simply a set of horizontal and vertical lines. To get them all parallel, I made sure that Flash's grid snap option was turned on. My final board graphic is in the Library, as a graphic symbol called grid.

The ball needs to know when it is no longer on the board, and for this we need to build up a **collision map**. This identifies the parts of the stage where the ball is not allowed to go. You can see the map below right – it's really just a shape telling Flash what areas are 'outside' the board. This system can be used in all sorts of advanced interfaces (and games, which are really just *very* advanced interfaces as far as I'm concerned) where you have intelligent or 'self-moving' elements and want to constrain their motion within an irregular area.

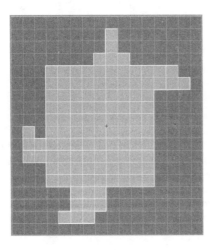 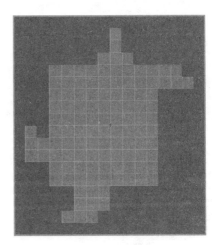

This technique is particularly useful, for example, when representing fake 3D views (such as isometric viewpoints) that are built up using Swift3D or judicious use of Flash's rotate and scale/skew controls. You can see how you might create a fake 3D interface in the next picture, but don't forget to skew the collision map as well! To keep this exercise simple, I'll stick to the 2D version, but it was a really close call because converting to the 3D interface requires little extra effort – as you'll find if you attempt it.

Hint: build the 2D interface, place it all within a single movie clip, and scale and skew it to give an isometric view. You'll have to shift the collision map up slightly as well, to fit in with the new view).

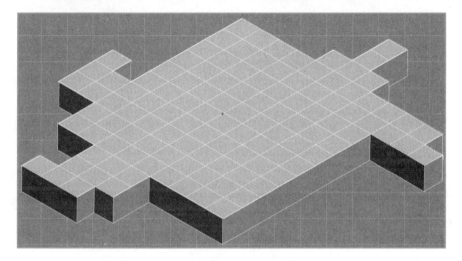

As for the programming, the interface works like this:

- The steel ball tries to reach the mouse position, but moves with a kind of inertia, making its reactions delayed (thus emulating a real steel ball).

- When the ball hits the collision map, a variable called _root.collision is set to true, and the ball is sent back to its original starting point. (Because collision is at _root, it's a **global** variable. It will need to be accessed from a number of different places, so making it global is a good idea.) There's really not much new about this variable – it's just another flag that's used to communicate a state to behavior movie clips, which is a programming device you've seen before.

- When the ball hits any of the four circular pads that you saw in the first picture, the interface jumps to a new scene representing a new part of the site. This is done via a simple goto. To add more goto jumps is just a case of adding more pads, so it's a pretty flexible system, and particular pads could be made to do other things as well.

The Steel Ball

The steel ball is simply a movie clip called ballBearing that's controlled by a behavior that makes it follow the mouse cursor:

The specular, ball, and shadow layers contain the graphics, while the code is contained in the behavior layer. I've created a modular behavior clip called followerBehavior to give me the mouse-following functionality; you can see it above as the little circle to the top left of the ball, and its timeline comprises the standard, three-keyframe ActionScript structure we discussed earlier:

Frame 1 asks for the starting point of the parent ballBearing clip, and assigns it to variables called xStart and yStart:

```
xStart = _parent._x;
yStart = _parent._y;
```

Frame 2 moves the ball towards the position of the mouse, as long as no collision with the map is detected (that is, as long as _root.collision is not true). If there is no collision, the code looks at where the ball is now (x, y), where it wants to go to (xHome, yHome, which is the current mouse position), and moves 1/32 of this distance every frame, making the ball's reaction to your movement pretty slow:

```
if (!_root.collision) {
    x = _parent._x;
    y = _parent._y;
    xHome = _root._xMouse;
    yHome = _root._yMouse;
    x = x + ((xHome - x) / 32);
    y = y + ((yHome - y) / 32);
    _parent._x = x;
    _parent._y = y;
} else {
    _parent._x = xStart;
    _parent._y = yStart;
```

```
        _root.collision = false;
    }
```

The `else` part handles what happens when a collision *is* seen, in which case all we need to do is send the ball back to its starting position (xStart, yStart, which we stored in frame 1). Since we've moved the ball away from its collision position, we must also reset the `collision` variable back to `false`, because the collision is no longer occurring.

Frame 3 is just our `goto` back to frame 2, so that our main script is carried out continuously:

```
        gotoAndPlay (2);
```

Notice that the steel ball's behavior was written without us knowing *how* `_root.collision` will be set to `true` when a collision takes place. This is the magic of using modular code within movie clips: you can simply *assume* the relationships with other behaviors, and tackle each part of the overall code in a bite-sized chunk. All I need to know about my collision detection routine at this time is that it will set `_root.collision` to `true` on a collision, and nothing else. In fact, I wouldn't even care if someone else were writing it, as long as they knew what it had to do. This makes for efficient team coding and delegation – go tell your boss!

The Collision Map

The collision map has exactly the same basic structure as the ball (which is no surprise, because it's a standard structure): a movie clip (called mazeHitMap) with an embedded behavior (mazeHitTestBehavior). Predictably, the map layer contains my collision map, and the behavior layer contains my collision detection code.

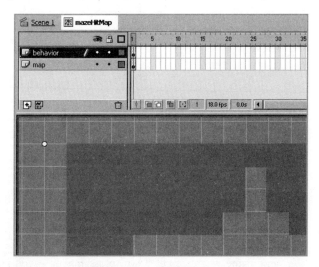

There is a myth that accurate, pixel-perfect collision detection is hard, and only top programmers should attempt it. However, this is just not true for Flash, because the functionality is there as a standard ActionScript function. Consequently, my collision detection behavior in mazeHitTestBehavior is precisely two frames long – this time, we don't even need an initialization frame:

Frame 1 contains the following code, which looks for a hit between the ball bearing and the collision map (Frame 2 just says `gotoAndPlay (1);`):

```
if (_parent.hitTest(_root.ball._x, _root.ball._y, true)) {
    _root.collision = true;
}
```

The `hitTest` is set up to detect a collision between mazeHitMap (the parent) and the (x, y) coordinates corresponding to the instance of the ball (`_root.ball._x, _root.ball._y`). The last argument to the `hitTest` method is a flag that tells Flash whether it needs to evaluate the movie clip's bounding box for collision, or the movie clip's actual *shape* (in other words, it looks for non-zero pixels within the bounding box). Setting it to `true` evaluates the shape, making for pixel-perfect collision detection.

There is a disadvantage to doing this though, which is that Flash can only perform shape-based collision detection between a movie clip and a point. You can't perform shape-based collision detection between two movie clips, which is why the ball bearing movie clip is defined here by its x, y coordinates. This isn't too much of a problem in this application, because the ball would only fall off the edge of the board when its center went over the edge, but it's something to remember. Sometimes, you might have to go for the less accurate bounding box detection (as we did in the MP3 download interface), because you want to detect an overlap between two movie clips. This will become clearer if you look at the diagram below, which shows the two possible ways of detecting collisions between two instances, A and B.

B.hitTest(A._x, B._y, true)

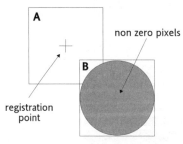

shape based detection; registration point of clip A has to overlap non zero pixels in clip B for collision detection to occur.

B.hitTest(A)

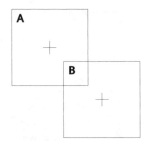

bounding boxes based detection; any overlap of the two clip bounding boxes (even if there are no pixels actually in collision) causes collision detection to occur.

Because we've assumed an instance name of `ball` for our steel ball bearing, we will have to remember to give it the same name when we get down to assembling everything on the stage, but for now we can jump straight to the last element in our design: the detection pads.

The Detection Pads

The detection pads (contained in the overSensor movie clip) are the circles in the four maze exits, and they perform collision detection between themselves and the steel ball's center point in much the same way as hitTestMap. This time, though, I decided not to use a behavior clip, because of the simplicity of the script.

Here, pad contains a simple circle, which is our collision area, while actions contains two frames of ActionScript:

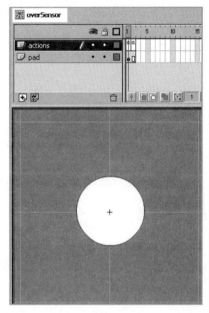

Frame 1 contains:

```
if (hitTest(_root.ball._x, _root.ball._y, true)) {
    _parent.gotoAndPlay (gotoLabel);
}
```

This is simply detecting a collision between our pad and the steel ball's (x, y) coordinates. If a collision occurs, the main timeline (which is the _parent) is made to jump to a location specified by gotoLabel. Since this label will be different for each of the four detection pads, that sounds like a job for a smart clip!

overSensor is a smart clip with one clip parameter: our gotoLabel variable:

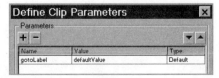

Frame 2 is just a simple goto:

```
gotoAndPlay (1);
```

That's all our pieces; the final step is putting it all together...

The Interface

The stage area consists of four layers: board, sensors, ball, and actions:

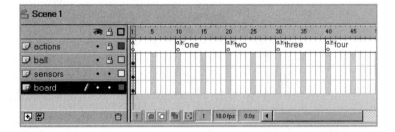

The board layer contains the game board, a graphic symbol called grid:

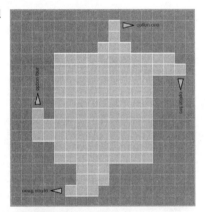

The sensors layer contains an instance of the mazeHitMap, and four instances of the overSensor smart clip:

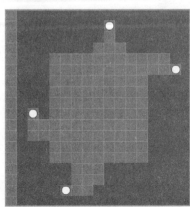

We want the mazeHitMap to be invisible, and we'll need to reference it in our scripts. I have therefore given it the instance name hitArea. The four overSensor smart clips need their clip parameters initializing, and I've given their respective gotoLabel parameters values of one to four. This corresponds to the labels one to four on the actions layer, so that the overSensor clips will cause a jump to their respective gotoLabel value when the steel ball rolls over them.

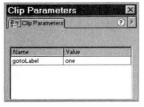

The ball layer contains the steel ball. Its initial position is important, because it will be read as the initial starting position by its embedded behavior followerBehavior, and the ball will start again from this position every time it falls off the edge of the grid. Don't forget to give it the instance name ball, because it's referred to by that name in some of the code.

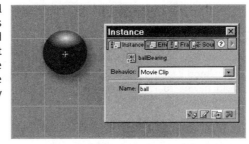

Finally, the code to string it all together is in the actions layer. Frame 1 has this attached:

```
collision = false;
hitArea._visible = false;
stop ();
```

This initializes our global variable collision, and makes our collision map invisible by setting its _visible property to false (this is why I gave it an instance name earlier). Note that using _visible instead of _alpha is a much less computationally intensive way of making something invisible (especially if there's animation going on over or including the movie clip in question), and should therefore be preferred.

The four labels one to four contain the navigation commands to make the timeline jump to four scenes called option 1 to option 4. Each labeled frame contains a command of the form:

```
gotoAndPlay ("option 1", 1);
```

Having this 'extra' step of redirection is a particularly flexible way of doing things, because you can attach all sorts of things to the four keyframes that you couldn't specify via smart clip parameters.

And that's everything. You could make the option scenes have further mazes, and you could even modify the interface to have 'ball dropping' and 'ball teleporting' animations for the two collision conditions. There's also the cool 3D interface which you could use as a starting point – so get your skates on and see what you can do with it, before all the other readers develop the idea! Alternatively, get your sketchpad out, and modify everything you've learned so far to build an interface that looks nothing like this one. That's what Flash is all about.

Conclusion

We've gone through only a few complete interface designs in this chapter, but we have examined many of the techniques behind them. I've tried to avoid the 'usual' list of interface designs (sideways-scrolling, window-based, etc.) because the programming know-how to generate these can get very specific, and I really wanted to show you the more basic ideas behind interface creation. I hope that I've been able to provide some insight into the thought processes and basic building blocks of successful interface design.

Flash 5 has given us many new tools, and I have intentionally used the ones that are relevant to interface design, particularly because the Flash documentation doesn't imply that they can be used in this way. Now that you've seen their usefulness, and the programming structures that work (modular design via behaviors, use of flags, property based control using relative paths to avoid having to know instance names, etc.), you'll hopefully have some ideas for some *really* complex interfaces.

Another part of advanced interface design is *inspiration*. Some designers (Josh Ulm, Brendan Dawes) have chosen cinematic themes and styles, while others (Josh Davis, Yugo) have gone for the emulation of physical motion and its internal relationships, and Slam Mathematics™, and chaos theory. Others still (James Paterson, Joe Cartoon) have opted for more surreal interfaces, complete with little stick men going through mangles, ninja hamsters, and other stuff too way-out to mention.

The point is that all the designers mentioned have a love for the direction they are going with their interfaces, and that shows through. This is something always to bear in mind.

My personal source of inspiration is video games, because I believe all the problems that developers of advanced interfaces come across have already been solved by the video game industry, and their systems of control, intelligence and movement are easily converted into Flash 5 – or at least, they are now that we have a structured, object-based language to work with.

The question you need to ask when starting out on an advanced interface is, "What can I see out there that hasn't been used in this way by Flash before?" Then you need to identify whether (or rather, *how*) it can be made into an intuitive and engaging interface. And that is fun in itself.

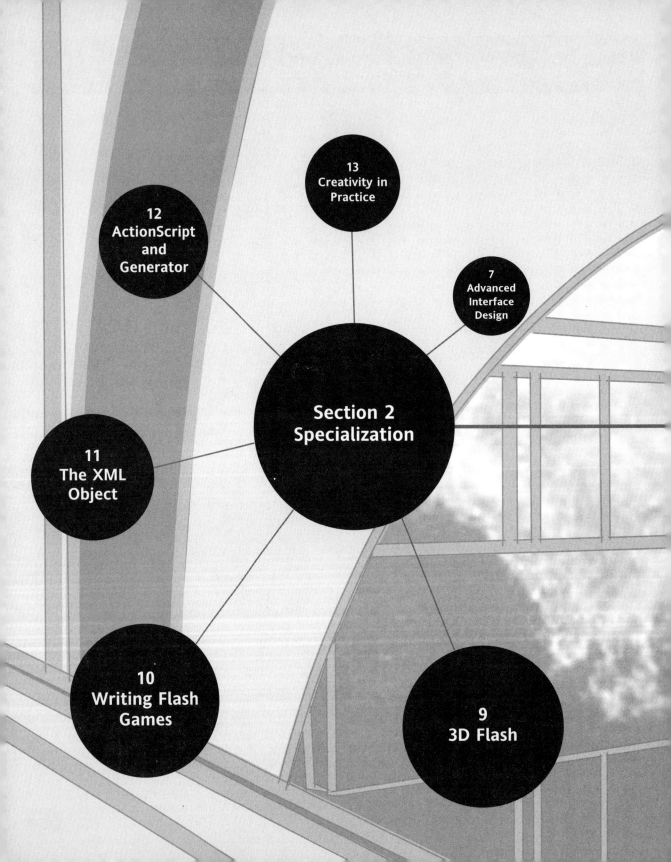

Chapter 8
Sound Control

In all but a few cases, sound is an essential component of entertainment media such as TV and cinema. As we seek to increase the richness of the web sites we produce, it seems reasonable to ask why, in the end, the Internet should be any different. The introduction of sound can add considerably to the impact and effectiveness of a site, but in the past it has been unpopular because of the demands it places on limited bandwidth. With the widespread acceptance of compression technologies such as MP3, however, sound is becoming an increasingly attractive proposition.

In this chapter, we'll examine the facilities for handling sound in Flash 5 ActionScript, which are provided in the methods of the Sound object. While we're at it, we'll look at a couple of issues that can prevent the new sound commands from working properly. Of course, we'll discuss fixes to get over these problems as we go along, and I'll try to introduce you to sound with ActionScript via a fairly gentle curve, because it's a path that can be somewhat fraught for the unwary.

> *This chapter will only look at event-driven sounds. Flash also lets you use streaming sounds, but experience suggests that using streaming sound within an ActionScript-heavy site is error prone. The reason for this is that once a streaming sound is initiated, Flash will 'lock' itself to that sound, rather than the timeline. If, for any reason, the timeline cannot keep up with the sound stream, Flash skips frames to keep up. This might be acceptable in a tween-based timeline, but one that uses ActionScript can't handle it: those missed frames might contain important initialization scripts, or vital algorithms. In addition, ActionScript-heavy sites tend to contain many small timeline loops, making them incompatible with a linear streaming sound.*

How sound works in Flash

Superficially quite simple looking, Flash 5's Sound object is actually extremely flexible, and there are a number of options open with regard to how you define and use it. Before we can begin to dissect it, though, it's important that you understand a few fundamental features of using sound in Flash, and it's these that we'll look at in this section.

To some extent, the techniques available for manipulating sound from within ActionScript map to the volume and pan (or 'balance') controls that you'd find on an average hi-fi. At least some of this first example is likely to be revision to you, but take a look at sound.fla to see how pan and volume controls work together in real life. It begins with a small box containing a couple of dials:

Don't worry about how this works in terms of ActionScript code just yet – we'll be examining that later on. For now, it's just something to play with. First, 'turn it on' by clicking the button. Then, as you move the right dial (click and hold near the dial dot, and move the cursor in the direction you want the dial to turn), you'll see two speakers appear. These represent the volume of the sound; as you turn the dial, the speakers grow larger or smaller accordingly.

Now try the same with the balance control. As you do so, an important point to note is that once the balance is moved to (say) the right of center, it no longer affects the right-hand speaker. Rather, it reduces the volume of the left-hand speaker. Gone unnoticed, this fairly subtle point can cause all sorts of conceptual problems when we come to plug numbers into Flash's digital controls, as we'll see later on.

Also notice how the volume and pan work together: the volume control sets the maximum volume for both speakers, and the pan control varies the volume of the individual speakers between zero and the maximum set by the volume control. Converting those dial settings into values that we'll use in Flash, we get something like the diagram below:

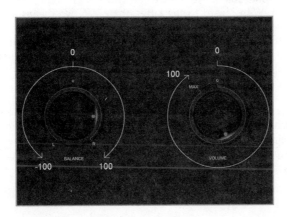

The volume control is straightforward: a value of zero gives no volume (or 0%), while maximum volume corresponds to a numerical value of 100. The pan control is a little trickier: at its center point (that is, equal speaker balance), it has a value of 0. The extreme left (when sound is only in the left speaker) is at a value of -100, while the extreme right (when sound is only in the right speaker) is at a value of 100.

In the picture above, the volume is at around 50%, while the pan control is giving full volume to the right speaker, and about 50% to the left speaker. Converting those into values to be used by the Flash 5 ActionScript Sound object, both the volume and the pan would be set to something close to 50. For the time being, that's about all you need to know; you can come back and see exactly how the movie works later on, but now we can start to make progress.

Creating a sound object

In this section, I'll lay down all the ground rules of sound object definition (and what they actually mean in real terms), so that you can move ahead with confidence. As far as ActionScript is concerned, there are three ways of generating sound from within Flash:

- The Flash 4 technique of attaching sounds to timelines, and controlling them with time-based sound envelopes

- The Flash 5 way, which is to attach sounds to ActionScript Sound objects

- A mixture of the two

By the nature of this book, it will come as no surprise that we won't be covering the first of these in any depth, and we'll assume that you already know something about it. The other two, however, are fair game, and you'll see numerous examples of both being used in the remainder of the chapter.

To obtain a usable sound object, we have to do two things: create the sound object itself, and 'attach' a sound to it. With regard to the latter, there are two means at your disposal: you can refer to an actual sound file, or to a timeline containing a sound. The first way is easier, but the second allows you to control multiple sounds from the same sound object (and, as we shall see later, to use the old Flash 4 sound features in unison with Flash 5's sound objects). The second way also has a couple of subtle bugs that you need to know about, but we'll tackle them as and when they arise.

The next few exercises use specialFX.fla as a starting point. This has a few sounds already imported into its Library, but you can just as well modify it to use your own sounds if you wish. The sounds in specialFX.fla were created for a Pac Man/Mario Bros type Flash game, and come complete with the added saccharine cuteness that was required of sound effects for platform games of the early 1980s.

Attaching sounds via linkage

Linking Flash 5 Sound objects to sound files in the Library is best used when you want to attach a single sound to each object, for the lifetime of the object in question. You might use this technique to create sound objects that drive the individual special effects in a game or an animated feature, for example.

Before you can attach, say, **Winner_02** to a sound object, you first have to give it a **linkage name.** This not completely unlike the idea of giving instance names to movie clips: the linkage name, not the Library name, is how you'll refer to the sound in your ActionScript code. To create a linkage name, you can:

■ Highlight the sound in the Library, and then select Linkage... from the Library's Options drop-down menu

■ Right-click on the sound, and select Linkage... from the menu that pops up

Either way, you'll see the Symbol Linkage Properties dialog box appear. To give the sound a linkage name, you need to select the Export this symbol radio button, and enter a unique name in the Identifier field (which will now be active). I called this one win2:

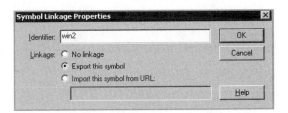

A word of warning is appropriate here. Flash appears to make no check on the uniqueness of the identifier you use, so keep notes or use some sort of naming convention, or you may experience some unwelcome effects.

With the sound now prepared, we're ready to attach it to a Sound object, which we create from ActionScript using code like this:

```
mySound = new Sound (target);
```

Where:

- *mySound* is the name of your sound object. This follows all the normal rules that govern ActionScript variables, so to access it from anywhere other than the timeline where it was defined, you'd use the standard dot notation paths.

- *target* is the path to the timeline on which this sound object will be created. It's usual not to specify anything for this parameter, in which case Flash will create the object on the current timeline. Sometimes, though, it can be useful to create all your sound objects in the same place (such as the main timeline, or a specific movie clip), so that you know where they all are, and at what point they will all be defined.

Using a sound from the Library

Using specialFX.fla as a starting point, and in frame 1 of the main timeline, add this line of code:

```
winSound = new Sound ();
```

As suggested above, if you wanted to create the sound object someplace other than the timeline we're on, you could add the path inside the parentheses. Make sure that the path exists when you issue the new Sound command, though, or the object will not be created at all. For this reason, it's usually better to create sound objects from the timeline to which you want them added.

Next, add the following command to attach the winSound object to our win2 sound file:

```
winSound.attachSound ("win2");
```

The quotation marks here mean that the linkage name is a string, and not a variable or an object. (If you don't use quotation marks, Flash will assume that you're referring to a path, as we'll see later in the chapter.) With that done, playing the sound requires a very simple third command:

```
winSound.start ();
```

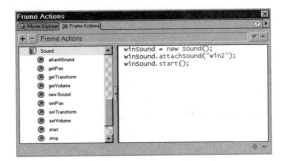

If you now test the movie, you'll hear the **Winner_02** jingle play once. If you want to stop the sound before it reaches its natural conclusion, you can add the following statement a few frames along the timeline:

```
winSound.stop();
```

The stop method stops the sound dead in its tracks, at the current frame. Once you're happy with how it works, delete the keyframe you just added (along with any additional frames) so that you're back to a single keyframe at frame 1.

> *It sounds unlikely, but there are actually some subtle aspects to the way* stop() *behaves. However, these don't become apparent until we start controlling multiple sound objects, so we'll come back to this method again when we reach those heady heights.*

The Sound.start method

Getting back to the start method, which we used *au naturel* in the last example, there are a couple of parameters that we can specify in order to gain more accurate control over how a sound is played:

```
mySound.start(offset, loops);
```

Here, *offset* is the number of seconds into the sound you want to start playing, and *loops* is the number of times the sound should replay. You can discover how long a sound is in seconds by selecting it and clicking on the Library window's Options > Properties menu item. I found, for example, that Winner_02 is 3.8s long, so if I wanted to start from the middle of the sound and play it twice, I would replace the earlier statement with:

```
winSound.start(1.9, 2);
```

Flash applies the *offset* to every loop, so this sound will start playing from the halfway point on both occasions it gets played, not just the first time. As far as *loops* is concerned, a value of 214748 is about as high as you can go, so specify that if you want a sound that effectively repeats forever.

> *In fact, for most practical purposes, setting a value for loops of something around 1000 is usually enough. But just in case you ever need to know the limit, now you do!*

Sometimes, you'll have a sound that has an unwanted delay at the beginning of the file, or perhaps some 'white noise' that you want to skip. If you're able to discern your preferred starting point by looking at the sound's waveform, a neat trick is *temporarily* to attach the sound to a frame, and then press Edit... in the Sound panel to bring up the Edit Envelope window. By selecting the icons at the bottom right of this window, you can:

- Find out the time in seconds at which particular features of the waveform start, and use that as the *offset*. In the waveform below, there's a 'gap' in the sound that ends just after 3 seconds in. By zooming in to the waveform (using the magnifying glass icons), you can find the end point of this gap precisely.

- Convert seconds into frames by making the Edit Envelope window show the timescale in frames. You can toggle between the two representations by pressing the third and fourth icons.

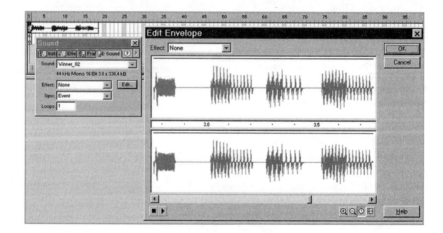

Controlling the volume and pan of a sound object

To vary the volume and pan levels of a sound object – which is what happened in the example that you stepped through at the start of the chapter – we can use the setVolume and setPan methods. In frame 1 of the same movie, add the new lines shown below:

```
vol = 100;
pan = 0;
winSound = new Sound ();
winSound.attachSound ("win2");
winSound.start (0, 214748);
```

Then, create new keyframes at frames 2 and 3, and rename the current layer actions. In frame 2, add:

```
winSound.setVolume (vol);
winSound.setPan (pan);
```

And in frame 3, add:

```
gotoAndPlay (2);
```

This set of scripts now creates variables called pan and vol, and then a sound object called winSound that plays in a constant loop. Frames 2 and 3 simply keep reapplying our vol and pan variables to set the volume and pan levels of the sound.

To vary vol and pan, create a new layer called text. In it, add two input text fields with their options specified as shown below, and give them variable names vol and pan respectively. Don't forget to add a minus sign in the text entry field at the bottom right, or you won't be able to enter negative values.

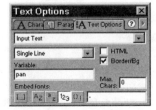

"vol" and "pan" are simply a couple of bits of static text to remind you which entry box is which. As a sanity check, your timeline should now look like this, and you can see the finished FLA as `specialFXTest.fla`:

> **Warning: The next step may create some very loud and distorted sounds. If you have an external amplifier connected to your computer, turn the volume down to about 10% before proceeding.**

If you run this movie, you'll hear the jingle play continuously, and you can change the current value of either the volume or the pan via the text entry boxes. Putting a value between 0 and 100 in the `vol` text box will result in the volume control varying between 0 and 100%; supplying a `pan` value of between -100 and 100 will split the sound between your left and right audio outputs.

> *I built this example with text boxes rather than sliders for a reason: Flash lets you go beyond the given maximum ranges for volume and pan. If you try entering 'out-of-range' values, you'll discover that Flash generates an overdriven version of the sound sample. This is not so great if you do it by mistake, but if you're using guitar samples or certain bass sounds, it's potentially really useful in a soundtrack composition!*

Generating a reverb effect

It may have crossed your mind that even the simple commands you've seen so far have the potential to create some fairly advanced effects, such as reverb. The following script, for example, gives you a slight reverb effect (use the original `specialFX.fla` as your starting point, and add the script to frame 1):

```
winSound = new Sound ();
winSound2 = new Sound ();
winSound.attachSound ("win2");
winSound2.attachSound ("win2");
winSound.start (0, 1);
winSound2.start (0.05, 1);
```

This creates two sound objects linked to the same sound, and plays them with a slight delay between them. Obviously, then, if you change the last line (as shown below), you'd expect to hear no delay at all:

```
winSound.start(0, 1);
winSound2.start(0, 1);
```

But if you try it, you'll find that you *do* still hear a delay!

The reason for this is that in Flash, event sounds and sounds triggered by ActionScript *are not synchronized*, so that two 'identical' sounds started on the same frame will not necessarily start or finish at the same time (or even last as long as they should!). This problem has caused all sorts of head scratching, and has put many Flash designers off the complex use of sound altogether, but the fix is actually very simple.

The Flash sound player can be forced into synch with the timeline whenever a *streaming* sound is played, because this type of sound *must* be closely tied to the timeline. The fix, then, involves playing a short streaming sound at the beginning of every timeline that requires synchronized sound.

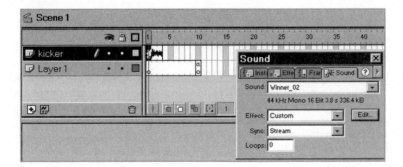

At frame 1 of your timeline, add a short streaming sound. It can be any sound at all, and to make it inaudible, set its volume to zero via the Edit Envelope window. It only needs to last a few frames, after which you can issue ActionScript sound commands safe in the knowledge that they are now properly synchronized. I always add the streaming sound in a new layer called kicker, because that's precisely what it does – it kicks the Flash sound player into working properly!

You'll need to move your code to somewhere after the kicker; I've deleted my initial code from frame 1, and placed the following at frame 10:

```
winSound = new Sound ();
winSound2 = new Sound ();
winSound.attachSound ("win2");
winSound2.attachSound ("win2");
winSound.start (0, 1);
winSound2.start (0.05, 1);
stop ();
```

As expected, my jingle plays with a 0.05 second reverb. To check that proper synchronization is taking place, setting the delays on both sound objects to zero should result in the original sound, signifying that the two sound files are now playing in perfect time – and this is exactly what happens. Because this fix is crucial to advanced sound creation in Flash, I've included an FLA containing the workaround as synchFix.fla for you to look at if you get stuck.

If you've got an electric guitar (I recorded a clean Fender Strat sound during testing), try sampling some of your sound and playing it back with an overdriven volume setting and the reverb effect. Cool! I remember a pleasant night in with my guitar, Flash, a few beers, and a hefty guitar amp after realizing all this was possible. I don't think it went down well with the neighbors, though.

Controlling multiple sound objects

Now that you've seen how to create basic sound objects, I'll demonstrate how to manage some simple, non timeline-based sounds in a practical example. Do you remember the old Space Invaders games? They had a deep 'heartbeat' sound in the background that got faster as the invaders got lower. We'll recreate that effect by looking at the position of a space invader, and selecting one of several different sounds to use, based on how far down the screen it is. We'll also create a master control to set the overall pan and volume levels.

The finished file is included as invader.fla, but if you want to follow along with this exercise and create the full FLA from scratch, you can use invaderSound.fla (which is a blank stage with the sound files imported into the Library) as a starting point. Whichever you choose, we'll split this exercise into two parts:

- Creation of the sound effect itself

- Addition of a master volume and pan control

A 'Space Invaders' sound effect

Looking at the Library, you'll see five sounds: Background_Heartbeat1 to 5. These sounds are our heartbeat getting progressively faster. We'll need to choose between them as our invader progresses down the screen:

Name	Kind
🔊 Background_Heartbeat1	Sound
🔊 Background_Heartbeat2	Sound
🔊 Background_Heartbeat3	Sound
🔊 Background_Heartbeat4	Sound
🔊 Background_Heartbeat5	Sound

Now, using the Symbol Linkage Properties dialog we met earlier, give these five sounds the linkage names heart1 to heart5. As noted, Flash will *not* check these identifiers against each other for uniqueness. Furthermore, should you misspell any of them, Flash won't give you any error messages at any time (the affected sound object simply will not work) – so take care!

In frame 1 of the main timeline, add the following code:

```
// Initialize sound objects
sound1 = new Sound ();
sound1.attachSound ("heart1");

sound2 = new Sound ();
sound2.attachSound ("heart2");

sound3 = new Sound ();
sound3.attachSound ("heart3");

sound4 = new Sound ();
sound4.attachSound ("heart4");

sound5 = new Sound ();
sound5.attachSound ("heart5");
```

This creates and attaches all the sound objects we need. Note that since we specified no path when creating the objects, all of these sounds will reside on the main timeline. This is something that we'll rely on later.

Next, we need to write the ActionScript code that will drive our sound effect. To do this, we'll create a movie clip that's made to move down the screen. As it does so, we'll switch between the five heartbeats, selecting faster ones as the invader gets closer to the bottom. Diagrammatically, our scheme looks something like this:

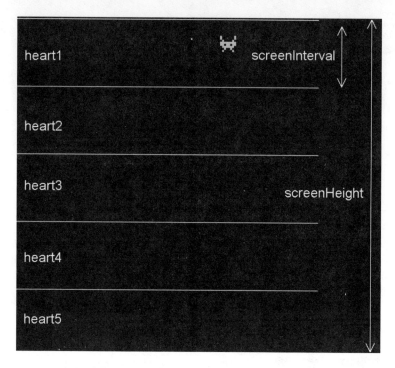

If we split the height of the screen into five equal intervals, each one equal to screenHeight / 5, we can begin by starting heart1 at the top interval, before switching it for heart2 as we cross the boundary into the next interval, and so on all the way down to heart5 in the bottom interval. To make our FLA simple, we'll create the alien's movement on this occasion simply by making it draggable.

To the script we've already created in frame 1, add the following:

```
// Initialize global variables
screenHeight = 400;
screenWidth = 550;
```

As well as the screen's height, I have also defined a variable to store its width, because I know that we'll most likely need it sooner or later.

To make our alien draggable, we'll need some kind of button, and what could be more suitable than an invisible one, such as you met in the previous chapter? Create one of these, and call it invisible button.

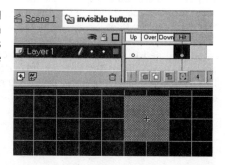

Now create a movie clip called alien1, and in frame 1 of layer 1, create a space invader graphic. (I went for the green-cathode-pixilated look, but feel free to be more creative!) Once you're happy, drag your invisible button over the top, scaling it to fit as necessary.

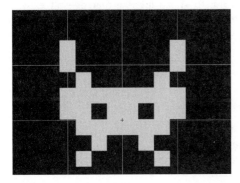 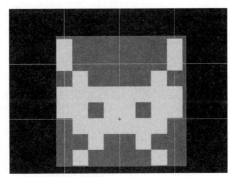

To make the movie clip draggable, attach the following script to the button:

```
on (press) {
    startDrag ("");
}

on (release, releaseOutside) {
    stopDrag ();
}
```

Finally, we need to add some code to convert the current position of our alien into a sound object selection. Drag an instance of the alien1 movie clip onto the stage in frame 1 of a new layer called graphic, and add the following code to it:

```
// Initialize
onClipEvent (load) {
    screenInterval = _root.screenHeight / 5;
    oldHeight = -1;
}
```

When this clip is loaded, Flash looks at the screenHeight global variable and creates a local variable called screenInterval. Incidentally, this is a better technique than the (apparently) simpler:

```
screenInterval = 400 / 5;
```

The reason for this is that if you build a number of movie clips that all use screenInterval (or variables derived from it), you'll have a big job to change them all should you ever change the screen size. Placing variables such as screenHeight in frame 1 of the main timeline gives you a single, sensible place to make such changes, saving time in the long run.

The second variable, oldHeight, represents the last known interval in which the alien was located. In interval 1, oldHeight is equal to 1, and you can probably guess what values it takes in intervals 2, 3, 4, and 5. By comparing this variable with the *current* height (which we'll work out in the next frame), we can tell whether the alien has crossed into a new interval, and therefore start a new sound effect. By initializing oldHeight to -1, an interval that doesn't exist, we're forcing Flash to start a sound straight away. Using a 'dummy' value to make sure your code does something on startup is another common technique in scripting, and another useful trick to learn.

After the initialization code, add:

```
onClipEvent (enterFrame) {
    height = Math.floor (_y / screenInterval) + 1;

    if (height != oldHeight) {
        _root.sound1.stop ("heart1");
        _root.sound2.stop ("heart2");
        _root.sound3.stop ("heart3");
        _root.sound4.stop ("heart4");
        _root.sound5.stop ("heart5");

        if (height == 1) {
            _root.sound1.start(0, 999);
        } else if (height == 2) {
            _root.sound2.start(0, 999);
        } else if (height == 3) {
            _root.sound3.start(0, 999);
        } else if (height == 4) {
            _root.sound4.start(0, 999);
        } else {
            _root.sound5.start(0, 999);
        }
        oldHeight = height;
    }
}
```

The first line of this event handler works out which interval we're in – the Math.floor part gives us a whole number value between 0 and 4, and adding 1 makes sure that height is a number between 1 and 5, corresponding to our five sounds heart1 to heart5.

The condition in the first if statement compares height with oldHeight, to see if the alien has crossed an interval boundary. This comparison will also always be true if this is the first time the script has been run, because oldHeight is -1 at that stage.

If a boundary has been crossed, the first thing we need to do is to turn off the current sound. We *could* use all sorts of clever arrays and other logic only to turn off the sound that's currently playing, but it's much easier (and faster) just to turn them all off.

> *Notice that the calls to* stop *here include a path to the timeline where the sound object was created:* _root. *You might reasonably assume that* _root.sound1.stop () *would turn off* sound1, *and* _root.sound2.stop () *would turn off* sound2, *but this is not how the* stop *method works. If you don't put anything in the parentheses, Flash will turn off all sounds currently playing, which is not usually what you'd want. To make Flash differentiate between the sound objects, and turn each one off separately, you have to include the linkage identifier in the parentheses, as shown. I'll say more on this subject later on.*
>
> *Of course,* _root.sound1.stop (), *which would stop all sound, actually is the effect we're trying to achieve on this occasion. However, I've gone to the trouble of referencing each sound object and turning it off individually to show how it must be done when you want to stop sounds from playing selectively.*

The final if...else if... statement then looks at the value of height to decide which sound object to restart, and finally we set oldHeight = height to set us up for the next iteration.

If you run this FLA now, you'll hear the dreaded invader heartbeat get faster as you drag the alien down the screen, and we've succeeded in our task: we've built a simple bit of code that provides selection between a number of different incidental sounds, based on conditional events. This can be much more powerful than the timeline-based sound structures we're forced to use if we *don't* use ActionScript, because we can now make our sound effects react to whatever we want, rather than playing linearly or being attached to simple button and movie clip events.

Attaching sounds using path names

So far, we've linked library sounds to Sound objects, but sound in Flash is *much* more flexible than that. We can actually link *anything* to a sound object, where "anything" includes:

- A timeline, such as _root or _parent

- A loaded level, such as _level34

- A movie clip timeline, such as _root.myMovie

This ability allows you to control *all* sounds in the named target, including Sound objects and any non-ActionScript-based sounds that are attached to keyframes. This explains why Flash insists on sound objects being owned by the timeline they are created on – you can add further nested levels of sound control, based on timelines!

A master volume control

In this example, we'll use Flash's ability to attach a timeline to a sound object to create a master volume control that will simultaneously affect all the sounds we've used so far. As usual, the finished movie for this section is included with the downloadable files as `invader2.fla`, but you can also follow on from where we just left off, if you wish.

In frame 1 of the main timeline, add two lines to the bottom of the listing, as shown:

```
// Initialize global variables
screenHeight = 400;
screenWidth = 550;

// Initialize sound objects
sound1 = new Sound ();
sound1.attachSound ("heart1");
sound2 = new Sound ();
sound2.attachSound ("heart2");
sound3 = new Sound ();
sound3.attachSound ("heart3");
sound4 = new Sound ();
sound4.attachSound ("heart4");
sound5 = new Sound ();
sound5.attachSound ("heart5");

soundAll = new Sound ();
soundAll.attachSound (_root);
```

This sound object is different from the others, because it's referring to the entire timeline, rather than to a specific sound. Because this target is now a path, rather than a string-based name, it no longer appears in quotes.

Any manipulation of the `soundAll` object will affect *all* sounds on `_root` – in this case, all the other sounds in the example. The individual sound object controls will still work, of course, but they will also go 'through' `soundAll`, which will define the overall maximum volume.

To see this in action, let's add some controls that make `soundAll` do some work. For the purposes of showing the basic concepts, I'll create some fairly simple draggable button sliders – of course, you'll use a super-duper pop-up window with metallic, photo-realistic sliders and LED bar graphs when you come to implement it on your site.

First, we'll create a volume widget that can be dragged up and down to change the volume. It will start at the bottom of the screen, 100 pixels from the right, and moving it towards the top will reduce the master volume towards 0%:

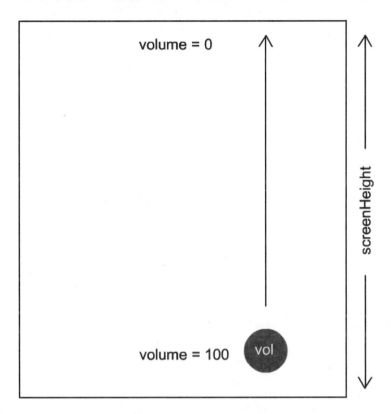

The widget is going to be a little draggable puck that works in similar fashion to the space invader. So, create a new movie clip called volWidget, rename its single layer to text, and add two more layers called button and graphic.

On the graphic layer, add a small circle, as shown below left. Make sure that the registration point corresponds to the center of this circle. On the button layer, add another instance of the invisible button, scaling it to cover the circle. Finally, on the text layer, add a bit of static text to label your widget with 'vol'.

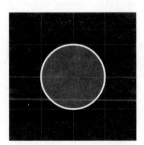
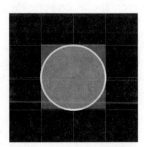

To make the widget draggable, you'll need to attach the following script to the invisible button:

```
on (press) {
    startDrag ("", false, x, 0, x, range);
}

on (release, releaseOutside) {
    stopDrag ();
}
```

Assuming that x and range are variables defined elsewhere as the horizontal position and permitted vertical range of the slider, this will constrain the drag within a bounding box of zero width (so that the widget can only be dragged up and down), and limits the up-down drag to the height of the screen.

Like the space invader, event handlers attached to an instance of this movie clip govern the effect of the widget on the sounds Flash produces:

```
onClipEvent (load) {
    range = _root.screenHeight;
    scale = range / 100;
    x = _root.screenWidth - 100;
    _x = x;
    _y = range;
}

onClipEvent (enterFrame) {
    vol = _y / scale;
    _root.soundAll.setVolume (vol);
}
```

In the handler for the load event, where x and range are also defined, scale is the factor we need to use with the current position of our widget in order to get a 0 to 100 range. The last two lines place the widget at its starting position, which is the bottom right of the screen, 100 pixels from the edge. Notice that the code is able to make use of the screen size variables (screenHeight, screenWidth) that we set up on the _root timeline.

In the enterFrame handler, the first line converts the widget's position to a value between 0 and 100 by dividing it by our scale factor. The second line then applies this volume value to every sound attached to the main timeline.

If you want to, you can test the movie now, but we also need a pan control that will be almost identical to the volWidget. A sensible starting point would seem to be to copy it, renaming the copy panWidget in the Library. The Library should now look something like this:

The pan control will move from side to side, 100 pixels from the bottom of the screen. When in the middle of the screen, the pan will be at its zero (balanced) position, while extreme left and right positions will correspond to left-only and right-only settings.

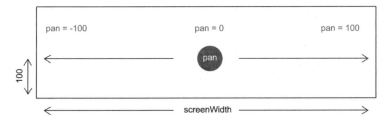

To code this up, we need to drag a copy of the new panWidget clip onto the stage, in the same frame and the same layer as the other two movie clips, and write a slightly different pair of event handlers:

```
onClipEvent (load) {
    range = _root.screenWidth;
    midPoint = range / 2;
    scale = range / 200;
    y = _root.screenHeight - 100;
    _x = midPoint;
    _y = y;
}

onClipEvent (enterFrame) {
    pan = (_x - midPoint) / scale;
    _root.soundAll.setPan (pan);
}
```

Here, `midPoint` is the center x position of the screen, and therefore the starting point of our widget in the x direction. This time, the scale runs from -100 to 100 (or 200 units), so we need to divide the range by 200 to get our scaling factor, `scale`.

The first line of the `enterFrame` handler converts the `_x` property of the movie clip to our -100 to 100 panning scale, while the second line applies the `pan` value to the `soundAll` object on the `_root` timeline.

The penultimate act is to change the script in the invisible button to read:

```
on (press) {
    startDrag ("", false, 0, y, range, y);
}

on (release, releaseOutside) {
    stopDrag ();
}
```

This constrains the widget to a horizontal strip that's 100 pixels above the base of the screen, and keeps it within the visible screen area.

A useful side-effect of handling the movement of the two widgets in this way is that it doesn't matter where on the stage you place them – they'll be moved to their correct positions by the `onClipEvent (load)` handlers. If you now test your movie (or my attempt, `invader2.fla`), you'll observe the following:

- Moving the invader selects between sound objects to be played

- Moving the two widgets varies the pan and volume settings, *irrespective of which sound is currently playing*

Additive effects of sound objects

The movie we just assembled is actually quite a complex one. On the main timeline, a selection is made between several sound objects, depending on the position of our alien. Clearly, this selection could be based upon much more arcane selection conditions, and we could have used the individual objects' pan/volume controls had we wanted to. The result of this selection is then passed through another sound object, `soundAll`. We have used this object as a master control, allowing us to manipulate the *overall* sound attached to `_root`, *irrespective of how many sound objects may be involved*. We're effectively using a hierarchy of controls, and the effects of successive levels of control are additive, raising the prospect of all sorts of interesting effects.

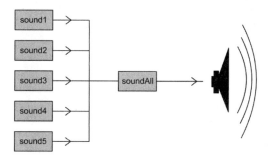

Our system works on the fact that sound1 to 5 control raw sound files, but the next sound in the sequence, soundAll, controls a *level* that contains all the sounds. By using sound objects to form hierarchies in this way, we can pass our sound through a number of different sound objects, thus emulating real electronic filter circuits in which the effect of each sound processor in the sequence is additive.

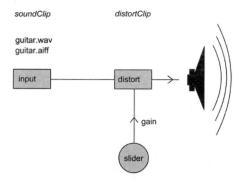

Consider the diagram above. The soundClip movie clip has a sound object defined on its timeline that's linked to a file containing guitar sounds. distortClip is another movie clip containing a sound object that targets soundClip's timeline as its input. This latter sound object overdrives its input by setting the volume greater than 100, based on a slider value. You don't have to stop there though, because you could build a third clip (say, reverbClip) that takes input from distortClip and adds a reverb effect by duplicating distortClip and then adding a slider-controlled delay between it and its instance copy.

The final output would be an overdriven version of the original sound with added reverb, all of which can be altered in real time with a couple of sliders! Who needs to play air guitar, when we have Flash?

Creating and controlling soundtracks

An advantage of being able to target *timelines* when defining a sound object is that doing so allows you to control a timeline with sound attached to its keyframes (using the Sound panel and its associated Edit Envelope window). By this process, you can arrange a set of sounds onto a timeline in a sequence, to build up soundtracks and other musical compositions from individual samples. Flash allows you to have up to eight sound channels playing at the same time, so using this method you can create what amounts to an eight-channel sample sequencer (often called a **tracker** by musicians).

Creating a soundtrack

Here, I'll quickly recap how to create a soundtrack using the *stun:arpeggio* composition, as seen in the friends Of ED book *Foundation ActionScript* (www.stundesign.com), but then quickly move on to advanced control of such a soundtrack via ActionScript. If you're particularly interested in creating soundtracks, Chapter 11 in the book *Foundation Flash* tells you how to go about it.

The soundtrack timeline should consist of a single scene (you'll lose synchronization if you cross over into another scene), and you need to start the timeline with a 'kicker' sound, as described earlier in the chapter.

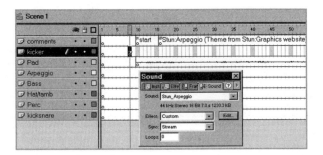

You can then start attaching sounds to the timeline, one per layer, as shown below. On the Sound panel, set Sync to Event for all of these sounds.

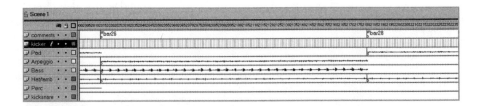

You can use the Edit Envelope window to fade or pan each sound. I used this feature at the end of the soundtrack as a fadeout effect, as shown below:

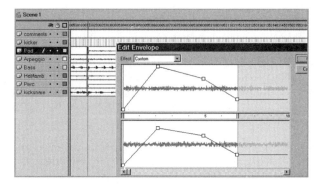

The important thing to realize here is that when we come to control the soundtrack with sound objects, the Edit Envelope window's volume envelopes will be *additive* with any controls we apply. This allows us to use the volume envelopes to control mix levels within our composition, and to control the overall sound via our sound object.

> *If you're intrigued by all of this, you might also like to take a look at killersound's way of implementing sound compositions in Flash. Their method uses the Edit Envelope to fade sounds that are all started simultaneously, and this can be a little better synchronized than the easier method shown above. (See* www.killersound.com, *choose* HTML version, *and go to* Tech Center > Goodies.*)*

To use our soundtrack, we need to create it either as a movie clip, or as a loaded level. For the latter, you'd use a script of this form:

```
loadMovie ("soundtrack.swf", 99);
soundtrack = new Sound ();
soundtrack.attachSound (_level99);
```

Note that you have to start the level loading before you can attach it to a Sound object (because a level doesn't exist until you start loading it). I tend to use level 99 as a soundtrack level because it's sufficiently far away from level 0 not to be affected (overwritten) by additional levels the main site may want to load.

To control your soundtrack if you decide to implement it as a movie clip, you would simply use:

```
soundtrack = new Sound();
soundtrack.attachSound(clip);
```

Where *clip* is the path to the soundtrack. Here are a couple of extra tips:

- If you decide to use a load level, consider using a load *target* (that is, an empty movie clip placed ready on the stage) instead. This lets you refer to the soundtrack timeline (and therefore link a sound object to it) before you actually start loading content. (This is a big advantage of load targets over load levels in general, when you're providing external control via ActionScript.)

- As well as allowing you to load sound separately from the main site, using a load level or a load target allows you to let the user select the soundtrack to be loaded without having to change the sound object (because the path remains the same). As well as giving the user flexibility in choosing the soundtrack, it also makes update of your sound files easier, because they're totally separate from the main site content.

Controlling a soundtrack

To control the sound objects above, you'd need to use scripts based upon the ones we'll look at next. I've included the commands necessary to control a soundtrack timeline that's implemented as a load level, but controlling a load target or a soundtrack timeline within a movie clip would be very similar.

Everything starts easily enough; to set the pan and the volume of a sound object representing a soundtrack, you simply call its setPan and setVolume methods, as before. Similarly, to stop the soundtrack, you'd use:

```
soundtrack.stop ();
```

However, you may also want to consider adding:

```
_level99.gotoAndStop (1);
```

This stops the running (but now silent) soundtrack timeline from imposing any further load on the processor. Also, if the user decides they don't want music at all, you could consider unloading the soundtrack level (via unloadMovieNum (99)) to free up bandwidth if it's still in the process of streaming in. (This can be checked by looking at the condition _level99._framesloaded == _level99._totalframes, which will be false during download and true once download has completed.)

To restart the soundtrack after the above stop, you would use:

```
soundtrack.start ()
_level99.gotoAndPlay (1);
```

This is necessary (rather than `soundtrack.start` alone) because the sound is attached to a timeline rather than a raw sound file, and we need the *timeline* to be playing in order to hear the soundtrack.

To restart the soundtrack from the beginning, assuming it is already playing, you would use:

```
soundtrack.stop ();
_level99.gotoAndPlay (1);
```

So far, then, this chapter has given a primer in how to use the Flash `Sound` object on its own and in conjunction with frame-based sounds. In the next section, we'll put it all together to build an oft-requested Flash project: a mixing desk with which users can build their own remixes.

Advanced sound control

The methods of the Flash 5 `Sound` object that we've looked at so far allow you roughly the amount of control that you'd expect from a portable radio or tape system with simple volume and balance knobs. However, there are two significant additional features that you may wish to add to your movies:

- Most serious hi-fi systems allow you to convert stereo sound into mono sound. This could soon be an issue for web authoring, because some portable or wireless devices (as well as office-based set-ups, or systems aimed at graphics production rather than sound – such as those used in many web design houses) may not have full stereo support.

- Sound systems intended for professional sound mixing allow you to alter the pan control without changing the overall volume (or more technically, the *power*) of a sound. This is to allow you to change the stereo image of a particular track, while maintaining the prominence that track has in the overall composition.

The method that lets you incorporate both of these features is `setTransform`. Although initially a little daunting to set up – as well as defining the sound object itself, you have to define a second object to act as the **sound control object** – `setTransform` can deliver a fine degree of control over the noises your movies make. Because the logic behind `setTransform` can be a little impenetrable, there are some who don't use it, on the basis that they don't see its usefulness over the more straightforward `setVolume`/`setPan` combination. Here, I hope that we will remedy this situation once and for all.

In the final example of this chapter, we'll go through what many consider to be the 'holy grail' of sound in Flash: building a movie that allows its users to produce their own mix of a set of sounds interactively. If you search the Web, there are a couple of sites that allow you to do this, but few if any of them make use of constant volume pan control, which is something that all professional DJs or recording equipment will have. First though, we need to examine how to set up and control a sound object using only `setTransform`.

Mixing sound digitally with setTransform

Take a look at the following illustration, which (in the loosest possible way) shows a sound transformation taking place:

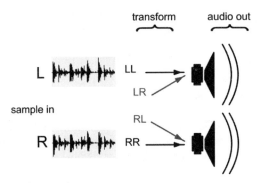

In terms of actions and terminology that you've already seen, and ignoring (for now) a couple of rather obvious features of this diagram, Flash's process for 'transforming' sound is:

- A sound sample is attached to a sound object. Flash allows this sample to be stereo (as represented above) or mono, which is the same except that the L or the R component will be zero.

- When you play the sound, a percentage of the L sample, LL, is fed into the left audio out channel.

- Similarly, a percentage of the R sample, RR, is fed into the right audio out channel.

- The percentage values LL and RR are dependent on the current volume and pan control values, as you saw in `sound.fla` right at the start of this chapter.

The difference with the `setTransform` method is that it allows you to manipulate not only everything mentioned above, but also two more components of the sound: LR and RL.

- LR is the percentage of the right sample that is played in the left speaker (or the amount of the right channel signal that is 'crossed over' to the left channel).

- RL is the percentage of the left sample that is played in the right speaker (or the amount of the left channel signal that is 'crossed over' to the right channel).

Furthermore, with `setTransform`, the LL and RR values are no longer linked (as they are with `setPan`, which will increase the right speaker pan if you decrease the left speaker pan). This means that you can create left/right pan combinations that would be impossible using `setPan`. For example, `setTransform` allows you to send a proportion of a mono sample to both speakers, so that you can create a 'stereo' effect using ActionScript:

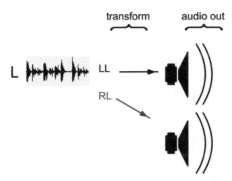

In this case, you might have a mono sound that emerges only from the left speaker. By defining a non-zero RL component, however, you can form a stereo signal. By varying LL and RL, you can also dynamically vary the stereo image.

As a further example, `setTransform` allows you to make a stereo signal into mono *without losing the sound information in either channel*. This is fundamentally different from simply setting the pan control hard left or hard right, because by using pan you:

- Lose the information in the channel you have muted to form the mono signal

- Halve the available volume, if a user has a system with both L and R channels connected to a single speaker (this is the usual setup for systems that only support one speaker)

- Allow the possibility that users with only one speaker connected will hear nothing at all, because you're sending a mono signal to the wrong channel!

Lastly, as mentioned above, `setTransform` allows you to make changes to the pan control *without affecting the overall sound power*. This is vital for the professional mixing of sound. Many home computers are now connected to a high quality amplifier and speakers, so any web site that takes the time to use quality sound processing that includes this functionality is bound to win musically-minded converts – and just maybe walk away with the 'sound' category that Flash competitions seem to include!

Controlling a sound object with setTransform

Creating a sound object for use with setTransform is exactly as you've seen before, but you also have to create a second object to control the setTransform operation itself. If you want to perform this experiment using the same sound sample as me, the project below is included as setTransform.fla. When you run it, you'll see nothing, but you'll hear what was originally a stereo sample playing both channels through the left speaker.

To create a sound object called soundA, with the intention of using it to control a sound in the Library with linkage name loop, we would use these actions:

```
soundA = new Sound (_root);
soundA.attachSound ("loop");
soundA.start ("loop");
```

There's nothing here that you haven't seen before – the last statement just starts the sound playing once. If you're using a different, short sound, you may have to make it play more than once in order to hear the effects of the set of commands we're about to add.

The thing to remember is that the setTransform method requires the LL, LR, RR, and RL values illustrated in the diagrams above, but they must exist *within a single object*. This object can be called anything you like (I'll call mine soundAtrans, because it will apply a transformation to soundA), but it must contain four properties called ll, lr, rr, and rl, representing our percentage values LL, LR, RR, and RL respectively. The next two lines of ActionScript code define a control object with its four properties set up so that all the sound in any sample it's applied to goes to the left speaker:

```
soundAtrans = new Object ();
soundAtrans = {ll:100, lr:100, rr:0, rl:0};
```

The last thing to do is to call soundA's setTransform method with our control object soundAtrans as the argument:

```
soundA.setTransform (soundAtrans);
```

To change the transformation so that it plays mono sound through *both* speakers (that is, to make rr and rl equal to 100, as well as ll and lr), you could add the following:

```
soundAtrans.rr = 100;
soundAtrans.rl = 100;
soundA.setTransform (soundAtrans);
```

If you like, you can create some different stereo effects by changing the properties of the sound. Try setting the control object in setTransform.fla to the following values. (At this stage, I recommend using my FLA, because I've selected my sound sample to illustrate some features that may not be obvious in all cases.)

```
soundAtrans = {ll:100, lr:0, rr:100, rl:0};
```

This will produce normal stereo sound, and is the sound without any transformations applied.

```
soundAtrans = {ll:50, lr:0, rr:50, rl:0};
```

This will produce the sound in stereo, at 50% of full volume.

```
soundAtrans = {ll:100, lr:-100, rr:0, rl:0};
```

You might like to try explaining this one for yourself before you read on. In fact, you hear nothing, because the left and right channels are *almost* identical. By selecting a value of -100 for the right speaker component that's fed into the left speaker, we're subtracting the waveforms, giving us near silence.

> *For the technically minded, a negative volume setting shifts the waveform of your sound by 180 degrees. By creating sounds that you actually want to mix in this way, you can create some pretty far-out effects, but most of the time this is something you're unlikely to want to do.*

```
soundAtrans = {ll:200, lr:0, rr:200, rl:0};
```

For those who like it noisy! This will give you thumping, overdriven bass, but make sure that your amplifier isn't set too high before trying it at home! I suspect you'll make few friends if you use this on a site without warning – especially among those users who are browsing the Net with a pair of headphones on, or looking at your site during a quiet office dinner break.

> *The use of overdriven volume is an unsupported feature, so it's OK to use in your own site, but be careful when using it for a client – it may not work in the next revision of the plug-in. Being a bit of a noise demon, I've used it myself on a site that had a volume dial that went up to 11 (in the best tradition of spoof rock 'n' roll movies) – with a little skull-and-crossbones symbol next to it as fair warning!*

Finally, try this one. You'll only hear the effect if you're listening through a properly set up stereo speaker system:

```
soundAtrans = {ll:100, lr:0, rr:-100, rl:0};
```

This is creating the same effect as wiring up a speaker system with the positive and negative wires to one speaker crossed, resulting in sounds from the two speakers canceling each other out rather than adding together. The bass sounds will disappear – but if you change the balance on your amplifier so that only one speaker is being driven, they will return. This is very similar to the 'no sound' effect we created a moment ago, but this time the phase shift is occurring not in the Flash Player, but in the speakers themselves. This is an effect that you would normally want to avoid, and in general ll and rr should have the same sign.

Dynamic sound transformations

The power of using setTransform only really starts to shine when you start to control the transformation dynamically. Doing so has two advantages:

- It is easy to define preset effects. By defining more than one control object, you can instantly swap between sound setups. For example, the following script defines two objects: stereo is set up to provide parameters for a stereo setTransform, and mono is set up for... well, you can probably guess the rest.

```
stereo = new Object();
    stereo = {ll:100, lr:0, rr:100, rl:0};
    mono = new Object();
    mono = {ll:100, lr:100, rr:100, rl:100};
```

By calling mysound.setTransform (stereo) or mysound.setTransform (mono), you can easily switch between stereo and mono output. This is the sort of thing that's likely to become increasingly necessary in the future, because some hardware (particularly wireless devices) may not support stereo. For sites in the here and now, you can easily add a mono/stereo control next to your sound's on/off control via simple button events:

```
on (release) {
    mysound.setTransform (mono);
}
```

- It is easy to define *variable* sound effects and sound transformations under the control of ActionScript. This is really the big one as far as we are concerned, so let's delve a bit deeper with a simple example.

This example is included with the files for download as setTransform2.fla. The FLA includes a movie clip that continuously alters the stereo image between the left and right speaker (that is, a pan effect), and does this without changing the overall volume of the total sound. It's really quite similar to setTransform.fla, to the extent that the code in frame 1 (in the actions layer) is almost identical:

```
soundA = new Sound (_root);
soundA.attachSound ("loop");
soundA.start (0, 999);

soundAtrans = new Object ();
soundAtrans = {ll:50, lr:0, rr:50, rl:0};
soundA.setTransform (soundAtrans);
```

The only real difference is that this time, I'm making the sound loop 999 times via the third line – more than long enough for you to hear the effect. I've also set the sound control object soundAtrans to give 50% volume in both left and right speakers.

On the control layer, there's an empty movie clip called soundcontrol (you'll see it just above the stage area, at the top left corner). Although it's empty, it has some clip event handlers attached to it. With the Actions window open, select the movie clip to see this code:

When the load event occurs, we set a variable called direction to 2. This is the rate at which our pan will take place: 2% per frame. (The load event occurs on the first occasion Flash sees our movie clip on the timeline. In this case, that's frame one, so this represents our initialization.)

The second event handled here, enterFrame, occurs on every frame of the running SWF (even if the FLA has only one frame, as in this case), and so I've attached the main code to this handler. It just adds direction to our control object's ll property, and subtracts the same amount from rr. This will create a pan towards the left channel. The if statement checks for either ll or rr hitting zero, which would mean that our pan has gone all the way to an 'end'. When this occurs, direction has its sign reversed, and the pan will instead move towards the right speaker. This will continue indefinitely (well, 999 times – if you can stand it for that long!). If you debug the movie, you can see the pan changing visually:

As noted in the introduction, this pan is different from the one we heard using the simpler `setPan` and `setVolume` methods (in `sound.fla`), because it allows us to change the stereo image *without* altering the overall volume. This system is not used in domestic hi-fi equipment, but it *is* used in sound mixing, because it allows changes to the stereo image independently of the stereo volume.

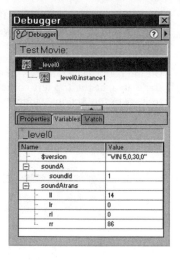

Advanced sound targeting

Targeting your sound commands correctly can be a tricky business; you have to understand when you're defining a *global* sound control (which acts on all sounds in the movie), a *local* sound control (which acts on a single timeline), and an *individual* sound control (which acts on a single linked sound file). The real killer is that if you don't define your sound objects properly, you may be assuming one type of control, when in fact you're applying something very different!

Global and local control

I've said this before, but I'll say it again: if you define a sound object on the main timeline without a target, any actions you apply to the object will affect *all sound in the movie*. This can be confusing, because it occurs even if you think you've provided enough information to point to a specific sound object.

```
soundA = new Sound ();
soundA.stop ();
```

If you attach these actions to the main timeline, they will stop *all* sounds, because *they don't have a target defined*. In fact, even if you define a sound object on the main timeline that's attached to an individual sound via linkage, such as

```
soundA = new Sound ("linkage_ID");
soundA.stop ();
```

the `stop` method will *still* act globally, which is even more confusing. As we saw in the example with the space invader, there's only way to stop a sound that's attached via linkage without stopping everything else on the same timeline. In the following script, the `stop` command only affects the second sound:

```
soundA = new Sound ();
soundA.attachSound ("acid");
soundA.start ("acid");

soundB = new Sound ();
soundB.attachSound ("bassline");
soundB.start ("bassline");
soundB.stop ("bassline");
```

The call to stop had to refer to the linkage name, so as a logical consequence, methods that don't allow you to specify a linkage name will always apply their actions to the whole timeline. This point is not documented anywhere, so it's one to remember – especially when you consider that the methods that *don't* let you define a linkage name include:

```
Sound.setPan
Sound.setVolume
Sound.setTransform
```

As you can see, this list features all the methods we've been using so far, and the implication is clear enough: you can't individually control multiple sounds defined via linkage if they are all on the same timeline. Unless you just want to start and stop a sound, don't use linkage to define your sound object, because the other commands listed above will give you unwelcome results.

Attaching sound objects to targets

To define a truly local sound control, you must define a target, as follows (from _root):

```
soundA = new Sound (myMovieClip);
soundA.stop ();
```

Here, soundA is attached to a **target**, which in this case is the movie clip instance called myMovieClip. The call to stop will now only stop those sounds that are attached to the myMovieclip timeline. If your movie clips are deeply nested, you can specify a path of any length in place of myMovieClip.

You could do the same thing by defining soundA within myMovieClip, which is fine – but because your object definitions are then spread all over the FLA, you won't be able to synchronize them! If synchronization is (or could be) a requirement, you should *define* the sounds in one place, even if they go to separate clips.

Advanced sound in Flash can be a tricky business, but my very last example in this chapter creates a fully functional advanced sound control interface. As well as demonstrating how to define truly separate sound objects and control each one locally, we've thrown in a modular, smart clip-based interface. Enjoy, and make the Web a noisier place!

A Flash mixing desk

Most recordings are made up of several **tracks** (where each track usually corresponds to one instrument or sound type) that are arranged together through a mixing desk, which allows you to assemble the sounds to form a composition. To do this effectively, you need to be able to do at least the following:

- Change the volume of each track

- Change the pan of each track

- Mute each track, or switch it in, instantaneously

These are the controls that we'll have in our mixing desk. The sensible way to go about building it is first to get the controls working for one track, and then to make the controls modular and create additional ones for each of our tracks.

The User Interface

Before we get into the actual sound management, let's have a look at how the dials work. There's an example of a typical dial set up in `dial.fla`, which you may find familiar:

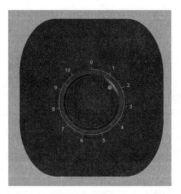

The dial is a movie clip that contains a circular dial shape, as shown above. It also has a dot and a chamfer on one side to signify where it's pointing (as is the current fashion in hi-fi dials – something that's also in line with my chosen black metal color scheme!). In Flash, though, the dot and chamfer have an additional function: they imply that to turn the dial, your mouse pointer must be near to them. That might sound a little unlikely when you read it from the page, but I've tested it on a number of people who weren't pre-warned, and they all managed to 'get it' straight away when faced with the Flash dial on screen.

Anyway, over the chamfer is an invisible button. The button is in the Dial movie clip, and has the following actions attached to it:

```
on (press) {
    buttonPress = true;
}

on (release, releaseOutside) {
    buttonPress = false;
}
```

This script simply sets a flag called buttonPress to true or false, depending on whether the user is over the button and has clicked and held the mouse button down. buttonPress remains true until the user releases the mouse button, and it stays true even if they move out of the button area. These actions are essentially checking for a 'press and hold'.

The instance of the Dial movie clip itself has the following actions attached:

```
onClipEvent (load) {
    angle = 0;
    buttonPress = false;
}

onClipEvent (enterFrame) {
    if (buttonPress) {
        if (_xmouse < 0) {
            angle -= 4;
            if (angle < 0) {
                angle = 0;
            }
        }
        if (_xmouse > 0) {
            angle += 4;
            if (angle > 324) {
                angle = 324;
            }
        }
    }
    _rotation = angle;
}
```

The load event handler initializes two variables: buttonPress (which we've already met) and angle, (which is the current angle the dial is at). Initially, it points straight up: zero degrees.

The `enterFrame` event handler performs the main task of rotating the dial. If we see a press-and-hold over the invisible button (via our friend `buttonPress`), we look at which side of the dotted line the mouse is on, and rotate the dial in that direction:

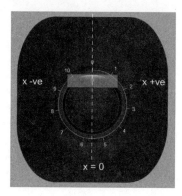

If we're to the left of the line (`_xmouse < 0`), we reduce the angle; if we're to the right of the line, we increase it. (To make the line go through the center of the button, the registration point of the movie has to be on the centerline of the dial – and preferably through the button's 'dot'.) The dial stops turning if we exceed the two end-stops: 0 or 324 degrees in this case.

If you're still not quite clear on how this would work, remember that the centerline rotates with the dial. This code essentially says, "Rotate the dial until the centerline goes through the current mouse position."

To use this dial in your own FLAs, you'll need to scale the angle of the dial into the range you want. If you wanted to have a range of 0 to 10 (as per the bezel), for example, you'd create another variable (say, `range`) and add the following immediately after the `_rotation = angle` line:

```
range = angle / 3.24;
```

If you'd named your dial instance `mydial`, and placed it on the main timeline, you could then access `range` from anywhere in the movie using `_root.mydial.range`.

When you experiment with `dial.fla`, you'll find that the dial doesn't go straight to your mouse, but moves at a constant rotation until it reaches the correct position. I did this to model professional sound equipment, which has damped dials to prevent you from making sudden changes, and to allow you to make smooth fade transitions. The dial also 'flickers' slightly when it reaches your mouse, but this effect is small enough not to affect our sound mixer later on.

Problems, Problems

Our eventual goal here requires us to solve a number of problems, and it would be best to develop some tactics for dealing with them now. As you'll see, some of them are far from trivial:

1. To synchronize sound to the level of accuracy we need, so that we can mix sounds with each other, we must define all the sound objects on the same timeline. We can attach them to other timelines via targets, but the definitions must be on the same frame in the same timeline.

2. Flash can handle up to eight tracks at the same time. Our per-track sound controls should ideally be modular, to allow us to handle that number of different dials. This may be difficult, though, because each control has to access a different sound object, and we have to be able to do it quickly to maintain accurate sequencing. Use of eval or string concatenation to vary the name of the target sound object can be a little slow (string handling in general is slow in Flash 5), so we have to be careful.

3. To build a credible mixing desk, we have to be able to cut sounds in or out immediately, not a couple of frames after the user has asked for it.

Let's take these in turn, although in fact you've already seen the solution to the first problem. To synchronize sounds accurately, it is best to attach them all to the same frame in the main timeline. Event sounds don't synchronize to the timeline (because they're designed for incidental effects that don't normally require close synch with each other), but you can fool the Flash sound player into thinking it's handling streaming sound (which does synchronize) by making the first sound on the timeline a streaming sound.

For the second, defining a path that contains a variable is actually very easy, although it's not documented in Macromedia's ActionScript Reference Guide. To add a variable into a dot notation path, you use syntax such as the following:

```
_root[path].something
```

Suppose that you had two movie clip instances, apple and banana. Both movie clips contain a variable called something, and you want to set one version of something to 5, conditionally. To access either _root.apple.something or _root.banana.something from the same statement, depending on a conditional term, you do this:

```
if (condition) {
    path = "apple";
} else {
    path = "banana";
}

_root[path].something = 5;
```

This is a really useful trick, because not only does it allow you to create smart clips that refer to unique objects without having to go through string concatenation (which is also rather slow), but also it provides for the creation of more general functions. Furthermore, it lets you quickly access objects or movie clips that are created at runtime (via duplicateMovieClip), making for lightning-fast game engines when you have a large number of collision detections to perform.

To cut sounds immediately, the best way is not to use stop, but simply to mute the sound by setting its volume to zero. As well as making the track disappear from the overall sound composition straight away, this has other advantages: the sound stays in synch with the other sounds (because it was never actually stopped) and the processor load of the Flash player stays constant because all the sounds are playing all the time. (This means that sounds will not become unsynchronized due to processing peaks or troughs.)

The finished article

Have a look at mixer.fla, which is our final project file. (You can tell it's a final version, because the bright background colors have finally gone!)

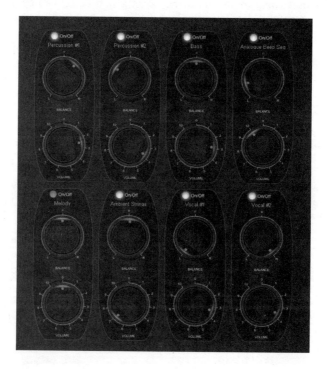

The movie is designed to be viewed full-screen, so get rid of the bandwidth profiler window if you want to read the text! Also, the FLA contains CD quality sound samples, and publishing the SWF file will take a long time on low-specification systems. (If you haven't got enough memory assigned to Flash on the Mac, it may even crash the computer.) If you're testing on a machine that isn't up to the job, try setting the Audio Event parameters (File > Publish Settings > Flash) lower; about 16-20kbps should do it, but the sound quality in the final SWF will be poor.

The final SWF requires a pretty high frame rate in order to create the close sound synchronization required, so that's been set to 24fps in Modify > Movie. Again, you might have trouble on a low-specification machine – advanced sound can be processor intensive, especially when we're not only handling eight MP3 streams at the same time, but also expecting the plug-in to mix them together dynamically!

If you haven't seen a mixing desk before:

- To bring in a track immediately, you have to set the volume and pan controls to the desired levels, and then switch the track in by clicking on the on/off LED.

- To fade a track in, switch it on via the LED, and then use the volume control.

- The stereo image of each track is altered via the balance control.

- Most popular music works in 4/4 time. The composition will sound odd unless you bring in each new change on the fourth beat of the fourth bar – unless of course you know enough about the rules to break them creatively! Otherwise, a good sense of rhythm is required...

Once you've finished creating your mega mix (which is harder than you think when not all the tracks are simple rhythms – the sounds need to be properly balanced in the overall composition if it is to sound any good), have a look at the FLA.

The kicker

The first thing to notice in the main timeline is how the Flash sound player is being forced to synchronize all our sound objects:

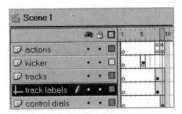

The kicker layer contains a short streaming sound that forces the rest of the sound in the movie to play in time. To hear what would happen without this trick, delete the kicker layer, and then try to sit through the resulting cacophony!

The code

The next stop on our tour is the actions layer. The sound objects are defined in frame 8:

```
// Set up a mute sound control object...
mute = new Object ();
mute = {ll:0, lr:0, rr:0, rl:0};

// Percussion1 track 1
perc1 = new Sound (track1);
perc1.setTransform (mute);

// Percussion2 track 2
perc2 = new Sound (track2);
perc2.setTransform (mute);

// Bass track 3
bass = new Sound (track3);
bass.setTransform (mute);

// Main melody track 4
mel = new Sound (track4);
mel.setTransform (mute);

// Ambient strings track 5
strings = new Sound (track5);
strings.setTransform (mute);

// Acid bleep track 6
acid = new Sound (track6);
acid.setTransform (mute);

// Vocal1 track 7
voc1 = new Sound (track7);
voc1.setTransform (mute);

// Vocal2 track 8
voc2 = new Sound (track8);
voc2.setTransform (mute);

// Note - max number of tracks is 8. Adding more tracks is
// possible, but only 8 at a time should be played.
```

We start by defining a sound control object called mute. This contains values to silence each sound as soon as it starts, via a call to setTransform. (Without this, we'd hear an initial sound 'blip'.)

The sounds are defined with targets track1 to track8. This ensures that each sound can be controlled independently; the setTransform actions we use throughout the FLA act not on the objects perc1 to voc2, but on the timelines track1 to track8. This is the only way we can perform individual control via the setTransform, setVolume, and setPan methods.

The track1 to track8 movie clips are at the top left of the stage, and appear in frame 8 of the tracks layer:

The track 1 2 3 4 5 6 7 8 static text is in a guide layer (track labels), so that I know which nameless, empty movie clip symbol is which. Each one contains a sound file that's attached directly to the first frame of its timeline, via the Sound panel:

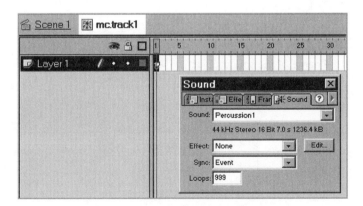

Now, you might well be thinking, "This is Flash 5; why don't you attach a Sound object instead of doing this?" Well, that's a good idea, but it doesn't work. As soon as you start defining sound objects outside the main timeline, you lose the synchronization that we gained with the kicker. To put that another way, the main timeline is the only one with synchronization. If you try the kicker trick on another timeline, the sounds will *not* be synchronized with the main timeline, but with their own kicker!

Frame 9 has a `stop` action in the actions *layer*, and we see our interface appear on this frame in the control dials layer. Each pair of dials you can see is an instance of the track controller smart clip, ms.trackController. This smart clip has two parameters:

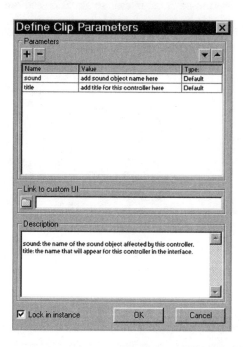

Here, `sound` is the name of the sound object we will be controlling, and `title` is the label that will appear on each track controller in the user interface. Looking inside ms.trackController, you'll see the following timeline:

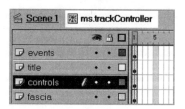

The dynamic text that's assigned to our `title` clip parameter is on the title layer, and the control dials themselves are on the controls layer. The code that implements the controller's logic is attached to a movie clip in the events layer.

The dial controls

The dial controls are almost identical to the ones in dial.fla, which you saw earlier. The balance control has this script attached to it:

```
onClipEvent (load) {
    angle = 0;
    buttonPress = false;
    pan = 0;
}

onClipEvent (enterFrame) {
    if (buttonPress) {
        if (_xmouse < 0) {
            angle -= 4;
            if (angle < -144) {
                angle = -144;
            }
        }
        if (_xmouse > 0) {
            angle += 4;
            if (angle > 144) {
                angle = 144;
            }
        }
        _rotation = angle;
        pan = Math.round (angle / 2.88);
    }
}
```

This gives us a value for pan (in the last line) that's between -50 and 50, which is what we'll be using in calls to setTransform later on. Unsurprisingly, the volume dial has an almost identical script attached:

```
onClipEvent (load) {
    angle = 0;
    buttonPress = false;
    volume = 0;
}

onClipEvent (enterFrame) {
    if (buttonPress) {
        if (_xmouse < 0) {
            angle -= 4;
            if (angle < 0) {
                angle = 0;
            }
        }
```

continues overleaf

```
                    if (_xmouse > 0) {
                        angle += 4;
                        if (angle > 324) {
                            angle = 324;
                        }
                    }
                    _rotation = angle;
                    volume = angle / 324;
                }
            }
```

This gives us a value for the `volume` variable that's between 0 and 1.

The LED on/off control

The controls layer also hides a rather nifty trick: the LED. Have a look at the LED movie clip, mc.lamp, whose timeline is shown below:

The clip toggles between an 'on' state and an 'off' state. To create something like this in Flash, you need two frames, both with a `stop` action attached. That's what the actions layer here provides.

The button layer contains a simple invisible button over the LED image. This has the following code attached:

```
on (press) {
    gotoAndPlay (1)
}
```

If we're currently on frame 1 and stopped, the button will make us go to frame 2, where we'll stop again. If we're currently on frame 2, the button will make us go to frame 1, but the `stop` action there will cause us to halt at that frame. Whichever frame we're currently on, the button makes us go to the other one.

The actions layer actually has another pair of actions attached to it: `led = 0` (off state, frame 1), and `led = 1` (on state, frame 2). We'll see how this value is used when we get to the final script that controls everything, round about now.

The controlling script

The script that controls each sound object is contained back in the events layer of our ms.trackController smart clip. It's attached to an empty movie clip called mc.dummy, which you can see above our controller (it's the little white dot):

When you're using movie clip events, you're sometimes stuck for something to attach your code to. We *could* attach it to ms.trackController, but then we'd have to remember to attach it to all eight instances. This is not only a chore, but it also stops our smart clip being truly modular (it requires you to attach the script, so it's no longer the 'drag me anywhere and I'll just work' type of smart clip). Also, adding eight identical scripts to our SWF file when we should be able to get away with just one feels downright shoddy.

The answer is to attach our script to an embedded movie clip, as we've done with mc.dummy. Because our script is attached *inside* ms.trackController, all our problems disappear. That's another sly trick to put away for later!

Anyway, back to the plot. The script looks like this:

```
onClipEvent (load) {
    sound = _parent.sound;
    controlSound = new Object ();
    controlSound = {ll:0, lr:0, rr:0, rl:0};
}

onClipEvent (enterFrame) {
    controlSound.ll = (50 - _parent.panControl.pan) *
                        _parent.volControl.volume *
_parent.lamp.led;
    controlSound.rr = (50 + _parent.panControl.pan) *
                        _parent.volControl.volume *
_parent.lamp.led;
     _root[sound].setTransform (controlSound);
}
```

As usual, the `load` event handler contains our initialization script. Because our smart clip parameter `sound` belongs to the parent movie clip ms.trackController, I've brought it into mc.dummy so that I don't have to bother with paths. This practice also helps with debugging – piping variables down from the parent allows you to check that they have actually been transmitted correctly, and can be seen by the child clip. The next thing is to define the sound control object that we'll be using in calls to `setTransform`. You'll recognize the initial values of `ll`, `lr`, `rr`, and `rl` as those required to mute our sound.

The `enterFrame` handler contains our main script, in which the sound control object's `ll` and `rr` properties are set in much the same way:

- The `(50 - _parent.panControl.pan)` term gives us our `ll` property value, which comes from the balance dial. (The `rr` value has to be 50 minus the `ll` value, hence the change of sign.).

- We then multiply the pan term by the volume dial's contribution, `_parent.volControl.volume`. Remember, this varies as a decimal number between 0 and 1. Multiplying the pan term above by a zero volume gives us zero, and multiplying by a volume of 1 (maximum volume) gives us the full contribution.

- Finally, we multiply by the LED's contribution, `_parent.lamp.led`. This can be either 0 (off) or 1(on). If the LED is off, we multiply by 0, which gives us zero for `ll` and `rr`. If it's on, we get the full contribution, so the LED term acts like a switch (as we would expect it to) on the signal so far.

All that remains is to use our newly calculated `ll` and `rr` values in the call to `setTransform`. The action below establishes the path to the timeline containing the sound in question, and then transforms that sound.

```
_root[sound].setTransform (controlSound);
```

This FLA contains a lot of tricks, so experiment a little and see what else you can discover. I've also made it easy to change the sounds used, so that you can easily add your own compositions. Make sure, though, that all the sounds are *exactly* the same length (using something like the *SoundForge* tracker software package) and are created for looping.

Flash sound resources

As well as the commercial angle, using sound in Flash is a popular pastime, and that's reflected in the quantity and diversity of related Internet sites. There are a lot of web-based resources for the non-musicians among us, and while many of the sound loops available out there are of poor quality (I hope they don't edit that out!), an oasis of real talent can be found at www.flashharmonics.co.uk

This is a music resource created specifically for Flash web designers, and there's more than just big bass dance sounds available (which must be a first). The sounds are not free, but they're so cheap you won't even notice!

As far as coding is concerned, another good resource exists at www.killersound.com. They introduced the 'kicker' fix that I used in this chapter, and while (at the time of writing) the tutorials use Flash 4, there are still some useful tips and tricks here. (Use the link to the Tech center to get to the 'killersound method' tutorials.)

For the latest word from the horse's mouth, try www.macromedia.com/support/flash, which usually has some new technical notes that are worth reading. In particular, TechNote#12046 contains the latest sound-related Flash links.

Lastly, some of the very best resources of all (if you can find them) are impoverished musicians with Steinberg Cubase and SoundForge on their computers. Find one, befriend it, promise it free beer, and you'll find a constant stream of suitable sounds. It works for me!

Hardware issues

Finally, I should mention that some hardware has known issues with the Flash player, and certain Windows 9x soundcard drivers will create a scratchy popping noise every now and again, particularly at high volumes. Persistent offenders are:

- Crystal Audio System (IBM Intellistation E Pro)

- Soundblaster Audio PCI 64D

- Soundblaster Audio PCI 128D

- ESS Maestro-2E (Dell Inspiron laptops)

> *This list was provided by Urami, a legendary Flash Guru who lives on the macromedia.flash newsgroup, and there are a number of other laptops that seem to suffer from the same problem. If you see this behavior, download the latest drivers, and if that doesn't do the trick, holler at the hardware manufacturers!*

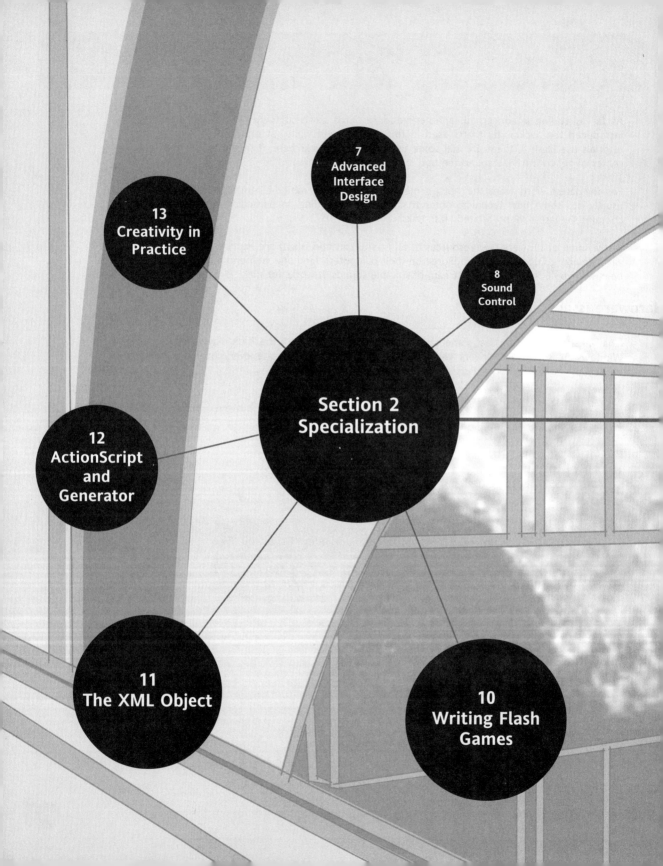

Chapter 9
3D Flash

We live in a three-dimensional world. Everything about the reality in which we live is three-dimensional. In fact, we are not capable of creating anything with less than three dimensions (although maybe a physicist or two will disagree). Many think of something like a piece of paper as being two-dimensional, but anyone who has done print production will tell you that any kind of paper has a specific thickness, not to mention texture. Any form of flat media has a texture to it, whether it's the grain of a canvas or the grid of a computer monitor. What we call 2D images are those images that appear on these media, for while they have a three-dimensional quality, that quality has no relationship to the nature of the image.

The challenge then is to accurately reproduce the feeling of our 3D world in a 2D image. Where a human artist might use paint and texture to add perspective, light, and shadows to an image, a computer achieves these aims using complex mathematical algorithms.

Flash is basically a 2D animation program. It has no support whatsoever for any type of 3D data. Therefore, the burden of creating anything three-dimensional is upon the developer. Luckily, Flash is an incredibly versatile environment, and in this chapter we will look at the two ways to make something look three-dimensional in Flash.

Faking 3D

Many people are interested in the best way to take material from their favorite 3D programs and bring it into Flash. Unfortunately, there is no perfect solution. If you simply want to import a still image of a 3D model, you need only render it in your 3D application and import the image into Flash as a bitmap, or vector, depending on what your 3D package supports.

If you need the object to have a transparent background, most 3D programs will allow you to render an alpha mask for an object, which you can bring into Photoshop with the rendered image to use as a layer mask. You can then use this composite image to create a transparent GIF or PNG that you can then bring into Flash.

If you want your 3D image to be able to move in a three-dimensional way however, you will need to bring an entire 3D animation into Flash. You could use almost any 3D program to render a series of bitmaps, but importing so many bitmap graphics into your Flash movie is seldom an option suitable for the web. Many packages however, now export vector information directly in the form of a SWF file. There are applications that specialize in 3D content for Flash, like Swift3D, as well as plug-ins for many of the more robust 3D environments, such as Flicker, a third party plug-in for Lightwave, and The Pro Pack for Poser, which includes Flash export. Still, all of these programs are rendering animated 3D content into a series of flat 2D images.

Creating 3D effects

However, there are other ways to get a 3D effect. Remember that you are dealing with a flat monitor screen here; the best that any technique can achieve is to make an image *look* three-dimensional, so whether you achieve that illusion with a real 3D model or not, is irrelevant, but maintaining the illusion of 3D can be a little more involved. We need to use some of the same tricks that an artist would use in a painting, things like depth, perspective, and light. I'm going to show you two examples of how you can use these tricks to make your Flash creations a little more three-dimensional.

3D orbit effect

This first effect is an old one. What we are going to do is create a ball that orbits around a word. All you need for this effect is a word written in a large font, and a ball graphic. I am actually using the first image from my 3D text animation, but you can just as easily create this effect with any text or object (the download file for this exercise is `orbit.fla`). For the ball, fill a circle with a radial gradient that goes from a color to transparent. We need to motion-tween the ball, so make it a graphic symbol. Now that we have our graphics, let's lay everything out on the timeline.

1. In the timeline, create two layers. Place the ball on the top layer and the text on the bottom.

2. Create a motion guide for the ball layer. Use the Pencil Tool to draw a circle around the text, like you can see in the picture. It is important that the circle almost closes, but not quite.

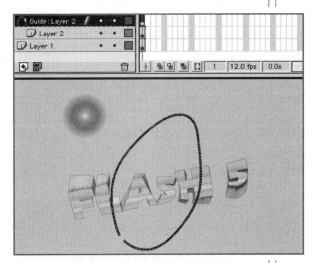

3. Position your ball so that it latches onto one end of the motion guide.

4. Add a keyframe to the ball layer where you want the animation to end. I've used 20 for this example, but somewhere in the region of 20-40 frames works well. Extend the number of frames in the motion guide layer to the same number of frames (an easy way to do this is by pressing F5). In this new keyframe on the ball layer, position the ball so that it latches on to the other end of the motion guide.

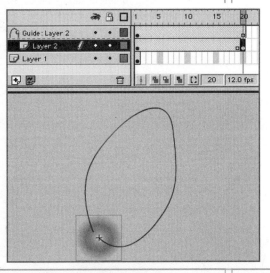

5. Create a motion tween for the ball layer and play the animation to see if our ball is…ahem…playing ball! You should see the ball follow the guide and move in a circular motion.

6. Now add a keyframe in the middle of the frame range of the ball layer. On this frame, set the scale of the ball to some percent of the original. I used 75%. The greater the difference in the scale, the more depth our animation will have, but too much will ruin the effect.

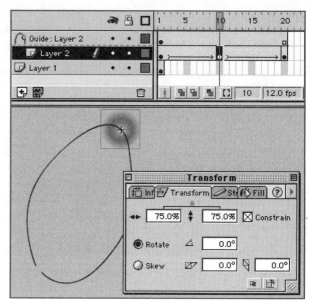

7. Add an action to the last keyframe on the ball layer. Tell the movie to:

    ```
    gotoAndPlay(1);
    ```

8. Lastly, extend the text layer to the last frame. Our timeline and stage should look like this:

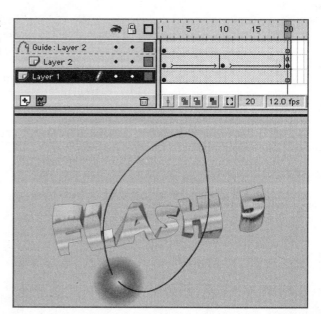

If you play the animation, you should see the ball fly around in a circle along your path, getting smaller and bigger as it goes along. This should give you a slight sense of 3D motion, but the ball is always on top of our text, which is definitely not what we want. What we need to do to solve this is get the ball to go around the text.

Thankfully, most of the work is already done. All that we need to do is create a duplicate of the text layer. Do this by creating a new layer, copying the content of the original text layer, and then selecting Edit > Paste in Place. Name this new layer TopText, and place it at the top so that the ball and guide layers are sandwiched between two text layers.

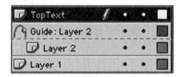

Here comes the trick. If you think about where the ball is compared to the text, it can only be in one of 4 places:

- Below the text

- Over the text for the first time

- Above the text

- Over the text for the second time

What we need to do is find a keyframe where the ball is neither below nor above the text graphic (for this example I've used frame 10), and then on each of the text layers, add a keyframe here. Then we need to delete the text on the TopText layer after that new keyframe, and delete the text on the bottom layer before that keyframe.

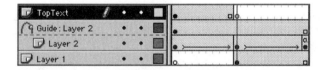

By doing this, the top text will be visible the first time the ball goes over the text, and the bottom text will be visible the second time. With the additional reference of the text, the ball really does look as though it's moving in 3D space.

Test the movie and watch our ball orbiting the text.

That is about as simple an example of pseudo-3D that we can try. Not only is it static, which means that it cannot change when it is playing, but it is also dependent on timeline animation, which is something we want to avoid in order to make reusable, interactive objects.

Spinning cube script

You can do a great deal of 3D work using keyframes and tweens. Drawing things out frame-by-frame tends to take a great deal of time, not to mention a fair amount of artistic talent, although we can often cheat by using a bit of ActionScript to aid our endeavors. If you can imagine trying to keyframe an object like a spinning cube, you will realize that while possible, such an animation would be a bit of work; especially if you want the cube to spin at different rates and in different directions.

It is possible, in controlled examples, to use ActionScript to help achieve a pseudo-3D effect, and in this example we are going to create a spinning cube that relies completely on ActionScript for its movement.

To create this illusion, we need a few pictures of an object. You can use any object you wish, as long as it is roughly the same size along at least two dimensions. To help emphasize the illusion of 3D, you will need four pictures of this object, one from each direction; front, back, left, right. I used a 3D modeler to generate pictures of a mannequin from each direction.

The ActionScript will use these four images, each placed on a square background, to create the illusion that the images are actually the sides of a cube. Try to find some kind of cubic object in your house, something that you can pick up easily. I have a tall block of notepaper on my desk that works wonderfully for this. Hold the block up to your eye level so that you cannot see the top or bottom, only the sides. Start the cube with one side facing you, and spin it slowly from left to right. What do you see? Try to imagine the cube as a picture on a 2D plane. You will notice that you can only see two sides of the cube at any given time. As soon as one side disappears over the edge, its opposite appears on the other side. Try to imagine visualizing this with two squares that always touch in the middle. What you end up with is that as one square gets wider, the other loses an equivalent width. In fact, if you were just describing shape without texture or light and shadow, the image of the cube spinning would simply look like a line moving across a rectangle's face, continually repeating a sweep from one side to the other.

Because only two sides are visible at any given time, we are only going to worry about two squares at a time. The other two will be kept hidden, waiting for their chance to become active. Therefore our script will basically say:

- Get a rotation increment. We will eventually be using the position of the mouse to extrapolate an amount by which to rotate.

- Increment the width of square one by that value, and likewise, decrement the width of square two.

- If either of the squares ends up with a width of greater that a 100%, do something to shift the images over by one square, and start the whole thing over again.

1.   Let's start out by assembling the things we will need for this effect. First, we need the four images that we will be using. These images should be the same size.

2.   Create a new movie clip to contain the main effect, call it Scripted Cube Effect. This movie clip needs to contain an Actions layer with three consecutive keyframes to contain our scripts. We'll also need an Images layer to hold our squares.

3.   Next, create a movie clip called shadow, and a movie clip called highlight. We will talk about these later.

4.   Create a movie clip called square to act as a template for the four squares you need to create. In the movie clip add three new layers. Call the top layer highlight, followed by shadow, image, and background. Place the shadow and highlight movie clips on their appropriate layers, making sure both are centered. Name the highlight movie clip instance `highlight`, and likewise the shadow movie clip instance `shadow`.

5.   In the background *layer*, drag one of the images in and center it. Draw an unfilled box the same size as the image and then delete the image. Set the stroke on the square to hairline width and color the stroke and fill as you wish.

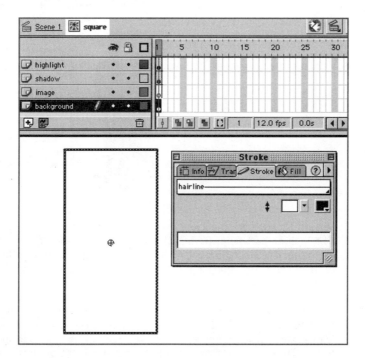

6.   So that is the base of our square movieclip finished. The next thing to do is to duplicate it. Go to your library and duplicate it four times. Do this by selecting the square movieclip and control-clicking/right clicking and selecting Duplicate from the drop-down menu. Name these new movie clips square1 through to square4.

7.   Now we need to centre our images on the Image layer of each of these new movie clips. Place the "front" image on square4, the "left" on square3, the "back" on square2,

and the "right" on square1. Make sure that no part of the image, visible or not, is outside of the box on the background layer.

8.   Now that we have all of our components created, we are ready to start laying them out in the Scripted Cube Effect movie clip. Open that movie clip and drag each of the numbered square movie clips onto the Images layer, centering them and giving each an instance name identical to their movie clip name.

The last of which should look a little like this:

The last thing to do to achieve the basic effect is to write the scripts. The effect uses a basic three-part script (to be placed on the Actions layer); the first frame initializing our setup, the second describing an iterative motion step, and the third looping back to the second. Thus our script will start on frame 1, and loop between frames 2 and 3 for the duration.

1.   Let's write the initialization script in frame one first. I want to create an array to hold our four square movie clips. While an array is not necessarily needed here, I think that it makes everything a lot neater, as well as making the code more reusable in the future. Therefore the first part of this script creates an array called "squares" and places the four square inside it.

```
//set up array to hold image movie clips
squares = new Array();
squares[1]=square1;
squares[2]=square2;
squares[3]=square3;
squares[4]=square4;
```

As we have learnt earlier in the book there is a shorter way to determine our arrays. We can use the `array` operator or `[]` to create a new array and initialize it in one line. The zero is there because arrays are numbered from zero, not one.

```
//set up array to hold image movie clips
squares=[0, square1, square2, square3, square4];
```

Remember that we already named the `square` movie clips, so either way this script is just placing those names inside of the array.

2. Next, we need to create a variable to hold the degree of incrementation. Right now, I am going to hardcode a value into this variable, but soon we will link it to the position of the mouse. Add this to our code:

```
rotNum=5;
```

3. Now we need to initialize the scale and visibility of each of the squares. Remember that only two of the squares will be visible at any one time. I randomly decided to make the third and fourth square the visible ones. The first and second squares will always be invisible. I also needed to pick a square to start off as fully revealed. Since square4 has the "front" image I decided to use that. This means that the third square will start off visible, but with a `_xscale` of zero. Here is the script.

```
squares[1]._xscale=0;
squares[2]._xscale=0;
squares[3]._xscale=0;
squares[4]._xscale=100;
squares[1]._visible=false;
squares[2]._visible=false;
```

That does it for the initialization script for now. We have set up an array of our squares, and we have prepared them for the next step, animation. The ActionScript for frame 1 should look like this:

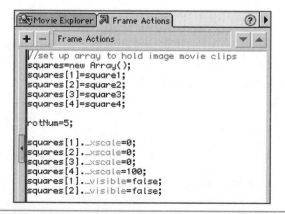

Let's move onto the motion script in frame 2. This script is written in three logical segments.

1.   The first uses the `rotNum` variable to adjust the scale of the two visible squares. Basically, we are deciding where to draw the dividing line between the two movie clips using their relative sizes at any give moment.

```
squares[3]._xscale += rotNum*(squares[4]._xscale/20);
squares[4]._xscale -= rotNum*(squares[3]._xscale/20);
```

Notice that the `rotNum` value is not being used as is, but rather is being modified by the scale of the other square. If we just said:

```
squares[3]._xscale+=rotNum;
squares[4]._xscale-=rotNum;
```

The scale of both of the moving squares combined would always equal the width of one square at 100%. If you pull out your cube again, you will notice that when the square is halfway through a turn, the 2D width of the cube is actually about half again as wide as one face of the cube. Thus, by using the scales as a multiplier on the widths, we create a more accurate illusion.

2.   The second segment uses two `if` statements to see if the cube has completed a turn. These segments are responsible for shifting the images in the array as necessary. The first `if` statement detects rightward turns and the second detects leftward turns. Each makes a copy of the `squares` array, and rearranges the squares appropriately. You can see each `if` statement below. Notice the conditional expressions. In the first statement, a right shift in the image array occurs when either the width of the fourth square hits zero, or the width of the third square exceeds 100. If you think about it, this is a little redundant, but it never hurts to be thorough. The use of `tempSquare` is necessary to be able to arrange the values in the array without destroying them in the process.

```
if (squares[4]._xscale<=0||squares[3]._xscale>100) {
        tempSquare=[0, squares[1], squares[2], squares[3],
    ➥ squares[4]];
        //
        squares[2]=tempSquare[1];
        squares[3]=tempSquare[2];
        squares[4]=tempSquare[3];
        squares[1]=tempSquare[4];
        //
        squares[1]._xscale=0;
        squares[2]._xscale=0;
        squares[3]._xscale=0;
        squares[4]._xscale=100;
        //
} else if (squares[3]._xscale<=0||squares[4]._xscale>100) {
        tempSquare=[0, squares[1], squares[2], squares[3],
    ➥ squares[4]];
        //
```

```
                squares[4]=tempSquare[1];
                squares[1]=tempSquare[2];
                squares[2]=tempSquare[3];
                squares[3]=tempSquare[4];
                //
                squares[1]._xscale=0;
                squares[2]._xscale=0;
                squares[3]._xscale=100;
                squares[4]._xscale=0;
            }
```

3.   The last section of the script first resets the visibility of the squares. Then it goes about positioning the two visible squares on the screen.

```
squares[1]._visible=0;
squares[2]._visible=0;
squares[3]._visible=1;
squares[4]._visible=1;
//
totalLength = squares[3]._width+squares[4]._width;
midpoint = (totalLength/2);
midpoint -= (totalLength);
//
squares[3]._x = midpoint+(squares[3]._width/2)
(squares[4]._x = _x = squares[3].x+
(squares[3]._width/2)+
(squares[4]._width/2);
```

To position the squares we need to first figure out how wide the cube is at that moment. We do this simply by adding the two widths together and storing the result in totalLength. We then take totalLength and halve it, to find the cube's midpoint. From that value, which is stored in the variable midpoint we subtract the totalLength. This gives us the _x we would use to position the cube so that the right side is at the centerline of the movie clip. With that value in hand, we place square3 so that is centered on the midpoint value. The last step is to position square4 so that is next to square3.

4.   The last step in this effect is to write the loop command in the third and final frame of the effect movie clip. Select the third frame on the Actions layer and enter:

```
gotoAndPlay(2);
```

5.   Place your Scripted Cube Effect movie clip on the main stage and test your movie. If everything went well, you should see the cube spin slowly rightward. If the effect is not working well, check your output for errors. If Flash is complaining that it cannot find something, you may not have named your squares properly.

Adding shadows to our cube

You might have noticed that our cube is not quite there yet. However, there is one thing we can do to make our cube look a lot more realistic. You probably remember the highlight and shadow movie clips that we created but never used. We are now going to use them to add an imaginary light source to our illusion of 3D. First, we need to go into our template square movie clip.

1. Select the box graphic on the background layer and copy it.

2. Now use the library to open the highlight movie clip. There should only be one layer and one frame, since we never touched this clip. Select Edit > Paste in Place to paste the square in the right place.

3. Set the fill color to white, fill the shape with the Paint Bucket Tool and then delete the outline, leaving only the fill.

   Repeat this process for the shadow movie clip, using black for the fill color.

4. That is all that needs to be done to the clips themselves. We do need however to add a little code to the scripts in the Scripted Cube Effect movie clip to deal with this new feature. Select the first frame of the Actions layer in that movie clip and add the following to the end of the script:

   ```
   for(i=1; i<=4; i++){
       squares[i].shadow._alpha=0;
       squares[i].highlight._alpha=0;
   }
   ```

   This will simply go through our square array and set the _alpha of the new shadows and highlights to zero.

5. Now select frame 2 and add this code to the end.

   ```
   squares[4].shadow._alpha=(100-squares[4]._xscale);
   squares[3].highlight._alpha=(100-squares[3]._xscale);
   //
   squares[1].shadow._alpha=0;
   squares[2].highlight._alpha=0;
   ```

   Examining this code, you will see that the highlight will only be visible on the third square; its opacity inversely proportional to the square's width. Likewise, the shadow layer is only visible in the fourth square. Now a light from the left will shade the squares when you play your movie.

6. The only problem now is that the squares are always rotating the same way and at the same rate. If you remember, we built the cube to rotate in either direction. To demonstrate this, let's link up the rotation of the cube to the _xmouse property. This is done on the second frame of the Actions layer. For this you need to know the width

of your main movie. For this example my movie is 500 pixels wide. Alter this figure to suit your movie if necessary. Insert the following code before the rest of the script on frame 2:

```
rotNum = (_xmouse) / (500/2);
```

Now test your movie and experiment by moving your mouse around. I think that it's with the interactivity of the effect that the illusion of 3D really comes alive.

This concludes our brief look at ways to create the illusion of 3D in Flash. The lesson to be learned here is that if you can simulate things like depth, perspective, and light, you often do not need to deal with true geometry. However, sometimes faking 3D is just not enough. This is often true when you need an object to move in a three dimensional way that you cannot predict. Imagine if you would, programming the spinning cube we just created to spin along more than one axis at a time. I will not say that anything is impossible within Flash, but if you could do it in a way that avoids traditional 3D math, I would say that it would be extremely complex. Therefore sometimes we have to really use 3D in order to achieve a 3D effect. The rest of this chapter is dedicated to taking you through the construction of a very simple 3D engine.

eal 3D in Flash

In order to work with three-dimensional information on the computer we need to do three basic things:

- Find a way to represent 3D data

- Find a way to manipulate 3D data

- Find a way to display 3D data.

It does not matter what type of 3D system we are trying to implement; whether we are building a 3D game or a ray-tracer for static images, we must come up with ways to define 3D information in a 2D space.

Representing 3D data in Flash

First, we need a way to represent and store 3D data, which will involve creating a data structure that can contain 3D information. The simplest such data structure we will be creating is a 3D point. A 3D point is a structure that defines a specific place in 3D space. The minimum amount of information we can associate with a 3D point for it to accomplish its intention is a set of three space coordinates. We are used to dealing with 2D points in Flash; that is points that have x and y values associated with them. To take this concept into three-dimensional space we need to add a coordinate to our 2D point, corresponding to a z-axis. Since Flash has no built in support for 3D, we need to make our 3D point as an object, and in this case we have two choices. We can either choose to define a point as an object, and then define variables x, y and z inside that object, or we can create an array object and use three spaces within the array as storage for the coordinate data.

For the examples in this chapter, I have chosen the latter approach to make iterating through the data a little easier. A simple point declaration may look like this:

```
// Point:
Point=new Array();
// x value
Point[1]=100;
// y value
Point[2]=100;
// z value
Point[3]=100;
// w value
Point[4]=1;
```

If you ever want to store any additional data per point, you can easily use the empty indexes of the array. For instance, if we wanted to associate a movie clip with a point to act as a graphic, you could use Point[5] to point to it (as I have already added a piece of data at index four). The w value for a point is used in some of the calculations that we will be using later, and essentially it is used to describe perspective.

Multi-dimensional arrays

Often, we will want to store our points in an array as well. This will allow us to create functions that will be able to access a set of points, and the variables contained within those points, using loop structures. In Flash, an array can contain any kind of data or object, including arrays. The term used to refer to an array inside of an array is **multi-dimensional array**. Think about using an array to represent a ten by ten grid. If we didn't know anything about multi-dimensional arrays, we might have to create an array with one hundred places, and multiply the index by the column to get at the right column data, but that certainly is not the smartest way to do it. Let's have a look at how we'd do it using a multi-dimensional array:

```
board=new Array();
for(i=1; i<=10;i++){
    board[i]=new Array();
}
```

Now, instead of using something like: (((row-1)*10)+column) to get a position in the array, we simply ask for board[row][column], which is a lot more logical. In this way, multi-dimensional arrays can be used to represent all kinds of data sets, from a 2D chessboard, to complicated spatial relationships.

Later, when we are defining 3D objects, a component we will need to create will be an array called points, which will itself store several point arrays like the one we defined earlier.

Matrices

As we get deeper and deeper into the technical aspects of 3D, we will be using a multi-dimensional array to represent a matrix. You might not think so now, but matrices are in fact, vital to any 3D manipulation, and we'll be taking a look at how this is so.

To get an idea of how this works, imagine being able to create an object that remembers every change you make to its properties. You could move this object, scale it, rotate it, edit its alpha, and the object would store a composite of all these changes. You could then apply this object to any other movie clip in your movie, and the composite of all of those changes would be applied to that movie clip. Well, this is analogous to what we will be doing with our matrices. We will create a matrix and then we'll apply **rotation**, **scaling**, and **translation** (linear movement) **transformations** to it, and one of the great things is that once we have this composite matrix, we can apply it to as many points as we want, and they will all move in a congruent way.

So what exactly is a matrix? Well, a matrix is a mathematical construct that is very similar to an array; the only difference being that a matrix is a **rectangular array of elements**, with each element relating to a given value. Not quite clear what I mean? Well, if you remember back to the Point array that we discussed just a few minutes ago, you could argue that we were already dealing with a matrix. Imagine if we were to put the contents of the array in a table that has a column for each element of the array, like this:

x	y	z	w
100	100	100	1

It doesn't look all that special, does it? In fact, it's quite straightforward, why even bother going to all the hassle of using a matrix? It doesn't look all that different from an array... Well, everything's just fine with arrays, but I ask you, what if we wanted to store the values for another point, how would we do that? Well, using matrices, it's simple; we just add another row to the matrix: (think about how messy this simple operation could be if we were using arrays), like this:

x	y	z	w
100	100	100	1
200	200	150	1

Matrices are described by their dimensions, thus an **m x n matrix consists of m rows and n columns**, so we could say that our earlier Point array is actually a 1 x 4 matrix, and similarly that the matrix shown in the above diagram is in fact a 2x4 matrix.

If ever you see a matrix written down somewhere else, you may notice something a little different about the way in which it is written, here's how you might see a 4x4 matrix appear:

$$\begin{Bmatrix} 75 & 168 & 99 & 1 \\ 88 & 100 & 70 & 1 \\ 75 & 50 & 60 & 1 \\ 200 & 45 & 175 & 1 \end{Bmatrix}$$

Hopefully, you'll have noticed that I've made two subtle changes, and they are more to do with presentation, as opposed to any kind of mathematical operation. Notice that I've encapsulated the matrix elements in some large curly braces (you may also see people using parentheses or other types of bracket too), and that I've omitted the column headings. This is just for convenience, as it makes things quicker to write down, we haven't lost any data, we've just written it in shorthand if you like. Providing we know what the columns of the matrix represent (which we should be able to deduce if we know in which context the matrix is being used), then we can see exactly what the information the matrix contains. So if, as in our discussion here, we knew that this matrix represented the contents of a number of point arrays, then we'd be able to see right away that each row correspond to the x, y, z, and w components of a point array object, with each column in the matrix relating to each specific property.

So, great... We've written the same data in a different form, what's the point? What can we do with it in this form? The answer to this is, in short, that we can do an awful lot. You see, over the years, academics with far too much time on their hands have seen fit to work on matrix theory, and thankfully, those clever (although often a little odd) individuals have come up with some very useful rules and results for manipulating matrices. The wonderful thing is that once we have our data in a matrix, we can perform all kinds of mathematical operations upon the matrix as a whole, thereby transforming and manipulating the data therein, to yield results that we can use. What kind of results? Remember I said about being able to apply scaling, rotations and translations? Well that's exactly what matrices enable us to do, and we'll see how we use them to carry out such operations a little later, as we progress through the chapter.

So just what do we do with a matrix to get these results? You might even be wondering what on earth we do to a matrix once we've got our data in it, for instance, can we multiply it? Can we add it to something? Just how do we go about using it? Well, this is a book about Flash, not math, and albeit you can add, subtract and carry out all kinds of other operations on matrices, for our purposes here, all we need concern ourselves with is **matrix multiplication**. "Hold it right there..." I hear you say, "I do not like the sound of that..." I can see your point. Probably two of the most intimidating words in mathematics, and they're both appearing in the same sentence. It got to be bad news, hasn't it? You'll be pleased to hear that matrix multiplication really isn't all that tough, so let's look at how we go about it...

Imagine we have a matrix which just four elements in it, a, b, c, and d (these would actually correspond to numbers, but for the clarity of this discussion, I've simply used letters), like this:

$$\begin{bmatrix} a & b \\ c & d \end{bmatrix}$$

Now suppose we wanted to multiply it (for whatever reason) by some number, let's say 2. Just how would we go about it? Easy, we simply write down what we have, like this:

$$2 \times \begin{bmatrix} a & b \\ c & d \end{bmatrix} = ??$$

But what is the answer? It's very straightforward. We multiply each matrix element by the factor we wish to multiply by, which in this case is simply 2:

$$2 \times \begin{bmatrix} a & b \\ c & d \end{bmatrix} = \begin{bmatrix} 2a & 2b \\ 2c & 2d \end{bmatrix}$$

Now for our purposes, it's unlikely that we would have to multiply a matrix by just a simple factor as we have just seen. Instead, the multiplication involved in the transformations used in 3D graphics usually requires the multiplication of our original matrix by another matrix. What is this other matrix? Well, that depends very much on the type of transformation that we want to carry out, as there are specific matrices for each type of transformation (and you'll see some of these matrices a little later), but for now, all we need to know is how we would actually go about multiplying two matrices. So let's suppose that for the transformation that we want to apply to our data has a matrix associated with it that looks like this:

$$\begin{bmatrix} e & f \\ g & h \end{bmatrix}$$

OK, fair enough, so what does our multiplication look like? Here it is:

$$\begin{bmatrix} a & b \\ c & d \end{bmatrix} \times \begin{bmatrix} e & f \\ g & h \end{bmatrix} = ??$$

But what is the answer? Well, remember those mathematicians? Well, they came with a rule for this matrix multiplication, which says that the product of these two matrices is another matrix, which looks like this:

$$\begin{bmatrix} a & b \\ c & d \end{bmatrix} \times \begin{bmatrix} e & f \\ g & h \end{bmatrix} = \begin{bmatrix} (ae+bg) & (af+bh) \\ (cd+dg) & (cf+dh) \end{bmatrix}$$

In order to multiply two matrices, you multiply the rows of the first matrix by the columns of the second. You traverse the rows and columns, adding up the products of the row/sum pairs.

Let's look at an example with some numbers in it, so you can see how the elements of the results matrix are formed:

$$\begin{bmatrix} 1 & 2 & 3 & 4 \\ 5 & 6 & 7 & 8 \\ 9 & 10 & 11 & 12 \\ 13 & 14 & 15 & 16 \end{bmatrix} \times \begin{bmatrix} a & b & c & d \\ e & f & g & h \\ i & j & k & l \\ m & n & o & p \end{bmatrix} = \begin{bmatrix} (a + 2e + 3i + 4m) & (b + 2f+ 3j +4n) & (c + 2g +3k + 4o) & (d +2h + 3l + 4p) \\ (5a + 6e + 7i + 8m) & (5b + 6f + 7j + 8n) & (5c + 6g + 7k + 8o) & (5d + 6h + 7l + 8p) \\ (9a + 10e + 11i + 12m) & (9b + 10f + 11j + 12n) & (9c + 10g + 11k + 12o) & (9d + 10h + 11l + 12p) \\ (13a + 14e + 15i + 16m) & (13b + 14f + 15j + 16n) & (13c + 14g + 15k + 16o) & (13d + 14h + 15l + 16p) \end{bmatrix}$$

Notice how the result of multiplying a 4x4 matrix by a 4x4 matrix is another 4x4 matrix. You may think this is obvious, but what happens if we try multiplying matrices of different sizes? Have a look; try multiplying a few different matrices of different sizes. Hopefully, you'll notice that it only makes sense to multiply certain combinations of matrices. This only being able to multiply "compatible" matrices is a property of matrix multiplication that we have to learn to live with. However, for our purposes here, we'll only be multiplying 4x4 matrices, so we won't be adversely affected by this characteristic. In short, the rule for matrix multiplication is this: the product of two matrices is only valid if the number of columns in the first matrix equals the number of rows in the second.

Have a look at this matrix:

$$\left\{ \begin{matrix} 0 & 0 & 0 & 1 \\ 0 & 0 & 1 & 0 \\ 0 & 1 & 0 & 0 \\ 1 & 0 & 0 & 0 \end{matrix} \right\}$$

This is actually a very special matrix, called the **identity matrix**. When we multiply any compatible matrix by the identity matrix we get the original matrix as the result; just as you can multiply any number by 1 to get that same number. Such an operation may seem a little ineffectual, but it's useful to know about this matrix should you start working with combinations of matrices.

As you can imagine, once you start dealing with larger matrices (remember how big our multiplication of 2 4x4 matrices was, just a minute ago?), calculating them by hand quickly becomes impractical. Luckily we can make the computer do all the work for us. Before we move on, let's look at an example by building a matrix calculator.

Matrix calculator

To create the calculator, we will need to write a few functions that will handle all of the calculations for us. We are going to write the functions so that they are reusable, thereby enabling us to copy and paste them into our 3D engine later on. We will also need two buttons, one to reset the matrix, the other to calculate the result. We are also going to need several input text fields, 48 to be exact, 16 for each of the three matrices.

1. Begin by creating a new movie clip to house the effect. Call this clip Rotating Cube Effect. Create a layer for Actions, one for the text fields (call it Fields), and one for the interface elements (call this layer, Boxes).

2. Create an input text field on the text field layer. Size it so that it can hold one character. Feel free to use a large font size. Name the variable of the text field a_0_0.

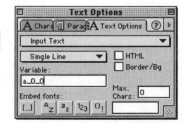

3. Duplicate the text field three times, and arrange the four text fields in a row. Name the variable in the second field, a_0_1, that in the third a_0_2, and the variable in the fourth field a_0_3. Use the Align panel to make them line-up nicely.

4. Select all four text fields and duplicate the row three times, lining the new rows up under the first, to form a grid. Again, use the Align panel to neaten up your grid. Go through and number the three new rows appropriately. The text fields in row two should all start with a_1_ followed by the corresponding column number.

5. Create a new button that contains a caption saying Identity as a graphic, and then place an instance of it under the grid of text fields. Your grid should be looking something like this:

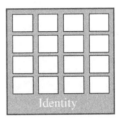

6. Select the grid and button; make a copy, and drag it to the right of the first grid. We need to rename each of the variables in each of the text fields in the new grid, and we do this by changing all of the a's to b's. So, our text fields in the second grid should range from b_0_0 through to b_3_3.

7. Copy the second grid, this time without the button, and paste it to the right again. Just as we did with the previous grid, we're going to have to assign new variables to each of the text fields. This time, our variables are going to have an r prefix, so assign variables to these text fields as such, using the variables names from r_0_0 through to r_3_3.

8. Make a new button labeled Calculate, and place it under the third grid. Your layout should now resemble that shown here:

That's all we need to get started.

Right, what's next? Well, the script to calculate the product of the arrays is actually very short, thanks to Flash 5's `for` loop structure.

1. In the keyframe of the Actions layer, we need to initialize a few arrays, and then define a function.

    ```
    array_1=new Array;
    array_1[0]=new Array;
    array_1[1]=new Array;
    array_1[2]=new Array;
    array_1[3]=new Array;

    array_2=new Array;
    array_2[0]=new Array;
    array_2[1]=new Array;
    array_2[2]=new Array;
    array_2[3]=new Array;
    ```

    This code should look familiar by now. All we are doing above is creating two 2D arrays, called `array_1` and `array_2`.

2. Now let's look at the function definition. The function, called `ArrayMult`, takes in two 4x4 arrays, and then returns the product. Inside the function, the first thing the function does is to create a new array to hold the result. Then there are three levels of nested `for` loops. I don't want to bore you to death, walking through the iterations of the loop structure, so let's just look at the main line in the center. It is basically saying that for each position (i, j) in the result matrix, multiply through using `k` to iterate through the rows of `array1`, and the columns of `array2`. If you compare the code to the examples we did by hand, you will see that it is doing exactly the same thing, and like I said just a minute ago, after all of this calculation, the function returns the product of these two matrices, as `result`.

    ```
    function ArrayMult(array1, array2) {
    result=new Array;
    result[0]=new Array;
    result[1]=new Array;
    result[2]=new Array;
    result[3]=new Array;

    for(i=0; i<=3; i++){
            for(j=0; j<=3; j++){
                    result[i][j]=0;
                    for(k=0; k<=3; k++){
                            result[i][j]+=array1[i][k]*array2[k][j];
                    }
            }
    }
    return (result);
    }
    ```

3. Now we need to add code to make our buttons functional. All the Identity buttons do is set the matrix above them to the identity matrix. This is just to save you time when you test your movie, as entering 32 numbers by hand can become a little tedious after a while. So, all the button script does is iterate through the text fields setting everything to zero, unless the row and column are equal, in which case it sets the matrix element to 1. Here's the handler for the Identity button below the leftmost (or "a") grid:

```
on (release) {
    for(l=0;l<=3;l++){
        for(m=0;m<=3;m++){
            this["a_"+ l + "_"+ m]=int(l==m);
        }
    }
}
```

Notice that this function does not affect the arrays we declared earlier – these are not set until you click the Calculate button.

4. Copy the script above and paste it into the center Identity button. Replace the a with a b-so the code looks like this:

```
on (release) {
    for(l=0;l<=3;l++){
        for(m=0;m<=3;m++){
            this["b_"+ l + "_"+ m]=int(l= =m);
        }
    }
}
```

5. Add the following code to the Calculate button, and then we should be set:

```
on (release) {
    for(l=0;l<=3;l++){
        for(m=0;m<=3;m++){
            array_1[l][m]=this["a_"+ l + "_"+ m];
            array_2[l][m]=this["b_"+ l + "_"+ m];
        }
    }
    theResult=this.ArrayMult(array_1,array_2);
    for(l=0;l<=3;l++){
        for(m=0;m<=3;m++){
            this["r_"+ l + "_"+ m]=theResult[l][m]
        }
    }
}
```

Test the movie. Try entering some numbers into the text fields; remember that if you multiply any matrix by the identity matrix, you should get your original matrix as the result. If you really want to test it out, try a few different matrices, and either sit down and do the math, or perhaps compare your output to that of a graphing calculator or some other device capable of matrix multiplication.

Calculating the product of two 4x4 matrices is a big part of the math required for our 3D engine. The other thing we need to do is write a function to calculate the product of a 4x4 matrix and a point (remember how a point is represented in terms of matrices), like the ones we talked about earlier. This function, called PointMult(array, point), takes in a 4x4 array and a 4x1 array. Using a structure similar to that of the previous function, nested for loops yield the result, which is of course a 4x1 array, or a point.

```
function PointMult(array, point) {
    result=new Array;
    for(i=0; i<=3; i++){
        for(j=0; j<=3; j++){
            result[i]+=array[i][j]*point[j];
        }
    }
    return result;
}
```

The PointMult calculator is available for your perusal in this chapter's FLA file, which is available for download.

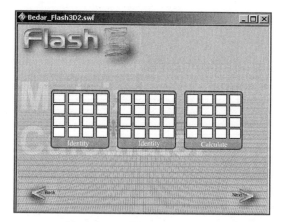

Matrix transformations

Now that we know what matrices are, and how to work with them, let's talk about why we need them. Matrix math is at the heart of modern runtime 3D graphics. Matrices are used in what's called a 3D transformation. A 3D transformation refers to an operation in which we take an object, represented as a set of points in three-dimensional space, and change it in some way. What do I mean, "change"? Well, examples of transformations include:

- Scaling: Making the object bigger or smaller.

- Rotation: Rotating the object around one of the three axes.

- Translation: Moving the object in a linear fashion.

Each of these transformations can be represented as a specific 4x4 matrix. For instance, there is a unique matrix for a rotation of 10 degrees around the y-axis, and this matrix is the same whether you are applying it to a single point or a 3D universe – pretty powerful stuff. However, the matrix for the 10 degree y-axis rotation is only good for that specific transformation; a rotation of 11 degrees about the y-axis corresponds to a completely different matrix.

In order to calculate a matrix for a rotation through a given angle, we start with a template of a rotation matrix, and then plug-in the angle, ϕ, through which we want the transformation to sweep. A few template transformations are shown below. Don't worry if they seem ridiculously complex, the elements of each matrix are the result of highly theoretical study, and for our purposes, we can just take them as given. We will end up making functions that use these templates to construct matrices based upon any given input value.

Transformation Matrix Templates

$$\begin{pmatrix} 1 & 0 & 0 & 0 \\ 0 & 1 & 0 & 0 \\ 0 & 0 & 1 & 0 \\ 0 & 0 & 0 & 1 \end{pmatrix}$$

Identity Matrix

$$\begin{pmatrix} 1 & 0 & 0 & \delta x \\ 0 & 1 & 0 & \delta y \\ 0 & 0 & 1 & \delta z \\ 0 & 0 & 0 & 1 \end{pmatrix}$$

Translation Matrix

$$\begin{pmatrix} \%x & 0 & 0 & 0 \\ 0 & \%y & 0 & 0 \\ 0 & 0 & \%z & 0 \\ 0 & 0 & 0 & 1 \end{pmatrix}$$

Scaling Matrix

$$\begin{pmatrix} 0 & 0 & 0 & 0 \\ 0 & \cos\phi & \sin\phi & 0 \\ 0 & -\sin\phi & \cos\phi & 0 \\ 0 & 0 & 0 & 0 \end{pmatrix}$$

X-Rotation Matrix

$$\begin{pmatrix} \cos\phi & 0 & -\sin\phi & 0 \\ 0 & 0 & 0 & 0 \\ \sin\phi & 0 & \cos\phi & 0 \\ 0 & 0 & 0 & 0 \end{pmatrix}$$

Y-Rotation Matrix

$$\begin{pmatrix} \cos\phi & \sin\phi & 0 & 0 \\ -\sin\phi & \cos\phi & 0 & 0 \\ 0 & 0 & 0 & 0 \\ 0 & 0 & 0 & 0 \end{pmatrix}$$

Z-Rotation Matrix

If you remember, a point is represented by a 4x1 matrix, and a given transformation can be applied to a point by multiplying the respective matrices, and we'll be using the `PointMult` function we defined earlier to perform this multiplication. Applying the transformation matrix to a point has the end result of moving that point in 3D space. Similarly, applying the same matrix to a group of points, will move the collection of points, 'en masse', in such a way that the points maintain the same relationship relative to one another.

The best thing about using matrices in 3D is the inherent ability they give you to combine transformations. Let's say that we wanted to rotate an object and then scale it. Instead of moving the object twice, we can create a **composite matrix** of the two transformations by multiplying the corresponding transformation matrices together. The point matrix is then multiplied by this composite matrix; resulting in the desired composite transformation being applied to the point. The great thing about using matrices in this way is that we can create large chains of complex transformations, and implement them relatively easily.

When deciding on a transformation to apply to an object, it is important to keep in mind where that object is in 3D space, and how that effects our transformation. All transformations transform objects in relation to the center of your space, or the **origin**. Thus, if we were to try to rotate an object that is off in space, some distance from the origin, the object will appear to orbit the axis of the transformation. If we want to rotate an object on it's own center, we must first translate the object to the origin, and this is where the composite transformations come in handy. Almost any transformation you construct will begin with a translation out from the origin, and end with one in to the origin. Everything else will be in between.

Now, before you write me a letter telling me about my sloppy typing, I think I should tell you that I actually did mean to say that you start by translating back out, and end by translating in. The last thing you need to know about transformations for our discussion here, is that composite matrices are constructed in reverse order. For example, let's say that we wanted to rotate an object by 10 degrees about the z-axis, and then scale it by 110%. Here, the order of transformations would begin by translating the object back to where it was, scaling the object, rotating it, translating it in to the origin, and end by multiplying the points describing the object.

This is just the way matrix multiplication works, and is something you have to keep in mind.

Rotating a cube

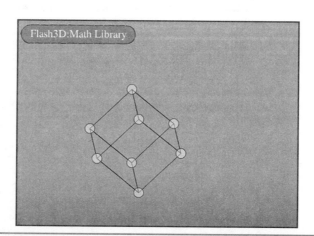

We now have all the tools necessary to begin constructing our first example of true 3D in Flash, and are going to construct a very simple 3D object: the cube. A cube has eight points, each of which we'll represent as an array. In turn, all of these points will be stored in a larger array, which will essentially be a 3D object.

Let's get started by creating all of the objects we need for this project:

1. First, let's create a movie clip called Rotating Cube to house the effect itself.

2. Inside the clip, we'll need a layer to hold our Actions, and we're going to need four consecutive keyframes on this layer.

3. Next, add one layer to hold an instance of our math movie clip (which we will be making in a moment), and another to hold all of the graphics that we will be using.

4. We will need a movie clip to be the visual representation of a data point. I've used a clip called Ball that contains a small circle graphic filled with 50% white, and more or less anything will work here, but ideally we should try to keep the graphic fairly simple. Place this clip on the graphics layer of the Rotating Cube movie clip, and give it an instance name of ball.

5. Lastly, we need a movie clip to hold all of our math functions. We could write these functions in the movie clip, but it will save us some work later on if we make a dedicated function library that can be moved from movie to movie. I am calling the movie clip 3DTransformations. There will be no visible component to the movie clip, but since we will be using it a great deal, I gave it a small icon that will appear on the stage.

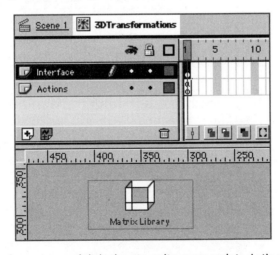

Now that we have all the pieces we need, it is time to write some scripts. Let's start by creating the function library.

Inside the 3DTransformations movie clip, click on the frame to bring up the Frame Actions window. All of the script in this frame will reside in various function definitions, and these functions will be called from other places in movie. The first two functions that we are going to write should look fairly familiar, as they are the ArrayMult and PointMult functions that we talked about earlier. Due to our care in writing functions that are reusable, we are able to use these functions again here, thereby saving ourselves work. Here are those functions again:

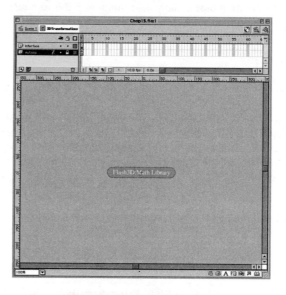

```
//Multiplies two 4x4 matrices
function ArrayMult(array1, array2) {
    result=new Array;
    result[0]=new Array;
    result[1]=new Array;
    result[2]=new Array;
    result[3]=new Array;

for(i=0; i<=3; i++){
        for(j=0; j<=3; j++){
            result[i][j]=0;
            for(k=0; k<=3; k++){
                result[i][j]+=array1[i][k]*array2[k][j];
            }
        }
}
}
return result;
}

//Multiplies a 4x4 matrix by a 4x1 array which represents a point
//in 3D space
```

```
function PointMult(array, point) {
    result=new Array;

    for(i=0; i<=3; i++){
        for(j=0; j<=3; j++){
            result[i]+=array[i][j]* point [j];
        }
    }
return result;
}
```

As you can see, there is nothing new here. These two functions will handle all of our matrix math for us. The remaining functions in this movie clip will focus on the construction of transformation matrices.

We need a function to build each of the types of transformation matrices that we want to use. This will include the three types of rotation matrix, a scaling matrix, and of course a translation matrix. Each of these functions will start by creating an empty 4x4 matrix to store the result in, and each function will then initialize that array to the identity matrix. Each function will end by returning the new matrix.

1.   Let's take a look at the translation matrix first. If you remember what the template for this matrix looked like, you will remember that the template provided for three variables, which are equivalent to the x, y, and z offsets. This means that the function will need to ask for those three variables as input. Let's look at the code now.

```
//Create a translation matrix based on a x,y,z offset
function createTransMatrix(x,y,z){
trans=new Array();
trans[0]=new Array();
trans[1]=new Array();
trans[2]=new Array();
trans[3]=new Array();

for(l=0;l<=3;l++){
        for(m=0;m<=3;m++){
                trans[l][m]= int(l==m);
        }
}

trans[0][3]=x;
trans[1][3]=y;
trans[2][3]=z;
return trans;
}
```

As you can see, most of the code above is involved solely in initializing the array. Only three out of the last four lines of the function actually have anything to do with translation.

2. Next we are going to create the function that makes scaling matrices. This function will also take in an x, y, and z value, but this time, instead of corresponding to distance, it refers to size as a percent. So for example, if we were to enter (1,1,1) into the function, it would give us a matrix that keeps the object the exact same size, which is in fact, equivalent to the identity matrix. However, if we were to enter (2,2,2) into the function, it would produce a matrix that doubles objects in size. Here, have a look at the code for this function, notice that it is almost identical to the last.

```
//Create a scaling matrix based on a x,y,z degree
function createScaleMatrix (x,y,z){
scale=new Array();
scale[0]=new Array();
scale[1]=new Array();
scale[2]=new Array();
scale[3]=new Array();

for(l=0;l<=3;l++){
        for(m=0;m<=3;m++){
                scale[l][m]= int(l==m);
        }
}
scale[0][0]=x;
scale[1][1]=y;
scale[2][2]=z;

return scale;
}
```

3. Now we need to create the three rotation functions. In terms of input, each of these functions takes in an angle, given as a degree, which can be any number from zero to positive 360. Inside the function, the degree is converted to radians, which is then used to construct the matrix. All three functions are similar, but each constructs a slightly different matrix. So, without further ado, here are the three functions:

```
//Creates a matrix to represent a rotation around the z-axis
function createZRotationMatrix (deg){
    deg*=(Math.PI/180);
    zrot=new Array();
    zrot[0]=new Array();
    zrot[1]=new Array();
    zrot[2]=new Array();
    zrot[3]=new Array();
    for(l=0;l<=3;l++){
            for(m=0;m<=3;m++){
                    zrot[l][m]= int(l==m);
            }
    }
    zrot[0][0]=Math.cos(deg);
    zrot[0][1]=((Math.sin(deg))*-1);
```

```
        zrot[1][0]=Math.sin(deg);
        zrot[1][1]=Math.cos(deg);
        return zrot;
    }

    //Creates a matrix to represent a rotation around the y-axis
    function createYRotationMatrix (deg){
        deg*=(Math.PI/180);
        yrot=new Array();
        yrot[0]=new Array();
        yrot[1]=new Array();
        yrot[2]=new Array();
        yrot[3]=new Array();
        for(l=0;l<=3;l++){
                for(m=0;m<=3;m++){
                        yrot[l][m]= int(l==m);
                }
        }
        yrot[0][0]=Math.cos(deg);
        yrot[0][2]=Math.sin(deg);
        yrot[2][0]=((Math.sin(deg))*-1);
        yrot[2][2]=Math.cos(deg);
        return yrot;
    }

    //Creates a matrix to represent a rotation around the x-axis
    function createXRotationMatrix (deg){
        deg*=(Math.PI/180);
        xrot=new Array();
        xrot[0]=new Array();
        xrot[1]=new Array();
        xrot[2]=new Array();
        xrot[3]=new Array();
        for(l=0;l<=3;l++){
                for(m=0;m<=3;m++){
                        xrot[l][m]= int(l==m);
                }
        }
        xrot[1][1]=Math.cos(deg);
        xrot[1][2]=((Math.sin(deg))*-1);
        xrot[2][1]=Math.sin(deg);
        xrot[2][2]=Math.cos(deg);
        return xrot;
    }
```

Again, we see that the functions are very similar, and that these functions are a bit more complex than the scaling and translation functions. In particular, the rotation functions make use of Flash's Math object to utilize its trigonometric functions. While these functions are necessary for any type of rotation, accessing them so often will tend to slow down our animation, so we'll discuss ways to reference them less a little bit later.

4. Here's the last matrix generation function that we need to create. This function creates a perspective matrix, which can be used to add depth to animations, and we'll use it a little bit later on.

```
//Creates a perspective matrix to represent the given distance
function createPerspectiveMatrix (d){

    perspective=new Array();
    perspective[0]=new Array();
    perspective[1]=new Array();
    perspective[2]=new Array();
    perspective[3]=new Array();

    for(l=0;l<=3;l++){
            for(m=0;m<=3;m++){
                    perspective[l][m]=Int(l==m);
            }
    }
    perspective[3][2]=(-1/d);
    perspective[3][3]=0;

    return perspective;
}
```

That's it; we're done adding functions to our math library for now. Add our math library to it's own layer in our Rotating Cube movie clip. Set its instance name to `transform`.

5. Click on the first keyframe of the Actions layer in the Rotating Cube movie clip. The first thing we need to do is set up our 3D points, and the ball graphics that will go along with them. We already have one copy of the ball on the stage, but we have eight points. Therefore we need to make a few copies of the ball movie clip. We are actually going to make eight copies, and then throw away the original. This is because we may want to change the level each ball resides on, to make it pass above or beneath another ball. Only dynamically placed movie clips can be moved from level to level, so the original is best left out of our model.

In the first part of the frame 1 script, we create a new array to hold the balls, and then populate it with copies of the ball movie clip.

```
num_balls=8;
balls=new Array();

for(i=0; i<num_balls; i++){
    duplicateMovieClip ( ball, "ball"+i, i+20);
    balls[i]=eval("ball"+i);
    balls[i]._x=0;
    balls[i]._y=0;
}
ball._visible=false;
```

I use a counter, called `num_balls` to iterate through a `for` loop, in which the duplication code is stored. The duplication code itself is fairly standard, with the possible exception of the last term in the duplication command itself; an `i+20` to designate the level. I wanted to leave plenty of levels for any additions that we will make to the code in the future. Notice also that we set the original ball's visibility to `false` after the code is done. It will always be there, but we can safely forget about it.

6. Next we hard code the initial positions of the balls. I decided to represent a 100x100 cube, although you can pick any size box you wish. More importantly, I placed the center of my cube at (0,0,0) so that I do not have to worry about translating the cube out and in every time I want to rotate it. We can seldom get away with this, but it should speed things up a little for this example. Before we start coding our points, we'll need an array to hold them. So, to deal with this we create an array called `ballcoord`, and initialize it to hold empty point objects. Then we simply pass through the array, assigning values to the points. As you can imagine, manually entering more complex models would be prohibitive.

```
ballcoord=new Array();
for(i=0; i<num_balls; i++){
    ballcoord[i]=new Array();
}
//Hard Code the Positions of the 8 balls

//x
ballcoord[0][0]=-50;
//y
ballcoord[0][1]=50;
//z
ballcoord[0][2]=50;
//w
ballcoord[0][3]=1;

ballcoord[1][0]=50;
ballcoord[1][1]=50;
ballcoord[1][2]=50;
ballcoord[1][3]=1;

ballcoord[2][0]=50;
ballcoord[2][1]=-50;
ballcoord[2][2]=50;
ballcoord[2][3]=1;

ballcoord[3][0]=-50;
ballcoord[3][1]=-50;
ballcoord[3][2]=50;
ballcoord[3][3]=1;

ballcoord[4][0]=-50;
ballcoord[4][1]=50;
```

```
ballcoord[4][2]=-50;
ballcoord[4][3]=1;

ballcoord[5][0]=50;
ballcoord[5][1]=50;
ballcoord[5][2]=-50;
ballcoord[5][3]=1;

ballcoord[6][0]=50;
ballcoord[6][1]=-50;
ballcoord[6][2]=-50;
ballcoord[6][3]=1;

ballcoord[7][0]=-50;
ballcoord[7][1]=-50;
ballcoord[7][2]=-50;
ballcoord[7][3]=1;
```

7.   Lastly, we have one function to define. This function will update the position of the balls at any time. We will call it every time we move the balls to redraw them.

```
function setPos(){
    for(i=0; i<num_balls; i++){
        balls[i]._x=ballcoord[i][0]/ballcoord[i][3];
        balls[i]._y=ballcoord[i][1]/ballcoord[i][3];
        //balls[i]._xscale=90+(ballcoord[i][2]/4);
        //balls[i]._yscale=balls[i]._xscale;
        //balls[i]._alpha=balls[i]._xscale;
    }
}
```

Notice that the last three expressions in the `for` loop are commented out. These lines use the depth information stored in our point objects to approximate the appearance of objects moving in the z plane. The first two lines adjust the ball's scale according to its z value, and the third adjusts the ball's opacity. Depending on the ball graphic you are using, you may want to try enabling one or both of these functionalities.

8.   We are now ready to write the transformation script. Go to frame 2 of your Actions layer. We already have all of the functions we need; we simply need to use them. For this example, we are going to hard code a rotation that uses all three types of rotation matrix. While transformations need to be applied in reverse order, the order in which we apply rotations does not matter. For readability, I am using temporary variables to store the intermediary matrices, but we could nest all of the commands into one monstrous line of code.

```
transZRot=transform.createZRotationMatrix(random(5));
transYRot=transform.createYRotationMatrix(random(5));
transXRot=transform.createXRotationMatrix(random(5));

temp=transform.ArrayMult(transYRot, transZRot);
finalTrans=transform.ArrayMult(temp, transXRot);
```

The first three lines of the above code create the three rotation matrices that we are going to use, and for each, a random number between 0 and 5 is being entered. The last two lines are combining the three rotation matrices using our matrix multiplication function. We will use the `finaltrans` matrix for our point multiplication in the next frame.

9. The script in the third keyframe is responsible for calculating the new position for each ball. The script starts with a simple `for` loop that iterates through the `balls` array and multiplies each point against the `finaltrans` matrix from the last frame. This is followed by some optional code that orders the balls' levels based on depth. If your balls are opaque and more complicated than a simple monochromatic dot, you will probably need to employ this code. Since my ball graphic is 50% transparent, it's very hard to tell which ball is actually on top, and as such, I can turn this code off to save time.

```
//Determine next position
for(i=0; i<num_balls; i++){
    ballcoord[i]=transform.PointMult(FinalTrans,ballcoord[i])

    //depth based reordering...turn off for more speed
    for(j=0; j<num_balls; j++){

if(ballcoord[i][2]>ballcoord[j][2]&&balls[i].depth<balls[j].depth)
{
                temp=balls[i].depth;
                balls[i].depth=balls[j].depth;
                balls[j].depth=temp;
                balls[i].swapDepths( balls[j])
        }
    }
}

//reposition balls
setPos();
```

The script ends with a call to the `SetPos` function that we defined in frame 1, which will redraw all of the balls in their new locations.

10. The last thing we need to do is place a `gotoAndPlay(3)` command on frame 4 of the actions layer. This will activate the loop necessary to animate the cube. With this done, you can test out your movie.

If all went well, your cube should be spinning in the center of your movie clip. How smoothly it is animating will depend upon the speed of your system, but it should be acceptable. This effect really pushes the boundaries of what Flash can do, and remember that Flash movies play better in the browser than they do in the Flash authoring environment.

Let's stop for a second and think about why we set the loop to go to frame 3. If you remember, in frame 2 we set the rotation matrices to random numbers. If we were to set the loop to go back to frame 2, the rotation would be slightly different each time. Try it and play your movie, you'll notice that the animation is much slower this time, which makes sense when you think of all the additional work the movie is doing in each cycle. We need to come up with ways to improve the performance of our script...

Optimizing performance
We can go about this by looking over our functions and frame scripts to see if any work is being wasted. One thing that strikes me is that our rotation transformation construction functions seem to do a lot of work, creating a new array, using trigonometric functions, converting degrees to radians; all to be thrown away. What if we were to save the results of all this work somehow, so that any given matrix would never be built twice? Up until now, we have been using a brute force approach to the problem of rotating a cube. While this may be perfectly ok for small problems, in this case we are simply asking the computer to do too much, hence the degradation of performance. By eliminating unnecessary work, and by thinking about how to do things more efficiently, we are making our code much more sophisticated.

1. To try this idea out, we are going to have to modify our transformation library a little. Open it up, and select the keyframe with all of the code. We need to first add a function that will give us some space to store all of this matrix information we will be gathering. We can place this function after all of the others. Let's call it `Init3D`. This function will set up three new arrays, one for each of the rotation functions. You might think that it would be a great idea to fill the arrays right now with matrices for each possible rotation, which is of course completely possible.

Unfortunately, it takes far too long, and a lot of the work we do might go unused. Instead, we are going to institute a *calculate once, use forever* policy, wherein the rotation functions only construct a new matrix if they do not have a matrix for that value already.

```
//init 3D
function init3D_func(){
rotx=new Array();
roty=new Array();
rotz=new Array();
            for(i=0; i<=360; i++){
                    rotx[i]=0;
                    roty[i]=0;
                    rotz[i]=0;
            }
trace("Init3D Done");
}
```

Notice how we use a `trace` function to tell us that the function has run successfully. We also, as I mentioned, need to modify the three rotation functions to make use of these new arrays. Let's look at the new x-rotation function, and highlight what has changed.

```
//Creates a matrix to represent a rotation around the X axis-deg
//must be between 0 and 360
function createXRotationMatrix (deg){
      input = deg;

      if(rotx[input] != 0){
              return(rotx[input]);

      }else{
              deg* = (Math.PI/180);
              xrot = new Array();
              xrot[0] = new Array();
              xrot[1] = new Array();
              xrot[2] = new Array();
              xrot[3] = new Array();
              for(l=0;l<=3;l++){
                      for(m=0;m<=3;m++){
                              xrot[l][m]=Int(l==m);
                      }
              }
              xrot[1][1] = Math.cos(deg);
              xrot[1][2] = ((Math.sin(deg))*-1);
              xrot[2][1] = Math.sin(deg);
              xrot[2][2] = Math.cos(deg);
              trace("XROT "add input);
              rotx[input] = xrot;
              return xrot;
      }
}
```

Basically, what we are doing is making the function act as one big if/else statement, with the else clause containing all of the code that the function contained earlier, and this is executed if this particular input has never been tried before. However, before we get to that point, we check to see if the place in the array that corresponds to the input has already been set. If it has, we simply return the previously calculated array. Notice that I also added a trace function so that we can see when the else clause is executed.

Looking over our new function, you may see another place where we are wasting work. In the process of setting up our matrices, we are calling four functions from the Math object. In fact, we are calling two functions, twice. While this may not seem like a huge waste of work, trigonometric functions are more costly than most. Therefore, we are going to calculate the values we need and store them as variables, which will then be used in the matrix. Add these lines to your function: access

```
SIN=Math.sin(deg);
COS=Math.cos(deg);
```

Then we use these new variables in the assignment statements like so:

```
xrot[1][1]=COS;
xrot[1][2]=(SIN*-1);
xrot[2][1]=SIN;
xrot[2][2]=COS;
```

I shall leave it up to you to edit the other two rotation functions. Just make the exact same changes as we made to the x-rotation function. The nice thing about doing things this way is that you do not have to edit the way your transformation calls work in the slightest. All you need to do in the main movie is add a call to init3D sometime before you use any of the rotation functions. I would suggest inserting a keyframe into the Actions layer for this purpose, between the first and second frame.

Before we move on, we can make one last optimization. Most of the work being done to animate our cube is done between the ArrayMult and PointMult functions. Obviously, any improvements we can make to these two will positively affect performance. If you look at either function, they seem fairly efficient. However, what may be surprising for some, is that while the nested looping structure is the most efficient way to write these functions as far as lines of code are concerned, setting-up and maintaining that looping structure is costing us some computing power. Speed-wise, we would be better off breaking out of the two nested loops, and writing out the statements by hand. Since this example is already pushing the limits of Flash, let's try this last optimization.

2. Go to your math library, and select the frame script. We are going to be replacing the ArrayMult and PointMult functions, so you can either delete them or comment them out. The new functions are, as mentioned, functionally equivalent, but with no for loops.

Here's the new `ArrayMult` function. You can see that it is setting every position in the result array manually.

```
//Multiplies two 4x4 matricies
function ArrayMult(m, n){
result=new Array;
result[0]=new Array;
result[1]=new Array;
result[2]=new Array;
result[3]=new Array;

result[0][0]=m[0][0]*n[0][0] + m[0][1]*n[1][0] +
            ➥m[0][2]*n[2][0] + m[0][3]*n[3][0];
result[0][1]=m[0][0]*n[0][1] + m[0][1]*n[1][1] +
            ➥m[0][2]*n[2][1] + m[0][3]*n[3][1];
result[0][2]=m[0][0]*n[0][2] + m[0][1]*n[1][2] +
            ➥m[0][2]*n[2][2] + m[0][3]*n[3][2];
result[0][3]=m[0][0]*n[0][3] + m[0][1]*n[1][3] +
            ➥m[0][2]*n[2][3] + m[0][3]*n[3][3];

result[1][0]=m[1][0]*n[0][0] + m[1][1]*n[1][0] +
            ➥m[1][2]*n[2][0] + m[1][3]*n[3][0];
result[1][1]=m[1][0]*n[0][1] + m[1][1]*n[1][1] +
            ➥m[1][2]*n[2][1] + m[1][3]*n[3][1];
result[1][2]=m[1][0]*n[0][2] + m[1][1]*n[1][2] +
            ➥m[1][2]*n[2][2] + m[1][3]*n[3][2];
result[1][3]=m[1][0]*n[0][3] + m[1][1]*n[1][3] +
            ➥m[1][2]*n[2][3] + m[1][3]*n[3][3];

result[2][0]=m[2][0]*n[0][0] + m[2][1]*n[1][0] +
            ➥m[2][2]*n[2][0] + m[2][3]*n[3][0];
result[2][1]=m[2][0]*n[0][1] + m[2][1]*n[1][1] +
            ➥m[2][2]*n[2][1] + m[2][3]*n[3][1];
result[2][2]=m[2][0]*n[0][2] + m[2][1]*n[1][2] +
            ➥m[2][2]*n[2][2] + m[2][3]*n[3][2];
result[2][3]=m[2][0]*n[0][3] + m[2][1]*n[1][3] +
            ➥m[2][2]*n[2][3] + m[2][3]*n[3][3];

result[3][0]=m[3][0]*n[0][0] + m[3][1]*n[1][0] +
            ➥m[3][2]*n[2][0] + m[3][3]*n[3][0];
result[3][1]=m[3][0]*n[0][1] + m[3][1]*n[1][1] +
            ➥m[3][2]*n[2][1] + m[3][3]*n[3][1];
result[3][2]=m[3][0]*n[0][2] + m[3][1]*n[1][2] +
            ➥m[3][2]*n[2][2] + m[3][3]*n[3][2];
result[3][3]=m[3][0]*n[0][3] + m[3][1]*n[1][3] +
            ➥m[3][2]*n[2][3] + m[3][3]*n[3][3];

return result;
}
```

Now that we have a new `ArrayMult` function, let's break out the `PointMult` function as well. Since there are many less things to multiply in this function, I rewrote it to set the result array in one line, we could've done the same for `ArrayMult`, but it would be incomprehensible.

```
//Multiplies a 4x4 matrix by a 4x1 array which represents a point
//in 3D space

function PointMult(m, n) {
result=new Array;
result=[m[0][0]*n[0] + m[0][1]*n[1] + m[0][2]*n[2] +
➥m[0][3]*n[3],m[1][0]*n[0] + m[1][1]*n[1] + m[1][2]*n[2] +
➥m[1][3]*n[3],m[2][0]*n[0] + m[2][1]*n[1] + m[2][2]*n[2] +
➥m[2][3]*n[3],m[3][0]*n[0] + m[3][1]*n[1] + m[3][2]*n[2] +
➥m[3][3]*n[3]];
return result;
}
```

Now that our optimizations are complete, test your new and improved effect. Hopefully you will notice an improvement in the performance.

3.   We are now ready to customize the rotation values a little. Up until now our cube has been spinning without any real logic. We are going to use the mouse position to determine the degree of rotation, so that the cube appears to spin towards the mouse. If you remember, the rotation functions can only accept values between 0 and 360 inclusively. Therefore, we cannot specify negative rotations directly, however, we can simulate negative rotations by taking a value that would correspond to a negative rotation and adding 360 to it. You may want to further limit your range of virtual degrees to plus or minus 20 or 30, simple because large numbers tend to make the animation look jumpy. Just to illustrate how to get usable mouse values, I have re-written the transformation script, which should now be on frame 3 with the addition of the keyframe to accommodate the initialization function. Here is the script:

```
//This Code links the rotation to the mouse position
x=int(_xmouse/25);
y=int(_ymouse/20)*-1;
if(x<0){
     x+=360;
}
if(y<0){
     y+=360;
}
//Transformation Generation
transYRot=transform.createYRotationMatrix(x);
transXRot=transform.createXRotationMatrix(y);

finalTrans=transform.ArrayMult(transYRot, transXRot);
```

Notice that I've gotten rid of the rotation around the z-axis, since that is hard to relate to mouse movement. The first two lines of the script capture the current mouse position and divide the coordinates by numbers that were selected based upon my movie size to get me close to 180 degrees of movement. Notice the use of the int function to strip away any decimals, which would not go well in our transformation functions. The y value was also inversed, because in Flash a positive y value is actually down, which is not really what we want in this case. We then convert any negative numbers to their positive equivalents by subtracting them from 360. Lastly, we simply plug the modified coordinates into the rotation functions. Depending on your system, this added code could be the proverbial last straw when it comes to performance, but hopefully your results will be acceptable.

Connecting the dots

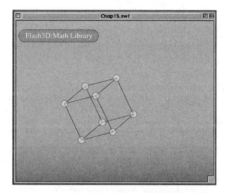

So far I have been purposely leaving out an important piece of functionality. We have had our 3D balls spinning around in the air for a while now, looking good, but not quite giving the illusion of a cube. What we really need to do is connect the dots. Unfortunately, Flash does not have any support for drawing lines dynamically; so we have to resort to some trickery. This will not make sense the first time through, but we are going to use a specially made movie clip to draw lines between our points. First, let's make the movie clip.

1. Create a new movie clip called line, and inside it draw a square of exactly 100 pixels. Use the rulers if you want, but make sure you use the Transform panel to check that the dimensions are exact. Align the square so that its upper left corner is in the exact center of the movie clip. Use the Align to stage option in the Align panel for precision. Select and delete the square's fill, and select the edges. Make the stroke color something dark, like black or dark blue.

2. Now, carefully draw a line from the upper left corner of the square to the lower right corner. Make this line red. Lastly, select all of the lines and make sure that each has their thickness set to hairline. When you are done, drag this movie clip into the effect movie clip and name it line.

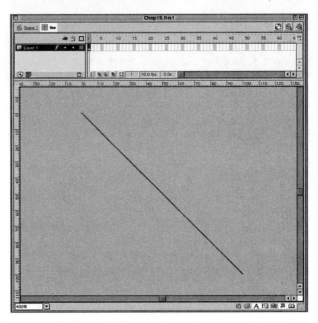

3.   Now that the movie clip is made, we need to write some code in frame 1 of the effect movie clip. Inside this script, we need to figure out how many lines we are going to need. Since we have a cube, we will need twelve lines to describe the edges of the shape. You may want to draw lines from one point to its diagonal as well, but that is up to you. For now, just as we did with the balls, we need to create an array to hold the lines, which we must then populate with copies of the line movie clip. This time we are going to use the original copy of the line movie clip, so right after we declare the array; we set the existing line as the first item.

```
lines=new Array();
lines[0]=line;
for (i=1; i<12; i++) {
    duplicateMovieClip (line, "line"+i, i);
    lines[i] = eval("line"+i);
}
```

The duplication script should look familiar. Notice that these lines will take up some of the space we left in the level structure below the balls.

4.   Now that we have our lines, we need to figure out how to use one to connect two points. We are going to write a function that will take in a line and two balls as input, and then stretch the line between the two points. The function starts by placing the upper left corner of the 100x100 line movie clip at the first point. It then uses the difference between the two points to scale the movie clip so that the lower right corner of the 100x100 clip is positioned at the second point. Now, since the hairline graphic in the line movie clip runs from the upper right to lower left, the net visual effect of all this is that the line appears to run from point one to point two. Here's the function:

```
function DrawLine(line, p1, p2){
    line._x = p1._x;
    line._y = p1._y;
    line._xscale = p2._x-p1._x;
    line._yscale = p2._y-p1._y;
    }
```

5. Before we can get lines to draw between the points, we need to establish a relationship between each line and a set of two points. We are going to do this by creating a function that draws the entire shape. This function, which we will call drawWireFrame, will simply call DrawLine twelve times, once for each line. As for which lines go with each point, I just use a pencil and paper to draw out the cube and the lines.

```
function drawWireFrame(){
    DrawLine(lines[0], balls[0], balls[4]);
    DrawLine(lines[1], balls[0], balls[1]);
    DrawLine(lines[2], balls[0], balls[3]);
    DrawLine(lines[3], balls[1], balls[2]);

    DrawLine(lines[4], balls[1], balls[5]);
    DrawLine(lines[5], balls[2], balls[6]);
    DrawLine(lines[6], balls[2], balls[3]);
    DrawLine(lines[7], balls[3], balls[7]);

    DrawLine(lines[8], balls[4], balls[5]);
    DrawLine(lines[9], balls[4], balls[7]);
    DrawLine(lines[10], balls[5], balls[6]);
    DrawLine(lines[11], balls[6], balls[7]);
}
```

Now that we have our drawing function, we can simply call it right after setPos in the second-to-last frame. Try viewing your movie. It's amazing how much realism a few simple lines can add. In fact, if you make the balls invisible altogether, the cube looks very realistic.

You can try different types of lines in your models. Sticking to hairlines is a good idea, because they are not affected by scale, but nothing restricts you to straight lines. As long as the beginning and end of the line are in the correct places, you can bend, split, and curve the line as much as you want, and you can get some nice effects this way.

By now you should have your cube spinning around nicely. We have one last optional feature to add before we move on to the next example, perspective. You may have noticed that it can be difficult to tell which way the cube is spinning. This is largely because we are not giving our eyes enough information about the depth of our cube to make visual sense of it. When objects get farther away from our eyes, they appear smaller. Likewise, points that are further away from us appear closer together than the same points when they are closer. This effect is called perspective, and we need to emulate it in order to make our cube look more realistic. If you remember, we already have created a function in our math library that creates a perspective matrix. We now need to modify our script so that we can apply a perspective effect.

Perspective transformations are slightly different than those we have touched upon previously. The main difference is that this transformation is destructive, meaning that we will be losing information about our points, specifically, the z values. If we look at the math behind the perspective matrix, we can see that the transformations are wiping out all of the z values, and creating a w value for the first time. This w value will be used to divide each point's x and y values, thus creating the perspective effect. The best way to think of a perspective transformation is that we are taking a 3D image and flattening it onto a 2D plane, which explains the loss of the z values. Unfortunately, once we apply a perspective transformation to a point, we can no longer use that point data in other transformations. Therefore, we will apply perspective transformations to a copy of our point data, after the points are set.

1. The first step in setting up our perspective effect is to copy the `ballcoord` array into an array called `perspectivePoint`. The following code placed in the first frame script after `ballcoord` is defined, accomplishes this simple procedure.

```
perspectivePoint=new Array();
for(i=0; i<num_balls; i++){
            perspectivePoint[i]=new Array();
            for(j=0; j<4; j++){
                    perspectivePoint[i][j]=ballcoord[i][j];
            }
}
```

2. We also need to edit our `setPos` function to use the new perspective data. Notice that our x and y values in `ballcoord` are now being divide by the w values in `perspectivePoint`.

```
function setPos(){
      for(i=0; i<num_balls; i++){

balls[i]._x=ballcoord[i][0]/perspectivePoint[i][3];

balls[i]._y=ballcoord[i][1]/perspectivePoint[i][3];
            }
}
```

3. Moving on to frame 2 of our Rotating Cube movie clip, we need to add one line to create a perspective matrix. This can be added anywhere among the other matrix initialization calls.

```
transPerspective=transform.createPerspectiveMatrix(250);
```

The value that you pass into the function describes the amount of perspective distortion applied. Values in the 100-300 range work well.

4. In frame 3 of our script, we take the result of our transformations, and multiply it by our perspective matrix, storing the result in a variable called `tempPerspective`.

```
tempPerspective=transform.ArrayMult( finalTrans,
    ➥transPerspective);
```

5. Finally, in the fourth frame of our script, we add one line to the loop that multiplies out all of our point data.

```
for(i=0; i<num_balls; i++){
ballcoord[i]=transform.PointMult(FinalTrans,ballcoord[i]);
perspectivePoint[i]=transform.PointMult(tempPerspective,
    ➥ballcoord[i]);
...
...
}
```

After these few simple changes, you should see a remarkable difference in the realism of your cube. You can experiment with more complicated shapes, although you will find that you'll always be trying to balance complexity and performance. Before you try to program any model, just get out a piece of paper and draw a quick sketch, being sure to label the points. The transformation library that we have built is very versatile, and you can use it again and again in your effects. We are now ready to move onto a more complex application of our 3D math functions.

Animated figure

To finish off our discussion of 3D in Flash, we are going to take a look at a more advanced 3D model, and how to manipulate it. Up until now, we have been animating one object, in one particular way at any given time. While this is a great way to try out our 3D code, it really does not take full advantage of it. In this example we are going to see how we can move different sets of points in different ways at the same time, by manipulating the transformation matrix for each point individually. While we could pick any type of shape to illustrate this functionality, it will be a little more interesting to look at a humanoid figure.

In this section we will see how we can represent a more complex object as an object, as well as how to use our matrix transformations to manipulate this object in 3D space. We will also take a peek at the type of code construct used to animate such a figure.

The figure model which we will be building, which I will be calling `stickMan` is much more complicated than our 3D cube. We therefore need more complexity in the data structure that we will be using to represent him. We will be creating three object types, the `stickMan` object itself, and the `point`, and `line` objects, of which he will be comprised.

1. Start by creating a new movie clip called CharAnimation Effect and placing it on the main stage. We will be working in this clip for this example. Let's start off by creating a point object.

If you recall a new object type is created by defining a constructor function for that object. In this case, we need to create a point object, so we will be creating a function called point. Open the CharAnimation Effect movie clip and rename the existing layer as Actions. We'll set up two variables, point_counter and points on the first frame of the layer:

```
//Point Definition
point_counter=0;
points=new Array();
```

As you may have guessed, points is an array that will hold every new point object that we create. No matter what type of object structure we create, it's always useful to have a list that we can iterate through should the need arise. The point_counter variable is just that; it is incremented every time a new point is created and more importantly, it is the index of the last point object in points.

2. With the variables initialized, we are ready to create our point object. point will take in our standard four-part point data: x, y, z, and, w. Once a point is made, the first thing it does is increment point_counter, which it then uses to set its own ID number, a number unique to each point. Then the point is inserted into the points array. Enter the following code after the last:

```
function point(x,y,z,w){
    point_counter++;
    this.id=point_counter;
    points[point_counter]=this;
    ...
```

3. Next, the point object stores the input parameters in like-named variables. These values will remain constant, and while they are probably not incredibly useful, they could come in handy if ever we need to reset a point to its original position. The real work will be done by the next two sets of points however, the tx, ty, and tz variable will store the current 3D positions of the point, and the dx and dy variables will store the current 2D position of the point, which, as we learned when talking about perspective, is not always the same thing.

```
    ...
    this.x=x;
    this.y=y;
    this.z=z;
    this.w=w;

    this.tx=x;
    this.ty=y;
    this.tz=z;

    this.dx=x;
    this.dy=y;
    ...
```

4. Each point will have a movie clip associated with it to act as the graphic representation of the point, when such an output is desired. Create a movie clip that has a 1 or 2 pixel point drawn inside it, name an instance of it pointMC, and place it in the CharAnimation Effect movie clip. This code duplicates that movie clip, and links it to the current point:

```
...
    duplicateMovieClip (pointMC, "point" + point_counter,
➥point_counter*100);
    this.graphic=eval("point" + point_counter);
...
```

5. Each point will also contain its own matrix, which will store the last matrix transformation applied to it, and this matrix will be used later to draw the point. To initialize a matrix, we set it to the identity matrix. Lastly, each point has a variable called delta, which is a Boolean variable that determines whether or not a point needs to be drawn. This is a work saving optimization to make sure that points that have not moved are not redrawn.

```
    ...
    this.temp=transform.createIdentityMatrix();
    this.delta=false;
    ...
```

6. To finish off the point object, we need to give it a few method functions. Once created, these functions will be available to every point we make. The drawPoint function sets the 2D position of each point's graphic movie clip using the 2D dx and dy values. The transform function takes a transformation matrix as input, and multiplies it by the stored matrix inside the point. This result matrix then replaces the point's own matrix.

```
    ...
    this.drawPoint=function () {
this.graphic._x=this.dx;
this.graphic._y=this.dy;}
    this.transform=function (matrix) {
            this.temp=transform.ArrayMult(this.temp,matrix);
    }

}
```

7. The line object is very similar to the point object, save instead of point information, the line object takes in two point objects to use to position a line movie clip. The line movie clip itself is exactly the same as the one used in the 3D cube example, so you can reuse that library item if you wish. Drag it into the CharAnimation Effect movie clip and name it lineMC.

Just as with the point object, we start off our line definition with an external array lines, and a counter, line_counter. As you can see, there are two parameters needed to make a new line, two points. This way, each line will know how to draw itself.

```
//Line Definition
line_counter=0;
lines=new Array();

function line(point1,point2){
    line_counter++;
    this.id=line_counter;
    lines[line_counter]=this;
    this.point1=point1;
    this.point2=point2;

...
```

8. The line object also makes a copy of a movie clip, in this case the lineMC we made earlier.

...

```
    duplicateMovieClip (lineMC, "line" + line_counter,
        ➥line_counter);
    this.line=eval("line" + line_counter);
...
```

9. line has a crucial method called drawLine. This function takes the two points that are associated with a particular line object and stretches the lineMC between them, as we saw in the 3D Cube example.

...

```
    this.drawLine=function () {
        this.line._x = this.point1.graphic._x;
        this.line._y = this.point1.graphic._y;
        this.line._xscale = this.point2.graphic._x-
            ➥this.point1.graphic._x;
        this.line._yscale = this.point2.graphic._y-
            ➥this.point1.graphic._y;
    }
}
```

Now that we have our two basic object types, it's time to define our main object, the stickMan object. This object actually has very little functionality in its variables, other than assembling a group of points and lines in order to draw a figure. It does however have some very important methods.

10. The stickMan object only stores one variable that is not a point or a line, and that is an overall transformation matrix, called trans, which is initialized to the identity matrix.

```
//stickMan Definition
function stickMan(){
this.trans=transform.createIdentityMatrix();
...
```

11. The rest of the data is a series of specific point and line declarations. These are grouped by body part, and are hard coded into the object. We can get away with this because we can always use transformations to affect our object if need be.

```
...
////BODY PARTS DEFINED
//hip
this.hip_right=new point(-10,-5,0,1);
this.hip_mid=new point(0,0,0,1);
this.hip_left=new point(10,-5,0,1);
this.hipLeft=new line(this.hip_mid, this.hip_right);
this.hipRight=new line(this.hip_mid, this.hip_left);
//shoulder
this.shoulder_right=new point(-10,48,0,1);
this.shoulder_mid=new point(0,50,0,1);
this.shoulder_left=new point(10,48,0,1);
this.shoulderLeft=new line(this.shoulder_mid,
    ➡this.shoulder_right);
this.shoulderRight=new line(this.shoulder_mid,
    ➡this.shoulder_left);
//l_arm
this.l_arm_1=new point(15,25,-10,1);
this.l_arm_2=new point(20,10,25,1);
this.LeftArmOne=new line(this.shoulder_left, this.l_arm_1);
this.LeftArmTwo=new line(this.l_arm_1, this.l_arm_2);
//r_arm
this.r_arm_1=new point(-15,25,-10,1);
this.r_arm_2=new point(-20,10,25,1);
this.RightArmOne=new line(this.shoulder_right, this.r_arm_1);
this.RightArmTwo=new line(this.r_arm_1, this.r_arm_2);
//l_leg
this.l_leg_1=new point(15,-40,10,1);
this.l_leg_2=new point(10,-100,10,1)
this.LeftLegOne=new line(this.hip_left, this.l_leg_1);
this.LeftLegTwo=new line(this.l_leg_1, this.l_leg_2);
//r_leg
this.r_leg_1=new point(-15,-40,10,1);
this.r_leg_2=new point(-10,-100,10,1);
this.RightLegOne=new line(this.hip_right, this.r_leg_1);
this.RightLegTwo=new line(this.r_leg_1, this.r_leg_2);
//head
```

```
this.l_head=new point(15,65,5,1);
this.r_head=new point(-15,65,5,1);
this.m_head=new point(0,80,-5,1);
this.neck_mid=new point(0,58,0,1);
this.HeadLeft=new line(this.l_head, this.m_head);
this.HeadRight=new line(this.r_head, this.m_head);
this.neck_midLeft=new line(this.l_head, this.neck_mid);
this.neck_midRight=new line(this.neck_mid, this.r_head);
//Body
this.BodyMain=new line(this.shoulder_mid, this.hip_mid);
this.Bodyneck_mid=new line(this.shoulder_mid, this.neck_mid);
...
```

There are a great many points involved, as you can see. In fact, there are really too many to animate very easily. Most 3D applications allow you to group sets of points into discrete parts to make them easier to animate.

We can do this by creating named arrays that will represent body parts, each of which will store the points that make up that body part. Most importantly, the first item in each array will be the point upon which that body part rotates. We will see why this is important in a minute. Here are the arrays that I am using:

```
...
// Animation Groups-Sets of points that can be moved as a unit

this.Head=[this.shoulder_mid,this.neck_mid,this.m_head,this.l_head
➡,this.r_head];
this.LeftArm=[this.shoulder_left,this.l_arm_1,this.l_arm_2];
this.RightArm=[this.shoulder_right,this.r_arm_1,this.r_arm_2];
this.LeftLeg=[this.hip_left,this.l_leg_1,this.l_leg_2];
this.RightLeg=[this.hip_right,this.r_leg_1,this.r_leg_2];
this.Body=[this.hip_mid];
this.Figure=[];
this.Figure=this.Figure.concat(this.Body,this.Head,this.LeftArm,
➡this.RightArm,this.LeftLeg,this.RightLeg);
this.LeftHand=[this.l_arm_1,this.l_arm_2];
this.RightHand=[this.r_arm_1, this.r_arm_2];
...
```

12. Now that we know what we will be animating, we can add the methods that make the stickMan object tick. The first is a function that moves the entire figure by adjusting the figures trans matrix. This function will be useful if we want to move or rotate the entire figure, and not individual parts. This function is almost identical to the transform function in the point object, save after this one multiplies the two matrices, it sets all the point's delta values to true.

```
...
this.transformFigure=function (matrix) {
    this.trans=transform.ArrayMult(this.trans,matrix);

    for(i in points){
  points[i].delta=true;}

}
...
```

13. The second function is designed to take in a matrix and a string, and to transform only the animation group specified by that string with the given matrix. This function will be used to do the real animating.

```
...
this.transform=function(group,matrix) {

    group=eval("this." + group);
    var dx=group[0].tx;
    var dy=group[0].ty;
    var dz=group[0].tz;
    var trans_out=transform.createTransMatrix(dx,dy,dz);
    var trans_in=transform.createTransMatrix(0-dx,0-dy,0-dz);

group[0].temp=transform.ArrayMult(trans_out,transform.ArrayMult
➥(matrix,trans_in));

    for(i in group){
            group[i].delta=true;
            group[i].temp=group[0].temp;

    }
}
...
```

Notice how the above function creates two translation matrices, one the opposite of the other. This is the same thing we did in the 3D cube example to ensure that we were rotating the cube about its center point, except that now we are using the first point in each array as the center point for that animation group, which is why the "joint" of each body part must be first in the array.

14. The last method of the stickMan object is the draw function. This function iterates through the points array, and if a particular point's delta is true, it multiplies the point's transformation matrix by the figure's matrix, and then uses the composite of those two matrices to transform the point. The point is then updated with this new information, and delta is set back to false. Now that each point is updated, each has its draw function called to update it graphic on the screen. As a last step in the function, every line in the lines array is drawn.

...

```
this.draw= function () {
    trace("Draw");
    for(i in points){
            if(points[i].delta==true){
            temp=transform.arrayMult(points[i].temp,this.trans);

tempPoint=[points[i].x,points[i].y,points[i].z,points[i].w];
            tempPoint=transform.pointMult(temp,tempPoint);

            points[i].tx=tempPoint[0];
            points[i].ty=tempPoint[1];
            points[i].tz=tempPoint[2];

            points[i].dx=points[i].tx;
            points[i].dy=points[i].ty;
            points[i].delta=false;
    }
points[i].drawPoint();
}

    for(i in lines){
            lines[i].drawLine();
    }

}
}
```

15. At this point, we have enough to start animating our figure. However, in order to make things a little easier, I wanted to create a function that will animate every body part in one call, but by different amounts. This function below accomplishes this by consolidating a call to the transform method of each body part. This function is purely a space saver, and introduces no new functionality.

```
function setFigure(model,Head, LeftArm, LeftHand, RightArm,
➥RightHand, LeftLeg,RightLeg, Body ,Figure){

if(Head!=0){model.transform("Head",Head)}
if(LeftArm!=0){model.transform("LeftArm",LeftArm)}
if(RightArm!=0){model.transform("RightArm",RightArm)}
if(LeftLeg!=0){model.transform("LeftLeg",LeftLeg)}

if(RightHand!=0){model.r_arm_2.transform(RightArm);}
if(LeftHand!=0){model.l_arm_2.transform(LeftArm);}

if(RightLeg!=0){model.transform("RightLeg",RightLeg)}
if(Body!=0){model.transform("Body",Body)}
if(Figure!=0){model.transform("Figure",Figure)}

model.draw();

}
```

That does it as far as the frame 1 script for this effect goes. We have done a great deal of work to set up this object, and hopefully learned a little about complex object design in the process. Now it's time to put our object in motion.

1. Move to the frame script for frame 2. We are going to set up a simple test animation to see if everything is working properly. We need to do a few things to to set up the animation in this frame. First, remember that before we can call functions from our 3D library we need to call init3D_func. Next, create a new stickman object called myGuy.

    ```
    transform.init3D_func();
    myGuy=new stickMan();
    ```

2. The way the figure was defined, it is actually upside down, thanks to Flash's unusual y-axis orientation. Therefore, the first thing we are going to do to myGuy is rotate him 180 degrees on the z-axis. After we create the appropriate matrix, w can use myGuy's transformFigure function to affect all of his points at the same time. Also by using this function, we only have to apply the matrix once.

    ```
    ZRotation=transform.createZRotationMatrix(180);
    myGuy.transformFigure(ZRotation);
    myGuy.draw();
    ```

3. Move on to frame 3. We are just going to spin the figure for now, to see if it is working. Therefore, we use code almost identical to the three lines above, except that this is a y-axis transformation, and it is going to be applied continuously.

    ```
    YRotation=transform.createYRotationMatrix(10);
    myGuy.transformFigure(YRotation);
    myGuy.draw();
    ```

4. On frame 4, write gotoAndPlay(3) to create a loop. Test your movie. Hopefully you will see a stick figure rotating in the middle of your screen. If some of the lines are not quite right, check the point declarations in the stickman object.

We did not do all this work however, just to spin the little guy. We could have done that by modifying our cube script to account for the new points and lines. So, let's create a simple animation that makes use of the figure's structure. We are going to make the character perform a rigorous set of jumping jacks, and we will do it within the confines of the frames we have set up.

1. The first step is to add the following few lines to the frame 2 script. These are just variables that need to be initialized before we start looping.

    ```
    test=true;
    degree=10;
    ```

2. In the frame 3 script, we have a bit of work to do. The challenge here, which is quite separate from any of our 3D considerations, is to create a cyclic degree variable, which will increment up to a certain value, and then decrement down to zero again. Most of this script does just that. This degree variable is then used to create matrices for the various body parts.

```
//JumpingJack Motion Script
step=20;

if((degree>45 && test )||(degree<=10 && !test )){
    if(test){
            test=0;
    }else{
            test=1
    }
trace(test)
}
degree1=degree;
degree2=360-degree;
degree3=degree*2;
degree4=360-(2*degree);

if(test){degree+=step;}else{degree-=step;}
```

Basically, the script starts off with test equal to one, and degree equal to ten. As the script progresses, degree is incremented or decremented by step, based on the value of test. To start out, it is being incremented. When degree is greater than 45 however, test gets set to zero, which causes degree to start to be decremented. This cycle continues indefinitely. Degree is split in each cycle into four related values, degree 1 to 4; degree2 is the opposite angle of degree1, as is degree4 of degree3. These values are used to build opposite rotation matrices below.

```
LeftLeg=transform.createZRotationMatrix(degree1);
RightLeg=transform.createZRotationMatrix(degree2);

LeftHand=transform.createZRotationMatrix(degree3);
RightHand=transform.createZRotationMatrix(degree4);

Jump=transform.createTransMatrix(0,0-(degree/10),0)
```

In order to make myGuy do a jumping jack, we are creating transformation matrices for each of the arms and legs, as well as a translation matrix called jump. The former will move the arms and legs, while the other will move the body up and down accordingly.

3. Finally, we use our setFigure function to apply these matrices to our figure. Notice that when we do not want to modify a certain part, we enter zero.

```
setFigure(myGuy, Jump, LeftHand, 0, RightHand, 0, LeftLeg,
➡RightLeg, Jump ,0);
```

If you test your movie, you should see myGuy doing his workout. This animation is about as simple as I could make it, while still transforming body parts separately, and it works well for cyclical motion. If however, you wanted myGuy to do something like walk halfway onto the stage and wave, you would be better off creating a keyframe in your timeline for every position, and letting Flash play them linearly.

nclusion

In this chapter we have looked at two ways to create the illusion of 3D within Flash. The first was to go ignore the math, and just go over the appearance of 3D. While this approach can lead to some very plausible results, it is difficult to develop a methodology in these effects, since every effect can require radically different tactics. The second approach we looked at tried to use true 3D calculations; the same basic math used in more advanced 3D applications. The benefits of this approach include versatility, and consistency. Unfortunately, we are pretty much limited to a wire frame engine, due to constraints in Flash's drawing abilities, and fairly small model sizes. Still, all limitations aside, it is amazing that we can take a multimedia tool and create a 3D engine, however restricted. Computers keep on getting faster, and Flash keeps on getting better, so perhaps we will be able to take this idea further sometime soon.

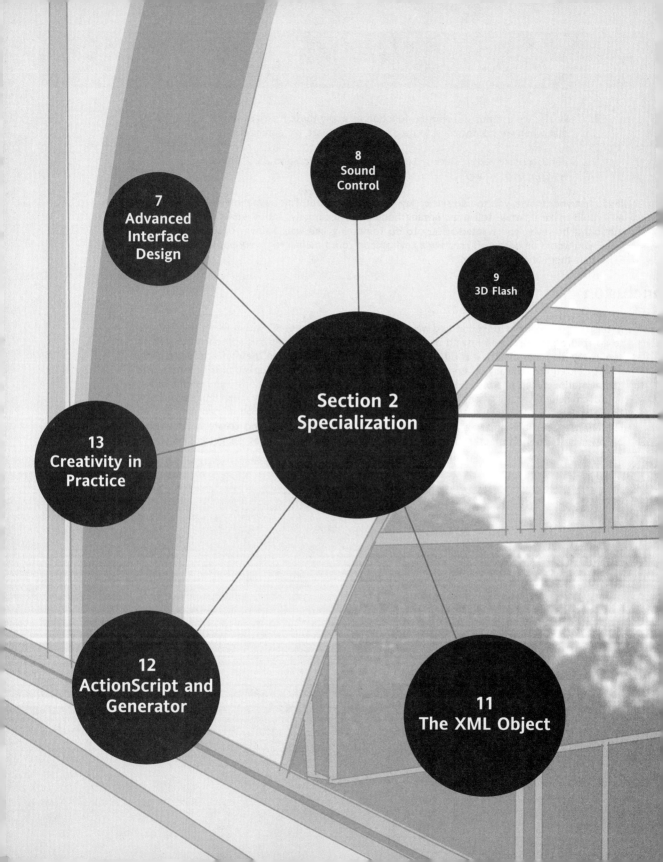

Chapter 10
Writing Flash
Games

Games are one of the best showcases for Flash scripting, and it is here that you will get to do a lot of scripting using all parts of ActionScript. In this chapter we'll be looking at game scripting, and we'll do this by examining a sample game. I've chosen to take a look at "Lunar Lander", which is hopefully a game that you are familiar with from the 80's. It started as a stand-up arcade game by Atari, but has been ported numerous other platforms, all the way down to some graphing calculators. We'll be continuing this venerable tradition by making it in Flash 5.

For those of you unfamiliar with the game, all it consists of is the player piloting a lunar landing module with the aim of making a controlled descent to land safely in the appropriate area. The player has only rotation and thrust controls at their disposal, with the trick being that if the module goes too fast, it will crash. Also, to throw in a bit more fun, the amount of fuel is finite, and the gravity effect varies between levels. As you'll see, since there aren't hundreds of things going on at once (we only have one ship, moving on a more or less static backdrop), the programming isn't too complicated, and even without lots of secondary elements to the game, I'm sure you'll find it fun, challenging, and highly addictive.

We'll start off by making the visual elements of the game, and then piece-by-piece we'll add functionality to the elements to make a working game. At several points along the way you'll be able to test your creation to see if you've got each piece working correctly, and once we've got a finished product, we'll talk about some enhancements you might want to try on your own.

During the course of the chapter, we'll cover some scripting elements that will be useful to you when developing many other types of games, and to make our ship move, we'll be looking at some basic physics and trigonometry. Those last couple of words may have made some of you wince, but having a basic understanding of those two topics will vastly increase your ability to make enjoyable arcade-style games. We'll also look at using the Key object to allow us to use multiple keys simultaneously, some minor collision detection, and otherwise setting properties using variables, functions, and conditionals.

etting up the file

Let's start the project by opening a new document in Flash. Go to the Movie Properties window where we'll want to set the frame rate, dimensions, and background color.

As a general rule, games are always more fun at a higher frame rate, in fact, thinking about it, everything in Flash is more fun at a higher frame rate. As a result, I've chosen to do this game at 30 frames per second (FPS), which is as high as I would go, given the performance of current computers. However, as with everything, there are some exceptions here, and a few warnings too, so take heed. Slower machines simply won't hit 30 FPS. Its not actually a big deal, the game may play a little more slowly, but as long as it's consistently playing slower, that's fine. Actually, the game we'll be making here should fare better than most, on account of it having very simple graphics and just one moving object.

Testing is always critical. If you or your client has a base processor speed in mind, check the prototypes of your game on a machine of that speed. By doing this, you will be able to see if the game is playing acceptably, and if not, make changes during the development process. If you don't have a testing environment, many of the Flash community sites have site check forums where you can post your work and get feedback from people (who hopefully have a machine of the same specification as your intended target machine).

The reason for wanting a higher frame rate is that it will make the game play more smoothly. Think of it as being like "connect the dots"; if we only had four dots to describe a circle it would be hard to guess what the shape is (in fact, it would look like a square). However, if we tried again, using 10 dots, the circular shape would be much more visible. The same holds true for a lot of arcade games. If the screen doesn't refresh very often, the movements will look jerky, and the overall effect of the game will be reduced.

Beyond its visual justification, a high frame rate also has other implications. Collision detection will become more accurate when we have an increased number of sampling points. For example, with too big a gap between frames, our module could travel further "into" an object between frames, and thus more of an overlap would occur between the colliding objects, resulting in a less plausible collision.

In the following illustration, we see a ship moving at a constant rate, on a collision course with the ground. To keep its apparent rate, a ship in a 15 FPS environment would have to travel twice as far per frame to reach the same point. Notice that with twice as many frames, the lunar module does not move down as far between frames, and how in the third frame of the top schematic, the ship is already embedded in the ground. For the higher frame rate example, the ship moved in smaller increments (more frequently) and detected the collision much closer to the actual surface.

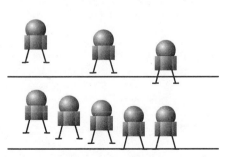

Because of this, keep in mind that the increments used in this project are based on animating at 30 FPS. If you choose to alter this value, you should also proportionally change all of the variables we use later in the file having to do with movement. For instance, from the example above, if you were to halve the frame rate, you would need to move the ship twice as far in each frame in order to move at the same overall rate.

The dimensions for this game should be 550 pixels wide and 400 pixels high. The dimensions for a game are completely arbitrary, but you should give some thought as to how the game should function, and of how the layout would accommodate this. Since the way this game works isn't hugely dependent of the dimensions of the screen, I just decided to stay with Flash's default movie size.

For the background color, since it's a game set in space, let's set it to black, well, near black anyway. Why? Well, in games with "black" backgrounds, generally, I set the background to be just a bit lighter than black, so that if I embed the movie on a black page, you can still see the edges of the screen. It also gives it a look closer to the old arcade games, whose "black" was not really all that dark. If you want to do this, you'll need to close the Movie Properties window, and go to the Mixer panel.

Once there, make a color that is just a little off black, and then select Add Swatch from the fly-out menu. Only colors that are listed in the color palette are available as background colors. To change the background color, just go back to Movie Properties and choose your new swatch from the color selector there. Keep in mind that if you're worried about staying in web safe colors, it's probably best to stay with black.

Now that we have a file all set, go ahead and save it. Next we'll start putting actual content in the file.

Visual elements

As a "Scripter" it pains me to say it, but the graphics you use for a game can end up being just as important (if not more so) than the actual coding. Most people just won't really give the time of day to a game that looks bad, and even a mediocre game can be helped dramatically by the skills of a good artist. This may sound a bit obvious, but it's the graphics that the player is staring at the whole time, not your code (no matter how lovely or elegant it may be!). This is definitely not to say that you have to go overboard on graphics, I'm still a fan of simplicity and clean design. In fact, too detailed a graphic can dramatically slow down a game. My point is that you should consider your graphics, whatever they may be, as an integral part of the game experience.

For Lunar Lander, we'll break this up into three sections:

- Assets for the ship
- Scenery
- Interface

I've kept the style pretty plain in my graphics for two reasons, the first being file size (the final game is 19K), and the second point being that this game is modeled after a game made in 1979 using only vectors, so keeping things to a minimum adds an air of authenticity to the project. I certainly have updated matters a bit though, by using gradients and transparency. I've kept the color palette down to grayscale, so as to be a little more faithful to what was available for games back then. Essentially, as with all stylistic decisions, do whatever you think looks good.

Remember, there doesn't need to be any artwork in your game that *has* to look exactly like the graphics in my version of the game (though for the sake of the speed of the game, you may want to stick with simple elements).

Building a Lunar Lander

It took NASA scientists many years to come up with the design for the Lunar Lander. You'll do it in a matter of minutes. If you can't even spare that much time to think about design, rest assured that you can always use the graphics in the FLA from the web site.

As you can see, the shape doesn't need to be very complex. The ship will be pretty small, so there isn't much point in adding a lot of detail. In the graphic above, the small ship on the right is the ship at its actual size on the stage. The one on the left is just a scaled-up version so you could get a better look at it. I made this just using the Oval, Rectangle, and Line tools. Do be sure that you draw it in the upright position, as this will be important when it becomes time to script.

Once you have your lunar module all set, select it and make it into a movie clip - the symbol name is unimportant, but be sure to give it an instance name of ship on the main stage.

Inside ship, we need to make the thrust effect (which if you remember was one of our player's two controls, the other controls being for rotation). It's eventually going to be controlled by scripting tied to the thrust controls; so let's make a shape on a new layer (beneath the current one) that looks like the full thrust. I should mention that the gradient of the thrust is based on transparency, not color change. If the ship passes in front of anything like a background, having a gradient that goes to black would not look good. You can change the alpha of a color in a gradient by selecting the Color tab under the gradient and then changing the Alpha value in the Mixer panel.

Make this shape into a movie clip with an instance name of thrust. Inside thrust we just need to make an animation of the thrust going from the "Off" position, to full-throttle. To do that, add a keyframe to frame 5, and then go back to frame 1. Resize the shape (or alter the gradient) until it looks invisible, and now you can simply add a shape tween between the two frames, which should give us the effect of a growing thrust. Below are the five frames of the thrust movie clip shown twice, once with the ship for reference, and the second by itself (the ship should not be inside the thrust movie clip).

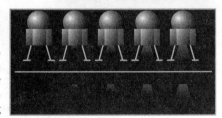

In frame 1 of the thrust movie clip, go ahead and add a stop action so that the movie waits until our scripts tell it what to do.

Congratulations! You are now the proud owner of a Lunar Lander. It's a shame you have to destroy it now...Our next step is to create the explosion that will occur if and when the ship crash-lands, hitting the ground badly. For this, we'll need to be in the ship movie clip again, not in thrust. Add a keyframe in frame 2 of the layer containing the ship. Then add a blank keyframe in frame 2 of the layer containing the thrust since it won't be needed when the ship is exploding. Feel free to handle the explosion however you like. I did mine by cutting the ship up into many irregular pieces then used a frame-by-frame animation to show them exploding out, and then I put a radial gradient behind it, tweening out.

Let's also add a `stop` action in frame 1 of this movie clip, as we wouldn't want the ship blowing-up prematurely. Also, add a label, crash, to frame 2, so that when the time comes to blow the ship up, we can just reference the frame label.

The last element of the ship is not actually in the `ship` movie clip. You see, when the ship explodes, it would be nice to have a screen-wide flash of light. This effect doesn't contribute anything to the functionality of the game, but it can enhance the perceived effect of the explosion quite dramatically, and it's also a pretty common effect that is good to know about.

To make the flash, let's go back to the main timeline, add a new layer called explosion flash, and then draw a rectangle bigger than the stage. The color should be white or light gray. Also make sure that it's an opaque color, since it's a very quick effect and we wouldn't want it chugging due to transparency. Select the rectangle and then make it into a movie clip, giving it an instance name of `flash`.

Go into `flash`, and drag the first frame over to frame four. Then add a keyframe at frame 6, and then finally blank keyframes in frames 5 and 7. This will cause two quick bursts of light. You may want to make the second burst slightly darker, so that it looks as though it's less intense than the first blast. Also add a `stop` action to frame one, as we've done with the other movie clips.

Your timeline should be looking something like this:

Feel free to adjust the actual frames later once we get the script that controls the explosion. You may want to adjust the timing of the light burst to coincide better with your explosion effect.

We're done with the ship now, so go back out to the main timeline so we can start on the scenery.

Building an environment

When the ship lands, part of the challenge of the game will be to land on a specific area of the ground marked-off as a landing pad. To make this environment, we'll need to create several elements. First is the land itself, then come the markers showing the edges of the landing area, followed by some sort of paved area for the pad itself. These are the elements of the environment that are essential to game functionality, but this would also be the stage at which we could add extra decorative elements, such as a backdrop or star effects.

Let's start with the land. For this version of the game, the ground is going to be uniformly flat, which will allow us to move the landing pad around easily (don't worry, we'll create the landing pad in just a minute). An easy way to do this is to draw a big, flat rectangle across the bottom of the stage, select it, and then make it into a movie clip, giving it an instance name of land.

We are going to be using land later, when we get to collision detection. Because of this, we are going to need an easy way to access the y coordinate of the top of the land. This can all be done very nicely by taking half the height of the movie clip, and adding it onto the position of the land movie clip, since new symbols are automatically centered on their registration marks. An easier way is to just go into land, and move it down until the top is right on the registration mark, this way we just need to look up the _y position of land when trying to find its edge.

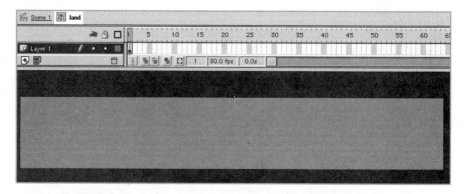

Back on the main timeline, we need to add the next element, which is the marker. The marker is just a small pylon, which will let you see the edges of the landing area more easily. Make whatever shape you want, and then convert it into a movie clip, with the instance name of leftMark. Copy and paste another copy of the marker onto the stage, and place it to the right of leftMark. Make the instance name of this rightMark. Feel free to add any effects you wish (perhaps a pulsing light?) to the Mark movie clips. Keep in mind though, that whatever you do to one is automatically updated in the other. The next screenshot illustrates how mine looks in the running movie and the large marker on the right is a scaled-up version (at 800% to be precise) so you can have a closer look.

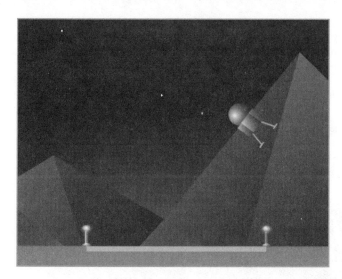

For now, before we add the scripting to position the markers, space them out more or less like the picture. The landing area will eventually be defined as the area between the markers, so placing them manually will allow us to have an initial landing area wide enough to test the ship with.

Next comes what is effectively the paving of the landing pad. This is just going to be a rectangle, dynamically fitted between the markers. I'd recommend against adding any detail or texture to the rectangle, as it will be distorted as it scales. Also, because of the scaling process, the width of the rectangle is irrelevant. Select your rectangle and make it into a movie clip with the instance name pad.

Much as we did with land, we need to position the rectangle inside the movie clip against the registration mark. This time though, the left side needs to touch the registration mark. This is so that we can position pad at the same point as leftMark, so we don't have to get into figuring out its position from the middle.

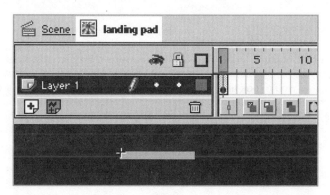

On the main timeline, feel free to add whatever background graphics you want. These will be purely decorative, though I should reiterate that being decorative is still pretty important. In my file I added some simple triangular mountains with a gradient glow behind them, although you could add anything from a bitmap all the way to an animated sequence.

Our main timeline, with our delightful mountain range, should look a little like this;

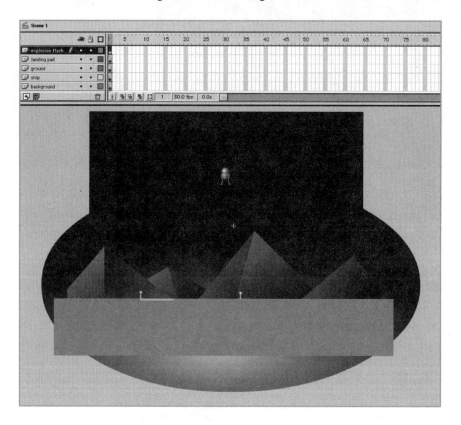

As you can see, there are a lot of rough edges, so while working on a file, I like to make a mat to block out the offstage area (but you could use a mask to do the same thing). This is just a big rectangular shape that is much larger than the screen with a hole in it the size of the stage. It serves a few purposes. First, it allows me to cover over the rough edges, so I can get an idea of what the final product would look like in Flash's testing player, and the other reason for using the mat is in case the SWF is viewed as a projector. You see, when you expand the window disproportionately, if there is no mat, it will expose the edges. The mat should be in its own layer at the very top, and don't worry about making it into a movie clip, although I would suggest locking the layer, so you don't accidentally move it.

To start us moving towards the actual scripting, we'll create the last major set of visual elements, the interface.

Building an interface

Depending upon the information, there are many different ways in which we can display information to the user, and we'll be covering several of them in this example game. Lunar Lander has a lot of information that we can report, and not all of it is absolutely necessary, so feel free to pick and choose amongst these if you want. We'll go through creating the visual elements for the:

- Main menu

- Level start screen

- Win level message

- Warnings (too much vertical, horizontal or rotational speed)

- Altitude

- Gravity amount

- Lives left

- Remaining fuel

- Ship's orientation

- Ship's motion vector

Main menu

The first interface element your user is ever going to see is the main menu. This is where you can link to the game itself, read instructions on how to play, and this is also a good spot for credits or for some more detailed, polished piece of art for your game. For me, I chose to stay with my simplicity theme, and do an opening screen reminiscent of an old arcade opening screen, blocky font and all. We just need to include the name of the game, a play button and some control instructions.

However, before we begin making the interface, we need to get the elements we've already built, out of the way. Lock the mat layer (if you haven't done so already) and grab all the keyframes on frame 1 of the timeline, and move them over several frames to frame 5. So now, if you go back to frame 1, you should have a clean stage to build your menu on.

To display the game instructions you can either make a link to another frame, or just state them on this screen, it's entirely up to you. Lunar Lander has three controls, left and right to rotate, and then a key to thrust, which for the sake of convenience, we'll use the respective cursor keys as controls. Since the controls aren't complicated, and the game objective is straightforward, there is really no need to write out in-depth directions.

To let the user play the game, we need to make a button shape and then actually convert it into a button symbol. If you choose to make your button consist of just text (as I did), make sure that you go into the button, and add a large shape over the text in the Hit frame. Adding such an overlay means that the user doesn't need to have their cursor directly on the letters to trigger the button. My menu looks like the following:

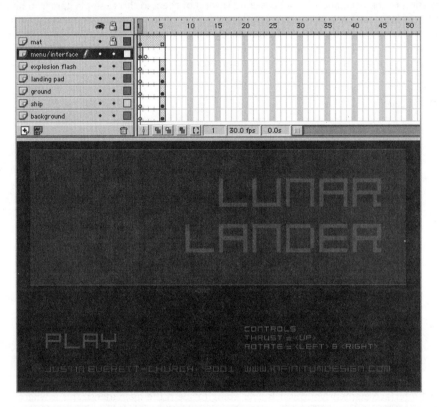

Be sure to add a blank keyframe in the frame that has your game assets in it, so the menu doesn't block them. Also, now that we have multiple frames in the timeline, let's add a stop action so that the player will stop on the menu when the file is opened. Since we already have a lot of layers to deal with, it's a good idea to create a dedicated actions layer, so that our actions are readily accessible. Go ahead, create this new layer, and add a stop action in frame 1.

Level

The next element of the interface is the "new level" screen. Instead of dumping our player directly into the game play, it's generally best to do a slight build-up/warning, if nothing more it will at least give the user a chance to move his hand from the mouse to the keyboard. While in this area, we can take the opportunity to display the level number, which would allow us to use this section for both the beginning of the game, and the buffer time between levels.

Let's create this screen in frame 5, where all of our game elements are. While we are displaying the level number, we don't want the ship to be there (since it will be controllable), so let's move the ship's keyframe to frame 10 for the moment. When the game is played, this delay will only be for a very brief amount of time, and we can adjust the timing later on if need be.

Go ahead and move the keyframes for the markers, the landing pad, and the flash over to frame 10 as well, so now at frame five we should only have the completely static items (the background and the land). On these layers insert some frames with F5 so that they extend to frame 10. Your timeline should look like this:

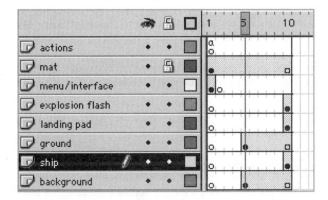

Frame 10 will be where the game is actually played. Add a stop action here as well, so that as we play through the level screen it will stop at the game area and not loop back to the menu.

Create a new layer and on frame 5, add a caption saying level, in the middle of the screen, and add a dynamic text field under it. Your text field should be for the variable, level, should be , and you should also click the button to embed only the number curves, since the level will always be a number.

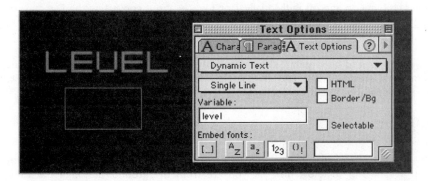

Finally, add a blank keyframe in frame 10, so that the level message doesn't show up during game play.

We are now ready to add the interface elements that provide the user with the essential information that they will need during the game. We'll be adding the following elements in a new layer, with a keyframe at frame 5. The interface will be present before the game begins so that the user becomes accustomed to it before the action begins.

Win message

Upon completing a level, it's a good idea to display a message before jumping to the next level screen, as this gives the player a moment to appreciate what they've achieved, and also won't leave them disoriented, as they would be with an immediate jump to the next level. So, in the layer with the level message in it, go to the blank keyframe at frame 10. We can add the win message here, making this layer a general message layer. Add a caption to the middle of the screen, saying something like "Excellent!", "Good Job!", or perhaps "Mission Complete", and then select it, and then make it into a movie clip. Give it the instance name win.

Go into win and move the keyframe at frame 1 to frame 2, this way, the message won't be visible by default. Also add a stop action to frame one to make sure it stays at the blank frame.

Warnings

While the game is being played, to our player these are the most important pieces of information. For example, an attempt to touchdown while one of the warning lights is on will result in the ship being destroyed and the loss of a player's life. As you can imagine, the landing of the ship must be controlled, and we could quantify this by stipulating that when making contact, the ship needs to be going very slowly, it mustn't be spinning, and it must also be oriented in an upright fashion. If any of these elements are out of whack, the player's ship could be at risk of crashing, and we need to display this information to the user.

So, to do this, begin by using the text tool to add the following as four different static text boxes: Dangers:, Vertical, Horizontal, Rotational. The reason for making them as different text boxes is that the last three will be made into separate movie clips. In this way, the scripting will be able to turn their visibility on and off individually. Don't worry about converting the Dangers: caption to a movie clip, as it won't ever need to be changed. If you want, you might want to add a divider line between the heading and the warnings.

Since we are going to be targeting these clips with scripting, they'll need instance names. I chose the names yDanger, xDanger and rDanger as these warnings will be associated with too much y, x, or rotational movement, respectively.

Altitude & gravity

Next, we will want to display a couple of pieces of dynamic text information. When trying to land the ship, it's helpful to know how far you are from the ground, although the value of this information will be most appreciated should our player use too much thrust, and go off the top of the screen. Normally, this sort of information is reported in meters or feet, but since this is Flash we'll be using pixels – but if anyone asks, just say you are doing a complicated analysis that is converting it to appropriately scaled feet.

To set up this interface element, create a static text box, with the caption: altitude:. Next to it, add a dynamic text box, much as we did with the level indicator (number curves embedded, not Selectable, Single Line and so on). The variable name for this won't be just a simple name as before. The ship is going to calculate the distance between itself and the ground as part of its normal collision detection operation, so there is no real point in reinventing the wheel.

With text boxes we can actually type in a path to a variable in another timeline; set the variable name to `ship.altitude`. This will automatically update the text field with the appropriate value, and if we are in the level screen, where the ship is purposefully absent, the field will simply display the last value that the variable had before the object disappeared.

Gravity is another useful piece of information that is best displayed by a text field. Like `altitude`, it will also be referencing a variable that exists inside `ship`. In addition to embedding the numeric curves, add the decimal point character, ".", in the field to the right of the embed font buttons. Gravity in this case will start out as a very small number, and will then increase. If you are at all confused about how the text field should be set up, the gravity field should look exactly like what's in the picture below.

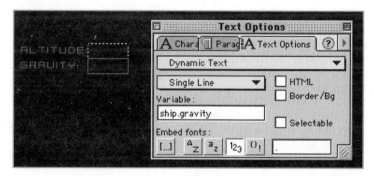

ives

As you play the game you'll find it difficult to get very far - not to mention frustrating - because, as it stands, one small mistake ends the game. Now, this is where our discretion comes into play. You see, to make the challenge of the game more palatable to our player, we'll give them a certain number of chances to successfully complete the landing. To do this, we need to create a movie clip that displays some sort of marker indicating the number of lives that our player has remaining. For now, create a marker, and make it into a movie clip. This clip should have the instance name `lives`. It's probably a good idea to add a text label below `lives` so the player knows what the marker means.

Go into `lives` so we can make the other markers, and then the progression of losing them one by one. Copy your marker, paste it back on the stage, and move it over a bit. Keep doing this for as many lives as you feel like giving the player. Being generous here is nice, but remember that if they lose, they'll also have to spend more time playing your game to get back to the same point, and that if the player can just keep trying the level until luck helps them land the ship, then a lot of the allure is taken away from the game. Think about it, if the player has fewer lives, they are more likely to play the game carefully, intrinsically making it a better game experience. Games that can be completed on account of luck, or by simply button-mashing your way through often lose their appeal prematurely.

So, you should now have one frame with several life icons in it. Add a keyframe in frame 2, and get rid of one of them on the end. Keep repeating the process until you have no more icons on the stage, and then add a `stop` action in frame 1 to keep the movie clip from cycling through its animation.

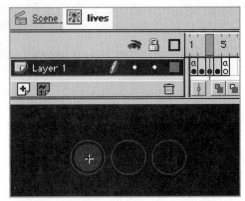

We now come to what is an age-old dilemma for arcade games. When you have one marker left, is that your last life? Or is it your last reserve life? Essentially, when the life indicator looks like the picture above, and you crash the ship, do you expect the game to end, or do you expect to get one more chance? I've always seen the life indicator as reserve lives, and not counting the ship I'm currently using. If you decide that is the way you want to go, add another blank keyframe at the end of your movie (so there should then be two frames with no markers). Otherwise, if you choose to be a little more miserly with the lives, don't add the frame. The reason for the extra frame will become clear when we add the scripting to end the game, but basically it's there so that if the game's in the extra frame, the player will get to play the level once with no markers showing, in other words, they get to play the "extra" life.

Fuel

That big thruster we built has to run on something you know, and since there is fuel, we need to make a fuel gauge. There are several ways of doing this. Fuel could be expressed as a finite number approaching 0, much like the altitude variable will, as a text-based percentage. However, it's a lot more visually interesting to implement it as a graphical indicator. Once again, we have options. The two most common ones would be a thermometer-style bar, that shrinks as the fuel stocks are depleted, and a gauge similar to what you would find in a car, with a needle pointing somewhere between "Full" and "Empty".

I decided to do something resembling a thermometer bar, but in a smaller space. The fuel gauge is a thermometer bar, behind a circular mask. As the fuel is used, the fill in the circle is lowered. To make the circle's fill lower, make a rectangle (preferably slightly transparent so it won't block the ship if it goes under the gauge), and add a line at the top in a contrasting color. Convert the rectangle and line into a movie clip. Then just set up a motion tween of the symbol moving down. After that, add a layer above the tween and draw a filled circle to act as the mask. Convert the layer to a mask, and we are then in business. I also chose to add the letter E at the end of the animation in a frame on a new layer to indicate that the fuel is empty.

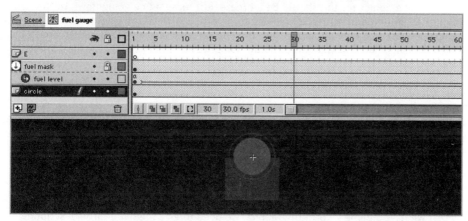

If you wanted to implement a needle-style gauge, the process is similar, but would involve a rotating needle instead of lowering a rectangle, and also wouldn't need the mask, since the needle should always be fully visible.

Orientation

I made an orientation gauge to show which direction the ship is pointing. This may seem pretty redundant since you can just look at the ship and see which way it's pointing. Well, it is and it isn't. If your ship is on the screen then everything is fine. However, imagine just how useful such an instrument would be, if you were to thrust your ship off the top of the screen. By working in conjunction with the altitude indicator and the motion vector (which we'll create next), it would be possible to control your ship completely by instruments alone (a possible twist to the game if you wanted, although you would have to be a pretty sadistic game developer to try that one!).

The graphics for the orientation gauge are pretty simple. Just draw an arrow, make it into a movie clip, and then add any decorative elements you want, perhaps a circle around it and a text label underneath it.

Motion vector

OK, this is the last interface element! This gauge will simply be a line indicating the direction in which the ship is moving (which is possibly different from the direction in which it is pointing), and will also infer the relative velocity by the length of the line.

Setting up the graphics for this should be a breeze. Just make a line going down to the right at a 45-degree angle (remember, if you hold down the SHIFT key while drawing the line, it will lock at the major angles). It is very important that the line be a hairline, since no matter how a hairline is scaled or manipulated, it will always be the same weight (whatever the smallest visible weight is), and you can set this property by using the Stroke panel.

The length of the line is unimportant for much the same reason the width of the landing pad was unimportant; we'll be using scripting to scale the line accordingly. However, to scale it, the instrument needs to be a movie clip. In the clip, the top-left point of the line needs to be aligned to the registration mark. This will allow us to have the line always pointing from the center. It might be a good idea to add a decorative circle, which will indicate maximum velocity.

Adding functionality through scripting

Now that we have a game's worth of graphics, we need to give them life through scripting. If you were to test your movie now, you'll see your menu but won't be able to get to the actual game area. So, let's start off by adding the scripts to the button in the menu, and then continue with the ship, and then finish up with the landing pad and interface scripting.

Before we start scripting, let's add one last organizational element. Now, because later on it may be useful later to shift frames around to change timing, let's add frame labels to the major events, so that when we do move the frames, we don't have to go back and change the code. In frame 1 (the menu), let's add a frame label to the actions layer called menu. Then in frame 5 (the level screen), add another called level. Finally, in frame 10 (the game play screen) add a frame label called game.

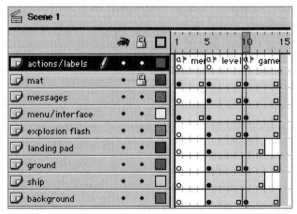

Scripting the menu

This section hardly deserves its own heading because it's so simple. We'll just be setting up an event handler on the play button, and then adding some simple commands. Add an `on(release)` handler to the play button. Inside this, we need to do two things: the first being to set the `level` variable to 1 (since it's a new game), and secondly, to actually start playing. Level is going to be a variable sitting on the main timeline. So, you won't need to specify a path to the variable when setting it.

```
on (release) {
    //the game should always start at level 1
    level = 1;
}
```

Then, to start the game, we will actually want to go to the `level` frame, and then play. By having set the `level` variable, the text field we set up earlier will now be populated. Keep in mind that when specifying a frame label that it is a string. If you don't use quotes, Flash will evaluate the word as a variable, and will then go to the frame based on that variable's value (not what you want to do!).

```
on (release) {
    //the game should always start at level 1
    level = 1;
    gotoAndPlay ("level");
}
```

That's pretty much it for the play button. If you wanted to add a continue button, the code would be the same except that you would omit the `level` assignment (that way, the game will continue at the same level). Remember, make sure that if someone clicks the continue button before they've ever played the game, the `level` variable will be undefined. To get around this, check to see if `level` has a value; if it doesn't, set the value to 1.

Scripting the ship

The ship is where everything is going to happen. We'll store most of the game's variables within this object, as well as defining many functions based on the activities of the ship. We'll start out with the planning stages, discussing what the ship will be doing and why, then breaking them up into logical groups. Following that, we'll set up the environment that the code will live in, set up the controls for the ship, and then tackle each major function. When were through, all that will be left is to list the functions as they need to be called, and at that point we'll be about 95% of the way to a finished game. By keeping most of the variables and work within the ship object, we are making our lives easier when it comes to modifying many aspects of the game, and it also makes for neat and easy-to-follow code.

Nailing down the game play details

At the beginning of this chapter we discussed very briefly how and what we'd like to happen during the game. Now it's time to make sure that we have the details straight, so that the code will make sense as we plan and implement it.

At the beginning of a level the ship will start out at the top center of the screen. It's going to start at a rotation of 0, in a good landing position, with zero velocity. From there, gravity will take over, and will start to pull the ship down. Our player will then have to use the thruster to slow and maneuver the ship, rotating it to provide the horizontal motion necessary to land on the landing pad, all using limited fuel (which once exhausted, will render the ship's controls useless).

The thrust will work according to the laws of physics, by adding speed to the current momentum of the ship. The strength of the thrust will be determined by the level number, just as the gravity will be. If the thrust strength were not increased steadily, the force of gravity would soon outstrip the power of the thruster, and it would not be possible to win a level.

The ship's rotation will work in much the same way as the thrust, though the rotational power will be constant throughout the game. Many users will have to get used to the fact that the rotation also has inertia (more closely simulating real life). The game is very difficult with the rotation modeled as perfect inertia, so to make it a more enjoyable game, the ship's rotational speed will be damped, and thus it will slowly stop spinning.

As the ship is moving around it will also be doing several other things. If the ship goes off the viewing area of the screen to the right or left, the ship will wrap to the other side, and the ship will also be checking its position relative to the ground to see if it needs to run the landing scripts.

When the time comes to touchdown, the ship must meet several requirements:

- Its motion must be within certain parameters

- Its rotation (if any) must be minimal

- The ship must be upright

- The ship must be within the designated landing markers

If even one of those conditions is not met, the ship will explode on impact, conversely, if everything is ok, the ship will stop, and we move on to the next level.

As I said earlier, Lunar Lander has three controls: thrust, clockwise rotation and counter-clockwise rotation. I've chosen to use the left and right arrow keys to rotate, and the up arrow key to apply thrust (although another fairly intuitive thrust key would be the space bar). How you choose the control mechanism is up to you, but there are a few things I would like to point out. The first and most obvious is that the player usually only has two hands, with ten fingers. If your controls require your user to draft their toes into service, you may want to re-think things a little. Essentially, try to keep it simple, think about what the user has to do. Control keys should be placed in ways that are intuitive and comfortable. If our player is uncomfortable, confused or has to move their hands a lot, something is wrong, and the end result is a less enjoyable gaming experience.

Now that we have a reference by which the general rules are set, we can begin determining just what sort of logical division to make in the ship's scripts.

Planning scripts

From the description above, there are several things our ship needs to be able to do:

- Accelerate

- Burn fuel

- Move

- Wrap

- Check speed/position

- Detect collisions

- Land safely

- Crash

All of these should be pretty straightforward, with the possible exception of the distinction between movement at a constant velocity, and acceleration (remember, acceleration only happens when the user uses the thrust key). We also need a maintenance movement script that keeps the ship moving regardless of what the user does. The items in this bulleted list work out to be our major functions:

- `accelerate()`

- `useFuel()`

- `move()`

- `wrap()`

- `dangerCheck()`

- `altitudeCheck()`

- `touchDown()`

- `crash()`

Functions can have several different purposes, the most common being their use in multi-purpose code. If you're trying to figure out whether or not you should use functions or not, a general rule would be that if you need several lines of code in more than one place, you should definitely be thinking about calling a function. For instance, `useFuel` will be called by all three of the control keys, and while we could just copy and paste the code from place to place, it's more efficient to write it once, and then reference the function as many times as we need.

In addition to that, functions make great organizational tools. Code is a lot more readable when you hit a line saying `accelerate()` than when the same thing is expressed as ten lines of code in the middle of a larger sea of code. Using a function, our code for acceleration is neatly contained inside a function sitting elsewhere, you can almost think of a function as a little black box that you press a button on, and it does its job. We don't need to care how it does it, as long as it works, and when we do our first pass at the code we can refer to these function names before we even define them.

In this way, we can break the project up into several smaller tasks, a process that is aptly referred to as **modularity**. Another key benefit of modular design is that by dividing the program into logical groups of actions, different functions can be assigned to different people thus enabling more than one person working on the same Flash program, thereby reducing development time. This way, when delegating tasks during a project, you could say, "make me a function that takes the following input, and by the time it's finished has done X to it", When the function is produced, it can simply be plugged into the larger program. Of course, a key point throughout this is that you have to decide what functions you need ahead of time.

Code set-up

Right, since we've done some dividing, it's now time to do some conquering. We need to decide where the code should live, and in this case, since it all has to do with the ship, it's best that we keep it there. In general, it's always a good idea to keep code near to what it is affecting. Just one example of the benefits of this would be that by storing the code for our ship, in the ship, there will be a lot less code to type since we will be able to call the ship's properties, using shorter paths, not to mention the benefits of having the code stored in such a logical manner.

In Flash 4, everything was done with looping movie clips, but I'm happy to say that this is a thing of the past. With Flash 5 came the `onClipEvent` event handler, so now we can attach code directly to an instance of a movie clip. The benefits of `onClipEvent` are enormous, but for this project it's enough that it gives us a good way to initialize functions and variables, while in the same place (although in a different `onClipEvent` statement), allowing us to write code that is executed constantly.

On the main timeline, select the ship and open the actions panel. In here, we need to add two `onClipEvent` statements, the first with the `load` event, which will only execute once when a movie clip appears in the movie (if it disappears then reappears, the code will run again). The second event will be `enterFrame`, which executes the code at the frame rate (even if the movie clip is stopped). The advantage to this style over a loop is that the code is in the **scope** of the movie, but more importantly, no matter what is going on inside the movie, this code just keeps running. The code should look something like this:

```
onClipEvent (load) {
}
onClipEvent (enterFrame) {
}
```

The load event will be used to initialize our functions and several variables. After that, the functions will be called from the enterFrame event, although before we build the functions, we need to set up the controls, as having the controls in place will facilitate testing as we tackle the functions.

Controls

In Flash 5 there are two ways of triggering code based upon the user pressing a specific key. The first is as an event on a button, but unfortunately there are a lot of limitations to this technique; perhaps the most noticeable being that you can only have one key triggering at any one time. Think of a button's trigger style as a word processor. When you hit two keys at once, it will sort them into an order, and then just repeat the latter key. Also as with word processors, there is a delay between the first keystroke and its repetition (set in the OS), and for the sensitive controls needed for this game, this method just isn't an option.

The way in which we can get multiple key inputs with no repetition delay is by using the Key object. Instead of using an event handler waiting for the key to be pressed, we will constantly be using the Key object to see whether or not the key in question is "down". So, instead of being an event in a handler, we'll be using the result from the Key object with the isDown method to denote a specific key as the condition of an if statement. Since this code needs to be checked through a condition, we need to have the condition running constantly. Let's add the following to the enterFrame statement:

```
onClipEvent (enterFrame) {
    // turn Counter-Clockwise
    if (Key.isDown(Key.LEFT)) {
    }
    // turn Clockwise
    if (Key.isDown(Key.RIGHT)) {
    }
    // thrust
    if (Key.isDown(Key.UP)) {
    }
}
```

The three if statements are for each of the different controls, the only difference between each one being the actual key that is referenced. The statements should be separate since we want to be able to call rotation and thrust simultaneously. If we set it up as a cascade of if and else statements, we could potentially block commands that should not be blocked.

Inside these statements, we need to add the code specific to the command. So, for the first two commands, that means dealing with the rotation. Even though we eventually want to rotate the ship, this command will only run when the key is down, and because of the rotational inertia that we are planning to add, we need the ship to keep rotating even after the key is released. To do this we can make a variable, which let's call rmove, which will describe how many degrees the ship needs to rotate in each frame.

When you decide how much you want to increase that variable by, keep in mind that it's a cumulative process, and that the amount needs to be pretty small so that if you hold the key down for several frames you won't completely spin out of control, I found a good speed to be 0.5. The difference between counter-clockwise and clockwise controls is just whether we subtract or add this amount onto the rmove:

```
onClipEvent (enterFrame) {
    // turn Counter-Clockwise
    if (Key.isDown(Key.LEFT)) {
        rmove -= .5;
    }
    // turn Clockwise
    if (Key.isDown(Key.RIGHT)) {
        rmove += .5;
    }
    // thrust
    if (Key.isDown(Key.UP)) {
    }
}
```

For thrust the idea is pretty similar, but the ship's movement will have an x and y component to it, which will require some math, so this is why we are going to be making the accelerate function. For now, we don't need to know what it does; we only need to trust that it will do its thing properly. Also, as you will hopefully recall, we built a thrust movie clip inside ship showing a smaller or larger thrust trail. Whenever we have the thrust key pressed we want the trail to get longer, and when it's not pressed, it should get shorter. Since the key checking code is going to execute on every frame, we can do this by adding a command telling thrust to go to the next frame. If you hold down the thrust key it will appear to play through its animation. When the key is not pressed it just needs to go to the previous frame. Since our condition is whether the key is down, to check if it's up, is simply the else case.

```
onClipEvent (enterFrame) {
    // turn Counter-Clockwise
    if (Key.isDown(Key.LEFT)) {
        rmove -= .5;
    }
    // turn Clockwise
    if (Key.isDown(Key.RIGHT)) {
        rmove += .5;
    }
    // thrust
    if (Key.isDown(Key.UP)) {
        accelerate();
        thrust.nextFrame();
    } else {
        thrust.prevFrame();
```

```
                }
            }
```

I should also mention here that I was careful when naming the `accelerate` function. An obvious name for it would be `thrust`, but since we have a movie clip named `thrust`, it would be very easy to run into problems. The same is true for variable names. Anything where you get to customize the name should be unique within that timeline amongst everything, not just objects/variables of the same type.

The last element to go inside these `if` statements is the `useFuel` function call. The ship being carried by inertia is not energy intensive, however, controlling the ship with thrusters for rotation or main thrust would be. When we make `useFuel`, we will make it have an input so that we can specify just how much fuel to use. Since it probably takes a lot less energy to nudge a ship into rotation than it does to get the whole object moving, let's specify a smaller amount of fuel consumption for the rotation.

Once again, we are going to call a function we haven't yet built, but don't worry, we have at least planned its general function. We'll worry about getting the function to act as advertised in just a little bit. The amount of fuel available is going to be specified in a variable soon, but since we have complete control over the number in that variable, let's say the thruster uses 2 fuel units, and rotation takes 1 fuel unit.

```
onClipEvent (enterFrame) {
    // turn Counter-Clockwise
    if (Key.isDown(Key.LEFT)) {
        rmove -= .5;
        useFuel(1);
    }
    // turn Clockwise
    if (Key.isDown(Key.RIGHT)) {
        rmove += .5;
        useFuel(1);
    }
    // thrust
    if (Key.isDown(Key.UP)) {
        accelerate();
        thrust.nextFrame();
        useFuel(2);
    } else {
        thrust.prevFrame();
    }
}
```

The controls are now ready, but there are times when we don't want them to be able to do anything. The reason for tracking fuel consumption is so that when we run out, we'll know to block the thrust and rotation controls. Also, when the ship has landed, whether crashed or not, the controls have to be blocked. We can't have the ship rotating while it's sitting on the ground; that would just be embarrassing.

To block the controls, we'll nest our `if` statements in a larger `if` statement checking against two variables. The variables are `empty` and `impact`. As you know, we haven't initialized either of these variables yet, but that's ok. We actually won't. `empty` is an indicator that the fuel is empty, and `impact` simply means that we've hit the ground. Neither of these should have a value until one of our functions sets them. Since they start off undefined, if we used them as the condition of an `if` statement, they would evaluate to `false`. Since we want the contents of the `if` statement to execute when these values are undefined, we just need to use the logical NOT operator (`!`) to change false (or `0`) to true (or `1`). Also, to check for two variables, we need to use the AND operator (`&&`). Your code should look something like the following:

```
onClipEvent (enterFrame) {
        // handle the control input only allow control if there is
fuel
        // and you haven't landed (or crashed)
        if (!empty && !impact) {
                // turn Counter-Clockwise
                if (Key.isDown(Key.LEFT)) {
                        rmove -= .5;
                        useFuel(1);
                }
                // turn Clockwise
                if (Key.isDown(Key.RIGHT)) {
                        rmove += .5;
                        useFuel(1);
                }
                // thrust
                if (Key.isDown(Key.UP)) {
                        accelerate();
                        thrust.nextFrame();
                        useFuel(2);
                } else {
                        thrust.prevFrame();
                }
        }
}
```

Central control

I'm giving this an impressive name, but as you'll see, its not very exciting code, although the fact that this isn't very exciting code though is a wonderful thing. Having decided to delegate the workings of the ship to functions, we just need a small block of code to call each of the functions in the right order. These are the sort of maintenance functions that keep the ship moving, and check for events such as collisions, amongst other things.

Having said that, much like the controls, there are times when we don't want these functions to run. Maintaining the ship's movement and the like is not tied to the fuel gauge; for instance, if your ship runs out of gas, that doesn't stop gravity, or make the ground any softer. Conversely, we do want the motion to stop once we've touched the ground, as otherwise any remnant of motion would keep the ship moving even though it's sitting on the ground. Not good. Once again we'll do this by negating impact.

```
onClipEvent (enterFrame) {
        // handle the control input only allow control if there is
        // fuel and you haven't landed (or crashed)
        if (!empty && !impact) {
                // turn Counter-Clockwise
                if (Key.isDown(Key.LEFT)) {
                        rmove -= .5;
                        useFuel(1);
                }
                // turn Clockwise
                if (Key.isDown(Key.RIGHT)) {
                        rmove += .5;
                        useFuel(1);
                }
                // thrust
                if (Key.isDown(Key.UP)) {
                        accelerate();
                        thrust.nextFrame();
                        useFuel(2);
                } else {
                        thrust.prevFrame();
                }
        }
        // this is central control. having broken the
        // tasks up into functions we can easily see what
        // is actually going on.
        if (!impact) {
                move();
                wrap();
                dangerCheck();
                altitudeCheck ();
        }
}
```

That's all there is for the onClipEvent (enterFrame). While playing the game frame (where the ship is present), all of this code will continually run. We now need to initialize the functions so that they can be called properly.

From now on, as we complete functions, you can test the movie to see how it adds to the functionality of the game. For now, don't worry about calling non-existent functions. It's something I don't recommend for a final product, but for testing, it will be fine. If you were to test now, the only reaction would be to see the thrust trail expand and contract as you press and release the thrust key. You are also setting the variables, but they just have no apparent effect yet.

Initialization

I'm finally starting to appreciate what my programming professors always taught. The best way to program is to organize meticulously, and *then* implement. It's very good advice, but it always seems to take longer to see the fun results doing it this way. This is essentially my way of saying that you've endured a lot of preparation (albeit worthwhile preparation!), and now it's time to see the game come together.

We'll go through each of the functions one by one, and also initialize any variables that the function may need. When we divided the main timeline into three different sections, you may have wondered why elements such as the ship are not in the level screen. The reason for this is that we are going to be initializing several variables that are specific to the level. When we load a new level and the movie is in a part of the timeline where the ship does not exist, its object is simply discarded. When we get back to the game frame, the ship reappears, but is freshly initialized.

All of this section will be taking place inside the onClipEvent (load). There will be quite a bit of code, so we'll tackle each function without seeing it in the context of the rest of the code until we've defined all the functions. For each function, just place the code under the previous one.

accelerate()

The first of our functions that we hit was accelerate. This function will run only when the thrust key is pressed, and will be used to determine how to divvy up the thrust's power between x movement and y movement based on which way the ship is pointing. For instance, in the ship's default position, pointing straight up, all of the thrust would be put into vertical (y) motion. At differing angles, the amount to x and the amount to y will change.

The distance of the thrust will be based on a variable that we need to set up. Let's call it power. The thrust always needs to allow the ship to overcome gravity, no matter how strong it is, because if it can't, there's no way to win the level. This means that we also now have to define the value of gravity, and then make thrust mathematically related to it.

In this case, gravity is simply the amount that is added to the y movement with every frame, and needs to be a very small. Why? Well, let's consider the situation where the user doesn't use the thrust. In such a case, the motion induced by gravity will grow quickly, rather like an avalanche, the instantaneous speed being the cumulative effect of gravity in all of the previous frames, which could then result in the ship moving quickly in no time. As you can imagine, this is highly dependent upon the amount added to the y movement with each passing frame, and hence the choice of a small value for this amount. However, part of the game is that the gravity needs to get stronger with each increasing level. So, this means that we need to make a gravity function that is a function of the level variable. Luckily, we have already defined this variable back in the play button on the main menu. Let's start gravity out with a base value of something like 0.05 pixels per frame and increment it by 0.01 for each level you've passed. To do that, gravity should be set to the value of 0.01 times the current level number, and then have 0.05 added on to it. level can be found up one level on the root.

```
//
// ***** ACCELERATION *****
gravity = .01*_parent.level + .05;
```

Now that we have gravity, we can figure out power. Having the power three times stronger than gravity will allow the ship to overcome its force pretty easily, while not being so powerful as to have an adverse affect upon the fine-control of the ship. It might seem counter-intuitive, but making the thrust stronger will actually make the game a fair bit harder.

```
//
// ***** ACCELERATION *****
gravity = .01*_parent.level + .05;
// acceleration rate
power = 3*gravity;
```

Any of the values we discuss in the initialization section can be altered to vary the game play. In fact, after we've completed the move function (coming up later on), why not experiment a little by changing these values, and seeing the effect upon the difficulty of the game?

Now that we have power, we can start to build the function definition itself. This function won't need to take any input, so the code should look like this:

```
//
// ***** ACCELERATION *****
gravity = .01*_parent.level + .05;
// acceleration rate
power = 3*gravity;
// given the direction your ship is moving, and the thrust power,
// it alters the xmove and ymove variables, altering your vector
function accelerate () {
}
```

In the function, we need to divide power between the x and y directions. The best way of doing this is with trigonometry, specifically the sine and cosine functions. Trigonometry enables us to use the known pieces of information about a right triangle to deduce the properties of any other side or angle of the triangle. In this case, our triangle is formed by power, rotated to the orientation of the ship with its two other sides being the x and y components.

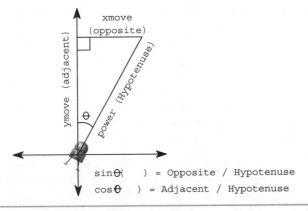

$$\sin\theta(\quad) = \text{Opposite} / \text{Hypotenuse}$$
$$\cos\theta(\quad) = \text{Adjacent} / \text{Hypotenuse}$$

Since we know the angle at which the ship is pointing, and we know the hypotenuse's length (power), we have enough information to find the length of the other two sides. These other two sides are the x and y components that make up power.

The **sine** of an angle (pronounced "sign", and you may also see it written as "sin") is just a ratio of two sides of the triangle (the **opposite** side and the **hypotenuse**). If you are asking yourself "the *opposite* of what exactly?", "opposite" refers to the side of the triangle that is opposite the angle describing the rotation of the ship.

So, great, we have a ratio, what now? Well, the reason this ratio is valuable to us because we already know the length of the hypotenuse, and we want to find out what the length of the opposite side is, in other words, xmove. To find this value, trigonometry dictates that we can just multiply the value of the hypotenuse (power) by the ratio, which cancels out the value of the hypotenuse in the ratio, leaving us with just the length of the side.

It's pretty much the same with **cos** (pronounced "co-sign", as "cos" is actually an abbreviation for "cosine"). The only difference here is that the ratio relates the adjacent side and the hypotenuse to the angle. You'll notice that the angle is contained between two lines, one is the **hypotenuse**, and the other is referred to as the **adjacent side**. This side is also rather conveniently the other side that we need to figure out (ymove), so much as we did with the sin function, we simply cancel out the value of hypotenuse and are left with the length of the side we need.

However, before we program this, there are two things we need to keep in mind. As you can see in the previous diagram, since power is going to be a positive number, when it is broken apart, the y component needs to be multiplied by -1, since "up" in Flash goes towards negative infinity. The second issue is that Flash deals with degrees, while trigonometry is based on a different measurement system for angles, called **radians**. To use the sin and cos, we will need to do a conversion to radians.

There are 360 degrees in a full circle, and there are 2 pi radians in a circle. Knowing this, we can move out of degrees by expressing an angle as a ratio of a circle (angle / 360); for instance, 90 degrees is 0.25 of a circle. Since we know how many radians go into a circle, we can multiply the ratio by that value, and what we are left with is an angle expressed in radians. When writing the code, to access the value of pi we can use the Math object, Math.PI.

```
//
// ***** ACCELERATION *****
gravity = .01*_parent.level + .05;
// acceleration rate
power = 3*gravity;
// given the direction your ship is moving, and the thrust power,
// it alters the xmove and ymove variables thus altering your
//vector
function accelerate () {
    // convert ship's rotation (in degrees) to radians
    angle = (_rotation/360)*2*Math.PI;
}
```

Now that we have an angle expressed in terms of radians stored in a variable, we can move on, and do the trigonometry. The actual theory behind trigonometry is much harder to get to grips with than the actual application. sin and cos are both methods of the Math object, in which we need only specify the angle. So, we're now all the way back to the situation we had with the rotational controls. This function only gets called when the thrust is on, but the ship, with its inertia, should keep going all the time. The solution here is going to be the same, that is: add the amount to a move variable, and then rely on the move function to do something with the value.

```
//
// ***** ACCELERATION *****
gravity = .01*_parent.level + .05;
// acceleration rate
power = 3*gravity;
// given the direction your ship is moving, and the thrust power,
// it alters the xmove and ymove variables thus altering your
//vector
function accelerate () {
        // convert ship's rotation (in degrees) to radians
        angle = (_rotation/360)*2*Math.PI;
        // then alter the movement variables
        xmove += power*Math.sin(angle);
        ymove += -power*Math.cos(angle);
}
```

useFuel()

This function is our fuel accounting system. As fuel is used in piloting the ship, it adds the amount used to a variable. If the amount of fuel used reaches the fuel maximum, it will set the empty variable we referenced in the controls section to 1, and will block the player from commanding the ship. This function will also control the appearance of the fuel gauge that we created earlier.

In order to compare the fuel used to a fuel maximum, we first need to decide what that amount is, I rather arbitrarily chose the value 1000, but it can be any constant you want, or it can be level dependant, like the gravity variable. However, by keeping this value constant, we implicitly increase the difficulty of the game. You see, as the gravity increases with each level, it takes more and more thrust/fuel to keep the ship from plummeting to the planet's surface. Let's set the maximum as the variable fuelMax outside of the function.

```
//
// ***** FUEL CONSUMPTION *****
// fuel variable: a common level technique
// is to reduce the fuel each level.
// I chose a constant since higher levels
// require a lot more thrust to counter increased gravity.
fuelMax = 1000;
```

Now we need to actually define the function, and unlike the last function, we will want to specify a parameter here. Since we need to specify the amount of fuel used, let's call it amount. We can then increment a variable like fuelUsed by the value of amount. When the ship initializes, fuelUsed is undefined, so evaluates to 0, giving a good starting point.

```
//
// ***** FUEL CONSUMPTION *****
// fuel variable: a common level technique
// is to reduce the fuel each level.
// I chose a constant since higher levels
// require a lot more thrust to counter increased gravity.
fuelMax = 1000;
// This function does the accounting on your fuel reserves
function useFuel (amount) {
    fuelUsed += amount;
}
```

If `fuelUsed` is greater than or equal to `fuelMax`, then it's time to cut off the controls. In addition though, we also need to return the `thrust` movie clip back to frame one, and once we've set `empty` to 1, the script will not even get to the `if` statement that backs the `thrust` animation up.

```
//
// ***** FUEL CONSUMPTION *****
// fuel variable: a common level technique
// is to reduce the fuel each level.
// I chose a constant since higher levels
// require a lot more thrust to counter increased gravity.
fuelMax = 1000;
// This function does the accounting on your fuel reserves
function useFuel (amount) {
    fuelUsed += amount;
    if (fuelUsed>=fuelmax) {
        empty = 1;
        thrust.gotoAndStop(1);
    }
}
```

If you are wondering why I suggest maintaining two variables to deal with fuel instead of just subtracting from the `fuelMax` variable, it's because we will need both values to determine what to do with the fuel gauge. Since the gauge is a long tween, we need to express the fuel state as a ratio of how much we've used, to how much there is in total, and we can arrange this by employing a variable, which we'll call `fuelRatio`. After that, we have to send the gauge to the appropriate frame by multiplying our `fuelRatio` variable by the total number of frames in the tween. But what happens when we haven't used the fuel that will make the ratio equal to 0? Since there is no frame 0 we have to adjust to take this into account. To do this, subtract 1 from the total number of frames, multiply this by the ratio, and then add 1 back in. We will then need to round this amount to the nearest integer value to ensure that we end up with an integer value for the frame number, since for example, there is also no frame 1.245.

```
//
// ***** FUEL CONSUMPTION *****
// fuel variable: a common level technique
// is to reduce the fuel each level.
// I chose a constant since higher levels
// require a lot more thrust to counter increased gravity.
```

```
fuelMax = 1000;
// This function does the accounting on your fuel reserves
function useFuel (amount) {
     fuelUsed += amount;
     if (fuelUsed>=fuelmax) {
           empty = 1;
           thrust.gotoAndStop(1);
     }
     fuelRatio = fuelUsed/fuelMax;
     _parent.fuelGauge.gotoAndStop(Math.round(fuelRatio *
  ➥(_root.fuelGauge._totalFrames-1))+1);
}
```

move()

After we complete this function, you'll have a Flash movie that you can actually test with a moving ship and everything. This function is going to both move the ship, and rotate it, based upon the values of the three move variables that we've already set. This function is called by the central control, and will be run constantly as long as the ship hasn't landed or crashed. Instead of just moving the ship, we are also going to check the current move values against a terminal linear and rotational velocity, as it's a pretty common oversight in many Flash games to fail to implement a limit on how fast something can move.

So for example, in the case of rotation, if I didn't set a maximum rotation rate, it could get to the point where the ship is rotating at 360 degrees per frame, giving the appearance of being still, but resulting in a crash upon landing in such a state.

The effect is even more extreme for movement. If there were no terminal velocity, it would be possible to end up moving hundreds of pixels per frame. With such a wide gap, it would be easy for the ship to completely miss a collision with the land, and just continue on its merry way down.

So, now that we've talked about what the extreme cases can be, let's set some reasonable maximums. For velocity, I like it at about 15 pixels per frame. 15 pixels is still quite a bit to move in one frame when you consider that the movie is running at 30 frames per second, and as for rotation, I personally like the rotation to stay below 10 degrees per frame.

The last variable we need to initialize is the friction for the rotation. I think having inertia on the ship makes for a more fun game, and a greater challenge. Several of the people I tested this game on didn't quite see it the same way. So, as is the nature of things, I compromised. The ship's rotation has inertia, but if you don't do anything, the rotation will settle out to a stop on its own. The amount of inertia you carry from frame to frame is up to you, and is determined by a variable we'll call rotationalFriction. This variable dictates how much of the inertia is kept between frames. The rest is lost to some (rather unnatural) friction. 1 means no degradation, 0 means no inertia - anything outside that range would send the ship spinning out of control. I chose a value of 0.95, as it seemed to be a good value to be challenging but not impossible.

```
//
// ***** MOVEMENT *****
maxVelocity = 15;
maxRotation = 10;
rotationalFriction = .95;
```

Now we can define the function, and start it off by adding the effect of gravity to the `ymove` variable. In this game, gravity pulls straight down, so it doesn't need to affect the `xmove` at all.

```
//
// ***** MOVEMENT *****
maxVelocity = 15;
maxRotation = 10;
rotationalFriction = .95;
// this applies gravity and rotational friction to
// the ship's vector then actually moves the ship
function move () {
    // apply gravity to the vertical movement
    ymove += gravity;
}
```

In `accelerate`, we spent our time taking a partial thrust vector and breaking it apart. Here we are going to be doing more or less the reverse, by taking the `xmove` and `ymove` values and reconstructing a single vector. We need to do this to make a single value to check against `maxVelocity`. However, to do this, we won't be using trigonometry, but will instead use some basic geometry.

From school, you'll probably remember something called Pythagoras' theorem, which relates the two shortest sides of a right triangle (so that's the opposite and adjacent sides) to the longest side, the hypotenuse. The theory states that the square of the hypotenuse equals the sum of the squares of the other two sides. Solving for the hypotenuse, we see that it equals the square root of the sum of the squares of the other two sides. So what has that got to do with what we're doing here? Well, look at it this way, if we apply the theorem to our project, we see that if we multiply `xmove` by itself, and then multiply `ymove` by itself, then add these two results together and take the square root, we end up with the length of the composite movement value.

```
//
// ***** MOVEMENT *****
maxVelocity = 15;
maxRotation = 10;
rotationalFriction = .95;
// this applies gravity and rotational friction to
// the ship's vector then actually moves the ship
function move () {
    // apply gravity to the vertical movement
    ymove += gravity;
    // check against maxVelocity
    hypotenuse = Math.sqrt((xmove*xmove)+(ymove*ymove));
}
```

We then just need to compare `hypotenuse` against `maxVelocity`. If `hypotenuse` is less than or equal to `maxVelocity`, nothing needs to happen since the speed is under this speed limit. On the other hand, if `hypotenuse` is larger than `maxVelocity`, then we have a really big hypotenuse, which also means a really big triangle. If we shrink the hypotenuse down to the size we need it to be (within the speed limit) then the right triangle formed from that triangle will have the lengths that we need. What we need to do is alter the `move` variables to bring `hypotenuse` back within the speed limit.

If we are just scaling a triangle, and are not messing with the angles, the sides will always remain in proportion. Knowing that, if we find out how much we had to shrink down the hypotenuse to make it equal the speed limit, we should also be able to deduce how much to shrink the other sides (the `move` variables).

To do this scaling, we need to set up a ratio of the `maxVelocity` to the `hypotenuse` value. This ratio is the proportion that we can use on the `move` variables to scale them down to the right size, an operation undertaken by simply multiplying each `move` variable by the ratio.

```
//
// ***** MOVEMENT *****
maxVelocity = 15;
maxRotation = 10;
rotationalFriction = .95;
// this applies gravity and rotational friction to
// the ship's vector then actually moves the ship
function move () {
    // apply gravity to the vertical movement
    ymove += gravity;
    // check against maxVelocity
    hypotenuse = Math.sqrt((xmove*xmove)+(ymove*ymove));
    if (hypotenuse>maxVelocity) {
        xmove *= maxVelocity/hypotenuse;
        ymove *= maxVelocity/hypotenuse;
    }
}
```

In the next step we're actually going to move the ship! Take the `move` variables and add them on to the current `_x` and `_y` values of the ship.

```
//
// ***** MOVEMENT *****
maxVelocity = 15;
maxRotation = 10;
rotationalFriction = .95;
// this applies gravity and rotational friction to
// the ship's vector then actually moves the ship
function move () {
    // apply gravity to the vertical movement
    ymove += gravity;
    // check against maxVelocity
```

```
        hypotenuse = Math.sqrt((xmove*xmove)+(ymove*ymove));
        if (hypotenuse>maxVelocity) {
                xmove *= maxVelocity/hypotenuse;
                ymove *= maxVelocity/hypotenuse;
        }
        // move the ship
        _x += xmove;
        _y += ymove;
    }
```

Just as setting the rotation variable, rmove, was easier than setting the xmove and ymove variables, checking it against its maximum will also be relatively easy. rmove can either be negative or positive; depending upon which direction the ship is going. Because of that, we need to check rmove against maxRotation to check for clockwise motion that is too fast, and similarly against negative maxRotation to check for counter-clockwise motion that is too fast. If the amount exceeds the limit, it then needs to be set to either positive or negative maxRotation.

```
        //
        // ***** MOVEMENT *****
        maxVelocity = 15;
        maxRotation = 10;
        rotationalFriction = .95;
        // this applies gravity and rotational friction to
        // the ship's vector then actually moves the ship
        function move () {
            // apply gravity to the vertical movement
            ymove += gravity;
            // check against maxVelocity
            hypotenuse = Math.sqrt((xmove*xmove)+(ymove*ymove));
            if (hypotenuse>maxVelocity) {
                    xmove *= maxVelocity/hypotenuse;
                    ymove *= maxVelocity/hypotenuse;
            }
            // move the ship
            _x += xmove;
            _y += ymove;
            // check against maxRotation
            if (rmove>maxRotation) {
                    rmove = maxRotation;
            } else if (rmove<-maxRotation) {
                    rmove = -maxRotation;
            }
        }
```

All that's left is to apply rmove and then degrade its value by multiplying it by rotationalFriction.

```
//
// ***** MOVEMENT *****
maxVelocity = 15;
maxRotation = 10;
rotationalFriction = .95;
// this applies gravity and rotational friction to
// the ship's vector then actually moves the ship
function move () {
      // apply gravity to the vertical movement
      ymove += gravity;
      // check against maxVelocity
      hypotenuse = Math.sqrt((xmove*xmove)+(ymove*ymove));
      if (hypotenuse>maxVelocity) {
            xmove *= maxVelocity/hypotenuse;
            ymove *= maxVelocity/hypotenuse;
      }
      // move the ship
      _x += xmove;
      _y += ymove;
      // check against maxRotation
      if (rmove>maxRotation) {
            rmove = maxRotation;
      } else if (rmove<-maxRotation) {
            rmove = -maxRotation;
      }
      // rotate the ship
      this._rotation += rmove;
      // degrade the rotational inertia
      rmove *= rotationalFriction;
}
```

If you test here, you'll find that you can now actually play with your ship, but be warned: keep it on the screen, since it won't detect the ground, nor will it do anything at the screen's edge.

wrap()

When the ship goes off the side of the screen, we need to move it to the other side of the screen so that it just doesn't get lost in the hinterlands of offstage. This function actually won't require us to define any variables ahead of time, in fact, all it's going to require is the width of the screen. Since that's not something that changes often at this point in a game's development process, I feel pretty comfortable hard coding the value into our code. If you feel otherwise, feel free to make a variable ahead of time, and simply reference it instead of the static value that I'm using.

To determine whether or not to wrap, we need to ask two questions:

- Is the ship completely off screen? – Is its center point off the screen by at least half of its width?

- Is the x motion for the ship still carrying it off screen?

The reason for checking the second element is because once we wrap the ship to the other side of the screen, it is going to be placed just off screen, with the caveat that it will be heading on to the screen now. So, if we didn't check that second part, we could potentially set up a loop, which would result in the ship constantly bouncing from edge to edge.

To check for the left edge, we just need to see if the ship's position is less than half of its width, since the boundary itself is 0. If it is, then we set the ship's _x property to the width of the movie (550) plus half the ship's width causing it to be just barely off screen. To check the horizontal movement, we just check to see if xmove is negative (moving to the left).

Let's make the width of the screen a variable so that if you should need to change the dimensions of the movie later, you only need to change this one variable.

```
//
// ***** WRAPPING *****
// if the ship has flown off the side of the screen,
// wrap it to the other side.
screenWidth = 550
function wrap () {
    if (_x<(-_width*.5) && xmove<0) {
        // if past left boundary, wrap to the right
        _x = screenWidth+_width*.5;
    }
}
```

The process is pretty much the same for checking the other boundary, more or less just swapping the condition's coordinate with the one for the wrapped location then checking to see if xmove is positive.

```
//
// ***** WRAPPING *****
// if the ship has flown off the side of the screen,
// wrap it to the other side.
screenWidth = 550
function wrap () {
    if (_x<(-_width*.5) && xmove<0) {
        // if past left boundary, wrap to the right
        _x = screenWidth+_width*.5;
    } else if (_x>(screenWidth+_width*.5) && xmove>0) {
        // if past right boundary, wrap to the left
        _x = -_width*.5;
    }
}
```

Try testing again here. You should be able to do laps across the screen by pointing sideways.

dangerCheck()

Now that we have the ship moving around, it's time to start thinking about landing. To land though, we need to know if our current motion/rotation is within tolerance. If not, we are going to need to display warnings specifying what flight characteristics to correct. Let's start by setting the motion limits for a safe landing. There are four limits we need to set: horizontal motion (shear), vertical motion, angular momentum and the ship's orientation. Here are the values I chose:

```
//
// ***** DANGER CHECK *****
// safety parameters: these may be adjusted to your
// preference or made level-dependant variables.
ysafety = 1.5;
xsafety = .6;
spinsafety = 1;
anglesafety = 8;
// this checks to see if the ship would be able to land
// safely given its current velocity and rotation
function dangerCheck () {
}
```

I came by these values by tracing the values of each of the movement variables in question, and just recording that which I thought best represented the maximum safe speed for each. In other words, they are pretty arbitrary. If you'd like to try this yourself, add a line such as trace(ymove) in the function. This will display the value of ymove in the output window whenever the function is called. If you can get the ship moving at a speed that you think seems to be the maximum safe vertical speed, remember the number and plug it in as the value of the appropriate safety variable. You can then repeat that process for the other movement variables.

As a result of having people test this game, I've had a reasonable amount of feedback suggesting that the values I chose are stingy, but then again, if the game isn't a challenge it will get boring fast. It's up to you, use what feels right to you.

xsafety and ysafety are expressed as pixels per frame. spinsafety is in degrees per frame, and anglesafety is the number of degrees, in either direction, that the ship can be pointing at, relative to the 0 degree, vertical origin line.

Inside the function, we'll start by setting up an error counter. This variable will be incremented each time one of the safety limits is exceeded. Setting this variable does not do anything in the function, but will be used later when we detect the collision with the ground. If errors equals 0 we're safe, otherwise the ship will have a rather dire fate. This variable has to initialize to 0 every time the function runs so that errors is constantly re-evaluated (if it were cumulative we couldn't get back to 0).

After that, we then go through each of the limits and check them against the properties of the ship. Since the ship's movement variables can be either positive or negative depending on the direction the ship is moving, we need to simplify the information so we just have to do one check.

By taking the absolute value of the property using `Math.abs`, the number will be positive, and then we can just check it using a less than or greater than condition.

I decided to combine the `spinsafety` and `anglesafety` into one check that falls under the rotation warning. Though they are independent conditions, I thought it best not to try and explain the distinction to the player. To make the condition pass if either of the conditions is true, we need to use the logical OR operator (`||`).

```
//
// ***** DANGER CHECK *****
// safety parameters: these may be adjusted to your
// preference or made level-dependant variables.
ysafety = 1.5;
xsafety = .6;
spinsafety = 1;
anglesafety = 8;
// this checks to see if the ship would be able to land
// safely given its current velocity and rotation
function dangerCheck () {
    // initialize an error counter
    errors = 0;
    // check all of the parameters, turning on the indicators as
    // needed
    if (Math.abs(ymove)>ysafety) {
    }
    if (Math.abs(xmove)>xsafety) {
    }
    if (Math.abs(rmove)>spinsafety || Math.abs(_rotation)>angle
    ➥ safety) {
    }
}
```

If the property is outside the limit, then we need to turn on the visibility of the appropriate warning. This is also where we should increment the `error` variable, indicating that a test has failed. After that, we need to add `else` statements to turn the visibility of the warning off if the test passed.

```
//
// ***** DANGER CHECK *****
// safety parameters: these may be adjusted to your
// preference or made level-dependant variables.
ysafety = 1.5;
xsafety = .6;
spinsafety = 1;
anglesafety = 8;
// this checks to see if the ship would be able to land
// safely given its current velocity and rotation
function dangerCheck () {
    // initialize an error counter
```

```
      errors = 0;
      // check all of the parameters, turning on the indicators as
      // needed
      if (Math.abs(ymove)>ysafety) {
              errors++;
              _parent.ydanger._visible = 1;
      } else {
              _parent.ydanger._visible = 0;
      }
      if (Math.abs(xmove)>xsafety) {
              errors++;
              _parent.xdanger._visible = 1;
      } else {
              _parent.xdanger._visible = 0;
      }
      if (Math.abs(rmove)>spinsafety ||
    ➥ Math.abs(_rotation)>anglesafety) {
              errors++;
              _parent.rdanger._visible = 1;
      } else {
              _parent.rdanger._visible = 0;
      }
}
```

There is one more condition that we need to check which isn't based on a movement limit, and that is whether or not the ship is over the landing pad. To determine this, we need to see if the ship's x position is either less than the position of the left marker or greater than the position of the right marker. If it is, this should also increment `errors`, however, there is not really a need to show a warning since the location of the pad is very easy to see.

```
      //
      // ***** DANGER CHECK *****
      // safety parameters: these may be adjusted to your
      // preference or made level-dependant variables.
      ysafety = 1.5;
      xsafety = .6;
      spinsafety = 1;
      anglesafety = 8;
      // this checks to see if the ship would be able to land
      // safely given its current velocity and rotation
      function dangerCheck () {
          // initialize an error counter
          errors = 0;
          // check all of the parameters, turning on the indicators as
          // needed
          if (Math.abs(ymove)>ysafety) {
                  errors++;
                  _parent.ydanger._visible = 1;
          } else {
                  _parent.ydanger._visible = 0;
```

```
        }
    if (Math.abs(xmove)>xsafety) {
            errors++;
            _parent.xdanger._visible = 1;
    } else {
            _parent.xdanger._visible = 0;
    }
    if (Math.abs(rmove)>spinsafety ||
        ➡Math.abs(_rotation)>anglesafety) {
            errors++;
            _parent.rdanger._visible = 1;
    } else {
            _parent.rdanger._visible = 0;
    }
    if (_x<_parent.leftMark._x+(_width*.5) || _x>_parent.right
    ➡ mark._X_x-(_width*.5)) {
            errors++;
    }
}
```

OK, now play around with your game – try to hover in mid-air to test your warning. If after you've gotten used to the control you can't seem to get all of the warnings to turn off, you may want to alter the limits to make the game a bit easier. It seems to come down to whether or not you played this game as a kid. If you did, these levels should be just fine, otherwise the game is going to be pretty difficult until you get the hang of it, but that's half the fun.

altitude()

This is the last major function called by the control script we made earlier. Here, we need to find the distance between the feet of the ship and the ground. If that amount is 0 or less, we've arrived, and it's time to see if we've had a good or bad landing. The altitude will also be set to a variable, which as you may recall is referenced in the interface by the altitude text field.

To find the position of the ship's feet, we just take the vertical position of ship and add on half its height (remember that vertical values increase in the downwards direction). Then, by finding the difference between that value and the y position of land (found up one level on the root), we deduce the altitude. Since this variable is going to be visible to the user, it would be a good idea to round the value to an integer, as any difference in the altitude less than one pixel isn't significant for our purposes anyway. The code for this should look like the following:

```
//
// ***** ALTITUDE CHECK *****
// this checks to see if we are at the ground yet, and as a side
// effect populates the altitude variable which is visible in the
// interface
function altitudeCheck () {
    // find the distance betweel the bottom of the ship and the
    //ground
    altitude = Math.round(_parent.land._y-(_y+(.5*_height)));
}
```

Now that we have `altitude`, we can implement collision detection with `land`. Normally we could do this with Flash 5's new `hitTest` method, but since we have `altitude` to display to the user, we might as well use it for collision as well. If you are interested in using `hitTest` instead the condition would look like this:

```
if ( this.hitTest ( _parent.land)) {}
```

If you're wondering why the land is completely flat, well, unfortunately there's a good explanation for it. Flash's collision detection is far better than it used to be, but it still has a long way to go. `hitTest` will either check a point against the actual shape of a movie clip or it will compare the bounding boxes of two movie clips (remember: a bounding box is the smallest rectangle that can surround an object with sides that are parallel to the sides of the screen).

There are some workarounds, such as making the shape of the landscape then expanding the shape out some number of pixels (half the height of the ship), then doing point-to-movie-clip collision with the expanded shape movie clip and the position point of the ship (although this method has several other quirks associated with it). So, for simplicity, we are going to stick with flat land, and will use the altitude to check the collision.

Using `altitude`, the code looks like the following:

```
//
// ***** ALTITUDE CHECK *****
// this checks to see if we are at the ground yet, and as a side
// effect populates the altitude variable which is visible in the
// interface
function altitudeCheck () {
     // find the distance betweel the bottom of the ship and the
     //ground
     altitude = Math.round( _parent.land._y-( _y+(.5*_height)));
     if (altitude<=0) {
     }
}
```

If the code inside this conditional is being executed it means we've hit the ground. In the controls and central control script we used a variable called `impact` as a test for whether or not this collision has occurred, so let's go ahead and set that variable now. Since it's used as the condition of `if` statements, we just need to set it to 1 to affect how it interacts with those `if` statements.

```
//
// ***** ALTITUDE CHECK *****
// this checks to see if we are at the ground yet, and as a side
// effect populates the altitude variable which is visible in the
// interface
function altitudeCheck () {
     // find the distance betweel the bottom of the ship and the
     //ground
     altitude = Math.round( _parent.land._y-( _y+(.5*_height)));
     if (altitude<=0) {
```

```
                // by setting impact to 1 we will block the ship from
                // moving or recieving commands from the controls
                impact = 1;
          }
     }
```

After that, we need to find out if it was a good or bad landing, and send it to the appropriate outcome. As we discussed in the `dangerCheck` function, we'll be using `errors` as our test for a good or bad landing. If `errors` is greater than zero, the ship crashes, otherwise it touches down safely. To make this clear, I decided to make these outcomes into our last two functions.

```
     //
     // ***** ALTITUDE CHECK *****
     // this checks to see if we are at the ground yet, and as a side
     // effect populates the altitude variable which is visible in the
     // interface
     function altitudeCheck () {
          // find the distance betweel the bottom of the ship and the
          //ground
          altitude = Math.round(_parent.land._y-(_y+(.5*_height)));
          if (altitude<=0) {
                // by setting impact to 1 we will block the ship from
                //moving or recieving commands from the controls
                impact = 1;
                // was the landing good?
                if (errors) {
                     // guess not
                     crash();
                } else {
                     // woo-hoo
                touchDown();
                }
          }
     }
```

If you test now, your ship should stop when it reaches the ground no matter if it was a good or bad landing, and since we haven't defined the outcome functions yet, everything just stops on impact. If you want to try again you'll have to rewind the movie.

touchdown()

This is the "please return your seatback and tray tables to their full upright and locked positions for landing" function. As that's a mouthful, I think `touchDown` will suffice. For a good landing, we really just need to clean up the details such as turning of the thrust and aligning the ship properly.

With safety limits, there is still a small amount of wiggle room for the ship to be turned slightly crooked, and we must also consider the possibility that the ship might have moved down into the ground slightly in the frame in which the collision was detected. We need to straighten the ship up by setting its rotation to 0, and we also need to set its vertical position to the position of land plus half the height of the ship. As we do that, it would also be a good idea to set altitude to exactly zero, since theoretically if you are on the ground that's what it should be. Up to this point the function should look like this:

```
//
// ***** GOOD LANDING *****
function touchDown () {
    // turn off the engine
    thrust.gotoAndStop(1);
    // straighten up the ship
    _rotation = 0;
    // move the ship so its sitting on top of the ground
    _y = _parent.land._y-(.5*_height);
    // make the altitude readout accurate
    altitude = 0;
}
```

After that, there are two administrative things that must be done. First you get promoted a level, which we do that by incrementing the level variable. Second, we need the win message to play. As you'll recall, it's sitting on the root and has the name, win.

```
//
// ***** GOOD LANDING *****
function touchDown () {
    // turn off the engine
    thrust.gotoAndStop(1);
    // straighten up the ship
    _rotation = 0;
    // move the ship so its sitting on top of the ground
    _y = _parent.land._y-(.5*_height);
    // make the altitude readout accurate
    altitude = 0;
    // you get to go to the next level
    _parent.level++;
    // display the win message
    _parent.win.gotoAndPlay(2);
}
```

What we haven't done yet is anything that actually takes the movie back to the level screen to start the new level. Once we are done with the next function we'll go into win and add code there. As useful as functions are, they can't execute a command off in the future. Telling the movie to go to the level screen from the function would just make it happen immediately, not giving the player even a moment to see a cheesy congratulations message and to savor victory.

crash()

Well, it's inevitable; your lovely ship is going to get turned into a pile of bits sooner or later, so we might as well make the function to let it go out with at least a little dignity. In this case we don't need to worry about alignment or any of the other niceties of a soft landing. We just need to set the altitude indicator to 0 (even if the ship is slightly embedded in the ground), and then make both our big screen-sized Flash and the ship's explosion play.

```
//
// ***** BAD LANDING *****
function crash () {
    // make sure the indicator is correct
    altitude = 0;
    // plays a screen sized flash that is more
    // efficient to have sitting outside the ship's MC
    _parent.flash.play();
    // play the crash sequence in this MC. At the end it will
    // remove a life and take us back to start the level.
    gotoAndPlay ("crash");
}
```

Well, that's it for our two event handlers. It's a fair amount of code, but keep in mind that we're almost completely done with the game and all of the coding took place in one place. What's left is really just dotting the I's and crossing the T's. However, before we move, here's how all of the code attached to ship should look:

```
onClipEvent (load) {
    //
    // ***** ACCELERATION *****
    gravity = .01*_parent.level+.05;
    // acceleration rate
    power = 3*gravity;
    // given the direction your ship is moving, and the thrust
    // power, it alters the xmove and ymove variables thus
    // altering your vector
    function accelerate () {
        // convert ship's rotation (in degrees) to radians
        angle = (_rotation/360)*2*Math.PI;
        // then alter the movement variables
        xmove += power*Math.sin(angle);
        ymove += -power*Math.cos(angle);
    }
    //
    // ***** FUEL CONSUMPTION *****
    // fuel variable: a common level technique
    // is to reduce the fuel each level.
    // I chose a constant since higher levels
    // require a lot more thrust to counter increased gravity.
    fuelMax = 1000;
```

```
// This function does the accounting on your fuel reserves
function useFuel (amount) {
        fuelUsed += amount;
        if (fuelUsed>=fuelmax) {
                empty = 1;
                thrust.gotoAndStop(1);
        }
        fuelRatio = fuelUsed/fuelMax;
        _parent.fuelGauge.gotoAndStop(Math.round(fuelRatio*
          ➥(_root.fuelGauge._totalFrames-1))+1);
}
//
// ***** MOVEMENT *****
maxVelocity = 15;
maxRotation = 10;
rotationalFriction = .95;
// this applies gravity and rotational friction to
// the ship's vector then actually moves the ship
function move () {
        // apply gravity to the vertical movement
        ymove += gravity;
        // check against maxVelocity
        hypotenuse = Math.sqrt((xmove*xmove)+(ymove*ymove));
        if (hypotenuse>maxVelocity) {
                xmove *= maxVelocity/hypotenuse;
                ymove *= maxVelocity/hypotenuse;
        }
        // move the ship
        _x += xmove;
        _y += ymove;
        // check against maxRotation
        if (rmove>maxRotation) {
                rmove = maxRotation;
        } else if (rmove<-maxRotation) {
                rmove = -maxRotation;
        }
        // rotate the ship
        this._rotation += rmove;
        // degrade the rotational inertia
        rmove *= rotationalFriction;
}
//
// ***** WRAPPING *****
// if the ship has flown off the side of the screen,
// wrap it to the other side.
screenWidth = 550
function wrap () {
        if (_x<(-_width*.5) && xmove<0) {
                // if past left boundary, wrap to the right
                _x = screenWidth+_width*.5;
```

```
              } else if (_x>(screenWidth+_width*.5) && xmove>0) {
                    // if past right boundary, wrap to the left
                    _x = -_width*.5;
              }
       }
       //
       // ***** DANGER CHECK *****
       // safety parameters: these may be adjusted to your
       // preference or made level-dependant variables.
       ysafety = 1.5;
       xsafety = .6;
       spinsafety = 1;
       anglesafety = 8;
       // this checks to see if the ship would be able to land
       // safely given its current velocity and rotation
       function dangerCheck () {
              // initialize an error counter
              errors = 0;
              // check all of the parameters, turning on the
              // indicators as needed
              if (Math.abs(ymove)>ysafety) {
                    errors++;
                    _parent.ydanger._visible = 1;
              } else {
                    _parent.ydanger._visible = 0;
              }
              if (Math.abs(xmove)>xsafety) {
                    errors++;
                    _parent.xdanger._visible = 1;
              } else {
                    _parent.xdanger._visible = 0;
              }
              if (Math.abs(rmove)>spinsafety ||
                 ➡Math.abs(_rotation)>anglesafety) {
                    errors++;
                    _parent.rdanger._visible = 1;
              } else {
                    _parent.rdanger._visible = 0;
              }
              if (_x<_parent.leftMark._x+(_width*.5) ||
                 ➡_x>_parent.rightmark._x-(_width*.5)) {
                    errors++;
              }
       }
       //
       // ***** ALTITUDE CHECK *****
       // this checks to see if we are at the ground yet, and as a
       // side effect populates the altitude variable which is
       // visible in the interface
       //
```

```
function altitudeCheck () {
// find the distance betweel the bottom of the ship
// and the ground
altitude = Math.round(_parent.land._y-(_y+(.5*_height)));
if (altitude<=0) {
        // by setting impact to 1 we will block the
        // ship from moving or recieving commands from
        // the controls
        impact = 1;
        // was the landing good?
        if (errors) {
                // guess not
                crash();
        } else {
                // woo-hoo
                touchDown();
        }
}
}
//
// ***** GOOD LANDING *****
function touchDown () {
        // turn off the engine
        thrust.gotoAndStop(1);
        // straighten up the ship
        _rotation = 0;
        // move the ship so its sitting on top of the ground
        _y = _parent.land._y-(.5*_height);
        // make the altitude readout accurate
        altitude = 0;
        // you get to go to the next level
        _parent.level++;
        // display the win message
        _parent.win.gotoAndPlay(2);
}
//
// ***** BAD LANDING *****
function crash () {
        // make sure the indicator is correct
        altitude = 0;
        // plays a screen sized flash that is more
        // efficient to have sitting outside the ship's MC
        _parent.flash.play();
        // play the crash sequence in this MC. At the end it will
        // remove a life and take us back to start the level.
        gotoAndPlay ("crash");
}
}
onClipEvent (enterFrame) {
    // handle the control input only allow control if there is
```

```
                // fuel and you haven't landed (or crashed)
            if (!empty && !impact) {
                // turn Counter-Clockwise
                if (Key.isDown(Key.LEFT)) {
                    rmove -= .5;
                    useFuel(1);
                }
                // turn Clockwise
                if (Key.isDown(Key.RIGHT)) {
                    rmove += .5;
                    useFuel(1);
                }
                // thrust
                if (Key.isDown(Key.UP)) {
                    accelerate();
                    thrust.nextFrame();
                    useFuel(2);
                } else {
                    thrust.prevFrame();
                }
            }
            // this is central control.  having broken the
            // tasks up into functions we can easily see what
            // is actually going on.
            if (!impact) {
                move();
                wrap();
                dangerCheck();
                altitudeCheck();
            }
        }
```

Whew! Okay, maybe a "fair amount of code" wasn't right. It's a heck of a lot of code considering it's Flash, but bear in mind that without the comments, it's only about 125 lines of code for a functional game, which, in the end I think is pretty good.

So, now to finish up the last details of the game so we can talk about completely changing it!

Pulling it all together

We were able to cram an amazing amount of functionality into one place, but there are still a few operations that are better placed elsewhere. Specifically, we still need to deal with what happens to the screen after you either land or crash, the placement of the landing pylons, and finally add some functionality to the remaining interface elements.

Outcomes

As long as we are still in the mindset of dealing with the ship's outcome, let's finish off those elements. In win, which is out on the main stage in the game frame, let's add about 50 frames (at 30 FPS this is still less than a 2 second delay). At the end, add a keyframe to which we can add the code to take us back to the level screen to start the new level. The code for this is:

```
_parent.gotoAndplay("level");
```

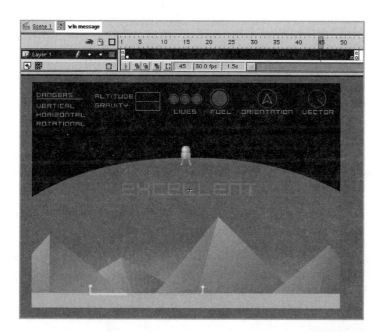

The process for after crashing is very similar. Go into ship and go to the end of your explosion animation. If there isn't already one, add a blank keyframe at the end (the ship is gone, we have to let go...). Next add about 50 frames once again, and add a keyframe to hold our code. This time we need to do two things: first we have to deduct one life, and then we need to go back to the level screen. Since we haven't incremented the level variable after crashing, it will load the same level. To remove one life we just have to tell the lives animation out on the root to go to the next frame.

```
_parent.lives.nextFrame();
_parent.gotoAndPlay("level");
```

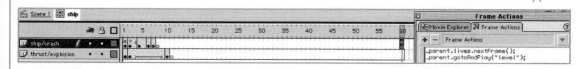

Since the ship does not exist in the level frame, it's important to save the command telling the main timeline to go to the level frame, until last. If you try it in the reverse order, it will go to the appropriate frame immediately, not even waiting to execute the rest of the actions in the frame.

Landing pad

Though you've been able to manually set the landing pylons, let's build the script now to randomly place them, and stretch the pad movie clip between them. When I say: "randomly place" the pylons I actually mean to do it in a controlled, random way. There are several cases we definitely would not want to have take place such as having the left marker on the right, and the right marker on the left, or by having them too close together to fit the ship between them.

What we can do though is to determine how far apart the pylons need to be, then place the left one randomly and just place the right one the appropriate distance from the left (although we will still have to be a little careful where we place the left marker so that the right one is not off the screen). The last important thing to mention about the pad is that the size is going to be level dependent. Yes, yes, one last mean trick to play on the unsuspecting player.

The code for the markers is going to be in the game frame of the actions layer. Right now, there should just be a stop action there. By making this code a frame action, the pylons will only be set when it enters the game screen. The first thing to do is to decide a base width that the pad can't go beneath. It's probably a good idea to do this as a function of the width of the ship. I thought the ship's width plus 10 pixels was pretty challenging but not impossible.

Next we need to decide how much we want to change the pad's width between levels, and over how many levels we want it to shrink. These two elements are strongly dependent on each other since the higher you make one, you need to make the other smaller, or else you'll end up with an enormous pad in the early levels. I found that 5 pixels per level for 20 levels was pretty good. That starts the pad at a width of 100 pixels plus the base amount. The code for these three variables should look something like this:

```
baseAmount= ship._width+10;
padIncrement = 5;
maxLevel = 20;
stop ();
```

From here, we can figure out just how wide the gap needs to be for any level. If we are at a level less than the maximum, the pad should be the value of padIncrement times maxLevel minus level, all added onto the base amount. The reason for subtracting level from maxLevel is that level starts out small and gets bigger; the pad needs to do the opposite. To achieve that, we take the initially small number of level and subtract it from the large number of maxLevel. That way, the difference will be big in early levels and small in later levels. If the level is greater than or equal to maxLevel though, the gap between the markers should just be the base value.

```
baseAmount= ship._width+10;
padIncrement = 5;
maxLevel = 20;
// place the markers by determining how far apart they need to be
if (level<maxLevel) {
```

```
            gap = baseAmount+(padIncrement*(maxLevel-level));
    } else {
            gap = baseAmount;
    }
    stop ();
```

The next step is to then place the left mark randomly along the x-axis on the stage, although we do want to make sure we leave enough room for the full pad to stay on screen. Since the width of the screen is 550, let's set the leftMark movie clip somewhere random between 0 and 550 minus the value of gap. We can then place rightMark at the position of leftMark plus the gap amount.

To do this we will use the random method of the Math object. Unlike in Flash 4, this code doesn't deal with integers. Instead, it will always return a decimal value between 0 and 1, and it's then up to us to multiply it by the number we want, and then make it into an integer if needed. That means getting the random value then multiplying it by the value of 550-gap (we can make it into a integer, but that's not necessary here).

```
    baseAmount= ship._width+10;
    padIncrement = 5;
    maxLevel = 20;
    // place the markers by determining how far apart they need to be
    if (level<maxLevel) {
            gap = baseAmount+(padIncrement*(maxLevel-level));
    } else {
            gap = baseAmount;
    }
    // then place one marker randomly,
    // but still allow for the width of the landing pad
    leftMark._x = Math.random() * (550-gap);
    rightMark._x = leftMark._x+gap;
    stop ();
```

After that, we need to position and scale the pad movie clip to fit between the markers. Given that the registration mark for the pad is at the left edge, we can align the movie clip with the leftMark movie. After that we just set its width the value of gap. In Flash 4, the _width property was a read-only property, but luckily that's no longer the case, since dealing with scale was much more complex.

```
    baseAmount= ship._width+10;
    padIncrement = 5;
    maxLevel = 20;
    // place the markers by determining how far apart they need to be
    if (level<maxLevel) {
            gap = baseAmount+(padIncrement*(maxLevel-level));
    } else {
            gap = baseAmount;
    }
    // then place one marker randomly,
    // but still allow for the width of the landing pad
    leftMark._x = Math.random() * (550-gap);
```

```
rightMark._x = leftMark._x+gap;
// then size the landing pad between the markers
pad._x = leftMark._x;
pad._width = gap;
stop ();
```

The last element in this script is to position the ship. If the pad is placed directly under the ship, the level is very easy since you don't have to steer. To check that it isn't over the pad, we just need to place the ship randomly along the x-axis and check whether it is between the markers. If it is, then we need to randomly place it again, and check the ship's location against the pad again. This process will continue until the ship is not over the pad.

The way to make this persistent script is to use a while loop. It will continue executing until its condition is no longer satisfied. I'd rather not let the ship get placed on the absolute edge of the screen as it would if we randomly set its position anywhere on the screen. So instead, let's cut off 25 pixels from both sides of the screen's width, and make the location be randomly between 25 and 525. To offset the value by 25, we would just need to find a value randomly between 0 and 500, and then add 25 on to that.

The condition for the loop should be to check if the ship's x position is greater than leftMark's and less than rightMark's.

```
baseAmount= ship._width+10;
padIncrement = 5;
maxLevel = 20;
// place the markers by determining how far apart they need to be
if (level<maxLevel) {
    gap = baseAmount+(padIncrement*(maxLevel-level));
} else {
    gap = baseAmount;
}
// then place one marker randomly,
// but still allow for the width of the landing pad
leftMark._x = Math.random() * (550-gap);
rightMark._x = leftMark._x+gap;
// then size the landing pad between the markers
pad._x = leftMark._x;
pad._width = gap;
// randomize the location of the ship so that it has been
// randomized at least once
ship._x = (Math.random() * 500) + 25;
// keep changing the ship's x position until it isn't directly
//over the pad
while (ship._x>leftMark._x && ship._x<rightMark._x) {
    ship._x = (Math.random() * 500) + 25;
}
stop ();
```

Lives

From here let's look at the final interface elements, specifically, the `lives` movie clip on the main timeline. When the ship crashes it will tell the movie clip to go to the next frame. That's just fine until you run out of frames. At that point we need to add some scripting to end the game. In the last frame (whether you chose to add an extra frame or not), tell the main timeline to go back to the main menu. Since the play button resets the game to level 1, starting the game again will erase your progress from the last game.

```
// the game is over
_root.gotoAndStop("menu");
```

Orientation

Let's now move over a couple places on the interface to the orientation gauge. This arrow just needs to point in the same direction the ship is pointing. It doesn't in any way reflect the direction the ship is moving. The code here is pretty simple. The rotation of the arrow just needs to be constantly set to the rotation of the ship. Anything that needs to be constantly done should raise a flag in your mind saying `onClipEvent (enterFrame)`. If you thought "looping movie clip", hold your hand out and then smack it with your other hand. In our `onClipEvent`, just be sure to reference the ship's rotation by going up a level. Even though the code is on the outside of the movie clip, it is still part of that movie clip's scope. The code should look like the following:

```
onClipEvent (enterFrame) {
    _rotation = _parent.ship._rotation;
}
```

Vector

I think this is by far the most interesting element of the interface. This shows what direction the ship is moving, and how fast it is moving. The way it does this is by stretching a movie clip so that it is the width of the ship's xmove variable, and is as tall as the ship's ymove variable. The movie clip it will be stretching is the one that has the diagonal hairline in it, and what we are actually doing is visually constructing a hypotenuse (the diagonal line) by setting the opposite and adjacent sides (the height and width).

The line can only ever be as long as the value of the maxVelocity variable set in the ship. If you decide to use a circle around this element like I did, the circle will need to have a height and width of two times maxVelocity. If that circle size doesn't work for you, you will need to proportionally shrink the height and width of the line in the code that we are getting ready to create.

On the main timeline, select the movie clip with the diagonal line, and open the Object Actions window. This is another piece of code that needs to be constantly running, so let's set up another onClipEvent (enterFrame). As I mentioned above, the first thing to do is to set the width and height of the movie clip to the values of xmove and ymove in the ship's timeline. Since an object can't have a negative height, we are going to need to account for the potential of xmove or ymove being negative.

```
onClipEvent (enterFrame) {
    // set the dimensions of the xmove and ymove variables.
    // height and width though only accept positive values
    // so we need to use absolute values
    _width = Math.abs(_parent.ship.xmove);
    _height = Math.abs(_parent.ship.ymove);
}
```

Having now made all of the values positive, the line would always point more or less down and to the right, but we need to make it stretch anywhere in the circle. To do that, we can multiply the appropriate scale element of the movie clip by –1 to flip its direction. So if xmove is negative, the _xscale of the movie clip should be negative. The same is true in terms of ymove and _yscale. Multiplying the scale by –1 won't always give us the desired effect. If we flip it once when the script runs again we wouldn't want the already negative value to be multiplied by –1. To get around this, we can use absolute values again. This way, if one of the move variables is negative we can take the current scale, make it positive (whether it was positive or negative before) then multiply that value by –1.

```
onClipEvent (enterFrame) {
    // set the dimensions of the xmove and ymove variables.
    // height and width though only accept positive values
    // so we need to use absolute values
    _width = Math.abs(_parent.ship.xmove);
    _height = Math.abs(_parent.ship.ymove);
    // the above code would always make the line point down
    // and to the right. We need to flip the scale of the
    // line if it needs to point another way
    if (_parent.ship.xmove<0) {
        _xscale = Math.abs(_xscale)*-1;
    }
    if (_parent.ship.ymove<0) {
        _yscale = Math.abs(_yscale)*-1;
    }
}
```

And with that, we're done with the game. Take it for a test drive; give yourself a pat on the back. Just because were done with the game development does not mean that you should be. In the next section we'll talk about some of the things you can try on your own to make the game even cooler.

me additions

I made this game as something I would like to play as well as taking us through some key game issues. Part of the fun of developing games though, is making the game your own way. As a sort of wrap up, I thought it might be a good idea to give you a few seed ideas of how to modify the game.

Scoring

Scores could be awarded upon the completion of levels based upon how close the ship landed to the center of the pad, or by how much fuel remains in the tank. Like `level`, this variable would need to exist in the main timeline so that it doesn't get deleted between levels. You would also need to add code to the play button to set the score back to 0 when a new game begins.

Once you set up a scoring system, there are several other possible bonuses such as additional lives awarded every so few many thousand points, or you could even use your score as a fuel reserve. Once the tank runs out, `maxFuel` would get set to the score and the score would decrease as you used fuel.

Meteorites

If the game is simply not challenging enough for you, you might want to add random falling meteorites that you need to dodge. To make falling objects, you'd just initialize the object with a random positive `ymove` variable, and just keep it moving by constantly adding it onto is current position. For collision detection you'll want to use the `hitTest` method between the ship and the meteor. A collision could then just trigger the `crash` function that you made in the ship.

Fuel bonus

Along the same line as the meteorite would be floating fuel bonuses. You could initialize `move` variables if you wanted to have the object in motion. Collision could then just lower the `fuelUsed` variable by a certain amount.

Landing accuracy bonus

How close you land to the exact center of the landing pad could give you a bonus of fuel for the next level, or you could keep track of a score using a dynamic text field. If you decide to use scoring, be sure that you reinitialize the score to 0 at the beginning of the game (which you would do in the play button where you initialize the level).

Updrafts

Gravity is constantly acting on the ship right now, but that doesn't have to be the case. You could add a graphic of something like a steam vent, and then if your ship is within a certain range of x coordinates, the ship's `ymove` variable could be altered to give it a bit of a lift. The amount of lift given could be inversely related to the altitude variable in the ship.

Docking with a ship

If you wanted to add a bit of a story to your game, you could turn the lunar module into a supply shuttle that has to go between a land base and a ship in the sky. Docking with the ship could be just like landing, except it's the top of the lunar module that has to gently touch the target instead of the feet. Then you could do supply runs back and forth where the longer you are able to stay docked with the shuttle, the more cargo you collect. Points can then be awarded for their successful delivery to the surface.

Retro-thrusters

So far we've used the up, right and left arrow keys. If you wanted, you could add a control to the down key to make a retro-thruster. This could be useful in cancelling out lift at the last moments in landing, or would be invaluable if you did the docking example above. If you were interested in setting up retro-thrusters, the structure would be very similar to the regular thrust controls. You would however, want to modify the `accelerate` function to allow you to specify the power as a parameter. If you are using a retro-thruster, `power` should be negative whatever its default is.

Summary

I hope some of the ideas will give you some inspiration to extend the functionality of the game. There is certainly a lot more that can be done with it. Even if none of these ideas appeal you, at least should be able to take elements of this game and make others.

I hope in this chapter that you've gotten a sense of what goes into making a game in Flash 5. Most of the code we used wasn't anything terribly new, but was just put together in a way to facilitate making a game. One thing I've noticed about the coolest of the Flash websites is using their interfaces is that just as entertaining as playing some games. It's this heightened interactivity that makes Flash such an exciting tool.

As we are at the end of this chapter you should now be familiar with how to:

- Re-purpose common interface elements such as dynamic text fields, thermometer bars, and line drawing effects to extend the usefulness and functionality of games

- Use the `Key` object to allow multiple keyboard inputs

- Divide complex scripting tasks into more manageable sub-tasks

- Use trigonometry, geometry and physics to simulate realistic movement

- Create inter-dependencies in variables so small changes in data are reflected by significant changes in game play and layout.

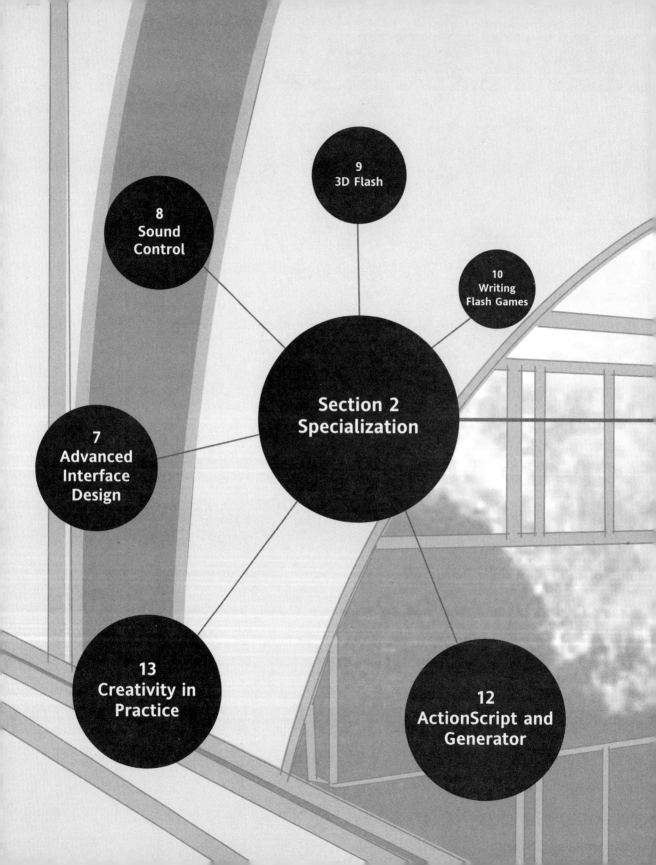

Chapter 11
The XML Object

XML (eXtensible Markup Language) is a means of representing data, and the relationships between the elements of data, within a document according to a few basic rules – rules that enable an XML document to be interpreted by all sorts of applications and processes. As we work through the examples presented in this chapter, you'll see that XML provides a very intuitive way of constructing and representing information in Flash.

Right at the start of this chapter, I should say that in order to put together some interesting demonstrations, and to get to the heart of Flash's support for XML, we're going to make the assumption that you've at least a little familiarity with XML already, and that you have a grasp of terms like "tag", "element", "attribute", "content", "well-formed", and "valid". If you're completely new to XML, you'll still be able to get a feel for what's going on, but you'll get most out the chapter by taking a quick look at an XML tutorial first.

> *The main reason why XML is so interesting for Flash designers is that it provides a way of separating presentation from content, allowing changes to data to not impinge upon its presentation, and vice versa.*

Because XML is a way of describing data that can then be used across a variety of platforms by various applications, it's becoming increasingly popular as a means of storing information. As the amount of data stored in XML form increases, it's going to become ever more important to learn how to utilize it in your development. Flash's superb display capabilities make it a prime candidate to be a leading way of providing shine to XML's ultra-useful, but rather drab, functionality.

In this chapter, we're going to examine Flash 5 ActionScript's XML object in detail. We'll see precisely what functionality it provides, we'll discover that it doesn't always behave exactly as we'd like, and we'll see what we can do to correct its little flaws. We'll also assemble a custom object that 'wraps' XML in order to provide enhanced functionality, and see a couple of examples of it being used in anger.

Before we get ahead of ourselves, though, and in keeping with my promise to take things slowly – at least at first – let's think about the kind of information that it might be useful to store in an XML document that's intended for use in a Flash application. Perhaps, for example, we might record the x coordinate of a Flash movie clip in an element like this:

```
<Xpos>273.95</Xpos>
```

Admittedly, it's not much to look at on its own, but the idea of using XML to tailor the appearance of a Flash movie, by storing initial property values, is a powerful one. It opens the door, for example, to the possibility of allowing users to customize the locations of menus and buttons in a Flash interface – does that sound more interesting?

To expand on this idea just a little, here's the line of XML we had above appearing in an XML document that describes the positions of four movie clips in a hypothetical Flash movie:

```
<FlashMovie>
    <MovieClip>
        <Xpos>273.95</Xpos>
        <Ypos>120</Ypos>
    </MovieClip>
    <MovieClip>
        <Xpos>275.65</Xpos>
        <Ypos>280.85</Ypos>
    </MovieClip>
    <MovieClip>
        <Xpos>357.35</Xpos>
        <Ypos>199.95</Ypos>
    </MovieClip>
    <MovieClip>
        <Xpos>192.7</Xpos>
        <Ypos>202.7</Ypos>
    </MovieClip>
</FlashMovie>
```

The FlashMovie element possesses four subordinate, 'child' MovieClip elements. In turn, these contain pairs of XPos and YPos elements that (obviously) describe the position of each movie clip in terms of its x and y coordinates on the stage. Our challenge now is to access this information from within a Flash movie – and that, of course, will require us to use the XML object. If you're a veteran of accessing the data in an XML document from other technologies – say, PHP, or JavaScript – you'll find that Macromedia's support is similar to that available in those environments, but not identical. If you're new to processing an XML document programmatically... well, there's plenty to learn!

ccessing an XML Document from Code

Broadly speaking, there are two widely used ways of examining an XML document programmatically, and both have analogies in Flash. In the first, your program starts 'reading' the XML document from the beginning, and an event is fired every time it comes across something new – a tag, an attribute, some content, anything at all. By keeping track of the sequence in which things are 'come across', it's possible to establish your current position in the document. This is an interesting and versatile technique, but it's not the one Flash uses, so we'll dwell no further on it here.

Instead of this, when you direct Flash's XML object to examine an XML document, it 'grabs' the whole thing at once, and performs some processing on it before it will allow you to perform any operations of your own. The purpose of this processing is to place the constituent pieces of the document into objects that can then be interrogated in a familiar way: just as you can have movie clips that are children of movie clips that are children of movie clips, so you can have XML elements that are children of XML elements that are children of XML elements. Dot syntax strikes again, and while there *is* a little more complexity than I've suggested here, this is a good place to start a more involved discussion.

> *The arrangement of elements within an XML document is often referred to as a tree. This derives from the fact that the hierarchical structure of an XML document, when represented graphically, resembles a tree – with the trunk representing the root element of the document, and its child elements forming the "branches". The contents of an element – that is, the textual information nested within a node – are referred to as the "leaves" of a given branch.*

The name given to Flash's way of representing an XML document is a **Document Object Model**, or just **DOM**. Unlike when you're dealing with movie clips, the objects that represent your document do not have names that match those of the elements they mirror. Instead, as we'll soon see, they take names that reflect their relative positions in the document – if you need to know the name of an element, you have to access it as a property of one of these objects.

Something else you'll need to get used to in order to use the XML object effectively is the idea of a **node**. More generic than an element, a node is the basic building block of the DOM, because every *node* in your original document is represented by an object. Elements are one type of node, but so too (for example) are attributes, and even the text or data an element contains. If you can start to think of the text or data of an element as being a 'child' of that element, you'll be a long way down the road to understanding how all this is going to work.

It's worth mentioning that because using the DOM in this way requires the creation objects that represent every part of an XML document, the available memory of an application can be absorbed rather quickly. While this isn't a tremendous concern within the desktop environment, it *can* be problematic for plug-ins such as Flash. It's advisable, therefore, that you pre-process large XML documents before they're transmitted to a Flash application. At it's simplest, this could just involve breaking the document down into multiple smaller elements – either by hand, or by developing a server side routine for the purpose.

For instance, a large document in which the root node (that is, the root element) of the document possessed four child nodes could be broken into four separate, well-formed XML documents. Most mature scripting languages (such as Perl, TCL, and Python) possess XML handling facilities that can be used to parse, analyze, and re-assemble XML documents when techniques like this become necessary.

ecap

In our very brief introduction to dealing with XML in Flash so far, we've said that:

- It's not difficult to find motivation for using XML documents in Flash, whether as a means for importing data, or a way of controlling the appearance of a movie

- Support for using XML in Flash 5 ActionScript is provided by the XML object

- The XML object represents the pieces of your document as a set of objects, arranged in a tree-like structure.

So far, though, the terms we've been using have been rather vague. What are the names of the objects that make up the DOM? How do the relationships between them work? How can any single set of objects successfully represent the infinite possible variety of XML documents? How, in a nutshell, are we to extract information in any way that we can use? It's about time we started talking specifics.

avigating XML Documents

It's worth mentioning that the DOM is a standard defined by the World Wide Web Consortium, whose web site you can find here:

http://www.w3c.org

That standard defined the names of the objects that are used in representing an XML document, as well as all the methods and properties they expose. This is precisely the reason why XML handling is similar in diverse programming environments: each has provided an implementation of the DOM for its own users. The names that we'll use in this section are those defined by the standard; as you'll see, they have exact counterparts in the methods and properties of Flash's XML object.

The imposed, tree-like structure of an XML document provides us with a context in which to navigate from one node to the next, by targeting the location of each node relative to its 'parent' nodes, its 'child' nodes, and its siblings (that is, those nodes with which it shares 'parents'). Within ActionScript, these relationships are expressed by using the properties and methods of the XML object. Each and every element node, for example, has a property called parentNode, through which it's possible to get access to details about its parent. The same element may also possess childNodes and siblings (nextSibling and previousSibling).

For instance, the node that begins with <MovieClip> below encompasses the childNodes <Xpos> and <Ypos>, as well as the children of these nodes: their nodeValues. We can say, for example, that the firstChild of <MovieClip> is <Xpos>:

```
<FlashMovie>
    <MovieClip>
        <Xpos>273.95</Xpos>    <!-- This is the firstChild -->
        <Ypos>120</Ypos>       <!-- This is the lastChild   -->
    </MovieClip>
    <MovieClip>
        <Xpos>275.65</Xpos>
        <Ypos>280.85</Ypos>
    </MovieClip>
    <MovieClip>
        <Xpos>357.35</Xpos>
        <Ypos>199.95</Ypos>
    </MovieClip>
    <MovieClip>
        <Xpos>192.7</Xpos>
        <Ypos>202.7</Ypos>
    </MovieClip>
</FlashMovie>
```

Just like a Flash movie clip, any node, no matter how far out on a limb of the tree it may be, can be addressed from the root node – as long as you're prepared to assemble the path involved! By using ActionScript's dot syntax, you can keep climbing as high as you like.

The following expression, for example, would target the nodeValue of the Xpos node associated with the third MovieClip, by addressing the document's root node (which we've earlier stored in a variable called FlashMovie:

```
FlashMovie.firstChild.nextSibling.nextSibling.firstChild.nodeValue
```

If you can't quite see how that works, take a look at the listing on the next page.

```
<FlashMovie>    <!-- This is FlashMovie.firstChild -->
<MovieClip>
   <Xpos>273.95</Xpos>   <Ypos>120</Ypos>
</MovieClip>    <!-- FlashMovie.firstChild.nextSibling -->
<MovieClip>
   <Xpos>275.65</Xpos>   <Ypos>280.85</Ypos>
</MovieClip>
<!--FlashMovie.firstChild.nextSibling.nextSibling -->
<MovieClip>
<!-- FlashMovie.firstChild.nextSibling.nextSibling.firstChild -->
   <Xpos>357.35</Xpos>   <Ypos>199.95</Ypos>
</MovieClip>
<MovieClip>
   <Xpos>192.7</Xpos>   <Ypos>202.7</Ypos>
</MovieClip>
</FlashMovie>
```

The parent/child hierarchy only extends to the immediate parents or children of a node. For example <Xpos> is the child of <MovieClip> but it's not addressable as a child node of <FlashMovie>. While this may be a bit confusing at first just remember that parents can have only one generation of children, and children one generation of parents – the DOM doesn't recognize grandparents or grandchildren!

Let's look at how Flash 5's XML parser renders a generic XML object in accordance with the DOM. We'll simply instantiate an XML object without actually loading an XML document into it and look at the resulting structure in Flash's debugger – this can be found by choosing Debug > List Variables from the command bar. By instantiating the XML object as such: foo = new XML ; and after choosing Control > Test Movie or Control > Debug Movie the following will appear in the debugger.

```
Variable _level0.foo = [object #1] {
    nodeType:1,
    nextSibling:null,
    previousSibling:null,
    parentNode:null,
    firstChild:null,
    lastChild:null,
    childNodes:[object #2] [],
    attributes:[object #3] {},
    nodeName:null,
    nodeValue:null,
    xmlDecl:undefined,
    docTypeDecl:undefined,
    status:0
}
```

You'll notice the Parent and Child Node assignments discussed earlier along with several new child types (firstChild, lastChild, previousSibling, and nextSibling). These identify the relative order of child nodes – again, these are referred to as node "properties". Also notice that childNodes is recognized as a type of array (childNodes:[object #2] [] represents an array primitive). When you request the child nodes of a parent node these children are indexed within an array. This makes it relatively easy to iterate through and locate child nodes as they're each assigned a numerical key from "0" through the index value of the last child. These properties are currently "null" because we haven't loaded a document into the XML object yet.

The other important properties apparent within the debugger read-out each deal with the characteristics and values assigned to individual nodes. Actually, node values are formally recognized as data nodes, but these must always be nested within a properly formed node element.

```
nodeType:1,
attributes:[object #3] {},
nodeName:null,
nodeValue:null,
```

The `nodeType` property carries a value of from 1 to 12, which correlate as follows.

1. **NODE ELEMENT** – This node represents an element. Returns: null

2. **NODE ATTRIBUTE** – This node represents an attribute of an element. Note that it is not considered a child of the element node. Returns: the value of the attribute

3. **NODE TEXT** – This node represents the text content of a tag, and are sometimes referred to as "Data Nodes". Returns: the content of the node

4. **NODE CDATA SECTION** – This node represents a CDATA (Character Data) element within the XML document. CDATA sections are used to notify the parser that the enclosed text should not be parsed. A CDATA element appears as such <![CDATA [...text...]]>. CDATA elements are useful for sending HTML documents, and JavaScript within an XML container. Returns: the content of the node

5. **NODE ENTITY REFERENCE** – This node represents a reference to an entity within the document. For example, the entity &HI is an entity reference to the text "Hello world"

    ```
    <!ENTITY HI "Hello World">
    <MESSAGE> &HI </MESSAGE>

    Returns: null
    ```

6. **NODE ENTITY** – Entities substitute for specific characters, text, objects, and resources within an XML document. There are three basic entity types :

    Internal Entities – reference entity values declared within the document

    External Entities – reference external resources such as XML files, or even image files

    Parameter Entities – substitute for parameters within a DTD (Document Type Definition)

Because most entities must be declared within a DTD, the only entities recognized by the Flash 5 parser are "character references" such as lt, gt, ampos, and quot. Returns: null

7. **NODE PROCESSING INSTRUCTION** – This node represents a processing instruction from the XML document. Processing Instructions (PI) are used to pass the parser, and other XML aware applications, directives relevant to the handling of a document. A "PI" is declared using the convention <? your_directive ?>, the XML declaration at the beginning of an XML document is an example of a processing instruction (<?xml version="1.0" ?>) Returns: the content of the node

8. **NODE COMMENT** – This node represents a comment in the XML document. Comments within XML documents appear as such <!—this is my comment >. Returns: the comment text

9. **NODE DOCUMENT** – This node represents the ROOT NODE of the document. Returns: null

10. **NODE DOCUMENT TYPE** – This node represents the document type declaration of the <!DOCTYPE> tag. Returns: null

11. **NODE DOCUMENT FRAGMENT** – This node represents a document fragment. A document fragment associates a node or subtree with a document, without having to represent the subtree in its expanded form. Returns: null

12. **NODE NOTATION** – This node represents a notation in the document type declaration. Node notation is often used to specify the location or handling of a specific resource. Returns: null

Even a simple XML document will generate a considerable amount of information in constructing its DOM representation. The DOM mapping of the document fragment that follows requires over fifty lines to describe. This highlights a key consideration when employing XML within Flash – the parsing of XML documents consumes resources in the form of RAM and processor cycles. Within the context of the Flash player this means that there is a threshold to the size of XML documents that can parsed. This is affected by the complexity of the document, which relates to the number of distinct nodes and how deeply they are nested. A complex document can be as taxing as a simple one several times larger.

If you attempt to parse an overly large/complex XML document while other processes are running, such as animations or frame loops, the performance of those processes will be impeded and they may even stall. You can overcome this obstacle by breaking larger documents into their constituent parts and by utilizing efficient methods for handling DOM structures once they've been rendered by the parser. The methods you use to access the DOM can be as resource intensive as parsing. For this reason, the adaptation of XML within Flash applications should be understood as an extension of ActionScript programming techniques and should be approached with a similar mindset. The Flash 5 parser essentially renders a data structure which is an object comprising subordinate arrays of objects – the nodes of the XML document. After a document is parsed, the process of extracting and manipulating data from that document falls within the realm of programming.

We'll review an example of such methods shortly, but just to demonstrate the point about how resource intensive XML in Flash can be, lets look at the DOM rendering of the following tiny XML document.

```
<?xmlversion="1.0"?><FlashMovie>
<MovieClip>
</FlashMovie>
```

The fragment above is rendered as.

```
Variable _level0.foo = [object #1] {
    nodeType:1,
    nextSibling:null,
    previousSibling:null,
    parentNode:null,

    firstChild:[object #2] {
      nodeType:1,
      nextSibling:null,
```

The "first child" of the whole document is our root element, FlashMovie. A nodeType of 1 confirms that this is an element node.

```
      previousSibling:undefined
      parentNode:[object #1],
      firstChild:[object #3] {
        nodeType:3,
```

Now we're inside the first child node of FlashMovie. Unfortunately, the parser has taken the line break in the document that appeared after the <FlashMovie> tag to be a text node (hence the nodeType of 3). We'll have more joy with the "next sibling" of this node:

```
        nextSibling:[object #4] {
          nodeType:1,
```

The nodeType of 1 here suggests that we have our MovieClip element, but before we can look at it in detail, the line break after that element results in another type 3 node:

```
          nextSibling:[object #5] {
            nodeType:3,
            nextSibling:null,
            previousSibling:[object #4],
            parentNode:[object #2],
            firstChild:null,
            lastChild:null,
            childNodes:[object #6] [],
            attributes:[object #7] {},
            nodeName:null,
            nodeValue:"\r\n"
```

```
                },
```

It's nodeValue that gives the game away here: the characters \r\n represent a carriage return, followed by a linefeed.

If we continue, however, we'll be back to that type-1 node we started earlier:

```
            previousSibling:[object #3],
            parentNode:[object #2],
            firstChild:null,
            lastChild:null,
            childNodes:[object #8] [],
            attributes:[object #9] {},
            nodeName:"MovieClip",
            nodeValue:null
            },
```

And the nodeName confirms that this is indeed our MovieClip element. If we go on, we'll see the remainder of the information about that first type-3 element we came across:

```
            previousSibling:null,
            parentNode:[object #2],
            firstChild:null,
            lastChild:null,
            childNodes:[object #10] [],
            attributes:[object #11] {},
            nodeName:null,
            nodeValue:"\r\n"
            },
```

Pausing to note only that we speculated earlier about this element is true (look at that nodeValues again), we arrive at last back in the information about FlashMovie:

```
            lastChild:[object #5],
            childNodes:[object #12] [
                0:[object #3],
                1:[object #4],
                2:[object #5]
            ],
```

This is the childNodes array of the FlashMovie node. Objects 3 and 5 are our 'rogue' text nodes, while object 4 was the MovieClip node. The rest of the information then plays out in a way that should be clear if you've got the hang of everything we've seen so far:

```
            attributes:[object #13] {},
            nodeName:"FlashMovie",
            nodeValue:null,
            },
        lastChild:[object #2],
        childNodes:[object #14] [
```

```
        0:undefined,
        1:[object #2]
    },
    attributes:[object #15] {},
    nodeName:null,
    nodeValue:null,
    xmlDecl:"<?xml version=\"1.0\"?>",
    docTypeDecl:undefined,
    status:0,
    loaded:true
    }
```

As you can see, the mapping of an XML document to a DOM representation produces a number of redundant structures (i.e. arrays of objects) and properties. These are all associated with the XML object instance which had parsed this document. A small document, such as our StateDoc sample, would produce approximately 120 discrete objects.

> *When the ActionScript interpreter renders the procedures of an XML handling routine, it has to maintain a memory of each object, variable, string and number that it encounters for as long as they are relevant to the process at hand. An XML document is rendered by the XML parser as a complex of arrays, which are recognized as an object within ActionScript. When navigating these arrays it's necessary for the interpreter to maintain each object associated with the document's DOM structure within memory. If the document is very complex, and/or there are many other objects created in the course of navigating the document, the amount of memory available to the interpreter can diminish to the point that the performance of your Flash application is affected. This is why it's a good idea to map a document's DOM structure to individual sets of arrays. When information is extracted from an array, only the elements of that array are held in memory. If the array represents the childNodes of a single node element of the document, then only the data of those child nodes is present.*

Let's demonstrate how to navigate our sample document, and introduce a few techniques.

```
<?xml version="1.0" ?>
  <FlashMovie>
    <MovieClip>
      <Xpos>273.95</Xpos>   <Ypos>120</Ypos>
    </MovieClip>
    <MovieClip>
      <Xpos>275.65</Xpos>   <Ypos>280.85</Ypos>
    </MovieClip>
    <MovieClip>
```

```
    <Xpos>357.35</Xpos>   <Ypos>199.95</Ypos>
  </MovieClip>
  <MovieClip>
    <Xpos>192.7</Xpos>   <Ypos>202.7</Ypos>
  </MovieClip>
</FlashMovie>
```

ethods and properties of the XML object

The Flash 5 XML object is native to the new Object–Oriented implementation of ActionScript. As with other objects, the XML Object gives you access to several pre-defined methods and properties for processing and writing XML documents. Let's look at some of them.

- **new XML** – The XML Object constructor. This instantiates an original XML object along with its attendant properties and methods. This is expressed as *foo = new XML;* The new XML constructor can also be written as *new XML(source)* where *source* is a either a previously loaded XML document, an XML document generated within the flash environment during runtime, or a previously instantiated XML object.

- **load** – loads the named XML document into the object instance created by new XML. This is expressed as *foo.load("yourXMLdoc.xml");*. The load method will accept document assignments as simple file names (eg. "XMLfile.xml"), URL assignments (ie. "http://yourDomain/XMLfile.xml"), and variables (eg. *bar = "XMLfile.xml" ; foo.load(bar);*).

- **onLoad** – We'll be implementing onLoad as an event handler which triggers its assigned function once the XML file named by the load method has been successfully loaded into the base XML object. This is expressed as *foo.onLoad = anyFunction;*. The default implementation of onLoad, which is not used in the following example, simply returns a Boolean value of true or false within a variable assigned as its argument. This is expressed as *foo.onLoad(success);* with the *success* variable carrying a true or false value depending on the status of the load method. This method would be employed within the context of a conditional statement (eg. *if (success) {...});* .

- **length** – length is an array property which returns the highest index value of the array plus one (ie. *length = index + 1*). Array indices begin with "0", so an index value of 3 actually means that there are four values in the array (eg. 0,1,2,3). Therefore, the length of the array is four.

- **nodeName** – The nodeName property returns the name of the target node or *null* if no node name is available or the targeted node is not a type 1 node.

- **childNodes** – This is formally recognized as a "collection" of XML object references that represent each of the child nodes of the targeted parent node. This collection of XML object references is passed as an array to the base object – this is why you can determine the node properties of an array index even though the array is not an XML object. For most practical purposes, the childNodes 'collectio' can be treated as a property that generates an array of child nodes.

The following presents three ActionScript functions – `root`, `strip`, and `valid`. These utilize the methods associated with the Flash 5 XML object to analyze and extract information from a document's DOM .

It would be a good idea to load the file `rootFunction_1.fla` within your Flash authoring environment so that you have a reference as you're following this section. Each of these functions contributes to a common XML handling routine. We'll first look at them individually.

First the XML object is instantiated with constructor 'new XML() .

```
xObj=new XML();   ..instantiate a new XML object named 'xObj'

xObj.onLoad=root; ..once the object has successfully loaded the
                    document 'stateEg', fire the root function.

xObj.load("stateEg.xml"); ..load 'stateEg.xml' into the XML parser
```

The root function is then utilized to isolate the root node of the document and return an array of validated nodes elements.

```
function root(){
var xMap=new Array();
xMap=this.childNodes;    load the array 'xMap' with the childNodes
                          of 'xObj'.

x=strip(xMap);    call the strip function (2) to determine the
                  first valid childNode of the document - the 'root
                  node'.
                  Pass the index value of this child to 'x'.

xMap=xMap[x].childNodes    now re-initialize xMap with the
                           childNodes of the root node.

trace("first Array.length = "+xMap.length);   what is the length
                                              of root's
                                              childNode array?

xMap=valid(xMap);   pass the xMap array to the valid
                    function(3) for cleaning.

trace("new Array.length = "+ xMap.length);   what is the true
                                             length of the
                                             childNode array and
                                             what are its elements?

  trace("Array elements = "+xMap);

}
```

Strip is encountered in the third line of the root function, it looks at the child elements of the xMap array and returns the first valid childNode after index 't'.

```
function strip (xob) {
// The temp property holds the last value of t for this object
t = xob.temp;

// This while loop iterates through the object's childNodes
// until a valid nodeName is found
while ((xob[t].nodeName == null) && (t < xob.length )) {
  t++;
}

// The index value of this node is returned to the caller
return t;
}
```

The valid function, encountered on the sixth line of the root function, creates an empty array, nodArr, and loads this with validated node elements. Because, as we've seen, the Flash 5 parser will register certain formating expressions as node instances, it's necessary to filter these instances to produce a proper array of child nodes. This is less of a problem when the tags of an XML document are concatenated (that is, end-to-end), but most documents aren't formatted in this way.

```
function valid(xMap){
  var nodArr=new Array();

//While iterator 'n', below, is less than the length of the array
//xMap, and the length of xMap doesn't exceed the value of its
//temp property +1, strip xMap and load any valid nodeNames into
//the nodArr array.

  for(n=0; n < xMap.length && xMap.length > xMap.temp+1 ;n++){
      xMap.temp=strip(xMap);
      nodArr[n]=xMap[xMap.temp].nodeName;
      xMap.temp++;
    }
  return nodArr;
}
```

The code below demonstrates how these functions, and the loading of the document, would be presented within your editing window. The action progresses in the following steps:

- The XML document is loaded, and once it has been parsed, the root function is called to extract an array of the childNodes of the root node.

- The root function isolates the root node by calling the strip function.

- The `strip` function finds the first valid child node of the subject array and returns the index value of this node.

- The `childNodes` of this child node – in this case, *the child nodes of the root node* – are then passed to the `valid` function as an array.

- The `valid` function then iterates through each apparent child node, and checks them using the `strip` function.

- When a valid child node is discovered, it is added to the `nodArr` array.

- The `nodArr` array is then passed back to the calling function: `root`.

```
Frame Actions                                                    ×
  Movie Explorer   Frame Actions                            ?  ▶
  + −   Frame Actions                                        ▽ △

function strip (xob) {
    t = xob.temp;
    while ((xob[t].nodeType != 1) && (t < xob.length)) {
        t++;
    }
    return t;
}

function valid(xMap) {
    var nodArr = new Array();
    for(n=0; n < xMap.length && xMap.length > xMap.temp+1; n++) {
        xMap.temp = strip(xMap);
        nodArr[n] = xMap[xMap.temp].nodeName;
        xMap.temp++;
    }
    return nodArr;
}

function root() {
    var xMap = new Array();
    xMap = this.childNodes;
    x = strip(xMap);
    xMap = xMap[x].childNodes
    trace("first Array.length = " + xMap.length);
    xMap = valid(xMap);
    trace("new Array.length = "+ xMap.length);
    trace("Array elements = " + xMap);
}

xObj=new XML();
xObj.onLoad = root;
xObj.load("example.xml");

 ◀                                                          ▶
  Line 1 of 33, Col 1                                        ⊕
```

Test `rootFunction_1.fla` to see the readout produced by the code above. When the `stateEg.xml` document is run through this process, the following trace reading will be presented. First, we find that nine child nodes were originally discovered:

```
first Array.length = 9
```

Then we discover that only four of these were valid element nodes:

```
new Array.length = 4
```

Finally, we find out what the names of these four valid nodes were:

```
Array elements = MovieClip,MovieClip,MovieClip,MovieClip
```

If we hadn't gone through this document to remove all the 'rogue' elements, the presentation of `childNodes` might appear something like this. You'll notice the presence of five invalid nodes.

```
first Array.length = 9
new Array.length = 9
Array elements = "\r\n",MovieClip,null,MovieClip,null,MovieClip,
null,MovieClip,"\r\n"
```

All of this nuisance data has been filtered out by the test:

```
while ((xob[t].nodeName == null) && (t<xob.length)) {
    t++;
}
```

If you wish, you can use other node properties to validate nodes as well. Here's an example of using the `nodeType` property to extract type 1 nodes – that is, element nodes. (For more about the kinds of things you can check for using `nodeType`, look back at the table of possible values it can take.)

```
function strip (xob) {
    t = xob.temp;
    // if the childNode is not type 1 , continue
    while ((xob[t].nodeType != 1) && (t<xob.length)) {
        t++;
    }

    return t;
}
```

The usefulness of examining XML nodes' properties derives from the fact that they provide a way of screening nodes that are encountered when processing an XML document. Much, if not most, of the data you'll extract from an XML document will be retrieved by iterating through an array of `childNodes` and extracting them according to name and/or type. For instance, a type-1 node is an element, and it can be expected to have a `nodeName` property and potentially attributes too. A type-3 node contains text, and it will ususally have something in its `nodeValue` property; this is usually the value you wish to extract for presentation to the user, or to a complementary application.

The use of identifying node properties can also be employed to step through the DOM structure adaptively. That is, they can direct the processing of the XML document in response to the characteristics of nodes encountered while the node tree is being analyzed. This enables XML handling to be generalized so that nodes don't have to be addressed explicitly and the same routine can therefore be used to process any XML document, or document sub-section. This usually requires the use of a recursive function.

> *Recursion is a technique in which the subject of a function call becomes the reference of that same function call over successive cycles. This occurs when the* `valid()` *function below calls itself to analyze the child node array that it has extracted* - `nodArr[n]=valid(nodArr[n])`. *The benefit in this technique is that a hierarchical, tree like, data structure such as XML can be broken down through recursion to produce successively more acute views of the XML data while retaining the context of that data – its parent and sibling nodes. The trace reading that follows demonstrates this on a simple document like* `StateDoc.xml`.

A simple modification to the `valid()` function will enable us to extract the `nodeName` of each valid node element within this document along with their `nodeValue`.

Load `rootFunction_2.fla` to test this example:

A new method:

- `haschildNodes` – a method which returns a Boolean true or false depending on whether the base XML Element has child Nodes.

- Here's how the operation proceeds in the new version of our valid function:

- The `for` loop has been modified with an internal condition which confirms whether a given element has child nodes.

- If it does, the nodeName and nodeValue properties of this element are retrieved.

- The child nodes of the element are then re-introduced to the valid() function, as its argument – `nodArr[n]=valid(nodArr[n]);`.

- This cycle proceeds through the last child node of the root node. `Valid()` demonstrates the construction of a recursive function.

```
Frame Actions                                                    ☒
🔲 Movie Explorer  🔳 Frame Actions                              ⑦ ▶
+ −  Frame Actions                                              ▼ ▲
function strip (xob) {
    t = xob.temp;
    while ((xob[t].nodeType != 1) && (t < xob.length)) {
        t++;
    }
    return t;
}

function valid(xMap) {
    var nodArr = new Array();
    for(n=0; n < xMap.length && xMap.length > xMap.temp+1; n++) {
        xMap.temp = strip(xMap);
        if (xMap[xMap.temp].hasChildNodes) {
            trace("element node : " + xMap[xMap.temp].nodeName);
            if (xMap[xMap.temp].firstChild.nodeValue != null) {
                trace(xMap[xMap.temp].nodeName + ".nodeValue =" +
                    xMap[xMap.temp].firstChild.nodeValue);
            }
            trace("~~~~~~~~~~~~~~~~~~~~~~~~~~~~~~~~o");
            nodArr[n] = new Array ();
            nodArr[n] = xMap[xMap.temp].childNodes;
            nodArr[n] = valid(nodarr[n]);
        }
        xMap.temp++;
    }
    return nodArr;
}

function root() {
    var xMap = new Array();
    xMap = this.childNodes;
    x = strip(xMap);
    xMap = xMap[x].childNodes
    trace("first Array.length = " + xMap.length);
    xMap = valid(xMap);
    trace("new Array.length = "+ xMap.length);
    trace("Array elements = " + xMap);
}

xObj = new XML();
xObj.onLoad = root;
xObj.load("example.xml");
◀                                                              ▶
Line 13 of 44, Col 1
                                                              ⊕
```

The trace reading is below.

```
Output                                                                    ×
Generator Installed                                                 Options
first Array.length = 9
element node : MovieClip
MovieClip.nodeValue =


~~~~~~~~~~~~~~~~~~~~~~~~~~~~~~~~~~~~~~o
element node : Xpos
Xpos.nodeValue =273.95
~~~~~~~~~~~~~~~~~~~~~~~~~~~~~~~~~~~~~~o
element node : Ypos
Ypos.nodeValue =120
~~~~~~~~~~~~~~~~~~~~~~~~~~~~~~~~~~~~~~o
element node : MovieClip
MovieClip.nodeValue =


~~~~~~~~~~~~~~~~~~~~~~~~~~~~~~~~~~~~~~o
element node : Xpos
Xpos.nodeValue =275.65
~~~~~~~~~~~~~~~~~~~~~~~~~~~~~~~~~~~~~~o
element node : Ypos
Ypos.nodeValue =280.85
~~~~~~~~~~~~~~~~~~~~~~~~~~~~~~~~~~~~~~o
element node : MovieClip
MovieClip.nodeValue =


~~~~~~~~~~~~~~~~~~~~~~~~~~~~~~~~~~~~~~o
element node : Xpos
Xpos.nodeValue =357.35
~~~~~~~~~~~~~~~~~~~~~~~~~~~~~~~~~~~~~~o
element node : Ypos
Ypos.nodeValue =199.95
~~~~~~~~~~~~~~~~~~~~~~~~~~~~~~~~~~~~~~o
element node : MovieClip
MovieClip.nodeValue =


~~~~~~~~~~~~~~~~~~~~~~~~~~~~~~~~~~~~~~o
element node : Xpos
Xpos.nodeValue =192.7
~~~~~~~~~~~~~~~~~~~~~~~~~~~~~~~~~~~~~~o
element node : Ypos
Ypos.nodeValue =202.7
~~~~~~~~~~~~~~~~~~~~~~~~~~~~~~~~~~~~~~o
new Array.length = 3
Array elements = ,,,,
```

So now, we've isolated each of the nodes within this document, and their node values, but there's yet another way to look at a node and decide whether it has any information that's actually going to be of any use to you.

A further way to determine whether a nodeValue actually contains real data, or is simply empty whitespace, is to compare its standard character encoding with its 'escaped' encoding, in which formatting expressions and reserved characters are selectively encoded. This is demonstrated in the following modification of the valid function; load rootFunction_3.fla to test this example:

```
if(xMap[xMap.temp].hasChildNodes) {
    trace("element node : " + xMap[xMap.temp].nodeName);

    enc =xMap[xMap.temp].firstChild.nodeValue;
    esc = escape(enc);
    trace(esc);
    trace(esc.length + "    :    " + enc.length);
```

The escaped encoding of whitespace is exactly three times the length of its unescaped form. Most numbers and characters aren't transcoded by 'escape', so only nodeValues comprised of whitespace and 'special' characters (such as <, >, ", etc.) will produce an escaped encoding that's exactly three times the length of the original. This is because their hexidecimal equivalent is represented as a three-character form (%nn), while unescaped characters are represented by a single character.

```
if((xMap[xMap.temp].firstChild.nodeValue != null) &&
            (esc.length / 3 != enc.length)) {
    trace(xMap[xMap.temp].nodeName + ".nodeValue = " +
        xMap[xMap.temp].firstChild.nodeValue);
}
trace("~~~~~~~~~~~~~~~~~~~~~~~~~~~~~~~~O");
nodArr[n] = new Array();
nodArr[n] = xMap[xMap.temp].childNodes;
nodArr[n] = valid(nodArr[n]);
}
```

When we run the sample with this new nodeValue filter in place, and additional trace statements, the following reading is produced. The nodeValue filter helps in determining which nodeValues actually contain data, and which are simply whitespace.

```
first Array.length = 9
element node : MovieClip
%0D%0A%20%20%20%20%20%20
24    :    8
~~~~~~~~~~~~~~~~~~~~~~~~~~~~~~O
```

The ratio of the escaped length to the unescaped length here – 24 to 8, or 3 to 1 – means that this is a 'bad' nodeValue.

```
element node : Xpos
273%2E95
8   :   6
Xpos.nodeValue = 273.95
~~~~~~~~~~~~~~~~~~~~~~~~~~~~~~~~O
element node : Ypos
120
3   :   3
Ypos.nodeValue = 120
~~~~~~~~~~~~~~~~~~~~~~~~~~~~~~~~O
```

Conversely, the ratios displayed by the values of these two nodes are less than 3 to 1, so we have 'good' values.

Now let's say that we wanted to apply the data we've extracted within a Flash application. The most practical way of doing this is to map these elements to a native ActionScript array object. When an array is loaded with the child nodes of an XML element, it is referred to as a collection, reflecting the fact that the XML object is actually passing the array references to a collection of XML objects that represent the element's child nodes. Once you have a document's nodes mapped to array structures, you can manipulate them as array indices while also accessing them as node elements.

Yet again, this can be accomplished with a simple modification to the `valid` function, so load `rootFunction_4.fla` to test this example:

```
xArr = new Array();
xObj = new XML();
xObj.onLoad = root;
xObj.load("example.xml");


    if(xMap[xMap.temp].hasChildNodes) {
        trace("element node : " + xMap[xMap.temp].nodeName);

        // Load each nodeName into xArr
        xArr.push(xMap[xMap.temp].nodeName);

        enc = xMap[xMap.temp].firstChild.nodeValue;
        esc = escape(enc);
```

```
            trace(esc);
            trace(esc.length + "    :    " + enc.length);
            if((xMap[xMap.temp].firstChild.nodeValue != null) &&
                        (esc.length / 3 != enc.length)) {
                xArr.push(xMap[xMap.temp].firstChild.nodeValue);
                trace(xMap[xMap.temp].nodeName + ".nodeValue = " +
                        xMap[xMap.temp].firstChild.nodeValue);
            }
            trace("~~~~~~~~~~~~~~~~~~~~~~~~~~~~~~~~~o");
            nodArr[n] = new Array();
            nodArr[n] = xMap[xMap.temp].childNodes;
            nodArr[n] = valid(nodArr[n]);
        }
```

After you've run the example, check your debugger to view the resulting array; the two lines of code we've added produce the following structure.

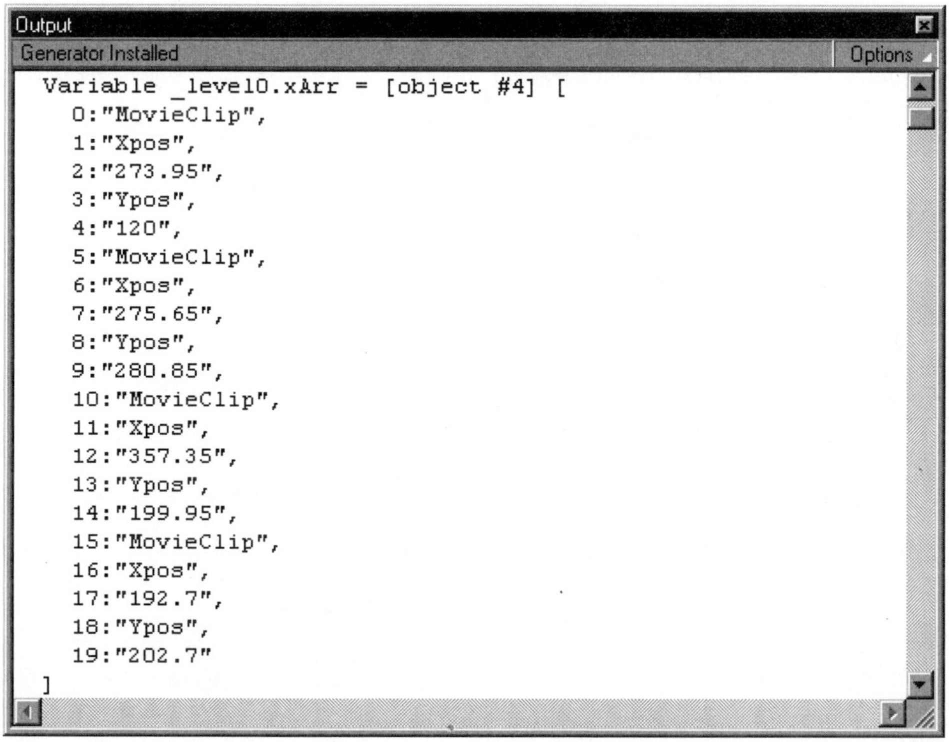

```
Output                                                          ×
Generator Installed                                      Options
  Variable _level0.xArr = [object #4] [
    0:"MovieClip",
    1:"Xpos",
    2:"273.95",
    3:"Ypos",
    4:"120",
    5:"MovieClip",
    6:"Xpos",
    7:"275.65",
    8:"Ypos",
    9:"280.85",
    10:"MovieClip",
    11:"Xpos",
    12:"357.35",
    13:"Ypos",
    14:"199.95",
    15:"MovieClip",
    16:"Xpos",
    17:"192.7",
    18:"Ypos",
    19:"202.7"
  ]
```

Once you've mapped the property values of your XML document to an array, you can determine the names and values of each node within the document simply by iterating through its elements. Unfortunately, this structure doesn't provide us with any information regarding the relationships of these values – if we weren't familiar with the sample document, it would be difficult simply to infer that Xpos was a child node of MovieClip. Also, reviewing these values by searching each element of the array is inefficient. Instead, we'll create an array that can be called by the name of the node it represents. The elements of this array will represent this node's values. Another modification to valid will do the trick; load rootFunction_5.fla to test this example:

```
xmlexample.txt - Notepad
File  Edit  Format  Help

function valid(xMap){
   var nodArr = new Array();
   for(n=0; n < xMap.length && xMap.length > xMap.temp+1; n++) {
      xMap.temp = strip(xMap);

      if(xMap[xMap.temp].hasChildNodes) {
         trace("element node : " + xMap[xMap.temp].nodeName);

         xArr.push(xMap[xMap.temp].nodeName);

         // Load the nodeName of each element into the variable xai
         var xai = xMap[xMap.temp].nodeName;

         // Create a new array under the nodeName of this element,
         // BUT first check to see whether this exists so that an
         // existing array isn't overwritten. A reference to a non-
         // existent object returns the value "undefined".
         if(typeof(eval(xArr[xArr.length - 1])) == "undefined") {
            eval(xai) = new Array();
         }
```

```
            enc = xMap[xMap.temp].firstChild.nodeValue;
            esc = escape(enc);


            if((xMap[xMap.temp].firstChild.nodeValue != null) &&
                            (esc.length / 3 != enc.length)) {
                xArr.push(xMap[xMap.temp].firstChild.nodeValue);


                // Load the nodeValue of this element
                //* into the new array
                eval(xai).push(xArr[xArr.length - 1]);
            }


            nodArr[n] = new Array();
            nodArr[n] = xMap[xMap.temp].childNodes;
            nodArr[n] = valid(nodArr[n]);
        }


        xMap.temp++;
    }
    return nodArr;
}
```

This produces the following arrays of nodeValues, indexed under the names of their parent nodes. The value of the first Xpos node can now be determined by examining _root.Xpos[0]. This is much easier than attempting to use DOM addressing to extract node names and values!

```
        Variable _level0.Xpos = [object #125] [
            0:"273.95",
            1:"275.65",
            2:"357.35",
            3:"192.7"
        ]

        Variable _level0.Ypos = [object #126] [
            0:"120",
            1:"280.85",
            2:"199.95",
            3:"202.7"
        ]
```

> *We've seen how an ActionScript function can be designed to step through an XML document adaptively by analyzing each node's properties (*nodeName, nodeValue, *and the Boolean method* hasChildNodes()*), and we've developed a set of routines which enable this process to be generalized across a range of documents using the principle of recursion. The previous example presents many new concepts in a short amount of space. Rather than focus on the specific base of code used to accomplish this, try to familiarize yourself with how these methods are applied, and what sorts of conditional and control structures are required to adapt them in general fashion. The subsequent examples in this chapter will apply these same methods to a more sophisticated example of Flash to Browser communication – you'll see that the same basic structures can be applied in a variety of situations*

So now that you have an idea of how to recurse and validate XML documents within Flash, we're going to introduce a practical example of XML integration. XML is gaining a tremendous momentum within the arena of web publishing. This is due, in part, to the fact that XML facilitates the separation of presentation and data layers within an application or web domain. An example of this is the use of XML 'Data Islands', which are XML documents embedded within a web page. The 'island' is not apparent on-screen, but can be used as a sort of local database by other facilities on the page – such as JavaScript, XSLT, and now Flash. Our example is going to demonstrate how an XML data island can be used to configure a Flash movie within the page. This is a simple implementation of the concept, but should give you an idea of how Flash elements can be integrated within XML driven publishing frameworks.

Data islands

This example is designed to be run within Internet Explorer 5/+ on a PC.

It is advisable that you load the file xmlisland.html within your browser to serve as a reference as you review this example.

Firstly, I'll introduce a new method:

- **parseXML** – The parseXML() method parses the XML document which is specified as its argument and passes this to the base XML object. This is implemented as *xmlObj.parseXML(xmlDoc)* where *xmlDoc* is a pre-parsed XML document. The parseXML() method behaves similarly to the load method.

The basic flow of control within this example initiates with the loading of the HTML document and XML data island into the browser.

■   A prompt is presented to the user asking for a command line entry of the word
'configure'. The original configuration of the Flash element is apparent on-screen.

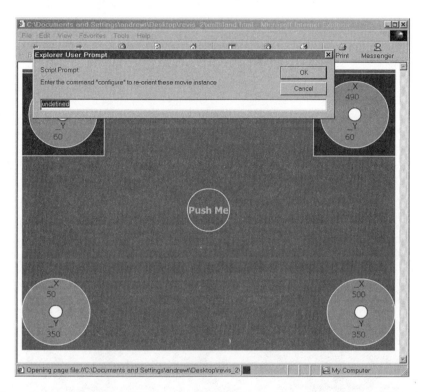

When the user enters "configure" at the prompt, the xmlFrag() function is fired.
xmlFrag() extracts the XML Data Island according to its id attribute and passes this to the
Flash application. The Flash application possesses a frame loop which monitors the state of
the variable _root.config. If _root.config possesses a value, the ActionScript function
configState() is fired and a callback is sent to the frame loop telling it to cease firing
configState(). If configState() were not prevented from firing, the performance of the
Flash movie would be adversely impacted.

The configState() function instantiates a new flaximal object and loads this with the
XML document passed from the HTML page. The flaximal object renders the XML
document as a compound set of arrays which are named for the node elements within the
document – we'll be reviewing flaXiMaL in the next section. Once the document has been
mapped to an array structure, configState() isolates the nodeNames of each movie
instance and evaluates these against their Xpos and Ypos values as below.

```
Instance=_root.code['StateDoc_parentof'][sd];
    if(eval(Instance)._parent==_level0){
        eval(Instance)._x=_root.code['Xpos'][sd];
        eval(Instance)._y=_root.code['Ypos'][sd];
```

```
        } else {
          eval(Instance)._parent._x=_root.code['Xpos'][sd];
          eval(Instance)._parent._y=_root.code['Ypos'][sd];
          }
```

Using eval() in this context allow us to treat the nodeNames of these elements as Flash object addresses and associate _x and _y properties with them. When this code is evaluated, the object referenced by the Instance variable above is repositioned to the values of its Xpos and Ypos nodes.

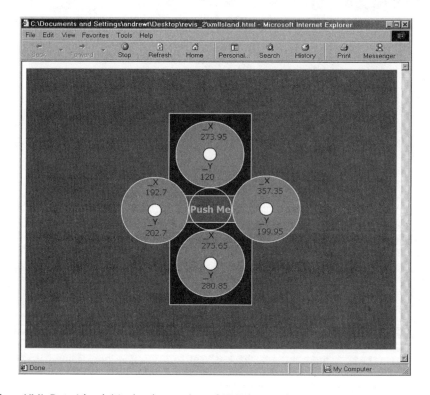

Here is an XML Data Island; it's simply a region of XML inserted at an appropriate point within an HTML or XHTML document. In this case, it's been placed below our Flash object to enforce their association.

```
        <body >
        <!—
         The Object Element below encapsulates a Flash Movie
         >
        <OBJECT classid="clsid:D27CDB6E-AE6D-11cf-96B8-444553540000"
        ➥
        codebase="http://download.macromedia.com/pub/shockwave/cabs/flash/
```

```
➥ swflash.cab#version=5,0,0,0"
 WIDTH=800 HEIGHT=600 id="example" name="example">
 .
 .
 .
</OBJECT>
<!--
   Below is the XML Data Island
>
<xml id="state">
  <StateDoc>
    <PrimaryInstanceB.SecondaryInstanceC>
      <Xpos>273.95</Xpos>
      <Ypos>120</Ypos>
    </PrimaryInstanceB.SecondaryInstanceC>
    <PrimaryInstanceA.SecondaryInstanceC>
      <Xpos>275.65</Xpos>
      <Ypos>280.85</Ypos>
    </PrimaryInstanceA.SecondaryInstanceC>
    <SecondaryInstanceB>
      <Xpos>357.35</Xpos>
      <Ypos>199.95</Ypos>
    </SecondaryInstanceB>
    <SecondaryInstanceA>
      <Xpos>192.7</Xpos>
      <Ypos>202.7</Ypos>
    </SecondaryInstanceA>
  </StateDoc>
</xml>
</body>
```

The <xml> tag used to delimit this region of XML is not an XML declaration; it's an XML specific tag used to encapsulate XML within XHTML and HTML documents.

The relevant code

We'll be using a JavaScript function to isolate the data island and pass this to our Flash movie.

```
<html>
<head>
<META HTTP-EQUIV="Expires" CONTENT="Mon, 04 Dec 1999 21:29:02
➥GMT" />
<script language="javascript">

// xml document is extracted by its 'id' attribute and passed to
Flash  // using the SetVariable method.

function xmlFrag() {
  try {
```

```
        var xmlFragment=document.getElementById("state").innerHTML ;
        Example = window.document.example;
        Example.SetVariable("config",xmlFragment);


        }
      catch(e){
        alert("XML ISLAND not recognized - reload this page");
        }
}
</script>
        .

        .
<script language="javascript">
input=prompt("Enter the command \"configure\" to re-orient these
➥movie instance");

if(input=="configure"){
   xmlFrag();
   }

</script>
```

Once the Flash movie receives the XML document, the configState() function is fired and the XML document is passed to the flaXiMaL object where it is mapped to a compound array structure. The configState() function then extracts these values and applies them to their relevant movie instance. This re-positions the instances on-stage according to the coordinates encoded within the XML data island.

FlaXiMaL

FlaXiMaL is an original object type which assists in mapping well formed XML documents to a set of arrays. These model both the relative and absolute hierarchies of the document's node name, child node, and node value properties, as well as its attributes. It's constructed using ActionScript's prototype mechanism. A significant benefit of using flaXiMaL is that the values used in naming these arrays derive from the node names of the subject XML document. This creates a map of the document which mirrors its own lexicon and enables multiple documents to be loaded into the same application. If a generic naming scheme were used in this situation, each new document would generate arrays which displaced those of the previous document.

Firstly, a new property to introduce:

- **parentNode** – returns the parent node of the target node. A parentNode is recognized as the parent of each of its child nodes. The syntax used is foo.parentNode.

Let's begin by looking at the array structures that FlaXiMaL produces from processing our sample document.

Notice that we've included an XML declaration to ensure that the document is well formed.

```
<?xml?>
<xml id="state">
  <StateDoc>
    <PrimaryInstanceB.SecondaryInstanceC>
      <Xpos>273.95</Xpos>
      <Ypos>120</Ypos>
    </PrimaryInstanceB.SecondaryInstanceC>
    <PrimaryInstanceA.SecondaryInstanceC>
      <Xpos>275.65</Xpos>
      <Ypos>280.85</Ypos>
    </PrimaryInstanceA.SecondaryInstanceC>
    <SecondaryInstanceB>
      <Xpos>357.35</Xpos>
      <Ypos>199.95</Ypos>
    </SecondaryInstanceB>
    <SecondaryInstanceA>
      <Xpos>192.7</Xpos>
      <Ypos>202.7</Ypos>
    </SecondaryInstanceA>
  </StateDoc>
</xml>
```

The document is loaded using the XML object's `load` method within the following code.

```
function loaded () {
   foo.generate();
}
c = 1;
foo = new flaximal("code");
foo.flaximal_obj.onLoad = loaded;
foo.load("ASstudioDoc.xml");
```

`foo` is actually established as a wrapper for the XML object `flaximal_obj` as apparent within the base `flaximal` function below.

```
function flaximal (name) {
   eval(name) = new Object ;
   this.flaximal_obj = new XML();
}
```

This relationship enables us to associate methods and properties with `flaximal` which possess distinct roles in XML handling. `Flaximal_obj` is a member of `flaximal` which initially parses the XML document. Notice that `foo` has inherited the `load` method associated with the XML object instance `flaximal_obj`.

After the XML document has been processed the following structures are apparent within the debugger.

Each node element within the document is represented by two arrays, one which indexes the node values of that element and another which indexes its child nodes. If an element does not have a node value it will only present a _parentof array.

```
Variable _level0.code = [object #14] { ~ the name given to the
                                            flaximal object.
xml_parentof:[object #15] [ ~ the xml tag from the Data Island
  0:"StateDoc"   ~ StateDoc is the childNode of 'xml'
],
xml_parentof_temp:0,
StateDoc_parentof:[object #16] [ ~ the _parentof array presents
                                     the childNodes of an
                                     element as
                                     its indices
  0:"PrimaryInstanceB.SecondaryInstanceC",
  1:"PrimaryInstanceA.SecondaryInstanceC",
  2:"SecondaryInstanceB",
  3:"SecondaryInstanceA"
],
StateDoc_parentof_temp:3,
```

The index values of the nodeValues of Xpos and Ypos correspond to the order in which they were encountered within the document. This enables you to reference the nodeValue according to the index value of its parent node.

```
Xpos:[object #17] [
  0:"273.95",
  1:"275.65",
  2:"357.35",
  3:"192.7"
],
Xpos_temp:3,

Ypos:[object #18] [
  0:"120",
  1:"280.85",
  2:"199.95",
  3:"202.7"
],
Ypos_temp:3,
```

Both Xpos and Ypos are the childNodes of the following elements

```
SecondaryInstanceB_parentof:[object #19] [
  0:"Xpos",
  1:"Ypos"
],
SecondaryInstanceB_parentof_temp:1,
SecondaryInstanceA_parentof:[object #20] [
```

```
            0:"Xpos",
            1:"Ypos"
        ],
        SecondaryInstanceA_parentof_temp:1
    }
```

You should be aware that there is actually a flaw in the mapping of our sample document. Because we're using Flash's native addressing syntax, it's not possible to create an array instance from the node names `"PrimaryInstanceB.SecondaryInstanceC"` and `"Primary InstanceA.SecondaryInstanceC"`. This problem can be rectified by not utilizing proper Flash instance names – by using `PrimaryInstanceB_SecondaryInstanceC` for instance – but for the purposes of our forthcoming example, we'll simply associate the `Xpos` and `Ypos` by their corresponding index values within the `StateDoc_parentof` array.

By using alternative node names the mapping would appear as such.

```
        Variable _level0.code = [object #14] {
            xml_parentof:[object #15] [
                0:"StateDoc"
            ],
            xml_parentof_temp:0,
            StateDoc_parentof:[object #16] [
                0:"PrimaryInstanceB_SecondaryInstanceC",
                1:"PrimaryInstanceA_SecondaryInstanceC",
                2:"SecondaryInstanceB",
                3:"SecondaryInstanceA"
            ],
            StateDoc_parentof_temp:3,
            PrimaryInstanceB_SecondaryInstanceC_parentof:[object #17] [
                0:"Xpos",
                1:"Ypos"
            ],
            PrimaryInstanceB_SecondaryInstanceC_parentof_temp:1,
            Xpos:[object #18] [
                0:"273.95",
                1:"275.65",
                2:"357.35",
                3:"192.7"
            ],
            Xpos_temp:3,
            Ypos:[object #19] [
                0:"120",
                1:"280.85",
                2:"199.95",
                3:"202.7"
            ],
            Ypos_temp:3,
            PrimaryInstanceA_SecondaryInstanceC_parentof:[object #20] [
                0:"Xpos",
                1:"Ypos"
```

```
        ],
        PrimaryInstanceA_SecondaryInstanceC_parentof_temp:1,
        SecondaryInstanceB_parentof:[object #21] [
          0:"Xpos",
          1:"Ypos"
        ],
        SecondaryInstanceB_parentof_temp:1,
        SecondaryInstanceA_parentof:[object #22] [
          0:"Xpos",
          1:"Ypos"
        ],
        SecondaryInstanceA_parentof_temp:1
      }
```

Now lets look at how FlaXiMaL processes a well formed XML document to extract the names and values of each node and generate array structures.

The loaded() function presented above calls flaXiMaL's generate() method.

```
function loaded () {
   foo.generate();
}
```

The generate() method is associated with the flax_gen function below through ActionScript's prototype mechanism.

For example:

```
flaximal.prototype.generate = flax_gen;
```

flax_gen is responsible for mapping the first instance of child nodes within a XML document and for establishing successive cycles of recursion which enable the discovery of deeply nested elements within the document.

```
function flax_gen () {

   // flax_root is created as an instance of the XML object

   flax_root = new XML();
   var flax_child = new Array();

   // it is then passed the child nodes of foo.flaximal_obj -
   // which isitself an instance of the XML object.

   flax_root = this.flaximal_obj.childNodes
   var frl = flax_root.length ; // 'frl' is an abbreviation for
                                //  flax_root.length
   prime = new Array ;
   // it is then passed the child nodes of foo.flaximal_obj -
   // which isitself an instance of the XML object.
```

```
strip(flax_root);    //the 'strip' function reads through an
                     //object's child nodes looking for non-null
                     //node names. When it finds one, the index
                     // of this child node is returned in a
                     //variable.

// now that we've found a valid node Element- the root node,
// we're  going to assign this to flax_root and proceed with
// mapping the document.

flax_root = this.flaximal_obj.childNodes[t];

if (flax_root.nodeName != null ) {

   //create an array instance named root_'root node name'

   eval("root_"+flax_root.nodeName) = new Array ;

   RootNode = flax_root.nodeName;
   root = eval("root_"+flax_root.nodeName) ;

   // the flax_child array had be instantiated in the 3rd line
   // of code. Below flax_child is passed the child nodes of the
   // root node.

   flax_child = flax_root.childNodes;

   // temp and t are used by the strip function to relate which
   // childnode of a node element is valid

   temp = 0;
   flax_child.temp = temp ;
   t=0;
```

Below we're establishing a loop within a loop, the for...loop is incrementing through the child nodes of flax_root and assigning the child nodes of each child node (for example. ele=flax_child[s].childNodes) of flax_root to a new array. Each subordinate set of child nodes is then passed to the while...loop where it is introduced to the map() function.

```
for(s=0;s <= frl;s++) {
   val = 0;
   elarray = new Array ;
   ele = new Array ;
```

```
                       ele = flax_child[s].childNodes ;
                       flax_occur = 0 ;
                        while (val < ele.length){
                       num = 0 ;
                       map(flax_child,elarray);
                       ++val }
                  }
               }
            }
```

map() receives two arrays; the second is used to store the child nodes of the first. When the map argument nodarr is received from flax_gen it's an empty array, subsequent calls to map() will provide a copy of nodarr, which represents a collection of child nodes. The strip() function is re-used within the map function and is presented below.

strip() receives a collection of child nodes and an array index value signified by temp. Each child node from the temp position forward is analyzed to determine whether there is a valid node name; when one is encountered its index value is passed back to the callee.

```
function strip (xob) {
    t = xob.temp
  while ((xob[t].nodeName == null) && (t<xob.length)) {
    ++t
    }
  return t}

function map (array,nodarr) {
  var  arr = new Array ;
    arr = array ;
  var  subarr = new Array ;
    subarr = nodarr ;

    // arr.temp is associated with the array argument passed to
    // map and indicates the current position of the child nodes
    // index within array.

  while (arr.temp <= arr.length ){

  arr.strip = strip(arr);
  arr.temp=t ;

    if (arr[arr.temp].nodeName != null) {
      flax_occur++ ;
      prime[flax_occur] = arr[arr.temp].nodeName;
      }

    if (arr[arr.temp].nodeName != null ) {
      vessel = arr[arr.temp].nodeName;
```

```
            var par = arr[arr.temp].parentNode.nodeName + "_parentof"
            prime[flax_occur] = vessel;
            flax_array(par,vessel,flax_occur);
        }
```

The following is the routine responsible for extracting and mapping attribute arrays to the `flaximal` object's native array structures:

```
    if (typeof(arr[arr.temp].attributes) != "undefined") {
        for (atts in arr[arr.temp].attributes) {
          var att_array = arr[arr.temp].attributes[atts];
          var attribute = arr[arr.temp].nodeName + "Attributes";
          flax_prop(atts, att_array);
          flax_array(attribute, atts, flax_occur);
          flax_array(attribute, att_array, atts);
        }
    }
```

Here, the keys of the `arr[arr.temp]` attributes collection are successively loaded into the `atts` variable. This variable is then processed by the series of statements contained within the `for..in` construct:

```
    subarr[arr.temp] = new Array;
    pr = arr[arr.temp].nodeName;


    if(arr[arr.temp].hasChildNodes()) {
        subarr[arr.temp] = arr[arr.temp].childNodes;


        var iti = 0;
        while(iti <= subarr[arr.temp].length) {
            subarr[arr.temp].temp = iti;
            strip_val(subarr[arr.temp]);
            iti= V;


            var enc = subarr[arr.temp][iti].nodeValue;
            var esc = escape(enc);

            if ((subarr[arr.temp][iti].nodeValue != null) &&
                        (esc.length / 3 != enc.length)) {
              var B = subarr[arr.temp][iti].nodeValue;
              flax_array(vessel, B, flax_occur);
            }
            iti++;
        }
```

```
                subarr[arr.temp].temp = 0;
                map(subarr[arr.temp], subarr);

            }

        primo = arr[arr.temp].nodeName;
        arr.temp++;
        }
    }
```

flax_gen and map are the functions responsible for processing the XML document and extracting valid nodeName, nodeValue, and attribute properties. These values are passed to the function flax_array, where they are mapped to complementary array structures.

```
    function flax_array (key, value, index) {
        ft = eval(flax);
        if(typeof(eval("ft." + key)) != "object") {
            eval("ft." + key) = new Array;
        }


        if(typeof(root[key]) != "object") {
            root[key] = new Array;
        }


        ktemp = key + "_temp";
        ev = eval("ft." + ktemp);
        if(typeof(ev) == "number") {
            kcount = ev;
            kcount++;
            flax_prop(ktemp, kcount);
            index = kcount;
        }
        else if(typeof(index) == "string") {
            eval("ft." + key)[index]= new Array;
            eval("ft." + key)[index] = value;
        }
        else if((typeof(eval(ev)) == "undefined") &&
                    (typeof(index)!= "string")) {
            flax_prop(ktemp, 0);
            index = 0;
        }


        root[key][index] = value;
        eval("ft." + key)[index] = value;
        root[flax_occur] = new Array;
```

```
        root[flax_occur] = root[key][index] ;
        delete(index);
    }
```

The FlaXiMaL object is found in its entirety in the file `flaxObject.as`.

The flow of control proceeds as follows.

- Instantiate the `flaximal` object

- Load a well formed XML document into its `flaximal_obj` member

- This fires the `flax_gen()` method associated with the. `onLoad()` method

- `flax_gen()` isolates the root node of this document using `strip()` and creates an array of root's `childNodes`

- Each child node is subject to the `map()` function according to their position within root's `childNode` array

- `map()` validates each received `childNode` and passes its values to the `flax_array()` method

- `flax_array()` creates a hierarchy of arrays from the values received via `map()`

- `map()` calls each array that it receives from `flax_gen()` recursively until there are no node elements remaining

- When this process is complete, a new compound data structure has been generated which represents a map of the XML document

ing XML to interact with external applications

This example utilizes the file `FlashApplication.html` – you should load this into your browser as a reference while you're reviewing this example. The corresponding FLA is `example.fla`.

This example will demonstrate a method for encoding ECMA scripts using XML and passing these to the browser for evaluation. This enables you to associate JavaScript programs with Flash objects and to execute these selectively, based on actions within the movie. It also enables Flash applications to be modularized in a manner which makes them more portable across various publishing frameworks and web application environments. The Flash movie is delivering the JavaScript necessary for its support which means that this code doesn't have to be pre-written into the HTML container. All that you need to do is provide the following function within the page.

```
function example_Dofscommand(command,args){
//IE
  if(command=="go"){
    args=unescape(args);
```

```
        eval(args);
    }
}
```

JavaScript's `eval()` method passes code directly to the JavaScript interpreter for evaluation. This enables you to load 'new' code into the interpreter after a page has been loaded.

Firstly, there's a new property to introduce.

- **firstChild** – returns the first child node of the subject parent node. The syntax for `firstChild` is *foo.firstChild*. It is important to remember that the first child node of a node element is always recognized in relation to its immediate parent element, and that this relationship only extends for one generation. Also, when an XML document is presented as a string (that is. a concatenated series of tags) the `firstChild` property can be used to retrieve the node value of an element. This method is often more effective than using the `nodeValue` property when XML objects are presented as strings.

Example 1:

```
<?xml version="1.0"?>
    <the_walls_of_my_house>
        <floor value="1">
            <rooms>
                <den>artificial wood panelling</den>
        cont...
```

The `firstChild` node of `<the_walls_of_my_house>` is `<floor>`; the `firstChild` node of `<floor>` is `<rooms>`.

Example 2:

```
<?xml version="1.0"?><the_walls_of_my_house><floor
value="1"><rooms><den>artificial wood panelling</den>
```

Here, `artificial wood panelling` can be recognized as the first child of `<den>`

- **lastChild** – returns the last child node of the subject parent node. This is expressed as *foo.lastChild*. The `lastChild` property is basically the inverse of the `firstChild` property, though it is not effective in extracting node values from XML objects in string form.

These following methods are used to write XML documents using ActionScript.

- **appendChild** – This method attaches a new child node to the subject parent node and is expressed as *foo.appendChild(node)*. The node value declaration is most effective when *node* reflects either an existing XML object, an Object property such the `childNode` of another XML object, or is written as a compound statement which instantiates a new XML object within the *node* argument. For example: *foo.appendChild((new XML()).createElement("element_name"))*

- **createElement** – The constructor method used in generating new XML node elements. The createElement method is expressed as *foo.createElement(name)* where *name* is the name of the element to be generated. The *foo* argument should reflect an existing XML object. In addition, createElement should be used in conjunction with appendChild as below. This is because the base XML object primitive is actually being appended with a new child node element relative to the XML Declaration.

  For example The following statements generate a new XML element named NODE.

  ```
  xmlObj = new XML();
  xmlObj.xmlDecl = "<?xml version=\"1.0\" ?>";
  xmlObj.appendChild((new XML).createElement("NODE"));
  trace(xmlObj);
  ```

  This produces : <?xml version="1.0" ?><NODE/>

- **createTextNode** – This is a constructor method used in creating new text nodes (also known as Data Nodes). The createTextNode method works similarly to the createElement constructor method by appending a new data node to the subject node element.

  ```
  xmlObj = new XML();
  xmlObj.xmlDecl = "<?xml version=\"1.0\" ?>";
  xmlObj.appendChild((new XML).createElement("NODE"));

  data_node="hello world";
  xmlObj.firstChild.appendChild((new
  XML).createTextNode(data_node));

  trace(xmlObj);
  ```

  This produces: <?xml version="1.0" ?><NODE>hello world</NODE>

You'll notice that that createTextNode is being appended to the firstChild node of xmlObj (ie.<NODE>). If firstChild were not utilized, hello world would be appended to the XML Declaration and create a poorly formed document.

There are a few other methods available for writing XML documents with ActionScript which aren't incorporated in the following example.

These are:

- **cloneNode(Boolean)** – This method is used to replicate the DOM structure of the target XML object, or node element, which is expressed as xmlObj.cloneNode(boolean). The Boolean value can be either true or false and specifies whether the target object or node is to be cloned or not. The purpose of the Boolean argument is to enable the clone node method to be switched either on or off selectively in response to rules applied to the XML document writing process. Boolean values can also be expressed as either 0 (false), or 1 (true), and as such may be manipulated by incrementing or de-incrementing a variable in the Boolean argument position.

An example:

```
xmlObj = new XML();
xmlObj.xmlDecl = "<?xml version=\"1.0\" ?>";
xmlObj.appendChild((new XML).createElement("NODE"));

data_node="hello world";
xmlObj.firstChild.appendChild((new
➥XML).createTextNode(data_node));

clone=xmlObj.cloneNode(true);
xmlObj.appendChild(clone);
trace(xmlObj);
```

This produces: `<?xml version="1.0" ?><NODE>hello world</NODE><NODE>hello world</NODE>`. If the statement `clone=xmlObj.cloneNode(true);` were modified to `clone=xmlObj.firstChild.firstChild.cloneNode(true);` the output of this routine would produce `<?xml version="1.0" ?><NODE>hello world</NODE>hello world`.

This is because the data node `hello world` is actually the first child node of the `<NODE>` element.

In this way, `cloneNode` enables you to either copy an entire XML document structure or to isolate elements of that structure using the document node tree model.

■ **removeNode** – The `removeNode` method erases the targeted node element.

```
xmlObj = new XML();
xmlObj.xmlDecl = "<?xml version=\"1.0\" ?>";
xmlObj.appendChild((new XML).createElement("NODE"));

data_node="hello world";
xmlObj.firstChild.appendChild((new
➥XML).createTextNode(data_node));

clone=xmlObj.cloneNode(true);
xmlObj.appendChild(clone);
trace(xmlObj);

xmlObj.lastChild.removeNode();
trace(xmlObj);
```

This action changes the previous output

`<?xml version="1.0" ?><NODE>hello world</NODE><NODE>hello world</NODE>`

to the following by removing the `lastChild` node.

```
<?xml version="1.0" ?><NODE>hello world</NODE>
```

■ **xmlDecl** – This is the XML Declaration property and is expressed as *foo.xmlDecl*. `xmlDecl` returns `<?xml version="1.0"?>`

ample in action

Once the HTML page has loaded, the Flash movie loads the document `ASstudioDoc.xml`.

This is passed to the `flaximal` object and rendered as a set of arrays under the object named `code`.

The user is intended to manipulate the movie instances by dragging them.

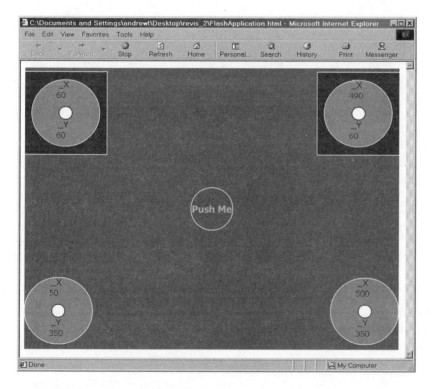

When the movie instance is released, the `reform_array()` method is passed the name of the movie instance and an array containing the code associated with the movie instances – `_root.code['code']`.

`reform_array()` correlates a capsule of JavaScript with its respective movie instance and creates a string of JavaScript code using the values of the movie instance, the arguments to the JavaScript function(s), and the function(s) itself.

This string is then passed to the JavaScript interpreter using `fscommand();`.

The code passed to the interpreter simply loads a function which records the coordinates of the movie instance and prints these using `alert()`.

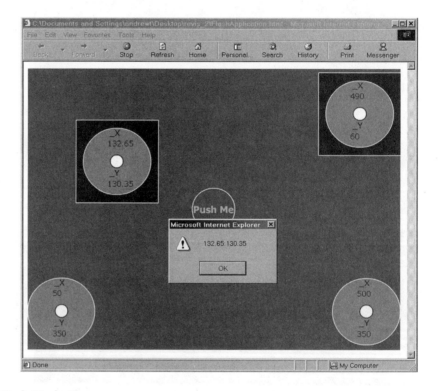

The Push-Me button

When the Push-Me button is pressed, coordinates held within `globalArray` are serialized and passed to the Flash movie to be rendered as an XML document.

The `encodeState()` function receives the serialized coordinates and parses these into an array. This array is passed to the `generateXML()` function.

`generateXML()` transforms the array to a well formed XML document and passes this to the JavaScript using `fscommand();`.

The rendered XML document is presented to the user.

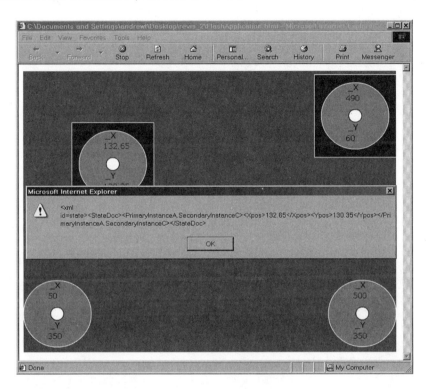

The JavaScript

```
<head>
<script language="JavaScript" for="example"
event="FSCommand(command, args)">
// test for IE vs. NN - this example is designed for IE
  if (navigator.appName.indexOf ("Microsoft") !='-1'){
      example_Dofscommand(command, args);
      }else{
      example_DoFSCommand(command,args);
      }
</script> <META HTTP-EQUIV="Expires" CONTENT="Mon, 04 Dec 1999
21:29:02 GMT" />
<script language="javascript">

/*
Flash passes the Javascript code below through fscommand()
```

```
instance="Instance Name";
xpos=MC._x;ypos=MC._y;
track(instance,xpos,ypos);

function track (instance,xpos,ypos){
globalArray[instance]=xpos+":"+ypos;
alert(globalArray[instance]);
 } ;
*/

globalArray=new Array();   // used to hold an array of MC
coordinates

function example_Dofscommand(command,args){
//     IE
if(command=="execute"){

  args=unescape(args);

// eval() receives and interperates code passed from the Flash
//element

  eval(args);
}

if(command=="load"){
  var arrString="0";

/*
each element of the globalArray is serialized below. This
produces a string of text similar to the following ..

0|PrimaryInstanceB.SecondaryInstanceC|:291.2:106.75|
➥PrimaryInstanceA.
➥
SecondaryInstanceC|:119.2:83.45|SecondaryInstanceB|:346.55:277.7|
➥ SecondaryInstanceA|:218.5:285.9

the name of each movie instance is followed by its coordinates
separated by a colon ":".
*/

for(ga in globalArray){
  arrString+="|"+ga+"|:"+globalArray[ga];
}
Example = window.document.example;
alert(arrString);

//passes the string to Flash's 'state' variable
```

```
Example.SetVariable("state",arrString);
}

if(command=="print"){          // prints the output from Flash
  alert(args);
  //eval(args);
  }
}
```

The Flash movie

The Flash component is identical to the one used in our previous example with the addition of the following code within the Push-Me button.

```
on(press){
  fscommand("load","dummyVar");
  _root.encodeState();

}
```

And this code within the drag buttons of each movie clip.

```
on (press) {
  if(_parent==_level0){
    startDrag (_self);
  } else {
    startDrag(_parent);
  }
}
```

`on..release` captures the coordinates of the movie clip and passes their value to corresponding global variables. It then calls `reform_array()` with the XML encoded JavaScript, and MC instance names as the arguments.

```
on (release) {
  stopDrag ();
  if(_parent==_level0){
  _root.xpos=_x;
  _root.ypos=_y;
  } else {
  _root.xpos=_parent._x;
  _root.ypos=_parent._y;
  }
  _root.reform_array(_root.code['code'],_target);

}
```

The `#include` directive in the first frame of this example loads the file `examCode.as` which contains several supporting ActionScript functions.

The function `reform_array()` is called from the drag button of each movie instance.

`reform_array()` re-writes the received instance name to a proper Flash 5 object address. It then extracts the JavaScript code elements appropriate to this instance and assembles a new block of JavaScript code to be sent to the browser.

```
function reform_array(elem,instance) {

// prepare a proper MC instance address

  target_array=new Array();
  target_array=instance.split("/");

  if(target_array[2]  != null){
    instance=target_array[1]+"."+target_array[2];
  } else {
    instance=target_array[1];
  }

// Instances and their correlating code elements are associated
//below.

  for(rpo in _root.code['root_parentof']){

    if(_root.code['root_parentof'][rpo]==target_array[1]){
      codeString=elem[rpo]+";";
    }
  }

// any arguments to the functions being passed are stored in
// 'arguments'

  arguments=_root.code['arguments'][rpo];

// codeString assembles the statements which are sent to the
//browser.

codeString="instance=\""+instance+"\";"+"xpos="+xpos+";"+"ypos="+y
pos  +";"+arguments+";"+codeString;
  trace(codeString);

// this string is then executed using eval()

  fscommand ("execute", codeString);
}
```

encodeState()

The function encodeState() is called from the Push-Me button with the code.

```
on(press){

    fscommand("load","dummyVar");

}
```

This retrieves the coordinates of each movie clip from the JavaScript globalArray as a serialized string.

```
if(_root.state!=null&  _root.stateReceived<1){

    _root.stateMod=_root.state;
    _root.encodeState();
}
```

encodeState() loads the serialized string held in the global variable state, which has been set from the browser, and proceeds to parse this into an array. This array contains both the instance names and the coordinates of each Flash movie instance. This string will resemble the following.

```
0|PrimaryInstanceB.SecondaryInstanceC|:291.2:106.75|
➡PrimaryInstanceA.SecondaryInstanceC|:119.2:83.45|
➡SecondaryInstanceB|:346.55:277.7|SecondaryInstanceA|:218.5:285.9

function encodeState(){
    stateReceived= 1;          // A flash-callback to the frameloop
    stateString=new String();
    stateString=state;
    stateArray=new Array();
    stateArray=stateString.split("|");// uses the
string.split()overload
    stateArray['instance']=new Array();
```

Each available MC instance name has been loaded into stateArray. Now an associative array stateArray['instance'] is created to hold the coordinates of each MC instance.

```
    for(sa=1;sa<stateArray.length;sa++){
        saStr=stateArray[sa];
        if(saStr.charAt(0)  !=":"){
            stateArray['instance'][sa]=stateArray[sa];
        } else {
            stateArray['instance'][sa]=stateArray[sa].split(":");
        }
    }
    /*
    we now have a multidimensional array containing the name of each
```

```
       movie instance and its coordinates on the stage.
       */
           generateXML();// call generateXML()
       }
```

generateXML()

generateXML() creates a new XML document based on the values carried with stateArray. Once completed, this document is passed to the browser for presentation to the user.

```
       function generateXML(){
         var genX=new XML();
         genX.xmlDecl="<xml id=state>";// registers the XML declaration
```

The appendChild method is used to add a childNode to a node element. Below appendChild is used to create the root element StateDoc.

The syntax appendChild((new XML()).createElement('name')) associates an XML object reference with the appended child node and names it using the createElement() method.

```
       genX.appendChild((new XML()).createElement('StateDoc'))

       for(s=1;s<stateArray['instance'].length;s++){
```

Test to determine whether each array element is a 'string' datatype, and thus a MC instance name. If it is, append a child node to the root node with the instance name as its nodeName.

```
       if(typeof(stateArray['instance'][s])=='string'){
         genX.firstChild.appendChild((new   XML()).
  ➡ createElement(stateArray['instance'][s]));
         } else {
```

If the array element is not a string then it is a number and requires that Xpos and Ypos nodes are generated to hold its value and the value of the next index element in sequence. These coordinate values are associated with Xpos and Ypos using the createTextNode() method.

Create the node Xpos within the child node associated with its MC instance. Assign Xpos a node value according to the corresponding position with the stateArray.

```
       parNode=genX.firstChild.childNodes.length-1;
       genX.firstChild.childNodes[parNode].appendChild((new
  ➡ XML()).createElement('Xpos'));

       // assign the corresponding coordinate value to Xpos.

       genX.firstChild.childNodes[parNode].firstChild.appendChild((new
  ➡ XML()).createTextNode(stateArray['instance'][s][1]));

       // create Ypos by the same method as Xpos and assign it a
       // corresponding node value.
```

```
    genX.firstChild.childNodes[parNode].appendChild((new
➡ XML()).createElement('Ypos'));
    genX.firstChild.childNodes[parNode].lastChild.appendChild((new
➡ XML()).createTextNode(stateArray['instance'][s][2]));
    }
  }
```

The rendered XML document is passed to the browser for display to the user.

```
        fscommand("print",genX.toString());
        trace(genX.toString());


    }
```

The previous example demonstrates a simple application of Flash to browser communication using XML. These methods enable Flash applications which require external script support to be developed independently of the specific HTML page in which they will be embedded. Such techniques are useful when incorporating Flash media within applications and web pages delivered from publishing and web application frameworks such as Cocoon and Enhydra. Essentially the Flash application is made portable by the fact that it carries and delivers script elements necessary to its function and is therefore much easier to incorporate into the page environment. The page author doesn't need to know how to write code which will successfully interface with the Flash element, they can simply embed the Flash application into their document and provide the necessary FSCOMMAND functions.

nmary

A few key points can be distilled from our review of XML handling within Flash.

- Use XML judiciously – XML handling consumes resources and can impact the performance of your application.

- Treat XML handling as a programming function – the Flash 5 XML parser presents a datastructure to your Flash application, to employ this effectively you'll need to use effective programming techniques.

- XML is a medium which can convey structured information across diverse environments.

- XML can be used to describe the application domain – the design of an XML document should complement the organization and processing of an application.

- XML can be used to store 'persistent' data much like a database.

I hope that in reading this chapter you've gained some insight into how XML can be incorporated within Flash applications, and how Flash applications can be extended using XML documents. If one point bears repeating, it is that XML handling within Flash should be treated as a programming technique. The success or failure of sophisticated XML driven Flash applications will depend on your ability to extract and organize XML data effectively.

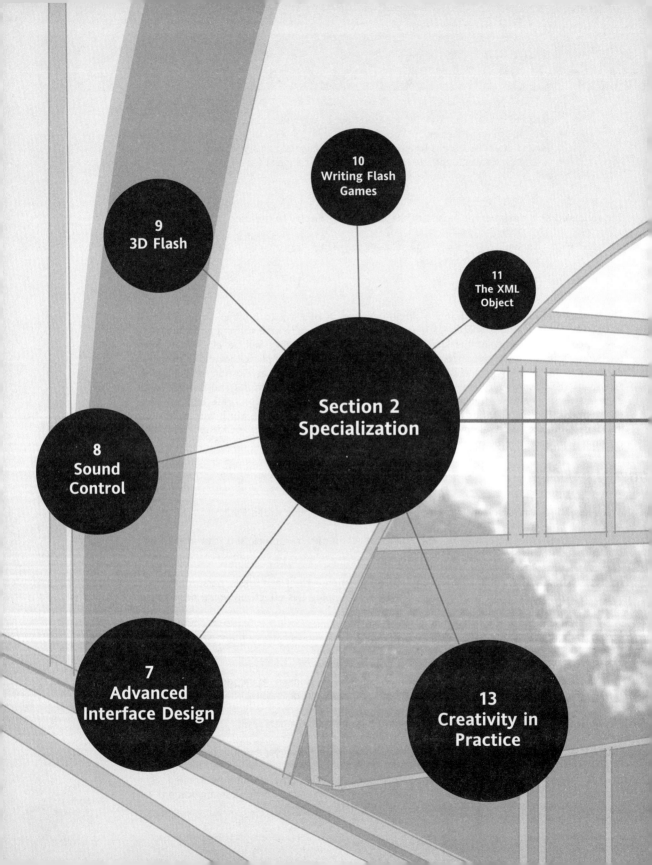

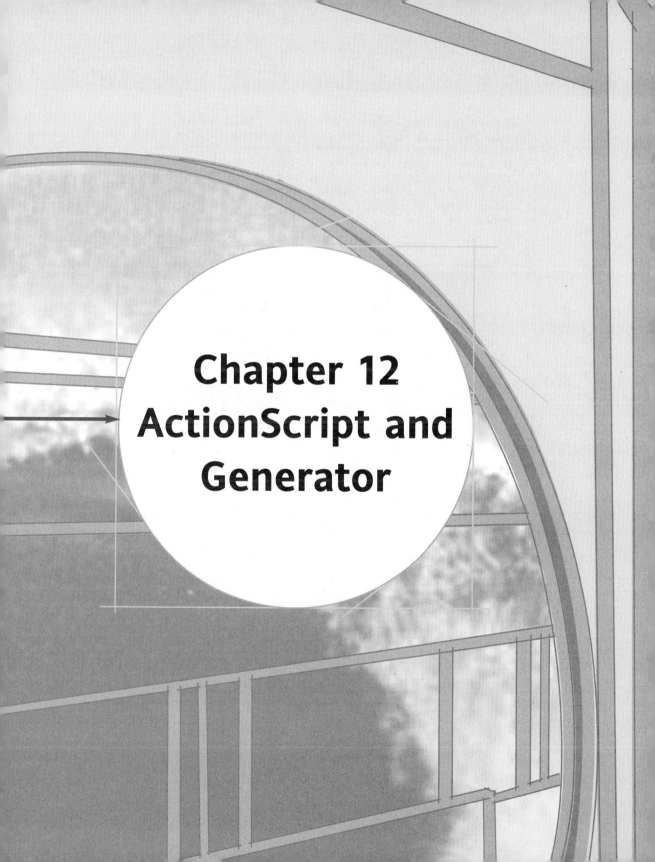

Chapter 12
ActionScript and Generator

If you've been using Flash for a while, you'll no doubt remember the jaw dropping moment when you first saw Yugo Nakamura's almost infamous scrolling, sliding, growing, shrinking, backward, forward, menu system on the old Mono*crafts site (www.yugop.com). I certainly do – it was the moment I thought two things: one, I need to put more hours into getting better at Flash, and two... this opens up a load of new horizons. Actually, at this point, I should pause. If you're not familiar with the menu system I'm referring to, you really should get acquainted with it. It's been discussed on many a Flash forum, and it's a fantastic demonstration of fluid motion using ActionScript.

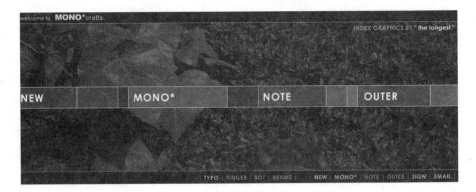

Why are we talking about this menu system here, in a Generator chapter? Well, like I said, it truly was absolutely awesome. Through the use of mathematics and some clever planning, the menu appeared to be never ending, hypnotically sliding back and forth according to the user's mouse movement. What if we wanted the same type of movement, but not satisfied with all of that, we wanted the items within it to be dynamic too? Say, for example, you wanted to display your portfolio, complete with the fluid sliding movement, but you were regularly adding, editing, and deleting items within the menu? It would be a nightmare to revisit your Flash file every time you wanted to amend content. The intention of this chapter, then, is twofold: to acquaint you with Generator, and to build just such a menu system.

In addition to building a dynamic menu system (genMenu), we'll also build an ActionScript-based introductory menu (preMenu), which will be used to gain access to our sliding navigation bar (nav, which lurks inside genMenu). This way, we can cover plenty of ActionScript, building main menus and submenus, using loading into levels, parking levels, and generally having a lot of fun with Flash and Generator. It may sound daunting, but I promise it won't be. First, we'll create a quick loader file; then it's headlong into our preMenu movie, which will be an all-ActionScript affair. Then we'll take a little time out to look at Generator before building our genMenu movie, which will use both ActionScript and Generator skills. Finally, we'll stitch the whole lot together. Are you ready?

redients

We'll be building three files during this chapter:

- `loader.swf`

- `preMenu.swf`

- `genMenu.swf`

ader.swf

The loader movie does precisely what it says it does: it loads the other two movies into levels. Why use a loader at all? In fact, I use this method quite often; it means that if I'm loading and unloading movies regularly, but I want to pass or store information, values, or settings, the base movie (loader.swf) is always there. It becomes a sort of storage area for variables and the like.

Start a new movie in Flash, and open up the Movie Properties window. Set the Background Color to a mid-gray (#999999) and, while you're there, also set the Width and Height to 750 x 400 pixels respectively, and the Frame Rate to 24. Save the file as `loader.fla`.

Now place the following actions in frame 1 of the movie:

```
loadMovieNum ("preMenu.swf", 1);
loadMovieNum ("genMenu.swf", 2);
```

These will just load our two menus into levels 1 and 2... and that's all there is to it! You can now test the movie, and although you'll just get a couple of errors in the Output window (because we haven't actually built the other two movies yet), this will leave a compiled SWF movie in the folder where you saved the FLA file.

That really is it for `loader.swf`. You can see that we're simply using it as a method of getting our other movies onto the screen. Now on to the bouncing introductory menu...

emenu.swf

The `preMenu` navigation system will be a free-floating menu that uses collision detection to bounce the menu items around the screen, and off each other. I'm sure that you've seen this kind of thing before, but maybe not used as a menu. Before I go further I'd like to give a credit to whoever came up with the original ball collision detection script – I've spent quite a bit of time trying to hunt down the elusive person, but to no avail. So, here and now I'd like to say a big thank you for making the very first example way back when, for others to use and improve upon. I hope you feel I've done it justice by bringing it up to date and Flash 5'izing it!

Start a new movie, give it the following parameters, and save the project as `preMenu.fla`.

- Background Color: **Mid-gray (#999999)**

- Width: **750**

- Height: **400**

- Frame Rate: **24**

Then add three new layers, and name the four layers you now have to match the ones in this screenshot:

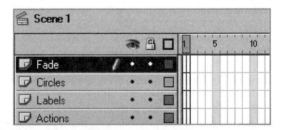

We'll start development proper by adding some frames to our Labels layer. Select frame 1, and give it a frame label "lblPlay". Add a keyframe at frame 6, and label it "lblOut". Lastly, add a keyframe at frame 30, and call that one "lblPark". I like to add a few blank frames after this, so that the last frame label is fully visible on the timeline, but it's your choice.

We'll be writing a function in frame 1 of our Actions layer that takes care of nav's movement and collisions. Before we start writing that though, we can get some easier stuff out of the way. Select the Actions layer, and add a keyframe at frame 5 that contains a simple `stop` action. Then, insert another keyframe at frame 28, and add the following action to it:

```
_level2.gotoAndPlay(_level2._currentframe + 1);
```

From our loader file, we know that genMenu will eventually be loaded into level 2, and I can tell you now that it will have a blank frame and a `stop` action in its first frame, which will keep it from playing. By adding this action to frame 28 of preMenu, genMenu will go to its next frame and start playing when the playhead passes this instruction. All that leaves us to do is to park preMenu on a blank frame, so that it doesn't interfere with genMenu. Add another keyframe at frame 30 with a `stop` action in it.

Shortly, we'll be building the circular menu elements you saw above, and giving them instance names of c1, c2, etc. These circles will float freely around the stage, bouncing off each other and the perimeters of the movie. When the circles are clicked, we'll make them disappear one by one, and this is where the Fade layer comes in. In advance of building our circle assets, let's set up our Fade layer to take care of the disappearing circles.

Select the Fade layer, and add a keyframe at frame 10. Add the following action to this frame:

```
_root.c1._visible = false;
```

Insert a new keyframe into frame 15 and put the same code in it, but alter the action to refer to c2 instead of c1. Once you've done that, do the same for frame 20 (changing the reference to c3) and then repeat the procedure one more time at frame 25 with a reference to c4.

When we click on one of the circles, the playhead will be sent to play past these frames. Each frame will set the visibility of one of the circles to false. Once past frame 25, the playhead will move on to frame 28, which will set genMenu on its way, before finally arriving at the blank lblPark frame, which has a stop action in it. By parking the menu, we're ensuring that we don't have to reload it if we decide to return to it. Had we unloaded it, we'd have had to reload it the next time we wanted to use it.

Next come the circular menu items. In the Circle layer, draw a simple circle on the stage, with the following parameters:

- Height: 50

- Width: 50

- Stroke Color: White

- Stroke Weight: Hairline

- Fill Color: Dull Gray (#666666)

> *If you like, you can use the assets from the accompanying source files, or make up your own design – as long as the dimensions are 50 x 50.*

Select the circle, convert it into a graphic symbol, and name it picCircle. Immediately reselect it, and this time turn it into a movie clip named movCircleInner. You should now have picCircle (the graphic symbol) nested inside of movCircleInner (the movie clip). Double-click the latter so that we can edit its contents, and give it a total of six layers named, from top to bottom, Circle1, Circle2, Circle3, Circle4, Labels, and Actions.

First, let's deal with the picCircle asset, which will be sitting somewhere on the stage. Move it from wherever it is into frame 1 of the Circle1 layer, and place a blank keyframe in frame 2 of this layer. Then, select the two frames (1 and 2), and copy them. Paste them into the Circle2 layer, then the Circle3 layer, and then the Circle4 layer. Once they're all in place, select and drag frames 1 and 2 from each layer to look like this:

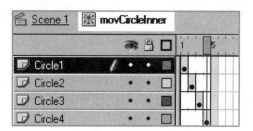

In order for the menu to be in any way useful, we need a way of distinguishing between the circles – four gray disks don't provide much information to the user. Revisit each circle and, using the Type tool, add a unique number or letter to their centers; I used P (portfolio), E (experiments), A (about), and C (contact).

To finish off this movie clip, select the Actions layer, and add keyframes to the first four frames, placing a stop action in each. Last, add a keyframe to the equivalent frames in the Labels layer, and name them lbl1, lbl2, lbl3, and lbl4 respectively:

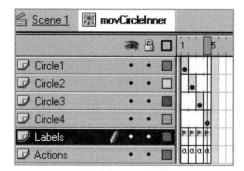

Now we need to come out of movCircleInner, and move up a level to the main timeline. Once there, reselect movCircleInner, and give it the instance name icon. Hit F8 to nest it inside a further movie clip, and call this one movCircle. Double-click movCircle, and add a layer to the timeline. Name the new layer Button, and then rename the layer that contains movCircleInner as Circle.

Create a 50 x 50 circular button in the Button layer that only contains a hit state – in other words, yet another invisible button – and name it in the Library as btnCircle. Center btnCircle and movCircleInner on the stage so that btnCircle is sitting on top of movCircleInner.

We need this button to do a couple of things. When the user runs their mouse over the button, we want the floating elements (which are normally moving around) to freeze in their current positions. When they move the mouse off the button, the circles will resume their random paths. We also want to give an indication of which menu element the user is over, but we can do that by adding a textual prompt to our loader movie later on. In the meantime, let's add some actions to the button:

```
on (rollOver) {
    _root.Over = true;
    _level0.txtReaction = subj;
}

on (rollOut) {
    _root.Over = false;
    _level0.txtReaction = "";
}

on (release) {
    _root.destination = subj;
    _root.gotoAndPlay (_root._currentframe + 1);
    _root.Over = false;
}
```

Let's examine these actions:

```
on (rollOver) {
    _root.Over = true;
    _level0.txtReaction = subj;
}
```

The circle function that we'll be writing shortly will check to see if the mouse is over any of our floating elements by testing the state of a variable called Over. So, on rollover, we want to set _root.Over to true. We also want to set our textual feedback (which we'll add later) to display a variable called subj.

Notice how we've used a mixture of _root and _level0 here. This is because _root refers to the root timeline of the movie from which it's called, while _level0 implicitly targets the base level – which, don't forget, is actually loader.swf. Next, we have the following:

```
on (rollOut) {
    _root.Over = false;
    _level0.txtReaction = "";
}
```

This simply resets what we set on rollover. The last piece of code is this:

```
on (release) {
    _root.destination = subj;
    _root.gotoAndPlay ("lblOut");
    _root.Over = false;
}
```

When the user clicks on a circle, we want genMenu to start playing, but not before our circles have disappeared one by one. We set a variable called destination on the root of this movie to equal whatever subj contains; this will simply hold a reference for the movie to be launched when the playhead passes frame 28. In this chapter, it will always be genMenu that gets told what to do, but if you were to build separate sliding menus for each of your headings (portfolio, experiments, about, contact), then this would go to them too. We then send the playhead off on its merry way along the root of the movie, to play past the frames that will set the visibility of the circles. Lastly, by setting _root.Over to false, we let the circles continue bouncing around until they disappear.

With that, we're through all the mundane-but-necessary parts, so let's return to the main timeline. At this point, we want to make sure that we have four circles, and that they each have an instance name. Copy and paste movCircle until you have four instances of it on the stage, and give them instance names c1, c2, c3, and c4. Insert a frame in frame 28 of the Circle layer, and your timeline and stage should look like this:

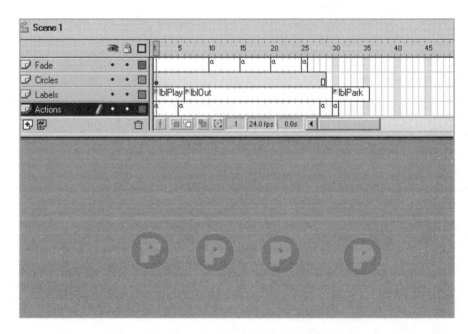

The only things that we have left to do are to add some onClipEvent actions to the circles, and to write the ActionScript for the random floating movement and collisions of the circles, which we'll wrap inside a single function. The first of these is quick and easy to do, so select each in turn, and add the following code:

```
onClipEvent (enterFrame) {
    _root.funcMover(this);
}
```

This code uses the enterFrame event, which creates a permanent loop to call the function we're about to write. It passes it one argument: this. Each circle will be calling the funcMover function, passing its own name to it for processing.

To write the function, make sure that you're on the main timeline, and select frame 1 of the Actions layer. I'll break this code into manageable chunks and explain each part as we proceed. Start by adding the following actions to frame 1:

```
// Define Variables
// movW & movH = Movie Width & Height
// circT = Total Circles
// circS = Circle Speed
movW = 750;
movH = 400;
_root.c1.subj = "portfolio";";
_root.c3.subj = "about";
_root.c4.subj = "contact";
circT = 4;
circS = 3;
```

The comments at the top of the code should explain these setup variables, so we'll swiftly move on:

```
for (i = 1; i < circT + 1; i++) {
    _root["c" + i].icon.gotoAndStop("lbl" + i);
    _root["c" + i].yMove = "";
    _root["c" + i].circR = _root["c" + i]._width / 2;
}
```

This for loop iterates from 1 to 4, telling each movie clip to gotoAndStop("lbl" + i). If you recall, we created four frames in movCircleInner named lbl1 to lbl4, and movCircleInner has the instance name icon. This is nested inside the movCircles, which have the instance names c1 thru c4, so we're saying (for example) _root.c1.icon.gotoAndStop("lbl1"). We're also setting a variable within c1 thru c4 called yMove that our function will check before continuing. The last line sets a variable within each of the circles to the width of the circle divided by 2 (in other words, the radius). Our function will need to use this information later.

Now we'll finally define that function. Carry on typing this ActionScript directly beneath the last piece:

```
// Circle Move Function
function funcMover (x) {
    // Set initial start positions and scale
    circX = x._x;
    circY = x._y;
    circN = x._name;
    x.icon._xscale = 100;
    x.icon._yscale = 100;
```

The first course of action in this function is to set `circX` and `circY` to `x._x` and `x._y` respectively. Here, the `x` before the period is the argument passed to it by each individual circle, so in the first three lines we're storing the x and y coordinates, and the name, of the clip that called this function in `circX`, `circY`, and `circN`.

The last two lines of the function so far may seem a little odd, and in truth, they are. I've included them because later on we'll want the circles to have rotation, and I can tell you that without these two lines, the circles will all very gradually shrink and deform. I'm pretty sure that somewhere out there is someone who can put their finger on the underlying reason, but for speed and ease I just included the lines.

```
if (!x.yMove) {
    // Distance
    x.xMove = random(circS) + 1;
    x.yMove = random(circS) + 1;

    // Direction
    if (random(2) - 1 == 0) {
        x.yMove *= -1;
    }
    if (random(2) - 1 == 0) {
        x.xMove *= -1;
    }
}
```

This nested `if` statement does a couple of things. First, it sets a random speed for each circle based on the variable `circS`. Second, it randomizes the direction in which the circle will begin to move. Having done that, we'd better deal with what happens when the circles reach the edge of the screen, as they assuredly will:

```
// Check Edges
if (circX <= (x.circR + circS)) {
    x.xMove *= -1;
    circX = (x.circR + circS);
} else if (circX >= (movW - x.circR) - circS) {
    x.xMove *= -1;
    circX = ((movW - x.circR) - circS);
```

```
        }

        if (circY <= (x.circR + circS)) {
            x.yMove *= -1;
            circY = (x.circR + circS);
        } else if (circY >= ((movH - x.circR) - circS)) {
            x.yMove *= -1;
            circY = ((movH - x.circR) - circS);
        }
```

This `if` statement simply checks the edges of the movie, so if `circX` (the `_x` position) is less than or equal to the circle radius plus the speed, then we know that we're going to hit the left hand wall. Similarly, if `circX` is greater than or equal to the movie width (`movW`) minus the circle radius and the speed, then we know that we'll hit the right hand wall. In each case, we simply change the direction of the circle by multiplying the x component of its speed by -1. We then repeat the procedure for the `_y` position.

Now that we've got some collision detection for the stage, we need to define what will happen when the circles hit each other:

```
            // Check for collision
            for (n = 1; n <= _root.circT; n++) {
                if ("c" + n != circN) {
                    nX = _root["c" + n]._x;
                    nY = _root["c" + n]._y;
                    nR = _root["c" + n].circR;
                    delta_x = ((circX + x.xMove) - nX);
                    delta_y = ((circY + x.yMove) - nY);

                    if (((delta_x * delta_x) + (delta_y * delta_y)) <
                        ➡((x.circR + nR) * (x.circR + nR))) {
                        // collision handling
                        nx = _root["c" + n].xMove;
                        ny = _root["c" + n].yMove;

                        // swap travel values with it.
                        tempx = x.xMove;
                        x.xMove = nx;
                        _root["c" + n].xMove = tempx;
                        tempy = x.yMove;
                        x.yMove = ny;
                        _root["c" + n].yMove = tempy;
                        _root["c" + n].collision = circN;
                    }
                }
            }
```

This loop iterates through each circle on the stage (checking first that it's not referring to itself), working out the distances between the `_x` and `_y` coordinates of the other circles, and its own `_x` and `_y` coordinates, adjusted for speed. It then uses Pythagoras' theorem to determine whether the distance between the circles' centers is less than the sum of their radii. If it is, the two circles must be in contact, and we have a collision to deal with.

Unlike the test, dealing with the collision is actually quite easy: we simply swap the movement values of one circle for the values of the circle it has collided with. If c1 is traveling to the right at '5', and c2 is traveling to the left at '10', then after the collision c1 will start traveling leftward at '10', and c2 will move rightward at '5'. This gives a similar type of effect to the Newton's Cradle executive toy that everyone had back in the 70s.

Lastly, once all of the testing has been done, we need actually to move the circles:

```
// move circle
if (_root.Over != true) {
    x._x = (circX + x.xMove);
    x._y = (circY + x.yMove);
    x.icon._rotation = (circY + circX);
}
}
```

If _root.Over (remember that this is set by a mouseOver on our button) does not equal true, then the _x and _y coordinates are set according to the existing values, plus the values of xMove and yMove. The icon is then rotated based on those values too.

That really is the final piece of code for frame 1 of the movie, so now you can test it. You should get some lovely floating movement for your circles that stops when you roll the mouse over one of them, and starts again when you remove it. Also, when you click on one, they should all disappear. It can almost become mesmerizing watching them... but let's not get hypnotized just yet. We have more to do.

Let's deal with our textual reaction to the mouseOver event of our circle buttons. Reopen loader.swf, and add a new layer to the main timeline. Name the original layer Actions, and the new layer Feedback. Select the Feedback layer and add a dynamic text field called txtReaction. Test your movie, and you should find that it loads preMenu.swf, and that you get textual feedback whenever you move the mouse over one of your menu circles.

Great. Save and close both loader.swf and preMenu.swf – they're done.

Now, before building the final part of this chapter, let's take that promised look at. If you're already familiar with some of the information here, then feel free to go ahead and skip through to building genMenu.swf.

cromedia Generator

Both Macromedia Generator and Macromedia Flash can be used to deliver customized visual content to a browser. However, they deliver different *types* of customized content, and each delivers it in a different way. Flash is an authoring tool, and Generator is a server side technology, like ASP or PHP. Developers use the Flash authoring environment (with the Generator authoring extensions installed) to add Generator objects to their Flash movies.

These Generator objects then get populated by content from by a data source, and Generator can output the result as a Flash movie (or in one of many other formats) – either when specifically requested by the user, or in a scheduled batch process. *Flash* customization occurs on the client browser, using the Flash Player, while *Generator* customization occurs on the server, and is delivered to the client in a variety of formats.

Generator extends Flash movies with Generator templates and objects. Generator and Flash work together to create powerful, customized, and automated web site graphics. How do *you* work with Generator? I thought you'd never ask.

nline and Offline Generation

Any Flash project you create that involves the use of Generator objects is called a **Generator template**, and project files of this type can be distinguished by their SWT extensions. After you've created a Generator template using Flash, you copy it to a web server along with any associated data sources and external media content. Once the template is on the server, Generator can process it either online, or offline.

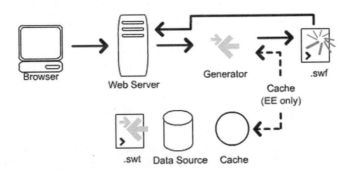

Online processing uses the **online generator**, which runs as an extension to a web server. (Versions of Generator are available for most common web servers, including Microsoft's Internet Information Server and Personal Web Server, Apache, Netscape Enterprise Server, and iPlanet Web Server.) The idea is that you insert a Generator template (SWT) file in an HTML document, and when the client browser opens the document, the web server starts an instance of Generator to process the embedded objects. It creates a SWF file on the fly, by combining the template with data from a data store.

> *Although the creation of SWF files will be our focus in this chapter, Generator is also capable of producing output in other formats, including QuickTime, GIF, JPEG, and PNG.*

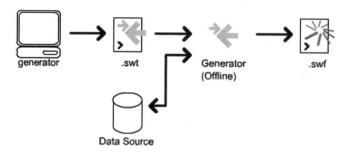

Offline processing uses the **offline generator**, which differs from the online generator in three main ways:

- It doesn't run as an extension of a web server. Rather, it's started directly from the command line.

- It directs output to a file on the web server, rather than sending it to a client browser. The web server can then serve this file, just as it would any other file of that type.

- It can be used to create image maps from Generator templates.

When the browser queries the server here, it is served a pre-generated SWF file. The SWF file is generated from the SWT and the data source on a regular basis – every week, every day, or even every few hours.

Choosing Between Online and Offline

From the descriptions above, it might appear that offline generation is a kind of poor cousin of online generation, but you should be wary of drawing that conclusion. It's a much more accurate reflection of the situation to say that the two techniques are targeted at different applications, and that the number of situations in which the two could truly be said to be in competition is really quite small.

Once you start to think about it, there are all kinds of applications for which Generator would be a useful tool, but creating real-time, dynamic content on the fly just isn't necessary. If the data on your site won't be updated more regularly than every couple of hours, do you really need

Generator to populate a template and deliver it to the user in response to every single request for that data – especially if the content hasn't changed for the last 24 hours? The process of offline generation is command-line driven, and writing batch files to create template-derived SWF files on a fairly frequent basis is not a difficult task.

Of course, if your business is providing real-time data such as news, weather, or stock values – anything that has to be absolutely current when the user hits it – you *will* need to use online processing... and you'll have another question to answer, too. Macromedia supplies Generator in two Editions, called Developer (DE) and Enterprise (EE), and you'll need to choose the right one for your business.

EE is the heavyweight of the two: it does everything that DE can do, and it includes more powerful features such as – crucially – multithreading. If your web site hosts a moderate amount of traffic, dynamic content creation with Generator is an extremely intensive process. EE is built to handle this situation in a way that DE is not (the latter can only process a single on-the-fly request at a time), and as you'd expect, you pay more for the product as a result.

Typically, the type of client that needs Enterprise performance will already have invested many thousands of dollars in their back end systems, and EE will be the natural choice. If you're just testing things at home, or delivering for a small online retailer who gets hundreds of hits per day, you may consider DE as a cost effective solution.

Why Use Generator?

Well, that's what Generator *is*, but what can it *do*? I think there are a couple of reasons why Generator is such a great tool to have in your armory. Firstly, you can use your favorite authoring tool (Flash) to build rich content that can be easily and quickly updated. Secondly, it relieves you from becoming the admin and upkeep person. Let me explain.

Point No. 1

CGI, ASP, JSP, PHP, ColdFusion, and XML are a few of the methods that enable developers to create dynamic, data-driven sites. They allow the developer to create personalized experiences for each user. Like many Flash developers, I want to deliver the same dynamic content, but in the high impact format that Flash allows me. Generator means that you don't have to make do with dynamic *HTML* content; instead, you can deliver personalized, dynamic, targeted, fresh, high impact content for each visitor, creating that all-important one-to-one experience. You don't need to give up high impact design and rich media for the sake of dynamic publishing. Best of all, you don't need to throw away the time and effort you've devoted to your Flash skills and learn an HTML-based scripting language. Generator is all authored from within Flash.

Point No. 2

You may recognize the next scenario. I've been asked many times by clients to produce visually engaging, rich Flash content. Once finished, it gets delivered... and then the client asks me to maintain and update the content whenever information changes. These requests can amount to simple alterations such as textual information, or slightly more involved changes such as new logos, or updated catalogue items.

This is where that little cartoon guy in my head starts jumping up and down, and steam starts firing out from his ears. Strictly speaking, these requests mean that I become reduced to an admin person. Whilst I want to please the client, I'm reluctant to spend more time administrating than designing, or developing new ideas and content. Although this kind of work can often be lucrative, be honest: we don't learn Flash and Generator so that we can create something once, then maintain it forever.

This is where Generator becomes invaluable. It allows developers to deliver the rich, engaging content that was requested, and then (impressively) *hand control to the client*. This relieves the developer of becoming the dreaded admin person, empowers the client, and only requires the developer to revisit the source files when a major design change is needed. The client is happy, because they don't have to endure escalating costs for each maintenance run. Updating content has been made very easy, and they haven't had to learn new skills or employ a specialist. The developer is happy, because they've been freed up to concentrate on new projects. Everyone's happy!

This section is aimed at Flash developers and designers who have a broad knowledge of Flash and who want to take the next step toward creating rich Flash content that can be dynamically updated from a variety of data sources. Developers that not only want the benefits of Flash, but also to enjoy the ability to update, change and freshen content with minimal time and effort, whenever and as often as they or their clients please.

Before we get down to the nitty-gritty, I should make it very clear that a single chapter is never going to suffice when it comes to covering a program like Generator. However, it's my intention to make you feel more comfortable with Generator, to give you some tips to help you avoid those 'screaming at everyone around you' moments, and to cover how well-written ActionScript and Generator code can complement one another. We'll also take a look at a couple of the more frequently used Generator objects, so that you can be up and running and producing templates in no time.

What Else Do I Need to Know?

Is there anything else standing in the way of us getting down to some examples? I should probably start to answer that question with something that may surprise you, which is that to follow the projects in this chapter, *you don't actually need to install Generator*. Here, we'll just be using the Generator authoring extensions that come in the box with Flash 5. Most users tend to install these at the same time as Flash itself – you're presented with an option to do so – but if you haven't, they're waiting for you on the product CD.

Now I'd better backtrack and explain about not needing Generator. It is certainly the case that if you want to test that your creations work when accessed from a web server, or you fancy trying your hand at some batch processing, you'll need a copy of Generator. In the short term, you can download a free, fully functional, trial version from the Macromedia web site at:

www.macromedia.com/software/generator/download

However, when you're creating Generator templates in the Flash environment, there are tools at your disposal that provide the ability to test your code on your local machine. This is called

authoring mode, and in it, static output for the file types selected in Flash's Publish Settings dialog box is created whenever you use the Publish or Test Movie commands. To answer my own question, then, our way is clear, and we can finally start to get some practical experience of working with Generator objects.

ere Do I Start?

I've just paused to read back over everything I've written so far, and I suddenly had a flashback to when *I* started using Generator. I know: it's a rather dizzying list of things to keep in mind at once, but don't panic. We'll examine all of this terminology, what it means, and how to use it during the chapter. It may appear daunting, but you can be confident that we'll take things step by step to make it clear.

When I started writing this chapter, I promised myself that I would do what I could to explain what I call the 'next step'. This is the one that comes after you've gone through the samples that came with Generator, you've scoured the Web to find better real world examples, and you've even hung around the user groups to try and understand how it works in real life. This is exactly where I became frustrated, but luckily I got involved in a project that forced me to discover how to access real data, from a real client's data source.

Where *do* you start with a Generator project? Do you build the data source first, or do you create the templates and then build the data source as you go along? Most of the time, you'll find that you're asked to make templates that interact with a client's existing data source, but it's important that we look at building a data source too. They're useful things to know about, and there are plenty of Flash developers who've never had to go near them before.

In this example, then, we'll look at things like web servers, building simple data sources, and discussing other file formats. We'll discover what ODBC connectivity is, how to build Generator templates and test them within Flash 5, and finally we'll look at publishing and how to test your project on a web server so that everything's ready for public consumption.

e Authoring Environment

It's time to become familiar with where things are, what they're called and how to use them, and we can start with the authoring environment. As stated above, Macromedia has shipped Flash 5 with the facility to author and perform limited testing of Generator templates without you having to buy Generator first. That probably sounds a little strange, but what it means is that you can install the Generator authoring extensions from the Flash CD (or download them from the Macromedia web site), and create SWT files (Generator templates) from within Flash 5.

Once you've installed the Generator authoring extensions in Flash, you can get to them via the Window > Generator Objects menu, which will open a panel like this:

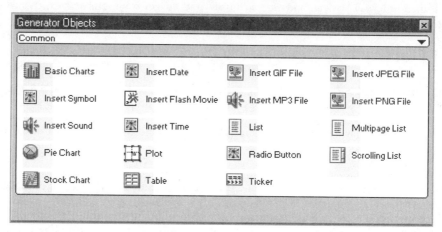

Just as you'd use the Library within a standard Flash movie, you use the Generator Objects dialog box to populate your templates. Developers create their templates within Flash by using these Generator objects which, explained simply, are just placeholders for content. Generator combines templates with content from a data source to create things like menu structures, lists, charts, animations, and graphics dynamically.

The data source that Generator gets its information from can be as simple as a text file that's stored on the local machine, or loaded by an HTTP request, or created by things like ASP and CGI. At the other end of the spectrum, we can use an industry-standard database, query it directly using the Structured Query Language (SQL), and populate our template with the result.

Say, for example, that we're running an online clothing store. Using SQL queries, we can populate our templates with specific content, based upon a user's request. If the user wants to see jackets, the Generator populates the template accordingly. If they want to see trousers, then we use the same template, and the same data source, but just pass it a different request. You can now see the beauty of Generator: instead of building hundreds of separate movies containing our shop's product lines, we need to build just one template that repopulates itself over and over again according to the user's request.

Data Sources

At the end of the day, any data source is just a container, and all we really care about here is getting data out of that container and into our projects. Generator demands that we deliver content in one of two forms: it will accept it from a plain text file, or an ODBC/JDBC connection. (Actually, there is a third form that's handy for testing purposes: you can type data straight into a Flash dialog box, as we'll see.)

A plain text file is exactly what it says, which means that you just need to use an application like Notepad (on a PC) or SimpleText (on a Mac) to type in your data. This method is very simple, and quick to get up and running, but it has its drawbacks. Using ODBC gives us far greater flexibility, because (as described above) we can *query* the data and therefore only populate our templates with targeted information. I think that deserves a little more explanation.

ODBC Connectivity

ODBC, or Open Database Connectivity, is the name of a technology that provides a standard 'link' between a data source and an application that wants to access the data it contains. It works by effectively placing a layer, called a database driver, between the two. The purpose of this layer is to accept the application's queries for data, and present the results back to it. The application doesn't need to know *how* the data was retrieved – and frankly, it doesn't care.

There are ODBC-compliant database drivers available for just about any kind of data source you can imagine, from a CSV (comma-separated values) file, to an Access, SQL Server, or Oracle database. Generator can issue commands to an ODBC driver, so it can use this data.

Of course, if I was worried about covering enough about Generator in a single chapter, it would be ambitious – to say the least – to try to give you a full introduction to ODBC as well. I'd recommend that once you've mastered the techniques in this chapter, you investigate using a fairly straightforward relational database, such as Microsoft Access. If you want to learn more about database theory and relational databases, use your favorite search engine and look for references to Dr E.F. Codd (the inventor of relational database theory), or just for relational database theory in general.

The Generator Interface Within Flash 5

Generator templates are created within Flash 5, using the Generator authoring extensions that are integrated seamlessly into the Flash 5 interface. They comprise:

- The Generator Objects palette

- The Generator panel

- The Generator environment variable button

- A new Generator Publish Settings tab

The Generator authoring extensions allow you to create, preview, and test Generator content. You don't need to install the Generator server component (Developer Edition or Enterprise Edition) in order to author Generator content, or to test it on your local machine. Using the software development kit that comes with the extensions, it's even possible to create custom Generator objects using Java. Many such objects can be found at the Macromedia Exchange at www.macromedia.com/exchange/flash.

The Generator Objects Palette

The Generator Objects palette, which you saw above, is used to place Generator objects onto the stage, or into symbols. In Flash, Generator objects appear as gray squares, and the object type appears in the top-left corner for identification:

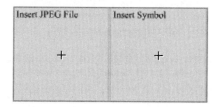

Adding Generator objects to your template is easy: just open the palette, and select and drag the object that you want to add to the stage. You'll now be able to move it around as if it were a symbol. If you double-click on the object, the Generator panel will appear. This is where parameters are entered.

The Generator Panel

The Generator panel is where you define the Generator object's parameters:

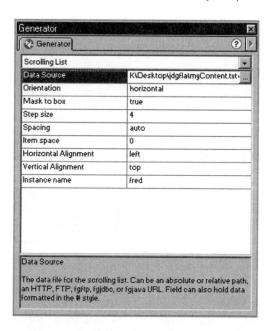

After you've positioned your Generator object on the stage, you can set its parameters by using this panel – you simply fill in the required settings according to your needs. We'll discuss these in detail later on.

e Generator Environment Variable Button

The Generator environment variable button sits quietly at the top right of your authoring environment, right next door to your Edit Scene and Edit Symbols buttons:

You can use this button to assign a data source to the timeline of the main movie, or a movie clip. Each timeline in a movie can have its own environment information. The Generator environment variable button opens the Set Environment dialog, from which you can set the environment data source for your templates:

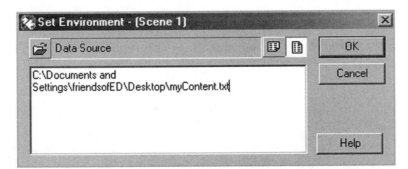

> Note that this dialog can assign data sources only to the timelines of the main movie, or a movie clip. It has no effect on the timelines of buttons or graphic symbols, even though the dialog box opens if you click the Generator environment variable button while inside them.

e Output Window

It might seem a little strange to mention it here, but the Output window is extremely useful for debugging your Generator templates. You can view errors and Generator output in this window, which makes it easy to find problems. Until you're very experienced with Generator, it's a good idea to leave the debug level set to Verbose. This will give you the most information about your template, which will make debugging much simpler.

Publish Settings

When you install the Generator authoring extensions, the Publish Settings dialog gains an extra tab named Generator:

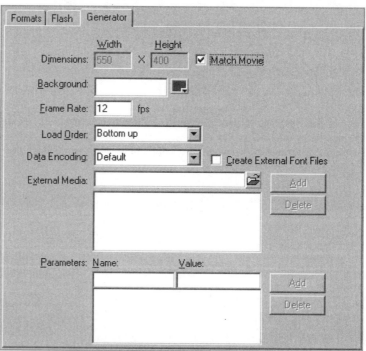

From here, you can set various options that will affect your SWT file when you publish it. They range from simple things like altering dimensions and background color, to changing the way data is encoded, and specifying parameters for testing templates locally.

We'll now take a look at what Generator can do, and run through a few basic examples.

A Rapid Introduction to Generator Variables

If you have indeed scoured the Net for examples, investigated the samples that shipped with Generator, and generally become confident enough to build something a little more involved, then you can feel free to skip this section. If you need a refresher, or some pointers to get you ready for our more advanced example, then let's take a look at some of the basics.

ow Your Tools

We've already taken a brief look at things like the Generator panel and the Generator Objects palette, but there's often more than one way to use them. For example, the Set Environment dialog box can be used in several ways: content can be written directly into it, or a reference to a data source, a SQL string, or a variable that will at some stage contain a reference to a data source can all be used. To demonstrate a couple of the options mentioned above, let's populate a variable using some different methods.

Simple as 1, 2, 3 (step 1)

Start a brand new project, ensure that Flash and Generator Template are checked in the Formats tab of the Publish Settings dialog, uncheck anything else that is checked, and click OK.

Next, select the Text tool, and type {myVariable} on the stage. Don't forget to include the braces {}, because these tell Flash that what you've just written is a **Generator variable**. Select the Generator environment variable button, and type the following into the dialog box that appears:

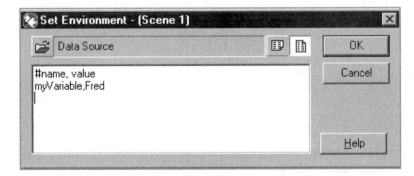

Choose OK, and test the movie. You should see something like this:

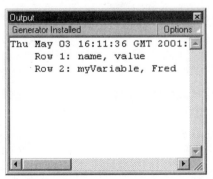

Now might be a good time to explain exactly what we just did.

What is a {variable}?

A Generator variable acts as a placeholder for the values that your data source will pass into Generator. They *always* appear between braces, and the main difference between Generator variables and ActionScript variables is that Generator variables get populated once, and then fixed, when Generator processes the template.

By placing # as the first character in the Set Environment dialog box, Generator understands that we're not referencing an external data source, and instead treats the entry the same way as if it had been written in a text file. As well as the convenience for testing purposes, this approach can also be useful in real templates, if you want to provide a few static values that are used repeatedly but aren't updated frequently. It saves the time and effort of managing a separate text file data source that would serve the same purpose.

Simple as 1, 2, 3 (step 2)

What happens if the values for the variables are stored in a 'real' data source, such as a text file, a database, or a Java class? We get exactly the same results! This time, we'll reference a text file containing our data, so create a text file on your desktop called `myContent.txt`, type in the following, and save it.

```
name, value
myVariable, Fred
```

Leave your {myVariable} text field on the stage, but select the Generator environment variable button, and delete the current content of the Set Environment dialog. Next, choose the Data Source file browser button, and navigate to the text file that you just created:

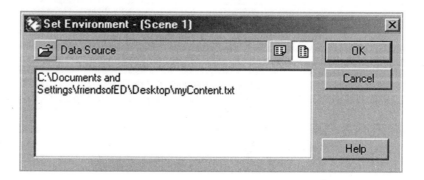

Once you've done this, choose OK and test the movie. You should see exactly the same thing as last time, the only difference being an extra line in the Output window telling you which text file the data was pulled from. Now that we're using a 'true' external data source, you'll note that we no longer precede name with the # symbol.

Simple as 1, 2, 3 (step 3)

Next, we'll try something a little different. We'll still use our text file to get the data from, but this time we'll use the Parameters field in the Generator Publish Settings tab. That means we're going to reference the text file by using a variable that will be populated with our data source's location.

Leave the text file called myContent.txt on your desktop, and leave {myVariable} on the stage. Next, select the Generator environment variable button, and replace the current content with {mySource}:

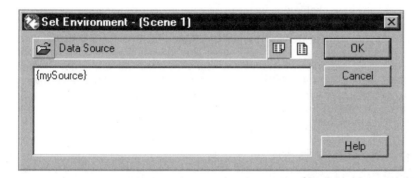

Now go to the Publish Settings dialog, and select the Generator tab. Type mySource into the Parameters Name field, and C:\WINDOWS\Desktop\myContent.txt (or the equivalent for your machine) into the Parameters Value field:

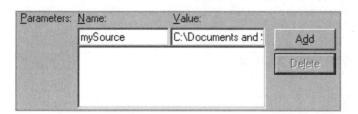

Finally, remember to click the Add button (I've been foiled by forgetting this important step many a time), then click OK and test the movie. Once again, you should get exactly the same result. Like last time, we're using a 'true' external source, but this time we're passing its location through a Generator variable placed in the Set Environment dialog box. This method is a particularly flexible one, because it means that you don't have to re-edit your movie if source filenames change.

> *The same methods we've just employed can also be used when filling in the Generator panel. The File Name field for any object can be populated using these techniques.*

Back to the Big Stuff

With the Generator basics behind us, we can start building our dynamic sliding menu system. This will be the most complicated of our three menus, but don't let that worry you. To make it, we'll be using a healthy mixture of Generator and ActionScript. I remember starting out with both, and one of the things that frustrated me most about learning was that although the tutorials I read worked, and helped me build whatever that tutorial covered, there was never a good enough explanation of why we did (or didn't) do certain things. As we start building, it may appear that I'm jumping backward and forward from object to object and clip to clip, adding ActionScript here and there, but this is because I want to be sure that we cover the reasons why we do and, sometimes more importantly, why we don't use particular methods. Please bear with me. By the end of the chapter, you should be confident not only that can you build a dynamic menu system, but also you can also understand exactly how it works.

If you study the accompanying source files for this chapter, you'll see that there are relatively few steps to building this menu system. Unfortunately, trying to articulate in print succinctly what is in the files can sometimes make it appear that building a project such as this is a laborious process. Whatever you do, don't think that. It takes many words to explain what you can do in a few seconds. My advice as you embark on this chapter is to have the source files to hand, and do a round robin between book, source files, and your files. You can then happily check everything as you go along.

Objects, Sources and Code

To complete our menu system, we'll be building a data source and a Flash template using the following Generator objects:

- Insert Symbol

- Insert JPG/GIF/PNG/SWF

- Replicate

As you'd expect, we'll investigate what each of these is, and what it does, when we encounter it. To keep your spirits up, here's a picture of what we'll be building:

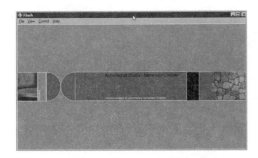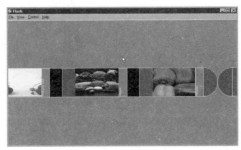

e Setup

This is another brand new project, and we can start the ball rolling by simply setting up the movie properties. Bring up the Movie Properties window, and set the following:

- Movie Width: 740

- Movie Height: 400

- Movie Background Color: Gray (#999999)

- Movie Speed: 24 fps

Now let's build some of our non-Generator specific visual content, starting with some of the menu's background elements. The finished nav menu will be split into 'left' and 'right' sections so that we can replicate one side and not the other. The first element that we'll create is the background for the left side of the nav; the entire nav, when finished, will look like this:

Draw a simple rectangle on the stage with these values:

- Stroke Color: #FFFFFF

- Stroke Weight: hairline

- Fill Color: #666666

- Height: 102.4

- Width: 400

Select the graphic and make it into a graphic symbol with the name picLeftNavBG:

Once you've made your rectangle into a symbol, you can delete it from the stage, as we won't need it for a while. Right now, we need to make a simple background for the right hand side of our nav. This side will have a slightly different look but it's essentially the same arrangement. As this side will contain images, it has an inner rectangle within an outer rectangle, like this:

You can either build your own rectangle with the following parameters, or use the symbol from the accompanying source files:

- Stroke Color: #FFFFFF

- Stroke Weight: hairline

- Outer Fill Color Left: #000000

- Outer Fill Color Right: #999999

- Inner Fill Color: #666666

- Outer rectangle Height: 102.4

- Outer rectangle Width: 275

- Inner rectangle Height: 102.4

- Inner rectangle Width: 200

However you got the rectangle, select the whole thing, and make it a graphic symbol called: picRightNavBG. Then delete it from the stage as you did for its partner.

Next, we'll quickly create another simple element: a 'back' button. This will have two purposes: to allow users to return from whence they came, and to 'link' the ends of the sliding menu to give a visual indication of where content starts to repeat. Once again, you can either use the one in the Library from the accompanying files, or make your own. To do this, first draw a circle:

- Stroke Color: #FFFFFF

- Stroke Weight: hairline

- Fill Color: #666666

- Height: 102.4

And then chop the circle in half vertically, positioning the two halves to look like this (I've also used the Line tool to add a white line to each side of the circle):

As with the rectangles, select the graphic, make it into a button named btnBack, and delete it from the stage. Finally, we need to create two assets that will be used later. One is a button; the other is a graphic that we'll use as a mask. Draw a simple white rectangle on the stage with no stroke, and the following width and height:

- Height: 155

- Width: 101.4

Select it, convert it into a graphic symbol and call it picImageMask. Now select that, but this time make it a button symbol, and name it btnImage. Double-click the latter so that you can edit its frames, and then simply drag the 'Up' keyframe to become the 'Hit' keyframe. This button should have no 'Up', 'Over', or 'Down' states. When you've finished, go back to the main stage and delete the button.

It may look complicated when you see it on the screen, but in terms of the visual components this project needs, that's about it. Later on, we'll create a couple of very simple icons to let our viewers know what section of our site they're viewing; these will be things like "Experiments", "Portfolio", "Contact", and "About". We'll be using Generator to populate our menu, and ActionScript to lay it out and deliver the fluid sliding motion, so believe it or not, our hard work is over.

Now to assemble our nav, and add ActionScript and Generator objects. We'll end up with a couple of nested movie clips within one main movie clip, but at the moment all you should see is an empty stage.

We'll start with the left hand side of our nav menu. Drag picLeftNavBG from the Library onto the stage. it's position is actually unimportant, because later we'll be scaling it and wrapping it inside a movie clip, but for ease you can put it at coordinates x=100, y=150, using the top-left registration point.

Select the graphic, and make it into a movie clip called movNavLeft. Double-click the movie clip so that we're back inside it, ready to add more elements to the background graphic. Name the layer that you've placed the graphic on as Gray BG, and then add two new layers called Back Button and ItemClip respectively.

Select the ItemClip layer, which will be where we add our first Generator object. Open up the Generator Object palette, and drag the Insert Symbol icon onto the stage. The Generator panel should automatically appear when you release the object onto the stage, but if not simply choose Window > Panels > Generator from the menu. This is where we'll be setting our parameters for this particular object, but first, move the Generator object so that it's right up against the left-hand side of the existing graphic. You can use the Info panel to do this, and while you're there you'll see the reason why we've been setting our objects to such seemingly odd sizes so far.

When you drag a Generator object onto the stage, it has the default dimensions of 102.4 x 102.4. I've no idea why – life would have been so much easier if they were nice round figures! So, rather than resizing the Generator objects and having then to worry about the further implications of scaling to fit, and the proportional scaling of imported objects, it seemed easier to do it this way.

If you don't see the Generator panel, or you've closed it, another quick method of launching it is to double-click a Generator object. Double-click the Insert Symbol object, and change the parameters to these:

- Symbol Name: {itemClip}

- Scale To Fit: true

- Instance Name: Icon

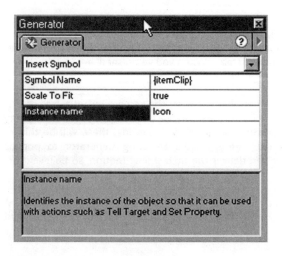

As a matter of fact, you could have left the instance name blank here, as there won't be any ActionScript or other movie clips referencing it. If you *did* need to reference it, then you could either enter a fixed name (as we have here), or a dynamic name using a Generator variable.

That neatly brings us on to look at what these parameters are, what we have entered, and what will happen when we publish our movie. Insert Symbol is another of those friendly things that does exactly what it says: it inserts a symbol into your movie from the Library. We want to display some kind of icon that denotes which section of our site our visitor is looking at. Later, we'll create some symbols representing the various sections of our site that will be placed on the stage by the Insert Symbol object, according to parameters passed to it by our data source.

Why did we use the Generator variable {itemClip} as our symbol name, rather than hard-coding it? Because we want to make our movie as flexible as possible. By referencing an external variable from our data source, we can change the name of the movie clip that will be brought in here without having to re-edit the movie.

Scale to fit is pretty easy to understand, although it's useful to know that it does not worry about proportional scaling, which isn't so hot. Of course, you could get around this by using ActionScript to re-scale the symbol, by referencing the Instance name that you assign in the last field of the panel.

Now it's time to populate the currently empty Back Button layer, and then finish building the stage elements. Drag btnBack from the Library onto the stage, and place it against the left-hand side of the Generator object. You should now have your elements lined up similar to the following illustration:

Now select the button, and add the following action to it (of course, you can change the URL to whatever you like):

```
on (release) {
    getURL ("http://www.developette.com", "_blank");
}
```

We now need to come out of our movie clip and get back to the main timeline. Do this, then select the movie clip, and give it the instance name NavLeft. Select the NavLeft movie clip, and then convert it to another movie clip called movInnerNav. Give this the instance name childNav.

Double-click movInnerNav, to get inside it. Rename the base layer as Nav Left, then add a new layer and call it Title Text. Use the Type tool and type {title} in a static text field on the stage. Make it black text, and 20 points high.

Add another layer called Description Text, again using a static text field, and type {description}. Make it white, and 14 points high. Align the text fields close to the Insert Symbol object, and extend them to fill the rectangle like this:

These fields are just Generator variables that will be populated by our data source. Before we go any further, quickly add two more layers: Actions and Nav Right. We'll add content to these later.

At this point, you may be wondering how we're going to populate these fields, and indeed the Insert Symbol object. Again, we'll make our movie as flexible as possible by setting our data source itself as a Generator variable, which will get its address for our data source fed to it externally.

Hit the Generator environment variable button, enter {source} into the text field, and be sure to select Column Name/Value data layout as our data source layout. This method allows us to use more than one column of data related to each record, as opposed to Name/Value data layout, which simply allows straight name/value pairs. When we build our data source, Column Name/Value data layout format requires that the first row of data specifies the variable names, and the following rows specify the values. This is how your Set Environment dialog box should look:

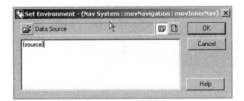

OK, let's take a deep breath, and review what we've done. If you take a second and go to the main timeline, you should now have a movie clip called movInnerNav (its library name) with the instance name childNav. Inside this movie clip, you should have five layers: Description Text, Title Text, Nav Left, Nav Right, and Actions. These contain your {description} text field, {title} text field, and movNavLeft movie clip (with the instance name NavLeft). Nav Right and Actions contain nothing at this stage, but they will do soon. Inside movNavLeft, you have three layers: Back Button, ItemClip, and Gray BG. These contain btnBack, an Insert Symbol Generator object, and picLeftNavBG respectively:

Let's crack on and add the right-hand side to the nav, then we can build our data source, add the ActionScript, and test it all! Drill down until you're inside movInnerNav, where you should see the empty layers Actions and Nav Right waiting for content. Select the latter, and then drag picRightNavBG from the Library onto the stage. Make sure that it's set to (550, 150), using the center registration point. Don't worry that it appears to be hanging off the right hand side of the stage at the moment, as this will be changed in a minute.

Select picRightNavBG, convert it into a movie clip named movNavRight, and give it the instance name imageWrapper1. Double-click the movie clip to get inside, name the layer that picRightNavBG is on as BG, then add a new layer named Image MC. Choose this, and drag btnImage from the Library onto the stage. Position it at the right-hand side of the inner rectangle, like this:

Add the following ActionScript to btnImage:

```
on (release) {
    getURL ("{largeImageURL}");
}
```

By now, you've probably noticed that when the user hits any of your images (which will each have an iteration of this button), they will fire off your getURL command and launch whatever appropriate link you have specified in your data source. For the sake of this example, though, if you wanted to get a 'round robin' thing going on (where any of the image buttons takes you back to the floating preMenu navigation), then comment out the on (release) code above, and add the following:

```
on (release) {
    _level1.gotoAndPlay ("lblPlay");
    _root.gotoAndStop ("lblPark");
}
```

This will send the movie to our blank frame (lblPark), and tell our parked movie to play.

Select btnImage, and make it into a movie clip called movImages, giving it the instance name images. Double-click movImages so that we're inside it, and name the layer that your button is on as Button. Add two new layers named Image and Image Mask, and then select the former. At this point, if the Generator Objects panel is not visible, open it. Drag the Insert JPEG File object from the panel onto the stage, and align it so that it's centered directly over the button. Select the Image Mask layer, and drag picImageMask from the Library onto the stage. Again, center it over the button.

You should now have three layers; from top to bottom, they are Button, Image Mask, and Image. Make the Image Mask layer into a mask layer, and move Image into it. Then, add three more layers named Image Credit, Labels, and Actions. Place them beneath the Image layer in that order, so that you end up with something like this:

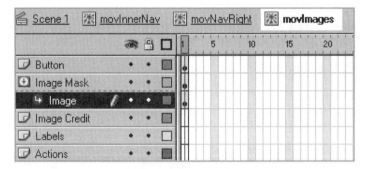

Select the Image Credit layer, and use the Type tool to type {credit} in a static text field on the stage. Make it white text and 10 points high. Rotate it 90 degrees counterclockwise, and position it in the bottom-left hand corner of the outer right-hand rectangle, like this:

We'll return to this movie clip to add content to the Labels and Actions layers shortly, but once again it's time for a breather, and a chance to look at what we've just created for the right-hand side of the nav.

Back up a couple of levels, so that you're looking at the contents of movInnerNav. You should see the movie clip called movNavRight sitting happily in the Nav Right layer. Double-click *this* movie clip, and you should then see two layers: Image MC, and BG, which contain movImages (with the instance name images) and picRightNavBG respectively. Double-click movImages so that you can see *its* contents, and you should find six layers, called Button, Image Mask (mask layer), Image (masked layer), Image Credit, Labels, and Actions. They contain the following: Button – btnImage, Image Mask – picImageMask, Image – **Generator Insert JPEG File object,**

Image Credit – rotated static text field containing {credit}, Labels – nothing yet, Actions – nothing yet. Your timelines should look like this:

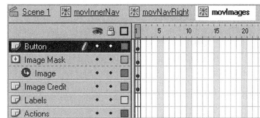

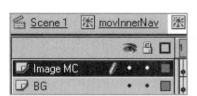

The final step before we build our data source and start adding the vital ActionScript to our movie is to select movNavLeft (instance name NavLeft), and scale the movie clip to 60% of its current size. Now select movNavRight (instance name imageWrapper1), and do the same. Reposition the two movie clips so that they butt up against each other, and everything will now be back on the stage. Double-click the stage to move up a level, select movInnerNav, and hit F8 to wrap it

inside a movie clip. Name this movNavigation, and give it the instance name parentNav. Save this file as genMenu.fla in the same directory as preMenu.fla and loader.fla.

> *If you want to, now might be a good time to check your file against the one on the web site, to make sure that your nested movie clips are the same.*

Let's briefly talk about why we have 'wrapped' so many nested movies, and kept the left and right parts of nav separate. On the main timeline, we have a movie clip (parentNav) that is essentially just a container. Inside this, we have childNav. We'll be using ActionScript to duplicate this childNav, and position the duplicated movie clips as if they were in one long line, so that it will stretch beyond the width of our stage. When we add code for it to start sliding, we can then create the illusion that it's continuous and has infinite length by clever repositioning of the parentNav movie clip.

Inside `childNav`, we separated the left and right side of `nav`. This is because we want the left side of the `nav` to display just once in each iteration of `childNav`, but we want to replicate the right side of the `nav` for each record in our data source. All this will result in the right side of the `nav` dynamically growing or shrinking, according to the number of records in our data source. Now you can see why there's a fairly complex setup procedure prior to adding our ActionScript.

Building the Data Source

To build our data source, we'll use a simple text editor. Earlier, we talked about a Generator variable called `{itemClip}`, which will contain the name of the movie clip within our Library that we would like to appear on the stage. This will be one of our field headings. We'll also need to differentiate records numerically, so we'll include a field that gives us a numerical identifier. On top of this, we'll have fields that contain data about where our images are, a title, a description, and a credit. We'll also include an external URL reference to a large version of the image (or this could be to some work that you've done). Create a new text file, and type in the following (dummy) data:

```
itemClip,imageNum, thumbImage, title, description, credit,
largeImageURL
Work,1,/images/image1.jpg,"Actionscript Studio - Generator
Chapter","Various images to accompany Generator chapter", "Baked
Earth",http://www.mydomain.com/image1.jpg
Work,2,/images/image2.jpg,,,"Cracking
Up",http://www.mydomain.com/image2.jpg
Work,3,/images/image3.jpg,,,"Rust",http://www.mydomain.com/
➡image3.jpg
Work,4,/images/image4.jpg,,,"Fruit",http://www.mydomain.com/
➡image4.jpg
Work,5,/images/image5.jpg,,,"Ornate",http://www.mydomain.com/
➡image5.jpg
Work,6,/images/image6.jpg,,,"Pick your
own",http://www.mydomain.com/image6.jpg
Work,7,/images/image7.jpg,,,"Veggie",http://www.mydomain.com/
➡image7.jpg
Work,8,/images/image8.jpg,,,"Peppers",http://www.mydomain.com/
➡image8.jpg
```

Save the text file as `dyn_menu_content.txt`, in the same directory as your FLA files. As usual, there's a copy of the file available on the web site, along with all the dummy images from this example for you to use. Make a folder named `images` in the folder where your Flash file and data source live, and copy the dummy images into it.

We now have our Flash movie laid out, our images waiting, and our data source built. All we need to do now is to add our ActionScript, and let our Flash movie know where its data source lives. A couple more minor bits and pieces, and we should be up and running!

You'll notice in our data source that the `itemClip` column makes reference to a movie clip called `Work`, but we haven't built this yet. In the source file included on the web site, you'll find four movie clips: `Work`, `Information`, `Contact`, and `Portfolio`. Drag these from the example file Library and into your movie. (Of course, you can always make some of your own if you'd prefer.) They will now be available for our Insert Symbol object.

Return to your Flash movie, make sure you're looking at the main timeline, and name the layer that contains `movNavigation` as Navigation. Then, add two new layers called Actions and dragControl:

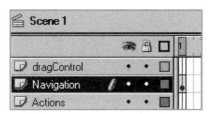

Select dragControl, and create an empty movie clip on the stage. Call it drag, and give it the instance name `dragControl`. Add the following ActionScript to it:

```
onClipEvent (enterFrame) {
    // Set parentNav width variable
    _root.parentNavWidth = _root.parentNav._width;

    // Establish mouse position
    _root.xPos = _root._xmouse;

    // Centre the menu drag to the screen
    _root.xPos = _root.xPos - (_root.screenWidth / 2);
    _root.parentNav._x = _root.parentNav._x -
        ➥_root.xPos / _root.slideSpeed;

    if (_root.parentNav._x < -_root.parentNavWidth / 2) {
        _root.parentNav._x = 0;
    } else if (_root.parentNav._x > 0) {
        _root.parentNav._x = (-_root.parentNavWidth / 2);
    }
}
```

Let's consider what this code does. Earlier, we discussed some clever code that would give the illusion of an infinitely long `nav` menu that continually slid left and right. This is how we do it. Imagine three identical images in a row, each 200 pixels wide. When they slide to the left, we want to determine when they reach -200, and then reposition them at 0, in the same way, if they are at +200 we want to reposition them at -200. This way, Flash will be resetting the x-coordinates of the images all the time, fooling the brain into believing that the three images are in fact a never-ending row of images.

To be honest, everything down to the `if` statement is pretty straightforward so we'll skip straight to that. The `if` statement evaluates whether the x-coordinate of the `parentNav` movie clip is further left than the width of `parentNav` divided by two. Now, you may be saying to yourself that you can see the `parentNav` clip on the stage, and it doesn't even fill the stage, let alone hang over the edges! Don't forget though, that we'll be duplicating the `childNav`, which in turn will have an 'expanded' `NavRight` movie clip, according to the number of records contained in our data source. Now let's add code to the first frame of the Actions layer on the main timeline:

```
startDrag ("dragControl", true);

// Set variables
_root.slideSpeed = 10;
_root.screenWidth = 740;
_root.screenHeight = 400;
_root.parentNav._x = 0;
_root.parentNav._xscale = 150;
_root.parentNav._yscale = 150;
_root.recordCount =
    ➥_root.parentNav.childNav.imageWrapper1.images._totalframes;
_root.navLeftWidth = _root.parentNav.childNav.navLeft._width;
_root.wrapperWidth =
    ➥_root.parentNav.childNav.imageWrapper1._width;
_root.childNavWidth = _root.parentNav.childNav._width;
```

Most of this sets up variables that are fairly self-explanatory, but one of the most important lines is the one that evaluates the `_totalframes` property of `imageWrapper1.images`, and it's certainly worth talking about. Generator offers more than just the objects from the Generator Object panel. We'll be using the Replicate function provided by Generator, which lets you display movie clips or graphics sequentially. This will literally iterate through a recordset, and create a new frame for each record. We'll then duplicate the `imageWrapper1` movie clip and tell each duplicated clip to go to a specific frame (thus displaying a new image), and position the duplicated movie clips with ActionScript to appear side by side. This way, we can use a single Insert JPEG File object that gets replicated as many times as there are records. With the use of the `duplicateMovie` command, we get to see the entire visual feast!

Generator delivers the ability to change movie clip properties, and even movie clips, with the following options: Replace, Replicate, Set Alpha, Set Brightness, Set Custom Color, Set Tint, and Transform. Now, you may be saying to yourself that you can do some of these with ActionScript, but don't forget that not only can these be set via external data sources, but they also all occur on the server side and not the client side, which means less strain on the user's machine, and fewer hits on the server by the user.

Double-click movNavigation, so that we can add actions to duplicate the childNav movie clip. Add a new layer, name it Actions, and add the following actions to frame 1:

```
for (n = 1; n < 4; n++) {
    newChild = "childNav" + n;
    duplicateMovieClip ("childNav", newChild, n);
    eval(newChild)._x = eval(newChild)._x +
    ➥n*(_root.navLeftWidth+(_root.wrapperWidth*_root.recordCount));
}
```

This simply duplicates the childNav movie clip three times, names it, and positions it. The clever line is the last one: This evaluates the width of the left part of the nav and adds the width of the right part of our nav, multiplied by the amount of records found in the data source. It then takes this value and repositions each subsequent duplicate to this value times the number of the loop.

Double-click childNav, so that we can add ActionScript to the Actions frame we left empty earlier. Add the following actions to frame 1 of the layer named Actions:

```
for (i = 2; i < _root.recordCount + 1; i++) {
    newWrapper = "imageWrapper" + i;
    duplicateMovieClip ("imageWrapper1", newWrapper, i);
    eval(newWrapper)._x = imageWrapper1._x +
    ➥imageWrapper1._width * (i - 1);
}

for (q = 1; q < _root.recordCount + 1; q++) {
    eval("imageWrapper" + q).images._name ="images" + q;
}

_root.newSize = this._width;
```

This code is worth dissecting in some detail, starting with the initialization of the for loop:

```
for (i = 2; i < _root.recordCount + 1; i++) {
```

This starts its count at 2 because imageWrapper1 already exists, and we want to keep it where it is. The loop will continue until it has iterated through all the records in the data source, and of course i++ simply increments our counter one at a time.

```
newWrapper = "imageWrapper" + i;
```

This line sets up a variable called newWrapper to equal the word imageWrapper plus the increment (i), so in the first iteration through the loop newWrapper is "imageWrapper2", in the second it will be "imageWrapper3", and so on.

```
duplicateMovieClip ("imageWrapper1", newWrapper, i);
```

This line duplicates the movie clip called `imageWrapper1`, and sets the name of the duplicated clip to whatever `newWrapper` is equal to in that iteration. Because we need to set a depth for the duplicated clip, the final parameter sets it to `i` (the current count number).

```
eval(newWrapper)._x = imageWrapper1._x +
➥imageWrapper1._width * (i - 1);
```

We need to set the x-coordinate of the duplicated clip to butt up neatly against the previous clip. We could simply say, "OK, the `imageWrapper1` clip is 200 pixels wide, and therefore we will set each new clip's x-coordinate to be whatever the previous x's position on the stage was, plus 200." However, if we're to make this a truly dynamic menu that can cope with bigger or smaller images, our code needs to be able to cope with these possible changes. We know that each duplicate is based upon `imageWrapper1`, and therefore we can happily use its width as our yardstick. We want to position subsequent duplicates at the edge of the last duplicate's right hand side. To find the right hand side coordinate of `imageWrapper1`, we use:

```
imageWrapper1._x + imageWrapper1._width
```

For the sake of simplicity, let's pretend that `imageWrapper1`'s width is 100, in which case we know that `imageWrapper2`'s `_x` property should be 100, `imageWrapper3`'s should be 200, and so on. Of course, a simple calculation that says, "Position each duplicate movie clip at a start point plus the original's width, and increment," will position each duplicate just where we want it. Hence:

```
imageWrapper1._x + imageWrapper1._width * (i - 1)
```

Finally, we need to tell Flash which movie clip to put in that position. We're not referring to an actual movie clip's instance name, but to a variable containing that name. We don't actually have an instance name called `newWrapper`, but we do know that the content of the variable `newWrapper` is an instance name, so we use `eval` to target the variable's content and not the variable itself: `eval(newWrapper)._x`.

This is very similar to when we duplicated the `childNav`. However, there is a subtle difference: in this case, we've added a further loop that will rename the movie clip images that live inside `imageWrapper` to have individual names.

Now let's take care of the population of the most important part of the whole movie: the images on the right side of our `nav`. Double-click `imageWrapper1`, and select the `images` movie clip. Now open up the Generator panel, and while `images` is selected, click on the drop-down and select Replicate. Then, set the following parameters:

- Data Source = {source}

- Expand Frames = false

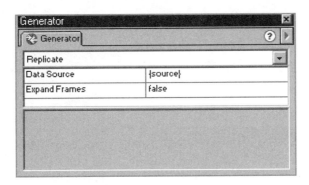

Double-click the `images` movie clip. We'll now add content to the Actions and Labels layers that we left empty earlier. Select the first frame of the Labels layer, and give it the label: `images{imageNum}`. This will gather information from our data source, and then literally create labels named `images1`, `images2`, and so on.

Now onto the first frame of the Actions layer, which contains possibly the most puzzling action of the whole movie. Add the following:

```
gotoAndStop (this._name);
```

What does this mean? We're simply telling the movie clip to go to the label that has the same as the movie clip itself. Don't forget, Generator has increased the number of frames within this movie clip, according to the amount of records it found in the data source. This code use is important because it ensures your movie will work no matter what Generator names the movie clips that it makes. We earlier created the frame label `images{imageNum}`, which will mean that we have a series of frame labels that match our duplicated movie names. There you have it: a quick and easy way to have as many movies as records, and each one with an image on each frame.

Finally (almost!), double-click the `movImages` movie clip that you've just been working on. You should now be able select the Insert JPEG File object, and change its parameters to these:

- File Name: `{thumbImage}`

- Cache: `false`

- Scale To Fit: `true`

- Export As: `JPEG`

- JPEG Quality: `75`

- Instance Name: `imageNumber{imageNum}`

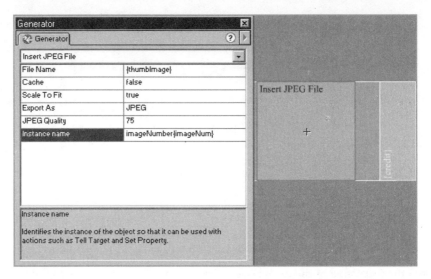

What haven't we done yet? We need to tell Flash where our data source lives! If this application were live on the Web, it could be passed along with the URL, or through a script. If it were offline, you could pass the data source address via the command prompt, or create a simple batch file to do it. For our test purposes, we'll use one of Flash's Publish Settings properties.

Go to the Publish Settings, and select the Generator tab. Type the following into the relevant fields, and remember to hit the Add button!

- Name: source

- Value: dyn_menu_content.txt

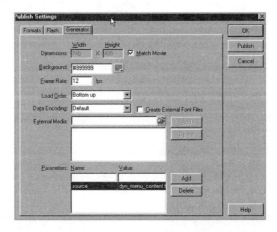

Now test your movie. If you've followed the steps, you should have a dynamically built, never-ending, backward-forward sliding menu!

Never content, we're going to change this slightly, as we don't want this nav to commence until it's called by preMenu. Make sure you're back at the main timeline, select the first frame in all four layers, and drag them over to frame 10. Add a new layer, and name it Labels. Select frame 1, and give it the frame label lblPark; then add a keyframe to frame 10 and name the frame label lblMenu. Select the Actions layer, and add a stop action to the first frame.

Test the movie, and don't worry that you can't see any movement – this is simply to populate it. Finally, go to the folder where you've saved your files, launch loader.swf, and see a successful test. Yes!

mmary

During your Generator development life, you will find yourself constantly switching between files: From data source to authoring environment, to browser, to testing, to editing, and re-testing. However, this kind of multitasking is very satisfying, and aren't we coming to expect it by now?

I hope very much that this chapter has helped get you started with Generator, and paved the way for you to investigate further the power that it offers. Don't forget: we've built a fairly impressive interface with just a couple of Generator objects in a short space of time. There are many more objects on offer. The best advice I can give is to make the Generator help files and manual your best friends!

ources

The files to accompany this chapter. Including all Flash source code, images, and text files are included in the source code download for this book. Once you've been through the chapter and understood how it works, start playing with the source, change some variables, add some more, try using other Generator objects, see what happens – but most important, have some fun.

eb

Some useful addresses to keep in your Favorites folder are:

www.markme.com	This is one of the best generator resources on the Web
www.flashgen.com	Some great examples and downloads here
www.gendev.net	The Generator Developer Network

wsgroup

macromedia.generator	This forum can be found here: forums.macromedia.com

Your Fingertips

Most importantly, don't forget the help files that come bundled with the Generator application itself. Many people overlook this resource, but I feel it is one of the most valuable of all!

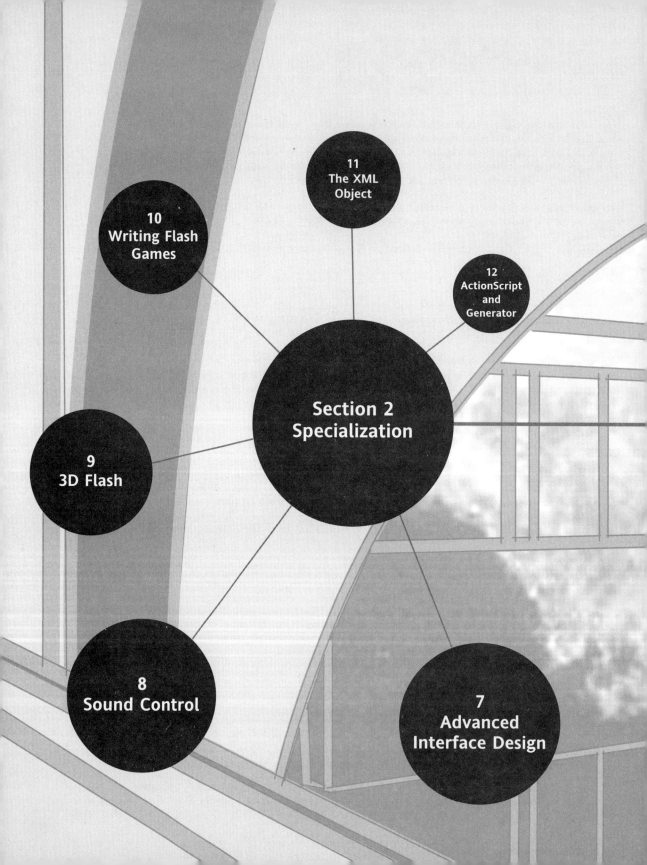

Chapter 13
Creativity in Practice

Although Flash 5 is a deep and powerful tool, its use for large-scale software development has been limited. This is partly because it's a relatively new product, but it's also partly because of the unprecedented integration of design and scripting capabilities that Flash 5 offers. This integration, though a boon to the independent designer/programmer/site maintainer, breaks traditional group software development models, which tend to rely on highly specialized roles and clearly differentiated design, development, and test phases. The purpose of this chapter is to explore some of the practical ways to use Flash for large projects, potentially with a group of people who may have different roles and skills.

Because this is a relatively new topic – until version 5, there wasn't enough scripting power in Flash to develop code-heavy applications – this section is presented as a set of tips and techniques, rather than as the last word on the subject. Most of this is a combination of common sense and personal experience, so the most important message of this chapter is probably that you should just spend some time thinking about the major issues that are presented here, even if you don't like these solutions. A little up-front planning can save days or even weeks at the end of a large project.

This chapter, then, is one way to look at the process of starting, building, and finishing a large Flash project. It is intended for anyone who wants to use the full power of ActionScript *and* Flash's unique graphical capabilities to maximum advantage – especially in situations where a group of people are sharing files, code, and ideas. The major phases outlined in this chapter are:

- Setting up a team a with sensitivity to the unique benefits and detriments of Flash development

- Starting a project, especially by prototyping

- Structuring a project, with a focus on strategies for concurrent group development

- An examination of some of the big issues encountered during the heart of the 'build' phase of a project

- Finishing a Flash project, with a review of techniques for optimization and debugging

Working With a Team

Using Flash with a team of developers and designers is still an evolving discipline. As Flash 5 becomes the standard for delivering web and device-based applications (and it should), Flash projects will grow in size and complexity, making it more common for a team of specialists to come together to create something in Flash. As this happens, our notions of the phases of software development, as well as those of our roles within a project, will need to change to fit Flash's unique capabilities.

ilding In Flexibility

Flash offers unprecedented flexibility. Want to change the way a screen looks? Go to the frame and move stuff around. Want to create a new animated button? Whip one up in a few minutes. Working in Flash is a joy because most of the things that have traditionally been difficult in software development (animating elements on screen, talking to servers, compiling) are built right into the tool. This makes it easy to take an original idea much further than ever before without committing extensive time and money to an unproven design.

Traditional software development is modeled after the process of real-world construction: you design it, then you figure out how to build it, then you go out and actually do it. As the process goes forward, the tolerances become slimmer, and it becomes more expensive and difficult to change decisions that have gone before. Flash development is more like a process of drafting and revision – some seemingly large changes can be made easily, and often a large chunk of the project can be built (or at least prototyped) in a relatively short period of time.

It is critical, then, to allow for this flexibility when scheduling a Flash project and assigning tasks. This often means dispensing with or modifying the formal design and feature requirements process that tend to precede standard software projects, in favor of an extended prototyping and early user-testing phase. This also means that quality analysis (QA) and user testing should be involved throughout a project's lifespan (rather than just at the end, as often happens with standard software development) because the software will be closer to its final form earlier in the development cycle.

le Definitions

The standard software development model uses developers and designers in highly specialized roles. Interaction designers are often separate from graphic designers, and user interface engineers are often separate from low-level code specialists. This is because these different roles require different skills, and more notably, familiarity with different tools. In the brave new world of Flash development, though, one tool does it all.

This is, of course, precisely the source of Flash's power. Like all power, though, it comes with responsibility. In a more traditional software development environment, engineers don't tend to tweak graphic designs, because they can't do it very easily – they probably don't even have Photoshop or a similar image-editing tool on their machines. With Flash, however, it's tempting and easy for *anyone* involved in a project to edit or change a design as they see fit. In general, this is a temptation that should be avoided.

This is not to say, though, that the quiet code geek who sits in the basement may not have a great user interface idea. The nice thing about Flash is that if they *do* have an idea, they should have no trouble mocking it up and demonstrating it. Instead, the point is that the best thing you can do when organizing your team to work on a project is to create clear role definitions at the outset. It doesn't matter who is ultimately responsible for a given feature or aspect of the project, but it's critically important that *someone* is.

Most software design issues ultimately boil down to matters of taste, and hoping for group consensus is a sure way to end up creating mediocre software. Consider having leads for different areas or aspects of your project, and then, after allowing everyone to offer an opinion, give them the final say. The consistency you will gain, in addition to the painfully long meetings you will avoid, will ultimately benefit the final product.

Of course, in the early phases of a project, it's fun and helpful to brainstorm and throw ideas around without a clear direction or leader. However, these brainstorming sessions can be a curse of sorts: no single design or implementation will ever compare to the unarticulated promise expressed in a freeform brainstorm. For this reason, it's usually best to curtail the open-ended phase of a project as much as possible. Talk is, after all, just talk.

Developers and Designers

We should take special note here of the ways that designers and developers can and should work together when using Flash. With the improvements in Flash 5's ActionScript, Flash went from a tool that was heavy on the visuals and light on the code, to one where it's possible to write almost any kind of software imaginable. Now, for the first time, people with strict development backgrounds are finding Flash to be an interesting and plausible solution for tricky client software problems. This is all great, but it means that the people doing the Flash development may no longer be the designers-cum-filmmakers-cum-all-around-digital-folks that they once were. Have no fear, though – Flash is great for letting developers and artists collaborate smoothly, as long as you set up your projects to accommodate this kind of collaboration from the beginning.

The most immediately effective thing you can do to work together well is to work in Flash as much as possible. If you're an artist who prefers to work in Adobe Illustrator, or Macromedia FreeHand, take the time to export your work to Flash and check it before sending it off to your developer. The export tools are still not perfect, and catching a problem early on will save you a ranting tirade later. Similarly, when exchanging notes, comments, sketches, revision requests, and pretty much any sort of idea related to the project, consider using Flash as the way to communicate whenever it's convenient. Flash is a great little presentation tool, and since it's so easy to just grab elements from one project and drop them into another, you can easily focus on the nitty-gritty elements of your design.

Developers working on a Flash project with a rapidly evolving visual design should try to identify the areas that are relatively fixed, and those likely to change, as early as possible. For the areas that *are* likely to change, pay special attention to encapsulating states as visually as possible – usually with individual frame locations – and try to make coherent pieces that can be understood even out of context. If your artist is working in a tool other than Flash, consider structuring your project so that the most rapidly changing parts of the UI contain no code at all, and can easily be completely replaced. Finally, a few well-placed smart clips can be a great boon to both developers and designers, allowing developers to free themselves from involved production tasks, and allowing designers to tweak to their hearts' content. In general, as a Flash developer working with a designer, you should look for ways to allow the designer to do as much of the final production work as possible – try not to spend your time matching your dynamic elements to a static screenshot, since you're duplicating work that the designer has already done.

For designers working on an ActionScript-heavy project, one piece of advice towers above all others: do not fear the code. The code is your friend. The code is ultimately what will bring your work to life, and it's never as complicated as it looks. If there's an element that's not working right, find the relevant ActionScript and skim it. If it makes absolutely no sense, give your developer a hard time – even a layperson should be able to glean *something* by looking the most complex ActionScript (if only by reading the comments). Don't be afraid to meddle (but make sure that you save a version first!) by adding a `trace` statement here, or modifying a constant there. Getting a feel for the code will not only make you more effective; it will enable you to understand how the project is built at a fundamental level. Among other things, this will give you an intuitive sense of the difficulty of the changes you will invariably propose as the deadline nears.

ys to Work Together

Once the finer points of your team's structure and role definitions have been established, spend some time plotting how, specifically, the team will work together. In addition to milestones and weekly meetings, consider the specifics of how your team will standardize and share their work.

hared Files

One obvious issue to resolve early on is the structure of the various servers and networks that will enable your team's collaboration. Since there aren't any group development tools (like Visual SourceSafe) for Flash, it's worth taking some real care to determine the best ways to store and back up your group's files. If it's important that you always have a working version of your software somewhere (for, say, a live web site) consider having two completely separate servers – one of them live, and one that's used exclusively for development and testing. If there are a lot of different files in your project that different developers or artists may need to edit at different times, create a locking system so that only one person has a file open for editing at a time. Locking systems can vary from the simple (yelling, "*Hey!* I'm working on `main.fla`, and if you touch it I'll smack you!") to the ornate (setting the file's properties to read-only while it's checked out), but any method is fine as long as it works.

ile Naming

When working as group, make sure that you have agreed on some kind of naming convention to facilitate the sharing and circulation of files. Never, under any circumstances, should you call a file `MyProject_newUI.fla`. Invariably, the next version of your project will be titled `MyProject_newnewUI.fla`. When you find yourself naming your latest version `MyProject_finalnewUIthistimeforreal.fla`, you'll see the wisdom of this prohibition. Better to just name files by date, using two digits for year, month, and day in that order: `MyProject010315.fla`. This has the added benefit of ensuring that the latest version of your project will appear at the end of your file list when you sort by name. Alternatively, you can just append a version number: `MyProject01.fla`. This has the advantage of allowing you only to change versions when you feel that the project is in some sort of sensible or working shape – if you have to go back a version, the project should at least still run.

To keep SWF filenames consistent, especially if you're testing with a pre-generated HTML page, or loading several files from Flash, use the Publish Settings controls under the File menu to specify the published filename. Even though the filename in the example below is `MyProject02.fla`, it will still output a SWF file named `MyProject.swf` when the File > Publish command is used.

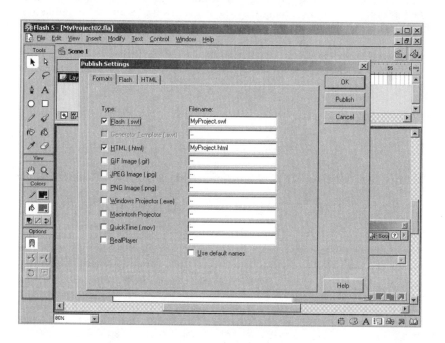

Stricter file naming conventions than this are generally only necessary for very large projects with a lot of assets. In this case, not only should the filename contain some sort of date or version control, but it should also have identifiers that indicate where it goes in the overall project.

Asset file names should generally follow the rules given above, and, if tools other than Flash are being used to generate assets, make sure to include the proper (dot) extension on the Macintosh, so that those working on PCs don't have to try all their programs to figure out how to read the file.

The general assumption here is that part of the advantage of working in Flash is that it accommodates a looser style of software development. Don't get too hung up on conventions – with Flash, if it works, it works. The kinds of strict conventions and formalized version control that are used for other types of software development are usually not necessary with Flash, because it's such a high-level tool.

Component Naming

Component naming conventions can make it much easier for other developers and designers to figure out how your project works. For instance, there can be several names for a single movie clip in Flash:

- It's name in the Library

- It's symbol name

- It's instance name

- It's symbol linkage identifier

Distinguishing between movie clips in the Library and those on the stage is important, and you should be consistent in your treatment of the issue. One common approach is simply to name instances of the movie clip the same as the library name, though clearly this will only work if there's just one instance of the clip on the stage at a time. Another option is to add mc as a prefix to the movie clip name. Whatever your solution, try to avoid making someone dig through dialog boxes and panels to figure out what you're doing. Here's an example of the sort of thing to be avoided:

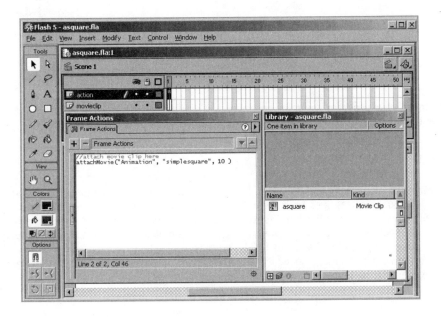

To understand what this code snippet actually does, you have to examine the linkage properties for the movie clip asquare, which are buried in a dialog box:

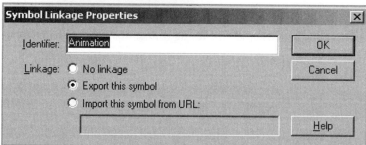

To make your program easier to understand, it's better to use a standard prefix, or to use the identical name for export identifiers as in the Library itself.

Getting Started

Perhaps the nicest thing about Flash is that it usually doesn't take much to get started: there are no low-level graphics routines to be written, or complicated infrastructure problems to be solved before you can put something on the screen. For this reason, though, Flash projects are often begun without much of a design document, prototype, or complete specification. If you're lucky enough to know exactly what you want to build, and have every detail worked out, then you should pat yourself on the back and go ahead and skip this section. If, on the other hand, you're like most Flash developers I've met, you probably think a design document would just spoil the fun.

At the beginning of a large Flash project, prototyping is the most important and powerful tool at your disposal. The final stages of software development can be tricky, and making big changes once your project is nearly done can be very difficult. Prototyping serves a few different purposes:

- It can help reveal and refine the user interface for your project.

- It can help you to explore the code architecture issues in your project, and test your ActionScript ideas to find the best way of doing something. This is particularly useful for the object-oriented approach, allowing you to test the objects in different situations before deciding to use them.

- It can also help to explain your intentions (and how much they will cost) to your team, clients, or superiors.

w Mapping

Many people like to jump right in with a few proposed screenshots or a simple code prototype, but it can sometimes be helpful just to doodle a proposed flow with paper and pencil. Sometimes, in a rush to prototype, important feature requirements are forgotten that are painful to reintroduce once the overall design has been put in place.

More formal tools, such as storyboards and flowcharts, can be helpful – especially when you're trying to pitch to a client, or explain a concept to a larger organization. However, be warned: a well-polished flowchart with animated, full color illustrations is just that and nothing more. There's no penalty for leaving a whole section or crucial logic step out of your flowchart; but there's a big one for leaving it out of your project. In general, these tools have a limited use that increases as the size of the team increases. Often, the more informal the early design process can be, the better. When you're just beginning a project, the smallest prototype will often tell you more than the most extensive design document.

de Prototyping

Prototyping tricky aspects of the code for your project may seem painful, because no one likes to write code that gets thrown away. Do it anyway. More than likely, you'll come across problems that you hadn't anticipated and, having written it once, you'll have some ideas about a much better way to deal with the issues you've uncovered. When you're working on code prototypes, don't worry about looks, performance, or optimization; just do what you have to do to make it work the way you want it to.

This is an example from the development of the Flatland Exports web site (http://flatlandexports.com). The goal for this project was to experiment with presenting a design company portfolio using a zoomable interface, rather than a system of modal screens and menus. The very first prototype was just a box that would zoom to full-screen when you ran the mouse over it.

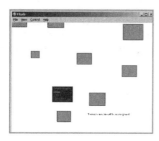 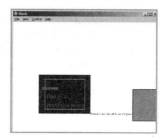 

As painful as it may be to look at, it was nonetheless extremely helpful. First, it communicated exactly what we were talking about when we said "zoomable interface". This was important for the simple reason that when people's heads are nodding in agreement, they are often each imagining something completely different. Building the core of the idea allows everyone to take a look and make sure that they're all picturing the same thing. Just as importantly, though, this prototype revealed some technical problems with keeping a piece centered on the mouse as it zoomed. These issues ended up having implications on how the whole project was structured. The code for this prototype was ultimately not used, but it paved the way for a cleaner, more refined approach to the final implementation.

Visual Prototyping

Prototyping for visual design is the easiest and most enjoyable kind of prototyping, and although it's simple, it is still a powerful technique. The simplest kind of prototype is just a series of screens drawn or imported into Flash that a user can step through by pressing the arrow keys – almost a working flow diagram. This can be remarkably effective. Slightly more complex, but also more revealing, is a visual design prototype that implements (say) just one button on each screen, and links it to the next screen with just one button.

In some cases, a few drawings next to one another – like a storyboard – can serve as a visual prototype, especially for animated sequences. That was the next phase of prototyping for the Flatland Exports site:

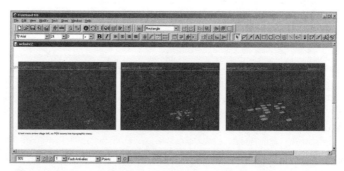

As you can see, it's just a series of screens, but it conveys a number of ideas. Unfortunately, when we looked at the code that would power this design, it proved too complicated. Still, this is a great example of how loose the back-and-forth can be in the prototyping phase. Don't worry about how it will ultimately look or work; just try to explore the all the aspects of your idea before jumping into development proper.

w Far Should a Prototype Go?

In all cases, the key to prototyping is doing as little as possible to communicate an idea – either to yourself, to your team, or to an audience. The art of good prototyping depends on laziness, and you should look for any and all shortcuts: hack, cheat, and steal code, if it makes things go faster. If you find that you're tearing your hair out on your prototype, stop. It should be fun and easy, and if, once you've learned and moved on from your mistakes, you have to throw the whole thing away, you shouldn't mind – in fact, you should expect to throw the whole thing away. In general, the hardest part of developing a new project is figuring out how it will work. Once you have a clear picture of that, doing the actual implementation should be relatively painless. Besides, you'll often find that you're able to cut and paste some of the routines from your prototype into a subsequent version.

Creating a prototype for an audience other than your team can be an important development milestone. Showing a prototype to a client can be an effective way of obtaining buy-off, of making sure that a project is headed in the right direction, or even of making a sale. Be warned, however: many clients are not trained to see the forest for the trees, so showing them the coolest bit of code you've developed with ugly stand-in graphics may not ultimately help your cause. When creating a prototype to show to clients, think about how you want your clients to react, and work backwards from there. This may sound manipulative, but remember: a prototype is built to show only a few aspects of the final project, so you should pick those aspects carefully, and make sure your clients understand exactly what you're showing them. If a prototype showed every aspect of the final project, it would be the real thing!

This exhortation to use caution when mixing prototypes and clients comes from hard-won personal experience. Flatland Exports once lost an account after showing a detailed interface prototype. We spent a considerable amount of time polishing the various linkages between screens, the choices of dropdowns versus scrolling lists, and the general flow of information through the application. We were happy with the work we'd done. When we showed it to the client, though, we got grimaces through our whole presentation. We later found out the problem: our prototype was in black and white. The client wanted something 'snazzy'.

Prototyping for user testing is an equally perilous, but slightly different case. User testing is an important part of refining any user interface: just because your design makes sense to you, it doesn't mean it will work for your target audience. Furthermore, user testing is all too often limited to the end of development cycle, when fixes are heavily constrained by schedule and the assumptions that were already built into the project. Creating a prototype that can be tested on users is a great way to highlight interface issues early on. When creating a prototype for user testing, you should begin with the results that you want to gather. "Does it work?" is not specific enough for a user-test prototype, but "Will users find the second-level menu options?" is. There are no hard-and-fast rules when it comes to what to focus on in your prototype, but you should try to concentrate on complex-but-important processes, and user interface elements that are unique to your application. For instance, if your site uses a relatively standard hierarchical menu system for high-level navigation, but has some tricky UI in the individual screens, consider only prototyping and testing the individual screens and not worrying about how users get from one screen to another.

Build just enough to get the answers you need, and interpret your feedback carefully. Did a certain test subject say they didn't like that feature because it's not useful, or because they didn't understand it? Finally, user testing does not have to be a formal process involving a one-way mirror and a clipboard. Sitting a friend or colleague in front of your computer and watching them play can be as enlightening as the most formal user test.

Structuring the Project

Once you get a good sense of the general size and shape of your Flash project, the next task is to break it down into small but sensible pieces. While this may not be necessary for small projects with a single developer, it is absolutely essential on larger projects, for two reasons:

- It makes the individual parts of your project easier to understand and test

- It allows for the greatest amount of concurrent development

There are as many ways to factor a project as there are projects, so first we'll examine the tools at your disposal for breaking up a project, and then we'll examine how they can be used together in a couple of case studies.

Planning for the Back End

Many large Flash projects have a back-end component, such as an online database or communications server, which provides core functionality to the Flash application. Often, the back-end and the Flash elements of the project cannot be integrated until late in the development cycle. In general, it's risky simply to wait for the back end to be ready before any kind of testing and integration, so an important part of your project structure is how you plan to accommodate your back end throughout the development cycle. The rest of this chapter deals only with Flash development, so the general goal here is to isolate the back-end issues from the majority of the Flash work.

The best way to deal with this is usually to create a dummy object, or a set of functions that handle all interaction with the back end, be that a database, a communications server, or whatever. Before the back end is live, it should be simulated by using routines that look information up in, say, a text file, and store it in a local data object. Once the back end is working, the routines should simply be rewritten to support it. Make sure that you follow all the rules of good object-oriented programming when you make your dummy server object: other objects should only interact with it via methods, and all of its data should be self-contained. You want it to be totally seamless when you replace the dummy calls with the real ones, and you want to allow for the internal data structure to change drastically without that impacting code anywhere else in your application.

Whenever possible, simulate the tricky aspects of your back end with your dummy server. For instance, if you know that there's going to be a lot of latency in server requests, build in a delay. You don't want to hook everything up and then find that you've failed to plan for slow server requests with only a week left in your project. Also, try and simulate the structure of the data coming from the server as closely as possible. The best text file to use to simulate server responses is an actual log of the server talking to another client. If that isn't available, be sure that you have agreed upon the basics of the server-client interaction and data structures with the relevant parties before building anything. Once you know what the structure is, follow it to the letter: if you know you're going to use XML to talk to the back end, use XML in your mockup. The time invested at the outset will easily be made up in a smooth integration phase.

Although it may seem like a lot of work to create a special object just to simulate your application's interaction with the back end, it is almost always worth it. First, if you build your dummy object well, it will make sure you're accounting for server issues early in your development cycle. Second, during middle phases of development, you may go back and forth between testing against the live server and testing against your dummy server several times. This is easy to do if you have a strongly encapsulated server object – you can just comment out one object, and uncomment another. Finally, with all but the simplest projects, it's often best to leave the server object in shipping code and change its internal workings to use live data, rather than trying to replace all of the server calls throughout your project. This has the added benefit of allowing you to add a server cache during your performance optimization phase.

ing #include

The #include command can be used to factor complex ActionScript code, or to isolate object definitions. In general, it's best to develop the ActionScript that will eventually be #included in its own FLA file, which usually also contains some scaffolding for testing the script. Once the script appears to be working well, it can then be copied into a text file and (traditionally) given the extension .as. A script called myscript.as would be included like this:

```
#include "myscript.as"
```

Although this is a powerful and often useful technique, it should be used sparingly for a couple of reasons. First, #included ActionScript throws off Flash's error reporting: the line numbers, and even the messages that you get in the output window when there's an error publishing your movie, will not accurately reflect the actual location of the error if it's in or after the #included ActionScript. Second, because of JavaScript's flexibility regarding data scope and type, it's generally a bad idea to include data definitions in #included code unless they are encapsulated in an object. Finally, it can be tough to implement good version control with #included ActionScript, because the name used with the #include action must be a literal. For all these reasons, it is usually best to factor scripts using #include after they are already relatively stable and well defined.

Factoring a project by using #include is best for:

- Isolating the code for complex algorithms

- Isolating an object definition

- Switching easily between two versions of an object or routine

This last use can be very powerful, functioning like the #ifdef statement in C. For instance, if your project relies on a heavy back end, but you've built a dummy server to test against, you may want to make it easy to switch back and forth between the dummy server and the real server. That could easily be accomplished like this:

```
var serverlive = true;
if (serverlive){
    #include "realserver.as";

    // Other code to initialize server included here
    ...

} else {
    #include "dummyserver.as";
}
```

During development, testing could switch between the dummy server and the live server simply by changing the value of serverlive.

Shared Libraries

Shared libraries offer a simple way to extract elements from a design. A shared library is simply a file containing one or more library elements that have symbol linkage identifiers, allowing them to be referred to even when they're not on the stage. You can incorporate shared library elements into your Flash file simply by choosing File > Open as Shared Library and dragging elements from the Library onto the stage. Shared elements behave like regular library elements at design time, but when the project is run the elements are actually loaded from a separate SWF file. Because the shared library elements live in a different file, that file can be revised and updated independently.

Shared libraries are good for factoring out largely independent UI or code elements that don't have complex interactions with one another. For instance, a shared library would be good for a palette of buttons that's reused throughout a project. Since factoring with shared libraries is so easy, and so well supported by Flash, it's an obvious first place to look to break down projects.

However, there are a few pitfalls to this approach. First, unlike normal library elements, once an item from a shared library is dragged into a project, its visual appearance in that FLA file is locked. This means that updates to the symbol in the shared library will not appear at build time, even though they will be reflected when you're viewing the SWF file at runtime. This is fine for an object with a simple user interface, or one that will stay at a fixed size, but it's no good for an object whose visual appearance may change dramatically, or need to line up accurately with other objects in the main movie. Of course, the shared library element may always be deleted and re-imported to reflect updates, but that can be a hassle – especially if the element appears in multiple places in the main movie. This can be especially problematic if the shared library symbol is a smart clip, in which case replacing the symbol also means copying whatever parameters had been set. For this reason, it's rarely a good idea to mix smart clips and shared libraries.

The second disadvantage to factoring a project by breaking it into shared libraries is that the individual pieces can be difficult to test, especially for unexpected interactions with other parts of the whole. This is because you need at least two movies in order to test shared library elements: the shared library itself, and then a movie that loads and uses it. Remember too that the entire shared library will be loaded at the moment its first element is called. If latency associated with loading the shared library may be an issue for you, be sure to account for this early in your test cycle, potentially by posting files to a development server to see how they'll run off the network. As with all approaches, early integration is the key to avoiding disaster when using shared libraries to factor a project. Create a location – usually on a server – where everyone can 'check-in' the latest version of their files, so that they can all be run together as soon as it's even remotely possible to do so. Developing libraries and features independently, and integrating late in a cycle, is a sure way to create unsolvable problems.

Because they can be hard to keep updated and test, shared libraries aren't the solution to every project factoring problem, but they are very useful in a couple of situations. Shared library files can be kept completely separate from the rest of a project, so they're usually best if:

- You have independent pieces that don't share any code, but need to be loosely bound together at runtime

- You are developing a set of independent pieces that you plan to reuse in different applications

- You want to create a palette of visual elements that are reused throughout one or more Flash projects

aded Movie Clips

Instead of keeping movie clips in a library (shared or otherwise) they can be loaded at runtime using the loadMovie command. There are a number of advantages to this approach, but chief among them is its transparency. A loaded movie clip behaves in all ways as if it were in the movie that loads it, except for the latency associated with pulling in the file.

An additional advantage of loaded movie clips is that they are, by their nature, highly separable from the rest of a project. This makes them easy to test and evolve without building extensive scaffolding to provide an environment where they can run.

Loaded movie clips can be used for just about anything where a piece of a project can be separated into a different movie clip. Among the most obvious applications, though, are elements with large independent pieces (like the levels of a game, the chapters in an interactive book, or the sections of an e-commerce web site).

A Theoretical Example: The "loader" Movie

Using a single movie to load others is a great way to factor a Flash project, and it can combine several of the techniques mentioned above. This approach provides a great deal of independence at build time, and tight integration at runtime.

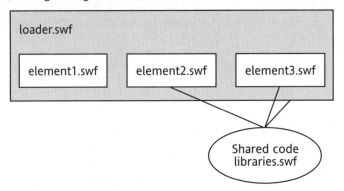

Here, the loader.swf movie contains a lot of essential code. Separable pieces of the project are broken into different files, which are each called as needed by the loader. These files may or may not share libraries (such as standard button elements) with one another or the master movie. Using this scheme, the loader can be responsible for lower-level tasks like directing key-input, creating new windows, or storing persistent data. The individual pieces can know as much or as little about their environment as necessary. Consider this example of a Flash movie that offers three relatively separate features: e-mail, news, and weather:

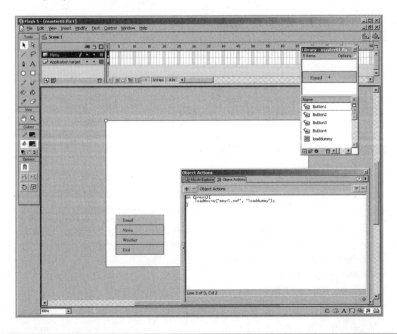

Here, the menu lives in the loader movie, and each button in the menu is capable of loading a different SWF file into the loaddummy target, which is the empty movie clip sitting at the top left corner of the stage (it's in the layer called Application target, underneath the menu). Using this scheme, the individual applications can be developed separately without worrying about how the user gets from one to another – the master movie takes care of that.

This is only the simplest example of the capabilities offered by this structure – loader movies can also allow for two elements to run concurrently, can coordinate the passing and storing of complex data among elements, and can override built-in Flash behaviors in a consistent way. For instance, in the example above, the loader movie could be responsible for storing all of the user's preferences for the different applications. The loader movie would save these preferences on the server, restoring them when necessary, and potentially even displaying the necessary UI to allow a user to enter their name and password. The benefits from this would be twofold: first, the code to do all this would live in only one place, and second, the UI would be completely consistent.

Much of the work that Flatland Exports has been doing involving devices such as TV set-top boxes has taken on this structure, since the environment in which Flash is running is relatively barren. By using this loader movie structure, we have been able to create what amounts to an operating system for device-based Flash applications. Since most of the devices that we're working with don't make use of standard input like the mouse and keyboard, we use the loader to do things like move the selection around the screen in response to key presses on the remote control. With this structure, we get total control of when and how applications are loaded, and we can abstract calls to the underlying hardware through objects that live in the loader.

Generally, we've found the most benefit from this style of run-time integration by making our individual elements as self-contained as possible. Ideally, they should run (perhaps with a few errors) outside of the context of the loader. Of course, this is not always possible when an extensive back end is involved, especially since a loader movie is often responsible for wrapping and simplifying outbound server calls. In this case, it sometimes helps to build small 'scaffold' loaders, which contain a stripped down feature set of the real loader movie, and offer just enough functionality to load and test an individual movie clip – perhaps using fake server data.

Practical Example: flatlandexports.com

In practice, most large Flash projects require a unique structure that uses a combination of the techniques above. The ideal structure of a Flash project ultimately depends on the demands of the project in question, as well as an eventual concession to performance. In general, your first pass at your project's structure will make use of some of these basic strategies for factoring a project, and will closely emulate the project's user experience. For instance, the user experience of the Flatland Exports site looks like this:

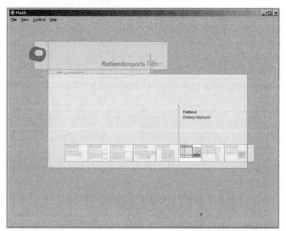

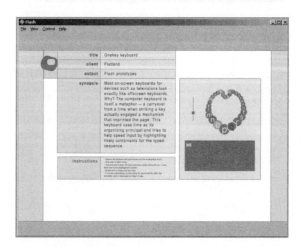

So our first pass at an architecture diagram might look like this:

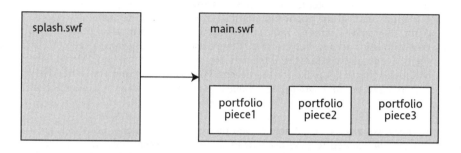

> *Upon examination, this structure actually has some built-in performance problems that we'll discuss in a moment, when we compare our proposed structure (above) with our final structure (below).*

In general, you should develop your projects with a focus on clarity and simplicity, and not worry too much about performance. Optimization is usually best left for the end. The one exception to this rule applies here, when you're working out the *structure* of your project. Because the structure will be difficult to change later, and because there are usually built-in performance trade-offs in any complex project structure, you should consider *these* performance issues up front. For instance, because of network latency, loading an additional file takes time – more time than it would take if that data were part of the original file. In relation to this, each section of the site has to be loaded when the user specifically requests it, rather than at the beginning, with the rest of the interface. Ordinarily, this could be a good thing, since it keeps the initial loading time down – but it also means there's a significant delay between clicking a link and viewing the associated section. On the other hand, there may be enough advantages to separating a given file that the extra time is justified. Only you can ultimately make that call, but you should consider the trade-offs from the start.

The ultimate structure of the Flatland Exports site is a compromise between optimization and ease. It looks like this:

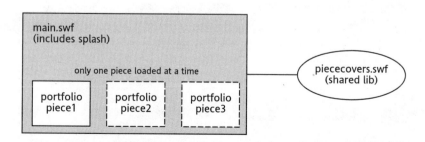

As you can see, the implemented structure is pretty different from what we initially proposed. This is for several reasons, not the least of which is performance. For instance, we were going to put the intro into a separate file, but we didn't want there to be any pause between the splash screen and the main part of the application. (In fact, we wanted the opposite: we wanted to load everything on the splash screen, without telling the user what was going on.) We also experimented with using scenes, but found that there wasn't any easy way to keep our data intact between them. Eventually, we put the intro and the main part of the program together in the same file. Although this didn't make for the neatest FLA (to get to the main code area, you have to scroll to frame 250 or so), it *did* make for quick loading and a smooth experience, and that's what we were after.

Similarly, we knew we wanted to be able to add pieces to our portfolio easily as it grew, but we *also* thought that we wanted to load the individual portfolio pieces only when the user actually wanted to view them, in order to avoid a long, aggravating initial load. This ultimately may or may not have been a good decision, but it allowed us the most flexibility, which can often be the deciding factor.

In any case, we decided to create two separate locations for each portfolio piece: one cover, which is loaded with the main file and lives in a shared library, and then the piece itself, which lives in its own Flash file. The shared library is responsible for keeping track of all the information that's shown in the main area (such as client names and project names) as well as the look of a piece before it gets loaded. That shared library file looks like this:

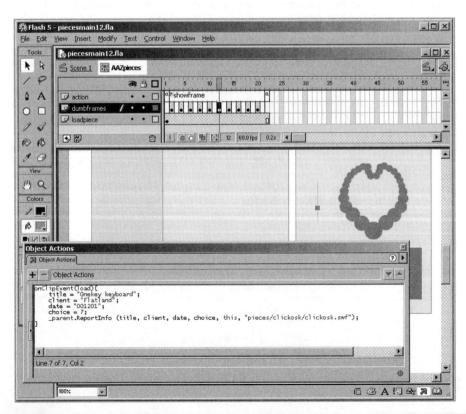

The individual pieces are kept in their own Flash files, and really know very little about the rest of the environment. They are only loaded when a piece comes to full size.

The problem with this structure is that when creating a new piece, we have to export an image out of the FLA file and import it into the shared library. It also means that any change we make to a piece requires a by-hand update to the shared library. It would be much easier if we just created the piece once, told the main movie about it, and then had the main movie load that file. We could have done it that way, but we were concerned about loading a lot of files concurrently – especially given the fact that some platforms (like the Macintosh) don't allow Flash to grab more memory if it needs it. We even experimented with loading pieces sequentially in the background, but found (unfortunately, again on the Macintosh) that a streaming load can significantly degrade Flash's performance.

As you can see, in the end we made several concessions in our structure to performance. Despite these, though, our final structure allowed us to work independently on the main movie even while we were putting together the individual pieces.

ne Key Flash Development Issues

So you know what you want to build, and you know generally how you're going to put it together. Now it's time to get to the meat of the issue: building it. Whether you're just slaving away late at night, or you're developing a component for a much larger project with a team of people, there are plenty of ways to help yourself along.

ing Out a Screen

At every Flash conference, you'll hear at least one speaker proudly announce, "...and when you open one of my Flash projects, you don't see a thing on the first frame. It's all done in code." These people usually emphasize the word 'code', as if to indicate its superiority over everything else in the world.

Although this is a valid approach, and it is sometimes the best one, it can also be over-used. One of the chief benefits of developing in Flash is its unprecedented ability to mix code and visuals. By taking advantage of this capability, you can make it easier to share projects and work on them with other people – even people who don't have technical skills.

In practice, all of this basically boils down to when and how much you use the attachMovie command. There are a number of cases where attaching a movie is the most sensible way to put a movie clip on the stage, but overusing it can yield Flash projects which are hard to follow – especially for non-technical people. Flash code can be hard to find at the best of times, because there are so many places for it to lurk: in frames, in on handlers, and nested inside movie clips. If you're working with a team that includes, say, a graphic designer, you should try to match the way your project looks at build time as closely as possible to the way it looks at runtime.

Consider the example of a simple menu bar navigation system. We want the menu to be built at runtime, so that we don't have to create separate assets for each button. We want the output to look like this:

Since we want the menu to build at runtime (that is, we want to reuse the same button for each menu option), we know that the project won't look the same as this at edit time. Still, we have some choices to make about how the menu is represented at edit time. At first blush, it may be tempting to use attachMovie, since we're creating a dynamic element. That would mean that in the example below, we would export the menubox symbol, and the stage would look this:

And we would have code in the first frame like this:

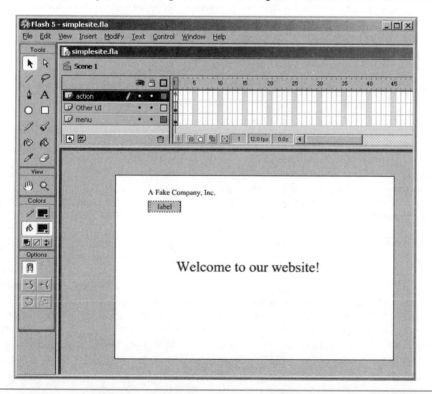

```
var menuxposition = 80;
var menuyposition = 50;

var menulist = new Array("Home", "Demos", "Products", "Portfolio", "Clients", "Contact");
var menudepth = 10;
for (var i = 0; i < menulist.length; i++){
    this.attachMovie("menubox", "box" + i, menudepth+i);
    eval("box" + i)._x += menuxposition + (eval("box" + i)._width * i ) - 1;
    eval("box" + i)._y += menuyposition;
    eval("box" + i).mylabel = menulist[i];
}
```

This is fine, and it works perfectly. However, if we're working on a team with a graphic designer, or it's likely that the design may change a lot as we revise, we'll have to go into the code to change the location of the menu. This is fine too, for a small example like this, but as projects get more complicated it may become harder to find the place where the position of this element is specified. Furthermore, a non-technical team member may not be comfortable looking through code to change the menu placement variables. As an alternative, we could put the first element of the menu on the stage, and use duplicateMovieClip to create the rest of the menu:

The code to create the menu then looks like this:

```
Frame Actions                                                    X
| Frame Actions |                                              ? ►
+  -  | Frame Actions |                                        ▼ ▲
var menulist = new Array("Home", "Demos", "Products", "Portfolio", "Clients", "Contact");
var menudepth = 10;
for (var i = 0; i < menulist.length; i++){
    if (eval("box" + i) == null){
        duplicateMovieClip("box" + (i-1), "box" + i, menudepth+i);
        eval("box" + i)._x += eval("box" + i)._width-1;
    }
    eval("box" + i).mylabel = menulist[i];
}
Line 10 of 10, Col 1
```

And we could reposition the entire menu by dragging its first element, since it appears on the stage.

This example is intended to make a general point: use the visual capabilities of Flash to your advantage. The same kind of logic can be applied to the use of frames, against the use of functions. Wherever possible, use Flash's built-in animation control (the timeline), rather than procedural animations. Reflect the state of an object with different frame locations, and don't be afraid to make deeply nested hierarchies of movie clips in order to allow for complex state combinations. Using these techniques, your projects will ultimately be simpler, cleaner, and easier to debug. There is rarely a performance or size bonus for doing things the hard way in code, so you should always try it the easy way first. In general, you should try to make your projects easy to decipher, even for someone who doesn't necessarily know ActionScript.

Good, Clear Code

The most important goal for any developer, after creating projects that work, should be to create projects that are clearly laid out and well put together. With few exceptions, the project that makes structural sense at build time will be smaller, faster, and easier to debug than a project with an opaque or complex internal structure. We have already discussed the importance of using the visual and time-based aspects of Flash to make your projects clearer, but here we consider the specifics of clear ActionScript. The ideal is to write *self-commenting code*, so that even if your explicit comments were deleted, someone could come in and quickly understand how the various pieces of your project work.

Consistency

The best way to make your projects clear is to be consistent. If you're someone who doesn't like code inside buttons, create functions for those buttons to call – but make sure that you do that *everywhere*. The one button that has its code inside the on (press) handler will invariably be the one that's generating the hard-to-trace errors. Similarly, if you mostly use onClipEvent (load) handlers to set clip properties, don't start using smart clips for the same thing, and certainly don't use a clip event handler to override or reset properties you've set in a smart clip.

Flexibility

After consistency, flexibility is the next most important attribute of good code. Although you may be creating an object or sub-system for a very particular purpose, you should take some time at the outset to consider how your work may be used across the project. Once you start writing, try to build in as few assumptions as possible.

The best example of a built-in assumption is the use of the _root keyword. Because Flash is so good at assembling object hierarchies at runtime, individual elements of a project often change scope considerably through the course of development. For instance, you may be building a feature for a large Flash project under the assumption that your feature will be loaded by the main movie, so every time you need to escape the feature's immediate context, or call into the parent movie, you use the _root keyword. Then, the person writing the loading system realizes that the feature you're building actually needs to be controlled by a separate 'feature controller', which will be a child of the root. Grumbling your way to your desk, you realize that you now have to go through your project and change every appearance of the _root keyword because your feature's scope has changed.

If you had just used relative pathnames all along, it wouldn't be a problem. If you find you absolutely must have a pointer to the top level of your project, consider including a line like this in each of your movie clips:

```
basepointer = _parent.basepointer;
```

And a line like this in the top-level movie:

```
basepointer = this;
```

This example is meant to illustrate a general point: *projects change*. Projects change scope, they change feature sets, they change UI, they change functionality, and sometimes, they change all of the above. The best thing you can do is to build in flexibility where it makes sense.

Clarity

Clear, clean ActionScript is the last element of good code. A lot of general texts have been written on the subject of good code, the best of which is *Code Complete* (Steve McConnell, Microsoft Press, 1993), which, despite its age, is still the definitive text on the low-level issues around writing good, clear code. Some key points are illustrated here. Take a look at this bit of ActionScript:

```
function ShowIt(param, flag) {
    s = param;
    v = flag;

    if (flag) {
        _visible = true;
        if (param == 4) {
```

```
            param = "special";
        }
        gotoAndStop(param);
    } else {
        _visible = flag;
    }
}
```

What on earth does it do? There are so many problems that it's hard to know where to begin. An obvious place to start, though, is the function definition. Function definitions should be specific – if possible, referring to who calls them and when. Parameter declarations should be as descriptive as possible. Let's change that first line to:

```
function ChangeState(newstate, bevisible) {
```

The next two lines are equally ugly. Use descriptive variable names, please! Also, we might want to indicate that leaving out the var declaration was intentional by using a prefix (such as 'static') to indicate that these are static variables.

```
staticMyStateNumber = newstate;
staticAmVisible = bevisible;
```

Next, let's clean up the way that the _visible property of the clip is set in the two if clauses. You should strive for parallelism in your ActionScript code, the same way that good writers use parallel grammar. If you use true in the first part of the if clause, use false in the next one. Better still, though, is to change the two lines into one simply by assigning the value of the variable directly to the property it represents, this way:

```
_visible = staticAmVisible;
```

Finally, let's take a look at the use of that param state variable. First of all, you should never set a parameter, unless that's the explicit intention of the function. Second, you shouldn't mix data types. In this example, param is passed as a number, and then changed to a name in a special case. This works because the gotoAndPlay command will accept number values (which resolve to frame references) and strings (which resolve to frame labels). But it's a bad habit because it means that you can no longer treat that variable in a consistent way. Let's replace this ugly mess with an array that keeps track of which frame corresponds to which internal state, like this:

```
var newframe = gStateFrameTable[staticMyStateNumber];
```

Our rewritten function now reads:

```
function ChangeState(newstate, bevisible) {
    staticMyStateNumber = newstate;
    staticAmVisible = bevisible;

    _visible = staticAmVisible;
    if (staticAmVisible) {
        var newframe = gStateFrameTable[staticMyStateNumber];
        gotoAndStop (newframe);
```

```
      }
    }
```

Much better! Of course, this is a labored and somewhat trivial example, but it illustrates some of the key aspects of clear ActionScript. Find your own style and develop it, but always try to make your code readable – the more it looks and sounds like your regular writing, the clearer, cleaner, and more efficient it will be.

One final note: many people suggest using comments to make code clearer. With rare exception, my personal experience has proven this to be ineffective. The best use for comments is to stand as placeholders for unimplemented functionality, to remember the reasons for a strange exception, or to document the reasons for a seemingly awkward approach. Well-written code shouldn't require comment. Often, the best way to find bugs in a program is to look for areas with a high density of comments, as that usually indicates that the original programmer wasn't sure exactly what was going on. By all means, comment your code, but do so sparingly. If your code has bugs in it, your comments will too!

Naming Conventions

One last way to make your code clearer, and to prevent certain kinds of errors, is to use a naming convention. Formal naming conventions are perhaps the most familiar – you may just have heard of the Hungarian naming convention, which was developed by Charles Simonyi and is in common use, especially in various Windows programming environments.

What seems to work better for some people is the use of simple prefixes for common data types, such as mc for a movie clip, and a for an array. Thus, mcShip is the name of the movie clip that contains the ship for your game, and aCollisionObjects is the array of objects on the screen with which it might collide. Again, it's a personal matter.

Finally, it should be noted that some people abhor convention and prefer simply to use descriptive names. The following code snippet follows no convention, but is eminently readable:

```
for (var count = 0; count < obstaclesArray; count++) {
    obstaclesArray[count].UpdatePosition();
}
```

At a minimum, try to use a few basic conventions to identify major data types, such as leadingLowerCase for variable names, LeadingUpperCase for function names, and Singleword for object names.

Finishing

So you're well on your way. You've got everything squared with your team. You're writing clear, consistent code in a well-structured project. Now comes the hard part: now you have to finish. You see, in the early phases of a project, everything goes smoothly. It seems like every day there's something new and exciting to see, the feature set grows rapidly, and everyone's happy. As time wears on, though, you find you spend whole days chasing the same bug; weeks seem to go by where nothing really changes; the stable areas of the project break; and it feels like you're taking two steps back for every one forward.

Don't worry – this is absolutely to be expected. It's a truism of software development that 80% of the work of a project is finishing that last 20%. This happens for several reasons:

- As a project's complexity grows, so does the trickiness of adding to it.

- Making something work correctly most of the time is much easier than making it work correctly *all* of the time. Adding error conditions and accommodating edge cases can take every bit as long as developing the original code, if not longer.

- As the project comes together, you will begin to see flaws in the original design that need to be addressed somehow. This can result in changes, from minor user interface tweaks, to drastic redesigns. Worse yet, at some point, you will doubtless consider the big fix.

The Big Fix

The big fix usually represents a crisis point for a development project. Not all projects have a big fix, but many do, and some have more than one. The big fix usually results from a fundamental assumption that has been proven wrong over the course of development, be that a user interface assumption, a code architecture assumption, or a performance assumption (which is why it's crucial to test assumptions in the prototyping stage!).

The big performance fix is usually the easiest type of big fix. The scenario is as follows: you've been working with a group on, say, a system with multiple independent features that talk to one another through a messaging system implemented in the loader movie. You happen to be responsible for the loader movie. You've been testing the capabilities of your messaging system all along, and you've been quite happy with it. You've added all sorts of nifty functionality, and you've even been through your code enough times to organize it into a well-commented, well-structured object library. The moment of truth comes (usually about 70% of the way into the project – too late by any standard, and a great argument for integrating early), and you finally get a chance to run your loader with the real features in the real target environment. You start your project, and... nothing happens. At least, not for a while. In short, you find that while your messaging system works perfectly, it is prohibitively slow.

Bear in mind that this is different from *optimization*, where you go through your code and find areas that perform acceptably, but could perform better. We'll get to that shortly. What we're talking about here is a problem where you're off by an order of magnitude. Still, the first and most important thing is: Don't panic. There's a reason why you built your code following all the rules of good object-oriented design. In all likelihood, your problem exists in one or two routines that you need to rethink and replace. Furthermore, these kinds of performance problems have just a handful of probable causes: unexpected server latency, unexpectedly large data sets, or unexpectedly rigorous drawing requirements. Note that the word 'unexpected' appears in all of these – good planning can often avoid this kind of problem.

Still, problems like this do arise, but the good news is that there are usually workarounds. Try dealing with server latency by creating an object in your Flash movie that acts as proxy for the server and keeps as much additional state as possible, so that requests that don't *need* to go all the way to server *don't*. If you already know the user's ID (because they input it earlier in the session), don't ask the server for it! Keep frequently accessed server data local if you can, but make sure that there's no way your program can get out of synch with the server.

If you find you're dealing with more data than you thought you would be, consider creating a new array or object that allows you to index the data more efficiently, before going through your whole program to change your basic data structures. Finally, when it comes to drawing problems, look for ways to make sure that objects aren't being drawn needlessly: Flash takes the time to draw each visible element, even if they're completely covered by a higher layer. If that doesn't help, consider omitting costly effects like alpha transparency, or dropping the quality to 'low' for brief periods of intensive screen update.

If none of these tips work for you, though, you may need to consider the big *code* fix. Big code fixes can sneak up on you, and for this reason they are the most pernicious type of big problem around. The danger of this kind of problem is that you've usually secretly known about it for a while, and you've probably invented a number of ways to work around it.

Let's say that you're writing an e-mail program. Good object-oriented programmer that you are, you've created a **Message** object to handle individual e-mail messages. Among other things, let's say that the Message object has an origin property, which tracks how the message was generated, and a messagetext property, which is the actual text of the message. Now let's say a lot of your routines look like this:

```
Message.prototype.EditText = function() {
    if (this.origin == "inbound") {
        this.AlertUser("Cannot edit incoming message.")
    } else if (this.origin == "outbound") {
        this.GotoEditScreen(this.messagetext);
    }
}
```

You're doing one thing if the message is an inbound message, and something else if it's outbound. It works – you've had it like this since day one – but there's something telling you that it's just not right. Furthermore, you've been finding that you're adding logic like this to more and more of your functions. Deep down, you know that you've really been working on two separate objects that share a base object. The first step is admitting you have a problem. Now, ask yourself, wouldn't it be nicer to create two separate message objects, one for inbound messages and one for outbound messages? The two clauses of the if statement above would then become two separate functions for two different classes, like this:

```
Inboundmessage.prototype.EditText = function () {
    this.AlertUser("Cannot edit incoming message.");
}

Outboundmessage.prototype.EditText = function () {
    this.GotoEditScreen(this.messagetext);
}
```

Common functionality could be inherited from a new common ancestor, called BasicMessage in this example, like this:

```
Inboundmessage.prototype.__proto__ = BasicMessage.prototype;
Outboundmessage.prototype.__proto__ = BasicMessage.prototype;
```

My advice is always to make the fix as soon as you start to sense that you have a problem, wherever and whatever the code that's troubling you. It never takes as long as you think it will, and it will almost always save you time in the end. Although it's tempting to work around problems like this in the name of finishing, you're almost guaranteed to spend hours chasing down problems related to a hacked implementation, and ultimately deciding to redo it the right way anyway.

Big code fixes usually take forms like this, where one object should be broken into a more refined hierarchy, where the nesting of movie clips should be reversed or redone, or where the fundamental encapsulation point of an object is slightly off. In general, they are the result of structural problems, but if your old thinking was clear (but wrong), and your new thinking is also clear, it shouldn't be that difficult to transform the old structure into the new one. Just go slowly, use the Movie Explorer, and make sure you save a version before you change anything!

The last kind of big fix, the big *user interface* fix, often seems more daunting than it really is. Assuming that most of your original user interface ideas are sound, the main challenge of implementing the big user interface fix is that it just seems like such a pain because of all the elements that need to be opened and jostled. While fixes like this often *are* a hassle, like most big fixes, they rarely take as long as you think they will.

The site for Flatland Exports had a big fix of this sort. The site was almost done, so we proudly posted a link announcing our 'beta'. At that time, the site looked like this:

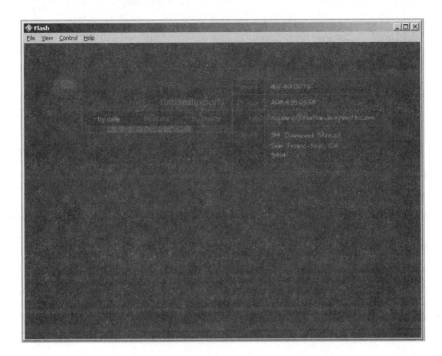

The folks on our beta list all responded favorably to the site's movement, and the general user interface scheme, but they all had a similar reaction: they found the text on the site either barely legible, or completely unreadable. After a fair amount of complaining, self-justification, and general unhappiness, we finally decided to pander to such base concerns as 'legibility'. We developed a new color palette, chose a new font, and spent an afternoon changing everything over. The results were dramatic (and hopefully favorable):

By definition, the big fix is usually worth making, but there are definitely some cases (especially when your project is intended for a very limited purpose and period of time) when it isn't. Even then, though, the big fix can speed up debugging and optimization enough to make it worthwhile. Keep your eye out for the big fix, and don't fear it: the sooner you make it, the easier it will be.

Optimizing

Assuming that you've made your big fix(es) – or even better, that you haven't had to make a big fix (yet) – you may want to take a little time for optimization, which comes in two flavors:

- Code optimization, which is the cleanup of anomalies and the consolidation of code as its purpose becomes clearer

- Speed optimization, which is experimentation with ways of making the code run faster

Code Optimization

Code optimization is a fun and worthwhile step in development, and it often behooves a programmer to spend a day or two just looking at the big ActionScript sections in a project (often, people prefer to print them out for this kind of work) and trying to find areas of overlap that can be made more efficient. Let's go back to that method we spent some time with in the section entitled 'Good, Clear Code':

```
function ChangeState(newstate, bevisible) {
    staticMyStateNumber = newstate;
    staticAmVisible = bevisible;

    _visible = staticAmVisible;
    if (staticAmVisible) {
        var newframe = gStateFrameTable[staticMyStateNumber];
        gotoAndStop (newframe);
    }
}
```

Now let's say that elsewhere in the code we find that the state of the clip has changed, and that we need to make sure it's reflected visually. The code snippet that does that looks like this:

```
    ...

    _visible = staticAmVisible;
    if (staticAmVisible) {
        var newframe = gStateFrameTable[staticMyStateNumber];
        gotoAndStop (newframe);
    }

    ...
```

Familiar, no? The fact this snippet appears in more than one place suggests that it may be best made into a method (called, say, ShowState) that just executes the snippet above. This may seem obvious, but some programmers resist changes like this, either precisely *because* they seem trivial, or because they think they will slow down program execution. As for the first argument, it's bogus: cleaning up code in small ways like this makes it much more readable, while reducing its susceptibility to hard-to-track bugs. As for the second argument, it rarely holds water, but it can usually be definitively proven one way or another.

Performance Optimization

Performance testing is fun for precisely that reason: measurable results. No longer do you have to rely on the insistence of the guy down the hall who swears he's been in the Flash player source code and knows for sure which routines are slow and which are fast. You can find out for yourself, and it's easy.

Working on a project recently, we came across a situation where we had to do some pretty intensive manipulation of some large arrays. We found that some of our operations were taking longer than we thought they should, so we decided to create a little script to test the methods we were using for adding an element to an array. The test script looked like this:

```
var testiterations = 100;

var testarray = new Array("b", "c", "d", "e");
var teststart = getTimer();

for (var iter = 0; iter < testiterations; iter++) {
    testarray.push("f");
}

var pushtimetaken = getTimer() - teststart;
pushtimetaken /= testiterations;

trace ("Time taken for push() = " + pushtimetaken);

var testarray = new Array("b", "c", "d", "e");
var teststart = getTimer();

for (var iter = 0; iter < testiterations; iter++) {
    testarray.unshift("a");
}

var unshifttimetaken = getTimer() - teststart;
unshifttimetaken /= testiterations;

trace ("Time taken for unshift() = " + unshifttimetaken);
```

This little script tests the time taken for two different operations on a small array: push and unshift. At the beginning of each test, a variable is set to the current time, using the getTimer function. The operation is then run a number of times (for more consistent results), and the total time is calculated by subtracting the current time from the start time. The time for each individual calculation is then computed by dividing the total time taken, by the number of iterations. Running on a decent Pentium III PC, the script produced the following in the output window:

```
Time taken for push() = 0.16
Time taken for unshift() = 2.68
```

Talk about a surprising result: unshift was over 15 times slower than push in this case! Now that we knew what the problem was, we just had to make sure we didn't use the unshift function.

Of course, performance testing doesn't always yield results like this, especially on a first try, but this is an idealized example to show how the general process works. The basic idea is to set a variable to the current time, run a process (usually repeatedly, for more reliable results), and subtract the start time from the current time. With the ease and power of using getTimer for performance testing, there's no excuse: if you even *suspect* that an area of your code is slow, you should do a definitive test. A word to the wise, though: if you can't set up a performance test directly in your code (which is the ideal), make sure that you're not introducing distortions in your test environment. For example, if you're not careful, you can easily find that you're testing the speed of Flash's for loop, or that a mistake in your code is introducing errors with your results. As always, use your *expected* results as a guideline – the more your observed results differ from what you thought you would see, the more careful you should be to make sure that you don't have an error in your test. Finally, always run performance tests as *comparisons* – absolute performance is hard to measure, and can depend on what tasks a given system has running in the background.

Depending on your project, performance optimization may not be necessary, and you should certainly do this kind of optimization last of all. The more information you have when you head into performance testing, the better off you'll be, since it's almost impossible to figure out what aspects of your program are slow until the whole thing is nearly assembled. Finally, the closer the program is to complete, the more accurately you'll be able to determine where and how to optimize performance.

It's important to note that speed of execution sometimes depends on the particular browser in which the movie is executed. Once you execute your project in the browser, there's a chance a few more errors will come to light. Test your program in as many browsers, and on as many platforms as you can. You don't have to make sure that your Flash file runs perfectly on *every* platform in *every* browser, but you definitely want to make sure it works on all of your *target* platforms, and there's no way to verify this other, than by trying.

With this kind of optimization, it's often helpful to pick a target low-end platform, and then test against that. Optimization is the kind of work that can go on forever, so you want to do just enough to make sure the program meets your performance goals.

bugging

Debugging is as much art as science, and the best thing you can do to aid the debugging process is to make sure that, at every level, your code and structure is sensible and clear. Still, when problems do arise (as inevitably they will) there are a few things you can do to make debugging easier and faster.

The hardest part of debugging is finding the problem, so the most important thing to do is to isolate. You have a suspicion about what might be causing the problem, so try to think of the way you would prove that. A great place to start is by using the trace command to print the value of a variable that you think may not be set properly.

When you're trying to isolate your problem, don't be afraid to add extra code, or even to copy suspicious routines into a new file and add some scaffolding to test them. Of course, you should keep track of your changes, and save often, but don't feel that time spent debugging isn't time spent programming: they're the same thing. Go slowly, change **one thing at a time**, and make sure that you understand *everything* – you understand exactly the problem you're trying to solve, you understand exactly how the current code works, and you understand exactly what you're trying to do to fix it.

The trace command is probably the easiest way to find bugs. For environments where trace can't be used (say, testing in a browser), it's often helpful to create one or more text fields in the main timeline, on a special layer above the rest of your UI. In the example below, you could print important state information with a line like:

```
_root.debugtext += "Value of menuarray is " +
menuarray.toString();
```

Best of all, while you're going back and forth between debug versions of your project, you can simply delete the debug layer and publish your file (without saving, of course), and you will have a build with none of the ugly debug information in it.

Finally, for browser-crashing bugs, where it's not even possible to figure out what's going on before something disastrous happens, try debugging using the browser's native JavaScript `alert` command. The basic way to do that looks like this:

```
getURL("javascript:alert(`" + debuginfo + "`)");
```

Which, when executed in your browser, will display a dialog like this:

The general pattern for debugging is: test, fix, test. Although it may be somewhat self-evident, it can be extremely motivating to set testing and debugging milestones at the end of a project, and it's important to make sure that all areas of your project receive their share of testing. Don't worry if you find that you're opening more bugs than you're fixing – that always happens early in the debugging phase. Just track them down one by one, and try to stay focused on the bugs. Though it may be tempting to break ground on the next project, or even to start version 2.0 of the current one, don't. You're not done coding until you're done with debugging.

Now for the list of debugging don'ts. Don't convince yourself that it's a problem with Flash. If you like, you can look at the support section on Macromedia's web site for known issues (http://macromedia.com/support/flash), but it's usually not worth the bother. It's rarely a problem with Flash — if it really is, you should be proud that you found it, and be able to reproduce it easily in a contained test environment. If you get to that stage, make sure you document it a little, and send it off to the good people at Macromedia as a bug report. Unless you feel confident doing that, it's unlikely that your bug arises from a problem with Flash.

Don't make the 'superstitious' fix. Most programmers have, at one time in their lives, made this kind of fix. This is the one where you seemingly change nothing relevant in the code, but it starts to work again. This leaves you with the conclusion that Flash has trouble with variables whose names start with '`i`', or doesn't properly ignore whitespace between commas. If you find yourself drawing conclusions like this, you've probably gone awry. In all likelihood, you're tired, or you're chasing a bug that isn't what you thought it was – or more likely, you fixed the problem in an earlier cycle but didn't realize it.

Finally, a special place in Hell is reserved for developers who create special cases to handle their bugs. For instance, let's say that you find a problem with this routine:

```
function SetRotation() {
    _rotation = GetNewClipAngle(sMyDirection);
}
```

It usually works, unless sMyDirection happens to equal 60. Here's the evil version of the 'fix':

```
function SetRotation() {
    if (sMyDirection != 60) {
        _rotation = GetNewClipAngle(sMyDirection);
    } else {
        _rotation = 22;
    }
}
```

This is not a fix! This is a new bug, as soon as someone changes any of the constants or routines that it depends on. In all likelihood, the bug results from a problem inside that GetNewClipAngle routine – if I had to guess, probably a division by zero error – but that's not the point. The point is that you should *always* understand your fixes, and except in extremely rare (and well commented) circumstances, you should never have to create a special case to handle a bug.

nch

So now you've *really* done it. You've prototyped, planned, and prepared. You've structured, coded, and collaborated. You've optimized, debugged, and done your big fix. What else could there be?

Well, that's often the problem. Here's the final piece of advice in this chapter: as soon as you feel like you maybe could see how you could sort of be finished, make a list of the last things that absolutely need to get done before you put up your project, and knock them off as quickly as possible. You don't have to make every last change before you put your files on your production server and let people start poking at what you made, but get the main ones covered. The feedback you get will be helpful, and by starting to think of the project as 'done', you will avoid the feature creep that can slow down or even torpedo a project as it nears completion.

With software developed for media other than the Internet, there are well-defined periods of alpha and beta leading up to the code freeze before ship. With software for the Internet, there is a kind of rolling beta that can last forever. This is a double-edged sword, though. On the one hand, you have the opportunity to make every last little change that your heart desires. On the other hand... you can actually end up making every last little change that your heart desires! Maybe there's a reason that traditional software development plans include a hard ship date!

Of course, if you're working for a client, you'll have to get their buy-off first, but the general point still applies: push it out the door. Focus your energies on getting it done, not making it perfect. You don't have to show it to everyone at first – just post it to, say, the site check board on FlashKit (http://flashkit.com) or FlashZone (www.flashzone.com) – but get some people to look at it as soon as possible. Unless you're developing for a distribution medium other than the Internet, you may have to try hard to resist the temptation to tweak forever. Do what you have to do to get it out there, and then sit with it for a few weeks, or even a month. If you still want to come back and revise, your fresh perspective will serve you well.

**Section 3
Case Studies**

**15
XML for Data
and Design**

Chapter 14
A Web Site from Scratch

Advanced Interface Design

I'll put my cards on the table straight away before we do anything. At the time of writing this introduction, none of the FLAs have been done, and I have Flash open on my computer with the default white 550x400 screen staring at me, waiting for me to do stuff. This is my choice because I don't want to just talk about writing one particular advanced interface, but the process involved in writing **any** advanced interface. I have no specification to start with. I'm just going to take it where it goes, and build myself an advanced ActionScript-based and ergonomic interface.

First off, I want to say a couple of things to set the scene; what constitutes an advanced interface, and how the're created in general terms?

So what's an advanced interface?

There's the standard Flash website, with its buttons and goto commands, where you are taking ideas from the 'standard book of interface concepts' (the place where all interface ideas eventually end up through overuse and familiarity), but we're not talking about those. We're talking about doing something *new*. Something where you take a few concepts and develop them, and then get them to the stage where they might be used commercially or creatively in a website. You'll probably have a shed full of ActionScripting ideas in there as well, because novel interfaces require novel coding; timeline based Flash has its place but by this point in the game we are probably looking towards wilder horizons. Those old static frame based concepts just don't hack it; we need event-driven code-hungry applications to break the plug-in and do things it was never meant to do.

You can copy someone else's ideas of course. The web is full of downloadable FLAs from other people, making this option very easy, but side scrollers, Swift3D rendered interfaces, and weird wobbly matrices are really only cool when there's one of them.

How do you create them?

All the advanced interfaces I have ever seen or created come about not only through meticulous design but by novel ideas appearing outside the design process. Advanced websites initially happen from creative thought. You tinker about for a bit, playing, experimenting, and building up a number of ideas. This may be all directionless stuff, but if you're anything like me, you'll be having a ball, enjoying the exploration, with no regard for the terrain covered. At the time, you might not realize it, but you are being *creative*. You build up a few disjointed ideas, some of which are good, some of which should be taken outside and shot.

All of the top Flash gurus I've ever spoken to or heard at Flash web design conferences seem to do the same thing – an initial expanding creative phase followed by a sifting and design phase. For many of them, the initial creative process starts a million miles away from Flash. It starts by looking at a worm, or a shell, or a car dashboard.

Then eventually a need for a new site comes along. That's the point when you stop being creative and you start *designing*. You have all these creative thoughts and ideas, and you just pick at them and say 'well, what if I designed something that used *that* graphics engine with *this* menu system?'.

You play about until you get something that fits, throwing in a couple of graphic effects or whatever, designing it all in so the ideas become *seamless*. That's the point of critical mass. You have something viable. You have an advanced interface.

In this chapter, I will document the journey up to the end of the initial creative phase, so we have a ready built interface incorporating a couple of ideas we developed on the way. I have teamed up with another designer and put the interface in with some content to build a final website. I won't talk much about the final step here (because we are teaching programming, and there's lots to fit in), but you can see the final site and associated readme file in the download.

rting on the journey...

Rather than start with the 'here's a bit of finished code I dreamed up' stage, I'll start from the initial 550x400 blank screen and work up. In many ways, this chapter is a journal showing you my thought processes and the design intent I went through. Of course the code is important, and that will appear as well (boy will it appear!) – but only in its correct context as part of an overall design.

So here's a few ideas, things I thought up while reading the IEEE Review or playing *Deus Ex* during a dinner break. Things that hit the periphery of memory, only to appear again when the dreaded 550x400 blank white stage appeared in front of me...

#1 – Adaptive Animation

Well, I don't know about you, but this title looked way too cool even before I knew what it meant. I saw it in a journal that was about neural nets and adaptive behavior, and someone said something about 'truly adaptive cybernetic motion was too costly to develop using real robots – better to simulate them via computers and adaptive animation'. Here it is again. I love it!

So then, I thought 'Within Flash, *what would you want to adapt animation to?*'

Well...

What if we could design a website that had an internal intelligence that allowed it to sense how fast the computer was, and to constantly alter the animations being played such that it always used the maximum processing power, whilst maintaining responsiveness?

This is a good idea to want to develop. I see questions every day from intermediate Flash designers who ask about performance and what should the frame rate be. There's no real answer of course, because it varies. If we could design something that actually looked at this problem constantly at run time, perhaps we would be onto something. That's the creative insight I started with at the beginning of day one. It's now early evening, and here's how I did...

First, the content. I've got to somehow build all of this into a real site, so I might as well start early on with some appropriate graphics. I know Jake Smith, creative director at Subnet (www.subnet.co.uk), is going to help out with this, and I also know he's hopelessly addicted to retro gaming (who isn't), complete with a Bubble Bobble arcade cabinet in his lounge, and a collection containing every other game console going. So I'll make life easy for him; the website will be called *Low Rez* (as in 'low resolution'). Here's a quick and easy graphic I thought up;

The alien shape is the *Low Rez* GameHead, in recognition of Jake's hopeless addiction.

I based a few initial animations on this, which you can check out if you want – they're graphics.fla. There's also some scratchy grunge animation in this FLA that I thought might be useful later on when we're ready to give the site some personality, (mc.grungeAnimation in the library) which are currently unused. (By the way, the only reason the text font has been broken apart is that I know most computers won't have it installed, so I've made the separate characters vectors rather than use the actual font. If you had it installed on your computer, I would not need to do this, and the final SWF would be smaller, and the FLA easier to update).

My initial thoughts on creating adaptive animation are that there are three essentials:

1. A variable that is constantly telling us how heavily loaded the Flash player is.

2. The animations. These need to be controlled entirely via ActionScript, otherwise we will not be able to adapt them on the fly.

3. Finally, we need some sort of additional code that creates a relationship between the animation and the variable; if the variable is telling us that the system is heavily loaded, the ActionScript needs to adapt its output, making the animation less complex, until we get an 'everything's running fine now' signal.

The variable I created is called optimum. This will sit on the root timeline and will be *true* if Flash isn't being heavily loaded, and *false* if it is. You can see how it is created by looking at frameRate.fla. The movieclip we are interested in is called performanceMonitor (it's in the misc folder). This movieclip works by first baselining your computer, and looks at how long it takes (on average) to render a blank frame, something that I will call the idle rate. It then multiplies this by 1.4 to arrive at the 'normal rate', which is how long a frame should take to render given that the plug-in is actually doing something. The 1.4 is an arbitrary value, and represents how loaded you are willing to accept Flash to become. As you increase this value, you are allowing the movie to become slower before adaptive animation kicks in, and you are reducing responsiveness to user actions.

Anyway, here's the code;

The timeline of performanceMonitor looks like this;

The first three keyframes baseline the computer (i.e. work out the 'normal rate'), and the last two keyframes constantly compare this value with the current performance.

Frame 1 (layer *actions*) has this script attached;

```
// If we have run this movie before,
// skip to the main monitoring loop,
// otherwise initialize and baseline now.
//
if (_root.normal >1) {
 gotoAndPlay ("loop");
} else {
 _root.stop();
 baselineLoop = 0;
 averageSample = 0;
 _root.optimum = false;
}
```

The if looks at whether we have run an instance of this movie clip before (I need to do this because I am using scenes and an instance cannot exist across scenes). We are doing this by looking at whether or not _root.normal, a variable that will be set later on, is greater than 1. If we see a value, then we know that the movie clip has been run before and we don't need to baseline again, otherwise we initialize for baselining.

Frames 2 and 3 perform the baselining. Frame 2 has this script attached;

```
sample = getTimer();
baselineLoop++;
```

... and frame 3 has this;

```
sample = getTimer() - sample;
averageSample += sample;
if (baselineLoop == 20) {
 normal = 1.4*(averageSample/20);
 _root.normal = normal;
 _root.play();
} else {
 gotoAndPlay ("baseline");
}
```

This two frame script measures the average time for a frame to complete, getTimer() – sample, and when it has measured the time to run through 20 frames, it takes an average 1.4*(averageSample/20), which is 1.4 times the average idle time per frame. This value is expressed in the same measurement as getTimer, which is in milliseconds. This value is called normal and I have popped a version of it on _root to make it global (that is, it will still be there even if the performanceMonitor movieclip disappears).

The final two frames, 5 and 6, compare the current value of frame duration with the normal value evaluated earlier. Frame 5 looks like this;

```
timer = getTimer();
```

... and frame 6 has this script attached;

```
sample = (getTimer()-timer+sample)/2
if (sample<_root.normal) {
 _root.optimum = true;
} else {
 _root.optimum = false;
}
gotoAndPlay ("loop");
```

This loop updates the global variable optimum, which is set to *true* if the movie is running at a reasonable speed (i.e. within 1/1.4 times its idle frame rate) or *false* if it isn't maintaining this frame rate (in which case the sampled frame duration will be higher than _root.normal). The only little trick here is that the sampled value is averaged with the last sampled value. This is to avoid 'spikes' which the Flash player seems to throw up a lot, probably because it is so low down in the pecking order of resources.

So now we have a means to adapt our SWF. How do we use it? Well, if _root.optimum is ever *false*, we have an overloading problem, and have to tell one or more of our animations to reduce complexity. On the other hand, if _root.optimum is ever *true*, we have the converse problem – our animations are not using the available processing bandwidth, so we will want our animations to become more complex.

I've used a simple starfield animation to illustrate the point here, the kind of thing you find in old dodgy '70s sci-fi, or in screensavers the world over. It'll work by increasing or decreasing the number of stars depending on the speed of the processor. Here's how it's done:

First there's a simple short white hairline in a movie clip called star, which is placed on the main stage with the instance name starStreak:

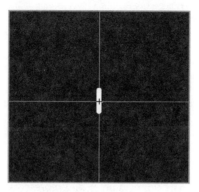

starStreak has the following script attached to it:

```
onClipEvent (load) {
  // get number of stars from _parent smartClip.
  numberOfStars = _parent.numberOfStars;
  // initialize me.
  speed = Math.random()*15+5;
  maxSize = speed/10;
  star._y = 0;
  star._yScale = 0;
  this._rotation = Math.random()*360;
  // duplicate me x stars
  if (this._name == "starStreak") {
    for (i=0; i<numberOfStars; i++) {
      duplicateMovieClip (this, "starStreak"+i, i);
    }
  }
}
onClipEvent (enterFrame) {
  // if I have reached my end-range, re-initialize me...
  if (star._y<-250) {
    speed = Math.random()*15+5;
    maxSize = speed/10;
    star._y = 0;
    star._yscale = 0;
    this._rotation = Math.random()*360;
  }
  // adapt how many of me there are to maintain framerate...
  if (this._name == "starStreak") {
    if (_root.optimum) {
      numberOfStars++;
      duplicateMovieClip (this, "starStreak"+numberOfStars,
➡ numberOfStars);
```

continues overleaf

```
        } else {
        removeMovieClip ("_parent.starStreak"+numberOfStars);
        if (numberOfStars>_parent.numberOfStars) {
          numberOfStars--;
        }
      }
    }
    // animate me...
    star._y = star._y-speed;
    star._yScale = -(star._y/2.5)*maxSize;
  }
```

Let's have a closer look at the `load` event script:

First off we get the variable `numberOfStars`, which is piped in from the parent movie clip. This value is coming in as a smart clip parameter, and represents the minimum number of stars we are happy with – there's no point in degrading our animation so far that the effect is lost, so the minimum number of stars makes sure that we don't end up with just one or two stars, which would ruin the effect.

The next command gives us a random speed between 5 and 20. We then use this to give us another variable, `maxSize`, which is intended to emulate the fact that slower stars will be further away, and therefore dimmer than the fast–moving (and therefore closer) stars. This line creates a maximum brightness for our star, based on its speed.

Then we simply place our star at its starting point and set the alpha to zero. The next few lines are the ones that may need some explaining. We apply a rotation transformation to starStreak's physical appearance, and rotate its x and y-axis, so that when we come to move it via its `_y` property, we won't be moving it up and down with respect to `_root`, but up and down a tilted internal y-axis; thus we end up with a starfield of stars traveling at all angles.

The final bit of code in this event duplicates our starStreak movie clip – but only if it's the original one. We do this in the `if` statement by comparing it with the name starStreak. Notice that this name is case sensitive, and that the script won't work if we use Starstreak or starstreak. If it turns out that this particular instance is the original, the `for` loop creates a number of instances named `starStreakNUM` where `NUM` is a number from 0 to our `numberOfStars` variable. Note that these duplicated instances *will not* create more instances, because their instance name is not `starStreak`.

The `enterFrame` script works by checking whether:

The star has moved more than 250 pixels (along its own y-axis), in the first `If` statement. If it has we re-initialize its variables ready for another trip out from the center.

Again, the key to this effect is the rotation. We don't just rotate the star graphic, remember we're also rotating its internal co-ordinate system as well, which means that internal to the star movie clip, the movement is downward, but because the whole movie clip is rotated, the actual movement relative to `_root` is at a variable angle.

The following diagram illustrates this:

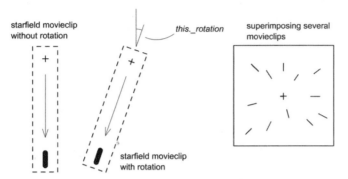

starfield movieclip without rotation

this._rotation

superimposing several movieclips

starfield movieclip with rotation

Finally we have the code that alters the number of stars displayed depending on the results of our baseline testing earlier. We either duplicate more movie clips if we haven't reached the optimum, or remove them if we have. Once we've done this, we animate the starfield.

Run the FLA in debug mode to see what's happening. Debug mode can be a little flaky, and I find I have to hit Control > Debug Movie twice before the debug window actually fires off correctly. If you don't see a movieclip called _Level0 as the first entry of the top pane of the debugger, and a proper hierarchy of clips being built up from it, you have to quit the SWF and do another Control > Debug Movie.

Once you have your debugger working, look for _level0.starfield.starStreak and hit the Variables tab.

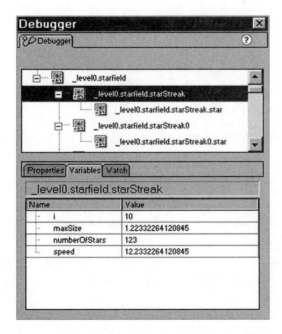

This will show you the variable `numberOfStars`. This value will move about as the loading varies. You can force the loading to vary by running the SWF in the standalone Flash player by varying the window size, which will cause the animation to degrade (bigger screen, less stars) or increase (smaller screen, more stars). This will change the loading on the Flash player, and simulates how the animation would adapt itself to changing circumstances. For a small screen area, I get about 150 stars on my machine, and about 90 for a big screen.

This animation will take advantage of the ever-spiralling power of computers – at the time of writing, I am using a 600MHz Pentium 3 PC, but I know there are far faster 1GHz+ machines out there. This SWF will give them an animation consistent with their hardware, making the animation more complex for users with hardware that can take it, and also making my site more future proof because of it. This doesn't work at the expense of increasing download time however, because it is being handled on the fly by ActionScript.

My animation takes account of the screen size the user tries to play it on. In particular, if I publish the movie such that it always scales to 100% of the browser window and then see it in full screen, the adaptive nature of the animation attempts to keep the starfield smooth by dropping stars, whereas a lot of other sites just get really *slow* when you attempt the same feat.

I could choose to actually turn off some effects altogether (such as Swift3D animations, multi-channel sound, etc.) if they were slowing down the prime content of my site (which would be the main content and the interface, resulting in a more responsive and focused site).

If this was a starfield being used in a video game, I could assume that the starfield background would never slow down my player and alien animations, which would again result in a responsive game whilst allowing the scalability of advanced future hardware to render a more graphically complete game. I don't have to resort to degrading the quality of the SWF itself (the Quality setting in the Publish windows HTML tab), which no web designer likes to do because at lower aliasing qualities everything just looks so *bad*.

Finally, the performanceMonitor movieclip provides some useful information that the bandwidth profiler doesn't, and I get the impression it will be something I will be dropping into my FLA timelines when I develop them in the future. It tells me how processor–intensive my animations are, and allows me to tweak them to drop the average frame duration, which is being presented to me via the debugger to millisecond precision. Cool!

As an aside, the performanceMonitor has shown up some really useful information, such as the fact that when I run multiple instances of the SWF, the window currently in focus gets the lion's share of the processing power, and it is not shared out between them. This is something to remember when creating framed Flash web pages that have more than one SWF embedded in them. It has also given me a better understanding of what frame rates and browser screen sizes actually do to an animation – try varying the frame rate of `frameRate.fla` and publishing it at different sizes and see what figures the performanceMonitor comes up with.

In fact, I like this concept of adaptive animation so much that I will attempt to use it in the main interface later on in this chapter by choosing what effects I do or do not render, and by selecting the animation complexity on the fly.

#2 – Non-Linear Navigation

Okay, so now I'm onto day two...

The idea of non-linear navigation is something I've had at the back of my mind for ages now, and it's something I have been put off developing because I wanted to save it for my own homesite. Anyway, the homesite has just not figured in my spare time activities because of my busy writing and design schedule, as well as learning Director, and the old version of my site has been down for ages because it was written in Flash 4 and is no longer any good. Might as well use my idea now then, because otherwise someone will have thought of it by the time I get round to implementing it, and by then it will be old news!

Web publishing has taken many analogies from print publishing. We have print related metaphors like web **pages** and **bookmarks** and HTML **paragraph** tags. A standard website navigation splits the content up into **sections** and these are accessed from a main or **contents** page. One of the two main differences between print and web based content amounts to one word; **links** (the other one is **multimedia**). Web pages have links that can exist anywhere in the document and these can quickly navigate you to a new and related page. This makes the Net much more versatile when you consider the entire World Wide Web, but when you are just looking at an individual website, I'm not so sure. Given the book in your hand and the website on your screen contain the same information, I'd say the book is always better, though of course you may have a different opinion.

Consider the online ActionScript Reference Guide and the printed version. Which one do you value the most? More importantly, which one lets you get to information on the `setProperty` command faster? For me, the printed book is faster, which is not usually the answer you would expect given that about 500 years of technology separate the two data retrieval systems.

I had a think about why this might be, and came up with this reason; the book has a truly non-linear data retrieval interface. I can jump from page to page and quickly home in on any bit of information because I take exactly the same time to get to a particular page as any other. There is no hierarchy or nested levels that I have to go through to get to a particular page *because the pages are arranged in a linear sequence*. This almost seems perverse; because the book is so simple and presents all its information in a sequential way, it is easier to use than the nested web pages of the online manual! The online version has information arranged in a non-sequential manner, with nested depths of information and links to related areas, but in many ways, that makes it harder and less intuitive because I have to follow a sequential path down the hierarchy – my *path* to the non-sequential information is actually *sequential!*

Furthermore, the book is a tactile system. If I know I want to go to page 361 (which is the page the `setProperty` action is described in my printed ActionScript Manual), I sort of know where that is straight away because I know something about the relationship between book thickness and page number.

When I get to the page I want, the information listing may be nested by way of tab spacing, box-outs, bullet points or whatever, but my eye can quickly take it all in without the need for anything as esoteric as a URL link because my eye moves far faster down a couple of pages of printed text than my mouse clicks down a hierarchy or nested, linked screens. The book wins again because it shows me all information on a single, simple un-nested level with no real navigation other than sequential text. Perverse!

Some of you may be muttering about the online version having a search facility as well, but I don't buy that based on experience – I can use the book index far quicker than the online search, and given that the manual is on your desk and the online manual is just a click away, I know of very few people who don't plum for the book.

Of course, there's a limit here, and after a certain bulk of data, the book loses out. My point is that for navigation within a modest amount of data, such as within the ActionScript Reference or a typical site, print would win.

I guess it all boils down to a book having all pages equally accessible at all times, whereas web sites work by having depths of information, where you have to go down a hierarchy to get to what you actually want – and in many cases you have to go down this route even if you know what the final destination point is.

So here's my second idea: what if we could make every page of a website equally accessible from the main page, and we totally did away with any semblance of hierarchy. Would that work? Would it now be as quick as my dog-eared ActionScript manual, with its coffee cup rings on the cover and scrawled side-notes in the margins? Well, I sort of tried it earlier in the day, and it didn't work. The thing is, the tactile parts of the printed book need to migrate across as well – the idea of 'I know roughly where this page is because as well as the order of pages I know about thickness' has to come in. It has to be a bit more precise than a scrollbar whose height gives some indication of position through the data (tried that idea as well, and my implementation was of the 'to be taken out and shot' variety).

And I was musing about this when it hit me. The only way I can get to any web page as quickly as any other is to always show all the web pages all the time, hierarchy and all.

Consider the following diagram:

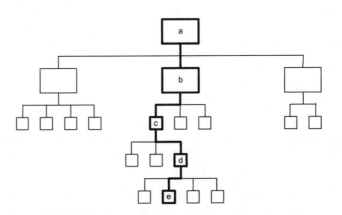

This is a typical hierarchy for a set of web pages. **a** is the main page, and then we have three links from that (of which **b** is one). We go down the hierarchy, zooming in to more specific pages until we get to the bottom, page **e**. Now here's a thing to think about. What if this was a site showing car parts? Page **a** was a page on my particular model, and page **b** was about the car interior, **c** was about seats, and **d** and **e** were zooming in to more and more basic parts. If I wanted to look at the screw thread that held together the knob that altered the pitch of my seat headrest, where would I start? If I couldn't see all the pages at once, I might go **a-b-c-d-e** but what if I could see them all? I might scan down the page without actually navigating to **a**, **b**, **c** or **d**, and just click on a page at around the level of **e**, because I know that the part we want is 'somewhere around that level'. That's the same concept as book thickness. In both, I am intuitively using spatial position to quickly jump to a place close to where I want to be using a non-linear search! I am not specifically searching on anything, but my human intuition tells me that my target is somewhere in that region. Being wrong doesn't matter that much, because my decision was so fast, I can just as quickly do another one.

The next problem is this... As I go down the hierarchy, there are more and more pages to show. In the diagram above, I naturally made them smaller. I can't therefore jump to any page as quickly as any other because the lower ones are harder to read. So I played about with that thought for a bit, and started thinking about **zooming**.

Normal web based navigation uses the metaphor of turning pages, but what if I discarded that altogether, because as discussed before, that only really works with a real book. What if I made the pages the same size irrespective of their position, but made them bigger based on how close they were to the mouse. Assuming the mouse moves to around where I am looking, I will be able to follow the path down to **e** and always be able to read what is on the page I am currently focusing on without actually selecting it – a process just like skimming down a page of written text.

I liked this train of thought. The concept of zooming in, visually skimming and navigating without buttons sounds a lot like using a book. The only question left was 'how do I actually select a page?'

There are three options:

- Click on a page.

- If you keep the mouse on a page, you keep zooming in until it fills the page and when that happens, the page becomes selected.

- All the pages are literally that; web pages. As soon as you have zoomed in sufficiently to read the text, look at the pictures, start using the buttons, or whatever, you can – they all work.

As soon as I'd thought up options 2 and 3 above, I knew I had invented my new interface. It seems such a natural thing to arrive at in hindsight – it doesn't look like a book, but if all my assumptions are correct, it will feel like one. The thought that having all the web pages active all the time worried me for a split second, but the previous idea on adaptive animation dovetailed with this so well. Instead of performance, what about degrading the web pages based on size. Web pages away from the mouse would have minimum active components through degradation, and would look like little more than icons. As the mouse moved towards them, they would grow in size and complexity, so that by the time they were big enough to be used, they were fully active.

Like Bones always says on Star Trek, 'It's a long shot, Jim, but it might just work....'

Interlude

Day three wasn't actually day three. There was a panic at the publishers; someone rang me and said they'd lost an author. I don't know how you can lose something as big and as slow as an author, but anyway, they were looking for volunteers (to replace him, not find him). I told them I was busy but I would take it on anyway, so that was that. This isn't an aside of course, it's what happens in real life, and you must document your work so that you can drag and drop jobs at a moments notice. It's not just good programming practice for propeller heads, it's a fact for anyone who wants to make good money out of this. My documentation so far is two sides of lined paper, and I've not wasted too much time in scribbling little diagrams and abrupt sentences on it like 'this goes here' and 'this needs a function writing'. I won't get lost because although I don't have a good map with the route inked in on it, I have a rough one of the terrain.

So day three was really day six by the time that little sideline was sorted out, but I hadn't lost anything. Time to start coding the idea up.

Rather than say 'here's the finished code', and you go away thinking 'I can see how this works, but not why he's gone down that route', I've included *all* my intermediate files as well. I'll just talk through the intermediate ones, and explain the first and last FLA in detail. Those with the time or inclination can look at the files that lead up to the final one, and laugh at all the little mistakes and box canyons I rode into.

The files are called `test1.fla` to `test7.fla`. Each one is separated from its predecessor by about 1-2 hours, so you have a good idea of my timescales as well as my coding.

Test1.fla

This is just a little FLA that scales a single page in and out when you move your mouse over it. Code wise though, it has some pretty cool features. The first one is that the coding is object oriented. By that, I don't mean I'm using modular movie clips or re-usable code segments, or even just 'object oriented thinking in a graphic environment'. I'm talking about the code itself;

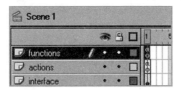

The interface layer includes my window graphic. Right now, it's just a simple frame, and we will look at it in a while. The actions layer defines an object that tells me about my screen area;

```
screen = new Object();
screen = {top:0, bottom:400, left:0, right:550};
```

The functions layer contains this little monster;

```
// Define window functions.
// These will be added to the local window
// object to create the window methods.
//
function scaleMe (me, meActive) {
 // if I am an active window, I need to grow,
 // otherwise I need to shrink.
 if (meActive) {
 if (_root[me]._xScale<100) {
 _root[me]._xScale = _root[me]._xScale*1.10;
 _root[me]._yscale = _root[me]._yScale*1.10;
 } else {
 _root[me]._xScale = 100;
 _root[me]._yScale = 100;
 }
 } else {
 if (_root[me]._xScale>10) {
 _root[me]._xScale = _root[me]._xScale*0.90;
 _root[me]._yScale = _root[me]._yscale*0.90;
 } else {
 _root[me]._xScale = 10;
 _root[me]._yScale = 10;
 }
 }
}
//
function cursorHit (me) {
 hit = false;
 if ((_root[me]._x-_root[me]._width/2)<_root._xMouse) {
 if ((_root[me]._x+_root[me]._width/2)>_root._xMouse) {
 if ((_root[me]._y-_root[me]._height/2)<_root._yMouse) {
 if ((_root[me]._y+_root[me]._width/2)>_root._yMouse) {
 hit = true;
```

continues overleaf

```
        }
        }
       }
      }
     return hit;
    }
```

This consists of two functions, scaleMe and cursorHit. The first one looks at the argument meActive, and depending on whether it is *true* or *false*, scales the target _root[me] up to 100% (me active) or down to 10% (me not active). At the extremes of scale factor, the code makes sure that I actually reach exactly 100% or 10% by explicitly setting these values.

The cursorHit function returns *true* if the cursor is over _root[me] and false if it isn't. It works by asking a set of nested if questions that check whether the cursor is on the correct side of all four window edges. If it is, then the cursor is within the window box.

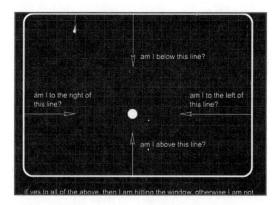

This seemed to me to be a better option than using a button hit or movie clip based hitTest because at the moment I don't know what is going to go into these windows, and using any of the 'standard' methods of detecting a rollover might interfere with the content I decide to put in the window frames later.

The important thing to notice is that neither of these functions have *any variables of their own*. They simply use the properties of the instance me to do whatever they do. We will see the importance of this in a moment.

The actual window movieclip is called mc.page. Open this, and have a look at the code that drives it, which you will find attached to a blank movieclip symbol on the top left inside corner of the window frame.

Hi Rez

```
onClipEvent (load) {
  // Define window object and methods.
  window = new Object();
  window.scale = _root.scaleMe;
  window.cursorHit = _root.cursorHit;
}
onClipEvent (enterFrame) {
active = window.cursorHit(_parent._name);
  window.scale(_parent._name, window.cursorHit(_parent._name));
}
```

The load event does something important to a true object oriented implementation; it attaches my functions to an object and turns them into *methods.* This creates a new object, window, which has two methods scaleMe and cursorHit. These can now be used in the rest of this script as any other method, (such as Math.abs or movieclip.gotoAndPlay). Put simply I have created new commands specific to this FLA, and when I am coding this FLA, I can treat them as additions to the ActionScript Reference guide.

What makes this object oriented is the fact that I no longer need to know about movie clips; the fact that my windows are actually movie clips with properties like _x and _y is no longer something I need to know because my new methods know that for me and handle all the properties. The new methods have ring-fenced the properties of the standard movieclip object (or put them inside a 'black box' that I no longer need to look into) and created a higher level object, the window that has methods tailored to my needs.

This 'moving to a higher level' or **abstraction** is a hallmark of object oriented coding, and something our code will use throughout this project. You may never have used it, but it is a very powerful technique. It also works by generalizing the problem in some cases, so instead of writing a specific 'move this there' routine, I write a 'move anything anywhere' routine.

You can see the new methods used in the enterFrame script. The variable active doesn't actually need to be there; it is just for diagnostics and shows that the cursorHit method is working properly when I look in the debug window.

A final thing to notice is our use of *idea #1* in a new guise. When the window is small, you might be able to see the words 'lo Rez' (you can zoom into a running SWF with the right-click or alt-click dropdown if you want to have a good look). As the window gets bigger, it switches to a window with 'hi Rez' in it. The window contents are being swapped based on size. Although there is no advantage in doing this now, when we have actual content, we can switch content for a low resolution, processor–friendly version when the window is unselected, and switch to the high resolution multimedia version, complete with animations and working buttons when the button is big enough for the user to appreciate it all. If we do it just right, the user will never detect our bluff, and will think that all the windows contain working content all the time!

The way this works is very simple, because as with all Good Ideas, the idea is the most complex thing; the code just follows from it. The switching occurs in the movieclip mc.frame, where the switching occurs based on the value of xscale. Frames 1 and 2 contain a hi-resolution and lo-resolution version of the frame, and a script attached to our empty movieclip shuffles between the two:

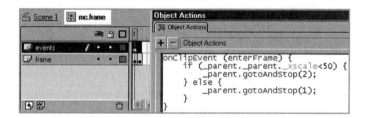

```
onClipEvent (enterFrame) {
  if (_parent._parent._xscale<50) {
  _parent.gotoAndStop(2);
  } else {
  _parent.gotoAndStop(1);
  }
}
```

My use of a movieclip property so soon after the discussion on abstracting away from the movieclip object seems like a bit of a *faux pas* here, but I really couldn't see the advantage in coding up a function just to look at whether _xscale<50. With Flash we always need to be careful of optimization, because it is designed for simple and low bandwidth web multimedia and not speed. As it happens, the solution of this little anomaly drops out later in the project, so don't worry too much. Take it as an early beta and enjoy the ride to the final polished code.

FLAs in between

By about `test03.fla`, the interface is starting to take shape. Here, I am starting to look at all sorts of ergonomic issues. The windows don't zoom in a linear way anymore, but rather start growing slowly, and once you have kept your cursor on one long enough to say 'yes, this is the one I want to see', the window 'snaps' up with a burst of speed. The transition between the two was selected so the user can 'browse', which is looking at a page quickly to see if it is the one they want. If it isn't, then the user will mouse over an adjacent one. Only when the user 'looks interested' does the interface actually provide a solid navigation transition.

Although it doesn't look like it visually, I am trying to emulate flicking through pages in a book. In doing this, the user looks at a lot of pages quickly until they get closer to their required content. Although the printed pages do not become 'low resolution' during the page flicking, our perception of them is low resolution because of the short timeslot we give each. When we finally get to our required page, we concentrate more, which makes it become 'high resolution'.

My system of being able to browse through *physically* low resolution images when initially selecting a page is trying to emulate this process, and the switch to high resolution emulates the 'aha – this looks interesting, let's take a closer look' moment.

There are still all sorts of issues that are unresolved at this point, (like what happens to unselected windows), but the interface is building up. If you have a quick look at the code, you will see something strange; the main code has stayed the same, but my methods (which are being defined by my functions) have grown considerably. That is because I am not actually really *changing code* so much as *developing my window object functionality*.

Another good thing is that all the code I am making changes to is in one place because all my basic window functionality is in one place. Although I am working within the event-driven and timeline system that is Flash, all my code changes are on a single script. This means I am not switching between frames saying 'damn, where is that pesky script attached', but rather going straight to one frame on the main timeline. To make it even easier, this frame is actually the first frame in the first layer!

This is due to the *structure* of my application. Although I have not decided to go down this route, the coding strategy I have chosen *makes* me go down it; I am using a structured approach, with the **definition** and the **use** (or application) of my functionality in two distinct places.

Before we leave `test3.fla`, notice that I have gone for a left-to-right graphic here. This was because I suspected drawing the table in the same direction we read might add something to it. It didn't, and you can see that this is one of those ideas that ended up being taken out and shot.

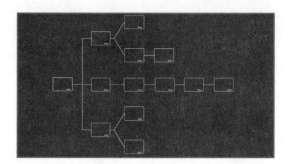

The idea I had of making visited pages a different color did work though, and made it to the finished version. Some you win, some you lose to the Wall.

The ideas in `test05.fla` are more or less the finished article (although the code needs polishing up).

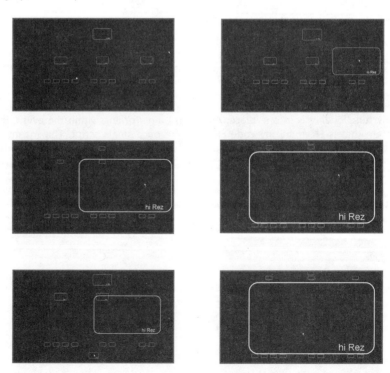

I realized that the interconnections between pages could just as easily be expressed by position (rather than a connected flow chart), as shown in the top left diagram, which is the navigation system with no window selected. The hierarchy is implied by both position and size.

Also, the concept of having all the windows available all the time has been implemented. The windows that are not selected auto-arrange themselves into a menu for the next step as soon as a page is selected. This is one of those ideas that just 'arrive' during the creative play part. I would have never thought;

 'I know, why don't I make the unselected windows arrange themselves into a new menu along the top and bottom when there is a full size window in the middle. This menu arrangement will be unique for each window, allowing you to do traditional page-to-page navigation when you have hit on the area you were 'flicking pages' to find'.

For a start, the coding would have been beyond me if I knew I had to create that sort of effect at step 1 (but having built it once, I suppose I have a good idea now!). But with my structured coding methods, each change soon becomes an easy incremental addition that is lagging only minutes behind my creative thought. By setting up the structures of my coding early on, I am forcing my final ActionScript to be structured despite whatever flights of fancy I throw at it. This allows my code to be easily modifiable, and it becomes quick to change rather than becoming a drudge that keeps fouling my creative vision.

t7.fla

In looking at the final test FLA for the interface, we will touch on a number of coding issues. As well as talking about how the code works, I want to touch on other issues to do with ActionScript heavy interface design in general.

The first of these issues is the ease of **content update**. A lot of ActionScript heavy interfaces are seen in sites aimed at other designers, and these are maintained by the designer who built the interface. If you want to actually build interfaces that are going to be updated by someone other than yourself, you need to think about making it sufficiently easy so that at a minimum, someone who understands Flash but not ActionScript can make the update. You need to be able to do this in a web design studio so that you can offload site update to a junior (although the rate will probably be the same as if you did it!).

I also want to think about **streaming issues**. Designer Flash interfaces have a bad reputation for taking an age to load, compounded by the fact that they don't use streaming, and I don't want mine to suffer from this double headed problem.

A more thorny issue is **performance**. A lot of interface designers skirt this issue by saying things like 'well if you want advanced multimedia on the web, you need a beefy machine'. Even worse for me is the hardcore elitist stance of 'The client's customers would typically have this system, and it works fine on that (and of course my client is a large record company/department store/car manufacturer whose goods are not bought by people with two year old hardware – but coincidentally they do tend to have the same beefy computer us designers at the swish downtown office tend to use)'. Well, I can live with all that, but if the hardcore Flash ActionScript designer about town doesn't even *attempt* to optimize his code, he will be part of the hardcore unemployed in my eyes...so we will look at code optimization as well before we let Jake loose on the content creation.

Okay, first things first, setting the scene.

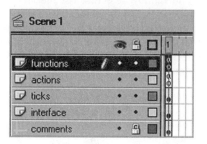

The layers are very similar to the previous FLAs. There is still an actions layer that defines the screen object. The functions layer still contains our methods, except they have grown considerably, and there is a few new features in there as well.

The main interface is on layer interface. The only new important layer is ticks. This contains a number of, well.... ticks. All will be explained in due course when we look at the stage area, which will happen almost immediately. The stage area looks like this:

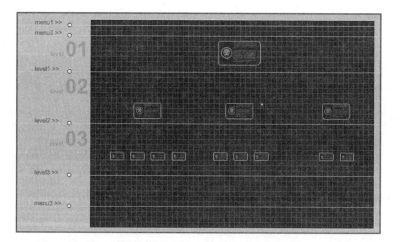

First, lets get the ticks out of the way. The interface needs a system of heights in the y direction that are important to the way the interface works. These are listed along the left edge as measurement point >>. Each point has a blank movieclip at that position, so Flash can read the position by looking at that movieclip's position. Such positions on graphs are usually called *ticks* so that is what I have called them.

These points could have been defined as variables or as the properties of an object (probably my old friend the `screen` object), but because they are part of the visual environment, I prefer to make them visual so I can drag them about by eye. The non-ActionScript friendly co-designer can understand them as well, so there will be less pestering when someone else has to update it. The guide lines are actually denoting where the separate levels of the site map are situated on the screen, and Flash will look at these positions when each window needs to decide where it should go to build the little top/bottom menus. They also tell the windows which level of the site map they are situated on.

Right, let's get the big bit over with; the functions that define the window methods. The methods are being called from the movie clips that house my window objects. These methods stop me having to think in terms of the movieclip objects because they handle all that low level stuff. Before we plough through the functions, let's have a look at what they are and where this code sits in the bigger picture:

My site is based around a new window object created specifically for it. It is a data object. This consists of two new methods `scaleMe()` and `cursorHit()`. These methods are used to control the underlying primitive movieclip object that my window object controls. The new object does not replace the movieclip, but sits between it and the main code.

The window object also creates some pseudo-properties, `instanceName.xs`, `instanceName ys`, `instanceName.homeX`, `instanceName.homeY`, which it places inside the movieclip. These properties define the starting position and scaling of the window, and the window object will cause its return to these values when it is not active. The window object has its own pseudo-constructor, which in Flash has been implemented as another method, `newWindowObject()`. This method generates the window properties noted above by looking at the underlying movieclip it is controlling.

Okay. Have a look at the first function. This defines my window properties, and more importantly, the comments in this function precede the whole listing with a brief description of what is actually going on in coding terms.

Although the comments don't give enough information for another programmer to take my code and use my object, it is enough for me, so that if I want to do something similar (or even if I later decide to build another object that lives on top of my window object in the same way that the window object lives on top of the movie clip) there is enough here to tell me what I need.

```
Frame Actions
Frame Actions
+ -   Frame Actions
function newwindowobject (me) {
    // define the properties of this window object by looking at the
    // movieclip primitive on which it is based...
    // Properties of the window object;
    //
    // xs,ys
    // The starting scale values of the window.
    // The window will return to these scale
    // values when inactive.
    //
    // homex,Y
    // The starting x,y values of the window.
    // The window will return to this position when
    // inactive.
    //
    // menu1,2,3
    // The three menu positions that the window will
    // go to if it is called to form a menubar.  These
    // are defined graphically.
    //
    // level1,2,3
    // The three areas corresponding to the three depths
    // of the website navigation chart.
    // These values are defined graphically.
    //
    // Implicit dependancies;
    // The window object requires there to be a screen object defined, and uses
    // the .xMiddle and .yMiddle properites of this object.
    // The window object requires there to be a winActive Object defined, and uses
    // the state, owner, fullwindow properties.  These should be initialized to;
    // state:false, owner:"none", fullwindow:false
    // The graphical components are created via dummy movieclip primitives positioned
    // on the stage.  These must be called menu1,2,3 and level1,2,3.
    //
    // Explicit dependancies;
    // The window object is based on the Flash movieclip primitive.
    //
    _root[me].xs = _root[me]._xScale;
    _root[me].ys = _root[me]._yScale;
    _root[me].homeX = _root[me]._x;
    _root[me].homeY = _root[me]._y;
}
```

Now we have looked at newWindowObject, which I have looked at first because it tells you what I am building, let's backtrack a half step and look at the variables at the top of the script...

```
// Define window functions.
// These will be added to the local window
// object to create the window.methods.
//
// set semaphores
winActive = new Object();
winActive = {state:false, owner:"none", fullWindow:false};
```

This object is needed so that the functions can talk to each other about things that the main code is not concerned about. The properties of winActive allow our functions to keep track of which window is currently active, and where it is. A *semaphore* is a low level variable that assigns ownership – only one window can be active, and if another pretender to this title comes along, it must wait until the title is up for grabs. The winActive object tells Flash if there is an active window, and points to its name.

The next function is called scaleMe, and it handles the scaling of the windows. Because this is a big bit of code, I will split it into two bite sized chunks: zooming in and zooming out. An important point to note is that although many of the lines here look long, they would be much shorter if it wasn't for the fact that almost everything in the function has a path attached to it, making for lots of text to describe what is essentially a simple property assignment.

Also, because I am using these functions to create methods rather than calling them as standard functions, the code will act as if it was situated at the frame in which the calling action occurs. I cannot therefore assume any relative paths because I don't always know where the function is actually being called, so all my paths are absolute. This again tends to make for long looking lines, but they will still reduce to a much simpler format when they are compiled.

```
Frame Actions
Frame Actions
+ - Frame Actions
//
function scaleMe (me, meActive) {
    // if I am an active window, I need to grow...
    if (meActive) {
        if (_root[me]._xScale<100) {
            _root[me]._xScale = _root[me]._xScale*1.10;
            _root[me]._yscale = _root[me]._yScale*1.10;
            _root.winActive.fullWindow = false;
        } else {
            _root[me]._xScale = 100;
            _root[me]._yScale = 100;
            _root.winActive.fullWindow = true;
        }
        // Because I am Active, I need to move
        // towards center stage.
        if (_root[me]._xscale>50) {
            _root[me]._x -= (_root[me]._x-_root.screen.xMiddle)/8;
            _root[me]._y -= (_root[me]._y-_root.screen.yMiddle)/8;
        }
    } else {
        // ... otherwise I am not the active window and need to shrink.
        if (_root[me]._xscale>_root[me].xs) {
            _root[me]._xScale = _root[me]._xscale*0.90;
            _root[me]._yScale = _root[me]._yscale*0.90;
        } else {
            _root[me]._xScale = _root[me].xs;
            _root[me]._yScale = _root[me].ys;
        }
        // If there is an active window that is not me
        // I need to get out of the way.
        if (_root.winActive.state && (_root[_root.winActive.owner]._xscale>40)) {
            _root.windowMenu(me, _root.winActive.owner);
        } else {
            // otherwise I need to go home.
            _root[me]._x -= (_root[me]._x-_root[me].HomeX)/8;
            _root[me]._y -= (_root[me]._y-_root[me].HomeY)/8;
        }
    }
}
```
Line 97 of 97. Col 1

Okay, first bit;

```
function scaleMe (me, meActive) {
// if I am an active window, I need to grow...
if (meActive) {
if (_root[me]._xScale<100) {
_root[me]._xScale = _root[me]._xScale*1.10;
_root[me]._yscale = _root[me]._yScale*1.10;
_root.winActive.fullWindow = false;
} else {
_root[me]._xScale = 100;
_root[me]._yScale = 100;
_root.winActive.fullWindow = true;
```

continues overleaf

```
        }
        // Because I am Active, I need to move
        // towards center stage.
        if (_root[me]._xscale>50) {
        _root[me]._x -= (_root[me]._x-_root.screen.xMiddle)/8;
        _root[me]._y -= (_root[me]._y-_root.screen.yMiddle)/8;
        }
```

This section contains the function head, which takes two arguments:

- me, which tells the function the name of the calling window

- meActive, which tells the function whether this window is active (ie the mouse is over it).

The first if simply scales the window up if it is active but not fully open. A fully open window is one at 100% scale factor. I am also setting a flag fullWindow, part of my winActive object. I have written this in because I am almost certain that this will be useful to know when I come to optimize my code, but I am not using it yet.

The else part of the if makes sure that the window never stays over 100% for too long. It does actually overshoot using the scale up formula we have just seen, but these lines quickly sort it out.

Finally, the last three lines move the window towards the center of the stage. This is done via an inertia equation. I considered making the inertia equation into a function itself because it is used so often, but I can see no point in doing something that is probably detrimental to overall performance. I have the same feeling about the with action. Although there are lots of lines where there looks to be an opportunity to use it, I believe that in many cases the saving is illusionary.

The second section of this function looks at the scaling down of a window. Because by this point in the if I know I am not working with an active window, I know that I have to scale it down to its original size. Because the windows all start at different sizes, the actual starting size is held by the originating window by our pseudo properties xs, ys.

The code here is actually the same as the scale up part, but the scale factor is less than 1. The more astute may be saying 'well, you have used the same functionality twice so why didn't you create a new function?' The answer is as simple as it is short; runtime performance.

The functionality that moves windows to make up menus at the top and bottom of the screen once there is an active window, is handled by the last part of this code. It looks for the existence of an active window that is not this window, and a new function windowMenu is called to create the menu. If you look at test5.fla you will see that windowMenu was actually called windowCollision initially. This ancestor of windowMenu checked for window collisions on the fly and was much more complicated than what we have now, but the tick system worked out much simpler and faster.

Finally, last else will capture situations where there are no active windows, and make each window go back to its starting point. These are held in two properties window.HomeX,Y

```
    } else {
        // otherwise I am not the active window and need to shrink.
        if (_root[me]._xScale>_root[me].xs) {
            _root[me]._xScale = _root[me]._xScale*0.90;
            _root[me]._yScale = _root[me]._yscale*0.90;
        } else {
            _root[me]._xScale = _root[me].xs;
            _root[me]._yScale = _root[me].ys;
        }
        // If there is an active window that is not me
        // I need to get out of the way.
        if
        (_root.winActive.state&&(_root[_root.winActive.owner]
➥._xscale>40)) {
            _root.windowMenu(me, _root.winActive.owner);
        } else {
            // otherwise I need to go home.
            _root[me]._x -= (_root[me]._x-_root[me].HomeX)/8;
            _root[me]._y -= (_root[me]._y-_root[me].HomeY)/8;
        }
    }
}
}
```

Some of you might be thinking that this is a lot of code for Flash to have to go through every frame for all of the windows. It's actually not as bad as it seems. If you actually follow the code through for all the conditions below;

- There is an active window and it is me.

- There is an active window and it is not me

- There are no active windows

You'll see that in each case very little code is actually run. The if else structures contain a lot of branches but only one is ever run, and the logic usually gets to it within two comparisons. The most lines that are ever actually seen are usually around five. We will look at this later in practical terms when we benchmark the code, because there are some hidden bottlenecks in this code we have to weed out.

Okay, on to our next function, cursorHit. As well as detecting collisions between a window and the cursor, this function also performs the important task of making sure only *one* window is actually ever defined as being hit, and therefore only one window is actually ever active. The function has to perform the following tasks:

- Check if there is already an active window, and if so, don't check for any more collisions.

- If no window is active currently, check for collisions, and if there is one, make the current window active.

● Release the current window from being active if it was active previously but is no longer under the cursor.

● Return a value that tells the originating window object whether it is active.

As you can see, although the functionality of this code is looking for collisions, its real task is to look at whether the current window meets the criteria to be active or not. Although the mouse position plays a major part in this as the users input into the process, the total functionality is looking at what other windows are doing as well.

Building up these rules was much harder than actually coding them up. They make sense when you read about them, but thinking them up from first principles is what makes a good coder; you can't code what you can't specify!

Firstly, if there already is an active window, the function returns *false*. The window is classed as 'not hit' irrespective of where the cursor is.

You might have wondered how the interface 'knows' what it is doing when occasionally you can see your cursor over windows that are currently underneath the window you just selected. This is how it happens

```
function cursorHit (me) {
  // If there is a window currently hit and it is
  // not me, I cannot be hit.
  if (_root.winActive.state && (_root.winActive.owner<>me)) {
    return false;
```

If a window is active (denoted by state = true) and it is not this window (owner <> me), then the function will return false. So, given that there is already an active window, this function will actually only run three lines of code for every window except the active one.

If the window gets past this point, then either there is no active window, or it is the active window. In either case, the function checks if the window is under the cursor. This is unchanged from test1.fla.

```
      } else {
          hit = false;
          // if I am currently under the cursor...
          if ((_root[me]._x-_root[me]._width/2)<_root._xMouse) {
             if ((_root[me]._x+_root[me]._width/2)>_root._xMouse) {
                if ((_root[me]._y-_root[me]._height/2)<_root._yMouse) {
                   if ((_root[me]._y+_root[me]._height/2)>_root._yMouse) {
```

If the window passes the collision test, then it is promoted to owner of the active window semaphore object, and its name is entered as the owner. If it already had this title, well, no matter – it's just told it still has it (this is as fast as doing it any other way, and simpler – there is no need to check if we are overwriting identical information, because checking and then not doing it if we don't have to takes more lines than not saving!)

```
                      // ...set me to hit, and lock other windows out.
                      hit = true;
                      _root.winActive.state = true;
                      _root.winActive.owner = me;
                   }
                }
             }
          }
```

By this point in the code, the only reason a window would get this far down would be that it is down as the active owner, but it is no longer under the cursor, or it is not active and neither is any other window. The semaphore is released if I was the previous owner but shouldn't be.

```
          // ... otherwise I was the last hit window, but I
          // am not anymore, so I should release control...
          if (!hit) {
             _root.winActive.state = false;
             _root.winActive.owner = "none";
          }
       }
```

Finally, if I have not dropped out of the nested if by now, it is because I am now active, or was previously active and still am. The function will return *false* except for this condition, where it returns *true;*

```
       return hit;
    }
```

Again, I should reiterate there is no clever code here. The commands used are almost boringly familiar; it is the conciseness of the code specification that is the real magic. The interaction of the semaphore and a few if statements has produced something that underpins the whole interface. The magic is not the scaling and scrolling animated windows you see when the FLA is running, it is the simplicity of the semaphore object and its contextual functionality that is applied to the mouse position.

The final function `windowMenu` does *not* get converted into a method later. It is an internal function called by the `scaleMe` method, and the user does not have to consider it. This function makes the non-active windows form menu strips above and below the active window. It is something the window object knows to do *itself*, and is one of the advantages in thinking in objects – as you code them up and your functions abstract away from the low level primitive objects that the functionality is rooted upon, you realize that you can leave them to do more and more by themselves.

A lot of people don't talk about this process when talking about Flash 5's new object based nature. Instead, the discussion is about the objects that control the graphic environment, such as movie clips, and sound and color, and it gets bogged down in setting properties and stuff. That isn't the object oriented part because you are concentrating on Flash's primitive objects rather than abstracting away from them, as our window methods do to the movie clip object by sitting between us and it so that we no longer have to consider it.

```
function windowMenu (me, you) {
    if (_root.winActive.owner<>"none") {
        // Am I level 1?
        _root[me]._xscale = 5;
        _root[me]._yscale = 5;
        if (_root[me].homeY<_root.level1._y) {
            yTarget = _root.menu1._y;
            // Am I level 2?
        } else if (_root[me].homeY<_root.level2._y) {
            yTarget = _root.menu2._y;
        } else {
            // then I must be level 3
            yTarget = _root.menu3._y;
        }
        _root[me]._y -= (_root[me]._y-yTarget)/4;
    }
}
```

The function simply looks at the position of the window, and based on where it sits in relation to the dummy movie clips that make up our ticks level1, level2, level3, the window will go to the corresponding menu position (which is also defined by the placement of dummy movie clips on the stage). Before all this happens, the window is scaled down to 5% in the first few lines.

Once the functions have been defined, they are attached to each of our window data objects as methods, and these are in turn used to control our animations. Have a look in mc.page. The script attached to the empty movieclip (top left corner) looks like this;

```
onClipEvent (load) {
    // Define my window methods.
    window = new Object();
    window.scale = _root.scaleMe;
    window.cursorHit = _root.cursorHit;
    window.newWindowObject = _root.newWindowObject;
    // create a new Window object here.
    window.newWindowObject(_parent._name);
}
onClipEvent (enterFrame) {
    window.scale(_parent._name, window.cursorHit(_parent._name));
}
```

The load event links our functions to the window object, and they are now methods. Think of the window object as a *wrapper* that covers the movie clip object to create a new graphic window object if you like – it's easier to visualize than the truth, which is that the window object is a *data* object that we talk to, and it in turn talks to the lower level (and harder to control) movie clip for us. The newWindowObject creates our window pseudo properties. I call them pseudo because I have not actually attached them to my data object, but rather as properties of the movie clip (or, if you want to step back for a minute into non-object terminology, they are variables on the movie clip timeline). This is easier to do because everything about the window object points to a movie clip rather than itself, so I thought I might as well place its properties there as well.

The enter event is almost all the main code. Yes. All of it! Because my methods do everything, there's not much else to have to do apart from call the methods.

The only other main code is my low resolution to high resolution switching. This occurs in the movieclip mc.frame.

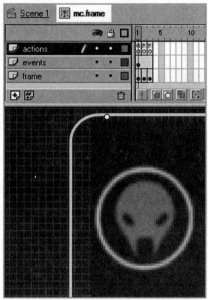

The event scripts attached to the blank movieclip at the top left contain the following script;

```
onClipEvent (enterFrame) {
  if (visited && (_parent._parent._xscale<50)) {
    _parent.gotoAndStop("loRez");
  }
  if (_parent._parent._xscale>50) {
    _parent.gotoAndStop("hiRez");
    visited = true;
  }
}
```

This is the only main application script that looks at a movie clip property. The window object wrapper should really be doing all the talking to the movie clip, but to be honest, I could not see a better application of this that didn't hit on performance. Although when I have my 'textbook structured programmer' head on, I don't like this situation, my 'structured programming head with added industrial experience' reminds me that I have seen this before on major projects where the defined objects have had to be tweaked slightly when added functionality outside the main object is required. This additional code goes by the name of *satellite logic*, and this is what I have here. The resolution switching function is not part of the window object (which is why I can't easily add it to that). I still can't help not liking this though and resolved to keep thinking of a way out of having to use this code.

Anyway, the code constantly looks at the scale factor and switches between the two content versions depending on how big the window is. The only slight complication over `test1.fla` is that when the `mc.frame` movieclip starts, it is kept on frame 1. The window border on that frame is green. Once the window has been selected and then unselected, the timeline doesn't return to this frame, but rather another frame, loRez, where the border is yellow. This allows the user to differentiate between visited pages (yellow) and unvisited pages (green). It's also why the two `if`s are not one `if else`; I don't want anything to happen until the 50% scaling point has been crossed and the window will then take up the 'visited' color.

With regard to the content, there were a number of options in deciding how the low resolution version of the content would be calculated. I could have used a system a bit like the starfield, where it is at full resolution when selected, and at whatever resolution the plug-in idle time allows during window inactive states. This is an idea to take away for later when I go and define the content for this site. For now, I chose a much simpler way out for this early beta; the high resolution version is the full Flash movie clip and the low resolution version is a small bitmap screen capture of the high resolution version. I created the low resolution version simply by taking the screen capture into Photoshop and reducing its dimensions;

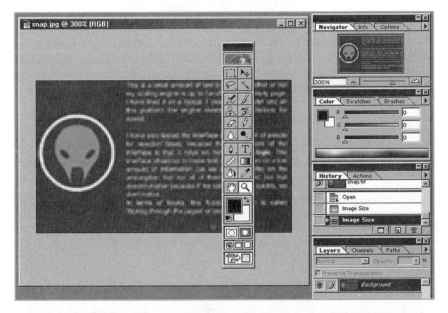

Useful web designer's Photoshop Tip; if you ever use blur or any of Photoshop's filter effects in this way, a better quality always results if you apply the filter many times with low values rather than once with high values. So performing a low pixel blur five times is much better than performing the blur once (with the blur setting set five times greater). This is because the first technique performs five times the number of samples during the filter application.

To work with bitmaps in Flash can potentially reduce performance, so to make sure that you minimize this effect unselect Allow smoothing in the bitmap properties window:

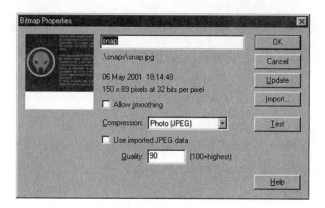

Because my images are particularly low resolution anyway, smoothing will have little effect in this particular case.

Okay, so now we have our interface up and running in isolation as `test7.fla`. We have gone through the creative phase and have thought up our code and graphic system. Time to add the all important patina of practicality and readiness for the real world into it before we start thinking about content

This is what I looked at during the first part of day 4...

Performance

Performance testing is something we usually do by eye. This is okay to show that the SWF works adequately overall, but it doesn't really tell us specifics. In particular, it doesn't help us to identify bottlenecks and places or transitions in the site that are particularly sluggish. Also, we can't tell if Flash is working really hard behind the scenes when there is nothing changing on the screen because our eyes have no point of reference.

A way forward is to use our performance monitor (or something like it).

I have tried to show you a formal method of testing for performance below that beats the 'checking it by eye method' hands down. Flash is a strange beast when it comes to performance; there are some difficult things it does really fast, but we usually find that there are other areas where it falls on its face for no apparent reason. I hear all sorts of people on the newsgroups saying 'why is my SWF so slow' when the answer is obvious; you did not design in performance checking in your development. This issue is particularly important when we are designing ActionScript–heavy sites and games, and we should know how to deal with it.

elining

First off, we need to know what the speed of the 'free-wheeling' plug-in is when nothing is happening. I have created a simple FLA (and you can see it as `test7_baseline.fla`) that contains my performance monitor movieclip from *idea #1* and a stop action at frame 6. The first few blank frames are to allow the plug-in to settle. I set the frame rate to the same as `test7.fla` (18fps), made sure no other applications were running and tested my movie.

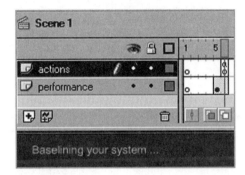

The movie came back with this;

My movie runs such that the average frame duration is 56ms. The *normal* value is just this x1.4, the value I will nominally accept as the frame duration of a SWF that is actually doing something. You will note that the movie is actually not making 18fps because; this is either my computer can't reach that value (which I doubt is the reason) or using the debugger and running the SWF within the Flash environment is a little slower than running it in a browser. Anyway, we will take the 56ms as our baseline figure because we are not really worried about the actual value, but by how much it changes.

Now I have some figures, time to see what my interface is up to...

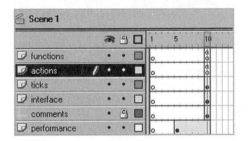

I dropped the performance monitor into the FLA into layer performance and had a look at the figures again. When you do this, don't change the screen size when you debug the movie (i.e. by changing the size of the bandwidth profiler) because this will mean you can't compare them to the previous FLA.

For the movie with the interface up and running, I get 57ms. 57ms! Even though my methods are being called all the time, the actual additional hit to the whole movie over that of an empty stage is *nothing*. Some of you might be pretty surprised by this, but I am not. It tells me that the code is just executing a couple of comparisons and the `if` statements are jumping straight to the small bits of code that have to run, and this is all happening before the next frame is required to start. Cool. So far so good.

When a window is actually selected, the figure goes up slightly to about 80ms, but we are not worried because this is still just below my *normal* value. The trouble comes when you have a look at what happens next...

Even though the screen is not doing anything once a window is selected and fully open, the frame duration has gone up to about 100ms (or down to 10fps). But nothing seems to be happening on the screen! What's going on?

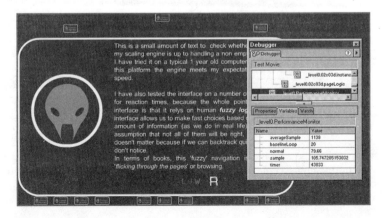

Well, I spent a while pruning a few milliseconds from the 100ms total by realizing that all the windows were being animated all the time. I realized that if I could decide when they should stop being animated, that would be something. I suspected that a property `active` might be useful. When it is `true`, the window is selected and being viewed by the user. When the window is unselected, this property would be `false`. This didn't quite work, because the unselected windows stopped animating too soon and never reached their menu positions in time. I therefore didn't stop animating them until the selected window was both:

- In the center of the screen

- Scaled to, 100%

To do this, I created a new property of `winActive` called `centeredWindow`. This is `true` when the window is at `screen.xMiddle, screen.yMiddle`. I created a new function that checked whether the current window needed animating, and called it `moveMeRequired`;

```
function moveMeRequired (me) {
  return !(_root.winActive.fullWindow &&
➥ _root.winActive.centeredWindow);
}
```

If the currently selected window is *not fully scaled up to 100% and not in the center*, all the windows need to continue animating as they move about. I tweaked the inertia values of all the animations so all the non-selected windows would be in position by the time the selected window was in position. I then changed my main code to reflect the use of the new method;

```
onClipEvent (load) {
  // Define my window methods.
  window = new Object();
  window.scale = _root.scaleMe;
  window.cursorHit = _root.cursorHit;
  window.newWindowObject = _root.newWindowObject;
  window.moveMeRequired = _root.moveMeRequired;
  // create a new Window object here.
  window.newWindowObject(_parent._name);
}
onClipEvent (enterFrame) {
  if (_parent.active || window.moveMeRequired(_parent._name)) {
    window.scale(_parent._name);
    window.cursorHit(_parent._name);
  }
}
```

The `enterframe` event script doesn't do anything to the window unless the window is active (in which case we have to run the methods, otherwise we will never know when it becomes unselected) or when the `moveMeRequired` method tells us that it is required to be animated.

Notice also that the `scale` method doesn't require the `activeMe` argument anymore; this has been superceded because we now have it as a property.

This all pulled my frame duration to 85ms, which was almost there. I could have stopped there but I know that when the content proper goes into these windows, there will be a major performance hit on top of this figure, which is not good. Ideally, I want this frame duration to be the same as the idle rate or very near.

It took a while to see where the rest of the performance was going, mainly because I could not see the wood for the trees, and it was actually glaringly obvious; the selected window is constantly being scaled *and* animated all the time! The inertia equations are forever moving my window closer to center-screen by smaller and smaller amounts and the window is always being scaled to 100%. Although you can't see the changes on screen, it is slowing Flash down. Because it is the largest window, the effect on performance of doing this (especially if it contains bitmaps) would have been enormous. I changed the code so that if the window is at its destination, no more animation will take place. I won't show you all the places I have done this (because the code changes are essentially the same) but will show you a single example;

Where previously I was doing this every time;

```
_root[me]._x -= (_root[me]._x-_root.screen.xMiddle)/8;
_root[me]._y -= (_root[me]._y-_root.screen.yMiddle)/8;
```

I now added the condition 'are we actually at xmiddle, ymiddle already?' as follows;

```
if ((Math.abs(_root[me]._x-_root.screen.xMiddle)>1) &&
➡ (Math.abs(_root[me]._y-_root.screen.yMiddle)>1)) {
```

All this reduced my original 100ms right down to the idle rate of 55ms, which means that the frame rate of 18fps is being more or less maintained, give or take the losses caused by using the debugger.

This process has made my original code a practical reality. I can use it in a navigation system safe in the knowledge that it only hogs processor time when windows are being moved around. When the content is finally being shown, my interface takes none of the processor time. If I hadn't gone through my code in this way, I would probably have given up and decided it was beyond Flash when my final content–laden site was being tested. I have resolved all problems that might cause this in my beta code stage, so I can add content with confidence later (and also allows me to suggest the interface to a client in a site mockup later – thus making a living out of all this tomfoolery).

You can see the result of this exercise as `test7_Performance.fla`. On my machine, it works well even in full screen browser mode, so our code is looking in much better shape already.

aming

I don't care what anyone else says. Flash is *not* a tool for creating broadband content. If you want to do broadband, get Director. A Flash site should stream in and avoid long periods of nothing happening. If you want to create a cool site to impress other Flash designers with a vested interest in looking up the cutting edge competition, go ahead, but don't expect the general public to stay for long. This applies just as well with 'designer' interfaces. I built the interface with this in mind, because the windows can still work even if they aren't all on screen yet (technically speaking, the interface is modular – it doesn't care how many windows there are). So all I have to do is this;

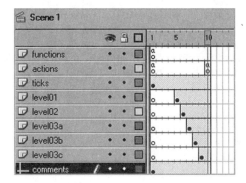

Layer level01 contains the windows in the stage area's level01 area, which works out at the top level page in the picture below. Layer level02 contains the windows in level02, which is the next three windows. So level01 will load up first, and then level02. Because a movie clip doesn't start playing until it's fully loaded, the user will see the top-level window appear first. If he selects it, he will see new levels appear as they are loaded up. I have split level three up into the three groups because there is rather too much content for one load.

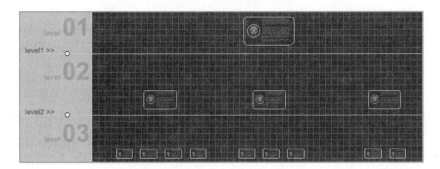

The only problem with this is that if there is already a window selected, newly loaded windows will not go to their menu bar position (because of the optimizations we made to speed up the code in the last section that prevents animation unless the window is in a state that requires it). So we need the windows to start off in one of two positions:

- In their home position if there is no active window at the point when our window loads up

- In their menu position if there is

To do this is much easier than it sounds because our method windowMenu almost does it already, except that it moves between the two positions gradually to create our animated movements. I want to create something very similar without the animations that I can call on the windows load event. The new method to do this, windowOnLoaded, took less than five minutes to create, because it is almost a straight copy and paste of the closely related windowMenu function. I could have altered windowMenu to handle both conditions, but I don't really want to compromise the wonderful performance figures I have now for this FLA, so I went down my chosen path of a separate method. It looks like this:

```
function windowOnLoaded (me) {
    if (_root.winActive.owner<>"none") {
        // iconize me
        _root[me]._xscale = 5;
        _root[me]._yscale = 5;
        // Am I level 1?
        if (_root[me].homeY<_root.level1._y) {
            yTarget = _root.menu1._y;
            // Am I level 2?
        } else if (_root[me].homeY<_root.level2._y) {
            yTarget = _root.menu2._y;
        } else {
            // then I must be level 3
            yTarget = _root.menu3._y;
        }
        _root[me]._x = _root[me].homeX;
        _root[me]._y = yTarget;
    }
}
```

It is exactly the same as the windowMenu function except the last two lines move the window to the menu position straight away rather than animate it towards it.

It is called in the main application code's load event (it's in mc.page, attached to the dummy movie clip if you need reminding);

```
onClipEvent (load) {
    // Define my window methods.
    window = new Object();
    window.scale = _root.scaleMe;
    window.cursorHit = _root.cursorHit;
    window.newWindowObject = _root.newWindowObject;
    window.moveMeRequired = _root.moveMeRequired;
    window.windowOnLoaded = _root.windowOnLoaded;
    // create a new Window object here.
    window.newWindowObject(_parent._name);
    // put me in the menu position if I've just loaded and there is
    // another window already selected...
    window.windowOnLoaded(_parent._name);
}
```

As well as defining my new method window.windowOnLoaded, the load event also runs it on the last line, moving it into its menu position as soon as it loads up if there is an active window. This produces a rather cool effect on the final SWF, because the menu items will appear around the selected window as soon as they are loaded, thus acting as a visual cue that there is more information to look at while the user is browsing the content that has already loaded in. You can emulate this condition by looking at the finished streaming-enabled FLA test7_streaming.fla and delaying the point that the separate levels load up by extending the timeline (or you can just run test7_streamingTrial.fla, where I have done it for you). You will see new windows magically appear in the correct position as soon as they appear on the timeline. As you play with the windows, new windows will appear, and always in the correct position for the current context. No pre-loader or other fancy screens required. Sometimes simplicity is the key!

By now, I'm into day four, evening. The interface test FLA is now a very advanced beta. I've done all my performance testing, I've addressed bandwidth issues, and the only thing left is to make sure that when Jake comes to add the content, he can do it easily and efficiently.

Before I look at building in ease of content update, I want to consolidate my position, tidy up what I have and look at where I am...

Consolidation

The first thing I wanted to do here is confirm it all works for a typical user. I have the advantage of having a very untypical user; Karen, my partner. The first time I ever tried to show her how to use an application (I was showing her how email works), I told her to 'move the mouse to the top of the screen', whereupon she lifted the mouse physically from the desk, and keeping it level, she lined it up with the top edge of the monitor. Web designers don't need to listen to web ergonomics experts telling them Flash is 99% rubbish, or usability engineers pontificating about what color buttons should be, web designers need people like Karen to test websites out on.

The second issue was a coding one. I was still unhappy about my satellite logic, because it is the only thing that spoils my object oriented approach. I can live with that, but if anyone comes to update the FLA, they will have to know what is going on because they will have to put content in the movieclip that contains it (mc.frame). The resolution switching occurs at 50%, which is also the point when scaleMe starts moving an active window towards the center of the screen. If I created a new property rezSwitch, and set it to true at this point, and then checked for the less than 50% when the window is zooming out, I could do away with the satellite logic altogether. Sounds like a plan.

The code snippet in scaleMe that sets rezSwitch is;

```
// Because I am Active, I need to move
// towards center stage.
if (_root[me]._xscale>50) {
  _root[me].switchRez = true;
```

The third line is the additional line. The code that resets it is (again, the last line is the addition):

```
// ... otherwise I am not the active window and need to shrink.
  if (_root[me]._xScale>_root[me].xs) {
    _root[me]._xScale = _root[me]._xScale*0.90;
    _root[me]._yScale = _root[me]._yscale*0.90;
    if (_root[me]._xscale<50) {
      _root[me].switchRez = false;
```

Finally, the event code in mc.frame, has to change to now reference the property switchRez.

```
onClipEvent (enterFrame) {
  if (visited && (!_parent._parent.switchRez)) {
    _parent.gotoAndStop("loRez");
  }
  if (_parent._parent.switchRez) {
    _parent.gotoAndStop("hiRez");
    visited = true;
  }
}
```

My main application code has now abstracted completely away from the movieclip object, and I am a happy programmer. I could have deleted this functionality and added it to mc.page (making it the only place in the interface that actually contains the main code). I have left it where it is because I can choose to delete it and instead use it as part of a single frame adaptive animation. For example, if I wanted to add the star animation in a window, I could set the number of stars to the minimum if the window was iconized (switchRez = false), and let it find its adaptive maximum when the window is fully opened (switchRez = true), which is a pretty cool thing to see if you place the star animation in all the windows in this way. Try it!

The final thing was to properly comment my code, which I have done in the final FLA (that now is my blank *Lo-Rez* website navigation system) blankSite.fla. If you want to use the navigation free from the *Lo-Rez* graphics, start with siteNavigation.fla.

ing Content

The final Lo-Rez site is included in the download for this chapter. This includes some content, including the ability to run Flash games from the windows. This is a hallmark of a good interface; it doesn't get in the way of intensive content, and you can't get much more 'hungry than ActionScript games!

The updating or adding content of the site was pretty easy. All that the content developer needs is a FLA that looks like this:

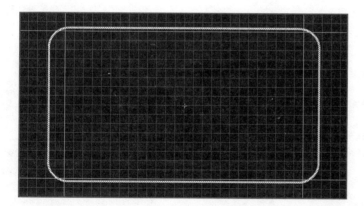

This shows the usable area of the zooming windows. The window can contain anything as long as it doesn't go outside the guidelines. Because the navigation system turns itself off to conserve processing power once a full window is seen, the content can assume it will have the lion's share of the plug-in. The content could easily be implemented as a load target, and contain SWFs that are mini sites in themselves. This may be the preferred way of working, because then the content developer doesn't have to see the site SWF; as long as he has the FLA of the window dimensions shown above.

If you need to keep everything as one SWF, then you need a separate movie clip that is based on mc.page and mc.frame. Because the performance monitor is a part of this site, like us you can include the performance variable and the switchRez property to create adaptive animations rather than a low resolution bitmap as we have used in this chapter. The graphics of the basic, empty site are pretty drab, but you can quickly spice the background up and add your own content. How about a main page that is your personal details, and the lower level windows contain example bitmaps and FLAs. Nice online portfolio potential...

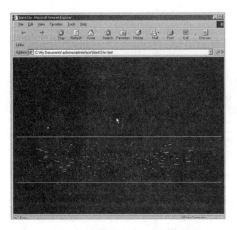

ving on...

There are all sorts of little tweaks to this basic interface that are made in the final design (which you can see in the download). For example, the menu bars just seem to move up and down rather than move to form real menus. This is because their menu position is currently just a squashed up version of their normal position, because the beta code simply creates something that works. My final design sets the menu positions for each window so that they are touching to form proper menustrip shapes that look like rows of icons;

The use of the adaptive degradation variable and resolution switching are used in the final content to create a site that is not only quick on today's hardware, but that will also look better with tomorrow's hardware. As the processor speeds go up, this site has the principles in place to update its content on the fly to take advantage.

The idea of flicking through pages in a book works, but like flicking quickly through a book, it requires a certain amount of skill. The site responsiveness has been tweaked so that a quick mouse user can roll onto an iconized window to see it grow just big enough to see whether it is what they want before moving on to another page or 'flicking'. Moving through the hierarchy is something that doesn't need to happen, because like in a book, you can go straight to any page. Just like in a book, it might not be the correct page, but it is so easy to realize where you are in the hierarchy (because of the tabular layout) and just start flicking between a few odd pages.

Karen is a non-experienced mouse user, but she likes it because it just looks so *nice* and fun to jump between windows and watch them grow and shrink. Hopefully though, this particular Flash site interface is not just eye candy, there is a solid ergonomic thought process to back it all up. My finishing point is not your finishing point however, because even now I have other ideas bubbling about. Play with it. Look at the example site that uses the interface... but most of all, develop ideas and try to add them to the interface and make it your own.

ing shots

The final site, complete with content, shows that object-oriented code written in Flash doesn't mean slow sluggish sites.

Also, if you look at the code for this site, you will see that there are no complex structures. There are no `hitTest` commands, or loops. Not even arrays. Although the object oriented approach may seem a little overly complex, once you get to grips with all these objects, methods and properties, your code will be much the same. Object oriented code is all about starting with a few basic objects, then building slightly more complex objects over the top of your existing ones, and gradually repeating this until you have something that has abstracted away from your low level system properties into data structures that describe your problem and not your hardware or authorware. No difficult commands, just concise, embedded structures.

At the end of this chapter you'll find full listings of the final versions of the three code sections that make up this interface. Play with the interface and see how it is all put together, and take away the route that caused me to arrive at it.

Most of all, have fun, and realize that big bits of ActionScript code are not there to confuse you. They are there to help you see your vision, and convert them into cool motion graphics...

Because after all, that is what Flash is for.

Code listings

Listing one; functions and their definition

```
// Define window functions.
// These will be added to the local window
// object to create the window.methods.

// set semaphore and tracking object;
// state: true when the window is selected.
// owner: instance name of the active window or "none" is no active window.
// fullWindow: true when the active window is fully open.
// centeredWindow: true when the active window is centered on the screen.

        winActive = new Object();
        winActive = {state:false, owner:"none", fullWindow:false,
        ➡ centeredWindow:false};

        function newWindowObject (me) {

// define the properties of this window object by looking at the
// movieclip primitive on which it is based...
// Properties of the window object;

// xs,ys The starting scale values of the window.
// The window will return to these scale
// values when inactive.
//
// homeX,Y
// The starting x,y values of the window.
// The window will return to this position when
// inactive.

// active Denotes whether the window is selected by the user (true)
// or iconized (false) menu1,2,3
// The three menu positions that the window will
// go to if it is called to form a menubar. These
// are defined graphically.
// level1,2,3
```

```
// The three areas corresponding to the three depths
// of the website navigation chart.
// These values are defined graphically.
//
// Implicit dependancies;
// The window object requires there to be a screen object defined, and uses
// the .xMiddle and .yMiddle properites of this object.
// The window object requires there to be a winActive Object defined, and uses
// the state, owner, fullWindow properties. These should be initialized to;
// state:false, owner:"none", fullWindow:false
//  The graphical components are created via dummy movieclip primitives

// positioned on the stage. These must be called menu1,2,3 and level1,2,3.
//
// Explicit dependancies;
// The window object is based on the Flash movieclip primitive.

        _root[me].xs = _root[me]._xScale;
        _root[me].ys = _root[me]._yScale;
        _root[me].homeX = _root[me]._x;
        _root[me].homeY = _root[me]._y;
        _root[me].active = false;
        _root[me].switchRez = false;
    }

    function scaleMe (me) {
        // if I am an active window, I need to grow...
        if (_root[me].active) {
          if (_root[me]._xScale<100) {
            _root[me]._xScale = _root[me]._xScale*1.10;
            _root[me]._yscale = _root[me]._yScale*1.10;
            _root.winActive.fullWindow = false;
          } else if (_root[me]._xscale<>100) {
            _root[me]._xScale = 100;
            _root[me]._yScale = 100;
            _root.winActive.fullWindow = true;
          }
          // Because I am Active, I need to move
          // towards center stage.
          if (_root[me]._xscale>50) {
            _root[me].switchRez = true;
            if ((Math.abs(_root[me]._x-_root.screen.xMiddle)>1) &&
➥ (Math.abs(_root[me]._y-_root.screen.yMiddle)>1)) {
                _root[me]._x -= (_root[me]._x-_root.screen.xMiddle)/8;
                _root[me]._y -= (_root[me]._y-_root.screen.yMiddle)/8;
                _root.winActive.centeredWindow = false;
            } else {
                _root.winActive.centeredWindow = true;
            }
          }
        }
```

```
        } else {
            // ... otherwise I am not the active window and need to
    shrink.
            if (_root[me]._xScale>_root[me].xs) {
              _root[me]._xScale = _root[me]._xScale*0.90;
              _root[me]._yScale = _root[me]._yscale*0.90;
              if (_root[me]._xscale<50) {
                _root[me].switchRez = false;
              }
            } else if (_root[me]._xScale<>_root[me].xs) {
              _root[me]._xScale = _root[me].xs;
              _root[me]._yScale = _root[me].ys;
            }
            // If there is an active window that is not me
            // I need to get out of the way.
            if (_root.winActive.state &&
➡ (_root[_root.winActive.owner]._xscale>40)) {
              _root.windowMenu(me);
            } else {
              // otherwise I need to go home.
              _root[me]._x -= (_root[me]._x-_root[me].HomeX)/16;
              _root[me]._y -= (_root[me]._y-_root[me].HomeY)/16;
            }
          }
        }
    }
    //
    function cursorHit (me) {
        // If there is a window currently hit and it is
        // not me, I cannot be hit.
        if (_root.winActive.state && (_root.winActive.owner<>me)) {
          return false;
        } else {
          _root[me].active = false;
          // if I am currently under the cursor...
          if ((_root[me]._x-_root[me]._width/2)<_root._xMouse) {
            if ((_root[me]._x+_root[me]._width/2)>_root._xMouse) {
              if ((_root[me]._y-_root[me]._height/2)<_root._yMouse) {
                if ((_root[me]._y+_root[me]._height/2)>_root._yMouse) {
          // ...set me to hit, and lock other windows out.

// Also, set properties/flags/semaphores as required for a newly non-active
// window.

                    _root.winActive.state = true;
                    _root.winActive.owner = me;
                    _root[me].active = true;
                }
              }
            }
          }
        }
    }
```

```
    // ... otherwise I was the last hit window, but I
    // am not anymore, so I should release control...
    if (!_root[me].active) {
      _root.winActive.state = false;
      _root.winActive.owner = "none";
      _root[me].active = false;
      _root.winActive.fullWindow = false;
    }
  }
  return hit;
}

function windowMenu (me) {
  if (_root.winActive.owner<>"none") {
    // Am I level 1?
    _root[me]._xscale = 5;
    _root[me]._yscale = 5;
    if (_root[me].homeY<_root.level1._y) {
      yTarget = _root.menu1._y;
      // Am I level 2?
    } else if (_root[me].homeY<_root.level2._y) {
      yTarget = _root.menu2._y;
    } else {
      // then I must be level 3
      yTarget = _root.menu3._y;
    }
    _root[me]._y -= (_root[me]._y-yTarget)/2;
    _root[me]._x -= (_root[me]._x-_root[me].homeX)/2;
  }
}
//
function moveMeRequired (me) {
  return !(_root.winActive.fullWindow &&
➥ _root.winActive.centeredWindow);
}
```

Listing two; Main application loop

```
onClipEvent (load) {
  // Define my window methods.
  window = new Object();
  window.scale = _root.scaleMe;
  window.cursorHit = _root.cursorHit;
  window.newWindowObject = _root.newWindowObject;
  window.moveMeRequired = _root.moveMeRequired;
  // create a new Window object here.
  window.newWindowObject(_parent._name);
}
onClipEvent (enterFrame) {
  if (_parent.active || window.moveMeRequired(_parent._name)) {
    window.scale(_parent._name);
    window.cursorHit(_parent._name);
  }
}
```

Listing three; Resolution switcher

```
onClipEvent (enterFrame) {
  if (visited && (!_parent._parent.switchRez)) {
    _parent.gotoAndStop("loRez");
  }
  if (_parent._parent.switchRez) {
    _parent.gotoAndStop("hiRez");
    visited = true;
  }
}
```

14
A Web Site
from Scratch

Section 3
Case Studies

Chapter 15
XML for Data and
Design

Since the advent of the Web, we've all been trying to make it come alive – and one way to do this is through the use of dynamic content. This is an aspect of web pages that is constantly championed by designers, programmers, and clients alike. Changing content on a monthly, weekly, or even daily basis has come to be expected.

In this chapter, we're going to take a look at an application for which dynamic content is particularly important: the news. Regardless of type, most web sites have some kind of 'news section' that contains announcements, press releases, information about site updates... anything that keeps visitors up to date with what has occurred recently. Often, however, web pages of this type could use a little help:

- For the viewer, news pages can be rather dry and wordy – and unless there's a particular story they're interested in, readers may not even bother with this area of the site.

- For the designer, news pages do little to stimulate the imagination, since they're mostly composed of dates and text. At best, they'll be forced to comply with some template handed down by the database administrator or programmer.

- For the programmer, news pages are a nightmare to update. Even if they create a template that can be updated through a database, this requires cooperation from the systems administrator, and may not be possible if the client or web host does not have database capabilities.

By the end of this chapter, you'll have seen how to apply many of the things this book has touched upon to create a dynamic news page that goes some way to satisfying viewer, designer, and programmer alike. You'll have an understanding of how the News and Development Links movie on my site (www.jrvisuals.com) works, and the design and programming issues that led me to choosing a Flash and XML solution. The movie incorporates use of the XML object, and some variable and MovieClip object manipulation.

Here is a quick peek at a sample frame of the final movie.

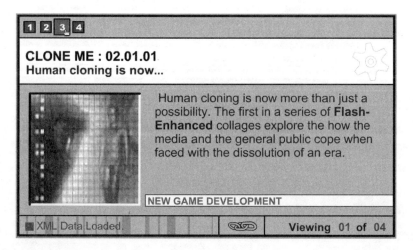

gn Issues

In my work, I try to incorporate design and programming as seamlessly as possible. A good web designer is aware of the intricacies and limitations of the delivery method they've chosen for the project at hand. In turn, a good programmer must be aware of the work that goes into a well-designed page, movie, or application. We've already discussed some of the design issues associated with the creation, maintenance, and presentation of news-type web pages in the earlier bullet points. In this section, we'll go into more detail, and contemplate some possible solutions.

The basic task at hand is to keep a body of information, in this case news and development stories, on a home page in an orderly and engaging fashion.

The body of information is going to be changing frequently, sometimes with short notice. For this reason, the information should be easy to update. It would also be nice if someone with a basic skill set – say, a junior programmer or production assistant – could update it. We don't want to have to call in the systems administrator, lead designer, and senior programmer in order to edit this portion of the site. Generally speaking, these are the reasons why most news pages end up being 'flat' HTML that's just updated by hand (sometimes from a basic template) as and when such changes are required.

Inevitably, there will a varying amount of data to represent, because news is always changing. This presents a problem when it comes to information architecture (explained below), and navigation. Both the architecture and the navigation will need a certain amount of flexibility to address this issue. In addition, the architecture will need to be thought out fairly well in order to be adaptable.

sible Solutions

One solution would be to have all the news items presented on a very long page. Alternatively, only the story titles (or the title and a brief) could be listed, along with links to pages containing the individual news stories. As far as architecture and navigation are concerned, this is a plausible solution. The problem in this case would be maintenance: the amount of work it would take to update, by hand, the title and brief page along with each individual content page and its links is far from trivial.

Perhaps you could get the programming team to build a database, and a page that dynamically builds the interface, title and brief, and story pages? This would address some of the maintenance issues – but it would also require additional skills and resources on the server side. These may not be available to the average person or client.

Unfortunately, these solutions either require more work than we want to have to do, or they're less-than-elegant ways to present the information we're trying to get across to the reader.

The news should also *look* good. Yes, it's just a bunch of text, but if you expect people to read it, it had better be attractive! One way of doing this would be to set up an HTML style sheet, and a layout template featuring tables. You could create graphics of all of the headlines and content (so that it would be anti-aliased), and use a font other than Arial or Times New Roman. You'd definitely want to include the occasional image, to enhance the look of the story. It would also be nice to have several 'standard' layouts, based on known situations that may arise: text-only press release, press release with photo, press release with multiple photos, etc.

The trouble is that regardless of appearance, all that would be pretty time consuming, and it could cause problems when it comes to updating. This way of doing it might also require the involvement of your graphics and programming departments – and even if, in your organization, this responsibility resides in one individual, they would still need to work in several applications in order to make even the smallest update to the news.

Old Attempts

Over the next couple of pages, I've reproduced some screenshots taken from previous versions of my site (and sites that I've worked on) that show the implementation of some of the designs described above. All of them work fairly well, but they definitely don't address all of our concerns. They're time consuming to update, and since they mostly comprise HTML text with style sheets, they don't quite have the design elegance we're looking for.

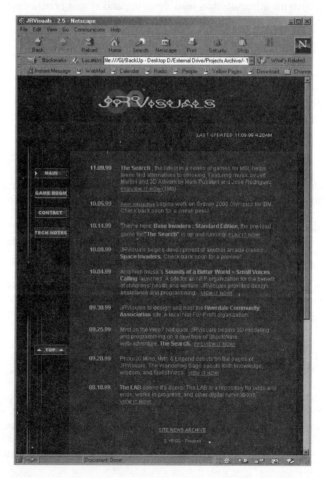

JRVisuals.com, version 2.5. This was a solution I tried in which the HTML was updated by hand. Two sets of pages had to be maintained: the front page housed the titles and briefs, and a unique sub-page was created for each story. It worked pretty well as far as layout and legibility were concerned, though some complained about the amount of scrolling. A simple style sheet maintained the look of the page, but adding, removing, and archiving news items was quite time consuming.

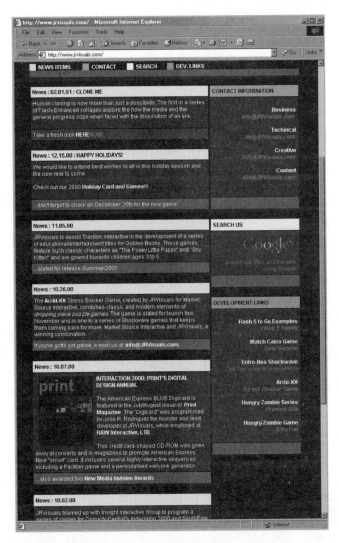

JRVisuals.com, version 3. I wanted a better-designed look to the news. Although still updated by hand, I enhanced the layout with a more intricate table, and some images. I also backed off on the two-page structure of the previous site. This page contains each news story in its entirety, with inline links to points of interest. It definitely cut down on the maintenance, but still left a bit to be desired in terms of presentation. I couldn't imagine having more than five or six stories on this page without thinking that the reader would have to scroll way too much to get to the older stories.

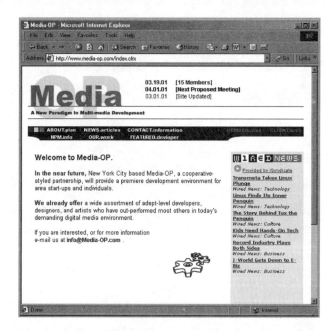

Media-OP.com, version 1.0. A third-party provider generates the news content on the right hand side of this page. The news items are served from a database, from where they are inserted into the Media-OP page. This is definitely the easiest way to go, but it limits the subjects and layout of the items to those available. Some news services and web sites provide this information in other portable formats such as XML. This is more of a programmer's concern, but think about it: as a designer, you can design once, and populate your design with content from various sources. Conversely, the news data, if created in XML, can easily be ported to another design or medium.

The Case for Flash

As you can see from the previous examples, I've invested a good deal of time in learning how to put together an HTML/CSS based news page. You may be wondering why on Earth I would decide to switch to another format. One reason, of course, is that Flash is just plain cool – everyone wants Flash these days – but that alone is unlikely to sell the idea to your clients.

There are some important design reasons why Flash won out over HTML for this project. Flash will allow for:

- A higher level of graphic design

- Embedded, anti-aliased text

- A more engaging user experience, through the addition of animation and sound

- A design that is more mindful of screen real estate

- A design that is dynamic and based on the content

- Dynamic (XML) data that can be updated by most anyone

Flash provides a lot of the flexibility we need to create an elegant interface that's both engaging and ergonomic. Being the fantastic designers that we are, it wouldn't take much effort on our part to put together something like this – maybe you've even done something like it already? Before we rush to begin, though, there's someone else to consider. We understand how Flash benefits the designer in us; let's now take a look at some of the programming issues that can be resolved, or at least reduced, by using Flash.

ramming Issues

Inevitably, we've already touched upon some of the programming issues surrounding this project, but we'll now look at these in more detail, and discuss possible solutions that will lead in the end to my final recommendation for the execution of this project. To recap, the main issues we want to address by building this movie are:

- Creating an engaging and easy-to-use user experience

- Making it easy to update and maintain

- Having dynamic content without a server-side application or database

- Creating portable data

If we can build a skeleton that contains all of the information we need to display, that can be ported easily to various designs and media, and at the same time minimize the amount of work we need to do in order to keep the information up to date, then we really will have achieved something excellent!

The support for XML in Flash 5 means that we can read and write data in a format that can come from or go to almost any other application. In addition, we can make this format as simple or as complex as we deem necessary. If we want our news pages to be updated by someone with basic skills, XML makes that possible.

Flash 5 also takes ActionScript to a level not attainable in previous versions. Aside from the addition of many new keywords, Flash 5 raises the bar with support for functions and a more object-oriented style of programming. With this in mind, we want to create an end product that may be useful beyond this application. We want to make sure that our ActionScript code is clean and easy to read, as well as easy to expand for future versions of this application.

The Deconstruction

In this section, I'm going to perform a step-by-step deconstruction of the News and Development Links movie that's featured on the www.jrvisuals.com web site, and whose picture you saw at the start of the chapter. Because you'll already have seen some of the more basic techniques, I'll be passing over those fairly quickly, in favor of detailing more intricate portions of the movie.

Design Sketches

Although at heart this is not a chapter on designing in Flash, you might want to consider the strengths and weaknesses of certain design styles in Flash.

Whenever possible, it's extremely helpful to sketch out some designs before beginning the production process. Traditionally, these sketches are done with pencil and paper, but if you're more comfortable sketching in Photoshop, Illustrator, Freehand, or even Flash itself, that's fine too. An important thing to keep in mind, though, is that it should be possible to create your final design – or something very close to it – in vector format; you don't want to weigh down your movie with bitmaps.

Here are some of the early sketches I drew for this project. I have also included some commentary on how I got to this point in the design process, and why a design was chosen or passed over for this particular project. In the end, you'll see that I chose the simplest 'external' design in order to concentrate on the XML programming and the appearance of the content – keeping in mind that I would be able to apply this code and logic to any design or 'skin' I might develop in the future.

This interface style has been roaming around in the back of my head for quite some time. I keep *trying* to apply it to the project at hand, but I have yet to find a perfect fit! You can see an old version, circa 1999, on one of my old pages (www.jrvisuals.com/lab/3dif.html). The idea is that you have an 'interface bot' that floats around displaying information related to the particular screen or page on view.

For this application, the center screen would display the current news item. The arrows on the right hand side would allow for scrolling of the current story. The buttons across the top and bottom would link to other news stories. The screen on the left would display either rollover information, or related links. I *still* like this design, but my main problem here is that the interface would detract from the content. Also, in order for the 'face' to be large enough to be useful for displaying news, the whole bot would have to be much bigger than the space I'm willing to set aside for news on my page. That said, if you develop an interface bot of your own, I'd be very interested to see how you did it – send me an e-mail and let me know!

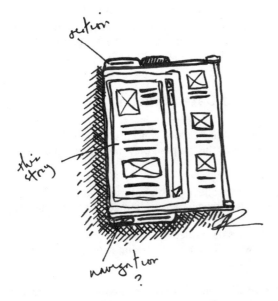

This particular design would be suited more to a standalone news application, than to one embedded in a web page. As with the previous one, it would need to take up quite a bit of screen real estate in order to be useful. My thinking here was that we could place briefs and images on the right hand side, and the full news story in a scrolling box on the left hand side. The tabs across the top of the interface would be used to separate types or sections of news.

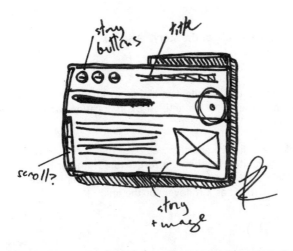

This last sketch represents the route I decided to follow – and it's obviously more compact and quite a bit simpler than the other designs. With a little more work, I think it will allow for a good number of news stories of varying length, with a couple of different layouts. I will also borrow the 'related link' idea from the first design. The basic wire frame graphics will also keep the movie small as far as downloads go, and will assure that the reader is focused on the story and not the interface.

The final design may change, but having a sketch like this to go by takes some of the pressure off designing on the fly. It's also a good idea, at this point, to ensure that there's room in the design for all of the information and functionality that will be needed on the page. At this stage, *all* aspects of your design are subject to change, so trying to keep it as flexible as possible is also a good idea.

Information Architecture and Data Modeling

There are a few different definitions of the concepts of **information architecture** and **data modeling**, but for the purposes of this chapter, they mean pretty much the same thing: how you organize your data.

More specifically, however, data modeling deals with the relationships between different pieces of data, and reaching an understanding of what information is 'contained by' or 'belongs to' other information. These concepts are very helpful when preparing an outline, or schema, for an XML document. A well thought out data model will ensure that you have little or no redundancy in your data. It will also help when it comes to making sure that your data is portable to other applications, sites, or media types.

The data model for this project is made up of several items, but it's fairly easy to identify that the main 'container' is the *Site News*. Within the Site News there can be any number of *Individual Stories*, themselves containers for all of the information necessary to display a single story. For the sake of simplicity, I have limited the items within an Individual Story to:

- One *Head* (the main title of the story). This is made up of text.

- One *Sub* (the sub-head or teaser). This is also made up of text.

- One *Body* (the main bulk of the story). Also text.

In addition to the text information for the story, we will have:

- An optional *Image* (a SWF file containing an image or animation pertaining to the story). The image needs to be defined by its location, which will be the path to the actual SWF file.

- An optional *Link* (a link to another web page that is related to this story). The link has three possible data items within it: a *Target* (the frame or browser window in which to display the link), a *URL* (the actual address of the link page), and a bit of text to describe the link (used as a rollover for the link).

The following diagram then illustrates the data model for this project:

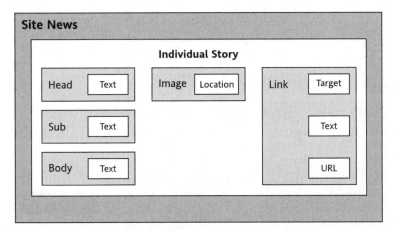

Seeing how these pieces of data are related should help you to conceptualize how the data should be organized. This may seem like overkill for something relatively simple like this, but the logic carries through to more complex data models. The better thought out your data model, the more accurate and effective your information architecture will be.

> *The usefulness of data modeling extends beyond the representation of information. Programmers use data modeling to help them figure out complex object-oriented problems, using a language called UML – the Unified Modeling Language.*

Information architecture has to do with how the data is placed in context and displayed to the viewer. As with data modeling, you may think that you can get away without considering this, but it's a very important part of your site. Good architecture ensures that your users don't become confused or lost within the information you're trying to relay. If you consider the pattern that your information follows, and decide upon the best way to group it visually, you're well on your way. The final definition can come in the form of a diagram, or a written specification – and with it, the necessary interface elements and screens you may need to display your information will become apparent.

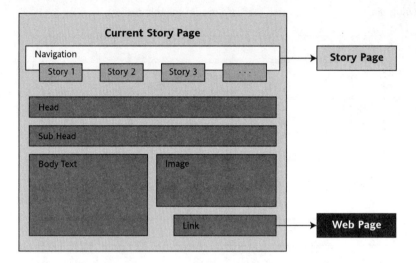

You may be wondering why the data model diagram and the information architecture diagram are so similar and, if they are indeed so similar, why we need both of them. The difference is that the data model will be transparent to the user, while the information architecture will be what the user comes in contact with. Another way to look at it is that the data model can be applied to any number of information architectures – the one shown above is just the one that happens to match our design concept, so why fight it? We can organize the way the user interacts with our data in various ways; this just happens to be the way I thought would be most user-friendly.

Do be aware that although I'm showing these concepts as graphics, and relating them specifically to our chosen design, I'm doing that simply to illustrate a point – the point being that you can look at data in ways that appeal to you or your clients. One of the beauties of using XML is its portability: the data, if well modeled, is not in any way tied to a specific design or medium. Our architecture is just a bit of logic that we can apply to *any* design that needs to display data in this manner. The data model, information architecture, and final design all work independently of each other, but in unison.

> *If you like, you can picture the data model as being the XML, and the information architecture as how we intend to have Flash display the XML data.*

At this point in a project, you might want to review or refine your design sketch, but here we're basically done: we have a detailed idea of the information we'll be displaying, and how we want to present it. Now we can start getting down to the business of assembling an XML file, and accessing and displaying that information from within Flash.

ting and Editing the XML File

Here's a skeleton XML document that's based on the data model I defined in the previous section, containing just one, empty, story. You should now be able to see clearly how the data model translates into XML. Keep in mind that within the <NEWS> element, you can have any number of stories.

```
<NEWS>
  <STORY>
    <HEAD></HEAD>
    <SUBHEAD></SUBHEAD>
    <BODY></BODY>
    <IMAGE></IMAGE>
    <LINK URL="" TARGET=""></LINK>
  </STORY>
</NEWS>
```

The next bit of code will show what this skeleton might look like when fleshed out. This is our XML document (news.xml), complete with all of the data that we will be using in this example. Keep in mind that although we're applying this XML to our specific information architecture and design, we *could* push this data through any XML-based interface, design, or platform.

```
<NEWS>
  <STORY>
    <HEAD>GAME LAUNCH : 10.26.00</HEAD>
    <SUBHEAD>Arrid-XX Stress Blocker </SUBHEAD>

    <BODY><![CDATA[The <a href='http://www.Arrid.com/'
target='_blank'><font color='#CC6600'>Arrid-XX</font></a>
Stress Blocker Game, created for
<a>href='http://www.MarketSource.com/'
target='_blank'><font color='#CC6600'>Market Source
Interactive</font></a> and their client <a
href='http://www.Arrid.com/' target='_blank'><font
color='#CC6600'>Carter Wallace</font></a>, combines classic and
modern elements of action puzzle games. The game is one in a
series of Shockwave games that keeps them coming back for
more.]]></BODY>
    <IMAGE>n_img_asb.swf</IMAGE>
    <LINK url="http://www.jrvisuals.com/j3_seg/PageView.cfm?pageID
      ➡=game&pageNum=2" target="_self">SEE MORE GAMES!</LINK>

  </STORY>

  <STORY>
    <HEAD>NEW GAME DEVELOPMENT</HEAD>
    <SUBHEAD>MatchCaixa Puzzler</SUBHEAD>
```

```
    <BODY><![CDATA[An original game created by <b>JRVisuals</b>
    and conceptualized in part by award winning designer <b>Terje
    Vist</b>. Match the patterns on a 3D grid, beat the clock,
    beat your friends, build and save new patterns to the web
    database for an endless number of challenges!]]></BODY>
      <IMAGE>n_img_caixa.swf</IMAGE>
      <LINK url="http://matchCaixa.cncdsl.com" target="_blank">VISIT
  ➡  THE DEVELOPMENT SITE</LINK>

    </STORY>

    <STORY>
      <HEAD>COMEDY CENTRAL SHOCKWAVE</HEAD>
      <SUBHEAD>Gotta Get Game?</SUBHEAD>

    <BODY><![CDATA[<b>JRVisuals</b> teamed up with <b>Insight
    Interactive Group</b> to program a series of games for <a
    href='http://www.ComedyCentral.com/' target='_blank'><font
    color='#CC6600'>Comedy Central's</font></a> Indecision 2000 and
    SouthPark mini-sites. The results were the highly acclaimed
    Slander Studio, Campaign Trail, and our personal favorite South
    Park Dodge Ball. These games combine the latest in
    <b>Macromedia Shockwave and FLASH</b> technologies to create a
    truly engaging interactive experience.]]></BODY>
      <IMAGE></IMAGE>
      <LINK url="http://www.jrvisuals.com/j3_seg/PageView.cfm?pageID
  ➡  =game&pageNum=2" target="_self">SEE MORE GAMES!</LINK>

    </STORY>

    <STORY>
      <HEAD>CLONE ME : 02.01.01</HEAD>
      <SUBHEAD>Human cloning is now...</SUBHEAD>

    <BODY><![CDATA[ Human cloning is now more than just a
    possibility. The first in a series of <b>Flash-Enhanced</b>
    collages explore the how the media and the general public cope
    when faced with the dissolution of an era.]]></BODY>
      <IMAGE>n_img_clone.swf</IMAGE>
      <LINK url="http://www.JRVisuals.com/j3_seg/PageView.cfm?pageID
  ➡  =here&amp;pageNum=2" target="_self">GO TO 'HERE NOW'</LINK>

    </STORY>
  </NEWS>
```

Once I'd written this file, I saved it in my working directory. (In order to keep the file structure simple, I'll be keeping all of the files in the same directory.) You can look at the finished version of this file (also called `news.xml`), which will contain a few more news stories, in the code that accompanies this chapter, downloadable from the friends of ED web site.

If we want to change the information that's displayed by Flash, we simply open this file in our text or HTML editor, and make the edits. To add a new story, we just set up another <STORY> element. The best way of doing this is just to copy and paste from another story block, and then edit the content and attributes to reflect what you want Flash to display.

Also keep in mind that although our structure and data model contain certain elements, our final data may not *require* all of these elements. For example, a news story may not have an image component, or there may be no related link for a particular item. In this case, the element can either be inserted but left empty, or omitted completely. Our code should be able to adjust accordingly – at the very least, it shouldn't be harmed by this turn of events.

There is one aspect of this XML code that may be of particular interest:

```
<BODY><![CDATA[ Human cloning is now more than just a
possibility. The first in a series of <b>Flash-Enhanced</b>
collages explore the how the media and the general public cope
when faced with the dissolution of an era.]]></BODY>
```

All of the <BODY> elements, of which this is simply the shortest, contain some regular HTML code. This particular element just has a pair of <b></b> tags, but in the others you can see things like <font> and <a> being used as well. In order for Flash to understand that this is HTML code that will be used to format the text (when placed in a dynamic HTML text box), we've had to frame the code within the following construct:

```
<![CDATA[ YOUR HTML FORMATTED TEXT HERE ]]>
```

This CDATA statement is very important, since it tells the Flash XML parser that the tags it contains are not to be treated as XML tags, but as nothing more than text.

The following HTML tags are supported by Flash (with optional tag attributes in brackets):

```
<A HREF='URL' >
<B>
<FONT [COLOR='#xxxxxx'] [FACE='Type Face'] [SIZE='Type Size']>
<I>
<P [ALIGN='LEFT'|'RIGHT'|'CENTER'] >
<U>
```

Keep in mind that you should use single quotes and not double quotes when specifying values for attributes within HTML tags. Using double quotes will confuse Flash.

Having HTML formatted text within your XML data is a great way to enhance the look of your final news application. You can add inline links, or change the color, size, and formatting of your text, all by using simple, familiar syntax. At the end of this chapter, in the resource list, there are a couple of links that will give you more information about using HTML within Flash.

Reading the XML File

At this point, you're probably starting to wonder when we'll start talking about the actual ActionScript code that will make this movie work. We'll get there in this very section!

Maybe you have a Flash movie built already, just waiting for some nice data? Or maybe you're familiar enough with Flash that you don't need the basics of this movie? If you're ready to get this XML file into Flash right away, we're going to go over the XML-specific ActionScript first. Later, in the overview section, I'll do a walkthrough of the movie, and touch upon all of the other components.

The Strategy

My basic strategy for handling the XML data is as follows:

- Initialize and prepare all of the variables that we will need in the global namespace.

- Load the XML file into Flash.

- Define the main set of XML functions that will be used throughout the movie.

- Wait for the XML data to load completely.

- Parse the data we want into a set of arrays. These arrays are kept in the global namespace to allow them to be read from within any other movie clip.

- Build the dynamic interface elements to suit the number of stories.

- Use the data in our arrays to display the story.

Organizing the Movie

The first thing you should know is that there's a scene in this movie that's placed before the main scene that does all of the above. The *first* scene of this movie (s_PreLoader) does nothing but preload all of the graphics information for the second scene (s_Main). All of the real action takes place in this second scene.

For organizational reasons, I put all of the XML-specific ActionScript code in a layer called > XML Actions. There's also a layer called > LABELS that holds all of the different keyframe labels that effectively divide the scene into its main areas.

The first label, INIT/FUNCTIONS, is arguably the most important. The ActionScript at this key frame initializes all the necessary variables and functions. It also creates the initial XML object global reference that will be used throughout this movie. The labels following INIT are discussed later in this section, so let's start looking at the code.

About the Code

If you look at the code from the web site and compare it with the listings below, you'll see a few small differences: for ease of reading, I removed some of the comments from this printed version. The companion source code is commented practically line-by-line, which (hopefully) will help you if you decide to re-purpose it for your own project. It would be a good idea to have these files available, and open, as you step through this chapter.

XML ActionScript Part 1: Initializing the variables and loading the file

First things first: before we begin loading the XML file, I want to define the variables that we will be using in this movie. Most important to this portion of the deconstruction are `timeout`, which will be used to judge if and when the XML file has taken too long to load; `txt_XMLstatus`, which is a dynamic textbox that will be used to display the status of the XML file (and any errors that may occur); and `XMLfilename`, which is a variable that holds the filename and path to our desired XML data file. The remainder of the variables will be discussed later on and have a variety of uses in our project.

```
// Initialize Global Variables

    // Initialize the Story Counters
    var tStoryCount = 0;
    var tCurrentStory = 0;

    // Initialize an Empty Array in which to store the stories.
    var aStories = new Array();

    // Initialize Story Index
    var tStoryIndex = 0;

    // Initialize Layout Frame
    var layoutFrame = 1;

    // Initialize TimeOut Variables; Time Out after 15 Seconds
    var timeOut = getTimer() + 15000;

    // Clear the XML Status Text Field
    var txt_XMLstatus = "";

    // Initialize XML File Name Variable
    var XMLfileName = "news.xml";
```

As you saw in Chapter 13, the first thing you have to do when working with the XML object in Flash is to initialize the variable that will contain the instance of the object. With that goal in mind, I placed the following code at the first frame (INIT/FUNCTIONS) of this scene (s_Main), in the > XML Actions layer:

```
// Create Initial Global XML Object Instance and Load it Up
var XMLobj = new XML();
```

```
XMLobj.load(XMLfileName);

// Display Loading Status
txt_XMLstatus = "Loading data from <font color='#CC6600'>" +
                XMLfileName + "</font>.";
```

To keep things simple, I named the XML object instance XMLobj. The second line then tells the object instance that it should load the XML data from a file called news.xml; this is the file that we created in the previous section, and whose location is defined in the variable XMLfileName.

Immediately after beginning to load the XML file, I display a message in the XML status text box that will let you and your users know that the loading process is progressing. Notice once again the use of HTML tags to format the text.

Similar to a standard Flash pre-loader, we now have to wait until the XML file is completely loaded. At the frame labeled WAIT, there is the following ActionScript:

```
// Check for Loaded XML
if (XMLobj.loaded) {

    <logic to be discussed in a moment>

}

// Check for Time Out
if (getTimer() > timeOut) {
    txt_XMLstatus = "XML Load Timed Out";
    gotoAndPlay("ERROR");
}
```

In the frame immediately after this one, I placed this code:

```
// Loop While Loading XML
gotoAndPlay ("WAIT");
```

In essence, the combination of these two frames of ActionScript keeps the movie looping between the WAIT frame and the subsequent frame while the XML file loads. If you're running the movie from your local folder, this will likely happen almost immediately, but it may take a second or two when access is taking place online.

Before we get into the logic, it's worth mentioning that the txt_XMLstatus variable refers to a text box on the screen. This will give the viewer some feedback, just in case it does take a while to load the XML file. (The project also features a layer called Blip that contains a small gray square in the WAIT frame, but not in the one after it. This will cause the square to blink on and off as the file loads.)

Here, now, is that first conditional statement in full:

```
if (XMLobj.loaded) {
```

```
// Initialize local variables
var XMLstatusList = new Array();

// Populate the Error Array
XMLstatusList = errorCheck(XMLobj);

// Display XML Status
txt_XMLstatus = XMLstatusList[1];

// Make sure there were no Errors Loading XML
if (XMLstatusList[0] == 0) {
    gotoAndPlay("DONE");
} else {
    gotoAndPlay("ERROR");
}
}
```

Getting down to business, the statement begins by checking to see if the loaded property of our XMLobj is true. If the XML document has *not* completely loaded, its value will be false, and the code will continue straight to the next frame – which will loop straight back to check the value of XMLobj.loaded once more.

When the value of loaded *is* true, the code will execute a function that I've defined called errorCheck. If this function finds no errors, the movie will jump to the frame labeled DONE. If there *are* errors, they will be displayed in the txt_XMLstatus text box, and the movie will jump to the frame labeled ERROR.

Here's the code for the errorCheck function, which can be found in the ActionScript located at the first frame.

```
function errorCheck(tOBJ) {

    // Init local variables
    var XMLstatusNumber = tOBJ.status;
    var XMLstatusDescript = "";
    var responseList= new Array();

    if (XMLstatusNumber == 0)
        { XMLstatusDescript = "XML Data Loaded."; }

    if (XMLstatusNumber == -2)
        { XMLstatusDescript = "Termination Error in CDATA."; }

    if (XMLstatusNumber == -3)
        { XMLstatusDescript = "Termination Error in DECLARATION.";
}

    if (XMLstatusNumber == -4)
        { XMLstatusDescript = "Termination Error in DOCTYPE."; }
```

```
if (XMLstatusNumber == -5)
    { XMLstatusDescript = "Termination Error in COMMENT."; }

if (XMLstatusNumber == -6)
    { XMLstatusDescript = "Malformed Error in XML."; }

if (XMLstatusNumber == -7)
    { XMLstatusDescript = "Out of memory Error."; }

if (XMLstatusNumber == -8)
    { XMLstatusDescript = "Termination Error in ATTRIBUTE."; }

if (XMLstatusNumber == -9)
    { XMLstatusDescript = "Error in START/END tag."; }

if (XMLstatusNumber == -10)
    { XMLstatusDescript = "Error in END/START tag."; }

responseList = [XMLstatusNumber, XMLstatusDescript];
return responseList;
}
```

The errorCheck function accepts a parameter called tOBJ, which will be an instance of the XML object. The status property of this object will contain zero if there is no error, or a numeric value that correlates to an error message. The set of if statements perform the task of mapping the numeric value to a text message (the values being tested come straight from the Flash documentation), and then the appropriate message is returned from the function – both the numeric and text values are returned in an array.

The ActionScript in the WAIT frame checks to see if the numeric value is anything other than a zero (which would indicate that the data was loaded successfully), and places the text message in the txt_XMLstatus text box.

The location of this message is highlighted in the following diagram of our final movie as area seven (7). You'll see more of this diagram further on in the chapter, when we discuss the layout of the movie.

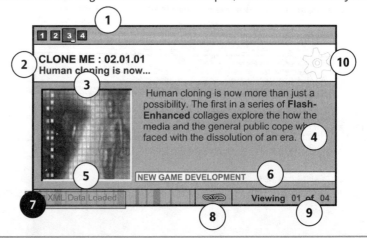

You may also have noticed that last bit of code at the bottom of the script on the WAIT frame:

```
// Check for Time Out
if (getTimer() > timeOut) {
    txt_XMLstatus = "XML Load Timed Out";
    gotoAndPlay("ERROR");
}
```

This code handles the possibility that the XML data is never loaded, due to a server error, an error in the path to the XML file, or some other reason. One of the variables initialized in the first frame of this scene was `timeOut`, which contains a number based on the time when the loading of the XML file was first attempted, plus 15 seconds. I figured that if the file has not been read within 15 seconds, there was probably an error and the ERROR frame should be called. This is a sample error screen:

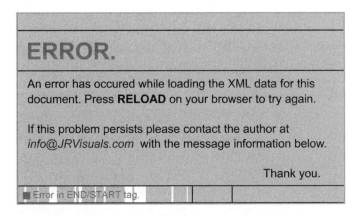

At this point, we have successfully loaded the XML data into `XMLobj`. The next step is to take this data and get it into a format that can be more readily used by our movie. If we wanted to, we could pull the data straight out of `XMLobj` as and when we required it, but as you'll see in the next section, it makes much more sense to put all the data we need into a neat little **array**. This occurs in the frame labeled DONE.

XML ActionScript Part 2: Parsing the data

Using the data in `XMLobj`, we're now going to build a multidimensional array that contains all of the information we'll need to display each of the news stories in our XML document. Later, we'll use the data stored in this array to lay out and populate the pages of our movie.

As mentioned earlier, after the XML data has been successfully read in, the movie jumps to the frame labeled DONE. The ActionScript code in this frame looks like this:

```
// Call Function to Build Story Data Arrays
buildStoryText(XMLobj);
```

Once again, we're passing our XML object as an argument to a function – `buildStoryText` – that was defined in the ActionScript for the frame labeled INIT/FUNCTIONS. It looks like this:

```
function buildStoryText(tXMLobj) {

    // Initialize container for news data
    // Pull the first node's child nodes into a variable
    // The child nodes are all the stories and their nested nodes
    var aNews = tXMLobj.firstChild.childNodes;

    // Loop through news nodes (stories)
    var newsN = 0;
    for (newsN in aNews) {

        // Found a story
        if ((aNews[newsN].nodeName) == "STORY") {

            var aStory = aNews[newsN].childNodes;
            var aStoryData = new Array();

            // Loop through this story's child nodes
            var storyN = 0;
            for (storyN in aStory) {

                // Step Through Story Data
                // HEAD (cdata)
                if ((aStory[storyN].nodeName) == "HEAD") {
                    aStoryData[0]=(aStory[storyN].firstchild.
                    ➥nodeValue);
                }

                // SUBHEAD (cdata)
                if ((aStory[storyN].nodeName) == "SUBHEAD") {
                    aStoryData[1]=(aStory[storyN].firstchild.
                    ➥nodeValue);
                }

                // BODY (cdata)
                if ((aStory[storyN].nodeName) == "BODY") {
                    aStoryData[2]=(aStory[storyN].firstchild.
                    ➥nodeValue);
                }

                // IMAGE (cdata)
                if ((aStory[storyN].nodeName) == "IMAGE") {
                    aStoryData[3]=(aStory[storyN].firstchild.
                    ➥nodeValue);
                }

                // LINK
                if ((aStory[storyN].nodeName) == "LINK") {

                    // LINK (cdata)
```

```
            aStoryData[4]=(aStory[storyN].firstchild.
            ➡nodeValue);

            // URL (attribute)
            aStoryData[5]=(aStory[storyN].attributes.URL);

            // TARGET (attribute)
            aStoryData[6]=(aStory[storyN].attributes.TARGET);
         }

      } // End Loop (storyN)

      // Store the story data array in the stories array
      aStories[tStoryCount] = aStoryData;
      tStoryCount = tStoryCount + 1;

   } // End If (STORY)

   } // End Loop (newsN)

} // End Function (buildStoryText)
```

You can probably get a pretty good idea of what this code does just by looking at it, and the comments. Still, it's a sizable chunk of ActionScript, so let's look through it in a little more detail.

```
function buildStoryText(tXMLobj) {

   // Initialize container for news data
   // Pull the first node's child nodes into a variable
   // The child nodes are all the stories and their nested nodes
   var aNews = tXMLobj.firstChild.childNodes;
```

After declaring the function, the first thing we do is to create and set the variable aNews. The value placed in this variable is an array containing all the children of the first node of our XML data, and their nested nodes. We retrieve this data from the XML object by using the childNodes property of the firstChild property of the function's parameter, tXMLobj.

Another way of thinking about this that makes it easier to understand (for me, at least!) is to translate the periods in this line of code to "of the", and read the line backwards. So, aNews is set to the childNodes of the firstChild of the tXMLobj. In this scenario, tXMLobj.firstChild will always contain the main element, <NEWS>, and so the childNodes comprise all of the nodes within the <NEWS> element.

At this point, it's worth recalling some of the variables that we initialized at the beginning of this movie, in INIT/FUNCTIONS:

```
   // Initialize the Story Counters
   var tStoryCount = 0;
   var tCurrentStory = 0;
```

```
// Initialize an Empty Array in which to store the stories.
var aStories = new Array();
```

The first variable, tStoryCount, will keep track of exactly how many stories we find. The other 'counter' variable, tCurrentStory, will be used to track which story is actually being displayed. The last one, aStories, is an empty array that will eventually store all of the data in aNews, but in more structured fashion.

```
// Loop through news nodes (stories)
var newsN = 0;
for (newsN in aNews) {

    // Found a story
    if ((aNews[newsN].nodeName) == "STORY") {

        var aStory = aNews[newsN].childNodes;
        var aStoryData = new Array();
```

This loop will step through each element in the aNews array – that is, as I mentioned above, each child node of the <NEWS> element. The loop counter is stored in the variable newsN, and we'll use this as the index for searching through the array.

What we're searching *for* are <STORY> elements, and that's the purpose of the condition in the if statement above. It gets the nodeName of the newsNth element of the aNews array, and compares it with "STORY". If no match is found, the code loops back to the beginning and tries the next node, until it has been through all the elements in the array.

When a match is found – that is to say, we hit a <STORY> element – the code inside the if statement continues to execute. At this point, we *know* that newsN is the index of a <STORY> element, and we can set the aStory variable to an array containing the child nodes of *that* element. We also want to create another empty array container, aStoryData, to store all of the data contained in these child nodes (in other words, the children of the <STORY> element).

Similar to what we did with the aNews array, we're going to begin another loop, inside the first, that will step through all of the nodes in our new array, aStory. The counter for this loop is stored in the variable storyN.

```
// Loop through this story's child nodes
var storyN = 0;
for (storyN in aStory) {

    // Step Through Story Data
    // HEAD (cdata)
    if ((aStory[storyN].nodeName) == "HEAD") {
        aStoryData[0]=(aStory[storyN].firstchild.
        ➡nodeValue);
    }

    // SUBHEAD (cdata)
    if ((aStory[storyN].nodeName) == "SUBHEAD") {
```

```
        aStoryData[1]=(aStory[storyN].firstchild.
        ➥nodeValue);
    }

    // BODY (cdata)
    if ((aStory[storyN].nodeName) == "BODY") {
        aStoryData[2]=(aStory[storyN].firstchild.
        ➥nodeValue);
    }

    // IMAGE (cdata)
    if ((aStory[storyN].nodeName) == "IMAGE") {
        aStoryData[3]=(aStory[storyN].firstchild.
        ➥nodeValue);
    }

    // LINK
    if ((aStory[storyN].nodeName) == "LINK") {

        // LINK (cdata)
        aStoryData[4]=(aStory[storyN].firstchild.
        ➥nodeValue);

        // URL (attribute)
        aStoryData[5]=(aStory[storyN].attributes.URL);

        // TARGET (attribute)
        aStoryData[6]=(aStory[storyN].attributes.TARGET);
    }

} // End Loop (storyN)
```

These lines look for matches with the element names we expect to find in our XML file. As each match is made, the value or content of that element is stored at a specific position in the aStoryData array. The table at the end of this section describes the tags, their indexes, and their contents.

The extra processing that's required for <LINK> elements is down to the fact that these contain more than just text content – they also have attributes pertaining to the link that we also need to extract. For the sake of simplicity, we just add two more items to the same array as the others, and store this information there. Notice that accessing the element's attributes requires us to use a different technique – a node's attributes property has a unique property for each attribute contained within that node. In our XML document, the <LINK> element was written with a URL and a TARGET attribute.

At the end of this loop, we'll have stepped through all of the data available for the current story being parsed. You'll notice that I've placed a comment at the end of the loop; I try to do this as often as possible with nested loops, or loops that contain if-else statements. I find that it helps immensely when it comes to reading through code quickly and efficiently.

Right now, if our code has executed correctly, and our XML document had the information that the code was seeking, we have in `aStoryData` an array containing all of the data for *one* news story. For one of the stories in our sample XML document, the seven elements of this array would look something like this:

```
"CLONE ME : 02.01.01",
"Human cloning is now...",
"Human cloning is now more than just a possibility. The first in
a series of <b>Flash-Enhanced</b> collages explore the how the
media and the general public cope when faced with the
dissolution of an era.",
"n_img_clone.swf",
"GO TO 'HERE NOW'",
"http://www.JRVisuals.com/j3_seg/PageView.cfm?pageID=here&amp;
    ➡pageNum=2",
"_self"
```

The next step is to put this array into our array of stories, `aStories`, and this takes place in the first line of the code reproduced below. On the next line, we increment `tStoryCount` so that the next time the code loops through this section, the next set of story data will be placed at the next index in the `aStories` array.

```
        // Store the story data array in the stories array
        aStories[tStoryCount] = aStoryData;
        tStoryCount = tStoryCount + 1;

    } // End If (STORY)

  } // End Loop (newsN)

} // End Function (buildStoryText)
```

After we've looped through all of the `<STORY>` elements inside the `<NEWS>` element, the function will end, and we'll be left with an array, `aStories`, containing all of our story information. Each element of this array contains a 'sub-array', so the overall arrangement is something like this:

```
[
    [HEAD, SUBHEAD, BODY, IMAGE, LINK, URL, TARGET],
    [HEAD, SUBHEAD, BODY, IMAGE, LINK, URL, TARGET],
    [HEAD, SUBHEAD, BODY, IMAGE, LINK, URL, TARGET]
]
```

Here's another way to look at this (you may want to take another look at this table when we start pulling information from these arrays, later in the chapter):

XML Tag	Tag Content	Array Index	Description
`<HEAD>`	Text data	0	The story title.
`<SUBHEAD>`	Text data	1	A brief, or sub-title.

XML Tag	Tag Content	Array Index	Description
`<BODY>`	Text data	2	The main text of the story.
`<IMAGE>`	Text data	3	The name and/or path to a SWF to illustrate this story.
`<LINK>`	Text data	4	Tool tip text for a link related to this story.
`<LINK URL>`	Attribute	5	The URL of this link.
`<LINK TARGET>`	Attribute	6	A valid target for this link.

At this stage, we have everything we need, formatted in a way that we like, to build all of the pages of the movie. Our XML data has now been fully parsed.

Laying Out the Scene Part 1: The layers and the library

I'm going to take a break from the code right now, and go over how and why I laid the scene out in the way I did. Inevitably, later in the discussion, we'll cover some ActionScript that's instrumental to how the data will be placed into the scene. Let's take it from the top, and look at the layers and library items in this movie.

The following screenshot shows the layers and labels used in the movie's main scene (we'll look at the preload scene on its own, in the next section).

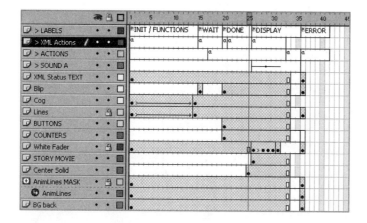

I like to use conventions in the layout and naming of my scenes, symbols, and library folders. I won't lie to you and say that I do it in exactly the same way for every project, but the more complex the movie, the more tightly I stick to them. The most important, in my opinion, is to have separate layers for labels, actions, and sounds. I start almost every movie by putting these layers in place – and to make absolutely sure that they stand out, I capitalize their names, prefix them with the > character, and keep them at the top of the scene.

On this occasion, since we have a set of actions and functions that are XML specific, I made another layer that holds all of the ActionScript of this type. On other occasions, I might make a separate layer that contains only functions. If frame labels begin to overlap, causing their names to be illegible, I add a second label layer and alternate the placement of labels so that they can all be seen clearly.

Another thing you'll notice here is that some layer names are written in capital letters. This helps me quickly distinguish between layer types and contents. The capitalized layers contain movie clips that I will likely edit more often, due to the intricate nature of their contents. Again, this is not necessary, but I find that it helps a great deal if you end up with more than about ten layers.

The following two screenshots show the Library used in this movie with all the folders open, and then all the folders closed, to show how tidy it is:

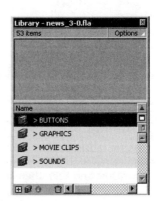

Here, you can see how I decided to organize my folders for this project. I usually break up the folders either by asset type, as I did here, or by component. (An example of the latter is the LINE MOVIE folder that you can see inside the > MOVIE CLIPS folder; this contains assets of all types that were used in the creation of the m_LINES movie clip.) As always, the purpose behind these folders stems from ease of use and ease of updating – it can be very difficult to find one symbol among hundreds, especially if they have the automatic names that Flash gives to them.

Another level of organization that should be apparent within the Library is my prefixing of asset types with an identifier. All movie clip symbols begin with m_, all graphic symbols begin with g_, and all button symbols begin with b_. As with the other guidelines in this section, using a convention like this is entirely at your discretion – but if you have multiple asset types in one folder, giving them these prefixes will sort them automatically, since they are displayed in alphabetical order by default.

Laying Out the Scene Part 2: The pre-load scene

As I mentioned earlier, we have two scenes in this movie. The first scene (s_PreLoader) is just a pre-loader, pure and simple. It makes sure that all of the graphics and text in the main movie have been downloaded to the client before the second scene (s_Main) is shown.

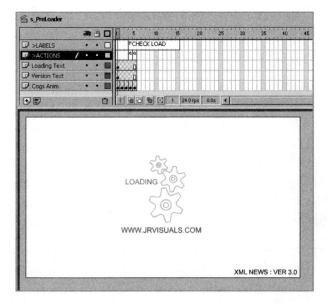

The layer labeled >ACTIONS does all of the work in this scene. The other layers contain animated and graphic elements that serve both as a distraction, and as an indication that the movie is doing *something*.

The frame labeled CHECK LOAD contains the following code, which simply uses the ifFrameLoaded action to see if the last possible frame of the scene s_Main is available locally, and therefore ready to be displayed.

```
// Check to see if all of the scene s_Main has been loaded.
ifFrameLoaded ("s_Main", 100) {
    gotoAndPlay ("s_Main", 1);
}
```

The frame immediately following this one sends the playback head back to the beginning of this scene and cycles through the sequence again. If the last frame had indeed been loaded, the movie will jump to the first frame of the scene s_Main. Although the last frame of s_Main isn't actually frame 100, Flash doesn't mind this, and just checks against the last frame with any content.

Laying Out the Scene Part 3: The main scene

The second scene in this movie, s_Main, contains everything else that's needed to make the movie work. As you saw earlier, when we discussed my tactics for organizing layers and the Library, it contains a number of ActionScript routines for handling the XML. Inevitably, it also has layers that contain the interface graphics, design elements, animations, masks, and sounds.

We have already covered the first chunk of functionality: the reading and parsing of the XML data. This occurs in the first 15 frames, between the labels INIT/FUNCTIONS and WAIT. We also discussed the function (buildStoryText) that's called from the frame labeled DONE and stores our XML data into the array aStories.

Before I detail the layers and contents of the remainder of the movie, I want to take a quick run through the last couple of ActionScript keyframes. We should also take another quick look at what a sample screen of the finished movie will look like. This will help us orient ourselves through what may be a tricky section of the chapter.

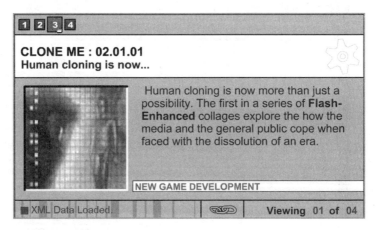

The frame immediately following DONE takes care of building our interface, which consists of a series of numbered buttons at the top of our movie that will link the user to each of the stories available at the time. It also deals with the 'related link' button at the bottom center of the movie. This is what the code looks like.

```
// Call function to create additional story buttons
// within movie clip "button host" (i_HOST)
buildButtonHost();
```

I will detail the `buildButtonHost` function a little later on.

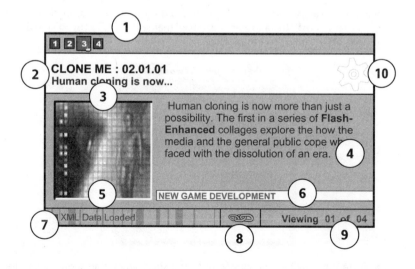

After the DONE frame, the playhead continues to DISPLAY, at which point the following code is executed.

```
// Call function to display current story
displayStory (tStoryIndex);

// Send STORY MOVIE to the current layout frame
i_STORY.gotoAndPlay(layoutFrame);
```

This basically populates all of the text fields, loads the image movie (if there is one) for this story, and tells the movie clip responsible for displaying the current layout to jump to the appropriate frame. This movie clip, named m_STORY, is in the layer labeled STORY MOVIE. Its instance is named i_STORY. After this, the playhead hits a `stop` action that has the movie wait in place until the user presses another story display button. I will also detail these functions later in this section.

The final label in this movie is ERROR, to which the movie jumps if there is a problem with the XML file. You'll probably remember this from earlier in the chapter, where the XML file load took place.

Now that we're aware of what's left ahead of us, let's define the areas of the movie, and break down the layers, movie clips, and actions responsible for what we see.

In this diagram, the interface areas of the movie are numbered according, more or less, to their positions on the screen. I've discussed some of them before, but going over them again in this way should aid your understanding of how the different areas interact with each other to create what looks like a complex scene layout

Area number one (1) in this diagram is the main user interface for the movie. These buttons, one for each story available, are created dynamically, based on the XML data in our arrays. As I mentioned earlier, the `buildButtonHost` function that was called in the frame immediately following DONE handles this. I should now tell you that most of the action pertaining to the creation of the buttons takes place is the layer named BUTTONS, which contains an instance (named i_HOST) of a movie clip called m_ButtonHost:

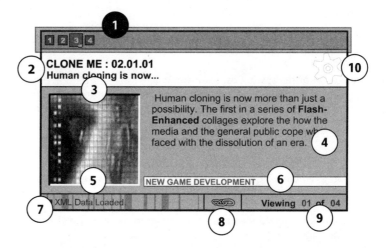

Let's take a look at how the `buildButtonHost` function uses i_HOST to build our interface. This movie clip is actually host to another instance (named i_BUT) of a movie clip called m_ButtonBase. The latter looks something like this.

As you can see from the timeline, the clip comprises a short animation sequence, followed by an action. The animation sequence basically pops the square outline of the button onto the screen, while the action stops the playback head. The last frame of this sequence contains a Flash button (b_BUT-1), while the element in the layer named Number is a dynamic text box named tButtonDisplay, set to the number one as a default value. Via its parent clip, this button will be duplicated a number of times, and each will have a unique number assigned to it. This number will be displayed in tButtonDisplay, used by the button to display its rollover text, and to execute the link to its related news story.

The buildButtonHost function takes this set of clips within clips (also known as 'nested' clips) and makes as many copies as are needed to deal with all the stories in the XML file. Let's take a closer look at this code.

```
function buildButtonHost() {

    // Set the first story button values
    i_HOST.i_BUT.tButtonIndex = 0;
    i_HOST.i_BUT.tButtonDisplay = 1;

    // Loop through stories
    for (var i = 1; i < aStories.length; i++) {

        // Create next story button
        duplicateMovieClip(i_HOST.i_BUT, "i_BUT" + i, i + 1);

        // Build dynamic target
        var tTarg = "i_BUT" + i;

        // Calculate gap between buttons
        var tGap = i * 15;

        // Set the first story button values
        i_HOST[tTarg]._x = tGap;              // Set gap
        i_HOST[tTarg].tButtonIndex = i;       // Set index
        i_HOST[tTarg].tButtonDisplay = i + 1; // Set display
    }
}
```

The first two lines of code set the default values for two variables contained within the nested button clip. tButtonIndex will be the array index value for the story associated with this button, and tButtonDisplay will be the number shown on the actual button.

```
function buildButtonHost() {

    // Set the first story button values
    i_HOST.i_BUT.tButtonIndex = 0;
    i_HOST.i_BUT.tButtonDisplay = 1;
```

Now we begin to loop through the stories, creating a button for each using the built-in duplicateMovieClip function. As you see, we are naming each new button using the loop counter, i. As the code loops, this index will be incremented by one, until it reaches the desired number of buttons.

```
// Loop through stories
for (var i = 1; i < aStories.length; i++) {

    // Create next story button
    duplicateMovieClip(i_HOST.i_BUT, "i_BUT" + i, i + 1);
```

In order to set the properties and variable values of this newly created button, we have to use its target name. The way I chose to address this issue was to build a string containing the path to the button most recently generated, and place it in a variable, tTarg.

```
    // Build dynamic target
    var tTarg = "i_BUT" + i;
```

The first thing we're going to want to do is space these buttons out. If we created duplicates without changing each button's _x property, they would be sitting on top of each other, and therefore useless. I calculated that 15 pixels per button would do the job, and produced the following:

```
    // Calculate gap between buttons
    var tGap = i * 15;
```

All we have left to do is set the properties. First, we set the horizontal location of the current button. Next, we set the button index, tButtonIndex – this is the variable that will be used by the on (release) mouse event in order to judge which story to display next. Finally, we set the value of the dynamic text field that exists over the button itself.

```
    // Set the first story button values
    i_HOST[tTarg]._x = tGap;                    // Set gap
    i_HOST[tTarg].tButtonIndex = i;             // Set index
    i_HOST[tTarg].tButtonDisplay = i + 1;       // Set display
    }
}
```

After this code is executed, we will have all of the buttons necessary to display each and every story in our original XML file. Each of the buttons has the following code attached to it:

```
// Handle ToolTip Text and Animation
on (rollOver) {
    if (_root.myToolTip(tButtonIndex) != "") {
        _root.i_STORY.i_TIP.txt_ToolTip =
                            _root.myToolTip(tButtonIndex);
        _root.i_STORY.i_TIP.gotoAndPlay("SHOW");
    }
}

on (press, release) {
    if (_root.myToolTip(tButtonIndex) != "") {
        _root.i_STORY.i_TIP.txt_ToolTip =
```

```
        _root.myToolTip(tButtonIndex);
        _root.i_STORY.i_TIP.gotoAndStop("ON");
    }
}

on (rollOut, releaseOutside) {
    _root.i_STORY.i_TIP.txt_ToolTip = "";
    _root.i_STORY.i_TIP.gotoAndStop("HIDE");
}

// Handle button click
on (release) {
    _root.tStoryIndex = tButtonIndex;
    _root.i_STORY.gotoAndStop("MT");
    _root.gotoAndPlay("DISPLAY");
}
```

These are pretty familiar functions. Before we discuss the rollOver and rollOut, let's look at the release handler. The first thing it does is to set the tStoryIndex variable at the root of the movie to the value stored in this button's tButtonIndex. This will make sure that the main timeline is aware of what story will be displayed next. The next line tells our story display movie clip (i_STORY) to sit and wait at an empty (MT) frame. (More on this clip coming up soon!). The last line of the release handler sends the main timeline back to the DISPLAY frame that, as I mentioned earlier, takes care of populating the screen with the elements of the news story at hand.

The other handlers here deal with displaying and removing the text that will tell the user the title of the news story that they would see, were they to click on the button. This takes place in the area of the movie numbered six (6) in our diagram, which I've called the 'tooltip'. The tooltip movie clip is named m_CurrToolTip, its instance is named i_TIP, and it sits in one of the layers of the movie clip instance i_STORY.

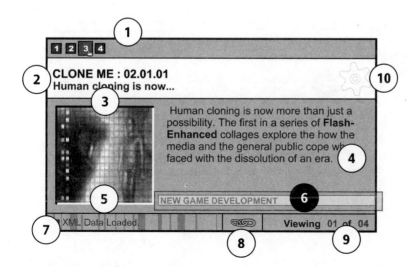

You've probably noticed that this bit of code is used in a couple of places:

```
if (_root.myToolTip(tButtonIndex) != "") {
```

This makes sure that there actually is some tooltip information to display. The `myToolTip` function is located at the root of this movie, and accepts a numeric parameter that identifies which story we're talking about. It then looks in our data array, and returns the text (if any exists) for the title of story identified by the index passed to it. This is the code for `myToolTip`:

```
// Return ToolTip (TITLE) for Story Button
function myToolTip (tIndex) {
    return aStories[tIndex][0];
}
```

In the case of `on (rollOver)`, the dynamic text field `txt_ToolTip` is populated with the value returned, and the tooltip movie clip is sent to a frame labeled SHOW, which actually animates the tooltip onto the screen.

In the case of the `on (press, release)` handler, the dynamic text field `txt_ToolTip` is populated with the value returned, and the tooltip movie clip is sent to a frame labeled ON, which displays the tooltip without animating it.

In the case of `on (rollOut, releaseOutside)`, the dynamic text field `txt_ToolTip` is cleared out, and the tooltip movie clip is sent to a frame labeled HIDE, which takes the tooltip off the visible area of the screen. This way, when the user moves the mouse off the button, the tooltip will not stay on the screen.

Remember, all of this functionality is given to each of the buttons created. The only difference between them is the number that's displayed on the actual button, and the number that's passed around as the story index.

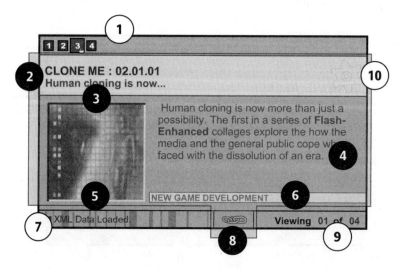

We've already mentioned the clip instance i_STORY several times. The areas of our diagram numbered two thru six, and eight, (2, 3, 4, 5, 6, 8) are all contained in the movie clip m_STORY. This sits on the main timeline, in the layer named STORY MOVIE. The displayStory function takes the current tStoryIndex as an argument, and populates all of these areas accordingly. (tStoryIndex, you may recall, is set when one of the interface buttons in area one is clicked.)

If we edit i_STORY in place, and keep the related numbers from our diagram as an overlay, it would look something like this.

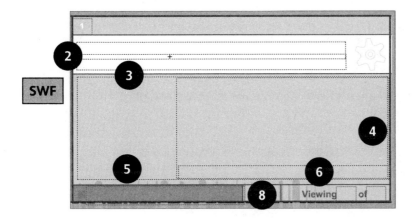

The following is a list of the layers, the movie clips, their instance names within this movie clip, and the XML elements from which they will get their values. It should be a helpful refresher.

Layer	Movie Clip	Instance	Text Box Var.	XML Element
HEAD	m_CurrHEAD	i_HEAD	txt_StoryTitle	<HEAD>
SUBHEAD	m_CurrSUBHEAD	i_SUBHEAD	txt_StoryBrief	<SUBHEAD>
BODY	m_CurrBODY	i_BODY	txt_StoryBody	<BODY>
BODY (text only)	m_CurrBODY (text only)	i_BODYTXT	txt_StoryBody	<BODY>
TOOLTIP	m_CurrTIP	i_TIP	txt_ToolTip	<HEAD>/<LINK>

Notice that the naming conventions are kept (more or less) consistent to each other, and to the element names in our XML document. This is a very important practice: it will save you time and confusion when you're trying to write and debug your ActionScript code.

Now we'll look at displayStory and how it affects each of these areas.

```
function displayStory (tStoryIndex) {

    // Display Current Story
    // Text Bits
    i_STORY.i_HEAD.txt_StoryTitle = aStories[tStoryIndex][0];
    i_STORY.i_SUBHEAD.txt_StoryBrief = aStories[tStoryIndex][1];
```

Keep in mind that this function is being called from the root of the movie and is placed in the first frame of this scene. Also note that each of the items in the movie clip m_STORY are nested within another movie clip. This allows for some flexibility should we later decide to animate or apply effects to these items.

Area number two (2) is where the story title, or head, is displayed. There is a dynamic text box named txt_StoryTitle, within a movie clip instanced as i_HEAD. This text box is populated with the story information in the first location of the array that's identified by aStories[tStoryIndex].

Area number three (3) is where the story teaser, or brief, is displayed. There is a dynamic text box named txt_StoryBrief, within a movie clip instanced as i_SUBHEAD. This text box is populated with the story information in the second location of the array that's identified by aStories[tStoryIndex].

Populating the next couple of areas is not as straightforward.

```
// SWF Image
if ((aStories[tStoryIndex][3]) != "") {
    loadMovie((aStories[tStoryIndex][3]), (i_STORY.i_IMAGE));
    i_STORY.i_BODY.txt_StoryBody = aStories[tStoryIndex][2];
    i_STORY.i_BODYTXT.txt_StoryBody = "";
    layoutFrame = "w_IMG";
```

The complexity comes from the fact that we're dealing with two possible layout scenarios here, based on whether we'll be displaying an image (actually, an external SWF). The path to the SWF file, if one exists, is stored in the fourth location in the story array, so our code checks to see if that location in the array contains anything other than an empty string.

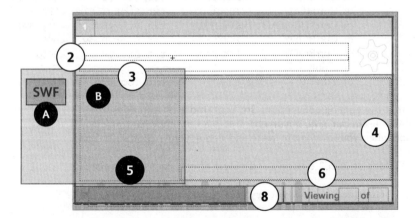

If a path or filename is found, the code continues by loading the external SWF file into our placeholder movie clip. This placeholder, instanced as i_IMAGE, contains nothing but a graphic indication that it is indeed a SWF placeholder. The diagram of area 5, above, indicates the location of this graphic as A.

Notice also the center point of this placeholder movie clip, indicated as B on the diagram of area 5. When the actual SWF is loaded in, its top left corner will land at that location. It took a bit of tweaking by hand to get it right, but this will guarantee that the SWF is positioned correctly. Using a SWF here allows us a great deal of flexibility. As long as we keep within the designated size (in the case of this layout, 100 by 100 pixels square) we can have anything that Flash can do in place of this image. Pretty powerful stuff!

After loading this external file, the dynamic text field in area number four (4) is populated – this is where the main story text, or body, is displayed. There is a dynamic text box named `txt_StoryBody`, within a movie clip instanced as `i_BODY`. This text box is populated with the story information in the third location of the array that's defined by `aStories[tStoryIndex]`.

The `layoutFrame` variable is also set to the particular frame label for this layout – in this case, `w_IMG`. The text box for the layout that's not being used is set to an empty string, so that nothing will be displayed in it.

In the event that there is no image component to this layout, the following code is executed:

```
        } else {
            i_STORY.i_BODYTXT.txt_StoryBody = aStories[tStoryIndex][2];
            i_STORY.i_BODY.txt_StoryBody = "";
            layoutFrame = "w_TXT"
        }
```

Area number four (4) is where the main story text, or body, is displayed. There's a dynamic text box named `txt_StoryBody`, within a movie clip instanced as `i_BODYTXT`. This text box is populated with the story information in the third location of the array that's defined by `aStories[tStoryIndex]`. `layoutFrame`, and the 'other' text box, are dealt with as before.

Notice that the dynamic text field is named the same in the case of both layouts – the difference is in the instance name of the movie clip that contains this text field. The other main difference is that the text box for the second layout covers the whole middle part of the movie. This is what the timeline for this movie clip looks like.

After seeing this, you should have a better idea of how the layouts work. Notice that the SWF image layer does not go out as far as the second layout, which is text only. Also notice the layer named blocker on the frame labeled MT. This is just a white box that hides all of our graphics and text boxes until a layout frame is called.

Getting back to the displayStory code, we were just on the verge of looking at the code for setting up the related link graphic and button in area eight (8):

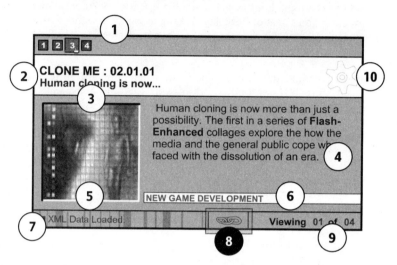

As with the image, the display of this link graphic is conditional on whether there actually is any content to display (or in this case, to link to):

```
// Related Link
// Display link button and graphic if there is a link.
if ((aStories[tStoryIndex][5]) != "") {
    i_STORY.i_LINK.gotoAndStop("LINK");
```

The link URL information is stored in the sixth location of the array that's defined by aStories[tStoryIndex]. If there *is* a URL to link to, our code tells the movie clip instanced as i_LINK to display the frame labeled LINK. This frame contains the button and the animated graphic for our link.

In the event that there's *no* link URL information, we don't want to display a link graphic or button, so our code tells the movie clip instanced as i_LINK to display the empty frame (MT):

```
} else {
    i_STORY.i_LINK.gotoAndStop("MT");
}
```

We've just got time for a quick look at how this related link movie works. This is what it looks like edited in place.

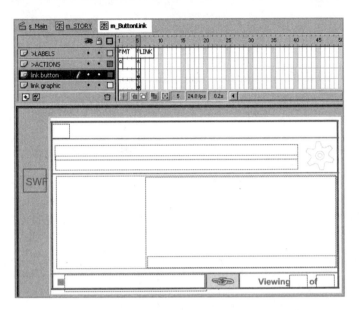

You can see the two labels and the link button, each on their own layer. The link graphic is just a simple animated movie clip of the links spinning in place, while the code on the link button looks like this:

```
on (rollOver) {
    _parent.i_TIP.txt_ToolTip = _root.myLinkTip();
    _parent.i_TIP.gotoAndPlay("SHOW");
}

on (rollOut,releaseOutside) {
    _parent.i_TIP.txt_ToolTip = "";
    _parent.i_TIP.gotoAndStop("HIDE");
}

on (release) {
    getURL (_root.myLinkURL(),_root.myLinkTip())
}
```

This button takes advantage of the tooltip movie clip that we discussed earlier (area 6 on our diagram). The only difference lies in where the text for the tooltip is actually coming from. Instead of myToolTip, it's being populated by the function myLinkTip.

In a similar way, when the button is clicked, a couple of functions return the values of the URL and the target window for this link. This information is used in conjunction with getURL to redirect the browser to the related link page or resource. Here's what these three simple functions look like.

```
// Return ToolTip (LINK) for Link Button
```

```
        function myLinkTip() {
            return aStories[tCurrentStory][4];
        }

        // Return URL (LINK-URL) for Link Button
        function myLinkURL() {
            return aStories[tCurrentStory][5];
        }

        // Return Target (LINK-TARGET) for Link Button
        function myLinkTarget() {
            return aStories[tCurrentStory][6];
        }
```

As you can see, these functions do nothing more than look into our story arrays and return the necessary values.

That does it for the related link; let's get back to the last part of displayStory, the final few lines which don't affect i_STORY. The text fields it is populating are out on the main timeline, in area nine (9).

```
        // COUNTER Current Story
        if (tStoryIndex < 9) {
            txt_CurrentStory = "0" + (tStoryIndex + 1);
        } else {
            txt_CurrentStory = tStoryIndex + 1;
        }

        // COUNTER Total Stories
        if (tStoryCount < 9) {
            txt_TotalStories = "0"+ tStoryCount;
        } else {
            txt_TotalStories = tStoryCount;
        }

    } // END * Function displayStory
```

This area of our movie displays a set of counters that tell the user which story they're viewing, and how many stories there are in total.

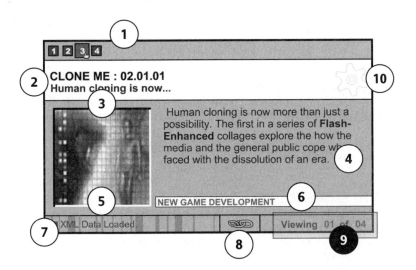

Before placing the value of tStoryIndex into the dynamic text box, I wanted to format it a bit. I figured that we'd never have more than 99 stories, so I know that both the number of the current story, and the total number of stories, will never be more than two digits long. For design purposes, as well as personal preference, I want to make sure that if we come up with a single digit number, as we do in this example, we prefix it with a zero. This way, our numbers will be displayed as 01, 02, 03, 04, 05, 06, 07, 08, 09, 10, 11, etc. We'll also be assured that the text in these boxes will always take up roughly the same amount of space, and therefore won't shift position when switching from a single- to a two-digit number.

We perform this formatting simply by checking the value of tStoryIndex. If this value is less than nine, then the value placed into the dynamic text box is the string literal "0" concatenated with the value of tStoryIndex incremented by one. Remember that arrays are zero-based, so when tStoryIndex is 9, we'll be looking at the *tenth* story – and we don't want to prefix a zero in that case. Also note that we have to specify "0" as a *string* here, so that the value in tStoryIndex is also treated as a string, giving us the result we want. Adding the *integer* zero to our current story number would not accomplish a great deal!

Finally, the result of these manipulations is placed into txt_CurrentStory, resulting in the appearance of our value in the dynamic text box with that name.

The second, similar piece of code in the above listing performs the same sort of formatting on the tStoryCount variable, which you may remember we created back in the buildStoryText function. This variable holds the total number of stories that we parsed and inserted into our story array. After checking to see if it needs a zero prefix, we place it into the dynamic text box variable txt_TotalStories.

The only section of our movie that I have yet to touch upon is area ten (10), but this is nothing more than a simple animated movie clip to add some more motion to our project. It is on the main timeline in a layer labeled Cog. With that, we've taken care of displayStory, and our deconstruction. The rest is up to you.

Review

In this chapter, we studied the creation of an XML-based news application built with nothing more than Flash and a text editor. We covered the design and programming issues, and how we came to the decision that Flash and XML was the combination of choice. We also considered some of the organizational issues involved with making a Flash movie of moderate complexity.

Let's go through those steps again, quickly. If you come to a step for which you feel the need to return and review, now is the time.

First, we considered the design and programming issues. We wanted something that was easy to update, yet had the flexibility of design that we get by using Flash. We took a look at the type of information we wanted to display, and broke it down into a couple of diagrams (data model and information architecture). These diagrams helped us decide how our XML data and our design would be structured. Once we had an XML file written, we used the XML object in Flash 5 to pull the data it contained into an easily accessible series of arrays. With these arrays, we had no problem populating our design with the necessary information.

Now I hand this movie and the knowledge I gained while creating it to you. If you should come up with great improvements, or even a simple adaptation of this code or the techniques used within it, I would love to hear from you. Please look in the resources section for a web site you can use to see the latest revisions of this code. There is also an e-mail address so that you can send me questions or comments you may have (I'll do my best to respond in a timely manner).

Where to go From Here

Here are some ideas and additional resources to help you take this to the next level.

Ideas

There are several things that I have not done, but may do in the future, with this movie.

I have considered adding more animation and effects to the text elements. For this reason, I have them embedded into movie clips.

It may be nice to have a few more different layouts as well. Right now I'm working with only two, but adding more would be pretty simple. I figure that if I had five different layouts, I could cover most of the different aspect ratios of images, and combinations of images and text.

Finally, as with any Flash project, I am always considering revisions to the code and layout of the movie that will make it more easily updateable and more portable. That is to say, there may be ways to make this movie more object-oriented than it is, which would allow us to use the bits and pieces we have created in a variety of different ways, and even in other projects.

Feel free to e-mail me at the address listed below if you come up with an interesting take on this project. You can also check my site (and the friends of ED site) for more information and updated files.

urces

Here are a few on-line resources that helped me out; they might help you.

ActionScript Studio – JRVisuals source files and e-mail:

www.JRVisuals.com/client/FoEd
actionScript@JRVisuals.com

Macromedia Tech Notes – New XML object features of Flash Player 5:

www.macromedia.com/support/flash/ts/documents/xml_content_type.htm

Macromedia Tech Notes – Using HTML text formatting in Flash 5:

www.macromedia.com/support/flash/ts/documents/htmltext.htm

Utilizing XML Data – Macromedia Tutorial:

www.macromedia.com/software/flash/productinfo/tutorials/intermediate/flash.pdf

Fig Leaf Software's Mailing List:

http://chattyfig.figleaf.com

XML – Extensible Markup Language:

www.w3c.org
http://www.xml.com
www.stars.com/Authoring/Languages/XML
www.macromedia.com/support/flash/interactivity/xml/xml.html

Index

The index is arranged hierarchically, in alphabetical order, with symbols preceding the letter A. Many second-level entries also occur as first-level entries. This is to ensure that users will find the information they require however they choose to search for it.

DESIGNER TO DESIGNER™

The New Masters Series – Advanced – *Showing it*
Where can you find out what inspires the top designers?
Where •can you learn the secrets of their design
techniques? New Masters is the ultimate showcase for
graphics pioneers from around the world, where they
write about what influences their design and teach the
cutting-edge effects that have made them famous.

The Studio Series – Intermediate – *Doing it*
The essence of the studio is the collective – a gathering
of independent designers who try out ideas and
explore techniques in finer detail. Each book in the studio
series assumes that the reader has learned the
fundamentals of the topic area. They want to grow their
skills with particular tools to a higher level, while at the
same time absorbing the hard-won creative experience of a
group of design experts.

The Foundation Series – Starting out – *Learning it*
Every web designer benefits from a strong foundation to
firmly establish their understanding of a new technology or
tool. The friends of ED foundation series deconstructs a
subject into step by step lessons – stand alone design
recipes that build together into a complete model project.
Practical, intuitive – a must-have resource.

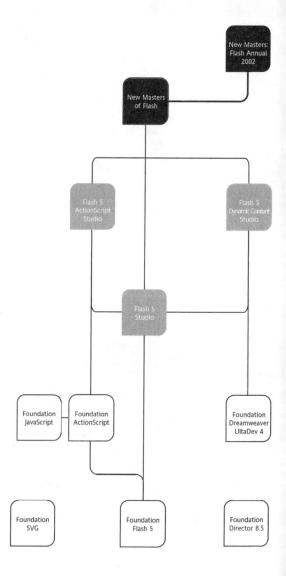

Books | D2D | Code | News | Contact | Home

Search

friendsof ⊘

DESIGNER TO DESIGNER™

Books

D2D

Code

News

Authors

Interviews

Web

Events

Contact

Home

You've read the book, now enter the community.

friendsofed.com is the online heart of the designer to designer neighbourhood.

As you'd expect the site offers the latest news and support for all our current and forthcoming titles – but it doesn't stop there.

For fresh exclusive interviews and videos every month with our authors – the new and future masters like Josh Davis, Yugo Nakamura, James Paterson and many other friends of ED – enter the world of D2D.

Stuck with a design problem? Need technical assistance? Our support doesn't end on the last page of the book. Just post your query on our message board and one of our moderators or authors will make sure you get the answers you need – fast.

New to the site is our EVENTS section where you can find out about schemes brewing in the ED laboratory. Forget everything you know about conferences and get ready for a new generation of designer happenings with a difference.

Welcome to friendsofed.com. This place is the place of friends of ED – designer to designer. Practical deep fast content delivered by working web designers.

Straight to your head.

www.friendsofed.com

freshfroot
motion web mindfood

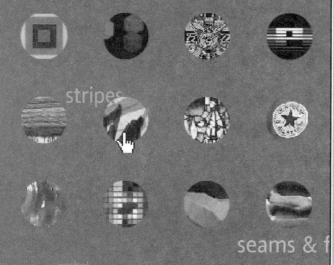

stripes

warhol

seams & f

my froot

my.froot

sheel

archive

a_z a-z

📅 date

? keyword

search for: inspiration

james pate

forward

urban

playground

hybrid   revolution   brendan dawes

http://www.freshfroot.com